THE DIVINE HOURS™

PRAYERS FOR SUMMERTIME

Ephesians 5:19 and 20:
Sing psalms and hymns and inspired songs among yourselves,
singing and chanting to the Lord in your hearts, always and everywhere giving
thanks to God who is our Father in the name of our Lord Jesus Christ.

THE
DIVINE HOURS™

PRAYERS FOR SUMMERTIME

Compiled and with Preface by
Phyllis Tickle

Image Books
Doubleday
New York London Toronto Sydney Auckland

AN IMAGE BOOK
PUBLISHED BY DOUBLEDAY
a division of Random House, Inc.

IMAGE, DOUBLEDAY, and the portrayal of a deer drinking from a stream
are registered trademarks of Random House, Inc.

The Divine Hours™ is a trademark of Tickle, Incorporated.

BOOK DESIGN BY RENATO STANISIC

The Library of Congress has cataloged the hardcover edition as follows:
Divine hours: prayers for summertime / compiled and with preface by
　　Phyllis Tickle.—1st ed.
　　　　p.　　cm.
　　　1. Prayers.　2. Church year prayer-books and devotions—English.
　　I. Tickle, Phyllis.
　　BV245.D64　2000
　　264'.15—dc21　　　　　　　　　　　　　　99-13200
　　　　　　　　　　　　　　　　　　　　　　CIP

ISBN-13: 978-0-385-50476-8
ISBN-10: 0-385-50476-4
Copyright © 2000 by Tickle, Incorporated

Contents

An Introduction to This Manual

From the beginning two things have been the necessary form and mystery of Christian spirituality. Two things, even before the closing events of resurrection, ascension, and commission, wove disparate and often renegade believers into an inspirited body of the whole, connected to God and each other.

Like a double helix rendered elegant by complexity and splendid by authority, the amalgam of gospel and shared meal and the discipline of fixed-hour prayer were and have remained the chain of golden connection tying Christian to Christ and Christian to Christian across history, across geography, and across idiosyncrasies of faith. The former is known as the food and sustenance of the Church, the latter as its work. *The Divine Hours* is about the second part of this double strand, the work; it is a manual for the contemporary exercise of fixed-hour prayer.

Although designed primarily for private use by individuals or by small groups, *The Divine Hours* may certainly be employed by larger and/or more public communities. Likewise, though designed primarily for lay use, it can as well be employed by the ordained in either private or corporate prayer.

Those already familiar with fixed-hour prayer (variously referred to as "The Liturgy of the Hours" or "keeping the hours" or "saying the offices") and with its tools (the breviaries of monastic worship and the Book of Hours manuals for laity that date from medieval times) will find some modifications and innovations here. They may wish to scan what follows for explication of these changes. Others, especially those for whom keeping the hours is a new practice, may wish to read the remainder of this introduction more thoroughly.

A Brief History of Fixed-Hour Prayer

The Age of the Apostles

Fixed-hour prayer, while it is with the Eucharist the oldest surviving form of Christian spirituality, actually had its origins in the Judaism out of which Christianity came. Centuries before the birth of Jesus of Nazareth, the Hebrew psalmist wrote that "Seven times a day do I praise you" (Ps. 119:164). Although scholars do not agree on the hours of early Judaism's set prayers (they were probably adjusted and readjusted many times), we do know that by the first century a.d. the ritual of daily prayer had assumed two characteristics that would travel down the millennia to us: The prayers had been set or fixed into something very close to their present-day schedule, and they had begun to assume something very close to their present-day intention.

By the beginning of the common era, Judaism and its adherents, already thoroughly accustomed to fixed hours for prayer, were scattered across the Roman Empire. It was an empire whose efficiency and commerce depended in no small part upon the orderly and organized conduct of each business day. In the cities of the Empire, the forum bell rang the beginning of that day at six o'clock each morning (prime or "first" hour); noted the day's progress by striking again at nine o'clock (terce or third hour); sounded the lunch break at noon (sext or sixth hour); called citizens back to work by striking at three o'clock (none or ninth hour); and closed the day's markets by sounding again at six o'clock in the afternoon (vespers or evening hour). Every part of daily life within Roman culture eventually came, to some greater or lesser extent, to be ordered by the ringing of the forum bells, including Jewish prayer and, by natural extension, Christian prayer as well.

The first detailed miracle of the apostolic Church, the healing of the lame man on the Temple steps by Sts. Peter and John (Acts 3:1), occurred when and where it did because two devout Jews (who did not yet know they were Christians as such) were on their way to ninth-hour (three o'clock) prayers. Not many years later, one of the great defining events of Christianity—St. Peter's vision of the descending sheet filled with both clean and unclean animals—was to occur at noon on a rooftop because he had gone there to observe the sixth-hour prayers.

The directive Peter received during his noon devotion—i.e., to accept all that God had created as clean—was pivotal because it became the basis of the ecumenism that rapidly thereafter expanded Church fellowship beyond Jewry. Peter was on the roof, however, not by some accident of having been in that spot when the noon bell caught him, but by his own intention. In Joppa and far from Jerusalem and the Temple, Peter had sought out the solitude of his host's rooftop as a substitute site for keeping the appointed time of prayer.

Such readiness to accommodate circumstance was to become a characteristic of fixed-hour prayer. So too were some of the words Peter must have used. We know, for instance, that from its very earliest days, the Christian community incorporated the Psalms in their prayers (Acts 4:23–30); and the Psalter has remained as the living core of the daily offices ever since. Likewise, by c. 60 a.d., the author of the first known manual of Christian practice, the *Didache*, was teaching the inclusion of the Lord's Prayer at least three times each day, a usage that was to expand quickly to include all the offices.

From the Apostles to the Early Fathers

As Christianity grew and, thanks to Peter's rooftop vision, as it spread, so too did the practice of formalized daily prayer. The process by which the fixed-hour prayers of the first century slowly recast themselves as the Divine Hours or Daily Offices of later Christians is blurred in some of its particulars, though we can attest to the approximate date and agency of many of them.

We know from their writings that by the second and third centuries the great Fathers of the Church—Clement (c. 150–215 a.d.), Origen (c. 185–254 a.d.), Tertullian (c. 160–225 a.d.), etc.—assumed as normative the observance of prayers in the morning and at night as well as the so-called "little hours" of terce, sext, and none . . . or in modern parlance, nine a.m., noon, and three p.m. These daily prayers were often said or observed alone, though they could be offered by families or in small groups.

Regardless of whether or not the fixed-hour prayers were said alone or in community, however, they were never individualistic in nature. Rather, they employed the time-honored and time-polished prayers and recitations of the faith. Every Christian was to observe the prayers; none was empowered to create them.

Within the third century, the Desert Fathers, the earliest monastics of the Church, began to pursue the universal Christian desideratum of living out St. Paul's admonition to "pray without ceasing" (I Th. 5:17). To accomplish this, they devised the stratagem, within their communities, of having one group of monks pass the praying of an office on seamlessly to another group of monks waiting to commence the next office. The result was the introduction into Christian thinking of the concept of a continuous cascade of prayer before the throne of God. That concept was to remain into our own time as a realized grace for many, many Christians, both monastic and lay.

Christians today, wherever they practice the discipline of fixed-hour prayer, frequently find themselves filled with a conscious awareness that they are handing their worship, at its final "Amen," on to other Christians in the next time zone. Like relay runners passing a lighted torch, those who do the work of fixed-hour prayer do create thereby a continuous cascade of praise before the throne of God. To participate in such a regimen with such an awareness is to pray, as did the Desert Fathers, from within the spiritual community of shared texts as well as within the company of innumerable other Christians, unseen but present, who have preceded one across time or who, in time, will follow one.

From St. Benedict to the Middle Ages

Once the notion of unbroken and uninterrupted prayer had entered monastic practice, so too, almost by default, did much longer prayers enter there. Yet for all their lengthiness and growing complexity and cumbersomeness, the monks' fixed-hour prayers became normative for the religious in both the Eastern and the Western branches of the Church. By the fourth century, certainly, the principal characteristics of the daily offices as we know them today were plainly in place, and their organization would be more or less recognizable as such to us today.

Meanwhile for secular (i.e., nonmonastic) clergy and for the laity, the prayers appointed for the fixed hours were of necessity much, much shorter, often confined to something not unlike the brief minutes of present-day observance. There were also many public churches or basilicas that, despite their uncloistered nature, were pastored by monastic orders, and in these there was some, almost inevitable, blending of the two forms—i.e., of the cumbersome monastic and the far more economical lay practices. St. Benedict, for example, fashioned his famous Rule after the offices as they were observed by monastics in the open basilicas of Rome.

It was, of course, St. Benedict whose ordering of the prayers was to become a kind of master template against which all subsequent observance and structuring of the divine hours was to be tested. It was also Benedict who first said, "*Orare est laborare, laborare est orare.*" "To pray is to work, to work is to pray." In so doing he gave form to another of the great, informing concepts of Christian spirituality—the inseparability of spiritual life from physical life. He also formalized the concept of "divine work."

"Office" as a word comes into modern usage from the Latin word *opus*, or "work." For most English speakers, it immediately connotes a place, rather than an activity. Yet those same speakers quite as naturally refer to professional functions—political ones, for example—as "offices," as in "He is running for office." Most of them readily refer to the voluntary giving up of the product of work as "offering" or "an offering." And those who govern or regulate work are routinely referred to as "officers" of a corporation or a civic unit. Thus in an earlier time that was much closer than we to the original possibilities of *opus*, it was entirely fitting that "office" should become the denominator for "the work of God."

For Benedict, as for many before him and almost all after him, fixed-hour prayer was and will always be *opus dei*, "the work of God," "the offices." As for the hours on whose striking the prayers are done, those belong to God and are, as a result, "divine." And the work is real, as fixed in its understanding of itself as it is in its timing.

Prayer is as variform as any other human activity. The Liturgy of the Hours, or the Divine Offices, is but one of those forms, yet it is the only one consistently referred to as "the work of God." The Divine Hours are prayers of praise offered as a sacrifice of thanksgiving and faith to God and as a sweet-smelling incense of the human soul before the throne of God. To offer them is to serve before that throne as part of the priesthood of all believers. It is to assume the "office" of attendant upon the Divine.

While the words and ordering of the prayers of the Divine Hours have changed and changed again over the centuries, that purpose and that characterization have remained constant. Other prayers may be petitionary or intercessory or valedictory or any number of other things, but the Liturgy of the Hours remains an act of offering . . . offering by the creature to the Creator. The fact that the creature grows strong and his or her faith more sinewy and efficacious as a result of keeping the hours is a by-product (albeit a desirable one) of that practice and not its purpose.

From the Middle Ages to Us

As the keeping of the hours grew in importance to become the organizing principle of both Christian spirituality and the Christian day, so too did the elaboration of the offices. By the eleventh century, saying an office required a veritable stack of books . . . a Psalter from which to sing the Psalms appointed for that day and hour, a lectionary from which to ascertain the appointed scripture reading, a sacred text from which to read the scripture thus discovered, a hymnal for singing, etc. As the growth of small communities took the laity away from the great cathedral centers where such tools and their ordering were available, it also created a need for some kind of unification of all the pieces and parts into a more manageable and more portable form. The result was the creation of a set of mnemonics, a kind of master list or, in Latin, *breviarium*, of how the fixed-hour prayers were to be observed and of the texts to be used.

From the less cumbersome listings of the *breviarium*, it was a short leap to incorporating into a book at least the first few words (and sometimes the whole) of all the texts required by the listing. This the officiants of the Papal Chapel did in the twelfth century, and the modern breviary was born. Breviaries, or manuals of prayer for keeping the daily offices, have varied over the subsequent centuries from order to order, from church to church, and from communion to communion within Christianity. So too has the ordering and number of the offices to be observed and even, in some cases, the setting of the appointed hours themselves.

The Anglican communion, for example, as one of its first acts of defiance in the time of the Reformation, created a new prayer book to govern the thinking and the practice of Christians in the new Church of England. That manual was given the intentionally populist name of *The Book of Common Prayer*. More often referred to affectionately today simply as the BCP, the manual has gone through many updates and revisions that have adjusted its language and even its theology to changing times and sensibilities. Despite those changes, however, and perhaps as a result of them, the BCP still orders, through one edition or another, the spiritual and religious lives of millions of Christians, many of them not Anglican by profession and all save a few of them certainly not English.

As one of its more "reforming" amendments, the first and subsequent editions of the BCP reduced or collapsed the Daily Offices into only two obligatory observances—morning prayer and evensong. Almost four hundred and fifty years later, in 1979, the U.S. (or Episcopal) Church bowed to the centuries and the yearning of many remembering hearts by restoring the noon office to its rightful place in the American BCP. In doing so, the Episcopal Church in the United States also acted within another abiding consistency of fixed-hour prayer—the enduring sense that the so-called Little Hours of terce, sext, and none, even when collapsed into one noontime observance, are as integral as are morning and evening prayer to the offices and to daily Christian practice, be it private or public.

Episcopal practice was not the first to undergo restructuring in the closing years of the twentieth century. In 1971 in accord with the directives of the Second

Vatican Council, Pope Paul VI issued The Liturgy of the Hours, which modified the offices to an ordering very similar to the one the American BCP would assume eight years later. Four offices were now suggested to laity and required of monastics, secular clergy, and those under orders: a morning office called still by its Latin name of Lauds; a noon office that allows the individual Christian to choose the hour of his or her workday (either terce, sext, or none) in which to pray the office and, as a result of that first choice, which of the three possible texts will be prayed; the early evening office of vespers; and before retiring, the simple, consoling office of compline. Under Paul VI's rubrics, there is also an obligatory Office of Readings that may be observed at any time of the believer's day that is most convenient.

Despite all the diversity that centuries and evolving doctrine have laid upon them, the Divine Hours have none the less remained absolute in their adherence to certain principles that have become their definition. The Daily Offices and the manuals that effect them are, as a result of that defining constancy, dedicated: to the exercise of praise as the work of God and the core of the offices; to the informing concept of a cascade of prayer being lifted ceaselessly by Christians around the world; to the recognition for every observant of an exultant membership with other observants in a communion of saints across both time and space; to the centrality of the Psalms as the informing text of all the offices (a centrality made doubly intense by the fact that theirs are the words, rhythms, and understandings that Jesus of Nazareth himself used in his own devotions while on earth); to the establishment in every breviary or manual of a fixed cycle that provides for the reading of at least some portion of all save three of the Psalms in the Hebrew/Christian Psalter (the present manual employs a six-week cycle and some portion of every Psalm); to the necessity of fixed components like the Our Father; to the formal ordering of each office's conduct; and to the efficacy of the repetition of prayers, creeds, and sacred texts in spiritual growth and exercise. It is on these principles and within the scope of these purposes that *The Divine Hours* is built.

Notes for the Use of This Manual

The Divine Hours: Prayers for Summertime, like most variations and revisions of established forms, is born out of contemporary need. In particular the manual strives for simplicity or familiarity of wording and ease of use. Not only will such an approach reassure those Christians who have not yet begun the practice of keeping the hours, but it will also provide even the liturgically accomplished with what one observer referred to as "a welcome lack of so many ribbons." With few exceptions, the entire text for each office is printed within that office, and the rubrics or headers of each part of each office are in contemporary rather than ecclesial English. The first evidence of this approach is in the manual's title itself. *Prayers for Summertime* uses the assignations of the physical year rather than those of the liturgical one. The rough correspondence in this case is between what the Western Church now calls Ordinary Time and what common speech calls summertime. The liturgical color appointed to Ordinary Time, however, is green; and in recognition of that, the rubrics and headers of each office are produced here in green.

The offices in this manual are appointed, as is often done now, not by the date of each individual day nor by the week of the liturgical year, but rather from the Sunday of each week of the physical calendar. The Church has long assigned certain prayers, readings, and intentions to certain days of the week. Thus, Friday is normally regarded as a penitential day, Saturday as a day of preparation for corporate worship, Sunday as a sabbath. Ordering the offices by numbered dates rather than from the first Sunday of each week obscures these historic rhythms.

Following current Church practice, the offices appointed for each day are four in number: morning, noon, vespers, and compline. Following the ancient principle of accommodation, there is flexibility about the hour or half hour within which each may be observed. The morning and vespers or evening prayers adhere to the general configurations of their antecedents, and the noon office is an amalgam of the Little Hours of terce, sext, and none into one whole. The fourth—compline—is frequently referred to as "the dear office." Unlike the others, compline is fixed by the individual and not by the clock, for it is observed just before retiring.

Because compline is indeed the dear office of rest and because it is freer in its timing, it is also more repetitive or fixed here in its structure. For this reason, there is only one week of compline texts for each month of the manual. Thus the compline for the first Monday in June is the compline for each Monday in June.

Each month's texts are preceded by a prefatory page that gives the page number for that month's compline texts; the physical or calendar date of saints' days and observances for the month; and the text of the Gloria and the Our Father. Most Christians are so absolutely familiar with both of these fixed prayers as to need no assistance in praying them. For that reason, they are the only parts of the daily offices not reproduced here within the texts of each office. On the other hand, new Christians or those just commencing the practice of the offices may find it reassuring to know that these two integral components are immediately available at the head of each month.

The Feasts and saints' days of the Church are so numerous as to be only rarely incorporated *in toto* by any breviary or manual. Rather, each selects for inclusion those holy days that are the major observances of the Church as well as some that seem most applicable to the volume's intended communion. Although this manual lists on each month's header the exact date of observation for each selected observance, it follows the pattern of celebrating the saint or feast on the Monday of the week within which the occasion falls. This system allows the user the flexibility to choose between precise commemoration or that of the memorializing week in general. In the event, as in third week of July, that there are two observances in one week; the later one is celebrated on Thursday.

To facilitate the Church's increasing emphasis on sacred texts, *The Divine Hours* incorporates readings into three offices—morning, noon, and compline. To make such incorporation possible, hymns are primary here only in the vespers office, just as some of the more repetitive practices of earlier manuals have been omitted. The list of the symbols and conventions used in this manual, which follows, will enrich the user's understanding of some of the other particulars of *The Divine Hours* as well.

The Symbols and Conventions Used in This Manual

Except where otherwise indicated, the texts for the sacred readings in this manual are taken from *The New Jerusalem Bible*. Thus, the conventions of that translation pertain here as well. For example, the italicizing of a segment within a reading indicates that those words or phrases have occurred previously elsewhere in scripture and probably constitute a direct quotation or incorporation by the current speaker.

On those few occasions when a sacred reading is from the King James Version rather than *The New Jerusalem Bible*, that change is noted at the reading's conclusion by the notation, "KJV." The texts for all save a handful of the Psalms and Psalm hymns employed here are from the Psalter of *The Book of Common Prayer*. These departures are marked with the appropriate citing words with one exception where, because of frequency and for aesthetic reasons, a symbol is used. ❖ indicates a medley or hymning of the canonical Psalms as assembled by Dr. Fred Bassett (c.f., Acknowledgments).

Unless otherwise indicated, the appointed prayers are taken from the BCP. Many of them have been adapted, however, for use here. Such texts are indicated by the symbol, †. Principally, the user already familiar with the BCP will note that many of the first person plural pronouns of "us, we, our" have been changed to the singular ones of "me, I, my." The sensibility informing these adaptations has been the desire to make each more immediately personal. Whether the offices as they are produced here are said in private (as will be by far the greater use) or in public, each observant prays both as an individual and as a participant in a praying community. Where the pronominal singulars of "me, I, my" are employed, the attention should be directed toward the individual. Where the plurals are employed, attention and intention are toward the larger community of the Church.

The Psalms are poetry, albeit a poetry that does not work on a poetics familiar to most English speakers. Few translations of that great body of devotion have come so close, however, as has the Psalter of the BCP to exposing and celebrating the rhythms, images, and aesthetic force of the originals; and it is for that reason that they have been used here. The BCP Psalter, like every other, has its own conventions, and they are followed here. This is particularly obvious in the presentations of the name of God. Long a problem for translators as well as readers, the presence in the Psalms of three different terms for the divine name requires carefully chosen English wording as well as a clearly defined rationale for the application of each term chosen. This rationale, while too lengthy for inclusion here, may be found in the prefatory material to the BCP Psalter.

The Psalms as reproduced here retain as well the *, or asterisks, that indicate the poetic breaks in the original Hebrew poem. Whether one is reading or chanting the Psalm, there should be a pause at this point in order for the rhythm of the poetry to be realized fully. Many Christians will want to chant the Psalms, since that most ancient of practices still extends to the observant the greatest and purest spiritual benefit personally. For the more chary, reading aloud will offer a similar benefit, since it too involves the body as well as the intellect in the keeping of the office.

Most contemporary observants, be they lay or ordained, keep the hours during the workday, a circumstance that means that the noon office in particular is observed within a space that is not only secular, but frequently populated. While one may withdraw to some removed space like an unoccupied room or a car, one still is rarely sufficiently secluded to be comfortable chanting or reading aloud. By contrast, for weekend days and for the offices of morning and evening, chanting or oral reading may be both possible and desirable.

Chanting an office is a complex exercise with an equally complex and intricate history. Those who are already informed in the art will find that the asterisks here furnish the necessary pointing. For those who have not previously chanted the offices but wish to add that exercise to their spiritual discipline and for those who are new observants, a few simple principles may be sufficient for basic proficiency.

In general, Psalms are sung or chanted along one single note or tone, one that is chosen by the observant as pleasing and comfortable to maintain over the course of the text. The pacing is natural, neither hurried nor pretentiously extended. By chanting, the observant is weaving in yet another part of the bouquet of prayer that is being offered to God, and a constant remembrance of this purpose will do much to make the discipline acceptable and pleasing. Each verse of the Psalm, by and large, constitutes a poetic unit and is interrupted or pointed by an asterisk. The asterisk signals not only the poetic break in the verse but also the point at which the chanter is to raise his or her tone one note. That raising occurs on the last accented syllable nearest to the asterisk. At the end of the second half of the verse—i.e., the sequence of words after the asterisk—the chanter lowers by one note the final, accented syllable. Pronouns like "me, he, thee," etc., are never elevated or lowered. The ear and the throat will soon show the new chanter as well that many English words are trisyllabic, having their accent on the first syllable. When such a word is the last one before an asterisk or a verse end, the first unaccented syllable goes up or down a note or half note as the case may be, and the second unaccented syllable goes up or down another similar gradation.

From such basic premises, the intrigued or impassioned chanter will discover rather quickly ways to elaborate the office to a rendering pleasing to him or her. Such elaborations, the chanter should be assured, have probably already been tried through the centuries by other Christians and may well be in full, current use by many of them. So also is there a range of options for rendering the prose or unpointed portions of each office. Readings or appointed prayers, for example, if chanted, are normally offered in a monotone with a lengthening of the final syllable of each breath-pause or sentence unit. The Our Father is frequently the exception to this principle, being offered silently by many worshipers.

The only necessary principle, in fact, is really to remember the words of St. Augustine, "Whoever sings, prays twice." In so saying, Augustine spoke to the attitude as well as the benefit of chanting the Psalms: That which deepens the observant's contemplation and that which increases the beauty of our devotion are, by definition, appropriate and good.

THE DIVINE HOURS

PRAYERS FOR SUMMERTIME

The Gloria
Glory be to God the Father, God the Son, and God the Holy Spirit. As it was in the beginning, so it is now and so it shall ever be, world without end. Alleluia. *Amen.*

The Lord's Prayer
Our Father, who art in heaven, hallowed be your Name.
May your kingdom come, and your will be done, on earth as in heaven.
Give us today our daily bread.
Forgive us our sins as we forgive those who sin against us.
Lead us not into temptation, but deliver us from evil;
for yours are the kingdom and the power and the glory
forever and ever. *Amen.*

Compline Prayers for June Are Located on Page 173

The Following Holy Days Occur in June:
Feast of St. Barnabas: *June 11*
Feast of St. Peter and St. Paul: *June 29*

June

The Morning Office　　　　　**To Be Observed on the Hour or Half Hour**
　　　　　　　　　　　　　　　　　　　Between 6 and 9 a.m.

The Call to Prayer
Come, let us sing to the LORD;* Let us rejoice this day in the strength of our salva-
　　tion.
Let us come into His presence with thanksgiving,* and raise a loud shout to Him
　　with psalms.

　　　　　　　　　　　　　　　　　　　　　　　　　　　　Psalm 95:1–2

The Request for Presence
Hear, O Shepherd of Israel, leading Joseph like a flock;* shine forth, you that are
　　enthroned upon the cherubim.
In the presence of Ephraim, Benjamin, and Manasseh,* stir up your strength and
　　come to help us,
Restore us, O God of hosts;* show the light of your countenance, and we shall be
　　saved.

　　　　　　　　　　　　　　　　　　　　　　　　　　　　Psalm 80:1–3

The Greeting
It is a good thing to give thanks to the LORD,* and to sing praises to your Name, O
　　Most High;
To tell of your loving-kindness early in the morning* and of your faithfulness in
　　the night season; for as it was in the beginning, it is now and it evermore shall
　　be. Alleluia.

　　　　　　　　　　　　　　　　　　　　　Psalm 92:1–2; Gloria

The Refrain for the Morning Lessons
Incline my heart, O God, to your ways.* Turn my eyes from longing after vanities.
　　　　　　　　　　　　　　　　　　　based on Psalm 119:36 and 37

A Reading
Jesus taught us, saying: 'And when you pray, do not imitate the hypocrites: they
　　love to say their prayers standing up in the synagogues and at the street cor-
　　ners for people to see them. In truth I tell you, they have had their reward. But
　　when you pray, go to your private room, shut yourself in, and so pray to your
　　Father who is in that secret place, and your Father who sees all that is done in
　　secret will reward you.'

　　　　　　　　　　　　　　　　　　　　　　　　　Matthew 6:5–6

The Refrain
Incline my heart, O God, to your ways.* Turn my eyes from longing after vanities.

The Morning Psalm　　　　　　　　*God's Gifts for Joyful Living*
The law of the LORD is perfect and revives the soul;* the testimony of the LORD is
　　sure and gives wisdom to the innocent.
The statutes of the LORD are just and rejoice the heart;* the commandment of the
　　LORD is clear and gives light to the eyes.

The fear of the LORD is clean and endures forever;* the judgments of the LORD are
    true and righteous altogether.
More to be desired are they than gold, more than much fine gold;* sweeter far than
    honey, than honey in the comb.
By them also is your servant enlightened,* and in keeping them there is great
    reward.

Psalm 19:7–11

The Refrain
Incline my heart, O God, to your ways.* Turn my eyes from longing after vanities.

The Gloria

The Lord's Prayer

The Prayer Appointed for the Week
Holy Father, creator and sustaining wisdom of all that is, both in heaven and on
    earth, take from me those thoughts, actions and objects that are hurtful. Give
    me instead those things that are profitable for me and all who seek rightly to
    praise you. I ask this grace in the company of all believers and through the
    name of Jesus Christ our Lord, who is, with you and the Holy Spirit, one God
    forever and ever. *Amen.*✝

The Concluding Prayer of the Church
Lord God, almighty and everlasting Father, you have brought me in safety to this
    new day: Preserve me with your mighty power, that I may not fall into sin, nor
    be overcome by adversity; and in all I do direct me to the fulfilling of your pur-
    pose; through Jesus Christ my Lord. *Amen.*✝

The Midday Office   **To Be Observed on the Hour or Half Hour
                                        Between 11 a.m. and 2 p.m.**

The Call to Prayer
Proclaim with me the greatness of the LORD;* let us exalt his Name together.

Psalm 34:3

The Request for Presence
LORD, hear my prayer,* and let my cry come before you
Incline your ear to me;* when I call, make haste to answer me,

Psalm 102:1ff

The Greeting
The LORD lives! Blessed is my Rock!* Exalted is the God of my salvation!
Glory to God the Father, God the Son, and God the Holy Spirit. As it was in the
    beginning, so it is now and so shall ever be, world without end. Alleluia. *Amen.*

Psalm 18:46; Gloria

The Refrain for the Midday Lessons

I will give thanks to you, O LORD, with my whole heart:* I will tell all of your marvelous works.

Psalm 9:1

A Reading

. . . if you declare with your mouth that Jesus is Lord and if you believe in your heart that God raised him from the dead, then you will be saved. It is by believing with the heart that you are justified, and by making the declaration with your lips that you are saved.

Romans 10:9–10

The Refrain

I will give thanks to you, O LORD, with my whole heart:* I will tell of all your marvelous works.

The Midday Psalm   *Happy Are Your People, LORD.*

Who is like you, LORD God of Hosts?* Mighty LORD, your faithfulness is all around you.

You rule the raging of the sea* and still the surging of the waves.

Yours are the heavens; the earth is yours also.* You laid the foundations of the universe and all that is in it.

You have made the north and the south;* the mountains rejoice in your name.

Righteousness and justice are the foundations of your power;* love and truth go before your face.

Happy are the people who know the festal shout!* they walk, O LORD, in the light of your presence.

They rejoice daily in your Name;* they are jubilant in your righteousness.

For you are the glory of their strength,* and by your favor is our might exalted.

Truly God is our ruler;* the Holy One of Israel is our King.

Psalm 89:8ff

The Refrain

I will give thanks to you, O LORD, with my whole heart:* I will tell of all your marvelous works.

The Gloria

The Lord's Prayer

The Prayer Appointed for the Week

Holy Father, creator and sustaining wisdom of all that is, both in heaven and on earth, take from me those thoughts, actions and objects that are hurtful. Give me instead those things that are profitable for me and all who seek rightly to praise you. I ask this grace in the company of all believers and through the name of Jesus Christ our Lord, who is, with you and the Holy Spirit, one God forever and ever. *Amen.†*

The Concluding Prayer of the Church
Lord, My God, King of heaven and of earth, for this day please direct and sanctify, set right and govern my heart and my body, my sentiments, my words and my actions in conformity with Your law and Your commandments. Thus I shall be able to attain salvation and deliverance, in time and in eternity, by Your help, O Savior of the world, who lives and reigns forever. *Amen.*

adapted from Divine Office

The Vespers Office **To Be Observed on the Hour or Half Hour Between 5 and 8 p.m.**

The Call to Prayer
Come let us bow down, and bend the knee* and kneel before the Lord our Maker. For he is our God* and we are the people of his pasture and the sheep of his hand.

Psalm 95:6–7

The Request for Presence
I call upon you, O God, for you will answer me;* incline your ear to me, and hear my words.

Psalm 17:6

The Greeting
You are God: I praise you;* you are the Lord: I acclaim you;
You are the eternal Father:* all creation worships you.
Throughout the world the holy Church acclaims you:* Father, of majesty unbounded,
your true and only Son,* worthy of all worship,
and the Holy Spirit,* advocate and guide.
As these have been from the beginning,* so they are now and evermore shall be. Alleluia.

based on the Te Deum and Gloria

The Hymn   *All Praise to Thee, My God, This Night*
All Praise to Thee, my God, this night,
For all the blessings of the light!
Keep me, O keep me, King of kings,
Beneath Thine own almighty wings.

Forgive me, Lord, for Thy dear Son,
The ill that I this day have done,
That with the world, myself, and Thee,
I, ere I sleep, at peace may be.

O may my soul on Thee repose,
And with sweet sleep my eyelids close,
Sleep that may me more vigorous make
To serve my God when I awake.

When in the night I sleepless lie,
My soul with heavenly thoughts supply;
Let no ill dreams disturb my rest,
No powers of darkness me molest.

O when shall I, in endless day,
For ever chase dark sleep away,
And hymns divine with angels sing,
All praise to thee, eternal king?

Praise God, from Whom all blessings flow;
Praise Him, all creatures here below;
Praise Him above, ye heavenly hosts;
Praise Father, Son, and Holy Ghost.

Thomas Ken

The Refrain for the Vespers Lessons
O, LORD, you are my portion and my cup;* it is you who uphold my lot.

Psalm 16:5

The Vespers Psalm   *An Evening Song*
I will bless the LORD who gives me counsel;* my heart teaches me, night after night.
I have set the LORD always before me;* because he is at my right hand I shall not
    fall.
My heart, therefore, is glad, and my spirit rejoices;* my body also shall rest in hope.
For you will not abandon me to the grave,* nor let your holy one see the Pit.
You will show me the path of life;* in your presence is fullness of joy, and in your
    right hand are pleasures for evermore.

Psalm 16:7–11

The Refrain
O, LORD, you are my portion and my cup;* it is you who uphold my lot.

The Lord's Prayer

The Prayer Appointed for the Week
Holy Father, creator and sustaining wisdom of all that is, both in heaven and on
    earth, take from me those thoughts, actions and objects that are hurtful. Give
    me instead those things that are profitable for me and all who seek rightly to
    praise you. I ask this grace in the company of all believers and through the
    name of Jesus Christ our Lord, who is, with you and the Holy Spirit, one God
    forever and ever. *Amen.*†

The Concluding Prayer of the Church
Lord Jesus, stay with me, for evening is at hand and the day is past; be my com-
    panion in the way, kindle my heart, and awaken hope, that I may know you as

you are revealed in Scripture and in the breaking of bread. Grant this for the sake of your love toward me. *Amen.*†

The Morning Office

To Be Observed on the Hour or Half Hour Between 6 and 9 a.m.

The Call to Prayer
Come, let us sing to the LORD;* let us shout for joy to the rock of our salvation.
Let us come before his presence with thanksgiving* and raise a loud shout to him with psalms.

Psalm 95:1–2

The Request for Presence
LORD, God of hosts, hear my prayer;* hearken, O God of Jacob.

Psalm 84:7

The Greeting
The LORD lives! Blessed is my rock!* Exalted is the God of my salvation!
Therefore will I extol you among the nations, O LORD,* and sing praises to your name.

Psalm 18:46ff

The Refrain for the Morning Lessons
My heart is firmly fixed, O God, my heart is fixed;* I will sing and make melody.

Psalm 57:7

A Reading
Jesus said: 'I am the Way, I am Truth and Life. No one can come to the Father except through me. If you know me, you will know my Father too. From this moment you know him and have seen him.'

John 14:6–7

The Refrain
My heart is firmly fixed, O God, my heart is fixed;* I will sing and make melody.

The Morning Psalm   *This Is the Gate of the LORD*
Open for me the gates of righteousness;* I will enter them; I will offer thanks to the LORD.
"This is the gate of the LORD;* he who is righteous may enter."
I will give thanks to you, for you answered me* and have become my salvation.
The same stone that the builders rejected* has become the chief cornerstone.
This is the LORD'S doing,* and it is marvelous in our eyes.
On this day the LORD has acted;* we will rejoice and be glad in it.

Psalm 118:19–24

The Refrain
My heart is firmly fixed, O God, my heart is fixed;* I will sing and make melody.

The Small Verse

Now thank we all our God
With hearts and hands and voices,
Who wondrous things has done,
In whom the world rejoices,

Who from our mothers' arms
Has blessed us on our way
With countless gifts of love
And still is ours today.

Martin Rinkart

The Lord's Prayer

The Prayer Appointed for the Week
Holy Father, creator and sustaining wisdom of all that is, both in heaven and on
earth, take from me those thoughts, actions and objects that are hurtful. Give
me instead those things that are profitable for me and all who seek rightly to
praise you. I ask this grace in the company of all believers and through the
name of Jesus Christ our Lord, who is, with you and the Holy Spirit, one God
forever and ever. *Amen.*†

The Concluding Prayer of the Church
Lord God, almighty and everlasting Father, you have brought me in safety to this
new day: Preserve me with your mighty power, that I may not fall into sin, nor
be overcome by adversity; and in all I do direct me to the fulfilling of your purpose; through Jesus Christ my Lord. *Amen.*†

The Midday Office **To Be Observed on the Hour or Half Hour
Between 11 a.m. and 2 p.m.**

The Call to Prayer
Hallelujah! Sing to the LORD a new song;* sing his praise in the congregation of the
faithful.
Let Israel rejoice in his Maker;* let the children of Zion be joyful in their King.
Let them praise his Name in the dance;* let them sing praise to him with timbrel
and harp.
For the LORD takes pleasure in his people* and adorns the poor with victory.

Psalm 149:1–4

The Request for Presence
Restore us, O God of hosts;* show me the light of your countenance, and we shall
be saved.

Psalm 80:7

The Greeting
Not to us, O LORD, not to us, but to your Name give glory;* because of your love
and because of your faithfulness.

Psalm 115:1

The Refrain for the Midday Lessons
Righteousness and justice are the foundations of your throne;* love and truth go
before your face.

Psalm 89:14

A Reading
Seek YAHWEH while he is still to be found, call to him while he is still near. Let the
wicked abandon his way, and the evil one his thoughts. Let him turn back to
YAHWEH who will take pity on him, to our God who is rich in forgiveness; for
my thoughts are not your thoughts and your ways are not my ways, declares
YAHWEH. For the heavens are as high above the earth as my ways are above
your ways, my thoughts above your thoughts.

Isaiah 55:6–9

The Refrain
Righteousness and justice are the foundations of your throne;* love and truth go
before your face.

The Midday Psalm   *A Song of Comfort*
With the faithful you show yourself faithful, O God;* with the forthright you show
yourself forthright.
With the pure you show yourself pure,* but with the crooked you are wily.
You will save a lowly people,* but you will humble the haughty eyes.

Psalm 18:26–28

The Refrain
Righteousness and justice are the foundations of your throne;* love and truth go
before your face.

The Gloria

The Lord's Prayer

The Prayer Appointed for the Week
Holy Father, creator and sustaining wisdom of all that is, both in heaven and on
earth, take from me those thoughts, actions and objects that are hurtful. Give
me instead those things that are profitable for me and all who seek rightly to
praise you. I ask this grace in the company of all believers and through the
name of Jesus Christ our Lord, who is, with you and the Holy Spirit, one God
forever and ever. *Amen.*†

The Concluding Prayer of the Church
God, you have prepared in peace the path I must follow today. Help me to walk
straight on that path. If I speak, remove lies from my lips. If I am hungry, take
away from me all complaint. If I have plenty, destroy pride in me. May I go
through the day calling on you, you, O Lord, who know no other Lord.

Ethiopian Prayer

The Vespers Office   **To Be Observed on the Hour or Half Hour**
                                         Between 5 and 8 p.m.

The Call to Prayer
Let us give thanks to the LORD for his mercy* and the wonders he does for his children.
For he satisfies the thirsty* and fills the hungry with good things.

adapted from Psalm 107:8–9

The Request for Presence
You are good and you bring forth good;* instruct me in your statutes.
For the law of your mouth is dearer to me* than thousands in gold and silver.

Psalm 119:68, 72

The Greeting
You are the LORD, most high over all the earth;* you are exalted far above all gods.

Psalm 97:9

The Hymn

God, who made the earth and heaven,
Darkness and light:
You the day for work have given,
For rest the night.
May your angel guards defend us,
Slumber sweet your mercy send us,
Holy dreams and hopes attend us
All through the night.

And, when morn again shall call us
To run life's way,
May we still, whate'er befall us,
Your will obey.
From the power of evil hide us,
In the narrow Pathway guide us,
Never be your smile denied us
All through the day.

Stanza 1: Reginald Heber
Stanza 2: William Mercer

The Refrain for the Vespers Lessons
The LORD, the God of gods, has spoken;* he has called the earth from the rising of the sun to its setting.

Psalm 50:1

The Vespers Psalm   *An Evensong*
You water the mountains from your dwelling on high;* the earth is fully satisfied by the fruit of your works.
You make grass grow for flocks and herds* and plants to serve mankind;
That they may bring forth food from the earth,* and wine to gladden our hearts,
Oil to make a cheerful countenance,* and bread to strengthen the heart.
You appointed the moon to mark the seasons,* and the sun knows the time of its setting.
You make darkness that it may be night,* in which all the beasts of the forest prowl.
The lions roar after their prey* and seek their food from God.
The sun rises, and they slip away* and lay themselves down in their dens.
Man goes forth to his work* and to his labor until the evening.

Psalm 104:13–16, 20–24

The Refrain
The LORD, the God of gods, has spoken;* he has called the earth from the rising of
the sun to its setting.

The Gloria

The Lord's Prayer

The Prayer Appointed for the Week
Holy Father, creator and sustaining wisdom of all that is, both in heaven and on
earth, take from me those thoughts, actions and objects that are hurtful. Give
me instead those things that are profitable for me and all who seek rightly to
praise you. I ask this grace in the company of all believers and through the
name of Jesus Christ our Lord, who is, with you and the Holy Spirit, one God
forever and ever. *Amen.*

The Concluding Prayer of the Church   *The Song of Simeon*
Now, Master, you are letting your servant go in peace as you promised; for my
eyes have seen the salvation which you have made ready in the sight of the
nations; a light of revelation for the gentiles and glory for your people Israel.
Glory to the Father, and to the Son, and to the Holy Spirit: as it was in the
beginning, is now, and will be forever. *Amen.*

                                                    Luke 2:29–32, Gloria

The Morning Office   **To Be Observed on the Hour or Half Hour**
                                      Between 6 and 9 a.m.

The Call to Prayer
Hallelujah! Praise the Name of the LORD;* give praise, you servants of the LORD,
Praise the LORD, for the LORD is good;* sing praises to his Name, for it is lovely.
For I know that the LORD is great,* and that our Lord is above all gods.

                                                    Psalm 135:1ff

The Request for Presence
Satisfy us by your loving-kindness in the morning;* so shall we rejoice and be glad
all the days of our life.

                                                    Psalm 90:14

The Greeting
Out of Zion, perfect in its beauty,* God reveals himself in glory.
Let the heavens declare the rightness of his cause;* for God himself is judge.

                                                    Psalm 50:2, 6

The Refrain for the Morning Lessons
Wake up, my spirit; awake, lute and harp;* I myself will waken the dawn.

                                                    Psalm 108:2

A Reading

Jesus taught us, saying: 'You must believe me when I say that I am in the Father and the Father is in me; or at least believe it on the evidence of these works.'

John 14:11–12

The Refrain

Wake up, my spirit; awake, lute and harp;* I myself will waken the dawn.

The Morning Psalm   *The Little Hills Like Young Sheep*

Hallelujah! When Israel came out of Egypt,* the house of Jacob from a people of strange speech,

Judah became God's sanctuary* and Israel his dominion.

The sea beheld it and fled;* Jordan turned and went back.

The mountains skipped like rams,* and the little hills like young sheep.

What ailed you, O sea, that you fled?* Jordan, that you turned back?

You mountains, that you skipped like rams?* You little hills like young sheep?

Tremble, O earth, at the presence of the Lord,* at the presence of the God of Jacob,

Who turned the hard rock into a pool of water* and flint stone into a flowing spring.

Psalm 114:1–8

The Refrain

Wake up, my spirit; awake, lute and harp;* I myself will waken the dawn.

The Gloria

The Lord's Prayer

The Prayer Appointed for the Week

Holy Father, creator and sustaining wisdom of all that is, both in heaven and on earth, take from me those thoughts, actions and objects that are hurtful. Give me instead those things that are profitable for me and all who seek rightly to praise you. I ask this grace in the company of all believers and through the name of Jesus Christ our Lord, who is, with you and the Holy Spirit, one God forever and ever. *Amen.*†

The Concluding Prayer of the Church

Lord God, almighty and everlasting Father, you have brought me in safety to this new day: Preserve me with your mighty power, that I may not fall into sin, nor be overcome by adversity; and in all I do direct me to the fulfilling of your purpose; through Jesus Christ my Lord. *Amen.*†

The Midday Office   **To Be Observed on the Hour or Half Hour**
Between 11 a.m. and 2 p.m.

The Call to Prayer

Worship the LORD in the beauty of holiness;* let the whole earth tremble before him.

Tell it among the nations: "The LORD is King!* He has made the world so firm that it cannot be moved; he will judge the peoples with equity."

Psalm 96:9–10

The Request for Presence
Be my strong rock, a castle to keep me safe,* for you are my crag and my stronghold; for the sake of your Name, lead me and guide me.

Psalm 31:3

The Greeting
I love you, O LORD my strength,* LORD my stronghold, my crag, and my haven.
My God, my rock in whom I put my trust,* my shield, the horn of my salvation, and my refuge; you are worthy of praise.

Psalm 18:1–2

The Refrain for the Midday Lessons
Be strong and let your heart take courage,* all you who wait for the LORD.

Psalm 31:24

A Reading
The partridge will hatch eggs it has not laid. No different is the person who gets riches unjustly: his days half done, they will desert him and he prove a fool after all.

Jeremiah 17:11

The Refrain
Be strong and let your heart take courage,* all you who wait for the LORD.

The Midday Psalm   Hear My Voice, O God
Hear my voice, O God, when I complain;* protect my life from fear of the enemy.
Hide me from the conspiracy of the wicked,* from the mob of the evildoers.
They sharpen their tongue like a sword,* and aim their bitter words like arrows,
That they may shoot down the blameless from ambush;* they will shoot without warning and are not afraid.
They hold fast to their evil course;* they plan how they may hide their snares.
They say, "Who will see us? Who will find out our crimes?* We have thought of the perfect plot."

Psalm 64:1–6

The Refrain
Be strong and let your heart take courage,* all you who wait for the LORD.

The Small Verse
Show me your mercy, O Lord;* And grant me your salvation.
Clothe your ministers with righteousness;* Let your people sing with joy.
Give peace, O Lord, in all the world;* For only in you can I live in safety.
Lord, keep this nation under your care;* And guide me in the way of justice and truth.

Let your way be known upon earth;* Your saving health among all nations.
Let not the needy, O Lord, be forgotten;* Nor the hope of the poor be taken away.
Create in me a clean heart, O God;* And sustain me with your Holy Spirit.†

The Lord's Prayer

The Prayer Appointed for the Week
Holy Father, creator and sustaining wisdom of all that is, both in heaven and on
    earth, take from me those thoughts, actions and objects that are hurtful. Give
    me instead those things that are profitable for me and all who seek rightly to
    praise you. I ask this grace in the company of all believers and through the
    name of Jesus Christ our Lord, who is, with you and the Holy Spirit, one God
    forever and ever. *Amen.*†

The Concluding Prayer of the Church
Heavenly Father, you have promised to hear what we ask in the Name of your
    Son: Accept and fulfill my petitions, I pray, not as I ask in my ignorance, nor as
    I deserve in my sinfulness, but as you know and love me in your Son Jesus
    Christ our Lord. *Amen.*†

The Vespers Office   **To Be Observed on the Hour or Half Hour**
                                              Between 5 and 8 p.m.

The Call to Prayer
Open my lips, O Lord,* and my mouth shall proclaim your praise.
Had you desired it, I would have offered sacrifice,* but you take no delight in
    burnt offerings.
The sacrifice of God is a troubled spirit;* and a broken and contrite heart, O God,
    you will not despise.

Psalm 51:16–18

The Request for Presence
Your word is a lantern to my feet* and a light upon my path.
Accept, O Lord, the willing tribute of my lips,* and teach me your judgments.

Psalm 119:105ff

The Greeting
You, O Lord, are my lamp;* my God, you make my darkness bright.

Psalm 18:29

The Hymn   *Come, Thou Long-Expected Jesus*
    Come, thou long-expected Jesus,   Born your people to deliver,
    Born to set your people free;   Born a child and yet a King,
    From our fears and sins release us;   Born to reign in us forever,
    Let us find our rest in thee.   Now your gracious kingdom bring.

By your own eternal Spirit
Rule in all our hearts alone;
By your all-sufficient merit
Raise us to your glorious throne.

Charles Wesley

The Refrain for the Vespers Lessons

Your love, O Lord, for ever will I sing;* from age to age my mouth will proclaim your faithfulness.

Psalm 89:1

The Vespers Psalm   He Shatters the Doors of Bronze

Give thanks to the Lord, for he is good,* and his mercy endures for ever.

Let all those whom the Lord has redeemed proclaim* that he redeemed them from the hand of the foe.

He gathered them out of the lands;* from the east and from the west, from the north and from the south.

He led them out of darkness and deep gloom* and broke their bonds asunder.

Let them give thanks to the Lord for his mercy* and the wonders he does for his children.

For he shatters the doors of bronze* and breaks in two the iron bars.

Let them give thanks to the Lord for his mercy* and the wonders he does for his children.

Let them offer a sacrifice of thanksgiving* and tell of his acts with shouts of joy.

Psalm 107:1ff

The Refrain

Your love, O Lord, for ever will I sing;* from age to age my mouth will proclaim your faithfulness.

The Gloria

The Lord's Prayer

The Prayer Appointed for the Week

Holy Father, creator and sustaining wisdom of all that is, both in heaven and on earth, take from me those thoughts, actions and objects that are hurtful. Give me instead those things that are profitable for me and all who seek rightly to praise you. I ask this grace in the company of all believers and through the name of Jesus Christ our Lord, who is, with you and the Holy Spirit, one God forever and ever. *Amen.*†

The Concluding Prayer of the Church

Protect me, Lord, as I stay awake; watch over me as I sleep, that awake I may watch with Christ, and asleep, rest in his peace. *Amen.*

The Morning Office   **To Be Observed on the Hour or Half Hour**
                                          Between 6 and 9 a.m.

The Call to Prayer
Bless our God, you peoples;* make the voice of his praise to be heard;
Who holds our souls in life,* and will not allow our feet to slip.

Psalm 66:7–8

The Request for Presence
Come to me speedily, O God. You are my helper and my deliverer;* Lord, do not
    tarry.

Psalm 70:5–6

The Greeting
You are my hope, O Lord God,* my confidence since I was young.
I have been sustained by you ever since I was born; from my mother's womb you
    have been my strength;* my praise shall be always of you.

Psalm 71:5–6

The Refrain for the Morning Lessons
"Be still, then, and know that I am God;* I will be exalted among the nations; I will
    be exalted in the earth."

Psalm 46:11

A Reading
Jesus taught us, saying: 'Whoever holds to my commandments and keeps them is
    the one who loves me; and whoever loves me will be loved by my Father, and I
    shall love him and reveal myself to him.'

John 14:21

The Refrain
"Be still, then, and know that I am God;* I will be exalted among the nations; I will
    be exalted in the earth."

The Morning Psalm   *Let the Hearts of Those Who Seek the Lord Rejoice*
Give thanks to the Lord and call upon his Name;* make known his deeds among
    the peoples.
Sing to him, sing praise to him,* and speak of all his marvelous works.
Glory in his holy Name;* let the hearts of those who seek the Lord rejoice.
Search for the Lord and his strength;* continually seek his face.
Remember the marvels he has done,* his wonders and the judgments of his
    mouth,
He is the Lord our God;* his judgments prevail in all the world.

Psalm 105:1–5, 7

The Refrain
"Be still, then, and know that I am God;* I will be exalted among the nations; I will
    be exalted in the earth."

The Cry of the Church
Lord, have mercy on us. Christ, have mercy on us. Lord, have mercy on us.

The Lord's Prayer

The Prayer Appointed for the Week
Holy Father, creator and sustaining wisdom of all that is, both in heaven and on
  earth, take from me those thoughts, actions and objects that are hurtful. Give
  me instead those things that are profitable for me and all who seek rightly to
  praise you. I ask this grace in the company of all believers and through the
  name of Jesus Christ our Lord, who is, with you and the Holy Spirit, one God
  forever and ever. *Amen.*†

The Concluding Prayer of the Church
Lord God, almighty and everlasting Father, you have brought me in safety to this
  new day: Preserve me with your mighty power, that I may not fall into sin, nor
  be overcome by adversity; and in all I do direct me to the fulfilling of your purpose; through Jesus Christ my Lord. *Amen.*†

The Midday Office   **To Be Observed on the Hour or Half Hour**
                                        Between 11 a.m. and 2 p.m.

The Call to Prayer
Praise the LORD, for the LORD is good;* sing praises to his Name, for it is lovely.
                                                                    Psalm 135:3

The Request for Presence
Hear the voice of my prayer when I cry out to you,* when I lift up my hands to
  your holy of holies.
                                                                     Psalm 28:2

The Greeting
  You are God: we praise you;
  You are the Lord: we acclaim you;
  You are the eternal Father:
  All creation worships you.
  To you all angels, all the powers of heaven,
  Cherubim and Seraphim, sing in endless praise:
      Holy, holy, holy Lord, God of power and might,
      heaven and earth are full of your glory.
  The glorious company of apostles praises you.
  The noble fellowship of prophets praises you.
  The white-robed army of martyrs praises you.
  Throughout the world the holy Church acclaims you;
      Father, of majesty unbounded,
      your true and only Son, worthy of all worship,
      and the Holy Spirit, advocate and guide.

You, Christ, are the king of glory,
the eternal Son of the Father.
When you became man to set us free,
you did not shun the Virgin's womb.
You overcame the sting of death
and opened the kingdom of heaven to all believers.
You are seated at God's right hand in glory.
We believe that you will come and be our judge.
Come then, Lord, and help your people,
bought with the price of your own blood,
and bring us with your saints
to glory everlasting.

Te Deum

The Refrain for the Midday Lessons
But it is good for me to be near God;* I have made the Lord GOD my refuge.

Psalm 73:28

A Reading
Since the practice of virtue and the observance of the commandments form part of
prayer, those who pray as well as work at the tasks they have to do, and com-
bine their prayer with suitable activity, will be "praying always." This is the
only way in which it is possible never to stop praying.

Origen of Alexandria

The Refrain
But it is good for me to be near God; I have made the Lord GOD my refuge.

The Midday Psalm   *In Truth God Has Heard Me*
Come and listen, all you who fear God,* and I will tell you what he has done for me.
I called out to him with my mouth,* and his praise was on my tongue.
If I had found evil in my heart,* the LORD would not have heard me;
But in truth God has heard me;* he has attended to the voice of my prayer.
Blessed be God, who has not rejected my prayer,* nor withheld his love from me.

Psalm 66:14–18

The Refrain
But it is good for me to be near God;* I have made the Lord GOD my refuge.

The Gloria

The Lord's Prayer

The Prayer Appointed for the Week
Holy Father, creator and sustaining wisdom of all that is, both in heaven and on
earth, take from me those thoughts, actions and objects that are hurtful. Give
me instead those things that are profitable for me and all who seek rightly to
praise you. I ask this grace in the company of all believers and through the

name of Jesus Christ our Lord, who is, with you and the Holy Spirit, one God forever and ever. *Amen.*†

The Concluding Prayer of the Church

Almighty and eternal God, ruler of all things in heaven and earth: Mercifully accept my prayers, and strengthen me to do your will; through Jesus Christ our Lord. *Amen.*†

The Vespers Office   **To Be Observed on the Hour or Half Hour**
                                          Between 5 and 8 p.m.

The Call to Prayer

Taste and see that the LORD is good;* happy are those who trust in him!

Psalm 34:8

The Request for Presence

Lord, hear my prayer, and let my cry come before you;* hide not your face from me in the day of my trouble.
Incline your ear to me;* when I call, make haste to answer me,
For my days drift away like smoke,* and my bones are hot as burning coals.
My heart is smitten like grass and withered,* so that I forget to eat my bread.
Because of the voice of my groaning* I am but skin and bones.
I have become like a vulture in the wilderness,* like an owl among the ruins.
I lie awake and groan;* I am like a sparrow, lonely on a house-top.

Psalm 102:1–7

The Greeting

To you, O LORD, I lift up my soul;* my God I put my trust in you . . .

Psalm 25:1

The Hymn

Lord Jesus Christ, abide with me,
Now that the sun has run its course;
Let hope not be obscured by night,
But may faith's darkness be as light.

Lord Jesus Christ, grant me your peace,
And when the trials of earth shall cease,
Grant me the morning light of grace,
The radiant splendor of your face.

Immortal, Holy, Threefold Light,
Yours be the kingdom, pow'r, and might;
All glory be eternally
To you, life giving Trinity!

Jerome Leaman

The Refrain for the Vespers Lessons
Oh, that Israel's deliverance would come out of Zion!* When God restores the fortunes of his people Jacob will rejoice and Israel be glad.

Psalm 53:6

The Vespers Psalm　　　　　　　　　　　*Turn Again to Your Rest, O My Soul*
The LORD watches over the innocent;* I was brought very low, and he helped me.
Turn again to your rest, O my soul.* For the LORD has treated you well.
For you have rescued my life from death,* my eyes from tears, and my feet from stumbling.
I will walk in the presence of the LORD* in the land of the living.

Psalm 116:5–8

The Refrain
Oh, that Israel's deliverance would come out of Zion!* When God restores the fortunes of his people Jacob will rejoice and Israel be glad.

The Cry of the Church
Lord, have mercy on us. Christ, have mercy on us. Lord, have mercy on us.

The Lord's Prayer

The Prayer Appointed for the Week
Holy Father, creator and sustaining wisdom of all that is, both in heaven and on earth, take from me those thoughts, actions and objects that are hurtful. Give me instead those things that are profitable for me and all who seek rightly to praise you. I ask this grace in the company of all believers and through the name of Jesus Christ our Lord, who is, with you and the Holy Spirit, one God forever and ever. *Amen*.†

The Concluding Prayer of the Church
Stay, O Lord, with those who wake, or watch, or weep tonight, and give your angels and saints charge over those who sleep.

The Morning Office　　　　　　**To Be Observed on the Hour or Half Hour**
Between 6 and 9 a.m.

The Call to Prayer
Open my lips, O LORD,* and my mouth shall proclaim your praise.

Psalm 51:16

The Request for Presence
Send out your light and your truth, that they may lead me,* and bring me to your holy hill and to your dwelling;
That I may go to the altar of God, to the God of my joy and gladness;* and on the harp I will give thanks to you, O God my God.

Psalm 43:3–4

The Greeting

Who is like you, LORD God of hosts?* O mighty LORD, your faithfulness is all
around you.
Righteousness and justice are the foundations of your throne;* love and truth go
before your face.

Psalm 89:8ff

The Refrain for the Morning Lessons

I will walk in the presence of the LORD* in the land of the living.

Psalm 116:8

A Reading

He was setting out on a journey when a man ran up, knelt before him and put this
question to him, 'Good master, what must I do to inherit eternal life?' Jesus said
to him, 'Why do you call me good? No one is good but God alone. You know
the commandments: *You shall not kill; You shall not commit adultery; You shall not
steal; You shall not give false witness;* You shall not defraud; *Honor your father and
mother.'* And he said to him, 'Master, I have kept all these since my earliest days.'
Jesus looked steadily at him and he was filled with love for him, and he said,
'You need to do one thing more. Go and sell what you own and give the money
to the poor, and you will have treasure in heaven; then come, follow me.' But his
face fell at these words and he went away sad, for he was a man of great wealth.
Jesus looked round and said to his disciples, 'How hard it is for those who have
riches to enter the kingdom of God! . . . It is easier for a camel to pass through
the eye of a needle than for someone rich to enter the kingdom of God.' They
were more astonished than ever, saying to one another 'In that case who can be
saved?' Jesus gazed at them and said, 'By human resources it is impossible, but
not for God: because for God everything is possible.'

Mark 10:17–27

The Refrain

I will walk in the presence of the LORD* in the land of the living.

The Morning Psalm   *In the Beginning, O Lord*

In the beginning, O LORD, you laid the foundations of the earth,* and the heavens
are the work of your hands;
They shall perish, but you will endure; they all shall wear out like a garment;* as
clothing you will change them, and they shall be changed;
But you are always the same,* and your years will never end.
The children of your servants shall continue,* and their offspring shall stand fast
in your sight.

Psalm 102:25–28

The Refrain

I will walk in the presence of the LORD* in the land of the living.

The Cry of the Church

In the evening, in the morning, and at noonday, I will complain and lament,* and he will hear my voice.

Psalm 55:18

The Lord's Prayer

The Prayer Appointed for the Week

Holy Father, creator and sustaining wisdom of all that is, both in heaven and on earth, take from me those thoughts, actions and objects that are hurtful. Give me instead those things that are profitable for me and all who seek rightly to praise you. I ask this grace in the company of all believers and through the name of Jesus Christ our Lord, who is, with you and the Holy Spirit, one God forever and ever. *Amen.*†

The Concluding Prayer of the Church

Lord God, almighty and everlasting Father, you have brought me in safety to this new day: Preserve me with your mighty power, that I may not fall into sin, nor be overcome by adversity; and in all I do direct me to the fulfilling of your purpose; through Jesus Christ my Lord. *Amen.*†

The Midday Office

To Be Observed on the Hour or Half Hour Between 11 a.m. and 2 p.m.

The Call to Prayer

Sing to God, O kingdoms of the earth;* sing praises to the Lord
He rides in the heavens, the ancient heavens;* he sends forth his voice, his mighty voice.

Psalm 68:33–34

The Request for Presence

May God be merciful to us and bless us,* show us the light of his countenance and come to us.
Let your ways be known upon the earth,* your saving health among all nations.

Psalm 67:1–2

The Greeting

Exalt yourself above the heavens, O God,* and your glory all over the earth.
So that those who are dear to you may be delivered,* save with your right hand and answer me.

Psalm 108:5–6

The Refrain for the Midday Lessons

Righteousness and justice are the foundations of your throne;* love and truth go before your face.

Psalm 89:14

A Reading

Blessed be the God and Father of our Lord Jesus Christ, the merciful Father and the God who gives every possible encouragement; he supports us in every hardship, so that we are able to come to the support of others, in every hardship of theirs because of the encouragement that we ourselves receive from God.

2 Corinthians 1:3–4

The Refrain

Righteousness and justice are the foundations of your throne;* love and truth go before your face.

The Midday Psalm   *In Your Goodness, O God*

God, when you went forth before your people,* when you marched through the wilderness,

The earth shook, and the skies poured down rain,* at the presence of God, the God of Sinai, at the presence of God, the God of Israel.

You sent a gracious rain, O God, upon your inheritance;* you refreshed the land when it was weary.

Your people found their home in it;* in your goodness, O God, you have made provision for the poor.

Psalm 68:7–10

The Refrain

Righteousness and justice are the foundations of your throne;* love and truth go before your face.

The Gloria

The Lord's Prayer

The Prayer Appointed for the Week

Holy Father, creator and sustaining wisdom of all that is, both in heaven and on earth, take from me those thoughts, actions and objects that are hurtful. Give me instead those things that are profitable for me and all who seek rightly to praise you. I ask this grace in the company of all believers and through the name of Jesus Christ our Lord, who is, with you and the Holy Spirit, one God forever and ever. *Amen.*†

The Concluding Prayer of the Church

Almighty God, to whom our needs are known before we ask. Help me to ask only what accords with your will; and those good things which I dare not, or in my blindness cannot ask, grant for the sake of your Son Jesus Christ our Lord. *Amen.*†

The Vespers Office   **To Be Observed on the Hour or Half Hour**
Between 5 and 8 p.m.

The Call to Prayer
Come, let us sing to the LORD;* let us shout for joy to the rock of our salvation.
Let us come before his presence with thanksgiving* and raise a loud shout to him
     with psalms.
For the LORD is a great God,* and a great king above all gods.
In his hands are the caverns of the earth,* and the heights of the hills are his also.
The sea is his, for he made it,* and his hands have molded the dry land.

Psalm 95:1–5

The Request for Presence
To you I lift up my eyes,* to you enthroned in the heavens.
As the eyes of servants look to the hand of their masters,* and the eyes of a maid to
     the hand of her mistress,
So our eyes look to the LORD our God,* until he shows his mercy.

Psalm 123:1–3

The Greeting
I put my trust in your mercy;* my heart is joyful because of your saving help.
I will sing to the LORD, for he has dealt with me richly;* I will praise the Name of
     the Lord Most High.

Psalm 13:5–6

The Hymn   *How Precious Is Your Steadfast Love, O God*
     How precious is your steadfast love, O God!
     All people may take refuge in the shadow of your wings.
     They feast on the abundance of your house,
     and you give them drink from the river of your delights.

     Happy are the people who know the festal shout,
     who walk in the light of your countenance;
     They exult your name all day long,
     and extol your righteousness.

     You are the glory of their strength;
     by your favor their horn is exalted.
     When deeds of iniquity overwhelm them,
     you forgive their transgressions.

     How precious is your steadfast love, O God!
     All people may take refuge in the shadow of your wings.
     O Lord my God, I will give thanks to you forever;
     I will exult and rejoice in your steadfast love.   ❖

The Refrain for the Vespers Lessons

For we are your people and the sheep of your pasture;* we will give you thanks
  for ever and show forth your praise from age to age.

Psalm 79:13

The Vespers Psalm   *Hosanna, LORD, Hosanna!*

Hosanna, LORD, hosanna!* LORD, send us now success.

Blessed is he who comes in the name of the LORD;* we bless you from the house of
  the LORD.

God is the LORD; he has shined upon us;* form a procession with branches up to
  the horns of the altar.

"You are my God, and I will thank you;* you are my God, and I will exalt you."

Give thanks to the LORD, for he is good;* his mercy endures for ever.

Psalm 118:25–29

The Refrain

For we are your people and the sheep of your pasture;* we will give you thanks
  for ever and show forth your praise from age to age.

The Cry of the Church

O God, come to my assistance! O Lord, make haste to help me!

The Lord's Prayer

The Prayer Appointed for the Week

Holy Father, creator and sustaining wisdom of all that is, both in heaven and on
  earth, take from me those thoughts, actions and objects that are hurtful. Give
  me instead those things that are profitable for me and all who seek rightly to
  praise you. I ask this grace in the company of all believers and through the
  name of Jesus Christ our Lord, who is, with you and the Holy Spirit, one God
  forever and ever. *Amen.*†

The Concluding Prayer of the Church

May God, the Lord, bless us with heavenly benediction, and make us pure and
  holy in his sight.

May the riches of his glory abound in us.

May He instruct us with the word of truth, inform us with the Gospel of salvation,
  and enrich us with his love, through Jesus Christ, our Lord.

Gelasian Sacramentary

The Morning Office   **To Be Observed on the Hour or Half Hour**
Between 6 and 9 a.m.

The Call to Prayer

Bless our God, you peoples;* make the voice of his praise to be heard;

Who holds our souls in life,* and will not allow our feet to slip.

Psalm 66:7–8

The Request for Presence
I call with my whole heart;* answer me, O Lord, that I may keep your statutes.
Hear my voice, O Lord, according to your loving-kindness;* according to your
    judgments, give me life.

Psalm 119:145ff

The Greeting
I am bound by the vow I made to you, O God;* I will present to you thank-
    offerings;
For you have rescued my soul from death and my feet from stumbling,* that I may
    walk before God in the light of the living.

Psalm 56:11–12

The Refrain for the Morning Lessons
The Lord has pleasure in those who fear him,* in those who await his gracious
    favor.

Psalm 147:12

A Reading   *The Song of Zechariah*
Blessed be the Lord, the God of Israel; for he has visited his people, he has set
    them free, and he has established for us a saving power in the house of his
    servant David, just as he proclaimed by the mouth of his holy prophets from
    ancient times, that he would save us from our enemies, and from the hands
    of all those who hate us, and show faithful love to our ancestors and so keep
    in mind his holy covenant. This was the oath he swore to our father
    Abraham, that he would grant us, free from fear, to be delivered from the
    hands of our enemies, to serve him in holiness and uprightness in his pres-
    ence all our days.
And you, little child, you shall be called the prophet of the Most High, for you will
    go before the Lord to prepare a way for him, to give his people knowledge of
    salvation through the forgiveness of their sins, because of the faithful love of
    our God in which the rising Sun has come from on high to visit us, to give light
    to those who live in darkness and the shadow dark as death, and to guide our
    feet into the way of peace.

Luke 1:68–79

The Refrain
The Lord has pleasure in those who fear him,* in those who await his gracious
    favor.

The Morning Psalm   *Proclaim the Greatness of Our God*
Proclaim the greatness of the Lord our God and fall down before his footstool;* he
    is the Holy One.
Moses and Aaron among his priests, and Samuel among those who call upon his
    Name,* they called upon the Lord and he answered them.
He spoke to them out of the pillar of cloud;* they kept his testimonies and the
    decree he gave them.

"O Lord our God, you answered them indeed;* you were a God who forgave
   them, yet punished them for their evil deeds."
Proclaim the greatness of the Lord our God and worship him upon his holy hill;*
   for the Lord our God is the Holy One.

Psalm 99:5–9

The Refrain
The Lord has pleasure in those who fear him,* in those who await his gracious
   favor.

The Cry of the Church
Lord, have mercy on us. Christ, have mercy on us. Lord, have mercy on us.

The Lord's Prayer

The Prayer Appointed for the Week
Holy Father, creator and sustaining wisdom of all that is, both in heaven and on
   earth, take from me those thoughts, actions and objects that are hurtful. Give
   me instead those things that are profitable for me and all who seek rightly to
   praise you. I ask this grace in the company of all believers and through the
   name of Jesus Christ our Lord, who is, with you and the Holy Spirit, one God
   forever and ever. *Amen.*†

The Concluding Prayer of the Church
Lord God, almighty and everlasting Father, you have brought me in safety to this
   new day: Preserve me with your mighty power, that I may not fall into sin, nor
   be overcome by adversity; and in all I do direct me to the fulfilling of your purpose; through Jesus Christ my Lord. *Amen.*†

The Midday Office   **To Be Observed on the Hour or Half Hour
                            Between 11 a.m. and 2 p.m.**

The Call to Prayer
Come, let us bow down, and bend the knee,* and kneel before the Lord our
   Maker.
For he is our God, and we are the people of his pasture and the sheep of his hand.

Psalm 95:6–7

The Request for Presence
Hear my prayer, O God;* do not hide yourself from my petition.
Listen to me and answer me.

Psalm 55:1–2

The Greeting
O God, you know my foolishness,* and my faults are not hidden from you.
Answer me, O Lord, for your love is kind;* in your great compassion, turn to me.

Psalm 69:6ff

The Refrain for the Midday Lessons
Our sins are stronger than we are,* but you will blot them out.
Psalm 65:3

A Reading
What god can compare with you for pardoning guilt and for overlooking crime? He does not harbor anger for ever since he delights in showing faithful love. Once more have pity on us, tread down our faults; throw all our sins to the bottom of the sea. Grant Jacob your faithfulness, and Abraham your faithful love, as you swore to our ancestors from the days of long ago.
Micah 7:18–20

The Refrain
Our sins are stronger than we are,* but you will blot them out.

The Midday Psalm   *For God Alone My Soul in Silence Waits*
For God alone my soul in silence waits;* truly, my hope is in him.
He alone is my rock and my salvation,* my stronghold, so that I shall not be shaken.
In God is my safety and my honor;* God is my strong rock and my refuge.
Put your trust in him always, O people,* pour out your hearts before him, for God is our refuge.
Those of high degree are but a fleeting breath,* even those of low estate can not be trusted.
On the scales they are lighter than a breath,* all of them together.
Put no trust in extortion; in robbery take no empty pride;* though wealth increase, set not your heart upon it.
God has spoken once, twice have I heard it,* that power belongs to God.
Steadfast love is yours, O Lord,* for you repay everyone according to his deed.
Psalm 62:6–14

The Refrain
Our sins are stronger than we are,* but you will blot them out.

The Cry of the Church
In the evening, in the morning, and at noonday, I will complain and lament,* and he will hear my voice.
Psalm 55:18

The Lord's Prayer

The Prayer Appointed for the Week
Holy Father, creator and sustaining wisdom of all that is, both in heaven and on earth, take from me those thoughts, actions and objects that are hurtful. Give me instead those things that are profitable for me and all who seek rightly to praise you. I ask this grace in the company of all believers and through the name of Jesus Christ our Lord, who is, with you and the Holy Spirit, one God forever and ever. *Amen.*†

The Concluding Prayer of the Church
Almighty God, whose most dear Son went not up to joy before he first suffered
   pain, and did not enter into glory before he was crucified: Mercifully grant that
   I, walking in the way of the cross, may find it to be none other than the way of
   life and peace; through Jesus Christ your Son my Lord. *Amen.*†

The Vespers Office   **To Be Observed on the Hour or Half Hour**
                                            Between 5 and 8 p.m.

The Call to Prayer
O tarry and await the LORD's pleasure; be strong, and he shall comfort your heart;*
   wait patiently for the LORD.

Psalm 27:18

The Request for Presence
Out of the depths have I called to you, O LORD; LORD, hear my voice;* let your ears
   consider well the voice of my supplication.

Psalm 130:1

The Greeting
For your Name's sake, O LORD,* forgive my sin, for it is great.

Psalm 25:10

The Hymn   *Just a Closer Walk with Thee*
   Just a closer walk with Thee;
   Grant it, Jesus, if you please,
   Daily walking close with Thee,
   Let it be, dear Lord, let it be.

   I am weak but You are strong,
   Jesus, keep me from all wrong.
   I'll be satisfied as long,
   As I walk—O let me walk—close with Thee.
   Please, dear Lord, let it be.

   When my feeble life is over,
   Time for me won't be no more,
   Guide me gently, safely over,
   To Thy kingdom's shore, to Thy shore.
   Please, dear Lord, let it be.
                              Spiritual

The Refrain for the Vespers Lessons
Let not those who hope in you be put to shame through me, Lord God of Hosts;*
   let not those who seek you be disgraced because of me, O God of Israel.

Psalm 69:7

The Vespers Psalm   *Against You Only Have I Sinned*
Have mercy on me, O God, according to your loving-kindness;* in your great
    compassion blot out my offenses.
Wash me through and through from my wickedness* and cleanse me from my sin.
For I know my transgressions,* and my sin is ever before me.
Against you only have I sinned* and done what is evil in your sight.
And so you are justified when you speak* and upright in your judgment.

Psalm 51:1–5

The Refrain
Let not those who hope in you be put to shame through me, Lord God of Hosts;*
    let not those who seek you be disgraced because of me, O God of Israel.

The Cry of the Church
Lord, have mercy on us. Christ, have mercy on us. Lord, have mercy on us.

The Lord's Prayer

The Prayer Appointed for the Week
Holy Father, creator and sustaining wisdom of all that is, both in heaven and on
    earth, take from me those thoughts, actions and objects that are hurtful. Give
    me instead those things that are profitable for me and all who seek rightly to
    praise you. I ask this grace in the company of all believers and through the
    name of Jesus Christ our Lord, who is, with you and the Holy Spirit, one God
    forever and ever. *Amen.*†

The Concluding Prayers of the Church
Almighty God, who has promised to hear the petitions of those who ask in your
    Son's Name: I beseech you mercifully to incline your ear to me who have made
    my prayers and supplications to you; and grant that those things which I have
    faithfully asked according to your will, may effectually be obtained, to the
    relief of my necessity, and to the setting forth of your glory; through Jesus
    Christ my Lord. *Amen.*†

May the souls of the faithful departed, through the mercy of God, rest in eternal
    peace. *Amen.*

The Morning Office   **To Be Observed on the Hour or Half Hour**
Between 6 and 9 a.m.

The Call to Prayer
Let us come before his presence with thanksgiving* and raise a loud shout to him
    with psalms.

Psalm 95:2

The Request for Presence
Lord God of hosts, hear my prayer;* hearken, O God of Jacob.

Psalm 84:7

The Greeting
My heart is firmly fixed, O God, my heart is fixed;* I will sing and make melody.
Wake up, my spirit; awake, lute and harp;* I myself will awaken the dawn.
I will confess you among the peoples, O Lord;* I will sing praise to you among the
nations.
For your loving-kindness is greater than the heavens,* and your faithfulness
reaches to the clouds.
Exalt yourself above the heavens, O God,* and your glory over all the earth.

Psalm 57:7–11

The Refrain for the Morning Lessons
On this day the Lord has acted;* we will rejoice and be glad in it.

Psalm 118:24

A Reading
Jesus taught us, saying: 'I shall not leave you orphans; I shall come to you. In a
short time the world will no longer see me; but you will see that I live and you
also will live. On that day you will know that I am in my Father and you in me
and I in you.'

John 14:18–20

The Refrain
On this day the Lord has acted;* we will rejoice and be glad in it.

The Morning Psalm   *All That Is Within Me, Bless His Holy Name*
Bless the Lord, O my soul,* all that is within me, bless his holy Name.
Bless the Lord, O my soul,* and forget not all his benefits.
He forgives all your sins* and heals all your infirmities;
He redeems your life from the grave* and crowns you with mercy and loving-
kindness;
He satisfies you with good things,* and your youth is renewed like an eagle's.

Psalm 103:1–5

The Refrain
On this day the Lord has acted;* we will rejoice and be glad in it.

The Small Verse
The Lord is a great God,* and a great King above all gods.
In his hand are the caverns of the earth,* and the heights of the hills are his also.
The sea is his, for he made it,* and his hands have molded the dry land.

Psalm 95:3–5

The Lord's Prayer

The Prayer Appointed for the Week
Holy Father, creator and sustaining wisdom of all that is, both in heaven and on
earth, take from me those thoughts, actions and objects that are hurtful. Give
me instead those things that are profitable for me and all who seek rightly to

praise you. I ask this grace in the company of all believers and through the name of Jesus Christ our Lord, who is, with you and the Holy Spirit, one God forever and ever. *Amen.*✝

The Concluding Prayer of the Church
Lord God, almighty and everlasting Father, you have brought me in safety to this new day: Preserve me with your mighty power, that I may not fall into sin, nor be overcome by adversity; and in all I do direct me to the fulfilling of your purpose; through Jesus Christ my Lord. *Amen.*✝

The Midday Office   To Be Observed on the Hour or Half Hour
                              Between 11 a.m. and 2 p.m.

The Call to Prayer
Bless God in the congregation;* bless the LORD, you that are of the fountain of Israel.

Psalm 68:26

The Request for Presence
I call upon you, O God, for you will answer me;* incline your ear to me and hear my words.

Psalm 17:6

The Greeting
You are my God, and I will thank you;* you are my God, and I will exalt you.

Psalm 118:28

The Refrain for the Midday Lessons
The LORD, the God of gods, has spoken;* he has called the earth from the rising of the sun to its setting.

Psalm 50:1

A Reading
Then I saw another angel, flying high overhead, sent to announce the gospel of eternity to all who live on the earth, every nation, race, language and tribe. He was calling, 'Fear God and glorify him, because the time has come for him to sit in judgment; worship *the maker of heaven and earth* and sea and the springs of water.'

Revelation 14:6–7

The Refrain
The LORD, the God of gods, has spoken;* he has called the earth from the rising of the sun to its setting.

The Midday Psalm   *He Has Led Captivity Captive*
The LORD gave the word;* great was the company of women who bore the tidings:
"Kings with their armies are fleeing away;* the women at home are dividing the spoils."

Though you lingered among the sheepfolds,* you shall be like a dove whose
   wings are covered with silver, whose feathers are like green gold.
When the Almighty scattered kings,* it was like snow falling in Zalmon.
O mighty mountain, O hill of Bashan!* O rugged mountain, O hill of Bashan!
Why do you look with envy, O rugged mountain, at the hill which God chose for
   his resting place?* Truly the LORD will dwell there for ever.
The chariots of God are twenty thousand, even thousands of thousands;* the LORD
   comes in holiness from Sinai.
You have gone up on high and led captivity captive; you have received gifts even
   from your enemies,* that the LORD God might dwell among them.
Blessed be the LORD day by day,* the God of our salvation, who bears our burdens.
He is our God, the God of our salvation;* God is the LORD, by whom we escape
   death.

Psalm 68:11ff

The Refrain
The LORD, the God of gods, has spoken;* he has called the earth from the rising of
   the sun to its setting.

The Gloria

The Lord's Prayer

The Prayer Appointed for the Week
Holy Father, creator and sustaining wisdom of all that is, both in heaven and on
   earth, take from me those thoughts, actions and objects that are hurtful. Give
   me instead those things that are profitable for me and all who seek rightly to
   praise you. I ask this grace in the company of all believers and through the
   name of Jesus Christ our Lord, who is, with you and the Holy Spirit, one God
   forever and ever. *Amen.*†

The Concluding Prayer of the Church
O God, the source of eternal light: Shed forth your unending day upon all of us
   who watch for you, that our lips may praise you, our lives may bless you, and
   our worship may give you glory; through Jesus Christ our Lord. *Amen.*†

The Vespers Office   **To Be Observed on the Hour or Half Hour**
Between 5 and 8 p.m.

The Call to Prayer
We will bless the LORD,* from this time forth for evermore. Hallelujah!

Psalm 115:18

The Request for Presence
Answer me when I call, O God, defender of my cause;* you set me free when I am
   hard-pressed; have mercy on me and hear my prayer.

Psalm 4:1

The Greeting
Be exalted, O LORD, in your might;* we will sing and praise your power.

Psalm 21:14

The Hymn
> God, creation's secret force,
> Yourself unmoved, yet motion's source,
> Who from the morn till evening's ray
> Through every change does guide the day:

> Grant me, when this short life is past,
> The glorious evening that shall last;
> That, by a holy death attained
> Eternal glory may be gained.

> Grant this, O Father ever one
> With Jesus Christ Your only Son
> And Holy Ghost, whom all adore,
> Reigning and blest forevermore. *Amen.*

adapted from THE SHORT BREVIARY

The Refrain for the Vespers Lessons
Among the gods there is none like you, O LORD,* nor anything like your works.

Psalm 86:8

The Vespers Psalm   *All Things Look to You, O LORD*
O LORD, how manifold are your works!* in wisdom you have made them all; the earth is full of your creatures.
Yonder is the great and wide sea with its living things too many to number,* creatures both small and great.
There move the ships, and there is that Leviathan,* which you have made for the sport of it.
All of them look to you* to give them their food in due season.
You give it to them; they gather it;* you open your hand, and they are filled with good things.
You hide your face, and they are terrified;* you take away their breath, and they die and return to their dust.
You send forth your Spirit, and they are created;* and so you renew the face of the earth.

Psalm 104:25–31

The Refrain
Among the gods there is none like you, O LORD,* nor anything like your works.

The Gloria

The Lord's Prayer

The Prayer Appointed for the Week
Holy Father, creator and sustaining wisdom of all that is, both in heaven and on
earth, take from me those thoughts, actions and objects that are hurtful. Give
me instead those things that are profitable for me and all who seek rightly to
praise you. I ask this grace in the company of all believers and through the
name of Jesus Christ our Lord, who is, with you and the Holy Spirit, one God
forever and ever. *Amen*.†

The Concluding Prayer of the Church
For an angel of peace, faithful guardian and guide of our souls and our bodies, we
beseech thee, O Lord.

Orthodox

ﮩﯿﮩ

The Morning Office   **To Be Observed on the Hour or Half Hour**
                                          Between 6 and 9 a.m.

The Call to Prayer
Ascribe to the LORD, you families of the peoples;* ascribe to the LORD honor and
power.
Ascribe to the LORD the honor due his Name;* bring offerings and come into his
courts.
Worship the LORD in the beauty of holiness;* let the whole world tremble before
him.

Psalm 96:7ff

The Request for Presence
Send out your light and your truth, that they may lead me,* and bring me to your
holy hill and to your dwelling;
That I may go to the altar of God, to the God of my joy and gladness;* and on the
harp I will give thanks to you, O God my God.

Psalm 43:3–4

The Greeting
As the deer longs for the water-brooks,* so longs my soul for you, O God.
My soul is athirst for God, athirst for the living God.

Psalm 42:1–2

The Refrain for the Morning Lessons
For who is God, but the LORD?* Who is the Rock except our God?

Psalm 18:32

A Reading

Jesus taught us, saying: 'Therefore, everyone who listens to these words of mine
and acts on them will be like a sensible man who built his house on rock. Rain
came down, floods rose, gales blew and hurled themselves against that house,
and it did not fall: it was founded on rock. But everyone who listens to these
words of mine and does not act on them will be like the stupid man who built
his house on sand. Rain came down, floods rose, gales blew and struck that
house, and it fell; and what a fall it had!'

Matthew 7:24–27

The Refrain

For who is God, but the Lord?* Who is the Rock except our God?

The Morning Psalm   *His Commandments Stand Fast Forever*

Great are the deeds of the Lord!* they are studied by all who delight in them.

His work is full of majesty and splendor,* and his righteousness endures for ever.

He makes his marvelous works to be remembered;* the Lord is gracious and full
of compassion.

He gives food to those who fear him;* he is ever mindful of his covenant.

He has shown his people the power of his works* in giving them the lands of the
nations.

The works of his hands are faithfulness and justice;* all his commandments are sure.

They stand fast for ever and ever,* because they are done in truth and equity.

He sent redemption to his people; he commanded his covenant for ever;* holy and
awesome is his Name.

Psalm 111:2–9

The Refrain

For who is God, but the Lord?* Who is the Rock except our God?

The Cry of the Church

Lord, have mercy on us. Christ, have mercy on us. Lord, have mercy on us.

The Lord's Prayer

The Prayer Appointed for the Week

O God, from whom all good proceeds: Grant that by your inspiration I may think
those things that are right, and by your merciful guiding may do them;
through Jesus Christ our Lord, who lives and reigns with you and the Holy
Spirit, one God for ever and ever. *Amen.†*

The Concluding Prayer of the Church

Lord God, almighty and everlasting Father, you have brought me in safety to this
new day: Preserve me with your mighty power, that I may not fall into sin, nor
be overcome by adversity; and in all I do direct me to the fulfilling of your purpose; through Jesus Christ my Lord. *Amen.†*

The Midday Office **To Be Observed on the Hour or Half Hour**
Between 11 a.m. and 2 p.m.

The Call to Prayer
Let us give thanks to the Lord for his mercy* and the wonders he does for his children.
For he satisfies the thirsty* and fills the hungry with good things.

adapted from Psalm 107:8–9

The Request for Presence
Let all who seek you rejoice in you and be glad;* let those who love your salvation
continually say, "Great is the Lord!"
Though I am poor and afflicted,* the Lord will have regard for me.
You are my helper and my deliverer;* do not tarry, O my God.

Psalm 40:17ff

The Greeting
I love you, O Lord my strength,* O Lord my stronghold, my crag, and my haven.
My God, my rock in whom I put my trust,* my shield, the horn of my salvation,
and my refuge; you are worthy of praise.

Psalm 18:1–2

The Refrain for the Midday Lessons
I will fulfill my vows to the Lord* in the presence of all his people.

Psalm 116:16

A Reading *The Second Song of Isaiah*
Seek out Yahweh while he is still to be found, call to him while he is still near. Let
the wicked abandon his ways and the evil one his thoughts. Let him turn back to
Yahweh, and he will take pity on him, to our God, for he is rich in forgiveness.
For my thoughts are not your thoughts and your ways are not my ways, declares
Yahweh. For the heavens are as high above the earth as my ways are above your
ways, and my thoughts above your thoughts. For, as the rain and the snow come
down from the sky and do not return before having watered the earth, fertilizing
it and making it germinate to provide seed for the sower and food to eat, so it is
with the word that goes from my mouth: it will not return to me unfilled or before
having carried out my good pleasure and having achieved what it was sent to do.

Isaiah 55:6–11

The Refrain
I will fulfill my vows to the Lord* in the presence of all his people.

The Midday Psalm *I Will Guide You with My Eye*
"I will instruct you and teach you in the way that you should go;* I will guide you
with my eye.
Do not be like a horse or mule, which have no understanding;* who must be fitted
with bit and bridle, or else they will not stay near you."

Psalm 32:9–10

The Refrain
I will fulfill my vows to the LORD* in the presence of all his people.

The Cry of the Church
O God, come to my assistance! O Lord, make haste to help me!

The Lord's Prayer

The Prayer Appointed for the Week
O God, from whom all good proceeds: Grant that by your inspiration I may think
    those things that are right, and by your merciful guiding may do them;
    through Jesus Christ our Lord, who lives and reigns with you and the Holy
    Spirit, one God for ever and ever. *Amen.*†

The Concluding Prayer of the Church
O God, you make me and your whole church glad with the weekly remembrance
    of the glorious resurrection of your Son our Lord: Give me this day such bless-
    ing through my worship of you, that the week to come may be spent in your
    favor; through Jesus Christ our Lord. *Amen.*†

The Vespers Office   **To Be Observed on the Hour or Half Hour**
                                                   Between 5 and 8 p.m.

The Call to Prayer
Let the Name of the LORD be blessed,* from this time forth for evermore.
From the rising of the sun to its going down* let the Name of the LORD be praised.

Psalm 113:2–3

The Request for Presence
As the eyes of servants look to the hand of their masters,* and the eyes of a maid to
    the hand of her mistress,
So our eyes look to you, O LORD our God,

adapted from Psalm 123:2–3

The Greeting
Blessed is the LORD!* for he has heard the voice of my prayer.

Psalm 28:7

The Hymn   *Sweet Hour of Prayer*
    Sweet hour of prayer, sweet hour of prayer,
    That calls me from a world of care,
    And bids me at my Father's throne,
    Make all my wants and wishes known!
    In seasons of distress and grief,
    My soul has often found relief,
    And often escaped the tempter's snare
    By your return, sweet hour of prayer.

Sweet hour of prayer, sweet hour of prayer,
Your wings shall my petition bear
To Him, whose truth and faithfulness
Engage the waiting soul to bless:
And since He bids me seek His face,
Believe His word, and trust His grace,
I'll cast on Him my every care,
And wait for you, sweet hour of prayer.

William W. Walford (adapted)

The Refrain for the Vespers Lessons

For you, O LORD, are good and forgiving,* and great is your love toward all who
call upon you.

Psalm 86:5

The Vespers Psalm   *Our Days Are Like the Grass*

The LORD has not dealt with us according to our sins,* nor rewarded us according
to our wickedness.
For as the heavens are high above the earth,* so is his mercy great upon those who
fear him.
As far as the east is from the west,* so far has he removed our sins from us.
As a father cares for his children,* so does the LORD care for those who fear him.
For he himself knows whereof we are made;* he remembers that we are but
dust.
Our days are like the grass;* we flourish like a flower of the field;
When the wind goes over it, it is gone,* and its place shall know it no more.
But the merciful goodness of the LORD endures for ever on those who fear him,*
and his righteous children's children;
On those who keep his covenant* and remember his commandments and do
them.
The LORD has set his throne in heaven,* and his kingship has dominion over all.
Bless the LORD, you angels of his, you mighty ones who do his bidding,* and hear-
ken to the voice of his word.
Bless the LORD, all you his hosts,* you ministers who do his will.
Bless the LORD, all you works of his, in all places of his dominion;* bless the LORD,
O my soul.

Psalm 103:10–22

The Refrain

For you, O LORD, are good and forgiving,* and great is your love toward all who
call upon you.

The Cry of the Church

Lord, have mercy on us. Christ, have mercy on us. Lord, have mercy on us.

The Lord's Prayer

The Prayer Appointed for the Week
O God, from whom all good proceeds: Grant that by your inspiration I may think
   those things that are right, and by your merciful guiding may do them;
   through Jesus Christ our Lord, who lives and reigns with you and the Holy
   Spirit, one God for ever and ever. *Amen.*†

The Concluding Prayer of the Church
In truth God has heard me;* he has attended to the voice of my prayer.
Blessed be God, who has not rejected my prayer,* nor withheld his love from me.
Psalm 66:17–18

The Morning Office

**To Be Observed on the Hour or Half Hour
Between 6 and 9 a.m.**

The Call to Prayer
Be strong and let your heart take courage,* all you who wait for the LORD.
Psalm 31:24

The Request for Presence
O LORD, watch over us* and save us from this generation for ever.
Psalm 12:7

The Greeting
Restore us, O God of hosts;* show the light of your countenance, and we shall be
   saved.
Psalm 80:3

The Refrain for the Morning Lessons
You strengthen me more and more;* you enfold me and comfort me.
Psalm 71:21

A Reading   *In remembrance of Barnabas, one of the circle of seventy who founded
   the Church. He was martyred for his faith, at Salamis, June 61 a.d.*

There was a Levite of Cypriot origin called Joseph whom the apostles surnamed
   Barnabas (which means 'son of encouragement').
Those who had scattered because of the persecution that arose over Stephen trav-
   eled as far as Phoenicia and Cyprus and Antioch, but they proclaimed the message only to Jews. Some of them, however, who came from Cyprus and Cyrene,
   went to Antioch where they started preaching to the Greeks, proclaiming the
   good news of the Lord Jesus to them. The Lord helped them, and a great number believed and were converted to the Lord.
The news of them came to the ears of the church in Jerusalem and they sent
   Barnabas out to Antioch. There he was glad to see for himself that God had
   given grace, and he urged them all to remain faithful to the Lord with heartfelt

devotion; for he was a good man, filled with the Holy Spirit and with faith. And a large number of people were won over to the Lord.

Barnabas then left for Tarsus to look for Saul, and when he found him he brought him to Antioch. And it happened that they stayed together in that church a whole year, instructing a large number of people. It was at Antioch that the disciples were first called 'Christians.'

Acts 4:36, 11:19–26

The Refrain
You strengthen me more and more;* you enfold me and comfort me,

The Morning Psalm   *I Love to Do Your Will, O My God*
In the roll of the book it is written concerning me:* 'I love to do your will, O my God; your law is deep in my heart.'

I proclaimed righteousness in the great congregation;* behold, I did not restrain my lips; and that, O LORD, you know.

Your righteousness have I not hidden in my heart; I have spoken of your faithfulness and your deliverance;* I have not concealed your love and faithfulness from the great congregation.

Let them be ashamed and altogether dismayed who seek after my life to destroy it;* let them draw back and be disgraced who take pleasure in my misfortune.

Let those who say "Aha!" and gloat over me be confounded,* because they are ashamed.

Let all who seek you rejoice in you and be glad;* let those who love your salvation continually say, "Great is the LORD!"

Psalm 40:9–11, 15–17

The Refrain
You strengthen me more and more;* you enfold me and comfort me.

The Gloria

The Lord's Prayer

The Prayer Appointed for the Week
O God, from whom all good proceeds: Grant that by your inspiration I may think those things that are right, and by your merciful guiding may do them; through Jesus Christ our Lord, who lives and reigns with you and the Holy Spirit, one God for ever and ever. *Amen.*†

The Concluding Prayer of the Church
Almighty God, who gave to your servant Barnabas boldness to confess the Name of Jesus Christ before the rulers of this world, and courage to die for his faith: Grant that I and all your Church may also be ready to give a reason for the hope that is in us, and to suffer gladly for the sake of our Lord Jesus Christ; who lives and reigns with you and the Holy Paraclete, one God, for ever and ever. *Amen.*†

The Midday Office   **To Be Observed on the Hour or Half Hour**
                                         Between 11 a.m. and 2 p.m.

The Call to Prayer
Give thanks to the LORD and call upon his Name;* make known his deeds among
  the peoples.
Sing to him, sing praises to him,* and speak of all his marvelous works.
Glory in his holy Name;* let the hearts of those who seek the LORD rejoice.
Search for the LORD and his strength;* continually seek his face.
Remember the marvels he has done,* his wonders and the judgments of his
  mouth.

Psalm 105:1–5

The Request for Presence
Teach me your way, O LORD, and I will walk in your truth;* knit my heart to you
  that I may fear your Name.
I will thank you, O LORD my God, with all my heart,* and glorify your Name for
  evermore.

Psalm 86:11–12

The Greeting
My mouth shall recount your mighty acts and saving deeds all the day long;*
  though I can not know the number of them.

Psalm 71:15

The Refrain for the Midday Lessons
I will confess you among the peoples, O LORD;* I will sing praises to you among
  the nations.

Psalm 108:3

A Reading
Lord YAHWEH has given me a disciple's tongue, for me to know how to give a
  word of comfort to the weary. Morning by morning he makes my ears alert to
  listen like a disciple. The Lord YAHWEH has opened my ear.

Isaiah 50:4

The Refrain
I will confess you among the peoples, O LORD;* I will sing praises to you among
  the nations.

The Midday Psalm   *In God the Lord, Whose Word I Praise*
In God the LORD, whose word I praise, in God I trust and will not be afraid,* for
  what can mortals do to me?
I am bound by the vow I made to you, O God;* I will present to you thank-
  offerings;
For you have rescued my soul from death and my feet from stumbling,* that I may
  walk before God in the light of the living.

Psalm 56:10–12

The Refrain
I will confess you among the peoples, O LORD;* I will sing praises to you among the nations.

The Small Verse
The Lord is my shepherd and nothing is wanting to me.* In green pastures He has settled me.

THE SHORT BREVIARY

The Lord's Prayer

The Prayer Appointed for the Week
O God, from whom all good proceeds: Grant that by your inspiration I may think those things that are right, and by your merciful guiding may do them; through Jesus Christ our Lord, who lives and reigns with you and the Holy Spirit, one God for ever and ever. *Amen.*†

The Concluding Prayer of the Church
O Lord my God, to you and your service I devote myself, body, soul, and spirit. Fill my memory with the record of your mighty works; enlighten my understanding with the light of your Holy Spirit; and may all the desires of my heart and will center in what you would have me do. Make me an instrument of your salvation for the people entrusted to my care, and let me by my life and speaking set forth your true and living Word. Be always with me in carrying out the duties of my salvation; in praises heighten my love and gratitude; in speaking of You give me readiness of thought and expression; and grant that, by the clearness and brightness of your holy Word, all the world may be drawn to your blessed kingdom. All this I ask for the sake of your Son my Savior Jesus Christ. *Amen.*†

The Vespers Office   **To Be Observed on the Hour or Half Hour**
                                                        Between 5 and 8 p.m.

The Call to Prayer
Love the LORD, all you who worship him;* the LORD protects the faithful, but repays to the full those who act haughtily.

Psalm 31:23

The Request for Presence
Teach me your way, O LORD, and I will walk in your truth;* knit my heart to you that I may fear your Name.

Psalm 86:11

The Greeting
Whom have I in heaven but you?* And having you I desire nothing upon earth.

Psalm 73:25

The Hymn   *Faith of Our Fathers*
> Faith of our Fathers! Living still
> In spite of dungeon, fire, and sword,
> O how our hearts beat high with joy
> whenever we hear that glorious word!
> Faith of our fathers, holy faith!
> We will be true to you till death.
>
> Faith of our fathers! We will love
> Both friend and foe in all our strife,
> And preach you, too, as love knows how
> By kindly words and virtuous life:
> Faith of our fathers, holy faith!
> We will be true to you till death.

> *Frederick W. Faber (adapted)*

The Refrain for the Vespers Lessons
Let the faithful rejoice in triumph;* let them be joyful on their beds.

> *Psalm 149:5*

The Vespers Psalm   *That the Generation to Come Might Know*
That which we have heard and known, and what our forefathers have told us,* we
    will not hide from their children.
We will recount to generations to come the praiseworthy deeds and the power of
    the LORD,* and the wonderful works he has done.
He gave his decrees to Jacob and established a law for Israel,* which he com-
    manded them to teach their children;
That the generations to come might know and the children yet unborn;* that they
    in their turn might tell it to their children;
So that they might put their trust in God,* and not forget the deeds of God, but
    keep his commandments;
And not be like their forefathers, a stubborn and rebellious generation,* a genera-
    tion whose heart was not steadfast, and whose spirit was not faithful to God.

> *Psalm 78:3–8*

The Refrain
Let the faithful rejoice in triumph;* let them be joyful on their beds.

The Gloria

The Lord's Prayer

The Prayer Appointed for the Week
O God, from whom all good proceeds: Grant that by your inspiration I may think
    those things that are right, and by your merciful guiding may do them;
    through Jesus Christ our Lord, who lives and reigns with you and the Holy
    Spirit, one God for ever and ever. *Amen.*†

The Concluding Prayer of the Church

God be in my head
    and in my understanding.
God be in mine eyes
    and in my looking.
God be in my mouth
    and in my speaking.

God be in my heart
    and in my thinking.
God be at mine end
    and my departing.

Sarum Primer, 1527

The Morning Office

**To Be Observed on the Hour or Half Hour
Between 6 and 9 a.m.**

The Call to Prayer

Sing praise to the LORD who dwells in Zion;* proclaim to the peoples the things he
has done.

Psalm 9:11

The Request for Presence

May God be merciful to us and bless us,* show us the light of his countenance and
come to us.

Psalm 67:1

The Greeting

Awesome things will you show us in your righteousness, O God of our salvation,*
O Hope of all the ends of the earth and of the seas that are far away.

Psalm 65:5

The Refrain for the Morning Lessons

From now onwards all generations will call me blessed, for the Almighty has done
great things for me.

Luke 1:48

A Reading

Mary set out at that time and went as quickly as she could to a town in the hill
country of Judah. She went into Zechariah's house and greeted her kinswoman
Elizabeth. Now as soon as Elizabeth heard Mary's greeting, the baby she was
carrying leapt in her womb and Elizabeth was filled with the Holy Spirit. She
gave a loud cry and said, "Of all women you are the most blessed, and blessed
is the fruit of your womb. Why should I be honored with a visit from the
mother of my Lord? For the moment your greeting reached my ears, the child
in my womb leapt for joy. Yes, blessed is she who believed that the promise
made her by the Lord would be fulfilled."

And Mary said:
>"My soul proclaims the greatness of the Lord
>and my spirit *exults in God my savior;*
>because *he has looked upon his lowly handmaid.*
>Yes, from this day forward all generations will call me blessed,
>for the Almighty has done great things for me.
>*Holy is his name,*
>and *his mercy reaches from age to age for those who fear him."*

Luke 1:39–50 KJV

The Refrain
From this day forward all generations will call me blessed, for the Almighty has done great things for me.

The Morning Psalm   *I Thank You with All I Am*

I thank you with all I am,
I join heaven's chorus.
I bow toward your holy temple,
to praise your name.

By your love and fidelity,
you display to all
the glory of your name and promise.
As soon as I call, you act,
renewing my strength.

Around the world,
rulers praise you
for your commanding word.
They sing of your ways,
"Great is your glory, Lord."

Though high up,
you see the lowly;
though far away,
you keep an eye on the proud.

When I face an opponent,
you keep me alive.
You reach out your hand,
your right hand saves me.

Lord, take up my cause,
Your love lasts for ever.
Do not abandon
what your hands have made.

Psalm 138:1–8 from THE PSALTER

The Refrain
From this day forward all generations will call me blessed, for the Almighty has done great things for me.

The Cry of the Church
O God, come to my assistance! O Lord, make haste to help me!

The Lord's Prayer

The Prayer Appointed for the Week
O God, from whom all good proceeds: Grant that by your inspiration I may think those things that are right, and by your merciful guiding may do them; through Jesus Christ our Lord, who lives and reigns with you and the Holy Spirit, one God for ever and ever. *Amen.†*

The Concluding Prayer of the Church
Lord God, almighty and everlasting Father, you have brought me in safety to this
   new day: Preserve me with your mighty power, that I may not fall into sin, nor
   be overcome by adversity; and in all I do direct me to the fulfilling of your purpose; through Jesus Christ my Lord. *Amen.*†

The Midday Office   **To Be Observed on the Hour or Half Hour**
                                        Between 11 a.m. and 2 p.m.

The Call to Prayer
Sing to him, sing praise to him,* and speak of all his marvelous works.
                                                    Psalm 105:2

The Request for Presence
Let your countenance shine upon your servant* and teach me your statutes.
                                                    Psalm 119:135

The Greeting
Let all who seek you rejoice and be glad in you;* let those who love your salvation
   say for ever, "Great is the Lord!"
                                                    Psalm 70:4

The Refrain for the Midday Lessons
Happy are those who act with justice* and always do right!
                                                    Psalm 106:3

A Reading
Every achievement rots away and perishes, and with it goes its author. Happy the
   man who meditates on wisdom, and reasons with good sense, who studies her
   ways in his heart, and ponders her secrets. He pursues her like a hunter, and
   lies in wait by her path; he peeps in at her windows, and listens at her doors; he
   lodges close to her house, and fixes his peg in her walls; he pitches his tent at
   her side, and lodges in an excellent lodging; he set his children in her shade,
   and camps beneath her branches; he is sheltered by her from the heat, and in
   her glory he makes his home. Whoever fears the Lord will act like this, and
   whoever grasps the Law will obtain wisdom. She will come to meet him like a
   mother, and receive him like a virgin bride.
She will give him the bread of understanding to eat, and the water of wisdom to
   drink. He will lean on her and will not fall, he will rely on her and be not put to
   shame. She will raise him high above his neighbors, and in full assembly she will
   open his mouth. He will find happiness and a crown of joy, he will inherit an
   everlasting name. Fools will not gain possession of her, nor will sinners set eyes
   on her. She stands remote from pride, and liars cannot call her to mind. Praise is
   unseemly in a sinner's mouth, since it has not been put there by the Lord. For
   praise should only be uttered in wisdom, and the Lord himself then prompts it.
                                                    Ecclesiasticus 14:20–15:10

The Refrain
Happy are those who act with justice* and always do right!

The Midday Psalm   *The Nations Make Much Ado*
There is a river whose streams make glad the city of God,* the holy habitation of
    the Most High.
God is in the midst of her; She shall not be overthrown;* God shall help her at the
    break of day.
The nations make much ado, and the kingdoms are shaken;* God has spoken and
    the earth shall melt away.
The LORD of hosts is with us;* The God of Jacob is our stronghold.

Psalm 46:5–8

The Refrain
Happy are those who act with justice* and always do right!

The Gloria

The Lord's Prayer

The Prayer Appointed for the Week
O God, from whom all good proceeds: Grant that by your inspiration I may think
    those things that are right, and by your merciful guiding may do them;
    through Jesus Christ our Lord, who lives and reigns with you and the Holy
    Spirit, one God for ever and ever. *Amen.*†

The Concluding Prayer of the Church
God of mercy,
this midday moment of rest
is your welcome gift.
Bless the work we have begun,
make good defects
and let us finish it in a way that pleases you.
Grant this through Christ our Lord. *Amen.*

THE LITURGY OF THE HOURS, VOL. III

The Vespers Office   **To Be Observed on the Hour or Half Hour**
Between 5 and 8 p.m.

The Call to Prayer
Sing to the LORD, you servants of his;* give thanks for the remembrance of his holi-
    ness.
For his wrath endures but the twinkling of an eye,* his favor for a lifetime.

Psalm 30:4–5

The Request for Presence

Hear my prayer, O LORD, and give ear to my cry; . . . For I am but a sojourner with you,* a wayfarer, as all my forbears were.

Psalm 39:13–14

The Greeting

O God, when you went forth before your people* when you marched through the wilderness,

The earth shook, and the skies poured down rain, at the presence of God, the God of Sinai* at the presence of God, the God of Israel.

You sent a gracious rain, O God, upon your inheritance;* you refreshed the land when it was weary.

The Lord gave the word;* great was the company of women who bore the tidings.

Psalm 68:7ff

The Hymn   *Your Hand, O Lord, in Days of Old*

Your hand, O Lord, in days of old
Was strong to heal and save;
You triumphed over pain and death,
O'er darkness and the grave.
To you they went, the blind, the mute,
The palsied and the lame,
The leper set apart and shunned,
The sick and those in shame.

And then your touch brought life and health,
Gave speech and strength and sight;
And youth renewed, with health restored,
Claimed you, the Lord of light.
And so, O Lord, be near to bless,
Almighty now as then,
In every street, in every home,
In every troubled friend.

O be our mighty healer still,
Lord of life and death;
Restore and strengthen, soothe and bless
With your almighty breath.
On hands that work and eyes that see,
Your healing wisdom pour,
That whole and sick, weak and strong
May praise you evermore.

Edward Plumptre

The Refrain for the Vespers Lessons

Weeping may spend the night,* but joy comes in the morning.

Psalm 30:6

The Vespers Psalm   *My Soul Is Quieted Within Me*
O Lord, I am not proud;* I have no haughty looks.
I do not occupy myself with great matters,* or do things that are too hard for me.
But I still my soul and make it quiet, like a child upon its mother's breast;* my soul
    is quieted within me.

Psalm 131:1–3

The Refrain
Weeping may spend the night,* but joy comes in the morning.

The Gloria

The Lord's Prayer

The Prayer Appointed for the Week
O God, from whom all good proceeds: Grant that by your inspiration I may think
    those things that are right, and by your merciful guiding may do them;
    through Jesus Christ our Lord, who lives and reigns with you and the Holy
    Spirit, one God for ever and ever. *Amen.*†

The Concluding Prayer of the Church
Hear, O Lord, your servants, offering evening praises to your Name. Through the
    silent hours of the night deign to watch over us, whom You have protected in
    all dangers of the day. Through Jesus Christ our Lord. *Amen.*

Anglo-Saxon, Traditional

The Morning Office   **To Be Observed on the Hour or Half Hour**
Between 6 and 9 a.m.

The Call to Prayer
Wake up, my spirit; awake lute and harp;* I myself will waken the dawn.

Psalm 57:8

The Request for Presence
O God of hosts,* show the light of your countenance, and we shall be saved.

Psalm 80:7

The Greeting
My lips will sing with joy when I play to you,* and so will my soul, which you
    have redeemed.

Psalm 71:23

The Refrain for the Morning Lessons
Send forth your strength, O God;* establish, O God, what you have wrought for us.

Psalm 68:28

A Reading
Jesus said: 'As long as the day lasts we must carry out the work of the one who
    sent me; the night will soon be here when no one can work. As long as I am in
    the world I am the light of the world.'

John 9:4–5

The Refrain
Send forth your strength, O God;* establish, O God, what you have wrought for us.

The Morning Psalm   *Your Testimonies Are Very Sure*
The waters have lifted up, O LORD, the waters have lifted up their voice;* the
    waters have lifted up their pounding waves.
Mightier than the sound of many waters, mightier than the breakers of the sea,*
    mightier is the LORD who dwells on high.
Your testimonies are very sure,* and holiness adorns your house, O LORD, for ever
    and for evermore.

Psalm 93:4–6

The Refrain
Send forth your strength, O God;* establish, O God, what you have wrought for us.

The Gloria

The Lord's Prayer

The Prayer Appointed for the Week
O God, from whom all good proceeds: Grant that by your inspiration I may think
    those things that are right, and by your merciful guiding may do them;
    through Jesus Christ our Lord, who lives and reigns with you and the Holy
    Spirit, one God for ever and ever. *Amen.*†

The Concluding Prayer of the Church
Lord God, almighty and everlasting Father, you have brought me in safety to this
    new day: Preserve me with your mighty power, that I may not fall into sin, nor
    be overcome by adversity; and in all I do direct me to the fulfilling of your pur-
    pose; through Jesus Christ my Lord. *Amen.*†

The Midday Office   **To Be Observed on the Hour or Half Hour**
                                         Between 11 a.m. and 2 p.m.

The Call to Prayer
Let us make a vow to the LORD, our God and keep it;* let all around him bring gifts
    to him who is worthy to be feared.

adapted from Psalm 76:11

The Request for Presence
Let the peoples praise you, O God;* let all the peoples praise you.

Psalm 67:3

The Greeting
Happy are the people whose strength is in you!* whose hearts are set on the pilgrims' way.

Psalm 84:4

The Refrain for the Midday Lessons
All the nations you have made will come and worship you, O Lord,* and glorify your Name.

Psalm 86:9

A Reading
. . . They all had harps from God, and they were singing the hymn of Moses, the servant of God, and the hymn of the Lamb: 'How great and wonderful are all your works, Lord God Almighty; just and true are all your ways, *King of Nations.* Who would not revere and *praise your name, O Lord?* For you alone are holy, *and all nations will come and adore you* for the many acts of saving justice you have shown.'

Revelation 15:2–4

The Refrain
All the nations you have made will come and worship you, O Lord,* and glorify your Name.

The Midday Psalm   *Your Wonders Are More Than I Can Count*
Great things are they that you have done, O Lord my God! How great your wonders and your plans for us!* there is none who can be compared with you.
Oh, that I could make them known and tell them!* but they are more than I can count.

Psalm 40:5–6

The Refrain
All the nations you have made will come and worship you, O Lord,* and glorify your Name.

The Small Verse
'I am the Alpha and the Omega,' says the Lord God, who is, who was, and who is to come, the Almighty.

Revelation 1:8

The Lord's Prayer

The Prayer Appointed for the Week
O God, from whom all good proceeds: Grant that by your inspiration I may think those things that are right, and by your merciful guiding may do them; through Jesus Christ our Lord, who lives and reigns with you and the Holy Spirit, one God for ever and ever. *Amen.†*

The Concluding Prayer of the Church
Let us bless the Lord God living and true! Let us always render him praise, glory,
honor, blessing, and all good things! Amen. Amen. So be it! So be it!

St. Francis of Assisi

The Vespers Office   **To Be Observed on the Hour or Half Hour**
                                          Between 5 and 8 p.m.

The Call to Prayer
Be glad, you righteous, and rejoice in the LORD;* shout for joy, all who are true of
heart.

Psalm 32:12

The Request for Presence
Exalt yourself above the heavens, O God,* and your glory over all the earth.

Psalm 57:11

The Greeting
May God give us his blessing,* and may all the ends of the earth stand in awe of
him.

Psalm 67:7

The Hymn   *O Worship the King, All Glorious Above!*
    O Worship the King, all glorious above!
    O gratefully sing his power and his love!
    Our shield and defender, the Ancient of Days,
    Pavilioned in splendor, and girded with praise.

    O tell of his might! O sing of his grace!
    Whose robe is the light, whose canopy space.
    His chariots of wrath the deep thunderclouds form,
    And dark is his path on the wings of the storm.

    The earth, with its store of wonders untold,
    Almighty, your power hath founded of old,
    And established it fast by a changeless decree,
    And round it hath cast, like a mantle the sea.

    Your bountiful care, what tongue can recite?
    It breathes in the air, it shines in the light;
    It streams from the hills; it descends to the plain,
    and sweetly distills in the dew and the rain.

    Frail children of dust, and feeble as frail,
    In you do we trust, nor find you to fail;
    Your mercies, how tender! How firm to the end!
    Our maker, defender, redeemer, and friend!

Robert Grant (adapted)

The Refrain for the Vespers Lessons
Let your ways be known upon earth,* your saving health among all nations.

Psalm 67:2

The Vespers Psalm   ***Sing Praises to His Name***
Sing to God, sing praises to his Name; exalt him who rides upon the heavens;*
    YAHWEH is his Name, rejoice before him!
Father of orphans, defender of widows,* God is his holy habitation!

Psalm 68:4–5

The Refrain
Let your ways be known upon earth,* your saving health among all nations.

The Cry of the Church
In the evening, in the morning, and at noonday, I will complain and lament,* and
    he will hear my voice.

Psalm 55:18

The Lord's Prayer

The Prayer Appointed for the Week
O God, from whom all good proceeds: Grant that by your inspiration I may think
    those things that are right, and by your merciful guiding may do them;
    through Jesus Christ our Lord, who lives and reigns with you and the Holy
    Spirit, one God for ever and ever. *Amen.*†

The Concluding Prayer of the Church
Almighty and eternal God, rulers of all things in heaven and earth: Mercifully
    accept the prayers of your people everywhere, and strengthen each of us to do
    your will; through Jesus Christ my Lord. *Amen.*†

The Morning Office   **To Be Observed on the Hour or Half Hour**
Between 6 and 9 a.m.

The Call to Prayer
Come, let us sing to the LORD; . . . For the LORD is a great God,* and a great King
    above all gods.

Psalm 95:1, 3

The Request for Presence
Gladden the soul of your servant,* for to you, O LORD, I lift up my soul.

Psalm 86:4

The Greeting
Exalt yourself above the heavens, O God,* and your glory over all the earth.

Psalm 57:6

The Refrain for the Morning Lessons
Let not those who hope in you be put to shame through me, Lord GOD of hosts;*
  let not those who seek you be disgraced because of me.

Psalm 69:7

A Reading
Jesus taught us, saying: 'Be on your guard, stay awake, because you never know
  when the time will come. It is like a man traveling abroad: he has gone from his
  home, and left his servants in charge, each with his own work to do; and he has
  told the doorkeeper to stay awake. So stay awake, because you do not know
  when the master of the house is coming, evening, midnight, cockcrow, or
  dawn; if he comes unexpectedly, he must not find you asleep. And what I am
  saying to you I say to all: Stay awake!'

Mark 13:33–37

The Refrain
Let not those who hope in you be put to shame through me, Lord GOD of hosts;*
  let not those who seek you be disgraced because of me.

The Morning Psalm   **Let the Earth Be Glad**
Let the heavens rejoice, and let the earth be glad; let the sea thunder and all that is
  in it;* let the field be joyful and all that is therein.
Then shall all the trees of the wood shout for joy before the LORD when he comes,*
  when he comes to judge the earth.
He will judge the world with righteousness* and the peoples with his truth.

Psalm 96:11–13

The Refrain
Let not those who hope in you be put to shame through me, Lord GOD of hosts;*
  let not those who seek you be disgraced because of me.

The Gloria

The Lord's Prayer

The Prayer Appointed for the Week
O God, from whom all good proceeds: Grant that by your inspiration I may think
  those things that are right, and by your merciful guiding may do them;
  through Jesus Christ our Lord, who lives and reigns with you and the Holy
  Spirit, one God for ever and ever. *Amen.*†

The Concluding Prayer of the Church
Lord God, almighty and everlasting Father, you have brought me in safety to this
  new day: Preserve me with your mighty power, that I may not fall into sin, nor
  be overcome by adversity; and in all I do direct me to the fulfilling of your purpose; through Jesus Christ my Lord. *Amen.*†

The Midday Office	To Be Observed on the Hour or Half Hour
	Between 11 a.m. and 2 p.m.

The Call to Prayer
"Come now, let us reason together," says the LORD.

Isaiah 1:18 KJV

The Request for Presence
Awake, O my God, decree justice;* let the assembly of peoples gather around you.
Let the malice of the wicked come to an end, but establish the righteous;* for you
    test the mind and heart, O righteous God.

Psalm 7:7, 10

The Greeting
Deliver me, O LORD, by your hand* from those whose portion in life is this
    world . . .

Psalm 17:14

The Refrain for the Midday Lessons
Righteousness shall go before him,* and peace shall be a pathway for his feet.

Psalm 85:13

A Reading
In my letter I wrote to you that you should have nothing to do with people living
    immoral lives. I was not including everybody in this present world who is sex-
    ually immoral, or everybody who is greedy, or dishonest, or worships false
    gods—that would mean you would have to cut yourselves off completely from
    the world. In fact what I meant was that you were not to have anything to do
    with anyone going by the name of brother who is sexually immoral, or is
    greedy, or worships false gods, or is a slanderer or a drunkard or dishonest;
    never even have a meal with anyone of that kind. It is no concern of mine to
    judge outsiders. It is for you to judge those who are inside, is it not? But out-
    siders are for God to judge.

I Corinthians 5:9–13

The Refrain
Righteousness shall go before him,* and peace shall be a pathway for his feet.

The Midday Psalm *Righteousness Is the Scepter of Your Kingdom*
Your throne, O God, endures for ever and ever,* a scepter of righteousness is the
    scepter of your kingdom; you love righteousness and hate iniquity.
Therefore God, your God, has anointed you* with the oil of gladness above your
    fellows.
All your garments are fragrant with myrrh, aloes, and cassia,* and the music of
    strings from ivory palaces makes you glad.
Kings' daughters stand among the ladies of the court;* on your right hand is the
    queen, adorned with the gold of Ophir.

Psalm 45:7–10

The Refrain
Righteousness shall go before him,* and peace shall be a pathway for his feet.

The Cry of the Church
Lord, have mercy on us. Christ, have mercy on us. Lord, have mercy on us.

The Lord's Prayer

The Prayer Appointed for the Week
O God, from whom all good proceeds: Grant that by your inspiration I may think
those things that are right, and by your merciful guiding may do them;
through Jesus Christ our Lord, who lives and reigns with you and the Holy
Spirit, one God for ever and ever. *Amen.*†

The Concluding Prayer of the Church
Renew in my heart, O God, the gift of your Holy Spirit, so that I may love you
fully in all that I do and love all others as Christ loves me. May all that I do proclaim the good news that you are God with us. *Amen.*†

The Vespers Office　　　　　　　**To Be Observed on the Hour or Half Hour**
Between 5 and 8 p.m.

The Call to Prayer
Exalt him who rides upon the heavens;* YAHWEH is his Name, rejoice before him!
Psalm 68:4

The Request for Presence
Hearken to my voice, O LORD, when I call;* have mercy on me and answer me.
You speak in my heart and say, "Seek my face."* Your face, LORD, will I seek.
Psalm 27:10–11

The Greeting
　　O gracious Light,
　　pure brightness of the everlasting Father in heaven,
　　O Jesus Christ, holy and blessed!

　　Now as we come to the setting of the sun,
　　and our eyes behold the vesper light,
　　we sing praises O God: Father, Son and Holy Spirit.

　　You are worthy at all times to be praised by happy voices,
　　O Son of God, O giver of life,
　　and to be glorified through all the worlds.
Phos Hilaron

The Hymn

We praise you, O God; we acknowledge you to be the Lord.
All earth worships you, the Father everlasting.
To you all Angels cry aloud,
the Heavens and all the Powers therein.
To you Cherubim and Seraphim continually cry:
  Holy, holy, holy, Lord God of Sabaoth;
  Heaven and earth are full of your majesty and your glory.
The glorious company of the apostles praise you.
The goodly fellowship of the prophets praise you.
The noble army of martyrs praise you.
The holy Church throughout all the world acknowledges you,
  the Father, of an infinite majesty,
  your adorable, true, and only Son,
  also the Holy Ghost the Comforter.

You are the King of Glory, O Christ.
You are the everlasting Son of the Father.
When you took it upon yourself to deliver man,
you humbled yourself to be born of a Virgin.
When you had overcome the sharpness of death,
you opened the kingdom of heaven to all believers.
You sit at the right hand of God, in the Glory of the Father.
We believe that you will come to be our judge.
  We therefore pray, help your servants,
  whom you have redeemed by your precious blood.
  Count them among your saints,
  in glory everlasting.

        adapted from the TE DEUM

The Refrain for the Vespers Lessons

The LORD is my light and my salvation: Whom then shall I fear?* The LORD is the
strength of my life; of whom then shall I be afraid?

        Psalm 27:1

The Vespers Psalm   *Bless the* LORD, *All You His Hosts*

Bless the LORD, you angels of his, you mighty ones who do his bidding,* and hear-
ken to the voice of his word.
Bless the LORD, all you his hosts,* you ministers of his who do his will.
Bless the LORD, all you works of his, in all places of his dominion;* bless the LORD,
O my soul.

        Psalm 103:20–22

The Refrain

The LORD is my light and my salvation: Whom then shall I fear?* The LORD is the
strength of my life; of whom then shall I be afraid?

The Cry of the Church
O Lamb of God, that takes away the sins of the world, have mercy upon me.
O Lamb of God, that takes away the sins of the world, have mercy upon me.
O Lamb of God, that takes away the sins of the world, grant me your peace.

The Lord's Prayer

The Prayer Appointed for the Week
O God, from whom all good proceeds: Grant that by your inspiration I may think
those things that are right, and by your merciful guiding may do them;
through Jesus Christ our Lord, who lives and reigns with you and the Holy
Spirit, one God for ever and ever. *Amen.*†

The Concluding Prayer of the Church
Protect me, Lord, as I stay awake; watch over me as I sleep, that awake I may
watch with Christ, and asleep, rest in his peace. *Amen.*†

The Morning Office   **To Be Observed on the Hour or Half Hour**
                                           Between 6 and 9 a.m.

The Call to Prayer
Come now and see the works of God,* how wonderful he is in his doing toward
all people.

Psalm 66:4

The Request for Presence
Satisfy us by your loving-kindness in the morning;* so shall we rejoice and be glad
all the days of our life.

Psalm 90:14

The Greeting
Save us, O LORD our God, and gather us from among the nations,* that we may
give thanks to your holy Name and glory in your praise.

Psalm 106:47

The Refrain for the Morning Lessons
Mercy and truth have met together;* righteousness and peace have kissed each
other.

Psalm 85:10

A Reading
Jesus taught us, saying: 'I have loved you just as the Father has loved me. Remain
in my love. If you keep my commandments you will remain in my love, just as
I have kept my Father's commandments and remain in his love. I have told
you this so that my own joy may be in you and your joy complete. This is my
commandment: love one another, as I have loved you. No one can have greater
love than to lay down his life for his friends.'

John 15:9–13

The Refrain

Mercy and truth have met together;* righteousness and peace have kissed each other.

The Morning Psalm   *The Fear of the Lord Is Clean and Endures For Ever*

The law of the Lord is perfect and revives the soul;* the testimony of the Lord is sure and gives wisdom to the innocent.

The statutes of the Lord are just and rejoice the heart;* the commandment of the Lord is clear and gives light to the eyes.

The fear of the Lord is clean and endures for ever;* the judgments of the Lord are true and righteous altogether.

More to be desired are they than gold, more than much fine gold;* sweeter far than honey, than honey in the comb.

By them also is your servant enlightened,* and in keeping them there is great reward.

Psalm 19:7–11

The Refrain

Mercy and truth have met together;* righteousness and peace have kissed each other.

The Cry of the Church

Lord, have mercy on us. Christ, have mercy on us. Lord, have mercy on us.

The Lord's Prayer

The Prayer Appointed for the Week

O God, from whom all good proceeds: Grant that by your inspiration I may think those things that are right, and by your merciful guiding may do them; through Jesus Christ our Lord, who lives and reigns with you and the Holy Spirit, one God for ever and ever. *Amen.†*

The Concluding Prayer of the Church

Lord God, almighty and everlasting Father, you have brought me in safety to this new day: Preserve me with your mighty power, that I may not fall into sin, nor be overcome by adversity; and in all I do direct me to the fulfilling of your purpose; through Jesus Christ my Lord. *Amen.†*

The Midday Office   **To Be Observed on the Hour or Half Hour**
Between 11 a.m. and 2 p.m.

The Call to Prayer

Worship the Lord in the beauty of holiness;* let the whole earth tremble before him.

Psalm 96:9

The Request for Presence

Remember not our past sins; let your compassion be swift to meet us;

Psalm 79:8

The Greeting
There is forgiveness with you;* therefore you shall be feared.

Psalm 130:3

The Refrain for the Midday Lessons
Keep watch over my life, for I am faithful;* save your servant whose trust is in you.

adapted from Psalm 86:2

A Reading
Hear the commandments of God to his people: I am the Lord your God who brought you out of bondage. You shall have no other gods but me. *Amen. Lord have mercy.*
You shall not make for yourself any idol. *Amen. Lord have mercy.*
You shall not invoke the Name of the Lord your God. *Amen. Lord have mercy.*
Remember the Sabbath day and keep it holy. *Amen. Lord have mercy.*
Honor your father and your mother. *Amen. Lord have mercy.*
You shall not commit murder. *Amen. Lord have mercy.*
You shall not commit adultery. *Amen. Lord have mercy.*
You shall not steal. *Amen. Lord have mercy.*
You shall not be a false witness. *Amen. Lord have mercy.*
You shall not covet anything that belongs to your neighbor. *Amen. Lord have mercy.*

The Refrain
Keep watch over my life, for I am faithful;* save your servant whose trust is in you.

The Midday Psalm   *Oh, How I Love Your Law, O Lord*
Oh, how I love your law, O Lord!
        It is my meditation all day long.
How sweet are your words to my taste,
        sweeter than honey to my mouth.
The law of your mouth is better to me
        than thousands of gold and silver pieces.
Your word is a lamp to my feet
        and a light to my path.
Your decrees are my heritage forever;
        they are the joy of my heart.
Your statutes have been my song
        wherever I make my home.
My lips will pour forth praise,
        because you teach me your statutes.
My tongue will sing of our promise,
        for all your commandments are right. ❖

The Refrain
Keep watch over my life, for I am faithful;* save your servant whose trust is in you.

The Small Verse
Create in me a clean heart, O God,* and renew a right spirit within me.
Cast me not away from your presence* and take not your holy Spirit from me.
Give me the joy of your saving help again* and sustain me with your bountiful
 spirit.

Psalm 51:11–13

The Lord's Prayer

The Prayer Appointed for the Week
O God, from whom all good proceeds: Grant that by your inspiration I may think
 those things that are right, and by your merciful guiding may do them;
 through Jesus Christ our Lord, who lives and reigns with you and the Holy
 Spirit, one God for ever and ever. *Amen.*†

The Concluding Prayer of the Church
Lord Jesus Christ, by your death you took away the sting of death: Grant me to so
 follow in faith where you have led the way, that I may at length fall asleep peacefully in you and wake in your likeness; for your tender mercies' sake. *Amen.*†

The Vespers Office   **To Be Observed on the Hour or Half Hour**

Between 5 and 8 p.m.

The Call to Prayer
Praise the Lord, all you nations;* laud him, all you peoples.
For his loving-kindness toward us is great,* and the faithfulness of the Lord
 endures for ever.

Psalm 117:1–2

The Request for Presence
Help us, O God our Savior, for the glory of your Name;* deliver us and forgive us
 our sins, for your Name's sake.

Psalm 79:9

The Greeting
You are to be praised, O God, in Zion . . . To you that hear prayer shall all flesh
 come,* because of their transgressions.

Psalm 65:1–2

The Hymn
 God has made an everlasting covenant with his people,
  and he never ceases to bless them.
 Grateful for these gifts, I confidently direct my prayer to him:
  Lord, bless your people.

Save your people, Lord,
　　and bless your inheritance.
Gather into one body all who bear the name of Christian,
　　that the world may believe in Christ whom you have sent.
Give my friends and loved ones a share in divine life,
　　let them be symbols of Christ before men.
Show your love to those who are suffering,
　　open their eyes to the vision of your revelation.
Be compassionate to those who have died,
　　welcome them into the company of the faithful departed.

THE LITURGY OF THE HOURS, VOL. III

The Refrain for the Vespers Lesson
Your love, O LORD, reaches to the heavens,* and your faithfulness to the clouds.

Psalm 36:5

The Vespers Psalm   *Renew a Right Spirit Within Me*
Create me in a clean heart, O God,* and renew a right spirit within me.
Cast me not away from your presence* and take not your holy Spirit from me.
Give me the joy of your saving help again* and sustain me with your bountiful
　　spirit.

Psalm 51:11–13

The Refrain
Your love, O LORD, reaches to the heavens,* and your faithfulness to the clouds.

The Small Verse
The people that walked in darkness have seen a great light; on the inhabitants of a
　　country in shadow dark as death light has blazed forth.

Isaiah 9:1

The Lord's Prayer

The Prayer Appointed for the Week
O God, from whom all good proceeds: Grant that by your inspiration I may think
　　those things that are right, and by your merciful guiding may do them;
　　through Jesus Christ our Lord, who lives and reigns with you and the Holy
　　Spirit, one God for ever and ever. *Amen.*†

The Concluding Prayers of the Church
Lord Jesus Christ, by your death you took away the sting of death: Grant me so to
　　follow in faith where you have led the way, that I may at length fall asleep peace-
　　fully in you and wake up in your likeness; for your tender mercies' sake. *Amen.*†

May the souls of the faithful departed, through the mercy of God, rest in eternal
　　peace. *Amen.*

The Morning Office   **To Be Observed on the Hour or Half Hour**
Between 6 and 9 a.m.

The Call to Prayer
I will call upon God, and the Lord will deliver me.
In the evening, in the morning, and at the noonday, he will hear my voice.
He will bring me safely back . . . God who is enthroned of old, will hear me.†

The Request for Presence
Show us your mercy, O Lord,* and grant us your salvation.
Psalm 85:7

The Greeting
Happy are those whom you choose and draw to your courts to dwell there!* they
will be satisfied by the beauty of your house, by the holiness of your temple.
Psalm 65:4

The Refrain for the Morning Lessons
How dear to me is your dwelling, O Lord of hosts!
Psalm 84:1

A Reading
Jesus said: 'I am the good shepherd; I know my own and my own know me, just as
the Father knows me and I know the Father; and I lay down my life for my
sheep. And there are other sheep I have that are not of this fold, and I must lead
these too. They too will listen to my voice, and there will be only one flock, one
shepherd.'
John 10:14–16

The Refrain
How dear to me is your dwelling, O Lord of hosts!

The Morning Psalm   *More Than Watchmen for the Morning*
I wait for the Lord; my soul waits for him;* in his word is my hope.
My soul waits for the Lord, more than watchmen for the morning,* more than
watchmen for the morning,
O Israel, wait for the Lord,* for with the Lord there is mercy;
With him there is plenteous redemption,* and he shall redeem Israel from all their
sins.
Psalm 130:4–7

The Refrain
How dear to me is your dwelling, O Lord of hosts!

The Small Verse
My soul has a desire and longing for the courts of the Lord;* my heart and my
flesh rejoice in the living God.
Psalm 84:1

The Lord's Prayer

The Prayer Appointed for the Week
O God, from whom all good proceeds: Grant that by your inspiration I may think
those things that are right, and by your merciful guiding may do them;
through Jesus Christ our Lord, who lives and reigns with you and the Holy
Spirit, one God for ever and ever. *Amen.*†

The Concluding Prayer of the Church
Lord God, almighty and everlasting Father, you have brought me in safety to this
new day: Preserve me with your mighty power, that I may not fall into sin, nor
be overcome by adversity; and in all I do direct me to the fulfilling of your purpose; through Jesus Christ my Lord. *Amen.*†

The Midday Office   **To Be Observed on the Hour or Half Hour**
Between 11 a.m. and 2 p.m.

The Call to Prayer
Let the righteous be glad and rejoice before God;* let them be merry and joyful.
Psalm 68:3

The Request for Presence
You are the LORD; do not withhold your compassion from me;* let your love and
your faithfulness keep me safe forever.
Psalm 40:12

The Greeting
Therefore I will praise you upon the lyre for your faithfulness, O my God;* I will
sing to you with the harp, O Holy one of Israel.
Psalm 71:22

The Refrain for the Midday Lessons
For the LORD God is both sun and shield;* he will give grace and glory.
Psalm 84:10

A Reading
How beautiful on the mountains, are the feet of the messenger announcing peace,
of the messenger of good news, who proclaims salvation, and says to Zion,
'Your God is king!' The voices of your watchmen! Now they raise their voices,
shouting for joy together, for with their own eyes they have seen Yahweh
returning to Zion.
Isaiah 52:7–8

The Refrain
For the LORD God is both sun and shield;* he will give grace and glory;

The Midday Psalm   *The Lord Is My Shepherd*
The LORD is my shepherd,* I shall not want.
He makes me lie down in green pastures* and leads me beside still waters.
He revives my soul* and guides me along right pathways for his Name's sake.
Though I walk through the valley of the shadow of death, I shall fear no evil;* for
    you are with me; your rod and your staff, they comfort me.
You spread a table before me in the presence of those who trouble me;* you have
    anointed my head with oil, and my cup is running over.
Surely your goodness and mercy shall follow me all the days of my life,* and I will
    dwell in the house of the LORD for ever.

Psalm 23:1–6

The Refrain
For the LORD God is both sun and shield;* he will give grace and glory.

The Gloria

The Lord's Prayer

The Prayer Appointed for the Week
O God, from whom all good proceeds: Grant that by your inspiration I may think
    those things that are right, and by your merciful guiding may do them;
    through Jesus Christ our Lord, who lives and reigns with you and the Holy
    Spirit, one God for ever and ever. *Amen.*†

The Concluding Prayer of the Church
Almighty God, who after the creation of the world rested from all works and
    sanctified a day of rest for all your creatures: Grant that I, putting away all
    earthly anxieties, may be duly prepared for the service of public worship,
    and grant as well that my Sabbath upon earth may be a preparation for the
    eternal rest promised to your people in heaven; through Jesus Christ our
    Lord. *Amen.*†

The Vespers Office   **To Be Observed on the Hour or Half Hour**
                                                        Between 5 and 8 p.m.

The Call to Prayer
Proclaim with me the greatness of the LORD;* let us exalt his Name together.

Psalm 34:3

The Request for Presence
. . . Come to me speedily, O God,
You are my helper and my deliverer;* O LORD, do not tarry.

Psalm 70:5–6

The Greeting
Blessed be the Lord GOD, the God of Israel,* who alone does wondrous deeds!
And blessed be his glorious Name for ever!* And may all the earth be filled with
his glory. Amen. Amen.

Psalm 72:18–19

The Hymn   *All Who Inhabit Planet Earth*
All who inhabit planet earth—
Join us in praising God with mirth:
Alleluia! Alleluia!
Shine, Brother Sun, with splendid ray,
And, Sister Moon, turn night to day:
Alleluia, Alleluia, Alleluia, Alleluia, Alleluia!

Come, Brother Wind, and bring your friends—
Calm Weather, Breeze, and wild West Winds—
Join our praises, Alleluia!
Shower down upon us, streams of rain,
Great ocean, and bounding main:
Sister Water, bring your laughter,
Alleluia, Alleluia, Alleluia!

Lighten our darkness, Brother Fire,
Lift up our spirits even higher:
Alleluia, Alleluia!
Sustain and feed us, Mother Earth,
Make all our music sing with mirth,
Alleluia, Alleluia, Tra-la-la-la, Tra-la-la-la, Alleluia!

St. Francis of Assisi

The Refrain for the Vespers Lessons
Let all peoples know that you, whose Name is YAHWEH,* you alone are the Most
High over all the earth.

Psalm 83:18

The Vespers Psalm   *Praise Him in the Heights*
Hallelujah! Praise the LORD from the heavens;* praise him in the heights.
Praise him, all you angels of his;* praise him, all his host.
Praise him, sun and moon;* praise him, all you shining stars.
Praise him, heaven of heavens,* and you waters above the heavens.
Let them praise the Name of the LORD;* for he commanded, and they were cre-
ated.
He made them stand fast for ever and ever;* he gave them a law which shall not
pass away.

Psalm 148:1–6

The Refrain
Let all peoples know that you, whose Name is Yahweh,* you alone are the Most
    High over all the earth.

The Small Verse
Save your people, Lord, and bless your inheritance;* Govern and uphold them,
    now and always.
Day by day I bless you;* I praise your Name for ever.
Lord, keep me from all sin today;* Have mercy on me, Lord, have mercy.
Lord, show me your love and mercy;* For I put my trust in you.
In you, Lord, is my hope;* And I shall never hope in vain.†

The Lord's Prayer

The Prayer Appointed for the Week
O God, from whom all good proceeds: Grant that by your inspiration I may think
    those things that are right, and by your merciful guiding may do them;
    through Jesus Christ our Lord, who lives and reigns with you and the Holy
    Spirit, one God for ever and ever. *Amen.†*

The Concluding Prayer of the Church
Glory to the Father, who has woven garments of glory for the resurrection; wor-
    ship to the Son, who was clothed in them at his rising; thanksgiving to the
    Spirit, who keeps them for all the Saints; one nature in three, to him be praise.

                                           Syrian Orthodox

The Morning Office   **To Be Observed on the Hour or Half Hour**
                                             Between 6 and 9 a.m.

The Call to Prayer
Sing to the Lord, you servants of his;* give thanks for the remembrance of his holi-
    ness.
For his wrath endures but the twinkling of an eye,* his favor for a lifetime.
Weeping may spend the night,* but joy comes in the morning.

                                             Psalm 30:4-6

The Request for Presence
I cry out to you, O Lord;* I say, "You are my refuge, my portion in the land of the
    living."

                                           Psalm 142:5

The Greeting

Glory to God in the highest, and peace to his people on earth. Lord God, heavenly King, almighty God and Father, we worship you, we give you thanks, we praise you for your glory. Lord Jesus Christ, only Son of the Father, Lord God, Lamb of God, you take away the sins of the world: have mercy on us; you are seated at the right hand of the Father: receive our prayer. For you alone are the Holy One, you alone are the Lord, you alone are the Most High, Jesus Christ, with the Holy Spirit, in the glory of God the Father. *Amen.*

Gloria in Excelsis

The Refrain for the Morning Lessons

"I will appoint a time," says God;* "I will judge with equity . . ."

Psalm 75:2

A Reading

He came to Nazara, where he had been brought up, and went into the synagogue on the Sabbath day as he usually did. He stood up to read, and they handed him the scroll of the prophet Isaiah. Unrolling the scroll he found the place where it is written:

The spirit of the Lord is on me,
for he has anointed me
to bring the good news to the afflicted.
He has sent me to proclaim liberty to captives,
sight to the blind
to let the oppressed go free,
to proclaim a year of favor from the Lord.

He then rolled up the scroll, gave it back to the assistant and sat down. And all eyes in the synagogue were fixed on him. Then he began to speak to them, 'This text is being fulfilled today even while you are listening.' And he won the approval of all, and they were astonished by the gracious words that came from his lips.

Luke 4:16–22

The Refrain

"I will appoint a time," says God;* "I will judge with equity . . ."

The Morning Psalm   *"I Will Rise Up," Says the* Lord

"Because the needy are oppressed, and the poor cry out in misery,* I will rise up," says the Lord, "and give them the help they long for."
The words of the Lord are pure words,* like silver refined from ore and purified seven times in fire.
O Lord, watch over us* and save us from this generation for ever.

Psalm 12:5–7

The Refrain

"I will appoint a time," says God;* "I will judge with equity . . ."

The Gloria

The Lord's Prayer

The Prayer Appointed for the Week
Keep, O Lord, your household the Church in your steadfast faith and love, that
　　through your grace each of us may proclaim your truth with boldness, and min-
　　ister your justice with compassion; for the sake of our Savior Jesus Christ, who
　　lives and reigns with you and the Holy Spirit, one God, now and for ever. *Amen.*†

The Concluding Prayer of the Church
Lord God, almighty and everlasting Father, you have brought me in safety to this
　　new day: Preserve me with your mighty power, that I may not fall into sin, nor
　　be overcome by adversity; and in all I do direct me to the fulfilling of your pur-
　　pose; through Jesus Christ my Lord. *Amen.*†

The Midday Office　　　　　　　**To Be Observed on the Hour or Half Hour**
　　　　　　　　　　　　　　　　　Between 11 a.m. and 2 p.m.

The Call to Prayer
Open my lips, O Lord,* and my mouth shall proclaim your praise.
Had you desired it, I would have offered sacrifice,* but you take no delight in
　　burnt-offerings.
The sacrifice of God is a troubled spirit;* and a broken and contrite heart, O God,
　　you will not despise.

Psalm 51:16–18

The Request for Presence
Show us the light of your countenance, O God,* and come to us.

based on Psalm 67:1

The Greeting
You, O Lord, are my lamp;* my God, you make my darkness bright.
With you I will break down an enclosure;* with the help of my God I will scale any
　　wall.

Psalm 18:29–30

The Refrain for the Midday Lessons
Happy are those who trust in the Lord!* They do not resort to evil spirits or turn to
　　false gods.

Psalm 40:4

A Reading
Come, simple souls, you who have no feeling of devotion, no talent, not even the
　　first elements of instruction—you who cannot understand a single spiritual
　　term, who stand astonished at the eloquence of the learned whom you admire;
　　come, and I will teach you a secret which will place you far beyond these clever
　　minds. I will make perfection so easy you will find it everywhere and in every-

thing. I will unite you to God, and He will hold you by the hand from the moment you begin to practice what I tell you. Come, not to learn the map of this spiritual country, but to possess it, to walk in it at your ease without fear of losing your way. Come, not to study the theory of God's grace, or to learn what it has done in the past and is still doing, but simply to be open yourself to what it can do. You do not need to know what it has said to others, or repeat words intended only for them which you have overheard. His grace will speak to you, yourself, what is best for you.

Jean-Pierre de Caussade

The Refrain
Happy are those who trust in the LORD!* They do not resort to evil spirits or turn to false gods.

The Midday Psalm   *The Lord of Hosts Is with Us*
God is our refuge and strength,* a very present help in trouble.

Therefore we will not fear, though the earth be moved,* and though the mountains be toppled into the depths of the sea;

Though its waters rage and foam,* and though the mountains tremble at its tumult.

The LORD of Hosts is with us;* the God of Jacob is our stronghold.

There is a river whose streams make glad the city of God,* the holy habitation of the Most High.

God is in the midst of her; she shall not be overthrown;* God shall help her at the break of day.

The nations make much ado, and the kingdoms are shaken;* God has spoken, and the earth shall melt away.

The LORD of Hosts is with us* the God of Jacob is our stronghold.

Come now and look upon the works of the LORD,* what awesome things he has done on earth.

It is he who makes war to cease in all the world;* he breaks the bow, and shatters the spear, and burns the shields with fire.

"Be still, then, and know that I am God;* I will be exalted among the nations; I will be exalted in the earth."

The LORD of Hosts is with us;* the God of Jacob is our stronghold.

Psalm 46:1ff

The Refrain
Happy are those who trust in the LORD!* They do not resort to evil spirits or turn to false gods.

The Cry of the Church
Even so, come Lord Jesus

The Lord's Prayer

The Prayer Appointed for the Week

Keep, O Lord, your household the Church in your steadfast faith and love, that through your grace each of us may proclaim your truth with boldness, and minister your justice with compassion; for the sake of our Savior Jesus Christ, who lives and reigns with you and the Holy Spirit, one God, now and for ever. *Amen.*†

The Concluding Prayer of the Church

O God, you make me glad with the weekly remembrance of the glorious resurrection of your Son my Lord: Give me this day such blessing through my worship of you, that the week to come may be spent in your favor; through Jesus Christ our Lord. *Amen.*†

The Vespers Office   **To Be Observed on the Hour or Half Hour Between 5 and 8 p.m.**

The Call to Prayer

Bless the LORD, you angels of his, you mighty ones who do his bidding,* and hearken to the voice of his word.

Bless the LORD, all you his hosts,* you ministers of his who do his will.

Bless the LORD, all you works of his,* in all places of his dominion; Bless the LORD, O my soul.

Psalm 103:20–22

The Request for Presence

Hear, O Shepherd of Israel, leading Joseph like a flock;* shine forth, you that are enthroned upon the cherubim.

Psalm 80:1

The Greeting

Praise God from whom all blessings flow;
Praise him all creatures here below;
Praise Him above, you heavenly hosts;
Praise Father, Son, and Holy Ghost.

Doxology

The Hymn   *Now Thank We All Our God*

Now thank we all our God	O may this bounteous God
With heart and hands and voices,	Through all our life be near us,
Who wondrous things has done,	With ever joyful hearts
In whom his world rejoices;	And blessed peace to cheer us;
Who, from our mothers' arms,	And keep us in God's grace,
Has blessed us on our way	And guide us when perplexed,
With countless gifts of love,	And free us from all ills
And still is ours today.	In this world and the next.

All praise and thanks to God,
Who reigns in highest heaven,
To Father and to Son
And Spirit now be given.
The one eternal God,
Whom heaven and earth adore
The God who was, and is,
And shall be evermore.

Martin Rinkart

The Refrain for the Vespers Lessons
I will be joyful in the LORD;* I will glory in his victory.

Psalm 35:9

The Vespers Psalm   *May the Lord Strengthen You Out of Zion*
May the LORD answer you in the day of trouble,* the Name of the God of Jacob
    defend you;
Send your help from this holy place* and strengthen you out of Zion;
Remember all your offerings* and accept your burnt sacrifice;
Grant your heart's desire* and prosper all your plans.
We will shout for joy at your victory and triumph in the Name of our God;* may
    the LORD grant all your requests.

Psalm 20:1–5

The Refrain
I will be joyful in the LORD;* I will glory in his victory.

The Gloria

The Lord's Prayer

The Prayer Appointed for the Week
Keep, O Lord, your household the Church in your steadfast faith and love, that
    through your grace each of us may proclaim your truth with boldness, and
    minister your justice with compassion; for the sake of our Savior Jesus Christ,
    who lives and reigns with you and the Holy Spirit, one God, now and for ever.
    Amen.†

The Concluding Prayer of the Church
Lord God, whose Son our Savior Jesus Christ, triumphed over the powers of death
    and prepared for us our place in the new Jerusalem: Grant that I, who have this
    day given thanks for his resurrection, may praise you in the City of which he is
    the light, and where he lives and reigns for ever and ever. *Amen.*†

The Morning Office   **To Be Observed on the Hour or Half Hour**
                                          Between 6 and 9 a.m.

The Call to Prayer
Worship the LORD in the beauty of holiness;* let the whole earth tremble before
   him.

Psalm 96:9

The Request for Presence   *Listen, Lord—A Prayer*
   O Lord, we come this morning
   Knee-bowed and body-bent
   Before thy throne of grace.
   O Lord—this morning—
   Bow our hearts beneath our knees,
   And our knees in the lonesome valley.
   We come this morning—
   Like empty pitchers to a full fountain,
   With no merits of our own.
   O Lord—open up a new window of heaven,
   And lean out far over the battlements of glory,
   And listen this morning.

James Weldon Johnson

The Greeting
The LORD lives! Blessed is my Rock!* Exalted is the God of my salvation!

Psalm 18:46

The Refrain for the Morning Lessons
The fool has said in his heart, "There is no God."

Psalm 14:1

A Reading
Jesus taught us, saying: 'This is what the kingdom of God is like. A man scatters
   seed on the land. Night and day, while he sleeps, when he is awake, the seed is
   sprouting and growing; how, he does not know. Of its own accord the land
   produces first the shoot, then the ear, then the full grain in the ear. And when
   the crop is ready, at once he starts to reap because the harvest has come.'

Mark 4:26–29

The Refrain
The fool has said in his heart, "There is no God."

The Morning Psalm   *Wait Upon the Lord*
Wait upon the LORD and keep his way;* he will raise you up to possess the land,
   and when the wicked are cut off, you will see it.
I have seen the wicked in their arrogance,* flourishing like a tree in full leaf.
I went by, and behold, they were not there;* I searched for them, but they could
   not be found.

Mark those who are honest; observe the upright;* for there is a future for the
 peaceable.
Transgressors shall be destroyed, one and all;* the future of the wicked is cut off.
But the deliverance of the righteous comes from the LORD;* he is their stronghold
 in time of trouble.
The LORD will help them and rescue them;* he will rescue them from the wicked
 and deliver them, because they seek refuge in him.

Psalm 37:36–42

The Refrain
The fool has said in his heart, "There is no God."

The Cry of the Church
O God, come to my assistance! O Lord, make haste to help me!

The Lord's Prayer

The Prayer Appointed for the Week
Keep, O Lord, your household the Church in your steadfast faith and love, that
 through your grace each of us may proclaim your truth with boldness, and
 minister your justice with compassion; for the sake of our Savior Jesus Christ,
 who lives and reigns with you and the Holy Spirit, one God, now and for ever.
 Amen.†

The Concluding Prayer of the Church
Lord God, almighty and everlasting Father, you have brought me in safety to this
 new day: Preserve me with your mighty power, that I may not fall into sin, nor
 be overcome by adversity; and in all I do direct me to the fulfilling of your purpose; through Jesus Christ my Lord. *Amen.*†

The Midday Office   **To Be Observed on the Hour or Half Hour**
Between 11 a.m. and 2 p.m.

The Call to Prayer
Sing to God, O kingdoms of the earth;* sing praises to the Lord.
He rides in the heavens, the ancient heavens;* he sends forth his voice, his mighty
 voice.
Ascribe power to God;* his majesty is over Israel; his strength is over the skies.
How wonderful is God in his holy places!* the God of Israel giving strength and
 power to his people! Blessed be God!

Psalm 68:33–36

The Request for Presence
May the glory of the LORD endure for ever;* may the LORD rejoice in all his works.

Psalm 104:32

The Greeting
Let the words of my mouth and the meditation of my heart be acceptable in your sight,* O LORD, my strength and my redeemer.

Psalm 19:14

The Refrain for the Midday Lessons
My tongue will proclaim your righteousness all day long.

Psalm 71:24

A Reading
We believe that the divine presence is everywhere and that "the eyes of the Lord are looking on the good and evil in every place." But we should especially believe this and hold it close without any doubt when we are assisting at the Work of God. To that end let us be mindful of the Prophet's words: "Serve the Lord in fear" and again "Sing praises wisely" and "In the sight of the Angels I will sing praise to You." Let us therefore consider how we ought to conduct ourselves in the sight of the Godhead and His angels, and let us take part in the singing of the psalms in such a way that our mind may be harmony with our voice.

St. Benedict

The Refrain
My tongue will proclaim your righteousness all day long.

The Midday Psalm   LORD, *Who May Dwell in Your Tabernacle?*
LORD, who may dwell in your tabernacle?* who may abide upon your holy hill?
Whoever leads a blameless life and does what is right,* who speaks the truth from his heart.
There is no guile upon his tongue; he does no evil to his friend;* he does not heap contempt upon his neighbor.
In his sight the wicked is rejected,* but he honors those who fear the LORD.
He has sworn to do no wrong* and does not take back his word.
He does not give his money in hope of gain,* nor does he take a bribe against the innocent.
Whoever does these things* shall never be overthrown.

Psalm 15:1–7

The Refrain
My tongue will proclaim your righteousness all day long.

The Gloria

The Lord's Prayer

The Prayer Appointed for the Week
Keep, O Lord, your household the Church in your steadfast faith and love, that through your grace each of us may proclaim your truth with boldness, and

minister your justice with compassion; for the sake of our Savior Jesus Christ, who lives and reigns with you and the Holy Spirit, one God, now and for ever. *Amen.*†

The Concluding Prayer of the Church
Direct me, O Lord, in all my doings with your most gracious favor, and further me with your continual help; that in all my work begun, continued, and ended in you, I may glorify your holy name, and finally, by your mercy, obtain everlasting life; through Jesus Christ my Lord. *Amen.*†

The Vespers Office   **To Be Observed on the Hour or Half Hour**
                          Between 5 and 8 p.m.

The Call to Prayer
Open my lips, O Lord,* and my mouth shall proclaim your praise.
Had you desired it, I would have offered sacrifice,* but you take no delight in
    burnt-offerings.
The sacrifice of God is a troubled spirit;* and a broken and contrite heart, O God,
    you will not despise.

Psalm 51:16–18

The Request for Presence
Give ear, O LORD, to my prayer,* and attend to the voice of my supplications.

Psalm 86:6

The Greeting
I give you thanks, O God, I give you thanks,* calling upon your Name and declaring all your wonderful deeds.

adapted from Psalm 75:1

The Hymn   *Holy Ghost, with Love Divine*

Holy Ghost, with love divine,   Holy Spirit, all divine,
Shine upon this heart of mine: Dwell within this heart of mine:
Chase the shades of night away,   Cast down every idol throne,
Turn my darkness into day.   Reign supreme—and reign alone.

A. Reed

Holy Ghost, with power divine,
Cleanse this guilty heart of mine:
Bid my many woes depart,
Heal my wounded, bleeding heart.

The Refrain for the Vespers Lessons
For you are my hope, O Lord GOD,* my confidence since I was young.

Psalm 71:5

The Vespers Psalm   *Turn Now, O God of Hosts*
You have brought the vine out of Egypt;* you cast out the nations and planted it.
You prepared the ground for it;* it took root and filled the land.
The mountains were covered by its shadow* and the towering cedar trees by its
    boughs.
You stretched out its tendrils to the Sea* and its branches to the River.
Why have you broken down its wall,* so that all that pass by pluck off its grapes?
The wild boar of the forest has ravaged it,* and the beasts of the field have grazed
    upon it.
Turn now, O God of hosts, look down from heaven; behold and tend your vine;*
    preserve what your right hand has planted.

                                                          Psalm 80:8–14

The Refrain
For you are my hope, O Lord GOD,* my confidence since I was young.

The Small Verse
The Lord is my shepherd and nothing is wanting to me. In green pastures He has
    settled me.

The Lord's Prayer

The Prayer Appointed for the Week
Keep, O Lord, your household the Church in your steadfast faith and love, that
    through your grace each of us may proclaim your truth with boldness, and
    minister your justice with compassion; for the sake of our Savior Jesus Christ,
    who lives and reigns with you and the Holy Spirit, one God, now and for ever.
    Amen.+

The Concluding Prayer of the Church
    Lord, take my heart,
    for I cannot give it to you.
    And when you have it,
    keep it.
    For I would not take it from you.
                        François Fénelon

The Morning Office   **To Be Observed on the Hour or Half Hour**
                                                    Between 6 and 9 a.m.

The Call to Prayer
God has gone up with a shout,* the LORD with the sound of the ram's horn.
Sing praises to God, sing praises;* sing praises to our King, sing praises.
For God is king of all the earth;* sing praises with all your skill.
God reigns over the nation;* God sits upon his holy throne.

                                                          Psalm 47:5–8

The Request for Presence
Early in the morning I cry out to you,* for in your word is my trust.

Psalm 119:147

The Greeting
Not to us, O LORD, not to us, but to your Name give glory;* because of your love
and because of your faithfulness.

Psalm 115:1

The Refrain for the Morning Lessons
Those who are planted in the house of the LORD* shall flourish in the courts of our
God.

Psalm 92:12

A Reading
To the Jews who believed in him Jesus said: 'If you make my word your home you
will indeed be my disciples, you will come to know the truth and the truth will
set you free.'

John 8:31–32

The Refrain
Those who are planted in the house of the LORD* shall flourish in the courts of our
God.

The Morning Psalm   *It Is Good for the Just to Sing Praises*
Rejoice in the LORD, you righteous;* it is good for the just to sing praises.
Praise the LORD with the harp;* play to him upon the psaltery and lyre.
Sing for him a new song;* sound a fanfare with all your skill upon the trumpet.
For the word of the LORD is right,* and all his works are sure.
He loves righteousness and justice;* the loving-kindness of the LORD fills the
whole earth.

Psalm 33:1–5

The Refrain
Those who are planted in the house of the LORD* shall flourish in the courts of our
God.

The Short Verse
'I am the Alpha and the Omega,' says the Lord God, who is, who was, and who is
to come, the Almighty.

Revelation 1:8

The Lord's Prayer

The Prayer Appointed for the Week
Keep, O Lord, your household the Church in your steadfast faith and love, that
through your grace each of us may proclaim your truth with boldness, and

minister your justice with compassion; for the sake of our Savior Jesus Christ, who lives and reigns with you and the Holy Spirit, one God, now and for ever. *Amen.*†

The Concluding Prayer of the Church
Lord God, almighty and everlasting Father, you have brought me in safety to this new day: Preserve me with your mighty power, that I may not fall into sin, nor be overcome by adversity; and in all I do direct me to the fulfilling of your purpose; through Jesus Christ my Lord. *Amen.*†

The Midday Office   **To Be Observed on the Hour or Half Hour**
Between 11 a.m. and 2 p.m.

The Call to Prayer
Clap your hands all you peoples;* shout to God with a cry of joy.
Psalm 47:1

The Request for Presence
Accept, O LORD, the willing tribute of my lips,* and teach me your judgments.
Psalm 119:108

The Greeting
I will offer you the sacrifice of thanksgiving* and call upon the Name of the LORD.
Psalm 116:15

The Refrain for the Midday Lessons
He shall say to the LORD, "You are my refuge and my stronghold,* my God in whom I put my trust."
Psalm 91:2

A Reading
And all these things which were written so long ago were written so that we, learning perseverance and the encouragement which the scriptures give, should have hope. Now the God of perseverance and encouragement give you all the same purpose, following the example of Christ Jesus, so that you may together give glory to the God and Father of our Lord Jesus Christ with one heart.
Romans 15:4–6

The Refrain
He shall say to the LORD, "You are my refuge and my stronghold,* my God in whom I put my trust."

The Midday Psalm   *Like Trees Planted by Streams of Water*
Happy are they who have not walked in the counsel of the wicked,* nor lingered in the way of sinners, nor sat in the seats of the scornful!

Their delight is in the law of the LORD,* and they meditate on his law day and night.

They are like trees planted by streams of water, bearing fruit in due season, with leaves that do not wither:* everything they do shall prosper.

It is not so with the wicked;* they are like the chaff which the wind blows away.

Therefore the wicked shall not stand upright when judgment comes,* nor the sinner in the council of the righteous.

For the LORD knows the way of the righteous,* but the way of the wicked is doomed.

Psalm 1:1–6

The Refrain

He shall say to the LORD, "You are my refuge and my stronghold,* my God in whom I put my trust."

The Gloria

The Lord's Prayer

The Prayer Appointed for the Week

Keep, O Lord, your household the Church in your steadfast faith and love, that through your grace each of us may proclaim your truth with boldness, and minister your justice with compassion; for the sake of our Savior Jesus Christ, who lives and reigns with you and the Holy Spirit, one God, now and for ever. *Amen.*†

The Concluding Prayer of the Church

Almighty and everlasting God, by whose Spirit the whole body of your faithful people is governed and sanctified: Receive my supplications and prayers which I offer before you for all members of your holy Church, that in our vocation and ministry we all may truly and godly serve you, through our Lord and Savior Jesus Christ. *Amen.*

The Vespers Office   **To Be Observed on the Hour or Half Hour**
Between 5 and 8 p.m.

The Call to Prayer

Blessed be the LORD, the God of Israel, from everlasting and to everlasting;* and let all people say, "Amen!" Hallelujah!

Psalm 106:48

The Request for Presence

Be my strong rock, a castle to keep me safe;* you are my crag and my stronghold.

Psalm 71:3

The Greeting

Your way, O God, is holy;* who is as great as our God?

Psalm 77:13

The Hymn   *A Song of Creation*

Glorify the Lord, all you works of the Lord,
    praise him and highly exalt him for ever.
In the firmament of his power, glorify the Lord,
    praise him and highly exalt him forever.

Glorify the Lord, you angels and powers of the Lord,
    O heavens and all waters above the heavens.
Sun and moon and stars of the sky, glorify the Lord,
    praise him and exalt him for ever.

Glorify the Lord, every shower of rain and fall of dew,
    all winds and fire and heat.
Winter and summer, glorify the Lord,
    praise him and highly exalt him forever.

Glorify the Lord, O chill and cold,
    drops of dew and flakes of snow.
Frost and cold, ice and sleet, glorify the Lord,
    praise him and highly exalt him forever.

Glorify the Lord, O nights and days,
    O shining light and enfolding dark.
Storm clouds and thunderbolts, glorify the Lord,
    praise him and highly exalt him forever.

Let the earth glorify the Lord,
    praise him and highly exalt him forever.
Glorify the Lord, O mountains and hills,
and all that grows upon the earth,
    praise him and highly exalt him forever.

Glorify the Lord, O springs of water, seas, and streams,
    O whales and all that move in the waters.
All birds of the air, glorify the Lord,
    praise him and highly exalt him forever.

Glorify the Lord, O beasts of the wild,
    and all you flocks and herds.
O men and women everywhere, glorify the Lord,
    praise him and highly exalt him forever.

Let the people of God glorify the Lord,
    praise him and highly exalt him forever.
Glorify the Lord, O priests and servants of the Lord,
    praise him and highly exalt him forever.

Glorify the Lord, O spirits and souls of the righteous,
    praise him and highly exalt him forever.

You that are holy and humble of heart, glorify the Lord,
    praise him and highly exalt him forever.

Let us glorify the Lord: Father, Son, and Holy spirit;
    praise him and highly exalt him forever.
In the firmament of his power, glorify the Lord,
    praise him and highly exalt him forever.

Song of the Three Young Men 35–65

The Refrain for the Vespers Lessons
Truth shall spring up from the earth,* and righteousness shall look down from
    heaven.

Psalm 85:11

The Vespers Psalm
Why are you so full of heaviness, O my soul?* And why are you so disquieted
    within me?
Put your trust in God;* for I will yet give thanks to him, who is the help of my
    countenance, and my God.

Psalm 43:5–6

The Refrain
Truth shall spring up from the earth,* and righteousness shall look down from
    heaven.

The Cry of the Church
In the evening, in the morning, and at noonday, I will complain and lament,* and
    he will hear my voice.

Psalm 55:18

The Lord's Prayer

The Prayer Appointed for the Week
Keep, O Lord, your household the Church in your steadfast faith and love, that
    through your grace each of us may proclaim your truth with boldness, and
    minister your justice with compassion; for the sake of our Savior Jesus Christ,
    who lives and reigns with you and the Holy Spirit, one God, now and for ever.
    Amen.†

The Concluding Prayer of the Church
Lord Jesus, stay with me, for evening is at hand and the day is past; be my com-
    panion in the way, kindle my heart, and awaken hope, that I may know you as
    you are revealed in Scripture and in the breaking of bread. Grant this for the
    sake of your love toward me. *Amen.*†

The Morning Office To Be Observed on the Hour or Half Hour
Between 6 and 9 a.m.

The Call to Prayer
I will call upon God* and the LORD will deliver me.
In the evening, in the morning, and at the noonday, I will complain and lament,*
and he will hear my voice.
He will bring me safely back . . . God, who is enthroned of old, will hear me.

Psalm 55:17ff

The Request for Presence
Show us the light of your countenance, O God,* and come to us.

based on Psalm 67:1

The Greeting
In you, O LORD, have I taken refuge; let me never be put to shame;* deliver me in
your righteousness.

Psalm 31:1

The Refrain for the Morning Lessons
Come and listen, all you who fear God,* and I will tell you what he has done for me.

Psalm 66:14

A Reading
Jesus taught us, asking: 'How can you believe, since you look to each other for
glory and are not concerned with the glory that comes from the one God?'

John 5:44

The Refrain
Come and listen, all you who fear God,* and I will tell you what he has done for
me.

The Morning Psalm *That Which We Have Heard and Known*
That which we have heard and known, and what our forefathers have told us,* we
will not hide from their children.
We will recount to generations to come the praiseworthy deeds and power of the
LORD,* and the wonderful works he has done.
He gave his decrees to Jacob and established a law for Israel,* which he com-
manded them to teach to their children;
That the generations to come might know, and the children yet unborn;* that they
in their turn might tell it to their children;
So that they might put their trust in God,* and not forget the deeds of God, but
keep his commandments;
And not be like their forefathers, a stubborn and rebellious generation,* a genera-
tion whose heart was not steadfast, and whose spirit was not faithful to God.

Psalm 78:3–8

The Refrain
Come and listen, all you who fear God,* and I will tell you what he has done for me.

The Cry of the Church
O God, come to my assistance! O Lord, make haste to help me!

The Lord's Prayer

The Prayer Appointed for the Week
Keep, O Lord, your household the Church in your steadfast faith and love, that
 through your grace each of us may proclaim your truth with boldness, and
 minister your justice with compassion; for the sake of our Savior Jesus Christ,
 who lives and reigns with you and the Holy Spirit, one God, now and for ever.
 Amen.†

The Concluding Prayer of the Church
Lord God, almighty and everlasting Father, you have brought me in safety to this
 new day: Preserve me with your mighty power, that I may not fall into sin, nor
 be overcome by adversity; and in all I do direct me to the fulfilling of your purpose; through Jesus Christ my Lord. *Amen.*†

The Midday Office   **To Be Observed on the Hour or Half Hour**
                            Between 11 a.m. and 2 p.m.

The Call to Prayer
Sing to the LORD with thanksgiving;* make music to our God upon the harp.
                                                        Psalm 147:7

The Request for Presence
Hear the voice of my prayer when I cry out to you,* when I lift up my hands to
 your holy of holies.
                                                        Psalm 28:2

The Greeting
You are the LORD, most high over all the earth;* you are exalted far above all gods.
                                                        Psalm 97:9

The Refrain for the Midday Lessons
Tell it out among all the nations: "The LORD is King!:* he has made the world so
 firm that it cannot be moved; he will judge all the peoples with equity."
                                                        Psalm 96:10

A Reading
Then I saw a *new heaven and a new earth;* the first heaven and the first earth had dis-
 appeared now, and there was no longer any sea. I saw the holy city, and the
 new Jerusalem, coming down out of heaven from God, prepared as a bride
 dressed for her husband. Then I heard a loud voice call from the throne, 'Here
 God lives among human beings. He will make *his home among them; they shall be*

his people, and he will be their God, *God-with-them. He will wipe away all tears from their eyes;* there will be no more death, and no more mourning or sadness or pain. The world of the past has gone.'

Then the One sitting on the throne spoke: 'Now I am making the whole of creation new. Write this, "What I am saying is trustworthy and will come true." ' Then he said to me, 'It has already happened. I am the Alpha and the Omega, the Beginning and the End, I will give water from the well of life free to anybody who is thirsty; anyone who proves victorious will inherit these things; and *I will be his God* and *he will be my son.* But the legacy for cowards, for those who break their word, or worship obscenities, for murderers and the sexually immoral, and for sorcerers, worshippers of false gods or any other sort of liars, is the second death in the burning lake of sulfur.'

Revelation 21:1ff

The Refrain
Tell it out among all the nations: "The LORD is King!:* he has made the world so firm that it cannot be moved; he will judge all the peoples with equity."

The Midday Psalm   *Be Joyful in the Lord*
Be joyful in the LORD all you lands;* serve the LORD with gladness and come before his presence with a song.

Know this, the LORD himself is God;* he himself has made us, and we are his; we are his people and the sheep of his pasture.

Enter his gates with thanksgiving; go into his courts with praise;* give thanks to him and call upon his Name.

For the LORD is good; His mercy is everlasting;* and his faithfulness endures from age to age.

Psalm 100:1–4

The Refrain
Tell it out among all the nations: "The LORD is King!:* he has made the world so firm that it cannot be moved; he will judge all the peoples with equity."

The Small Verse
Happy are the people whose strength is in you!* whose hearts are set on the pilgrims' way,

For one day in your courts is better than a thousand in my own room,* and to stand at the threshold of the house of my God than to dwell in the tents of the wicked.

Psalm 84:4, 9

The Lord's Prayer

The Prayer Appointed for the Week
Keep, O Lord, your household the Church in your steadfast faith and love, that through your grace each of us may proclaim your truth with boldness, and

minister your justice with compassion; for the sake of our Savior Jesus Christ, who lives and reigns with you and the Holy Spirit, one God, now and for ever. *Amen.*†

The Concluding Prayer of the Church

Let us bless the Lord God living and true! Let us always render him praise, glory, honor, blessing, and all good things! Amen. Amen. So be it! So be it!

St. Francis of Assisi

The Vespers Office   **To Be Observed on the Hour or Half Hour**
                                         Between 5 and 8 p.m.

The Call to Prayer

Give thanks to the LORD, for he is good;* his mercy endures for ever.

Psalm 118:29

The Request for Presence

As the eyes of servants look to the hand of their masters,* and the eyes of a maid to the hand of her mistress,

So my eyes look to you, O LORD my God.

adapted from Psalm 123:2–3

The Greeting

My heart sings to you without ceasing;* O LORD my God, I will give you thanks for ever.

Psalm 30:13

The Hymn   *O Love That Will Not Let Me Go*

O Love that will not let me go,   O light that follows all my way,
I rest my weary soul in you;   I yield my flickering torch to you;
And give you back the life I owe,   My heart restores its borrowed ray,
That in your ocean depths its flow   That in your sunshine's blaze its day
May richer, fuller be.   May brighter, fairer be.

George Matheson (adapted)

The Refrain for the Vespers Lessons

But you, O LORD, are gracious and full of compassion,* slow to anger, and full of kindness and truth.

Psalm 86:15

The Vespers Psalm   *My Soul Is Athirst for God*

As the deer longs for the water-brooks,* so longs my soul for you, O God.

My soul is athirst for God, athirst for the living God;* when shall I come to appear before the presence of God?

My tears have been my food day and night,* while all day long they say to me, "Where now is your God?"

I pour out my soul when I think on these things:* how I went with the multitude
and led them into the house of God,

With the voice of praise and thanksgiving,* among those who keep holy-day.

Why are you so full of heaviness, O my soul?* and why are you so disquieted
within me?

Put your trust in God;* for I will yet give thanks to him, who is the help of my
countenance, and my God.

Psalm 42:1–7

The Refrain

But you, O Lord, are gracious and full of compassion,* slow to anger, and full of
kindness and truth.

The Cry of the Church

Lord, have mercy on us. Christ, have mercy on us. Lord, have mercy on us.

The Lord's Prayer

The Prayer Appointed for the Week

Keep, O Lord, your household the Church in your steadfast faith and love, that
through your grace each of us may proclaim your truth with boldness, and
minister your justice with compassion; for the sake of our Savior Jesus Christ,
who lives and reigns with you and the Holy Spirit, one God, now and for ever.
Amen.†

The Concluding Prayer of the Church

I thank you, my God, for your care and protection this day, keeping me from physical harm and spiritual ignorance. I now place the work of the day into Your
hands, trusting that You will redeem my mistakes, and transform my accom-
plishments into works of praise.

And now I ask that You will work within me while I sleep, using the hours of my
rest to create in me a new mind and heart and soul.

May my mind, which during the day was directed to my work and activities,
through the night be directed wholly to You.

Jacob Boehme

The Morning Office

**To Be Observed on the Hour or Half Hour
Between 6 and 9 a.m.**

The Call to Prayer

Hallelujah! Give thanks to the Lord for he is good,* for his mercy endures for ever.

Psalm 106:1

The Request for Presence

I call with my whole heart;* answer me, O Lord, that I may keep your statutes.

Psalm 119:145

The Greeting
To you, O LORD, I lift up my soul; my God, I put my trust in you;* let me not be
  humiliated, nor let my enemies triumph over me.
Let none who look to you be put to shame.

Psalm 25:1–2

The Refrain for the Morning Lessons
No good things will the LORD withhold* from those who walk with integrity.

Psalm 84:11

A Reading
Jesus taught us, saying: 'Remain in me, as I in you. As a branch cannot bear fruit
  all by itself, unless it remains part of the vine, neither can you unless you
  remain in me. I am the vine, you are the branches. Whoever remains in me,
  with me in him, bears fruit in plenty; for cut off from me you can do nothing.'

John 15:4–5

The Refrain
No good things will the LORD withhold* from those who walk with integrity.

The Morning Psalm   *I Will Lift Up the Cup of Salvation*
How shall I repay the LORD* for all the good things he has done for me?
I will lift up the cup of salvation* and call upon the name of the LORD,
I will fulfill my vows to the LORD* in the presence of all his people.

Psalm 116:10–12

The Refrain
No good things will the LORD withhold* from those who walk with integrity.

The Cry of the Church
Lord, have mercy on us. Christ, have mercy on us. Lord, have mercy on us.

The Lord's Prayer

The Prayer Appointed for the Week
Keep, O Lord, your household the Church in your steadfast faith and love, that
  through your grace each of us may proclaim your truth with boldness, and
  minister your justice with compassion; for the sake of our Savior Jesus Christ,
  who lives and reigns with you and the Holy Spirit, one God, now and for ever.
  Amen.†

The Concluding Prayer of the Church
Lord God, almighty and everlasting Father, you have brought me in safety to this
  new day: Preserve me with your mighty power, that I may not fall into sin, nor
  be overcome by adversity; and in all I do direct me to the fulfilling of your purpose; through Jesus Christ my Lord. *Amen.*†

The Midday Office

**To Be Observed on the Hour or Half Hour
Between 11 a.m. and 2 p.m.**

The Call to Prayer
Come, let us sing to the LORD;* let us shout to the rock of our salvation.

Psalm 95:1

The Request for Presence
May God be merciful to us and bless us,* show us the light of his countenance and
come to us.

Psalm 67:1

The Greeting
Splendor and honor and kingly power are yours by right, O Lord our God, for you
created everything that is, and by your will they were created and have their
being

Revelation 4:11

The Refrain for the Midday Lessons
But I shall always wait in patience,* and shall praise you more and more.

Psalm 71:14

A Reading
Just as with the human body which is a unity although it has many parts—all the
parts of the body, though many, still making up one single body—so it is with
Christ. We were baptized into one body in a single spirit, Jews as well as Greeks,
slaves as well as free men, and we were all given the same Spirit to drink.

I Corinthians 12:12–13

The Refrain
But I shall always wait in patience,* and shall praise you more and more.

The Midday Psalm　　　　　　　　　*You Crown the Year with Your Goodness*
You make fast the mountains by your power;* they are girded about with might.
You still the roaring seas,* the roaring of their waves, and the clamor of their peoples.
Those who dwell at the ends of the earth will tremble at your marvelous signs;*
you make the dawn and the dusk to sing for joy.
You visit the earth and water it abundantly; you make it very plenteous;* the river
of God is full of water.
You prepare the grain,* for so you provide for the earth.
You drench the furrows and smooth out the ridges;* with heavy rain you soften
the ground and bless its increase.
You crown the year with your goodness,* and your paths overflow with plenty.
May the fields of the wilderness be rich for grazing,* and the hills be clothed with
joy.
May the meadows cover themselves with flocks, and the valleys cloak themselves
with grain;* let them shout for joy and sing.

Psalm 65:6–14

The Refrain
But I shall always wait in patience,* and shall praise you more and more.

The Gloria

The Lord's Prayer

The Prayer Appointed for the Week
Keep, O Lord, your household the Church in your steadfast faith and love, that
through your grace each of us may proclaim your truth with boldness, and
minister your justice with compassion; for the sake of our Savior Jesus Christ,
who lives and reigns with you and the Holy Spirit, one God, now and for ever.
Amen.†

The Concluding Prayer of the Church
You gather us together in faith, O God, as a loving mother and a gentle father.
Help us to remember that your dwelling place is built upon love and peace,
and that to bring about your reign on earth we must follow your way of peace.
We pray for all governments and legislatures that they may be mindful of the
rights of all peoples of this world to live in peace and dignity. Grant this in the
name of Jesus. *Amen.*

The New Companion to the Breviary

The Vespers Office **To Be Observed on the Hour or Half Hour**
Between 5 and 8 p.m.

The Call to Prayer
Come let us sing to the LORD;* Let us shout for joy to the Rock of our salvation.
Let us come before his presence with thanksgiving* and raise a loud shout to him
with psalms.
For the LORD is a great God,* and a great king above all gods.
In his hands are the caverns of the earth,* and the heights of the hills are his also.
The sea is his, for he made it,* and his hands have molded the dry land.

Psalm 95:1–5

The Request for Presence
Accept, O LORD, the willing tribute of my lips,* and teach me your judgments.

Psalm 119:108

The Greeting
O LORD of hosts,* happy are they who put their trust in you!

Psalm 84:12

The Hymn   *Joyful, Joyful, We Adore Thee*

Joyful, joyful, we adore thee,
God of glory, Lord of love;
Hearts unfold like flowers before thee,
Praising thee, their sun above.
Melt the clouds of sin and sadness;
Drive the dark of doubt away;
Giver of immortal gladness,
Fill us with the light of day.

All thy works with joy surround thee,
Earth and heaven reflect thy rays,
Stars and angels sing around thee,
Center of unbroken praise.
Field and forest, vale and mountain,
Blooming meadow, flashing sea,
Chanting bird and flowing fountain,
Call us to rejoice in thee.

Thou art giving and forgiving,
Ever blessing, ever blest,
Wellspring of the joy of living,
Ocean depth of happy rest!
Thou our Father, Christ our brother
All who live in love are thine;
Teach us how to love each other,
Lift us to thy joy divine.

Henry Van Dyke

The Refrain for the Vespers Lessons
The LORD will indeed grant prosperity,* and our land will yield its increase.

Psalm 85:12

The Vespers Psalm   ***Sing Praises with All Your Skill***
Clap your hands all you peoples;* shout to God with a cry of joy.
God has gone up with a shout,* the LORD with the sound of the ram's horn.
Sing praises to God, sing praises.* Sing praises to our King, sing praises.
For God is King of all the earth;* sing praises with all your skill.
God reigns over the nations;* God sits upon his holy throne.
The nobles of the peoples have gathered together* with the people of the God of
    Abraham.
The rulers of the earth belong to God,* and he is highly exalted.

Psalm 47:1, 5–10

The Refrain
The LORD will indeed grant prosperity,* and our land will yield its increase.

The Gloria

The Lord's Prayer

The Prayer Appointed for the Week
Keep, O Lord, your household the Church in your steadfast faith and love, that
    through your grace each of us may proclaim your truth with boldness, and
    minister your justice with compassion; for the sake of our Savior Jesus Christ,
    who lives and reigns with you and the Holy Spirit, one God, now and for ever.
Amen.†

The Concluding Prayer of the Church

O holy God, as evening falls remain with us, remember our good deeds and forgive our failings. Help us to reflect upon and live according to your covenant of love. Be with our lonely and elderly sisters and brothers in the evening of their lives. May all who long to see you face to face know the comfort of your presence. This we ask in union with Simeon and Anna and all who have gone before us blessing and proclaiming you by the fidelity of their lives. *Amen.*

THE NEW COMPANION TO THE BREVIARY

The Morning Office   **To Be Observed on the Hour or Half Hour**
Between 6 and 9 a.m.

The Call to Prayer

Taste and see that the LORD is good;* happy are those who trust in him!

Psalm 34:8

The Request for Presence

Be my strong rock, a castle to keep me safe;* you are my crag and my stronghold.

Psalm 71:3

The Greeting

O LORD, I cry to you for help;* in the morning my prayer comes before you.

Psalm 88:14

The Refrain for the Morning Lessons

God is a righteous judge;* God sits in judgment every day.

Psalm 7:12

A Reading

Jesus taught us, saying: 'Why do you call me, "Lord, Lord" and not do what I say? Everyone who comes to me and listens to my words and acts on them—I will show you what such a person is like. Such a person is like the man who, when he built a house dug, and dug deep, and laid the foundations on rock; when the river was in flood it bore down on that house but could not shake it, it was so well built. But someone who listens and does nothing is like the man who built a house on soil, with no foundations: as soon as the river bore down on it, it collapsed; and what a ruin that house became!'

Luke 6:46–49

The Refrain

God is a righteous judge;* God sits in judgment every day.

The Morning Psalm   *The LORD Is Known by His Acts of Justice*

The ungodly have fallen into the pit they dug,* and in the snare they set is their own foot caught.

The LORD is known by his acts of justice;* the wicked are trapped in the works of their own hands.

The wicked shall be given over to the grave,* and also the peoples that forget God.
Rise up, O LORD, let not the ungodly have the upper hand;* let them be judged
before you.
Put fear upon them, O LORD;* let the ungodly know they are but mortal.

Psalm 9:15ff

The Refrain
God is a righteous judge;* God sits in judgment every day.

The Cry of the Church
O God, come to my assistance! O Lord, make haste to help me!

The Lord's Prayer

The Prayer Appointed for the Week
Keep, O Lord, your household the Church in your steadfast faith and love, that
through your grace each of us may proclaim your truth with boldness, and
minister your justice with compassion; for the sake of our Savior Jesus Christ,
who lives and reigns with you and the Holy Spirit, one God, now and for ever.
Amen.†

The Concluding Prayer of the Church
Lord God, almighty and everlasting Father, you have brought me in safety to this
new day: Preserve me with your mighty power, that I may not fall into sin, nor
be overcome by adversity; and in all I do direct me to the fulfilling of your purpose; through Jesus Christ my Lord. *Amen.*†

The Midday Office
**To Be Observed on the Hour or Half Hour
Between 11 a.m. and 2 p.m.**

The Call to Prayer
"Come now, let us reason together," says the Lord.
Isaiah 1:18 KJV

The Request for Presence
O God, be not far from me;* come quickly to help me, O my God.
Psalm 71:12

The Greeting
"You are my God, and I will thank you;* you are my God and I will exalt you."
Psalm 118:28

The Refrain for the Midday Lessons
The same stone that the builders rejected* has become the chief cornerstone.
This is the LORD's doing,* and it is marvelous in our eyes.
Psalm 118:22–23

A Reading

Jesus has many lovers of His heavenly kingdom, but few bearers of His cross. He
has many seekers of consolation, but few of tribulation. He finds many companions at His feasting, but few at His fasting. All desire to rejoice in Him; Few are
willing to endure anything for Him. Many follow Jesus as far as the breaking of
bread, but few to the drinking of the cup of His passion. Many reverence His
miracles, but few will follow the shame of His cross. Many love Jesus as long as
no adversaries befall them. Many praise and bless Him so long as they receive
some consolation from Him. But if Jesus hide Himself and leave them but for a
brief time, they begin to complain or become overly despondent in mind.

Thomas à Kempis

The Refrain

The same stone that the builders rejected* has become the chief cornerstone.
This is the LORD's doing,* and it is marvelous in our eyes.

The Midday Psalm   *The Song of the Messiah*

My God, my God, why have you forsaken me?* and are so far from my cry and
    from the words of my distress?
I am poured out like water; all my bones are out of joint;* my heart within my
    breast is like melting wax.
My mouth is dried like a pot-shard; my tongue sticks to the roof of my mouth;*
    and you have laid me in the dust of the grave.
Packs of dogs close me in, and gangs of evildoers circle around me;* they pierce
    my hands and my feet; I can count all my bones.
They stare and gloat over me;* they divide my garments among them; they cast
    lots for my clothing.
Be not far away, O LORD;* you are my strength; hasten to help me.

Psalm 22:1ff

The Refrain

The same stone that the builders rejected* has become the chief cornerstone.
This is the LORD's doing,* and it is marvelous in our eyes.

The Cry of the Church

Lord, have mercy on us. Christ, have mercy on us. Lord, have mercy on us.

The Lord's Prayer

The Prayer Appointed for the Week

Keep, O Lord, your household the Church in your steadfast faith and love, that
    through your grace each of us may proclaim your truth with boldness, and
    minister your justice with compassion; for the sake of our Savior Jesus Christ,
    who lives and reigns with you and the Holy Spirit, one God, now and for ever.
    Amen.✝

The Concluding Prayer of the Church
Lord Jesus Christ, by your death you took away the sting of death: Grant me to so
follow in faith where you have led the way, that I may at length fall asleep
peacefully in you and wake in your likeness; for your tender mercies' sake.
Amen.†

The Vespers Office   To Be Observed on the Hour or Half Hour
                                      Between 5 and 8 p.m.

The Call to Prayer
I will call upon God,* and the LORD will deliver me.
In the evening, in the morning, and at the noonday, I will complain and lament,*
and he will hear my voice.
He will bring me safely back . . . ,* God, who is enthroned of old, will hear me.

Psalm 55:17ff

The Request for Presence
For God alone my soul in silence waits;* truly, my hope is in him.

Psalm 62:6

The Greeting
Out of Zion, perfect in its beauty,* God reveals himself in glory.

Psalm 50:2

The Hymn   *Prayer Is the Soul's Sincere Desire*
Prayer is the soul's sincere desire,   Prayer is the simplest form of speech
Unuttered or expressed,   That infant lips can try;
The motion of a hidden fire   Prayer the sublimest strains that reach
That trembles in the breast.   The Majesty on high.

Prayer is the burden of a sigh,   Prayer is the contrite sinners' voice,
The falling of a tear,   Returning from their way,
The upward glancing of an eye,   While angels in their songs rejoice
When none but God is near.   And cry, "Behold, they pray!"

James Montgomery

The Refrain for the Vespers Lessons
Let my mouth be full of your praise* and your glory all the day long.

Psalm 71:8

The Vespers Psalm   *Happy Are They Whom You Teach Out of Your Law*
He that planted the ear, does he not hear?* he that formed the eye, does he not see?
He who admonishes the nations, will not punish?* he who teaches all the world,
has he no knowledge?
The LORD knows our human thoughts:* how like a puff of wind they are.
Happy are they whom you instruct, O LORD!* whom you teach out of your law;
To give them rest in evil days,* until a pit is dug for the wicked.

For the LORD will not abandon his people,* nor will he forsake his own.
For judgment will again be just,* and all the true of heart will follow it.

Psalm 94:9–15

The Refrain

Let my mouth be full of your praise* and your glory all the day long.

The Cry of the Church

In the evening, in the morning, and at noonday, I will complain and lament,* and
he will hear my voice.

Psalm 55:18

The Lord's Prayer

The Prayer Appointed for the Week

Keep, O Lord, your household the Church in your steadfast faith and love, that
through your grace each of us may proclaim your truth with boldness, and minister your justice with compassion; for the sake of our Savior Jesus Christ, who
lives and reigns with you and the Holy Spirit, one God, now and for ever. *Amen.*†

The Concluding Prayers of the Church

Almighty God, who has promised to hear the petitions of those who ask in your
Son's Name: I beseech you mercifully to incline your ear to me who have made
my prayers and supplications to you; and grant that those things which I have
faithfully asked according to your will, may effectually be obtained, to the
relief of my necessity, and to setting forth of your glory; through Jesus Christ
my Lord. *Amen.*†

May the souls of the faithful departed, through the mercy of God, rest in eternal
peace. *Amen.*

The Morning Office   **To Be Observed on the Hour or Half Hour
Between 6 and 9 a.m.**

The Call to Prayer

Bless the LORD, you angels of his, you mighty ones who do his bidding,* and hear-
ken to the voice of his word.
Bless the LORD, all you hosts,* you ministers of his who do his will.
Bless the LORD, all you works of his, in all places of his dominion;* bless the LORD,
O my soul.

Psalm 103:20–22

The Request for Presence

Give ear to my words, O LORD;* consider my meditation.
Hearken to my cry for help, my King and my God,* for I make my prayer to you.
In the morning, LORD, you hear my voice;* early in the morning I make my appeal
and watch for you.

Psalm 5:1–3

The Greeting

O God, you will keep in perfect peace those whose minds are fixed on you; for in returning and rest we shall be saved; in quietness and trust shall be our strength.

Isaiah 26:3, 30:15

The Refrain for the Morning Lessons

The LORD's will stands fast for ever,* and the designs of his heart from age to age.

Psalm 33:11

A Reading

The Jews then said, 'You are not fifty yet, and you have seen Abraham!' Jesus replied: I tell you most solemnly, before Abraham ever was, I am.

John 8:57–58

The Refrain

The LORD's will stands fast for ever,* and the designs of his heart from age to age.

The Morning Psalm   *A Song About the Messiah*

The LORD said to my Lord, "Sit at my right hand,* until I make your enemies your footstool."

The LORD will send the scepter of your power out of Zion,* saying, "Rule over your enemies round about you.

Princely state has been yours from the day of your birth;* in the beauty of holiness have I begotten you, like dew from the womb of the morning."

The LORD has sworn and he will not recant:* "You are a priest for ever after the order of Melchizedek."

Psalm 110:1–4

The Refrain

The LORD's will stands fast for ever,* and the designs of his heart from age to age.

The Small Verse

The people that walked in darkness have seen a great light; on those who have lived in a land of deep shadow a light has shown.

Isaiah 9:1

The Lord's Prayer

The Prayer Appointed for the Week

Keep, O Lord, your household the Church in your steadfast faith and love, that through your grace each of us may proclaim your truth with boldness, and minister your justice with compassion; for the sake of our Savior Jesus Christ, who lives and reigns with you and the Holy Spirit, one God, now and for ever. *Amen.*†

The Concluding Prayer of the Church

Lord God, almighty and everlasting Father, you have brought me in safety to this new day: Preserve me with your mighty power, that I may not fall into sin, nor be overcome by adversity; and in all I do direct me to the fulfilling of your purpose; through Jesus Christ my Lord. *Amen.*†

The Midday Office   **To Be Observed on the Hour or Half Hour**
                               Between 11 a.m. and 2 p.m.

The Call to Prayer
Ascribe to the LORD, you families of the peoples;* ascribe to the LORD honor and
   power.
Ascribe to the LORD the honor due his Name;* bring offerings and come into his
   courts.
Worship the LORD in the beauty of holiness;* let the whole earth tremble before
   him.
Tell it out among the nations: "The LORD is King!"* he has made the world so firm
   that it cannot be moved; he will judge the peoples with equity.

Psalm 96:7–10

The Request for Presence
Hear, O Shepherd of Israel, leading Joseph like a flock;* shine forth, you that are
   enthroned upon the cherubim.
In the presence of Ephraim, Benjamin, and Manasseh,* stir up your strength and
   come to help us.
Restore us, O God of hosts;* show the light of your countenance, and we shall be
   saved.

Psalm 80:1–3

The Greeting
Into your hands I commend my spirit,* for you have redeemed me, O LORD, O
   God of truth.

Psalm 31:5

The Refrain for the Midday Lessons
Happy is the nation whose God is the LORD!* happy the people he has chosen to be
   his own!

Psalm 33:12

A Reading
Do not be afraid, for I have redeemed you; I have called you by your name, you
   are mine. Should you pass through the waters, I shall be with you; or through
   rivers, they will not swallow you up. Should you walk through fire, you will
   not suffer and the flames will not burn you. For I am YAHWEH, your God, the
   Holy One of Israel, your Savior.

Isaiah 43:2

The Refrain
Happy is the nation whose God is the LORD!* happy the people he has chosen to be
   his own!

The Midday Psalm   *The Sparrow Has Found a Nest*

. . . My soul has a desire and longing for the courts of the LORD;* my heart and my
flesh rejoice in the living God.

The sparrow has found her a house and the swallow a nest where she may lay her
young;* by the side of your altars, O LORD of hosts, my King and my God.

Psalm 84:1–2

The Refrain

Happy is the nation whose God is the LORD!* happy the people he has chosen to be
his own!

The Gloria

The Lord's Prayer

The Prayer Appointed for the Week

Keep, O Lord, your household the Church in your steadfast faith and love, that
through your grace each of us may proclaim your truth with boldness, and minister your justice with compassion; for the sake of our Savior Jesus Christ, who
lives and reigns with you and the Holy Spirit, one God, now and for ever. *Amen.*†

The Concluding Prayer of the Church

Almighty God, who after the creation of the world rested from all your works and
sanctified a day of rest for all your creatures: Grant that I, putting away all
earthly anxieties, may be duly prepared for the service of public worship, and
grant as well that my Sabbath upon earth may be a preparation for the eternal
rest promised to your people in heaven; through Jesus Christ our Lord. *Amen.*

The Vespers Office   **To Be Observed on the Hour or Half Hour
                                      Between 5 and 8 p.m.**

The Call to Prayer

The LORD is my strength and my shield;* my heart trusts him, and I have been
helped;

Therefore my heart dances for joy,* and in my song I will praise him.

Psalm 28:8–9

The Request for Presence

Hear, O LORD, and have mercy upon me;* O LORD, be my helper.

Psalm 30:11

The Greeting

Your righteousness, O God, reaches to the heavens;* you have done great things;
who is like you, O God?

Psalm 71:19

The Hymn

Dear Lord and Father of mankind,	Drop your still dews of quietness
Forgive our foolish ways!	Till all our strivings cease:
Reclothe us in our rightful mind;	Take from our lives the strain and stress,
In purer lives your service find,	And let our ordered lives confess
In deeper reverence, praise.	The beauty of your peace.

John G. Whittier

The Refrain for the Vespers Lessons

Remember me, O LORD, with the favor you have for your people,* and visit me
with your saving help.

Psalm 106:4

The Vespers Psalm   *The LORD Is My Light and My Salvation*

The LORD is my light and my salvation; whom then shall I fear?* the LORD is the
strength of my life; of whom then shall I be afraid?

When evildoers came upon me to eat up my flesh,* it was they, my foes and adversaries, who stumbled and fell.

Though an army should encamp against me,* yet my heart shall not be afraid;
And though war should rise up against me,* yet will I put my trust in him.

One thing have I asked of the LORD; one thing I seek;* that I may dwell in the
house of the LORD all the days of my life;

To behold the fair beauty of the LORD* and to seek him in his temple.

For in the day of trouble he shall keep me safe in his shelter;* he shall hide me in
the secrecy of his dwelling and set me high upon a rock.

Even now he lifts up my head* above my enemies round about me.

Therefore I will offer in his dwelling an oblation with sounds of great gladness;* I
will sing and make music to the LORD.

Psalm 27:1–9

The Refrain

Remember me, O LORD, with the favor you have for your people,* and visit me
with your saving help.

The Gloria

The Lord's Prayer

The Prayer Appointed for the Week

Keep, O Lord, your household the Church in your steadfast faith and love, that
through your grace each of us may proclaim your truth with boldness, and
minister your justice with compassion; for the sake of our Savior Jesus Christ,
who lives and reigns with you and the Holy Spirit, one God, now and for ever.
Amen.†

The Concluding Prayer of the Church
Give me courage to resist, patience to endure, constancy to persevere. Grant, in place of all consolations of the world, the most sweet unction of Thy Spirit, and in place of carnal love, pour into me the love of Thy Name.

Thomas à Kempis

⌁⌁⌁

The Morning Office   **To Be Observed on the Hour or Half Hour**
                                                                   Between 6 and 9 a.m.

The Call to Prayer
Enter his gates with thanksgiving; go into his courts with praise;* give thanks to him and call upon his Name.

Psalm 100:3

The Request for Presence
Satisfy us by your loving-kindness in the morning* so shall we rejoice and be glad all the days of our life.

Psalm 90:14

The Greeting
I will give thanks to you, O LORD, with my whole heart;* I will tell of all your marvelous works.
I will be glad and rejoice in you;* I will sing your Name, O Most High.

Psalm 9:1–2

The Refrain for the Morning Lessons
In God the LORD, whose word I praise, in God I trust and will not be afraid,* for what can mortals do to me?

Psalm 56:10

A Reading
Jesus taught his disciples, saying: 'This is why I am telling you not to worry about your life and what you are to eat, nor about your body and how you clothe it. For life is more than food, and the body more than clothing. Think of ravens. They do not sow or reap; they have no store houses and no barns; yet God feeds them. And how much more are you worth than the birds! Can any of you, however much you worry, add a single cubit to your span of life? If a very small thing is beyond your powers, why worry about the rest? Think how the flowers grow; they never have to spin or weave; yet, I assure you not even

Solomon in all his royal robes was clothed like one of them. Now if that is how God clothes a flower which is growing wild today and is thrown in the furnace tomorrow, how much more will he look after you, who have so little faith! But you must not set your hearts on things to eat and things to drink; nor must you worry. It is the gentiles of the world who set their hearts on all these things. Your Father well knows you need them. No, set your hearts on his kingdom, and these other things will be given you as well.'

Luke 12:22–31

The Refrain

In God the Lord, whose word I praise, in God I trust and will not be afraid,* for what can mortals do to me?

The Morning Psalm   *You Have Made Me Glad by Your Acts, O Lord*

It is a good thing to give thanks to the Lord,* and to sing praises to your Name, O Most High;

To tell of your loving-kindness early in the morning* and of your faithfulness in the night season;

On the psaltery, and on the lyre,* and to the melody of the harp.

For you have made me glad by your acts, O Lord;* and I shout for joy because of the works of your hands.

Psalm 92:1–4

The Refrain

In God the Lord, whose word I praise, in God I trust and will not be afraid,* for what can mortals do to me?

The Gloria

The Lord's Prayer

The Prayer Appointed for the Week

Lord, make me have perpetual love and reverence for your holy Name, for you never fail to help and govern those whom you have set upon the sure foundation of your loving-kindness; through Jesus Christ our Lord, who lives and reigns with you and the Holy Spirit, one God, for ever and ever. *Amen.*†

The Concluding Prayer of the Church

Lord God, almighty and everlasting Father, you have brought me in safety to this new day: Preserve me with your mighty power, that I may not fall into sin, nor be overcome by adversity; and in all I do direct me to the fulfilling of your purpose; through Jesus Christ my Lord. *Amen.*†

The Midday Office   **To Be Observed on the Hour or Half Hour**
                                         Between 11 a.m. and 2 p.m.

The Call to Prayer
Sing to the Lord and bless his Name;* proclaim the good news of his salvation
    from day to day.
Declare his glory among the nations* and his wonders among all peoples.
                                                         Psalm 96:2–3

The Request for Presence
Let my cry come before you, O Lord;* give me understanding, according to your
    word.
Let my supplication come before you;* deliver me according to your promise.
                                                         Psalm 119:169–170

The Greeting
Lord, you have been our refuge* from one generation to another.
Before the mountains were brought forth, or the land and the earth were born,*
    from age to age you are God.
                                                         Psalm 90:1–2

The Refrain for the Midday Lessons
Let me announce the decree of the Lord;* he said to me, "You are my son; this day
    have I begotten you. . . ."
                                                         Psalm 2:7

A Reading
This is the gospel concerning his Son who, in terms of human nature was born a
    descendant of David and who, in terms of the Spirit and of holiness was desig-
    nated Son of God in power by resurrection from the dead: Jesus Christ our
    Lord, through whom we have received grace and our apostolic mission of win-
    ning obedience of faith among all the nations for the honor of his name. You
    are among these, and by his call you belong to Jesus Christ. To you
    all, . . . grace and peace from God our Father and the Lord Jesus Christ.
                                                         Romans 1:3–7

The Refrain
Let me announce the decree of the Lord;* he said to me, "You are my son; this day
    have I begotten you. . . ."

The Midday Psalm   *I Love to Do Your Will, O My God*
Great things are they that you have done, O Lord, my God! how great your won-
    ders and your plans for us!* there is none who can be compared with you.
Oh, that I could make them known and tell them!* but they are more than I can
    count.
In sacrifice and offering you take no pleasure* (you have given me ears to hear you);
Burnt-offering and sin-offering you have not required,* and so I said, "Behold, I
    come.

In the roll of the book it is written concerning me* 'I love to do your will, O my
    God; your law is deep in my heart.' "

Psalm 40:5–9

The Refrain
Let me announce the decree of the LORD;* he said to me, "You are my son; this day
    have I begotten you. . . ."

The Small Verse
Let us bless the Lord. And all that is within me, forget not his benefits.

The Lord's Prayer

The Prayer Appointed for the Week
Lord, make me have perpetual love and reverence for your holy Name, for you
    never fail to help and govern those whom you have set upon the sure founda-
    tion of your loving-kindness; through Jesus Christ our Lord, who lives and
    reigns with you and the Holy Spirit, one God, for ever and ever. *Amen.*†

The Concluding Prayer of the Church
O God, you make me glad with the weekly remembrance of the glorious resurrec-
    tion of your Son my Lord: Give me this day such blessing through my worship
    of you, that the week to come may be spent in your favor; through Jesus Christ
    our Lord. *Amen.*†

The Vespers Office   **To Be Observed on the Hour or Half Hour
Between 5 and 8 p.m.**

The Call to Prayer
Hallelujah! Praise the Name of the LORD;* give praise, you servants of the LORD,
You who stand in the house of the LORD,* in the courts of the house of our God.
Praise the LORD, for the LORD is good;* sing praises to his Name, for it is lovely.

Psalm 135:1–3

The Request for Presence
Incline your ear to me;* make haste to deliver me.

Psalm 31:2

The Greeting
The Lord is in his holy temple;* let all the earth keep silence before him. *Amen.*

Psalm 11:4

The Hymn

Now thank we all our God,	O may this bounteous God
With hearts and hands and voices,	Through all our life be near us,
Who wondrous things has done,	With ever joyful hearts
In whom the world rejoices;	And blessed peace to cheer us;
Who from our mothers' arms	And keep us in his grace,
Has blessed us on our way	And guide us when perplexed,
With countless gifts of love	And free us from all ills
And still is ours today.	In this world and the next.

Martin Rinkart

The Refrain for the Vespers Lessons

Give thanks to the Lord, for he is good,* and his mercy endures for ever.

Psalm 107:1

The Vespers Psalm   *He Teaches Sinners His Way*

Gracious and upright is the Lord;* therefore he teaches sinners his way.

He guides the humble in doing right* and teaches his way to the lowly.

All the paths of the Lord are love and faithfulness* to those who keep his
covenant and his testimonies.

Psalm 25:7–9

The Refrain

Give thanks to the Lord, for he is good,* and his mercy endures for ever.

The Gloria

The Lord's Prayer

The Prayer Appointed for the Week

Lord, make me have perpetual love and reverence for your holy Name, for you
never fail to help and govern those whom you have set upon the sure foundation of your loving-kindness; through Jesus Christ our Lord, who lives and
reigns with you and the Holy Spirit, one God, for ever and ever. *Amen.*†

The Concluding Prayer of the Church

Lord God, whose Son our Savior Jesus Christ, triumphed over the powers of death
and prepares for us our place in the new Jerusalem: Grant that I, who have this
day given thanks for the resurrection, may praise you in the City of which he is
the light, and where he lives and reigns for ever and ever. *Amen.*†

The Morning Office   **To Be Observed on the Hour or Half Hour**
                                      Between 6 and 9 a.m.

The Call to Prayer

Let my mouth be full of your praise* and your glory all the day long.

Do not cast me off in my old age;* forsake me not when my strength fails.

Psalm 71:8–9

The Request for Presence
O LORD, my God, my Savior,* by day and night I cry to you.
Let my prayer enter into your presence . . .

Psalm 88:1–2

The Greeting
Show me your ways, O LORD,* and teach me your paths.
Lead me in your truth and teach me,* for you are the God of my salvation; in you
    have I trusted all the day long.

Psalm 25:3–4

The Refrain for the Morning Lessons
Deliverance belongs to the LORD.* Your blessing be upon your people!

Psalm 3:8

A Reading
Jesus taught his disciples, saying: 'I still have many things to say to you but they
    would be too much for you to bear now. However, when the Spirit of truth
    comes he will lead you to the complete truth, since he will not be speaking of
    his own accord, but will say only what he has been told; and he will reveal to
    you the things to come. He will glorify me, since all he reveals to you will be
    taken from what is mine. Everything the Father has is mine; that is why I said:
    All he reveals to you will be taken from what is mine. In a short time you will
    no longer see me, and then a short time later you will see me again.'

John 16:12–16

The Refrain
Deliverance belongs to the LORD.* Your blessing be upon your people!

The Morning Psalm   ***His Lightnings Light Up the World***
The LORD is King; let the earth rejoice;* let the multitude of the isles be glad.
Clouds and darkness are round about him,* righteousness and justice are the
    foundations of his throne.
A fire goes before him* and burns up his enemies on every side.
His lightnings light up the world; the mountains melt like wax at the presence of
    the LORD,* at the presence of the LORD of the whole earth.
The heavens declare his righteousness,* and all the peoples see his glory.

Psalm 97:1–6

The Refrain
Deliverance belongs to the LORD.* Your blessing be upon your people!

The Gloria

The Lord's Prayer

The Prayer Appointed for the Week
Lord, make me have perpetual love and reverence for your holy Name, for you
    never fail to help and govern those whom you have set upon the sure founda-

tion of your loving-kindness; through Jesus Christ our Lord, who lives and reigns with you and the Holy Spirit, one God, for ever and ever. *Amen.*†

The Concluding Prayer of the Church

Lord God, almighty and everlasting Father, you have brought me in safety to this new day: Preserve me with your mighty power, that I may not fall into sin, nor be overcome by adversity; and in all I do direct me to the fulfilling of your purpose; through Jesus Christ my Lord. *Amen.*†

The Midday Office

**To Be Observed on the Hour or Half Hour
Between 11 a.m. and 2 p.m.**

The Call to Prayer

All who take refuge in you will be glad;* they will sing out their joy forever.
You will shelter them,* so that those who love your Name may exult in you.
For you, O LORD, will bless the righteous;* you will defend them with your favor
as with a shield.

Psalm 5:13–15

The Request for Presence

You are the LORD; do not withhold your compassion from me;* let your love and
your faithfulness keep me safe for ever.

Psalm 40:12

The Greeting

O LORD, what are we that you should care for us?* mere mortals that you should
think of us?
We are like a puff of wind;* our days are passing like a shadow.

Psalm 144:3–4

The Refrain for the Midday Lessons

Protect my life and deliver me;* let me not be put to shame, for I have trusted in
you.
Let integrity and uprightness preserve me,* for my hope is in you.

Psalm 25:19–20

A Reading

I know, YAHWEH, no one's course is in his control, nor is it in anyone's power, as he
goes his way, to guide his own steps. Correct me, YAHWEH, but in moderation,
not in your anger or you will reduce me to nothing.

Jeremiah 10:23–24

The Refrain

Protect my life and deliver me;* let me not be put to shame, for I have trusted in
you.
Let integrity and uprightness preserve me,* for my hope is in you.

The Midday Psalm   *The Upright Will See This and Rejoice*
The LORD changed rivers into deserts,* and water-springs into thirsty ground.
A fruitful land into salt flats,* because of the wickedness of those who dwell there.
He changed deserts into pools of water* and dry land into water-springs.
He settled the hungry there,* and they founded a city to dwell in.
They sowed fields, and planted vineyards,* and brought in a fruitful harvest.
He blessed them, so that they increased greatly;* he did not let their herds decrease.
Yet when they were diminished and brought low,* through stress of adversity and
     sorrow,
(He pours out contempt on princes* and makes them travel in trackless wastes)
He lifted up the poor out of misery* and multiplied their families like flocks of sheep.
The upright will see this and rejoice,* but all wickedness will shut its mouth.
Whoever is wise will ponder these things,* and consider well the mercies of the
     LORD.

Psalm 107:33–43

The Refrain
Protect my life and deliver me;* let me not be put to shame, for I have trusted in
     you.
Let integrity and uprightness preserve me,* for my hope is in you.

The Cry of the Church
O God, come to my assistance! O Lord, make haste to help me!

The Lord's Prayer

The Prayer Appointed for the Week
Lord, make me have perpetual love and reverence for your holy Name, for you
     never fail to help and govern those whom you have set upon the sure founda-
     tion of your loving-kindness; through Jesus Christ our Lord, who lives and
     reigns with you and the Holy Spirit, one God, for ever and ever. *Amen.*†

The Concluding Prayer of the Church
Lord Jesus Christ, you have prepared a quiet place for us in your Father's eternal
     home. Watch over our welfare on this perilous journey, shade us from the
     burning heat of day, and keep our lives free of evil until the end. *Amen.*

THE LITURGY OF THE HOURS, VOL. III

The Vespers Office   **To Be Observed on the Hour or Half Hour**
                                                          Between 5 and 8 p.m.

The Call to Prayer
It is a good thing to give thanks to the LORD* and to sing praises to your Name, O
     Most High;
To tell of your loving-kindness early in the morning* and of your faithfulness in
     the night season.

Psalm 92:1–2

The Request for Presence
Hear my prayer, O God;* give ear to the words of my mouth.

Psalm 54:2

The Greeting
I will thank you, O Lord my God, with all my heart,* and glorify your Name for
evermore.

Psalm 86:12

The Hymn   *He Leadeth Me: O Blessed Thought!*

He leadeth me: O blessed thought!
O words with heavenly comfort fraught!
Whate'er I do, where'er I be,
Still 'tis God's hand that leadeth me.

And when my task on earth is done,
When by thy grace the victory's won,
E'en death's cold wave I will not flee,
Since God through Jordan leadeth me.

Sometimes mid scenes of deepest gloom,
Sometimes where Eden's bowers bloom,
By water still, o'er troubled sea,
Still 'tis his hand that leadeth me.

He leadeth me, he leadeth me,
By his own hand he leadeth me;
His faithful follower I would be,
For by his hand he leadeth me.

Joseph H. Gilmore

Lord, I would place my hand in thine,
Nor ever murmur nor repine;
Content, whatever lot I see,
Since 'tis my God that leadeth me.

The Refrain for the Vespers Lessons
I will bless the Lord who gives me counsel;* my heart teaches me, night after
night.

Psalm 16:7

The Vespers Psalm   *The Eyes of the Lord Are Upon the Righteous*
The eyes of the Lord are upon the righteous,* and his ears are open to their cry.
The face of the Lord is against those who do evil,* to root out the remembrance of
them from the earth.
The righteous cry, and the Lord hears them* and delivers them from all their
troubles.
The Lord is near to the broken hearted* and will save those whose spirits are
crushed.
Many are the troubles of the righteous,* but the Lord will deliver him out of
them all.

Psalm 34:15–19

The Refrain
I will bless the Lord who gives me counsel;* my heart teaches me, night after night.

The Small Verse
Happy are the people whose strength is in you!* whose hearts are set on the pilgrim's way,

For one day in your courts is better than a thousand in my own room,* and to
   stand at the threshold of the house of my God than to dwell in the tents of the
   wicked.

Psalm 84:4, 9

The Lord's Prayer

The Prayer Appointed for the Week
Lord, make me have perpetual love and reverence for your holy Name, for you
   never fail to help and govern those whom you have set upon the sure foundation of your loving-kindness; through Jesus Christ our Lord, who lives and
   reigns with you and the Holy Spirit, one God, for ever and ever. *Amen.*✝

The Concluding Prayer of the Church
Save me, O Lord, while I am awake, and keep me while I sleep. That I may wake
   in Christ and rest in peace.

adapted from THE SHORT BREVIARY

The Morning Office   **To Be Observed on the Hour or Half Hour**
                                  Between 6 and 9 a.m.

The Call to Prayer
Some went down to the sea in ships* and plied their trade in deep waters;
They beheld the works of the LORD* and his wonder in the deep.
Then he spoke, and a stormy wind arose,* which tossed high the waves of the sea.
They mounted up to the heavens and fell back to the depths;* their hearts melted
   because of their peril.
They reeled and staggered like drunkards* and were at their wits' end.
Then they cried to the LORD in their trouble,* and he delivered them from their dis-
   tress.
He stilled the storm to a whisper* and quieted the waves of the sea.
Then they were glad because of the calm,* and he brought them to the harbor they
   were bound for.
Let them give thanks to the LORD for his mercy* and the wonders he does for his
   children.
Let them exalt him in the congregation of the people* and praise him in the coun-
   cil of the elders.

Psalm 107:23–32

The Request for Presence
Open my eyes, that I may see* the wonders of your law.

Psalm 119:18

The Greeting
With my whole heart I seek you;* let me not stray from your commandments.

Psalm 119:10

The Refrain for the Morning Lessons
I hate those who have a divided heart,* but your law do I love.

Psalm 119:113

A Reading
Jesus taught us, saying: 'It is not anyone who says to me, "Lord, Lord," who will
enter the kingdom of heaven, but the person who does the will of my Father in
heaven. When the day comes many will say to me, "Lord, Lord, did we not
prophesy in your name?" Then I shall tell them to their faces: "I have never
known you; *away from me all evildoers!*" '

Matthew 7:21–23

The Refrain
I hate those who have a divided heart,* but your law do I love.

The Morning Psalm   *The Dullard Does Not Know*
Lord, how great are your works!* Your thoughts are very deep.
The dullard does not know, nor does the fool understand,* that though the wicked
grow like weeds, and all the workers of iniquity flourish,
They flourish only to be destroyed forever;* but you, O Lord, are exalted for ever-
more.

Psalm 92:5–7

The Refrain
I hate those who have a divided heart,* but your law do I love.

The Small Verse
The Lord is my shepherd and nothing is wanting to me. In green pastures He has
settled me.

The Short Breviary

The Lord's Prayer

The Prayer Appointed for the Week
Lord, make me have perpetual love and reverence for your holy Name, for you
never fail to help and govern those whom you have set upon the sure foundation of your loving-kindness; through Jesus Christ our Lord, who lives and
reigns with you and the Holy Spirit, one God, for ever and ever. *Amen.*†

The Concluding Prayer of the Church
Lord God, almighty and everlasting Father, you have brought me in safety to this
new day: Preserve me with your mighty power, that I may not fall into sin, nor
be overcome by adversity; and in all I do direct me to the fulfilling of your purpose; through Jesus Christ my Lord. *Amen.*†

The Midday Office   **To Be Observed on the Hour or Half Hour**
                                         Between 11 a.m. and 2 p.m.

The Call to Prayer
Sing to the LORD and bless his Name;* proclaim the good news of his salvation
    from day to day.
Declare his glory among the nations* and his wonders among all peoples.
For great is the LORD and greatly to be praised;* he is more to be feared than all
    gods.

Psalm 96:2–4

The Request for Presence
I have gone astray like a sheep that is lost;* search for your servant, for I do not
    forget your commandments.

Psalm 119:176

The Greeting
When your word goes forth it gives light;* it gives understanding to the simple.

Psalm 119:130

The Refrain for the Midday Lessons
He will not let your foot be moved* and he who watches over you will not fall
    asleep.

Psalm 121:3

A Reading
Now the spirit we have received is not the spirit of the world, but God's own
    spirit, so that we may understand the lavish gifts God has given us. And these
    are what we speak of, not in terms learnt from human philosophy, but in terms
    learnt from the Spirit: fitting spiritual language to spiritual things.

I Corinthians 2:12–13

The Refrain
He will not let your foot be moved* and he who watches over you will not fall
    asleep.

The Midday Psalm   *God Leads His People Like a Flock*
The waters saw you, O God; the waters saw you and trembled;* the very depths
    were shaken.
The clouds poured out water; the skies thundered;* your arrows flashed to and fro;
The sound of your thunder was in the whirlwind; Your lightnings lit up the
    world;* the earth trembled and shook.
Your way was in the sea, and your paths in the great waters,* yet your footsteps
    were not seen.
You led your people like a flock* by the hand of Moses and Aaron.

Psalm 77:16–20

The Refrain
He will not let your foot be moved* and he who watches over you will not fall
asleep.

The Gloria

The Lord's Prayer

The Prayer Appointed for the Week
Lord, make me have perpetual love and reverence for your holy Name, for you
never fail to help and govern those whom you have set upon the sure foundation of your loving-kindness; through Jesus Christ our Lord, who lives and
reigns with you and the Holy Spirit, one God, for ever and ever. *Amen.†*

The Concluding Prayer of the Church
God of mystery, God of love, send your Spirit into our hearts with gifts of wisdom
and peace, fortitude and charity. We long to love and serve you. Faithful God,
make us faithful. This we ask through the intercession of all your saints. *Amen.*

THE NEW COMPANION TO THE BREVIARY

The Vespers Office **To Be Observed on the Hour or Half Hour
Between 5 and 8 p.m.**

The Call to Prayer
Know that the LORD does wonders for the faithful;* when I call upon the LORD, he
will hear me.
Tremble, then, and do not sin;* speak to your heart in silence upon your bed.
Offer the appointed sacrifices* and put your trust in the LORD.

Psalm 4:3–5

The Request for Presence
O LORD, do not forsake me;* be not far from me, O my God.
Make haste to help me,* O Lord of my salvation.

Psalm 38:21–22

The Greeting
As the deer longs for the water-brooks,* so longs my soul for you, O God.

Psalm 42:1

The Hymn   O Love That Will Not Let Me Go
O Love that will not let me go,
I rest my weary soul in Thee;
I give Thee back the life I owe,
That in Thine ocean depths its flow
May richer, fuller be,
May richer, fuller be.

O light that followest all my way,
I yield my flickering torch to Thee;
My heart restores its borrowed ray,
That in Thy sunshine's blaze its day
May brighter, fairer be,
May brighter, fairer be.

O joy that seekest me through pain,
I cannot close my heart to Thee;
I trace the rainbow through the rain,
And feel the promise is not in vain
That morn shall tearless be,
That morn shall tearless be.

O cross that lifts up my head,
I dare not ask to fly from Thee;
I lay in dust life's glory dead,
And from the ground there blossoms red
Life that shall endless be,
Life that shall endless be.

Rev. George Matheson

The Refrain for the Vespers Lessons

The same stone that the builders rejected* has become the chief cornerstone.

Psalm 118:22

The Vespers Psalm   *Into Your Hands I Commend My Spirit*

In you, O LORD, have I taken refuge; let me never be put to shame;* deliver me in
  your righteousness.

Incline your ear to me;* make haste to deliver me.

Be my strong rock, a castle to keep me safe, for you are my crag and my stronghold;* for the sake of your Name, lead me and guide me.

Take me out of the net that they have secretly set for me,* for you are my tower of
  strength.

Into your hands I commend my spirit, for you have redeemed me,* O LORD, O
  God of truth.

Psalm 31:1–5

The Refrain

The same stone that the builders rejected* has become the chief cornerstone.

The Small Verse

Save your people, Lord, and bless your inheritance; Govern and uphold me, now
  and always. Day by day I bless you; I praise your Name for ever. Lord, keep me
  from all sin today; Have mercy on me, Lord, have mercy. Lord, show me your
  love and mercy; For I put my trust in you. In you, Lord, is my hope; And I shall
  never hope in vain.

The Lord's Prayer

The Prayer Appointed for the Week

Lord, make me have perpetual love and reverence for your holy Name, for you
  never fail to help and govern those whom you have set upon the sure foundation of your loving-kindness; through Jesus Christ our Lord, who lives and
  reigns with you and the Holy Spirit, one God, for ever and ever. *Amen.*†

The Concluding Prayer of the Church

Blessed be God, who has not rejected my prayer,* nor withheld his love from me.

Psalm 66:18

The Morning Office   To Be Observed on the Hour or Half Hour
                                     Between 6 and 9 a.m.

The Call to Prayer
Love the Lord, all you who worship him;* the Lord protects the faithful, but
   repays to the full those who act haughtily.

Psalm 31:23

The Request for Presence
O Lord, I call to you; my Rock, do not be deaf to my cry;* lest, if you do not hear
   me, I become like those who go down to the Pit.

Psalm 28:1

The Greeting
Your way, O God, is holy;* who is as great as our God?

Psalm 77:13

The Refrain for the Morning Lessons
Protect my life and deliver me;* let me not be put to shame, for I have trusted in you.

Psalm 25:19

A Reading
Jesus taught the crowds, saying: 'Is it not written in your Law: *I said, you are gods?*
   So it uses the word "gods" of those people to whom the Word of God was
   addressed—and scripture cannot be set aside. Yet to someone the Father has
   consecrated and sent into the world, you say, "You are blaspheming," because I
   said, "I am Son of God." If I am not doing my Father's work, there is no need to
   believe in me; but if I am doing it, then even if you refuse to believe in me, at
   least believe in the work I do; then you will know for certain that the Father is
   in me and I am in the Father.'

John 10:34–38

The Refrain
Protect my life and deliver me;* let me not be put to shame, for I have trusted in
   you.

The Morning Psalm   *You Have Made the Son of Man Strong for Yourself*
Let your hand be upon the man of your right hand,* the son of man you have
   made so strong for yourself.
And so will we never turn away from you;* give us life, that we may call upon
   your name.
Restore us, O Lord God of Hosts;* show the light of your countenance, and we
   shall be saved.

Psalm 80:16–18

The Refrain
Protect my life and deliver me;* let me not be put to shame, for I have trusted in
   you.

The Cry of the Church
In the evening, in the morning, and at noonday, I will complain and lament, and
he will hear my voice.

Psalm 55:18

The Lord's Prayer

The Prayer Appointed for the Week
Lord, make me have perpetual love and reverence for your holy Name, for you
never fail to help and govern those whom you have set upon the sure foundation of your loving-kindness; through Jesus Christ our Lord, who lives and
reigns with you and the Holy Spirit, one God, for ever and ever. *Amen.*†

The Concluding Prayer of the Church
Lord God, almighty and everlasting Father, you have brought me in safety to this
new day: Preserve me with your mighty power, that I may not fall into sin, nor
be overcome by adversity; and in all I do direct me to the fulfilling of your purpose; through Jesus Christ my Lord. *Amen.*†

The Midday Office   **To Be Observed on the Hour or Half Hour**
                                Between 11 a.m. and 2 p.m.

The Call to Prayer
Sing praise to the LORD who dwells in Zion;* proclaim to the peoples the things he
has done.

Psalm 9:11

The Request for Presence
Send out your light and your truth, that they may lead me,* and bring me to your
holy hill and to your dwelling;
That I may go to the altar of God, to the God of my joy and gladness;* and on the
harp I will give thanks to you, O God, my God.

Psalm 43:3–4

The Greeting
How glorious you are!* more splendid than the everlasting mountains!

Psalm 76:4

The Refrain for the Midday Lessons
Away from me, you wicked!* I will keep the commandments of my God.

Psalm 119:115

A Reading
'Look, today I set before you life and prosperity, death and disaster. If you obey
the commandments of YAHWEH your God which I am laying down for you
today, if you love YAHWEH your God and follow his ways, if you keep his commandments, his laws, and his customs, you will live and grow numerous, and
YAHWEH your God will bless you in the country which you are about to enter

and make your own. But if your heart turns away, if you refuse to listen, if you let yourself be drawn into worshipping other gods and serving them, I tell you today, you will most certainly perish; you will not live for long in the country which you are crossing the Jordan to enter and possess. Today, I call heaven and earth to witness against you: I am offering you life or death, blessing or curse. Choose life, then, so that you and your descendants may live, in the love of YAHWEH your God, obeying his voice, holding fast to him; for in this your life consists, and on this depends the length of time that you stay in the country which YAHWEH swore to your ancestors Abraham, Isaac and Jacob he would give them.'

Deuteronomy 30:15–20

The Refrain
Away from me, you wicked!* I will keep the commandments of my God.

The Midday Psalm   *Happy Are They Who Put Their Trust in You*
One day in your courts is better than a thousand in my own room,* and to stand at
    the threshold of the house of God than to dwell in the tents of the wicked.
For the LORD God is both sun and shield;* he will give grace and glory;
No good thing will the LORD withhold* from those who walk with integrity.
O LORD of hosts* happy are they who put their trust in you!

Psalm 84:9–12

The Refrain
Away from me, you wicked!* I will keep the commandments of my God.

The Gloria

The Lord's Prayer

The Prayer Appointed for the Week
Lord, make me have perpetual love and reverence for your holy Name, for you
    never fail to help and govern those whom you have set upon the sure founda-
    tion of your loving-kindness; through Jesus Christ our Lord, who lives and
    reigns with you and the Holy Spirit, one God, for ever and ever. *Amen.*†

The Concluding Prayer of the Church
May our sons be like plants well nurtured from their youth,* and our daughters
    like sculptured corners of a palace.
May our barns be filled to overflowing with all manner of crops;* may the flocks
    in our pastures increase by thousands and tens of thousands; may our cattle be
    fat and sleek.
May there be no breaching of the walls, no going into exile,* no wailing in the pub-
    lic square.
Happy are the people of whom this is so!* happy are the people whose God is the
    LORD!

Psalm 144:13–16

The Vespers Office   **To Be Observed on the Hour or Half Hour**
                                          Between 5 and 8 p.m.

The Call to Prayer
Sing to God, O kingdoms of the earth;* sing praises to the Lord.
He rides in the heavens, the ancient heavens;* he sends forth his voice, his mighty
    voice.

Psalm 68:33–34

The Request for Presence
Protect me, O God, for I take refuge in you;* I have said to the LORD, "You are my
    Lord, my good above all others."

Psalm 16:1

The Greeting
Praise God from whom all blessings flow; Praise Him all creatures here below;
    Praise Him above, you heavenly hosts; Praise Father, Son, and Holy Ghost.

Doxology

The Hymn   *When Morning Gilds the Skies*
When morning gilds the skies,   You nations of mankind,
My heart awaking cries,   In this your concord find:
May Jesus Christ be praised!   May Jesus Christ be praised!
When evening shadows fall,   Let all the earth around
This rings my curfew call: Ring joyous with the sound.
May Jesus Christ be praised!   May Jesus Christ be praised!

When mirth for music longs,   Sing, suns and stars of space,
This is my song of songs: Sing you that see his face,
May Jesus Christ be praised!   Sing, Jesus Christ be praised!
God's holy house of prayer   God's whole creation o'er,
Has none that can compare   Both now and evermore,
With "Jesus Christ be praised!"   Shall Jesus Christ be praised!

No lovelier antiphon   *German (unknown)*
In all high heaven is known   *translated by Robert S. Bridges*
Than "Jesus Christ be praised!"
There to the eternal Word
The eternal psalm is heard:
May Jesus Christ be praised!

The Refrain for the Vespers Lessons
I will bear witness that the LORD is righteous;* I will praise the Name of the LORD
    Most High.

Psalm 7:18

The Vespers Psalm　　　　　　*They Shall Make Known to a People Yet Unborn*

All the ends of the earth shall remember and turn to the Lord,* and all the families
　　of the nations shall bow before him.

For kingship belongs to the Lord;* he rules over the nations.

To him alone all who sleep in the earth bow down in worship;* all who go down to
　　the dust fall before him.

My soul shall live for him; my descendants shall serve him;* they shall be known
　　as the Lord's forever.

They shall come and make known to a people yet unborn* the saving deeds that
　　he has done.

Psalm 22:26–30

The Refrain

I will bear witness that the Lord is righteous;* I will praise the Name of the Lord
　　Most High.

The Cry of the Church

Even so, come Lord Jesus!

The Lord's Prayer

The Prayer Appointed for the Week

Lord, make me have perpetual love and reverence for your holy Name, for you
　　never fail to help and govern those whom you have set upon the sure founda-
　　tion of your loving-kindness; through Jesus Christ our Lord, who lives and
　　reigns with you and the Holy Spirit, one God, for ever and ever. *Amen.*†

The Concluding Prayer of the Church

Spirit of God, promise of Jesus, come to our help at the close of this day. Come
　　with forgiveness and healing love. Come with life and hope. Come with all
　　that we need to continue in the way of your truth. So may we praise you in the
　　Trinity forever. *Amen.*

The New Companion to the Breviary

The Morning Office　　　　　　**To Be Observed on the Hour or Half Hour**
　　　　　　　　　　　　　　　　　　Between 6 and 9 a.m.

The Call to Prayer

Let us bless the Lord, from this time forth for evermore. Hallelujah!

adapted from Psalm 115:18

The Request for Presence

Turn to me and have mercy upon me;* give your strength to your servant; and
　　save the child of your handmaid.

Psalm 86:16

The Greeting
You are my hiding-place; you preserve me from trouble;* you surround me with shouts of deliverance.

Psalm 32:8

The Refrain for the Morning Lessons
Behold, God is my helper;* it is the Lord who sustains my Life.

Psalm 54:4

A Reading
When he went into Capernaum a centurion came up and pleaded with him. 'Sir,' he said, 'my servant is lying at home paralyzed and in great pain.' Jesus said to him, 'I will come myself and cure him.' The centurion replied, 'Sir, I am not worthy to have you under my roof; just give the word and my servant will be cured. For I am under authority myself, and have soldiers under me; and I say to one man: "Go," and he goes; to another: "Come here," and he comes; to my servant: "Do this," and he does it.' When Jesus heard this he was astonished and said to those following him, 'In truth I tell you, in no one in Israel have I found faith as great as this. And I tell you that many will come from east and west and sit down with Abraham and Isaac and Jacob at the feast in the kingdom of heaven; but the children of the kingdom will be thrown out into the darkness outside, where there will be weeping and grinding of teeth.' And to the centurion Jesus said, 'Go back, then; let this be done for you, as your faith demands.' And the servant was cured at that moment.

Matthew 8:5–13

The Refrain
Behold, God is my helper;* it is the Lord who sustains my Life.

The Morning Psalm   A Song to the Father
But let the righteous be glad and rejoice before God;* let them be merry and joyful.
Sing to God, sing praises to his Name; exalt him who rides upon the heavens;*
  YAHWEH is his Name, rejoice before him!
Father of orphans, defender of widows,* God in his holy habitation!

Psalm 68:3–5

The Refrain
Behold, God is my helper;* it is the Lord who sustains my Life.

The Gloria

The Lord's Prayer

The Prayer Appointed for the Week
Lord, make me have perpetual love and reverence for your holy Name, for you never fail to help and govern those whom you have set upon the sure foundation of your loving-kindness; through Jesus Christ our Lord, who lives and reigns with you and the Holy Spirit, one God, for ever and ever. *Amen.*†

The Concluding Prayer of the Church
Lord God, almighty and everlasting Father, you have brought me in safety to this
new day: Preserve me with your mighty power, that I may not fall into sin, nor
be overcome by adversity; and in all I do direct me to the fulfilling of your purpose; through Jesus Christ my Lord. *Amen.*†

The Midday Office   **To Be Observed on the Hour or Half Hour**
Between 11 a.m. and 2 p.m.

The Call to Prayer
Be strong and let your heart take courage,* all you who wait for the LORD.

Psalm 31:24

The Request for Presence
Hear my cry, O God,* and listen to my prayer.
I call upon you from the ends of the earth.

Psalm 61:1–2

The Greeting
I love you, O LORD of my strength,* O LORD my stronghold, my crag, and my
haven.

Psalm 18:1

The Refrain for the Midday Lessons
Though my father and my mother forsake me,* the LORD will sustain me.

Psalm 27:14

A Reading
. . . If God is for us, who can be against us? Since he did not spare his own Son, but
gave him up for the sake of all of us, then can we not expect that with him he
will freely give us all his gifts? Who can bring any accusation against those that
God has chosen? When God grants saving justice, who can condemn? Are we
not sure that it is Christ Jesus who died—yes and more who was raised from
the dead and is at God's right hand—and who is adding his plea for us? Can
anything cut us off from the love of Christ . . . I am certain of this: neither death
nor life, nor angels, nor principalities, nothing already in existence and nothing
still to come, nor any power, nor the heights nor the depths, nor any created
thing whatever, will be able to come between us and the love of God, known to
us in Christ Jesus our Lord.

Romans 8:31ff

The Refrain
Though my father and my mother forsake me,* the LORD will sustain me.

The Midday Psalm   *Your Love, O Lord, For Ever Will I Sing*
Your love, O LORD, for ever will I sing;* from age to age my mouth will proclaim
your faithfulness.

For I am persuaded that your love is established for ever;* you have set your faithfulness firmly in the heavens.

Psalm 89:1–2

The Refrain
Though my father and my mother forsake me,* the LORD will sustain me.

The Cry of the Church
In the evening, in the morning, and at noonday, I will complain and lament,* and he will hear my voice.

Psalm 55:18

The Lord's Prayer

The Prayer Appointed for the Week
Lord, make me have perpetual love and reverence for your holy Name, for you never fail to help and govern those whom you have set upon the sure foundation of your loving-kindness; through Jesus Christ our Lord, who lives and reigns with you and the Holy Spirit, one God, for ever and ever. *Amen.*†

The Concluding Prayer of the Church
God of mercy,
this midday moment of rest
is your welcome gift.
Bless the work we have begun,
and make good its defects
and let us finish it in a way that pleases you.
Grant this through Christ our Lord.

THE LITURGY OF THE HOURS, VOL. III

The Vespers Office   **To Be Observed on the Hour or Half Hour Between 5 and 8 p.m.**

The Call to Prayer
Bless our God, you peoples;* make the voice of his praise to be heard;
Who holds our souls in life,* and will not allow our feet to slip.

Psalm 66:7–8

The Request for Presence
Show me the light of your countenance, O God, and come to me.

adapted from Psalm 67:1

The Greeting
Whom have I in heaven but you?* And having you I desire nothing upon earth.

Psalm 73:25

The Hymn   *The Third Song of Isaiah*
Arise, shine, for your light has come,* and the glory of the Lord has dawned upon
    you.
For behold, darkness covers the land;* deep gloom enshrouds the peoples.
But over you the Lord will rise,* and his glory will appear upon you.
Nations will stream to your light,* and kings to the brightness of your dawning.
Your gates will always be open* by day or night they will never shut.
They will call you the City of the Lord,* The Zion of the Holy One of Israel.
Violence will no more be heard in your land,* ruin or destruction within your bor-
    ders.
You will call your walls, Salvation,* and all your portals, Praise.
The sun will no more be your light by day;* by night you will not need the bright-
    ness of the moon.
The Lord will be your everlasting light,* and your God will be your glory.
Glory to the Father, and to the Son, and to the Holy Spirit: as it was in the begin-
    ning, is now, and will be for ever. *Amen.*

Isaiah 60:1ff

The Refrain for the Vespers Lessons
I have been sustained by you ever since I was born; from my mother's womb you
    have been my strength;* my praise shall be always of you.

Psalm 71:6

The Vespers Psalm   *Light Shines in Darkness for the Upright*
Light shines in the darkness for the upright;* the righteous are merciful and full of
    compassion.
It is good for them to be generous in lending* and to manage their affairs with jus-
    tice.
For they will never be shaken;* the righteous will be kept in everlasting remem-
    brance.
They will not be afraid of evil rumors;* their heart is right; they put their trust in
    the Lord.
Their heart is established and will not shrink,* until they see their desire upon
    their enemies.
They have given freely to the poor,* and their righteousness stands fast for ever;
    they will hold up their head with honor.
The wicked will see it and be angry;* they will gnash their teeth and pine away;
    the desires of the wicked will perish.

Psalm 112:4–10

The Refrain
I have been sustained by you ever since I was born; from my mother's womb you
    have been my strength;* my praise shall be always of you.

The Cry of the Church
O God, come to my assistance! O Lord, make haste to help me!

The Lord's Prayer

The Prayer Appointed for the Week
Lord, make me have perpetual love and reverence for your holy Name, for you
never fail to help and govern those whom you have set upon the sure foundation of your loving-kindness; through Jesus Christ our Lord, who lives and
reigns with you and the Holy Spirit, one God, for ever and ever. *Amen.*†

The Concluding Prayer of the Church
Almighty Father, you have given us strength to work throughout this day. Receive
our evening sacrifice of praise in thanksgiving for your countless gifts. We ask
this through our Lord Jesus Christ, your Son, who lives and reigns with you
and the Holy Spirit, one God, for ever and ever. *Amen.*

THE LITURGY OF THE HOURS, VOL. III

The Morning Office   **To Be Observed on the Hour or Half Hour**
                                Between 6 and 9 a.m.

The Call to Prayer
Sing to the LORD a new song,* for he has done marvelous things.
With his right hand and his holy arm* has he won for himself the victory.

Psalm 98:1–2

The Request for Presence
Let your loving-kindness be my comfort,* as you have promised to your servant.
Let your compassion come to me, that I may live,* for your law is my delight.

Psalm 119:76–77

The Greeting
I will confess you among the peoples, O LORD;* I will sing praises to you among
the nations
For your loving-kindness is greater than the heavens,* and your faithfulness
reaches to the clouds.

Psalm 108:3–4

The Refrain for the Morning Lessons
So teach us to number our days* that we may apply our hearts to wisdom.

Psalm 90:12

A Reading
In his honor Levi held a great reception in his house, and with them at table was a
large gathering of tax collectors and others. The Pharisees and their scribes
complained to his disciples and said, 'Why do you eat and drink with tax collectors and sinners?' Jesus said to them in reply, 'It is not those who are well
who need the doctor, but the sick. I have not come to call the upright, but sinners to repentance.'

Luke 5:29–32

The Refrain
So teach us to number our days* that we may apply our hearts to wisdom.

The Morning Psalm   ***He Shall Deliver the Poor Who Cry Out in Distress***
Give the king your justice, O God,* and your righteousness to the King's son . . .
For he shall deliver the poor who cries out in distress,* and the oppressed who has
    no helper.
He shall have pity on the lowly and the poor;* he shall preserve the lives of the
    needy.
He shall redeem their lives from oppression and violence,* and dear shall their
    blood be in his sight.
Long may he live! And may there be given to him the gold of Arabia;* may prayer
    be made for him always, and may they bless him all the day long.
May there be abundance of grain on the earth, growing thick even on the hilltops;*
    may its fruit flourish like Lebanon, and its grain like grass upon the earth.
May his Name remain for ever and be established as long as the sun endures;*
    may all the nations bless themselves in him and call him blessed.
Blessed be the Lord God, the God of Israel,* who alone does marvelous deeds!
And blessed be his glorious Name for ever!* And may all the earth be filled with
    his glory. Amen. Amen.

Psalm 72:1, 12–19

The Refrain
So teach us to number our days* that we may apply our hearts to wisdom.

The Small Verse
Create in me a clean heart, O God,* and renew a right spirit within me.
Cast me not away from your presence* and take not your holy Spirit from me.
Give me the joy of your saving help again* and sustain me with your bountiful
    spirit.

Psalm 51:11–13

The Lord's Prayer

The Prayer Appointed for the Week
Lord, make me have perpetual love and reverence for your holy Name, for you
    never fail to help and govern those whom you have set upon the sure founda-
    tion of your loving-kindness; through Jesus Christ our Lord, who lives and
    reigns with you and the Holy Spirit, one God, for ever and ever. *Amen.*†

The Concluding Prayer of the Church
Lord God, almighty and everlasting Father, you have brought me in safety to this
    new day: Preserve me with your mighty power, that I may not fall into sin, nor
    be overcome by adversity; and in all I do direct me to the fulfilling of your pur-
    pose; through Jesus Christ my Lord. *Amen.*†

The Midday Office **To Be Observed on the Hour or Half Hour**
Between 11 a.m. and 2 p.m.

The Call to Prayer
Hosanna, Lord, hosanna!* Lord, send us now success.
Blessed is he who comes in the name of the Lord;* we bless you from the house of
the Lord.
God is the Lord; he has shined upon us;* form a procession with branches up to
the horns of the altar.

Psalm 118:25–27

The Request for Presence
Set watch before my mouth, O Lord, and guard the door of my lips;* let not my
heart incline to any living thing.
Let me not be occupied in wickedness with evildoers,* nor eat of their choice
foods.
Let the righteous smite me in friendly rebuke; let not the oil of the unrighteous
anoint my head.

Psalm 141:3–5

The Greeting
Remember your word to your servant,* because you have given me hope.
This is my comfort in my trouble,* that your promise gives me life.

Psalm 119:49–50

The Refrain for the Midday Lessons
For God alone my soul in silence waits;* from him comes my salvation.

Psalm 62:1

A Reading
So it is proof of God's own love for us, that Christ died for us while we were still
sinners. How much more can we be sure, therefore, that, now that we have
been justified by his death, we shall be saved through him from the retribution
of God. For if, while we were enemies, we were reconciled to God through the
death of his Son, how much more can we be sure that being now reconciled, we
shall be saved by his life. What is more, we are filled with exultant trust in God,
through our Lord Jesus Christ, through whom we have already gained our reconciliation.

Romans 5:8–11

The Refrain
For God alone my soul in silence waits;* from him comes my salvation.

The Midday Psalm   *You Are My Refuge and My Stronghold*

He who dwells in the shelter of the Most High,* abides under the shadow of the
    Almighty.

He shall say to the LORD, "You are my refuge and my stronghold,* my God in
    whom I put my trust."

He shall deliver you from the snare of the hunter* and from the daily pestilence.

He shall cover you with his pinions, and you shall find refuge under his wings;*
    his faithfulness shall be a shield and a buckler.

You shall not be afraid of any terror by night,* nor of the arrow that flies by day;

Of the plague that stalks in the darkness,* nor of the sickness that lays waste at
    mid-day.

A thousand shall fall at your side* and ten thousand at your right hand, but it shall
    not come near you.

Your eyes have only to behold* to see the reward of the wicked.

Because you have made the LORD your refuge,* and the Most High your habita-
    tion,

There shall no evil happen to you,* neither shall any plague come near your
    dwelling.

                                                            Psalm 91:1–10

The Refrain

For God alone my soul in silence waits;* from him comes my salvation.

The Cry of the Church

In the evening, in the morning, and at noonday, I will complain and lament,* and
    he will hear my voice.

                                                            Psalm 55:18

The Lord's Prayer

The Prayer Appointed for the Week

Lord, make me have perpetual love and reverence for your holy Name, for you
    never fail to help and govern those whom you have set upon the sure founda-
    tion of your loving-kindness; through Jesus Christ our Lord, who lives and
    reigns with you and the Holy Spirit, one God, for ever and ever. *Amen.*†

The Concluding Prayer of the Church

Almighty God, whose most dear Son went not up to the joy before he first suffered
    pain, and did not enter into glory before he was crucified: Mercifully grant that
    I, walking in the way of the cross, may find it to be none other than the way of
    life and peace; through Jesus Christ your Son my Lord. *Amen.*†

The Vespers Office   **To Be Observed on the Hour or Half Hour**
Between 5 and 8 p.m.

The Call to Prayer
O tarry and await the LORD's pleasure; be strong, and he shall comfort your heart;*
wait patiently for the LORD.

Psalm 27:18

The Request for Presence
I have said to the LORD, "You are my God;* listen, O LORD, to my supplication."

Psalm 140:6

The Greeting
I am bound by the vow I made to you, O God;* I will present to you thank-
offerings;
For you have rescued my soul from death and my feet from stumbling,* that I may
walk before God in the light of the living.

Psalm 56:11–12

The Hymn   *A Song of Penitence*
O Lord and Ruler of the hosts of heaven,
        God of Abraham, Isaac, and Jacob,
        and of all their righteous offspring:
You made the heavens and the earth,
        with all their vast array.
All things quake with fear at your presence;
they tremble because of your power.
But your merciful promise is beyond all measure;
        it surpasses all that our minds can fathom.
O Lord, you are full of compassion,
        long-suffering, and abounding in mercy.
You hold back your hand;
        you do not punish as we deserve.
In your great goodness, Lord,
you have promised forgiveness to sinners,
        that they may repent of their sin and be saved.
And now, O Lord, I bend the knee of my heart,
        and make my appeal, sure of your gracious goodness.
I have sinned, O Lord, I have sinned,
        and I know my wickedness only too well.
Therefore I make this prayer to you:
        Forgive me, Lord, forgive me.
Do not let me perish in my sin,
        nor condemn me to the depths of the earth.
For you, O Lord, are the God of those who repent,
        and in me you will show forth your goodness.

Unworthy as I am, you will save me,
in accordance with your great mercy,
    and I will praise you without ceasing all the days of my life.
For all the powers of heaven sing your praises,
    and yours is the glory to ages of ages. Amen.

Prayer of Manasseh

The Refrain for the Vespers Lessons
Purge me from my sin, and I shall be pure;* wash me, and I shall be clean indeed.

Psalm 51:8

The Vespers Psalm   *You Forgave Me the Guilt of My Sin*
While I held my tongue, my bones withered away,* because of my groaning all
    day long.
For your hand was heavy upon me day and night;* my moisture was dried up as
    in the heat of the summer.
Then I acknowledged my sin to you,* and did not conceal my guilt.
I said, "I will confess my transgressions to the LORD."* Then you forgave me the
    guilt of my sin.
Therefore all the faithful will make their prayers to you in time of trouble;* when
    the great waters overflow, they shall not reach them.

Psalm 32:3–7

The Refrain
Purge me from my sin, and I shall be pure;* wash me, and I shall be clean indeed.

The Cry of the Church
Lord, have mercy on us. Christ, have mercy on us. Lord, have mercy on us.

The Lord's Prayer

The Prayer Appointed for the Week
Lord, make me have perpetual love and reverence for your holy Name, for you
    never fail to help and govern those whom you have set upon the sure founda-
    tion of your loving-kindness; through Jesus Christ our Lord, who lives and
    reigns with you and the Holy Spirit, one God, for ever and ever. *Amen.*†

The Concluding Prayers of the Church
Almighty God, who has promised to hear the petitions of those who ask in your
    Son's Name: I beseech you mercifully to incline your ear to me who have made
    my prayers and supplications to you; and grant that those things which I have
    faithfully asked according to your will, may effectually be obtained, to the
    relief of my necessity, and to the setting forth of your glory; through Jesus
    Christ my Lord. *Amen.*†

May the souls of the faithful departed, through the mercy of God, rest in eternal
    peace. *Amen.*

The Morning Office **To Be Observed on the Hour or Half Hour**
Between 6 and 9 a.m.

The Call to Prayer
Hallelujah! Praise the Name of the LORD;* give praise, you servants of the LORD.
Psalm 135:1

The Request for Presence
In your righteousness, deliver and set me free;* incline your ear to me and save me.
Psalm 71:2

The Greeting
O LORD, I am your servant;* I am your servant and the child of your handmaid;
you have freed me from my bonds.
Psalm 116:14

The Refrain for the Morning Lessons
This is the LORD's doing,* and it is marvelous in our eyes.
Psalm 118:23

A Reading
Thomas, called the Twin, who was one of the Twelve, was not with them when
Jesus came. So the other disciples said to him, 'We have seen the Lord,' but he
answered, 'Unless I can see the holes that the nails made in his hands and I can
put my finger into the holes that they made, and unless I can put my hand into
his side, I refuse to believe.' Eight days later the disciples were in the house
again and Thomas was with them. The doors were closed, but Jesus came in
and stood among them. 'Peace be with you,' he said. Then he spoke to Thomas,
'Put your finger here; look, here are my hands. Give me your hand; put it into
my side. Do not be unbelieving any more but believe.' Thomas replied, 'My
Lord and my God!' Jesus said to him: 'You believe because you can see me.
Blessed are those who have not seen and yet believe.'
John 20:24–29

The Refrain
This is the LORD's doing,* and it is marvelous in our eyes.

The Morning Psalm *He Has Not Dealt with Us According to Our Sins*
He has not dealt with us according to our sins,* nor rewarded us according to our
wickedness.
For as the heavens are high above the earth,* so is his mercy great upon those who
fear him.
As far as the east is from the west,* so far has he removed our sins from us.
As a father cares for his children,* so does the LORD care for those who fear him.
For he himself knows whereof we are made;* he remembers that we are but dust.
Psalm 103:10–14

The Refrain
This is the Lord's doing,* and it is marvelous in our eyes.

The Gloria

The Lord's Prayer

The Prayer Appointed for the Week
Lord, make me have perpetual love and reverence for your holy Name, for you
never fail to help and govern those whom you have set upon the sure foundation of your loving-kindness; through Jesus Christ our Lord, who lives and
reigns with you and the Holy Spirit, one God, for ever and ever. *Amen.*†

The Concluding Prayer of the Church
Lord God, almighty and everlasting Father, you have brought me in safety to this
new day: Preserve me with your mighty power, that I may not fall into sin, nor
be overcome by adversity; and in all I do direct me to the fulfilling of your purpose; through Jesus Christ my Lord. *Amen.*†

The Midday Office   **To Be Observed on the Hour or Half Hour**
Between 11 a.m. and 2 p.m.

The Call to Prayer
Hallelujah! How good it is to sing praises to our God!* how pleasant it is to honor
him with praise!

Psalm 147:1

The Request for Presence
Remember me, O Lord, with the favor you have for your people,* and visit me
with your saving help;
That I may see the prosperity of your elect and be glad with the gladness of your
people,* that I may glory with your inheritance.

Psalm 106:4–5

The Greeting
In you, O Lord, have I taken refuge;* let me never be ashamed.

Psalm 71:1

The Refrain for the Midday Lessons
Your statutes have been like songs to me* wherever I have lived like a stranger.

Psalm 119:54

A Reading
Yahweh says this: 'Accursed be the one who trusts in human beings, who relies on
human strength, and whose heart turns from Yahweh. Such a person is like
scrub in the wastelands: when good comes, it does not affect him since he lives
in the parched places of the desert, uninhabited, salt land. Blessed is the man
who trusts in Yahweh, with Yahweh for his reliance. He is like a tree by the

waterside that thrusts its roots to the stream: when the heat comes it has
nothing to fear, its foliage stays green; untroubled in a year of drought, it never
stops bearing fruit.'

Jeremiah 17:5–8

The Refrain
Your statutes have been like songs to me* wherever I have lived like a stranger.

The Midday Psalm   *I Am the Lord Your God*
Hear, O my people, and I will admonish you:* O Israel, if you would but listen to
me!
There shall be no strange god among you;* you shall not worship a foreign god.
I am the Lord your God, who brought you out of the land of Egypt and said,*
"Open your mouth wide, and I will fill it."

Psalm 81:8–10

The Refrain
Your statutes have been like songs to me* wherever I have lived like a stranger.

The Cry of the Church
Lord, have mercy on us. Christ, have mercy on us. Lord, have mercy on us.

The Lord's Prayer

The Prayer Appointed for the Week
Lord, make me have perpetual love and reverence for your holy Name, for you
never fail to help and govern those whom you have set upon the sure foundation of your loving-kindness; through Jesus Christ our Lord, who lives and
reigns with you and the Holy Spirit, one God, for ever and ever. *Amen.*†

The Concluding Prayer of the Church
Almighty God, who after the creation of the world rested from all your works and
sanctified a day of rest for all your creatures: Grant that I, putting away all
earthly anxieties, may be duly prepared for the service of public worship, and
grant as well that my Sabbath upon earth may be a preparation for the eternal
rest promised to your people in heaven; through Jesus Christ our Lord. *Amen.*†

The Vespers Office   **To Be Observed on the Hour or Half Hour
Between 5 and 8 p.m.**

The Call to Prayer
Great is the Lord and greatly to be praised;* there is no end to his greatness.

Psalm 145:3

The Request for Presence
"Hide not your face from your servant;* be swift and answer me, . . .
Draw near to me and redeem me . . ."

Psalm 69:19–20

The Greeting
> O gracious Light,
> pure brightness of the everlasting Father in heaven,
> O Jesus Christ, holy and blessed!
>
> Now as we come to the setting of the sun,
> and our eyes behold the vesper light,
> we sing your praises O God: Father, Son and Holy Spirit.
>
> You are worthy at all times to be praised by happy voices,
> O Son of God, O giver of life,
> and to be glorified through all the worlds.

Phos Hilaron

The Hymn   ***God Is Working His Purpose Out***
> God is working his purpose out
> As year succeeds to year;
> God is working his purpose out,
> And the time is drawing near;
> Nearer and nearer draws the time,
> The time shall surely be,
> When the earth shall be filled with the glory of God
> As the waters cover the sea.
>
> March we forth in the strength of God,
> With the banner of Christ unfurled,
> That the light of the glorious gospel of truth
> May shine throughout the world:
> Fight we the fight with sorrow and sin
> To set their captives free,
> That the earth may be filled with the glory of God
> As the waters cover the sea.
>
> All we can do is nothing worth
> Unless God blessed the deed;
> Vainly we hope for the harvest-tide
> Till God gives life to the seed;
> Yet nearer and nearer draws the time,
> The time shall surely be,
> When the earth shall be filled with the glory of God
> As the waters cover the sea.

Arthur C. Ainger

The Refrain for the Vespers Lessons
O God, you have taught me since I was young,* and to this day I tell of your wonderful works.

Psalm 71:17

The Vespers Psalm   *The Wicked Shall Be No More*

In a little while the wicked shall be no more;* you shall search out their place, but
they will not be there.

But the lowly shall possess the land;* they will delight in abundance of peace.

The wicked plot against the righteous* and gnash at them with their teeth.

The Lord laughs at the wicked,* because he sees that their day will come.

The wicked draw their sword and bend their bow to strike down the poor and
needy,* to slaughter those who are upright in their ways.

Their sword shall go through their own heart,* and their bow shall be broken.

The little that the righteous has* is better than the great riches of the wicked.

For the power of the wicked shall be broken,* but the Lord upholds the righteous.

Psalm 37:11–18

The Refrain

O God, you have taught me since I was young,* and to this day I tell of your wonderful works.

The Gloria

The Lord's Prayer

The Prayer Appointed for the Week

Lord, make me have perpetual love and reverence for your holy Name, for you
never fail to help and govern those whom you have set upon the sure foundation of your loving-kindness; through Jesus Christ our Lord, who lives and
reigns with you and the Holy Spirit, one God, for ever and ever. *Amen.*†

The Concluding Prayer of the Church

O God, the source of eternal light: Shed forth your unending day upon all of us
who watch for you, that our lips may praise you, our lives may bless you, and
our worship may give you glory; through Jesus Christ our Lord. *Amen.*†

❧

The Morning Office   **To Be Observed on the Hour or Half Hour
Between 6 and 9 a.m.**

The Call to Prayer

Let the peoples praise you, O God;* let all the peoples praise you.

Let the nations be glad and sing for joy,* for you judge the peoples with equity and
guide all nations upon the earth.

Let the peoples praise you, O God;* let all the peoples praise you.

Psalm 67:3–5

The Request for Presence
Hear my voice, O LORD, according to your loving-kindness;* according to your
judgments, give me life.

Psalm 119:149

The Greeting
Hosanna, LORD, hosanna!* LORD, send us now success.
Blessed is he who comes in the name of the LORD;* we bless you from the house of
the LORD.

Psalm 118:25–26

The Refrain for the Morning Lessons
I was glad when they said to me,* "Let us go to the house of the LORD."

Psalm 122:1

A Reading
Jesus taught us, saying: 'There is no need to be afraid, little flock, for it has pleased
your Father to give you the kingdom.'

Luke 12:32

The Refrain
I was glad when they said to me,* "Let us go to the house of the LORD."

The Morning Psalm   *Who Is Like You, O God?*
Your righteousness, O God, reaches to the heavens;* you have done great things;
who is like you, O God?
You have showed me great troubles and adversities,* but you will restore my life
and bring me up again from the deep places of the earth.
You strengthen me more and more;* you enfold me and comfort me,
Therefore, I will praise you upon the lyre for your faithfulness, O my God;* I will
sing to you with the harp, O Holy One of Israel.
My lips will sing with joy when I play to you,* and so will my soul, which you
have redeemed.
My tongue will proclaim your righteousness all day long,* for they are ashamed
and disgraced who sought to do me harm.

Psalm 71:19–24

The Refrain
I was glad when they said to me,* "Let us go to the house of the LORD."

The Cry of the Church
In the evening, in the morning, and at noonday, I will complain and lament,* and
he will hear my voice.

Psalm 55:18

The Lord's Prayer

The Prayer Appointed for the Week
Almighty God, you have built your Church upon the foundation of the apostles
and prophets, Jesus Christ himself being the chief cornerstone: Grant that all of
us may be joined together in unity of spirit by their teaching, that we may be
made a holy temple acceptable to you; through Jesus Christ our Lord, who lives
and reigns with you and the Holy Spirit, one God, for ever and ever. *Amen*.†

The Concluding Prayer of the Church
Lord God, almighty and everlasting Father, you have brought me in safety to this
new day: Preserve me with your mighty power, that I may not fall into sin, nor
be overcome by adversity; and in all I do direct me to the fulfilling of your purpose; through Jesus Christ my Lord. *Amen*.†

The Midday Office   **To Be Observed on the Hour or Half Hour**
Between 11 a.m. and 2 p.m.

The Call to Prayer
The LORD is King; let the earth rejoice;* let the multitude of the isles be glad.
Psalm 97:1

The Request for Presence
Hear, O Shepherd of Israel, leading Joseph like a flock;* shine forth, you that are
enthroned upon the cherubim.
Psalm 80:1

The Greeting
Yours is the day, yours also is the night;* you established the moon and the sun.
You fixed all the boundaries of the earth;* you made both summer and winter.
Psalm 74:15–16

The Refrain for the Midday Lessons
The earth, O LORD, is full of your love;* instruct me in your statutes.
Psalm 119:64

A Reading
Yes, you love all that exists, and nothing that you have made disgusts you, since if
you had hated something, you would not have made it. And how could a thing
subsist, had you not willed it? Or how be preserved, if not called forth by you?
No, you spare all, since all is yours, Lord, lover of life! For your imperishable
spirit is in everything! And thus, gradually, you correct those who offend; you
admonish and remind them of how they have sinned, so that they may abstain
from evil and trust in you, Lord.
Wisdom 11:24ff

The Refrain
The earth, O LORD, is full of your love;* instruct me in your statutes.

The Midday Psalm   *One Day Tells Its Tale to Another*
The heavens declare the glory of God,* and the firmament shows his handiwork.
One day tells its tale to another,* and one night imparts its knowledge to another.
Although they have no words or language,* and their voices are not heard,
Their sound has gone out into all the lands,* and their message to the ends of the
    world.
In the deep has he set a pavilion for the sun;* it comes forth like a bridegroom
    from his chamber; it rejoices like a champion to run its course.
It goes forth from the uttermost edge of the heavens and runs about to the end of it
    again;* nothing is hidden from its burning heat.

Psalm 19:1–6

The Refrain
The earth, O LORD, is full of your love;* instruct me in your statutes.

The Gloria

The Lord's Prayer

The Prayer Appointed for the Week
Almighty God, you have built your Church upon the foundation of the apostles
    and prophets, Jesus Christ himself being the chief cornerstone: Grant that all of
    us may be joined together in unity of spirit by their teaching, that we may be
    made a holy temple acceptable to you; through Jesus Christ our Lord, who
    lives and reigns with you and the Holy Spirit, one God, for ever and ever.
    Amen.†

The Concluding Prayer of the Church
O God, you make me glad with the weekly remembrance of the glorious resurrec-
    tion of your Son my Lord: Give me this day such blessing through my worship
    of you, that the week to come may be spent in your favor; through Jesus Christ
    our Lord. *Amen.*†

The Vespers Office   **To Be Observed on the Hour or Half Hour**
                                   Between 5 and 8 p.m.

The Call to Prayer
Behold now, bless the LORD, all you servants of the LORD,* you that stand by night
    in the house of the LORD.

Psalm 134:1

The Request for Presence
For God alone my soul in silence waits;* truly, my hope is in him.

Psalm 62:6

The Greeting
I remember your Name in the night, O LORD,* and dwell upon your law.

Psalm 119:55

The Hymn　　　　　　　　　*God Himself Is with Us*

God himself is with us;	Come abide within me;
Let us all adore him,	Let my soul, like Mary,
And with awe appear before him.	Be your earthly sanctuary.
God is here within us;	Come, indwelling spirit,
Soul, in silence fear him,	With transfigured splendor;
Humbly, fervently draw near him.	Love and honor I will render.
Now, his own who have known	Where I go here below,
God, in worship lowly,	Let me bow before you,
Yield their spirits wholly.	Know you, and adore you.

Gerhardt Tersteegen

The Refrain for the Vespers Lessons
Behold, he who keeps watch over Israel* shall neither slumber nor sleep.

Psalm 121:4

The Vespers Psalm　　　　　　　*He Brought Me Out into an Open Place*
I called upon the LORD in my distress* and cried out to my God for help.
He heard my voice from his heavenly dwelling;* my cry of anguish came to his ears.
The earth reeled and rocked;* the roots of the mountains shook; they reeled because of his anger.
Smoke rose from his nostrils and a consuming fire out of his mouth;* hot burning coals blazed forth from him.
He parted the heavens and came down* with a storm cloud under his feet.
He mounted on cherubim and flew;* he swooped on the wings of the wind.
He wrapped darkness about him;* he made dark waters and thick clouds his pavilion.
From the brightness of his presence, through the clouds,* burst hailstones and coals of fire.
The LORD thundered out of heaven;* the Most High uttered his voice.
He loosed his arrows and scattered them;* he hurled thunderbolts and routed them.
The beds of the seas were uncovered, and the foundations of the world laid bare,* at your battle cry, O LORD, at the blast of the breath of your nostrils.
He reached down from on high and grasped me;* he drew me out of the great waters.
He delivered me from my strong enemies and from those who hated me;* for they were too mighty for me.
They confronted me in the day of my disaster;* but the LORD was my support.
He brought me out into an open place;* he rescued me because he delighted in me.

Psalm 18:6–20

The Refrain
Behold, he who keeps watch over Israel* shall neither slumber nor sleep.

The Gloria

The Lord's Prayer

The Prayer Appointed for the Week
Almighty God, you have built your Church upon the foundation of the apostles
and prophets, Jesus Christ himself being the chief cornerstone: Grant that all of
us may be joined together in unity of spirit by their teaching, that we may be
made a holy temple acceptable to you; through Jesus Christ our Lord, who
lives and reigns with you and the Holy Spirit, one God, for ever and ever.
Amen.†

The Concluding Prayer of the Church
Protect me, Lord, as I stay awake; watch over me as I sleep, that awake I may
watch with Christ, and asleep, rest in peace. *Amen.*

The Morning Office **To Be Observed on the Hour or Half Hour**
Between 6 and 9 a.m.

The Call to Prayer
Hallelujah! Give praise, you servants of the LORD;* praise the Name of the LORD.

Psalm 113:1

The Request for Presence
Test me, O LORD, and try me;* examine my heart and mind.
For your love is before my eyes;* I have walked faithfully with you.
I have not sat with the worthless,* nor do I consort with the deceitful.
I have hated the company of evildoers;* I will not sit down with the wicked.
I will wash my hands in innocence, O LORD,* that I may go in procession round
your altar,
Singing aloud a song of thanksgiving* and recounting all your wonderful deeds.

Psalm 26:2–7

The Greeting
All your works praise you, O LORD,* and your faithful servants bless you.
They make known the glory of your kingdom* and speak of your power;
That the peoples may know of your power* and the glorious splendor of your
kingdom.

Psalm 145:10–12

The Refrain for the Morning Lessons
Those who sowed with tears* will reap with songs of joy.
Those who go out weeping, carrying the seed,* will come again with joy, shoul-
dering their sheaves.

Psalm 126:6–7

A Reading

When they had eaten, Jesus said to Simon Peter, 'Simon, son of John, do you love me more than these others do?' He answered, 'Yes, Lord, you know I love you.' Jesus said to him, 'Feed my lambs.' A second time he said to him, 'Simon son of John, do you love me?' He replied, 'Yes, Lord, you know I love you.' Jesus said to him, 'Look after my sheep.' Then he said to him a third time, 'Simon, son of John, do you love me?' Peter was upset that he asked him a third time, 'Do you love me?' and said, 'Lord, you know everything; you know I love you.' Jesus said to him, 'Feed my sheep. In all truth I tell you, when you were young, you put on your own belt and walked where you liked; but when you grow old, you will stretch out your hands, and somebody else will put a belt around you and take you where you would rather not go.' In these words he indicated the kind of death by which Peter would give glory to God. After this he said, 'Follow me.'

John 21:15–19

The Refrain

Those who sowed with tears* will reap with songs of joy.
Those who go out weeping, carrying the seed,* will come again with joy, shouldering their sheaves.

The Morning Psalm　　　　*Glorious Things Are Spoken of You, O City of Our God*

On the holy mountain stands the city he has founded;* the LORD loves the gates of Zion more than the dwellings of Jacob.
Glorious things are spoken of you,* O City of our God.
I count Egypt and Babylon among those who know me;* behold Philistia, Tyre, and Ethiopia: in Zion were they born.
Of Zion it shall be said, "Everyone was born in her,* and the Most High himself will sustain her."
The LORD will record as he enrolls the peoples,* "These also were born there."
The singers and the dancers will say,* "All my fresh springs are in you."

Psalm 87:1–6

The Refrain

Those who sowed with tears* will reap with songs of joy.
Those who go out weeping, carrying the seed,* will come again with joy, shouldering their sheaves.

The Cry of the Church

In the evening, in the morning, and at noonday, I will complain and lament,* and he will hear my voice.

Psalm 55:18

The Lord's Prayer

The Prayer Appointed for the Week

Almighty God, you have built your Church upon the foundation of the apostles and prophets, Jesus Christ himself being the chief cornerstone: Grant that all of us may be joined together in unity of spirit by their teaching, that we may be made a holy temple acceptable to you; through Jesus Christ our Lord, who lives and reigns with you and the Holy Spirit, one God, for ever and ever. *Amen.*+

The Concluding Prayer of the Church
Lord God, almighty and everlasting Father, you have brought me in safety to this new day: Preserve me with your mighty power, that I may not fall into sin, nor be overcome by adversity; and in all I do direct me to the fulfilling of your purpose; through Jesus Christ my Lord. *Amen.*+

The Midday Office	To Be Observed on the Hour or Half Hour
	Between 11 a.m. and 2 p.m.

The Call to Prayer
Hallelujah! Praise the LORD, O my soul!* I will praise the LORD as long as I live; I
will sing praises to God while I have my being.

Psalm 146:1

The Request for Presence
Bow your heavens, O LORD, and come down;* touch the mountains, and they shall
smoke.
Hurl the lightning and scatter them;* shoot out your arrows and rout them.
Stretch out your hand from on high;* rescue me and deliver me from the great
waters, from the hand of foreign peoples,
Whose mouths speak deceitfully* and whose right hand is raised in falsehood.

Psalm 144:5–8

The Greeting
To you I lift up my eyes,* to you enthroned in the heavens.
As the eyes of the servants look to the hand of their masters,* and the eyes of a
maid to the hand of her mistress,
So our eyes look to the LORD our God,* until he shows us his mercy.

Psalm 123:1–3

The Refrain for the Midday Lessons
Blessed be the LORD!* for he has shown me the wonders of his love in a besieged city.

Psalm 31:21

A Reading	*A homily in remembrance of Sts. Peter and Paul,*
	believed to have been martyred for their faith in late
	June, 64 a.d. by the Emperor Nero.

O holy Apostles, how shall we thank you, you who have labored so much for us! I
am filled with admiration whenever I think of you, Peter; when I remember
you, Paul, I am moved to tears. My lips are mute when I consider your suffer-

ings. How many prisons you have sanctified! How many chains you have
adorned! How many pains you have suffered! How many curses you have
borne! YOU bore Christ in your hearts; you refreshed the Christian communities through your sermons. Praised be the work of your tongues. For the sake
of the Church your garments were sprinkled with blood. You imitated Christ
in all; your voices penetrated a world, and your message crossed all boundaries of the earth. Rejoice, O Peter, that you were worthy to partake of the Cross
of Christ; you desired to hang upon the Cross after the pattern of your Master
Christ, not upright like the Lord, but head downward, as if you wished to journey from earth to heaven. Rejoice, O Paul, you who were beheaded with a
sword. This sword which severed your neck, this instrument of the Lord, is
admired by heaven and revered by earth. For me this sword should be a
crown, and the nails of Peter's cross, diamonds for a diadem.

St. John Chrysostom

The Refrain
Blessed be the LORD!* for he has shown me the wonders of his love in a besieged
city.

The Midday Psalm   *Who Can Ascend the Hill of the LORD?*
"Who can ascend the hill of the LORD?* and who can stand in his holy place?"
"Those who have clean hands and a pure heart,* who have not pledged them-
selves to falsehood, nor sworn by what is fraud.
They shall receive a blessing from the LORD* and a just reward from the God of
their salvation."
Such is the generation of those who seek him,* of those who seek your face, O God
of Jacob.

Psalm 24:3–6

The Refrain
Blessed be the LORD!* for he has shown me the wonders of his love in a besieged
city.

The Cry of the Church
Lord, have mercy on us. Christ, have mercy on us. Lord, have mercy on us.

The Lord's Prayer

The Prayer Appointed for the Week
Almighty God, you have built your Church upon the foundation of the apostles
and prophets, Jesus Christ himself being the chief cornerstone: Grant that all of
us may be joined together in unity of spirit by their teaching, that we may be
made a holy temple acceptable to you; through Jesus Christ our Lord, who
lives and reigns with you and the Holy Spirit, one God, for ever and ever.
Amen.†

The Concluding Prayer of the Church
Lord Jesus Christ, you said to your apostles, "Peace I give to you; my own peace I
 leave with you": Regard not my sins, but my faith, and give to me and all of us
 the peace and unity of that heavenly City, where with the Father and the Holy
 Spirit you live and reign, now and for ever. *Amen.*†

The Vespers Office   **To Be Observed on the Hour or Half Hour**
                                         Between 5 and 8 p.m.

The Call to Prayer
The LORD is in his holy temple.* Let all the earth keep silence before him.

based on Psalm 11:4

The Request for Presence
O LORD, I call to you; come to me quickly;* hear my voice when I cry to you.
Let my prayer be set forth in your sight as incense,* the lifting up of my hands as
 the evening sacrifice.

Psalm 141:1–2

The Greeting
O Lamb of God, that takes away the sins of the world, have mercy on us.
O Lamb of God, that takes away the sins of the world, have mercy on us.
O Lamb of God, that takes away the sins of the world, grant us your peace.

The Hymn   *Forth in the Peace of Christ We Go*
  Forth in the peace of Christ we go,
  Christ to the world with joy we bring;
  Christ in our minds, Christ on our lips,
  Christ in our hearts, the world's true King.

  Christ's are our lips, his words we speak;
  Prophets are we whose deeds proclaim
  Christ's truth in love that we may be
  Christ in our world, to spread Christ's name.

  We are the church: Christ bids us show
  That in his church all nations find
  Their hearth and home, where Christ restores
  True peace, true love, to all mankind.

James Quinn

The Refrain for the Vespers Lessons
He who dwells in the shelter of the Most High,* abides under the shadow of the
 Almighty.
He shall say to the LORD, "You are my refuge and my stronghold,* my God in
 whom I put my trust."

Psalm 91:1–2

The Vespers Psalm   *He Who Watches Over You Will Not Fall Asleep*

I lift up my eyes to the hills;* from where is my help to come?

My help comes from the LORD,* the maker of heaven and earth.

He will not let your foot be moved* and he who watches over you will not fall
   asleep.

Behold, he who keeps watch over Israel* shall neither slumber nor sleep;

The LORD himself watches over you;* the LORD is your shade at your right hand,

So that the sun shall not strike you by day,* nor the moon by night.

The LORD shall preserve you from all evil;* it is he who shall keep you safe.

The LORD shall watch over your going out and your coming in,* from this time
   forth for evermore.

Psalm 121:1–8

The Refrain

He who dwells in the shelter of the Most High,* abides under the shadow of the
   Almighty.

He shall say to the LORD, "You are my refuge and my stronghold,* my God in
   whom I put my trust."

The Gloria

The Lord's Prayer

The Prayer Appointed for the Week

Almighty God, you have built your Church upon the foundation of the apostles
   and prophets, Jesus Christ himself being the chief cornerstone: Grant that all of
   us may be joined together in unity of spirit by their teaching, that we may be
   made a holy temple acceptable to you; through Jesus Christ our Lord, who
   lives and reigns with you and the Holy Spirit, one God, for ever and ever.
   Amen.†

The Concluding Prayer of the Church

Father, as you made springs in valleys to form streams between mountains, so you
   made living streams of grace to flow from the apostles that their teaching may
   bring salvation to all nations. May I have practical knowledge of their doctrine,
   be obedient to their commands, obtain remission of sins through their prayers,
   and finally receive the reward of eternal happiness. *Amen.*

THE LITURGY OF THE HOURS, VOL. III

The Morning Office   **To Be Observed on the Hour or Half Hour**
                                          Between 6 and 9 a.m.

The Call to Prayer

Search for the LORD and his strength;* continually seek his face.

Psalm 105:4

The Request for Presence
Show your goodness, O Lord, to those who are good* and to those who are true of heart.

Psalm 125:4

The Greeting
Seven times a day do I praise you,* because of your righteous judgments.

Psalm 119:164

The Refrain for the Morning Lessons
Our days are like the grass;* we flourish like a flower of the field;
When the wind goes over it, it is gone,* and its place shall know it no more.

Psalm 103:15–16

A Reading
He put another parable before them. 'The kingdom of heaven may be compared to a man who sowed good seed in his field. While everybody was asleep his enemy came, sowed darnel among the wheat, and made off. When the new wheat sprouted and ripened, the darnel appeared as well. The owner's laborers went to him and said, "Sir, was it not good seed that you sowed in your field? If so, where does the darnel come from?" He said to them, "Some enemy has done this." And the laborers said, "Do you want us to go and weed it out?" But he said, "No, because when you weed out the darnel you might pull up the wheat with it. Let them both grow till the harvest; and at harvest time I shall say to the reapers: First collect the darnel and tie it into bundles to be burnt, then gather the wheat into my barn." '

Matthew 13:24–30

The Refrain
Our days are like the grass;* we flourish like a flower of the field;
When the wind goes over it, it is gone,* and its place shall know it no more.

The Morning Psalm   *He That Planted the Ear, Does He Not Hear?*
How long shall the wicked, O Lord,* how long shall the wicked triumph?
They bluster in their insolence;* all evildoers are full of boasting.
They crush your people, O Lord,* and afflict your chosen nation.
They murder the widow and the stranger* and put the orphans to death.
Yet they say, "The Lord does not see,* the God of Jacob takes no notice,"
Consider well, you dullards among the people;* when will you fools understand?
He that planted the ear, does he not hear?* he that formed the eye, does he not see?
He who admonishes the nations, will he not punish?* he who teaches all the world, has he no knowledge?
The Lord knows our human thoughts:* how like a puff of wind they are.
Happy are they whom you instruct, O Lord!* whom you teach out of your law.

Psalm 94:3–12

The Refrain
Our days are like the grass;* we flourish like a flower of the field;
When the wind goes over it, it is gone,* and its place shall know it no more.

The Small Verse
Lord, have mercy; Christ, have mercy; Lord, have mercy.

The Lord's Prayer

The Prayer Appointed for the Week
Almighty God, you have built your Church upon the foundation of the apostles
   and prophets, Jesus Christ himself being the chief cornerstone: Grant that all of
   us may be joined together in unity of spirit by their teaching, that we may be
   made a holy temple acceptable to you; through Jesus Christ our Lord, who lives
   and reigns with you and the Holy Spirit, one God, for ever and ever. *Amen.*†

The Concluding Prayer of the Church
Lord God, almighty and everlasting Father, you have brought me in safety to this
   new day: Preserve me with your mighty power, that I may not fall into sin, nor
   be overcome by adversity; and in all I do direct me to the fulfilling of your purpose; through Jesus Christ my Lord. *Amen.*†

The Midday Office   **To Be Observed on the Hour or Half Hour**
                                       Between 11 a.m. and 2 p.m.

The Call to Prayer
Know this, the Lord himself is God;* he himself made us, and we are his; we are
   his people and the sheep of his pasture.

Psalm 100:2

The Request for Presence
I am a stranger here on earth;* do not hide your commandments from me.

Psalm 119:19

The Greeting
I restrain my feet from every evil way,* that I may keep your word.

Psalm 119:101

The Refrain for the Midday Lessons
The heaven of heavens is the Lord's,* but he entrusted the earth to its peoples.

Psalm 115:16

A Reading
Whatever you eat, then, or drink, whatever else you do, do it all for the glory of
   God. Never be a cause of offense either to Jews or to Greeks or to the Church of
   God.

I Corinthians 10:31–32

The Refrain
The heaven of heavens is the Lord's,* but he entrusted the earth to its peoples.

The Midday Psalm *I Was Pressed So Hard That I Almost Fell*
All the ungodly encompass me;* in the name of the Lord I will repel them.
They hem me in, they hem me in on every side;* in the name of the Lord I will
repel them.
They swarm about me like bees; they blaze like a fire of thorns;* in the name of the
Lord I will repel them.
I was pressed so hard that I almost fell,* but the Lord came to my help.

Psalm 118:10–13

The Refrain
The heaven of heavens is the Lord's,* but he entrusted the earth to its peoples.

The Small Verse
Create in me a clean heart, O God,* and renew a right spirit within me.
Cast me not away from your presence* and take not your holy Spirit from me.
Give me the joy of your saving help again* and sustain me with your bountiful
spirit.

Psalm 51:11–13

The Lord's Prayer

The Prayer Appointed for the Week
Almighty God, you have built your Church upon the foundation of the apostles
and prophets, Jesus Christ himself being the chief cornerstone: Grant that all of
us may be joined together in unity of spirit by their teaching, that we may be
made a holy temple acceptable to you; through Jesus Christ our Lord, who lives
and reigns with you and the Holy Spirit, one God, for ever and ever. *Amen.*†

The Concluding Prayer of the Church *The Privilege Is Ours to Share in the Loving*
Almighty God, our heavenly Father, the privilege is ours to share in the loving,
healing, reconciling mission of your Son Jesus Christ, our Lord, in this age
and wherever we are. Since without you we can do no good thing.
May your Spirit make us wise;
May your Spirit guide us;
May your Spirit renew us;
May your Spirit strengthen us;
So that we will be:
Strong in faith,
Discerning in proclamation,
Courageous in witness,
Persistent in good deeds.
This we ask through the name of the Father.

Church of the Province of the West Indies

The Vespers Office   **To Be Observed on the Hour or Half Hour**
                                          Between 5 and 8 p.m.

The Call to Prayer
Let Israel rejoice in his Maker;* let the children of Zion be joyful in their King.
Let them praise his Name in the dance;* let them sing praise to him with timbrel
    and harp.
For the LORD takes pleasure in his people* and adorns the poor with victory.
Let the faithful rejoice in triumph;* let them be joyful on their beds.

Psalm 149:2–5

The Request for Presence
Show us your mercy, O LORD,* and grant us your salvation.

Psalm 85:7

The Greeting
Zion hears and is glad, and the cities of Judah rejoice,* because of your judgments,
    O LORD.

Psalm 97:8

The Hymn   *Holy, Holy, Holy*
    Holy, holy, holy, Lord God Almighty!
    Early in the morning our song shall rise to Thee;
    Holy, holy, holy, merciful and mighty,
    God in Three Persons, blessed Trinity!

    Holy, holy, holy, all the saints adore Thee,
    Casting down their golden crowns around the glassy sea;
    Cherubim and seraphim falling down before Thee,
    Which were and are, and evermore shall be.

    Holy, holy, holy, though the darkness hide Thee,
    Though the eye of sinful man Thy glory might not see;
    Only Thou art holy, there is none beside Thee,
    Perfect in power, in love, and purity.

    Holy, holy, holy, Lord God Almighty!
    All Thy works shall praise Thy name, in earth, and sky, and sea;
    Holy, holy, holy, merciful and mighty,
    God in Three Persons, Blessed Trinity!

Reginald Heber

The Refrain for the Vespers Lessons
For one day in your courts is better than a thousand in my own room,* and to
    stand at the threshold of the house of my God than to dwell in the tents of the
    wicked.

Psalm 84:9

The Vespers Psalm   *Out of Zion, Perfect in Its Beauty*

The LORD, the God of gods, has spoken;* he has called the earth from the rising of
    the sun to its setting.
Out of Zion, perfect in its beauty,* God reveals himself in glory.
Our God will come and will not keep silence;* before him there is a consuming
    flame, and round about him is a raging storm.
He calls the heavens and the earth from above* to witness the judgments of his
    people.
"Gather before me my loyal followers,* those who have made a covenant with me
    and sealed it with a sacrifice."
Let the heavens declare the righteousness of his cause;* for God himself is judge.

Psalm 50:1–6

The Refrain

For one day in your courts is better than a thousand in my own room,* and to stand
    at the threshold of the house of my God than to dwell in the tents of the wicked.

The Gloria

The Lord's Prayer

The Prayer Appointed for the Week

Almighty God, you have built your Church upon the foundation of the apostles
    and prophets, Jesus Christ himself being the chief cornerstone: Grant that all of
    us may be joined together in unity of spirit by their teaching, that we may be
    made a holy temple acceptable to you; through Jesus Christ our Lord, who
    lives and reigns with you and the Holy Spirit, one God, for ever and ever.
    Amen.†

The Concluding Prayer of the Church

Father, all-powerful and ever-living God,
we do well always and everywhere to give you thanks.
All things are of your making,
all times and seasons obey your laws,
but you chose to create us in your own image,
setting us over the whole world in all its wonder.
You made us the steward of creation,
to praise you day by day for the marvels of your wisdom and power.

THE ROMAN MISSAL

The Morning Office   **To Be Observed on the Hour or Half Hour**
                                Between 6 and 9 a.m.

The Call to Prayer

Sing to the LORD with the harp,* with the harp and the voice of song.
With trumpets and the sound of the horn* shout with joy before the King, the LORD.

Psalm 98:6–7

The Request for Presence
Our soul waits for the LORD;* he is our help and our shield.
Indeed, our heart rejoices in him,* for in his holy Name we put our trust.
Let your loving-kindness, O LORD, be upon us,* as we have put our trust in you.

Psalm 33:20–22

The Greeting
How deep I find your thoughts, O God!* how great is the sum of them!
If I were to count them, they would be more in number than the sand;* to count
them all, my life span would need to be like yours.

Psalm 139:16–17

The Refrain for the Morning Lessons
The LORD has sworn an oath to David;* in truth, he will not break it:
"A son, the fruit of your body* will I set upon your throne."

Psalm 132:11–12

A Reading
Jesus said: (to Martha) 'I am the resurrection. Anyone who believes in me, even
though that person dies, will live, and whoever lives and believes in me will
never die. Do you believe this?' 'Yes, Lord,' she said. 'I believe that you are the
Christ, the Son of God, the one who was to come into this world.'

John 11:25–27

The Refrain
The LORD has sworn an oath to David;* in truth, he will not break it:
"A son, the fruit of your body* will I set upon your throne."

The Morning Psalm   *I Will Establish His Line For Ever*
You spoke once in a vision and said to your faithful people;* "I have set the crown
upon a warrior and have exalted one out of the people.
I have found David my servant;* with my holy oil I have anointed him.
My hand will hold him fast* and my arm will make him strong.
No enemy shall deceive him,* nor any wicked man bring him down.
I will crush his foes before him* and strike down those who hate him.
My faithfulness and love shall be with him,* and he shall be victorious through
my Name.
I shall make his dominion extend* from the Great Sea to the River.
He will say to me, 'You are my Father,* my God, and the rock of my salvation.'
I will make him my firstborn* and higher than the kings of the earth.
I will keep my love for him for ever,* and my covenant will stand firm for him.
I will establish his line for ever* and his throne as the days of heaven."

Psalm 89:19–29

The Refrain
The LORD has sworn an oath to David;* in truth, he will not break it:
"A son, the fruit of your body* will I set upon your throne."

The Gloria

The Lord's Prayer

The Prayer Appointed for the Week
Almighty God, you have built your Church upon the foundation of the apostles
and prophets, Jesus Christ himself being the chief cornerstone: Grant that all of
us may be joined together in unity of spirit by their teaching, that we may be
made a holy temple acceptable to you; through Jesus Christ our Lord, who lives
and reigns with you and the Holy Spirit, one God, for ever and ever. *Amen.*†

The Concluding Prayer of the Church
Lord God, almighty and everlasting Father, you have brought me in safety to this
new day: Preserve me with your mighty power, that I may not fall into sin, nor
be overcome by adversity; and in all I do direct me to the fulfilling of your purpose; through Jesus Christ my Lord. *Amen.*†

The Midday Office   **To Be Observed on the Hour or Half Hour**
                                              Between 11 a.m. and 2 p.m.

The Call to Prayer
Hallelujah! Sing to the LORD a new song;* sing his praise in the congregation of the
faithful.

Psalm 149:1

The Request for Presence
You are good and you bring forth good;* instruct me in your statutes.

Psalm 119:68

The Greeting
Be exalted, O LORD, in your might;* we will sing and praise your power.

Psalm 21:14

The Refrain for the Midday Lessons
It is better to rely on the LORD* than to put any trust in flesh.
It is better to rely on the LORD* than to put any trust in rulers.

Psalm 118:8–9

A Reading
YAHWEH, my strength, my stronghold, my refuge in time of distress! To you the
nations will come from the remotest parts of the earth and say, 'Our fathers
inherited nothing but Delusion, Futility of no use whatever. Can anyone
human make his own gods? These are not gods at all!'

Jeremiah 16:19–20

The Refrain
It is better to rely on the LORD* than to put any trust in flesh.
It is better to rely on the LORD* than to put any trust in rulers.

The Midday Psalm   *Kingship Belongs to the Lord*

Praise the LORD, all you who fear him;* stand in awe of him, O offspring of Israel;
     all you of Jacob's line, give glory.

For he does not despise nor abhor the poor in their poverty; neither does he hide
     his face from them;* but when they cry he hears them.

My praise is of him in the great assembly;* I will perform my vows in the presence
     of those who worship him.

The poor shall eat and be satisfied,* and those who seek the LORD shall praise him:
     "May your heart live for ever."

All the ends of the earth shall remember and turn to the LORD,* and all the families
     of the nations shall bow before him.

For kingship belongs to the LORD;* he rules over the nations.

To him alone all who sleep in the earth bow down in worship:* all who go down to
     the just fall before him.

My soul shall live for him; my descendants shall serve him;* they shall be known
     as the LORD's for ever.

They shall come and make known to a people yet unborn* the saving deeds that
     he has done.

                                      Psalm 22:22–30

The Refrain

It is better to rely on the LORD* than to put any trust in flesh.
It is better to rely on the LORD* than to put any trust in rulers.

The Gloria

The Lord's Prayer

The Prayer Appointed for the Week

Almighty God, you have built your Church upon the foundation of the apostles
     and prophets, Jesus Christ himself being the chief cornerstone: Grant that all of
     us may be joined together in unity of spirit by their teaching, that we may be
     made a holy temple acceptable to you; through Jesus Christ our Lord, who
     lives and reigns with you and the Holy Spirit, one God, for ever and ever.
     Amen.†

The Concluding Prayer of the Church

God of justice, God of mercy, bless all those who are surprised with pain this day
     from suffering caused by their own weakness or that of others. Let what we
     suffer teach us to be merciful; let our sins teach us to forgive. This I ask through
     the intercession of Jesus and all who died forgiving those who oppressed them.
     Amen.†

The Vespers Office   **To Be Observed on the Hour or Half Hour**
                                Between 5 and 8 p.m.

The Call to Prayer
Come, let us bow down, and bend the knee,* and kneel before the LORD, our
  Maker.
For he is our God,* and we are the people of his pasture and the sheep of his
  hand.

Psalm 95:6–7

The Request for Presence
To you I lift up my eyes,* to you enthroned in the heavens.

Psalm 123:1

The Greeting
How priceless is your love, O God!* your people take refuge under the shadow of
  your wings.
They feast upon the abundance of your house;* you give them drink from the
  river of your delights.
For with you is the well of life,* and in your light we see light.

Psalm 36:7–9

The Hymn   *In the Garden*
I come to the garden alone,   I'd stay in the garden with Him
While the dew is still on the roses;   Though the night around me is falling,
And the voice that I hear,   But He bids me go;
Falling on my ear;   Through the voice of woe,
The Son of God discloses.   His voice to me is calling.
And He walks with me,   And He walks with me,
And He talks with me,   And He talks with me,
And He tells me I am His own,   And He tells me I am His own,
And the joy we share as we tarry there, And the joy we share as we tarry there,
None other has ever known.   None other has ever known.

                                                    C. Austin Miles

He speaks, and the sound of his voice
Is so sweet the birds hush their singing,
And the melody
That He gave to me,
Within my heart is ringing.
And He walks with me,
And He talks with me,
And He tells me I am His own,
And the joy we share as we tarry there,
None other has ever known.

The Refrain for the Vespers Lessons
Turn again to your rest, O my soul,* for the LORD has treated you well.
For you have rescued my life from death,* my eyes from tears, and my feet from
stumbling.

Psalm 116:6-7

The Vespers Psalm   *He Gives to His Beloved Sleep*
Unless the LORD builds the house,* their labor is in vain who build it.
Unless the LORD watches over the city,* in vain the watchman keeps his vigil.
It is in vain that you rise so early and go to bed so late;* vain, too, to eat the bread
of toil, for he gives to his beloved sleep.

Psalm 127:1-3

The Refrain
Turn again to your rest, O my soul,* for the LORD has treated you well.
For you have rescued my life from death,* my eyes from tears, and my feet from
stumbling.

The Small Verse
Show me your mercy, O Lord;* And grant me your salvation.
Clothe your ministers in righteousness;* Let your people sing with joy.
Give peace, O Lord, in all the world;* For only in you can I live in safety.
Lord, keep this nation under your care;* And guide me in the way of justice and
truth.
Let your way be known upon the earth;* Your saving health among all nations.
Let not the needy, O Lord, be forgotten;* Nor the hope of the poor be taken away.
Create in me a clean heart, O God;* And sustain me in your Holy Spirit.

The Lord's Prayer

The Prayer Appointed for the Week
Almighty God, you have built your Church upon the foundation of the apostles
and prophets, Jesus Christ himself being the chief cornerstone: Grant that all of
us may be joined together in unity of spirit by their teaching, that we may be
made a holy temple acceptable to you; through Jesus Christ our Lord, who
lives and reigns with you and the Holy Spirit, one God, for ever and ever.
Amen.†

The Concluding Prayer of the Church
Lord Jesus, stay with me, for evening is at hand and the day is past; be my companion in the way, kindle my heart, and awaken hope, that I may know you as
you are revealed in Scripture and the breaking of bread. Grant this for the sake
of your love. *Amen.*†

The Morning Office   **To Be Observed on the Hour or Half Hour**
                                                          Between 6 and 9 a.m.

The Call to Prayer
The LORD is King; let the people tremble;* he is enthroned upon the cherubim; let
the earth shake.

Psalm 99:1

The Request for Presence
Be seated on your lofty throne, O Most High;* O LORD, judge the nations.

Psalm 7:8

The Greeting
Save us, O LORD our God, and gather us from among the nations,* that we may
give thanks to your holy Name and glory in your praise.

Psalm 106:47

The Refrain for the Morning Lessons
Happy the nation whose God is YAHWEH,* the people he has chosen for his heritage.

Psalm 33:12

A Reading
So they awaited their opportunity and sent agents to pose as upright men, and to
catch him out in something he might say and so enable them to hand him over
to the jurisdiction and authority of the governor. They put to him this question,
'Master, we know that you say and teach what is right; you favor no one, but
teach the way of God in all honesty. Is it permissible for us to pay taxes to
Caesar or not?' But he was aware of their cunning and said, 'Show me a denar-
ius. Whose portrait and title are on it?' They said, 'Caesar's.' He said to them,
'Well then, pay Caesar what belongs to Caesar—and God what belongs to
God.' They were unable to catch him out in anything he had to say in public;
they were amazed at his answer and were silenced.

Luke 20:20–26

The Refrain
Happy the nation whose God is YAHWEH,* the people he has chosen for his heritage.

The Morning Psalm   *The Lord Beholds All People*
YAHWEH looks down from heaven,* he sees the whole human race;
From where he sits he watches* all who live on the earth,
He who molds every heart* and takes note of all that men do.
A large army will not keep a king safe,* nor does the hero escape by his great
strength;
It is delusion to rely on the horse for safety,* for all its power, it cannot save.
But see how the eye of YAHWEH is on those who fear him, on those who rely on his
love,* to rescue their souls from death and keep them alive in famine.
Our soul awaits YAHWEH,* he is our help and shield;

Our hearts rejoice in him,* we trust in his holy name.
YAHWEH, let your love rest on us* as our hope has rested in you.

Psalm 33:13–22

The Refrain
Happy the nation whose God is YAHWEH,* the people he has chosen for his heritage.

The Small Verse
'I am the Alpha and the Omega,' says the Lord God, who is, who was, and who is to come, the Almighty.

Revelation 1:8

The Lord's Prayer

The Prayer Appointed for the Week
Almighty God, you have built your Church upon the foundation of the apostles and prophets, Jesus Christ himself being the chief cornerstone: Grant that all of us may be joined together in unity of spirit by their teaching, that we may be made a holy temple acceptable to you; through Jesus Christ our Lord, who lives and reigns with you and the Holy Spirit, one God, for ever and ever. *Amen.*†

The Concluding Prayers of the Church
Lord God, almighty and everlasting Father, you have brought me in safety to this new day: Preserve me with your mighty power, that I may not fall into sin, nor be overcome by adversity; and in all I do direct me to the fulfilling of your purpose; through Jesus Christ my Lord. *Amen.*†

Lord God Almighty, you have made all the peoples of the earth for your glory, to serve you in freedom and in peace: Give to the people of our country a zeal for justice and the strength of forbearance, that we may use our liberty in accordance with your gracious will; through Jesus Christ our Lord, who lives and reigns with you and the Holy Spirit, one God, for ever and ever. *Amen.*†

The Midday Office   **To Be Observed on the Hour or Half Hour Between 11 a.m. and 2 p.m.**

The Call to Prayer
Be joyful in the LORD, all you lands;* serve the LORD with gladness and come before his presence with a song.

Psalm 100:1

The Request for Presence
May God be merciful to us and bless us,* show us the light of his countenance and come to us.

Psalm 67:1

The Greeting

I will confess you among the peoples, O Lord;* I will sing praise to you among the
nations.

For your loving-kindness is greater than the heavens,* and your faithfulness
reaches to the clouds.

Psalm 57:9–10

The Refrain for the Midday Lessons

Whoever is wise will ponder these things,* and consider well the mercies of the
Lord.

Psalm 107:43

A Reading

The sagacious ruler educates his people, and he makes his subjects understand
order. As the magistrate is, so will his officials be; as the governor is, so will be
the inhabitants of his city. An undisciplined king will be the ruin of his people,
a city owes its prosperity to the intelligence of its leading men. The govern-
ment of the earth is in the hands of the Lord, he sets the right leader over it at
the right time. Human success is in the hands of the Lord, it is he who invests
the scribe with honor. Do not resent your neighbor's every offense, and never
act in a fit of passion. Pride is hateful to God and humanity, and injustice is
abhorrent to both. Sovereignty passes from nation to nation because of injustice, arrogance and money.

Ecclesiasticus 10:1–8

The Refrain

Whoever is wise will ponder these things,* and consider well the mercies of the
Lord.

The Midday Psalm   *He Gathered Them Out of the Lands*

Give thanks to the Lord, for he is good,* and his mercy endures for ever.

Let all those whom the Lord has redeemed proclaim* that he redeemed them from
the hand of the foe.

He gathered them out of the lands;* from the east and from the west, from the
north and from the south.

He put their feet on a straight path* to go to a city where they might dwell.

Let them give thanks to the Lord for his mercy* and the wonders he does for his
children.

For he satisfies the thirsty* and fills the hungry with good things.

He led them out of darkness and deep gloom* and broke their bonds asunder.

Let them give thanks to the Lord for his mercy* and the wonders he does for his
children.

He sent forth his word and healed them* and saved them from the grave.

Let them give thanks to the Lord for his mercy* and the wonders he does for his
children.

Let them offer a sacrifice of thanksgiving* and tell of his acts with shouts of joy.

Psalm 107:1ff

The Refrain
Whoever is wise will ponder these things,* and consider well the mercies of the
  LORD.

The Small Verse
Truth shall spring up from the earth,* and righteousness shall look down from
  heaven.

Psalm 85:11

The Lord's Prayer

The Prayer Appointed for the Week
Almighty God, you have built your Church upon the foundation of the apostles
  and prophets, Jesus Christ himself being the chief cornerstone: Grant that all
  of us may be joined together in unity of spirit by their teaching, that we may
  be made a holy temple acceptable to you; through Jesus Christ our Lord, who
  lives and reigns with you and the Holy Spirit, one God, for ever and ever.
  Amen.†

The Concluding Prayer of the Church
Lord God Almighty, you have made all the peoples of the earth for your glory, to
  serve you in freedom and in peace: Give to the people of our country a zeal for
  justice and the strength of forbearance, that we may use our liberty in accordance with your gracious will; through Jesus Christ our Lord, who lives and
  reigns with you and the Holy Spirit, one God, for ever and ever. *Amen.*†

The Vespers Office   **To Be Observed on the Hour or Half Hour**
                                      Between 5 and 8 p.m.

The Call to Prayer
Rejoice in the LORD, you righteous,* and give thanks to his holy Name.

Psalm 97:12

The Request for Presence
Send forth your strength, O God;* establish, O God, what you have wrought for us.

Psalm 68:28

The Greeting
One generation shall praise your works to another* and shall declare your power.

Psalm 145:4

The Hymn   *Battle Hymn of the Republic*
Mine eyes have seen the glory of the coming of the Lord;
He is trampling out the vintage where the grapes of wrath are stored;
He has loosed the fateful lightning of his terrible, swift sword;
His truth goes marching on.
Glory! Glory, hallelujah!
Glory! Glory, hallelujah!
Glory! Glory hallelujah!
Our God is marching on.

I have seen Him in the watchfires of a hundred circling camps;
They have built Him an altar in the evening dews and damps;
I can read His righteous sentence by the dim and flaring lamps;
His day is marching on.
Glory! Glory, hallelujah!
Glory! Glory, hallelujah!
Glory! Glory hallelujah!
Our God is marching on.

He has sounded forth the trumpet that shall never sound retreat;
He is sifting out the hearts of men before his judgment seat;
O be swift, my soul, to answer Him! be jubilant my feet!
Our God is marching on!
Glory! Glory, hallelujah!
Glory! Glory, hallelujah!
Glory! Glory hallelujah!
Our God is marching on.

In beauty of the lilies, Christ was born across the sea,
With a glory in his bosom that transfigures you and me;
As He died to make men holy, let us die to make men free,
While God is marching on!
Glory! Glory, hallelujah!
Glory! Glory, hallelujah!
Glory! Glory hallelujah!
Our God is marching on.

Julia W. Howe

The Refrain for the Vespers Lessons
The hills stand about Jerusalem;* so does the LORD stand round about his people,
from this time forth for evermore.

Psalm 125:2

The Vespers Psalm   *The LORD Shall Reign For Ever*
Happy are they who have the God of Jacob for their help!* whose hope is in the
LORD their God;

Who made heaven and earth, the seas, and all that is in them;* who keeps his
    promise for ever;
Who gives justice to those who are oppressed,* and food to those who hunger.
The LORD sets prisoners free; the LORD opens the eyes of the blind;* the LORD lifts
    up those who are bowed down;
The LORD loves the righteous; the LORD cares for the stranger;* he sustains the
    orphan and widow, but frustrates the way of the wicked.
The LORD shall reign for ever,* your God, O Zion, throughout all generations.
    Hallelujah!

Psalm 146:4–9

The Refrain

The hills stand about Jerusalem;* so does the LORD stand round about his people,
    from this time forth for evermore.

The Small Verse

But if you will not serve the Lord, choose today whom you wish to serve, whether
    the gods that your ancestors served beyond the River, or the gods of the
    Amorites in whose land you are now living. As for me and my House, we will
    serve YAHWEH.

Joshua 24:15

The Lord's Prayer

The Prayer Appointed for the Week

Almighty God, you have built your Church upon the foundation of the apostles
    and prophets, Jesus Christ himself being the chief cornerstone: Grant that all of
    us may be joined together in unity of spirit by their teaching, that we may be
    made a holy temple acceptable to you; through Jesus Christ our Lord, who
    lives and reigns with you and the Holy Spirit, one God, for ever and ever.
    Amen.†

Concluding Prayer of the Church

Lord God Almighty, you have made all the peoples of the earth for your glory, to
    serve you in freedom and in peace: Give to the people of our country a zeal for
    justice and the strength of forbearance, that we may use our liberty in accor-
    dance with your gracious will; through Jesus Christ our Lord, who lives and
    reigns with you and the Holy Spirit, one God, for ever and ever. *Amen.*†

The Morning Office

**To Be Observed on the Hour or Half Hour
Between 6 and 9 a.m.**

The Call to Prayer

Proclaim the greatness of the LORD our God and worship him upon his holy hill;*
    for the LORD our God is the Holy One.

Psalm 99:9

The Request for Presence
Be pleased, O Lord, to deliver me;* O Lord make haste to help me.

Psalm 40:14

The Greeting
But you, O Lord my God, Oh, deal with me according to your Name;* for your
   tender mercy's sake, deliver me.
For I am poor and needy,* and my heart is wounded within me.

Psalm 109:20–21

The Refrain for the Morning Lessons
The Lord is full of compassion and mercy,* slow to anger and of great kindness.

Psalm 103:8

A Reading
Jesus taught us, saying: 'For God sent his Son into the world not to judge the
   world, but so that through him the world might be saved. No one who believes
   in him will be judged; but whoever does not believe is judged already, because
   that person does not believe in the name of God's only Son. And the judgment
   is this: though the light has come into the world people have preferred darkness to light because their deeds are evil.'

John 3:17–19

The Refrain
The Lord is full of compassion and mercy,* slow to anger and of great kindness.

The Morning Psalm   *He Put a New Song in My Mouth*
I waited patiently upon the Lord;* he stooped to me and heard my cry.
He lifted me out of the desolate pit, out of the mire and the clay;* he set my feet
   upon a high cliff and made my footing sure.
He put a new song in my mouth, a song of praise to our God;* many shall see, and
   stand in awe.
And put their trust in the Lord.

Psalm 40:1–3

The Refrain
The Lord is full of compassion and mercy,* slow to anger and of great kindness.

Cry of the Church
In the evening, in the morning, and at noonday, I will complain and lament,* and
   he will hear my voice.

Psalm 55:18

The Lord's Prayer

The Prayer Appointed for the Week
Almighty God, you have built your Church upon the foundation of the apostles
   and prophets, Jesus Christ himself being the chief cornerstone: Grant that all of

us may be joined together in unity of spirit by their teaching, that we may be made a holy temple acceptable to you; through Jesus Christ our Lord, who lives and reigns with you and the Holy Spirit, one God, for ever and ever. *Amen.*†

The Concluding Prayer of the Church

Lord God, almighty and everlasting Father, you have brought me in safety to this new day: Preserve me with your mighty power, that I may not fall into sin, nor be overcome by adversity; and in all I do direct me to the fulfilling of your purpose; through Jesus Christ my Lord. *Amen.*†

The Midday Office

To Be Observed on the Hour or Half Hour Between 11 a.m. and 2 p.m.

The Call to Prayer

Sing to the LORD, you servants of his;* give thanks for the remembrance of his holiness.
For his wrath endures but the twinkling of an eye,* his favor for a lifetime.

Psalm 30:4–5

The Request for Presence

Look upon your covenant;* the dark places of the earth are haunts of violence.

Psalm 74:19

The Greeting

O LORD, your love endures for ever;* do not abandon the works of your hands.

Psalm 138:9

The Refrain for the Midday Lessons

He has not dealt with us according to our sins,* nor rewarded us according to our wickedness.

Psalm 103:10

A Reading

. . . 'Here is the message of the Amen, the trustworthy, the true witness, the Principle of God's creation: I know about your activities: how you are neither cold nor hot. I wish you were one or the other, but since you are neither hot nor cold, but only lukewarm, I will spit you out of my mouth. You say to yourself, "I am rich, I have made a fortune, and have everything I want," never realizing that you are wretchedly and pitiably poor, and blind and naked too. I warn you, buy from me the gold that has been tested in the fire to make you really rich, and white robes to clothe you and hide your shameful nakedness, and ointment to put on your eyes to enable you to see. I *reprove and train those whom I love:* so repent in real earnest. Look, I am standing at the door, knocking. If one hears me calling and opens the door, I will come to share a meal at that person's side. Anyone who proves victorious I will allow to share my throne, just as I have myself overcome and have taken my seat with my Father on his throne. Let anyone who can hear, listen to what the Spirit is saying to the churches.'

Revelation 3:14–22

The Refrain
He has not dealt with us according to our sins,* nor rewarded us according to our wickedness.

The Midday Psalm   *To Those Who Keep in My Way*
But to the wicked God says:* "Why do you recite my statutes, and take my covenant upon your lips;

Since you refuse discipline,* and toss my words behind your back?

When you see a thief, you make him your friend,* and you cast in your lot with adulterers.

You have loosed your lips for evil,* and harnessed your tongue to a lie.

You are always speaking evil of your brother* and slandering your own mother's son.

These things you have done, and I kept still,* and you thought that I am like you."

"I have made my accusation;* I have put my case in order before your eyes.

Consider this well, you who forget God,* lest I rend you and there be none to deliver you.

Whoever offers me a sacrifice of thanksgiving honors me;* but to those who keep in my way will I show the salvation of God."

Psalm 50:16–24

The Refrain
He has not dealt with us according to our sins,* nor rewarded us according to our wickedness.

The Cry of the Church
O God, come to my assistance! O Lord, make haste to help me!

The Lord's Prayer

The Prayer Appointed for the Week
Almighty God, you have built your Church upon the foundation of the apostles and prophets, Jesus Christ himself being the chief cornerstone: Grant that all of us may be joined together in unity of spirit by their teaching, that we may be made a holy temple acceptable to you; through Jesus Christ our Lord, who lives and reigns with you and the Holy Spirit, one God, for ever and ever. *Amen.*†

The Concluding Prayer of the Church
Almighty God, whose most dear Son went not up to joy before he first suffered pain, and did not enter into glory before he was crucified: Mercifully grant that I, walking in the way of the cross, may find it to be none other than the way of life and peace; through Jesus Christ your son my Lord. *Amen.*†

The Vespers Office

**To Be Observed on the Hour or Half Hour
Between 5 and 8 p.m.**

The Call to Prayer
I will call upon God,* and the Lord will deliver me.
In the evening, in the morning, and at the noonday, I will complain and lament,*
  and he will hear my voice.
He will bring me safely back . . . God, who is enthroned of old, will hear me.

Psalm 55:17ff

The Request for Presence
Teach me your way, O Lord, and I will walk in your truth;* knit my heart to you
  that I may fear your Name.

Psalm 86:11

The Greeting
To you, O Lord, I lift up my soul;* my God I put my trust in you; . . .

Psalm 25:1

The Hymn   *Take My Life*
  Take my life, and let it be   Take my voice, and let me sing,
  Consecrated, Lord, to thee.   Always, only, for my King.
  Take my moments and my days;   Take my lips, and let them be
  Let them flow in ceaseless praise.   Filled with messages from thee.

  Take my hands, and let them move   Take my love; my Lord I pour
  At the impulse of your love.   At your feet its treasured store.
  Take my feet, and let them be   Take myself, and I will be
  Swift and beautiful for thee.   Ever, only, all for thee.

Frances R. Havergal

The Refrain for the Vespers Lessons
As far as the east is from the west,* so far has he removed our sins from us.

Psalm 103:12

The Vespers Psalm   *My Iniquities Overwhelm Me*
There is no health in my flesh, because of your indignation;* there is no soundness
  in my body, because of my sin.
For my iniquities overwhelm me;* like a heavy burden they are too much for me
  to bear.
My wounds stink and fester* by reason of my foolishness.
I am utterly bowed down and prostrate;* I go about in mourning all day long.
My loins are filled with searing pain;* there is no health in my body.
I am utterly numb and crushed;* I wail, because of the groaning of my heart.
O Lord, you know all my desires,* and my sighing is not hidden from you.
For in you, O Lord, have I fixed my hope;* you will answer me, O Lord my God.

Psalm 38:3–9, 15

The Refrain
As far as the east is from the west,* so far has he removed our sins from us.

The Cry of the Church
O God, come to my assistance! O Lord, make haste to help me!

The Lord's Prayer

The Prayer Appointed for the Week
Almighty God, you have built your Church upon the foundation of the apostles
and prophets, Jesus Christ himself being the chief cornerstone: Grant that all of
us may be joined together in unity of spirit by their teaching, that we may be
made a holy temple acceptable to you; through Jesus Christ our Lord, who lives
and reigns with you and the Holy Spirit, one God, for ever and ever. *Amen.†*

The Concluding Prayers of the Church
Almighty God, who has promised to hear the petitions of those who ask in your
Son's Name: I beseech you mercifully to incline your ear to me who have made
my prayers and supplications to you; and grant that those things which I have
faithfully asked according to your will, may effectually be obtained, to the
relief of my necessity, and to the setting forth of your glory; through Jesus
Christ my Lord. *Amen.†*

May the souls of the faithful departed, through the mercy of God, rest in eternal
peace. *Amen.*

The Morning Office   **To Be Observed on the Hour or Half Hour**
                                          Between 6 and 9 a.m.

The Call to Prayer
Ascribe to the LORD the glory due his Name;* worship the LORD in the beauty of
    holiness.
The voice of the LORD is upon the waters; the God of glory thunders;* the LORD is
    upon the mighty waters.
The voice of the LORD is a powerful voice;* the voice of the LORD is a voice of
    splendor.
The voice of the LORD breaks the cedar trees;* the LORD breaks the cedars of
    Lebanon;
He makes Lebanon skip like a calf,* and Mount Hermon like a young wild ox.
The voice of the LORD splits flames of fire; the voice of the LORD shakes the wilder-
    ness;* the LORD shakes the wilderness of Kadesh.
The voice of the LORD makes the oak trees writhe* and strips the forest bare.
And in the temple of the LORD* all are crying, "Glory!"
The LORD sits enthroned above the flood;* the LORD sits enthroned as King for
    evermore.
The LORD shall give strength to his people;* the LORD shall give the blessing of peace.

Psalm 29:2–11

The Request for Presence

O God, you are my God; eagerly I seek you;* my soul thirsts for you, my flesh
    faints for you, as in barren and dry land where there is no water.
Therefore I have gazed upon you in your holy place,* that I might behold your
    power and your glory.
For your loving-kindness is better than life itself;* my lips shall give you praise.
So will I bless you as long as I live* and lift up my hands in your Name.

Psalm 63:1–4

The Greeting

We have heard with our ears, O God, our forefathers have told us,* the deeds you
    did in their days, in the days of old.
How with your hand you drove the peoples out and planted our forefathers in the
    land;* how you destroyed nations and made your people flourish.
For they did not take the land by their sword, nor did their arm win the victory for
    them;* but your right hand, your arm, and the light of your countenance,
    because you favored them.

Psalm 44:1–3

The Refrain for the Morning Lessons

Arise, O God, and rule the earth,* for you shall take all nations for your own.

Psalm 82:8

A Reading

Asked by the Pharisees when the kingdom of God was to come, he gave them this
    answer, 'The coming of the kingdom of God does not admit of observation and
    there will be no one to say, "Look, it is here! Look, it is there!" For look, the
    kingdom of God is among you.'

Luke 17:20–21

The Refrain

Arise, O God, and rule the earth,* for you shall take all nations for your own.

The Morning Psalm   *This God Is Our God For Ever and Ever*

Your praise, like your Name, O God, reaches to the world's end;* your right hand
    is full of justice.
Let Mount Zion be glad and the cities of Judah rejoice,* because of your judgments.
Make the circuit of Zion; walk round about her;* count the number of her towers.
Consider well her bulwarks; examine her strongholds;* that you may tell those
    who come after.
This God is our God for ever and ever;* he shall be our guide for evermore.

Psalm 48:9–13

The Refrain

Arise, O God, and rule the earth,* for you shall take all nations for your own.

The Gloria

The Lord's Prayer

The Prayer Appointed for the Week
Almighty God, you have built your Church upon the foundation of the apostles
and prophets, Jesus Christ himself being the chief cornerstone: Grant that all of
us be joined together in unity of spirit by their teaching, that we may be made a
holy temple acceptable to you; through Jesus Christ our Lord, who lives and
reigns with you and the Holy Spirit, one God, for ever and ever. *Amen.*†

The Concluding Prayer of the Church
Lord God, almighty and everlasting Father, you have brought me in safety to this
new day: Preserve me with your mighty power, that I may not fall into sin, nor
be overcome by adversity; and in all I do direct me to the fulfilling of your purpose; through Jesus Christ my Lord. *Amen.*†

The Midday Office　　　　　　　**To Be Observed on the Hour or Half Hour
Between 11 a.m. and 2 p.m.**

The Call to Prayer
Hallelujah! Praise God in his holy temple;* praise him in the firmament of his
power.
Praise him for his mighty acts;* praise him for his excellent greatness.
Praise him with the blast of the ram's-horn;* praise him with lyre and harp.
Praise him with timbrel and dance;* praise him with strings and pipe.
Praise him with resounding cymbals;* praise him with loud-clanging cymbals.
Let everything that has breath* praise the Lord. Hallelujah!

Psalm 150:1–6

The Request for Presence
Lord, hear my prayer, and in your faithfulness heed my supplications;* answer
me in your righteousness.

Psalm 143:1

The Greeting
My eyes are fixed on you, O my Strength;* for you, O God, are my stronghold.

Psalm 59:10

The Refrain for the Midday Lessons
Blessed be the Lord God of Israel,* from age to age. Amen. Amen.

Psalm 41:13

A Reading
Glory be to him whose power, working in us, can do infinitely more than we can
ask or imagine; glory be to him from generation to generation in the Church
and in Christ Jesus for ever and ever. Amen.

Ephesians 3:20–21

The Refrain
Blessed be the LORD God of Israel,* from age to age. Amen. Amen.

The Midday Psalm   *May the LORD Grant You All Your Requests*
May the LORD answer you in the day of trouble,* the Name of the God of Jacob
    defend you;
Send you help from his holy place* and strengthen you out of Zion;
Remember all your offerings* and accept our burnt sacrifice;
Grant you your heart's desire* and prosper all your plans.
We will shout for joy at your victory and triumph in the Name of our God;* may
    the LORD grant all your requests.
                                                                Psalm 20:1–5

The Refrain
Blessed be the LORD God of Israel,* from age to age. Amen. Amen.

The Gloria

The Lord's Prayer

The Prayer Appointed for the Week
Almighty God, you have built your Church upon the foundation of the apostles
    and prophets, Jesus Christ himself being the chief cornerstone: Grant that all of
    us be joined together in unity of spirit by their teaching, that we may be made a
    holy temple acceptable to you; through Jesus Christ our Lord, who lives and
    reigns with you and the Holy Spirit, one God, for ever and ever. *Amen.*†

The Concluding Prayer of the Church
O God, the source of light: Shed forth your unending day upon all of us who
    watch for you, that our lips may praise you, our lives may bless you, and our
    worship may give you glory; through Jesus Christ our Lord. *Amen.*†

The Vespers Office   **To Be Observed on the Hour or Half Hour**
                                          Between 5 and 8 p.m.

The Call to Prayer
Sing with joy to God our strength* and raise a loud shout to the God of Jacob.
Raise a song and sound the timbrel,* the merry harp and the lyre.
Blow the ram's-horn at the new moon,* and at the full moon, the day of our feast.
                                                                Psalm 81:1–3

The Request for Presence
O God, do not be silent;* do not keep still nor hold your peace, O God . . .
                                                                Psalm 83:1

The Greeting
I will sing of mercy and justice;* to you, O LORD, will I sing praises.
                                                                Psalm 101:1

The Hymn   *Sweet Hour of Prayer*

Sweet hour of prayer, sweet hour of prayer,
That calls me from a world of care,
And bids me at my Father's throne,
Make all my wants and wishes known!
In seasons of distress and grief,
My soul has often found relief,
And oft escaped the tempter's snare
By your return, sweet hour of prayer.

Sweet hour of prayer, sweet hour of prayer,
Your wings shall my petition bear
To Him, whose truth and faithfulness
Engage the waiting soul to bless:
And since He bids me seek His face,
Believe His word, and trust His grace,
I'll cast on Him my every care,
And wait for you, sweet hour of prayer.

                                        W. W. Walford

The Refrain for the Vespers Lessons
I am like a green olive tree in the house of God;* I trust in the mercy of God for
ever and ever.

                                        Psalm 52:8

The Vespers Psalm   *The Lord Is in His Holy Temple*
The Lord is in his holy temple;* the Lord's throne is in heaven.
His eyes behold the inhabited world;* his piercing eye weighs our worth.
The Lord weighs the righteous as well as the wicked,* but those who delight in
violence he abhors.
For the Lord is righteous; he delights in righteous deeds;* and the just shall see his
face.

                                        Psalm 11:4ff

The Refrain
I am like a green olive tree in the house of God;* I trust in the mercy of God for
ever and ever.

The Small Verse
The Lord is my shepherd and nothing is wanting to me. In green pastures He hath
settled me.

                                        The Short Breviary

The Lord's Prayer

The Prayer Appointed for the Week
Almighty God, you have built your Church upon the foundation of the apostles
and prophets, Jesus Christ himself being the chief cornerstone: Grant that all of

us be joined together in unity of spirit by their teaching, that we may be made a holy temple acceptable to you; through Jesus Christ our Lord, who lives and reigns with you and the Holy Spirit, one God, for ever and ever. *Amen.*†

The Concluding Prayer of the Church

Almighty God, who after the creation of the world rested from all your works and sanctified a day of rest for all your creatures: Grant that I, pulling away all earthly anxieties, may be duly prepared for the service of public worship, and grant as well that my Sabbath upon earth may be a preparation for the eternal rest promised to your people in heaven; through Jesus Christ our Lord. *Amen.*†

June Compline

Sunday
The Night Office   To Be Observed Before Retiring

The Call to Prayer
May the Lord Almighty grant me and those I love a peaceful night and a perfect
     end. *Amen.*†

The Request for Presence
Our help is in the Name of the LORD;* the maker of heaven and earth.

Psalm 124:8

The Greeting
Almighty God, my heavenly Father: I have sinned against you, through my own
     fault, in thought, and word, and deed, and in what I have left undone. For the
     sake of your Son our Lord Jesus Christ, forgive me all my offenses; and grant
     that I may serve you in newness of life, to the glory of your Name. *Amen.*†

The Reading
Zechariah was filled with the Holy Spirit and spoke this prophecy: '*Blessed be the
     Lord, the God of Israel,* for he has visited his people, he has come to their rescue
     and he has raised up for us a power for salvation in the House of his servant
     David, even as he proclaimed, by the mouth of his holy prophets from ancient
     times . . .'

Luke 1:67–70

The Gloria

The Psalm   *Mercy and Truth Have Met Together*
I will listen to what the LORD God is saying,* for he is speaking peace to his faithful
     people and to those who turn their hearts to him.
Truly, his salvation is very near to those who fear him,* that his glory may dwell in
     our land.
Mercy and truth have met together;* righteousness and peace have kissed each
     other.
Truth shall spring up from the earth,* and righteousness shall look down from
     heaven.
The LORD will indeed grant prosperity,* and our land will yield its increase.
Righteousness shall go before him,* and peace shall be a pathway for his feet.

Psalm 85:8–13

The Gloria

The Small Verse
Into your hands, O Lord, I commend my spirit; for you have redeemed me, O
     Lord, O God of truth. Keep me, O Lord, as the apple of your eye; hide me
     under the shadow of your wings.†

The Lord's Prayer

The Petition
Lord, hear my prayers; And let my cry come to you.†

The Final Thanksgiving
Lord, you now have set your servant free to go in peace as you have promised; for
these eyes of mine have seen the Savior, whom you have prepared for all the
world to see: a Light to enlighten the nations, and the glory of your people
Israel. Glory to the Father, and to the Son, and to the Holy Spirit: as it was in the
beginning, is now, and will be for ever. *Amen.*

☙✦❧

Monday
The Night Office   **To Be Observed Before Retiring**

The Call to Prayer
May the Lord Almighty grant me and those I love a peaceful night and a perfect
end. *Amen.*†

The Request for Presence
Our help is in the Name of the LORD;* the maker of heaven and earth.

Psalm 124:8

The Greeting
Almighty God, my heavenly Father: I have sinned against you, through my own
fault, in thought, and word, and deed, and in what I have left undone. For the
sake of your Son our Lord Jesus Christ, forgive me all my offenses; and grant
that I may serve you in newness of life, to the glory of your Name. *Amen.*†

The Reading
YAHWEH, you are in our midst, we are called by your name. Do not desert us! O
our God, you are our hope.

Jeremiah 14:9, 22

The Gloria

The Psalm   *You Shall Find Refuge Under His Wings*
He who dwells in the shelter of the Most High,* abides under the shadow of the
Almighty.
He shall say to the LORD, "You are my refuge and my stronghold,* my God in
whom I put my trust."

He shall deliver you from the snare of the hunter* and from the deadly pestilence.

He shall cover you with his pinions, and you shall find refuge under his wings;*
his faithfulness shall be a shield and buckler.

You shall not be afraid of any terror by night,* nor of the arrow that flies by day;

Of the plague that stalks in the darkness,* nor of the sickness that lays waste at
mid-day.

A thousand shall fall at your side and ten thousand at your right hand,* but it shall
not come near you.

Your eyes have only to behold* to see the reward of the wicked.

Because you have made the LORD your refuge,* and the Most High your habitation,

There shall no evil happen to you,* neither shall any plague come near your
dwelling.

For he shall give his angels charge over you,* to keep you in all your ways.

They shall bear you in their hands,* lest you dash your foot against a stone.

You shall tread upon the lion and adder;* you shall trample the young lion and the
serpent under your feet.

Because he is bound to me in love, therefore will I deliver him;* I will protect him,
because he knows my Name.

He shall call upon me, and I will answer him;* I am with him in trouble; I will rescue him and bring him to honor.

With long life will I satisfy him,* and show him my salvation.

Psalm 91

The Gloria

The Small Verse

Into your hands, O Lord, I commend my spirit; For you have redeemed me, O
Lord, O God of truth. Keep me, O Lord, as the apple of your eye; Hide me
under the shadow of your wings.†

The Lord's Prayer

The Petition

Lord, hear my prayers; And let my cry come to you.†

The Final Thanksgiving

Lord, you now have set your servant free to go in peace as you have promised; for
these eyes of mine have seen the Savior, whom you have prepared for all the
world to see: a Light to enlighten the nations, and the glory of your people
Israel. Glory to the Father, and to the Son, and to the Holy Spirit: as it was in the
beginning, is now, and will be for ever. *Amen.*

Tuesday
The Night Office   **To Be Observed Before Retiring**

The Call to Prayer
May the Lord Almighty grant me and those I love a peaceful night and a perfect
end. *Amen.*†

The Request for Presence
Our help is in the Name of the LORD;* the maker of heaven and earth.

Psalm 124:8

The Greeting
Almighty God, my heavenly Father: I have sinned against you, through my own
fault, in thought, and word, and deed, and in what I have left undone. For the
sake of your Son our Lord Jesus Christ, forgive me all my offenses; and grant
that I may serve you in newness of life, to the glory of your Name. *Amen.*†

The Reading
Jesus taught us, saying: 'Come to me, all you who labor and are overburdened,
and I will give you rest. Shoulder my yoke and learn from me, for I am gentle
and humble in heart, *and you will find rest for your souls.* Yes, my yoke is
easy and my burden light.'

Matthew 11:28–30

The Gloria

The Psalm   *Into Your Hands I Commend My Spirit*
In you, O LORD, have I taken refuge; let me never be put to shame;* deliver me in
your righteousness.
Incline your ear to me;* make haste to deliver me.
Be my strong rock, a castle to keep me safe, for you are my crag and my strong-
hold;* for the sake of your Name, lead me and guide me.
Take me out of the net that they have secretly set for me,* for you are my tower of
strength.
Into your hands I commend my spirit,* for you have redeemed me, O LORD, O
God of truth.

Psalm 31:1–5

The Gloria

The Small Verse
Into your hands, O Lord, I commend my spirit; For you have redeemed me, O
Lord, O God of truth. Keep me, O Lord, as the apple of your eye; Hide me
under the shadow of your wings.†

The Lord's Prayer

The Petition
Lord, hear my prayers; And let my cry come to you.†

The Final Thanksgiving

Lord, you now have set your servant free to go in peace as you have promised; for
these eyes of mine have seen the Savior, whom you have prepared for all the
world to see: a Light to enlighten the nations, and the glory of your people
Israel. Glory to the Father, and to the Son, and to the Holy Spirit: as it was in the
beginning, is now, and will be for ever. *Amen.*

Wednesday
The Night Office   **To Be Observed Before Retiring**

The Call to Prayer

May the Lord Almighty grant me and those I love a peaceful night and a perfect
end. *Amen.*†

The Request for Presence

Our help is in the Name of the LORD;* the maker of heaven and earth.

Psalm 124:8

The Greeting

Almighty God, my heavenly Father: I have sinned against you, through my own
fault, in thought, and word, and deed, and in what I have left undone. For the
sake of your Son our Lord Jesus Christ, forgive me all my offenses; and grant
that I may serve you in newness of life, to the glory of your Name. *Amen.*†

The Reading

Be calm but vigilant, because your enemy the devil is prowling round like a roaring
lion, looking for someone to eat. Stand up to him, strong in faith and in the
knowledge that your brothers all over the world are suffering the same things.

I Peter 5:8–9

The Gloria

The Psalm   *The LORD Accepts My Prayer*

Have pity on me, LORD, for I am weak;* heal me, LORD, for my bones are racked.
My spirit shakes with terror;* how long, O LORD, how long?
Turn, O LORD, and deliver me;* save me for your mercy's sake.
For in death no one remembers you;* and who will give you thanks in the grave?
I grow weary because of my groaning;* every night I drench my bed and flood my
couch with tears.
My eyes are wasted with grief* and worn away because of all my enemies.
Depart from me, all evildoers,* for the LORD has heard the sound of my weeping.
The LORD has heard my supplication;* the LORD accepts my prayer.

Psalm 6:2–9

The Gloria

The Small Verse
Into your hands, O Lord, I commend my spirit; For you have redeemed me, O
Lord, O God of truth. Keep me, O Lord, as the apple of your eye; Hide me
under the shadow of your wings.†

The Lord's Prayer

The Petition
Lord, hear my prayers; And let my cry come to you.†

The Final Thanksgiving
Lord, you now have set your servant free to go in peace as you have promised; for
these eyes of mine have seen the Savior, whom you have prepared for all the
world to see: a Light to enlighten the nations, and the glory of your people
Israel. Glory to the Father, and to the Son, and to the Holy Spirit: as it was in the
beginning, is now, and will be for ever. *Amen.*

❦

Thursday
The Night Office   **To Be Observed Before Retiring**

The Call to Prayer
May the Lord Almighty grant me and those I love a peaceful night and a perfect
end. *Amen.*†

The Request for Presence
Our help is in the Name of the LORD;* the maker of heaven and earth.

Psalm 124:8

The Greeting
Almighty God, my heavenly Father: I have sinned against you, through my own
fault, in thought, and word, and deed, and in what I have left undone. For the
sake of your Son our Lord Jesus Christ, forgive me all my offenses; and grant
that I may serve you in newness of life, to the glory of your Name. *Amen.*†

The Reading
There is no need to worry; but if there is anything you need, pray for it, asking
God for it with prayer and thanksgiving, and that peace of God, which is so
much greater than we can understand, will guard your hearts and your
thoughts, in Christ Jesus.

Philippians 4:6–7

The Gloria

The Psalm   *Only You, LORD, Make Me Dwell in Safety*

Answer me when I call, O God, defender of my cause;* you set me free when I am
    hard-pressed; have mercy on me and hear my prayer.

"You mortals, how long will you dishonor my glory;* how long will you worship
    dumb idols and run after false gods?"

Know that the LORD does wonders for the faithful;* when I call upon the LORD, he
    will hear me.

Tremble, then, and do not sin;* speak to your heart in silence upon your bed.

Offer the appointed sacrifices* and put your trust in the LORD.

Many are saying, "Oh, that we might see better times!"* Lift up the light of your
    countenance upon us, O LORD.

You have put gladness in my heart,* more than when grain and wine and oil
    increase.

I lie down in peace; at once I fall asleep;* for only you, LORD, make me dwell in
    safety.

Psalm 4:1–8

The Gloria

The Small Verse

Into your hands, O Lord, I commend my spirit; For you have redeemed me, O
    Lord, O God of truth. Keep me, O Lord, as the apple of your eye; Hide me
    under the shadow of your wings.†

The Lord's Prayer

The Petition

Lord, hear my prayers; And let my cry come to you.†

The Final Thanksgiving

Lord, you now have set your servant free to go in peace as you have promised; for
    these eyes of mine have seen the Savior, whom you have prepared for all the
    world to see: a Light to enlighten the nations, and the glory of your people
    Israel. Glory to the Father, and to the Son, and to the Holy Spirit: as it was in the
    beginning, is now, and will be for ever. *Amen.*

❧

Friday
The Night Office   **To Be Observed Before Retiring**

The Call to Prayer

May the Lord Almighty grant me and those I love a peaceful night and a perfect
    end. *Amen.*†

The Request for Presence
Our help is in the Name of the LORD;* the maker of heaven and earth.

Psalm 124:8

The Greeting
Almighty God, my heavenly Father: I have sinned against you, through my own fault, in thought, and word, and deed, and in what I have left undone. For the sake of your Son our Lord Jesus Christ, forgive me all my offenses; and grant that I may serve you in newness of life, to the glory of your Name. *Amen.*†

The Reading
I pray that the God of peace, *who brought* our Lord Jesus *back* from the dead *to become the great Shepherd of the sheep by the blood that sealed an eternal covenant,* may make you ready to do his will in any kind of good action; and turn us all into whatever is acceptable to himself through Jesus Christ, to whom be glory for ever and ever. *Amen.*

Hebrews 13:20–21

The Gloria

The Psalm   *My Heart Teaches Me Night After Night*
O LORD, You are my portion and my cup;* it is you who uphold my lot.
My boundaries enclose a pleasant land;* indeed, I have a goodly heritage.
I will bless the LORD who gives me counsel;* my heart teaches me, night after night.
I have set the LORD always before me;* because he is at my right hand I shall not fall.
My heart, therefore, is glad, and my spirit rejoices;* my body also shall rest in hope.
For you will not abandon me to the grave,* nor let your holy one see the Pit.
You will show me the path of life;* in your presence there is fullness of joy, and in your right hand are pleasures for evermore.

Psalm 16:5–11

The Gloria

The Small Verse
Into your hands, O Lord, I commend my spirit; for you have redeemed me, O Lord, O God of truth. Keep me, O Lord, as the apple of your eye; hide me under the shadow of your wings.†

The Lord's Prayer

The Petition
Lord, hear my prayers; And let my cry come to you.†

The Final Thanksgiving
Lord, you now have set your servant free to go in peace as you have promised; for these eyes of mine have seen the Savior, whom you have prepared for all the

world to see: a Light to enlighten the nations, and the glory of your people Israel. Glory to the Father, and to the Son, and to the Holy Spirit: as it was in the beginning, is now, and will be for ever. *Amen.*

⌁❧⌁

Saturday
The Night Office   To Be Observed Before Retiring

The Call to Prayer
May the Lord Almighty grant me and those I love a peaceful night and a perfect end. *Amen.*†

The Request for Presence
Our help is in the Name of the LORD;* the maker of heaven and earth.

Psalm 124:8

The Greeting
Almighty God, my heavenly Father: I have sinned against you, through my own fault, in thought, and word, and deed, and in what I have left undone. For the sake of your Son our Lord Jesus Christ, forgive me all my offenses; and grant that I may serve you in newness of life, to the glory of your Name. *Amen.*†

The Reading
And Mary said: 'My soul proclaims the greatness of the Lord and my spirit *exults in God my savior; because he has looked upon his lowly handmaid.* Yes, from this day forward all generations will call me blessed, for the Almighty has done great things for me. *Holy is his name, and his mercy reaches from age to age for those who fear him.* He has shown the power of his arm, he has routed the proud of heart. *He has pulled down princes* from their thrones *and exalted the lowly. The hungry he has filled with good things,* the rich sent empty away. *He has come to the help of Israel his servant, mindful of his mercy*—according to the promise he made to our ancestors—of his mercy to Abraham and to his descendants for ever.'

Luke 1:46–55

The Gloria

The Psalm   *All You That Stand by Night*
Behold now, bless the LORD, all you servants of the LORD,* you that stand by night in the house of the LORD.
Lift up your hands in the holy place and bless the LORD;* the LORD who made heaven and earth bless you out of Zion.

Psalm 134

The Gloria

The Small Verse

Into your hands, O Lord, I commend my spirit; For you have redeemed me, O
Lord, O God of truth. Keep me, O Lord, as the apple of your eye; Hide me
under the shadow of your wings.†

The Lord's Prayer

The Petition

Lord, hear my prayers; And let my cry come to you.†

The Final Thanksgiving

Lord, you now have set your servant free to go in peace as you have promised; for
these eyes of mine have seen the Savior, whom you have prepared for all the
world to see: a Light to enlighten the nations, and the glory of your people
Israel. Glory to the Father, and to the Son, and to the Holy Spirit: as it was in the
beginning, is now, and will be for ever. *Amen.*

The Gloria

Glory be to God the Father, God the Son, and God the Holy Spirit. As it was
in the beginning, so it is now and so it shall ever be, world without end.
Alleluia. *Amen.*

The Lord's Prayer

Our Father, who art in heaven, hallowed be your Name.
May your kingdom come, and your will be done, on earth as in heaven.
Give us today our daily bread.
Forgive us our sins as we forgive those who sin against us.
Lead us not into temptation, but deliver us from evil;
for yours are the kingdom and the power and the glory
forever and ever. *Amen.*

Compline Prayers for July Are Located on Page 315

The Following Holy Days Occur in July:
Feast of St. Mary Magdalene: *July 22*
Feast of St. James and St. John: *July 25*

July

The Morning Office　　　　　**To Be Observed on the Hour or Half Hour**
　　　　　　　　　　　　　　　　　　　　　Between 6 and 9 a.m.

The Call to Prayer
Praise God from whom all blessings flow; Praise Him all creatures here below;
Praise him above, you heavenly hosts; Praise Father, Son, and Holy Ghost.

Traditional Doxology

The Request for Presence
Hear, O Shepherd of Israel, leading Joseph like a flock;* shine forth, you that are
enthroned upon the cherubim.

Psalm 80:1

The Greeting
Let all who seek you rejoice and be glad in you;* let those who love your salvation
say for ever, "Great is the LORD!"

Psalm 70:4

The Refrain for the Morning Lessons
My heart is firmly fixed, O God, my heart is fixed;* I will sing and make melody.

Psalm 108:1

A Reading
Jesus said: 'But the hour is coming—indeed is already here—when true worshippers will worship the Father in spirit and truth; that is the kind of worshipper
the Father seeks. God is spirit, and those who worship must worship in spirit
and truth.'

John 4:23–24

The Refrain
My heart is firmly fixed, O God, my heart is fixed;* I will sing and make melody.

The Morning Psalm　　　　　　　　　　　　**God Has Anointed You**
My heart is stirring with a noble song; let me recite what I have fashioned for the
　　king;* my tongue shall be the pen of a skilled writer.
You are the fairest of men;* grace flows from your lips, because God has blessed
　　you forever.
Strap your sword upon your thigh, O mighty warrior,* in your pride and your
　　majesty.
Ride out and conquer in the cause of truth* and for the sake of justice.
Your right hand will show you marvelous things;* your arrows are very sharp, O
　　mighty warrior.
The peoples are falling at your feet,* and the king's enemies are losing heart.
Your throne, O God, endures for ever and ever,* a scepter of righteousness is the
　　scepter of your kingdom; you love righteousness and hate iniquity.
Therefore, God, your God, has anointed you* with the oil of gladness above your
　　fellows.

All your garments are fragrant with myrrh, aloes, and cassia,* and the music of
strings from ivory palaces makes you glad.
King's daughters stand among the ladies of the court;* on your right hand is the
queen, adorned with the gold of Ophir.

Psalm 45:1–10

The Refrain
My heart is firmly fixed, O God, my heart is fixed;* I will sing and make melody.

The Small Verse
The people that walked in darkness have seen a great light; on those who live in a
land of deep shadow a light has shone.

Isaiah 9:1

The Lord's Prayer

The Prayer Appointed for the Week
O God, you have taught me to keep all your commandments by loving you and
my neighbor: Grant me the grace of your Holy Spirit, that I may be devoted to
you with my whole heart, and united to others with pure affection; through
Jesus Christ our Lord, who lives and reigns with you and the Holy Spirit, one
God, for ever and ever. *Amen.*†

The Concluding Prayer of the Church
Lord God, almighty and everlasting Father, you have brought me in safety to this
new day: Preserve me with your mighty power, that I may not fall into sin, nor
be overcome by adversity; and in all I do direct me to the fulfilling of your purpose; through Jesus Christ my Lord. *Amen.*†

The Midday Office   To Be Observed on the Hour or Half Hour
                          Between 11 a.m. and 2 p.m.

The Call to Prayer
Come, let us sing to the LORD;* let us shout for joy to the Rock of our salvation.
Let us come before his presence with thanksgiving* and raise a loud shout to him
with psalms.
For the LORD is a great God,* and a great king above all gods.
In his hands are the caverns of the earth,* and the heights of the hills are his also.
The sea is his, for he made it,* and his hands have molded the dry land.

Psalm 95:1–5

The Request for Presence
May God give us his blessing,* and may all the ends of the earth stand in awe of
him.

Psalm 67:7

The Greeting
You, O LORD, are a shield about me;* you are my glory, the one who lifts up my head.
I call aloud upon the LORD,* and he answers me from his holy hill;
I lie down and go to sleep;* I wake again, because the LORD sustains me.

Psalm 3:3–5

The Refrain for the Midday Lessons
May the glory of the LORD endure for ever;* may the LORD rejoice in all his works.

Psalm 104:32

A Reading
Sing a new song to YAHWEH! Let his praise be sung from the remotest parts of the
earth, by those who sail the sea and by everything in it, by the coasts and the
islands and those who inhabit them.

Isaiah 42:10

The Refrain
May the glory of the LORD endure for ever;* may the LORD rejoice in all his works.

The Midday Psalm   *Let Them Praise the Name of the* LORD
Praise the LORD from the earth,* you sea-monsters and deeps;
Fire and hail, snow and fog,* tempestuous wind doing his will;
Mountains and hills,* fruit trees and cedars;
Wild beasts and all cattle, kings of the earth and all peoples,* princes and all rulers
of the world;
Young men and maidens,* old and young together.
Let them praise the Name of the LORD,* for his Name only is exalted, his splendor
is over earth and heaven.
He raised up strength for his people and praise for all his loyal servants,* the chil-
dren of Israel, a people who are near him. Hallelujah!

Psalm 148:7–14

The Refrain
May the glory of the LORD endure for ever;* may the LORD rejoice in all his works.

The Cry of the Church
O God, come to my assistance! O Lord, make haste to help me!

The Lord's Prayer

The Prayer Appointed for the Week
O God, you have taught me to keep all your commandments by loving you and
my neighbor: Grant me the grace of your Holy Spirit, that I may be devoted to
you with my whole heart, and united to others with pure affection; through
Jesus Christ our Lord, who lives and reigns with you and the Holy Spirit, one
God, for ever and ever. *Amen.*†

The Concluding Prayers of the Church
O God, on this first day of the week, I join all creation and people of all ages in

praising you. Your kindness and forgiveness flow like a river through the centuries refreshing our faith, our hope and our love. May you be forever praised throughout all the ages. *Amen.*

adapted from THE NEW COMPANION TO THE BREVIARY

The Vespers Office   **To Be Observed on the Hour or Half Hour Between 5 and 8 p.m.**

The Call to Prayer
Bless the LORD, O my soul,* and all that is within me, bless his holy Name.
Bless the LORD, O my soul,* and forget not all his benefits.

Psalm 103:1–2

The Request for Presence
The LORD will hear the desire of the humble;* you will strengthen their heart and
   your ears shall hear.

Psalm 10:18

The Greeting
   O gracious Light,
   pure brightness of the everlasting Father in heaven,
   O Jesus Christ, holy and blessed!

   Now as we come to the setting of the sun,
   and our eyes behold the vesper light,
   we sing your praises O God: Father, Son and Holy Spirit.

   You are worthy at all times to be praised by happy voices,
   O Son of God, O giver of life,
   and to be glorified through all the worlds.

Phos Hilaron

The Hymn   *Be for Us a Moon of Joy*
   May you be for us a moon of joy and happiness.
   Let the young become strong
   and the grown man maintain his strength,
   the pregnant woman be delivered
   and the woman who has given birth suckle her child.
   Let the stranger come to the end of his journey
   and those who remain at home dwell safely in their houses.
   Let the flocks that go to feed in the pastures return happily.
   May you be a moon of harvest and of calves.
   May you be a moon of restoration and of good health.

Ethiopian Prayer

The Refrain for the Vespers Lessons
The LORD has heard my supplication;* the LORD accepts my prayer.

Psalm 6:9

The Vespers Psalm *If the LORD Had Not Been on Our Side*

If the LORD had not been on our side,* let Israel now say;
If the LORD had not been on our side,* when enemies rose up against us;
Then would they have swallowed us up alive* in their fierce anger toward us;
Then would the waters have overwhelmed us* and the torrent gone over us;
Then would the raging waters* have gone right over us.
Blessed be the LORD!* he has not given us over to be prey for their teeth.
We have escaped like a bird from the snare of the fowler;* the snare is broken, and
　　we have escaped.
Our help is in the Name of the LORD,* the maker of heaven and earth.

Psalm 124

The Refrain
The LORD has heard my supplication;* the LORD accepts my prayer.

The Small Verse
The Lord is my shepherd and nothing is wanting to me.* In green pastures He has
　　settled me.

A SHORT BREVIARY

The Lord's Prayer

The Prayer Appointed for the Week
O God, you have taught me to keep all your commandments by loving you and
　　my neighbor: Grant me the grace of your Holy Spirit, that I may be devoted to
　　you with my whole heart, and united to others with pure affection; through
　　Jesus Christ our Lord, who lives and reigns with you and the Holy Spirit, one
　　God, for ever and ever. *Amen.*†

Concluding Prayers of the Church
Lord God, whose Son our savior Jesus Christ, triumphed over the power of death
　　and prepared for us our place in the new Jerusalem: Grant that I, who have this
　　day given thanks for his resurrection, may praise you in the City of which he is
　　the light, and where he lives and reigns for ever and ever. *Amen.*†

The Morning Office **To Be Observed on the Hour or Half Hour**
Between 6 and 9 a.m.

The Call to Prayer
"Come now, let us reason together," says the Lord.

Isaiah 1:18 KJV

The Request for Presence
Be my strong rock, a castle to keep me safe;* you are my crag and my stronghold.

Psalm 71:3

The Greeting

The words of the LORD are pure words,* like silver refined from ore and purified
seven times in the fire.

Psalm 12:6

The Refrain for the Morning Lessons

"Because the needy are oppressed, and the poor cry out in misery,* I will rise up,"
says the LORD, "And give them the help they long for."

Psalm 12:5

A Reading

'Be compassionate just as your Father is compassionate. Do not judge, and you
will not be judged yourselves; do not condemn, and you will not be condemned; forgive, and you will be forgiven. Give, and there will be gifts for you:
a full measure, pressed down, shaken together, and overflowing, will be
poured into your lap; because the standard you use will be the standard used
for you.'

Luke 6:36–38

The Refrain

"Because the needy are oppressed, and the poor cry out in misery,* I will rise up,"
says the LORD, "And give them the help they long for."

The Morning Psalm   *He Shall Defend the Needy*

Give the King your justice, O God,* and your righteousness to the King's Son;
That he may rule your people righteously* and the poor with justice;
That the mountains may bring prosperity to the people,* and the little hills bring
righteousness.
He shall defend the needy among the people;* he shall rescue the poor and crush
the oppressor.
He shall live as long as the sun and moon endure,* from one generation to another.
He shall come down like rain upon the mown field,* like showers that water the
earth.
In his time shall the righteous flourish;* there shall be abundance of peace till the
moon shall be no more.
He shall rule from sea to sea,* and from the River to the ends of the earth.
For he shall deliver the poor who cries out in distress,* and the oppressed who has
no helper.
He shall have pity on the lowly and poor;* he shall preserve the lives of the needy.
He shall redeem their lives from oppression and violence,* and dear shall their
blood be in his sight.
May his Name remain for ever and be established as long as the sun endures;*
may all nations bless themselves in him and call him blessed.

Psalm 72:1ff

The Refrain
"Because the needy are oppressed, and the poor cry out in misery,* I will rise up,"
says the LORD, "And give them the help they long for."

The Cry of the Church
Even so, come Lord Jesus.

The Lord's Prayer

The Prayer Appointed for the Week
O God, you have taught me to keep all your commandments by loving you and
my neighbor: Grant me the grace of your Holy Spirit, that I may be devoted to
you with my whole heart, and united to others with pure affection; through
Jesus Christ our Lord, who lives and reigns with you and the Holy Spirit, one
God, for ever and ever. *Amen.*†

The Concluding Prayer of the Church
Lord God, almighty and everlasting Father, you have brought me in safety to this
new day: Preserve me with your mighty power, that I may not fall into sin, nor
be overcome by adversity; and in all I do direct me to the fulfilling of your purpose; through Jesus Christ my Lord. *Amen.*†

The Midday Office **To Be Observed on the Hour or Half Hour**
Between 11 a.m. and 2 p.m.

The Call to Prayer
Bless our God, you peoples;* make the voice of his praise to be heard;
Who holds our souls in life,* and will not allow our feet to slip.

Psalm 66:7–8

The Request for Presence
Show us the light of your countenance, O God,* and come to us.

based on Psalm 67:1

The Greeting
Happy are the people whose strength is in you!* whose hearts are set on the pilgrims' way.

Psalm 84:4

The Refrain for the Midday Lessons
Happy are they who fear the LORD,* and who follow in his ways!
You shall eat the fruit of your labor;* happiness and prosperity shall be yours.

Psalm 128:1–2

A Reading
And Laban said: Now therefore come, let us make a covenant, you and I: and let it
be for a witness between us. And Jacob took a stone, and set it up for a pillar.

And Jacob said to his brethren, Gather stones; and they took stones, and made a heap: and they ate there upon the heap. And Laban said, This cairn is a witness between you and me this day. Therefore was the name of it called Galeed; and Mizpah; for he said, The Lord watch between me and thee, when we are absent from one another. The God of Abraham, and the God of Nahor, the God of their Father, judge between us. And Jacob swore by the Fear of his father Isaac. Then Jacob offered sacrifice upon the mount and called his brethren to eat bread: and they ate bread, and then tarried all night in the mount. And early in the morning Laban rose up, and blessed them: and Laban departed, and returned unto his place.

adapted from Genesis 31:44ff KJV

The Refrain
Happy are they who fear the LORD,* and who follow in his ways!
You shall eat the fruit of your labor;* happiness and prosperity shall be yours.

The Midday Psalm   *There the LORD Has Ordained the Blessing*
Oh, how good and pleasant it is,* when brethren live together in unity!
It is like fine oil upon the head* that runs down upon the beard,
Upon the beard of Aaron,* and runs down upon the collar of his robe.
It is like the dew of Hermon* that falls upon the hills of Zion.
For there the LORD has ordained the blessing* life for evermore.

Psalm 133:1–5

The Refrain
Happy are they who fear the LORD,* and who follow in his ways!
You shall eat the fruit of your labor;* happiness and prosperity shall be yours.

The Small Verse
Blessed be the Name of the Lord and blessed be the people who are called by it.

The Lord's Prayer

The Prayer Appointed for the Week
O God, you have taught me to keep all your commandments by loving you and my neighbor: Grant me the grace of your Holy Spirit, that I may be devoted to you with my whole heart, and united to others with pure affection; through Jesus Christ our Lord, who lives and reigns with you and the Holy Spirit, one God, for ever and ever. *Amen.*†

The Concluding Prayer of the Church
Lord, my God, King of heaven and of earth, for this day please direct and sanctify, set right and govern my heart and my body, my sentiments, my words and my actions in conformity with Your law and Your commandments. Thus I shall be able to attain salvation and deliverance, in time and in eternity, by Your help, O Savior of the world, who lives and reigns forever. *Amen.*

adapted from DIVINE OFFICE, II

The Vespers Office   **To Be Observed on the Hour or Half Hour
                                          Between 5 and 8 p.m.**

The Call to Prayer
The righteous will be glad . . .
And they will say, "Surely, there is a reward for the righteous;* surely, there is a
God who rules in the earth."

Psalm 58:10–11

The Request for Presence
Make me understand the way of your commandments,* that I may meditate on
your marvelous works.

Psalm 119:27

The Greeting
You have made me glad by your acts, O Lord;* and I shout for joy because of the
works of your hands.

Psalm 92:4

The Hymn
Give thanks to the Lord, for he is good,* for his mercy endures for ever.
Give thanks to the God of gods,* for his mercy endures for ever.
Give thanks to the Lord of lords,* for his mercy endures for ever.
Who only does great wonders,* for his mercy endures for ever.
Who by wisdom made the heavens,* for his mercy endures for ever.
Who spread out the earth upon the waters,* for his mercy endures for ever.
Who created great lights,* for his mercy endures for ever.
The sun to rule the day,* for his mercy endures for ever.
The moon and the stars to govern the night,* for his mercy endures for ever.
Who struck down the firstborn of Egypt,* for his mercy endures for ever.
And brought out Israel from among them,* for his mercy endures for ever.
With a mighty hand and a stretched out arm,* for his mercy endures for ever.
Who divided the Red Sea in two,* for his mercy endures for ever.
And made Israel to pass through the midst of it,* for his mercy endures for ever.
But swept Pharaoh and his army into the Red Sea,* for his mercy endures for ever.
Who led his people through the wilderness,* for his mercy endures for ever.
Who remembered us in our low estate,* for his mercy endures for ever.
And delivered us from our enemies,* for his mercy endures for ever.
Who gives food to all creatures,* for his mercy endures for ever.
Give thanks to the God of heaven,* for his mercy endures forever.

Psalm 136:1ff

The Refrain for the Vespers Lessons
My mouth shall speak of wisdom,* and my heart shall meditate on understanding.

Psalm 49:2

The Vespers Psalm   *Having You I Desire Nothing Upon Earth*

Whom have I in heaven but you?* and having you I desire nothing upon earth.

Though my flesh and heart should waste away,* God is the strength of my heart
   and my portion for ever.

Truly, those who forsake you will perish;* you destroy all who are unfaithful.

But it is good for me to be near God;* I have made the Lord God my refuge.

Psalm 73:25–28

The Refrain

My mouth shall speak of wisdom,* and my heart shall meditate on understanding.

The Gloria

The Lord's Prayer

The Prayer Appointed for the Week

O God, you have taught me to keep all your commandments by loving you and
   my neighbor: Grant me the grace of your Holy Spirit, that I may be devoted to
   you with my whole heart, and united to others with pure affection; through
   Jesus Christ our Lord, who lives and reigns with you and the Holy Spirit, one
   God, for ever and ever. *Amen.*†

Concluding Prayer of the Church

O God, the King eternal, whose light divides the day from the night and turns the
   shadow of death into the morning: Drive far from me all wrong desires, incline
   my heart to keep your law, and guide my feet into the way of peace; that, having done your will with cheerfulness during the day, I may, when night comes,
   rejoice to give you thanks; through Jesus Christ my Lord. *Amen.*†

The Morning Office   **To Be Observed on the Hour or Half Hour**
Between 6 and 9 a.m.

The Call to Prayer

Come, let us sing to the Lord;* let us shout for joy to the Rock of our salvation.

Let us come before his presence with thanksgiving* and raise a loud shout to him
   with psalms.

Psalm 95:1–2

The Request for Presence

Early in the morning I cry out to you,* for in your word is my trust.

Psalm 119:147

The Greeting

I put my trust in your mercy;* my heart is joyful because of your saving help.

Psalm 13:5

The Refrain for the Morning Lessons
Yours are the heavens, the earth is also yours;* you laid the foundations of the
world and all that is in it.

Psalm 89:11

A Reading
Meanwhile the eleven disciples set out for Galilee, to the mountain where Jesus
arranged to meet them. When they saw him they fell down before him, though
some hesitated. Jesus came up and spoke to them. He said, 'All authority in
heaven and on earth has been given to me. Go therefore, make disciples of all
the nations; baptize them in the name of the Father and of the Son and of the
Holy Spirit, and teach them the commands I gave you. And know that I am
with you always; yes, to the end of time.'

Matthew 28:16–20

The Refrain
Yours are the heavens, the earth is also yours;* you laid the foundations of the
world and all that is in it.

The Morning Psalm   *He Has Made the Whole World So Sure*
The LORD is King; he has put on splendid apparel* the LORD has put on his apparel
and girded himself with strength.
He has made the whole world so sure* that it cannot be moved;
Ever since the world began, your throne has been established;* you are from ever-
lasting.

Psalm 93:1–3

The Refrain
Yours are the heavens, the earth is also yours;* you laid the foundations of the
world and all that is in it.

The Gloria

The Lord's Prayer

The Prayer Appointed for the Week
O God, you have taught me to keep all your commandments by loving you and
my neighbor: Grant me the grace of your Holy Spirit, that I may be devoted to
you with my whole heart, and united to others with pure affection; through
Jesus Christ our Lord, who lives and reigns with you and the Holy Spirit, one
God, for ever and ever. *Amen.*✝

The Concluding Prayer of the Church
Lord God, almighty and everlasting Father, you have brought me in safety to this
new day: Preserve me with your mighty power, that I may not fall into sin, nor
be overcome by adversity; and in all I do direct me to the fulfilling of your purpose; through Jesus Christ my Lord. *Amen.*✝

The Midday Office   **To Be Observed on the Hour or Half Hour**
                                         Between 11 a.m. and 2 p.m.

The Call to Prayer
Let the words of my mouth and the meditation of my heart be acceptable in your
   sight,* O LORD, my strength and my redeemer.

Psalm 19:14

The Request for Presence
Open my eyes, that I may see* the wonders of your law.

Psalm 119:18

The Greeting
My God, my rock in whom I put my trust,* my shield, the horn of my salvation,
   and my refuge; you are worthy of praise.

Psalm 18:2

The Refrain for the Midday Lessons
When I called, you answered me;* you increased my strength within me.

Psalm 138:4

A Reading
Finally, grow strong in the Lord, with the strength of his power. Put on the full
   armor of God so as to be able to resist the devil's tactics. For it is not against
   human enemies that we have to struggle, but against the principalities and the
   ruling forces who are masters of the darkness in this world, the spirits of evil in
   the heavens. That is why you must take up all God's armor, or you will not be
   able to put up any resistance on the evil day, or stand your ground even though
   you exert yourselves to the full. So stand your ground, with *truth a belt around
   your waist,* and *uprightness a breast plate,* wearing for shoes on your feet *the
   eagerness to spread the gospel of peace* and always carrying the shield of faith so
   that you can use it to quench the burning arrows of the Evil One. And then you
   must take *salvation as your helmet* and the sword of the Spirit, that is, the word
   of God.

Ephesians 6:10–17

The Refrain
When I called, you answered me;* you increased my strength within me.

The Midday Psalm   *You Lengthen My Stride Beneath Me*
It is God who girds me about with strength* and makes my way secure.
He makes me sure-footed like a deer* and lets me stand firm on the heights.
He trains my hands for battle* and my arms for bending a bow of bronze.
You have given me your shield of victory;* your right hand also sustains me; your
   loving care makes me great.
You lengthen my stride beneath me,* and my ankles do not give way.

Psalm 18:33–37

The Refrain
When I called, you answered me;* you increased my strength within me.

The Gloria

The Lord's Prayer

The Prayer Appointed for the Week
O God, you have taught me to keep all your commandments by loving you and
my neighbor: Grant me the grace of your Holy Spirit, that I may be devoted to
you with my whole heart, and united to others with pure affection; through
Jesus Christ our Lord, who lives and reigns with you and the Holy Spirit, one
God, for ever and ever. *Amen.*†

The Concluding Prayer of the Church
Heavenly Father, in you I live and move and have my being: I humbly pray you so
to guide and govern me by your Holy Spirit, that in all cares and occupations
of my life I may not forget you, but may remember that I am ever walking in
your sight; through Jesus Christ my Lord. *Amen.*†

The Vespers Office **To Be Observed on the Hour or Half Hour**
Between 5 and 8 p.m.

The Call to Prayer
Taste and see that the LORD is good;* happy are those who trust in him!
Psalm 34:8

The Request for Presence
O Lamb of God, that takes away the sins of the world, have mercy upon me.
O Lamb of God, that takes away the sins of the world, have mercy upon me.
O Lamb of God, that takes away the sins of the world, grant me your peace.

The Greeting
Happy are those whom you choose and draw to your courts to dwell there!* they
will be satisfied by the beauty of your house, by the holiness of your temple.
Psalm 65:4

The Hymn

Somebody's knocking at your door
Somebody's knocking at your door
Oh, sinner, why don't you answer,
Somebody's knocking at your door

Knocks like Jesus,
Somebody's knocking at your door
Oh, sinner, why don't you answer,
Somebody's knocking at your door

Can't you hear him,
Somebody's knocking at your door
Oh, sinner, why don't you answer,
Somebody's knocking at your door

Answer Jesus
Somebody's knocking at your door
Oh, sinner, why don't you answer,
Somebody's knocking at your door

Jesus calls you,	Can't you trust him,
Somebody's knocking at your door	Somebody's knocking at your door
Oh, sinner, why don't you answer,	Oh, sinner, why don't you answer,
Somebody's knocking at your door	Somebody's knocking at your door

African-American Spiritual

The Refrain for the Vespers Lessons

Weeping may spend the night,* but joy comes in the morning.

Psalm 30:6

The Vespers Psalm *A Broken and Contrite Heart, O God, You Will Not Despise*

Had you desired it, I would have offered sacrifice,* but you take no delight in
burnt-offerings.

The sacrifice of God is a troubled spirit;* a broken and contrite heart, O God, you
will never despise.

Psalm 51:17–18

The Refrain

Weeping may spend the night,* but joy comes in the morning.

The Cry of the Church

In the evening, in the morning, and at noonday, I will complain and lament,* and
he will hear my voice.

Psalm 55:18

The Lord's Prayer

The Prayer Appointed for the Week

O God, you have taught me to keep all your commandments by loving you and
my neighbor: Grant me the grace of your Holy Spirit, that I may be devoted to
you with my whole heart, and united to others with pure affection; through
Jesus Christ our Lord, who lives and reigns with you and the Holy Spirit, one
God, for ever and ever. *Amen.*†

Concluding Prayers of the Church

Almighty Father,
you have given me the strength
to work throughout this day.
Receive my evening sacrifice of praise
in thanksgiving for your countless gifts.
I ask this through my Lord Jesus Christ, your Son,
who lives and reigns with you and the Holy Spirit,
one God, for ever and ever.

THE LITURGY OF THE HOURS, VOL. III

The Morning Office   **To Be Observed on the Hour or Half Hour**
                                          Between 6 and 9 a.m.

The Call to Prayer
Bless the LORD, you angels of his, you mighty ones who do his bidding,* and hear-
    ken to the voice of his word.
Bless the LORD, all you his hosts,* you ministers of his who do his will.
Bless the LORD, all you works of his,* in all places of his dominion;
Bless the LORD, O my soul.

Psalm 103:20–22

The Request for Presence
Let those who seek you rejoice and be glad in you;* let those who love your salva-
    tion say forever, "Great is the LORD!"

Psalm 70:4

The Greeting
O LORD my God, I cried out to you,* and you restored me to health.
You brought me up, O LORD, from the dead;* you restored my life as I was going
    down to the grave.

Psalm 30:2–3

The Refrain for the Morning Lessons
May you be blessed by the LORD,* the maker of heaven and earth.

Psalm 124

A Reading
In the course of their journey he came to a village, and a woman named Martha
    welcomed him into her house. She had a sister called Mary, who sat down at
    the Lord's feet and listened to him speaking. Now Martha who was distracted
    with all the serving said, 'Lord, do you not care that my sister is leaving me to
    do the serving all by myself? Please tell her to help me.' But the Lord answered:
    'Martha, Martha,' he said, 'you worry and fret about so many things, and yet
    few are needed, indeed only one. It is Mary who has chosen the better part, it is
    not to be taken from her.'

Luke: 10:38–42

The Refrain
May you be blessed by the LORD,* the maker of heaven and earth.

The Morning Psalm   *Great Peace Have They Who Love Your Law*
Seven times a day do I praise you,* because of your righteous judgments.
Great peace have they who love your law:* for them there is no stumbling block.

Psalm 119:165

The Refrain
May you be blessed by the LORD,* the maker of heaven and earth.

The Small Verse
The Lord is my shepherd and nothing is wanting to me.* In green pastures He has
settled me.

THE SHORT BREVIARY

The Lord's Prayer

The Prayer Appointed for the Week
O God, you have taught me to keep all your commandments by loving you and
my neighbor: Grant me the grace of your Holy Spirit, that I may be devoted to
you with my whole heart, and united to others with pure affection; through
Jesus Christ our Lord. *Amen.*†

The Concluding Prayer of the Church
Lord God, almighty and everlasting Father, you have brought me in safety to this
new day: Preserve me with your mighty power, that I may not fall into sin, nor
be overcome by adversity; and in all I do direct me to the fulfilling of your purpose; through Jesus Christ my Lord. *Amen.*†

The Midday Office

**To Be Observed on the Hour or Half Hour
Between 11 a.m. and 2 p.m.**

The Call to Prayer
Open my lips, O Lord,* and my mouth shall proclaim your praise.

Psalm 51:16

The Request for Presence
Bow down your ear, O LORD and answer me . . .
Keep watch over my life, for I am faithful.

Psalm 86:1–2

The Greeting
I will offer you the sacrifice of thanksgiving* and call upon the Name of the LORD.

Psalm 116:15

The Refrain for the Midday Lessons
The angel of the LORD encompasses those who fear him,* and he will deliver them.

Psalm 34:7

A Reading
Give a welcome to anyone whose faith is not strong, but do not get into arguments
about doubtful points. One person may have faith enough to eat any kind of
food; another, less strong will eat only vegetables. Those who feel free to eat
freely are not to condemn those who are unwilling to eat freely, nor must the
person who does not eat freely pass judgment on the one who does—because
God has welcomed him. And who are you, to sit in judgment over someone
else's servant? Whether he deserves to be upheld or to fall is for his own master
to decide; and he shall be upheld, for the Lord has the power to uphold him.

One person thinks that some days are holier than others, and another thinks them all equal. Let each of them be fully convinced in his own mind. The one who makes special observance of a particular day observes it in honor of the Lord. So the one who eats freely, eats in honor of the Lord, making his thanksgiving to God; and the one who does not, abstains from eating in honor of the Lord, and makes his thanksgiving to God. For none of us lives for himself and none of us dies for himself; while we are alive, we are living for the Lord; and when we die, we die for the Lord: and so, alive or dead, we belong to the Lord.

Romans 14:1–8

The Refrain
The angel of the Lord encompasses those who fear him,* and he will deliver them.

The Midday Psalm   *The Lord Is a Friend to Those Who Fear Him*
Who are they who fear the Lord?* he will teach them the way that they should choose.
They shall dwell in prosperity,* and their offspring shall inherit the land.
The Lord is a friend to those who fear him* and will show them his covenant.
My eyes are ever looking to the Lord,* for he shall pluck my feet out of the net.

Psalm 25:11–14

The Refrain
The angel of the Lord encompasses those who fear him,* and he will deliver them.

The Cry of the Church
O God, come to my assistance!* O Lord, make haste to help me!

The Lord's Prayer

The Prayer Appointed for the Week
O God, you have taught me to keep all your commandments by loving you and my neighbor: Grant me the grace of your Holy Spirit, that I may be devoted to you with my whole heart, and united to others with pure affection; through Jesus Christ our Lord, who lives and reigns with you and the Holy Spirit, one God, for ever and ever. *Amen.*†

The Concluding Prayer of the Church
Most gracious God and Father, you are with me as I make my journey throughout this day. Help me to look lovingly upon all people and events that come into my life today and to walk gently upon this land. Grant this through Jesus who lives and walks among us ever present at each moment. *Amen.*†

The Vespers Office   **To Be Observed on the Hour or Half Hour Between 5 and 8 p.m.**

The Call to Prayer
Come now and see the works of God,* how wonderful he is in his doing toward all people.

Psalm 66:4

The Request for Presence
Let your countenance shine upon your servant* and teach me your statutes.

Psalm 119:135

The Greeting
I will praise you upon the lyre for your faithfulness, O my God;* I will sing to you
with the harp, O Holy one of Israel.

based on Psalm 71:22

The Hymn   *You, Lord, Are Both Lamb and Shepherd*

You, Lord are both lamb and shepherd,
You, Lord are both prince and slave,
You, peace-maker and sword-bringer,
Of the way you took and gave.
You, the everlasting instant,
You whom we both scorn and crave.

Clothed in light upon the mountain,
Stripped of might upon the cross,
Shining in eternal glory,
Beggared by a soldier's toss.
You, the everlasting instant,
You who are our gift and cost.

You who walk each day beside us,
Sit in power at God's side,
You who preach a way that's narrow,
Have a love that reaches wide.
You, the everlasting instant,
You who are our pilgrim guide.

Worthy is our earthly Jesus,
Worthy is our cosmic Christ,
Worthy your defeat and victory,
Worthy still your peace and strife.
You, the everlasting instant,
You who are our death and life.

Sylvia G. Dunstan

The Refrain for the Vespers Lessons
The LORD, the God of gods, has spoken;* he has called the earth from the rising of
the sun to its setting.

Psalm 50:1

The Vespers Psalm   *The LORD Beholds All People*
The LORD looks down from heaven,* and beholds all the peoples in the world.
From where he sits enthroned he turns his gaze* on all who dwell on earth.
He fashions all the hearts of them* and understands all their works.

Psalm 33:13–15

The Refrain
The LORD, the God of gods, has spoken;* he has called the earth from the rising of
the sun to its setting.

The Small Verse
Create in me a clean heart, O God,* and renew a right spirit within me.

Psalm 51:11

The Lord's Prayer

The Prayer Appointed for the Week
O God, you have taught me to keep all your commandments by loving you and
my neighbor: Grant me the grace of your Holy Spirit, that I may be devoted to

you with my whole heart, and united to others with pure affection; through Jesus Christ our Lord, who lives and reigns with you and the Holy Spirit, one God, for ever and ever. *Amen.*†

Concluding Prayers of the Church

Protect us, Lord, as we stay awake; watch over us as we sleep, that awake we may watch with Christ, and asleep, rest in his peace. *Amen.*

The Morning Office

To Be Observed on the Hour or Half Hour Between 6 and 9 a.m.

The Call to Prayer

Wake up, my spirit; awake lute and harp;* I myself will waken the dawn.

Psalm 57:8

The Request for Presence

You are the LORD; do not withhold your compassion from me;* let your love and your faithfulness keep me safe forever.

Psalm 40:12

The Greeting

My heart is firmly fixed, O God, my heart is fixed;* I will sing and make melody.

Psalm 57:7

The Refrain for the Morning Lessons

Cast your burden upon the LORD, and he will sustain you;* he will never let the righteous stumble.

Psalm 55:24

A Reading

The apostles said to the Lord, 'Increase our faith.' The Lord replied, 'If you had faith like a mustard seed you could say to this mulberry tree, "Be uprooted and planted in the sea," and it would obey you.'

Luke 17:5–6

The Refrain

Cast your burden upon the LORD, and he will sustain you;* he will never let the righteous stumble.

The Morning Psalm

He Shall Give His Angels Charge Over You

For he shall give his angels charge over you,* to keep you in all your ways.
They shall bear you in their hands,* lest you dash your foot against a stone.
You shall tread upon the lion and adder;* you shall trample the young lion and the serpent under your feet.

Psalm 91:11–13

The Refrain

Cast your burden upon the LORD, and he will sustain you;* he will never let the righteous stumble.

The Small Verse
My soul thirsts for the strong, living God and all that is within me cries out to him.

The Lord's Prayer

The Prayer Appointed for the Week
O God, you have taught me to keep all your commandments by loving you and
my neighbor: Grant me the grace of your Holy Spirit, that I may be devoted to
you with my whole heart, and united to others with pure affection; through
Jesus Christ our Lord, who lives and reigns with you and the Holy Spirit, one
God, for ever and ever. *Amen.*†

The Concluding Prayer of the Church
Lord God, almighty and everlasting Father, you have brought me in safety to this
new day: Preserve me with your mighty power, that I may not fall into sin, nor
be overcome by adversity; and in all I do direct me to the fulfilling of your purpose; through Jesus Christ my Lord. *Amen.*†

The Midday Office   **To Be Observed on the Hour or Half Hour
Between 11 a.m. and 2 p.m.**

The Call to Prayer
I will offer you a freewill sacrifice* and praise your Name, O Lord, for it is good.
Psalm 54:6

The Request for Presence
Look well whether there be any wickedness in me* and lead me in the way that is
everlasting.
Psalm 139:23

The Greeting
O God, you know my foolishness,* and my faults are not hidden from you.
Psalm 69:6

The Refrain for the Midday Lessons
So teach us to number our days* that we may apply our hearts to wisdom.
Psalm 90:12

A Reading
In all your prayer and entreaty keep praying in the Spirit on every possible occasion. Never get tired of staying awake to pray for all God's holy people; and
pray for me to be given an opportunity to open my mouth and fearlessly make
known the mystery of the gospel of which I am an ambassador in chains; pray
that in proclaiming it I may speak as fearlessly as I ought to.
Ephesians 6:18–20

The Refrain
So teach us to number our days* that we may apply our hearts to wisdom.

The Midday Psalm   *Let the Words of My Mouth Be Acceptable in Your Sight*
Who can tell how often he offends?* Cleanse me from my secret faults.
Above all keep your servant from presumptuous sins; let them not get dominion
    over me;* then shall I be whole and sound, and innocent of a great offense.
Let the words of my mouth and the meditation of my heart be acceptable in your
    sight,* O LORD, my strength and my redeemer.

Psalm 19:12–14

The Refrain
So teach us to number our days* that we may apply our hearts to wisdom.

The Cry of the Church
Lord, have mercy on us. Christ, have mercy on us. Lord, have mercy on us.

The Lord's Prayer

The Prayer Appointed for the Week
O God, you have taught me to keep all your commandments by loving you and
    my neighbor: Grant me the grace of your Holy Spirit, that I may be devoted to
    you with my whole heart, and united to others with pure affection; through
    Jesus Christ our Lord, who lives and reigns with you and the Holy Spirit, one
    God, for ever and ever. *Amen.*†

The Concluding Prayers of the Church
Almighty and eternal God, ruler of all things in heaven and earth: Mercifully
    accept the prayers of your people everywhere, and strengthen each of us to do
    your will; through Jesus Christ my Lord. *Amen.*†

The Vespers Office   **To Be Observed on the Hour or Half Hour**
                                Between 5 and 8 p.m.

The Call to Prayer
O tarry and await the LORD's pleasure; be strong, and he shall comfort your heart;*
    wait patiently for the LORD.

Psalm 27:18

The Request for Presence
Open my eyes, that I may see* the wonders of your law.
I am a stranger here on earth;* do not hide your commandments from me.
My soul is consumed at all times* with longing for your judgments.

Psalm 119:18–20

The Greeting
Your statutes have been like songs to me* wherever I have lived as a stranger.
I remember your Name in the night, O LORD,* and dwell upon your law.
This is how it has been with me,* because I have kept your commandments.

Psalm 119:54–56

The Hymn   *O Zion, Haste*

O Zion, haste, thy mission, high fulfilling,
To tell to all the world that God is Light;
That he who made all nations is not willing
One soul should perish, lost in shades of night.
Publish glad tidings, tidings of peace,
Tidings of Jesus, redemption and release.

Behold how many thousands are still lying,
Bound in the dark-some prison house of sin,
With none to tell them of the Savior's dying.
Or of the life He died for them to win.
Publish glad tidings, tidings of peace,
Tidings of Jesus, redemption and release.

Proclaim to every people, tongue, and nation
That God, in whom they live and move, is Love:
Tell how He stooped to save His lost creation,
And died on earth that man might live above.
Publish glad tidings, tidings of peace,
Tidings of Jesus, redemption and release.

Give of thy sons to bear the message glorious;
Give of thy wealth to speed them on their way;
Pour out thy soul for them in prayer victorious;
And all you spend Jesus will repay.
Publish glad tidings, tidings of peace,
Tidings of Jesus, redemption and release.

Mary A. Thomson

The Refrain for the Vespers Lessons

'I am the Alpha and the Omega,' says the Lord God, who is, who was, and who is
to come, the Almighty.

Revelation 1:8

The Vespers Psalm   *If I Forget You, O Jerusalem*

By the waters of Babylon we sat down and wept,* when we remembered you, O
Zion.
As for our harps, we hung them up* on the trees in the midst of that land.
For those who led us away captive asked us for a song, and our oppressors called
for mirth:* "Sing us one of the songs of Zion."
How shall we sing the LORD's song* upon an alien soil?
If I forget you, O Jerusalem,* let my right hand forget its skill.
Let my tongue cleave to the roof of my mouth if I do not remember you,* if I do
not set Jerusalem above my highest joy.

Psalm 137:1–6

The Refrain
'I am the Alpha and the Omega,' says the Lord God, who is, who was, and who is
    to come, the Almighty.

The Gloria

The Lord's Prayer

The Prayer Appointed for the Week
O God, you have taught me to keep all your commandments by loving you and
    my neighbor: Grant me the grace of your Holy Spirit, that I may be devoted to
    you with my whole heart, and united to others with pure affection; through
    Jesus Christ our Lord, who lives and reigns with you and the Holy Spirit, one
    God, for ever and ever. *Amen.*✝

The Concluding Prayer of the Church
Lord Jesus Christ, you said to your apostles, "Peace I give to you; my own peace I
    leave with you": Regard not my sins, but my faith, and give to me a place in the
    peace and unity of that heavenly City, where with the Father and the Holy
    Spirit you live and reign, now and forever. *Amen.*✝

The Morning Office   **To Be Observed on the Hour or Half Hour**
Between 6 and 9 a.m.

The Call to Prayer
I will call upon God,* and the Lord will deliver me.
In the evening, in the morning, and at the noonday, I will complain and lament,*
    and he will hear my voice.
He will bring me safely back . . .* God, who is enthroned of old, will hear me.

Psalm 55:17

The Request for Presence
Our God will come and will not keep silence;* before him there is a consuming
    flame, and round about him a raging storm.

Psalm 50:3

The Greeting
For your Name's sake, O Lord,* forgive my sin, for it is great.

Psalm 25:10

The Refrain for the Morning Lessons
Help me, O Lord my God;* save me for your mercy's sake.

Psalm 109:25

A Reading
Jesus taught us, saying: 'For as the Father has life in himself, so he has granted the
    Son also to have life in himself; and, because he is the Son of man, has granted
    him power to give judgment. Do not be surprised at this, for the hour is com-

ing when the dead will leave their graves at the sound of his voice: those who did good will come forth to life; and those who did evil will come forth to judgment. By myself I can do nothing; I can only judge as I am told to judge, and my judging is just, because I seek not to do my own will, but the will of him who sent me.'

John 5:26–30

The Refrain
Help me, O LORD my God;* save me for your mercy's sake.

The Morning Psalm   *Truly God Is Good to Those Who Are Pure of Heart*
Truly God is good to . . .* those who are pure at heart.
But as for me, my feet had nearly slipped;* I had almost tripped and fallen;
Because I envied the proud* and saw the prosperity of the wicked:
For they suffer no pain,* and their bodies are sleek and sound;
In the misfortunes of others they have to share;* they are not afflicted as others are;
Therefore they wear pride like a necklace* and wrap their violence about them
     like a cloak.
Their iniquity comes from gross minds,* and their hearts overflow with wicked
     thoughts.
They scoff and speak maliciously;* out of their haughtiness they plan oppression.
They have set their mouths against the heavens,* and their evil speech runs
     through the world.
And so the people turn to them* and find in them no fault.
They say, "How should God, know?* is there knowledge in the Most High?"
So then, these are the wicked;* always at ease, they increase their wealth.
In vain have I kept my heart clean,* and washed my hands in innocence.
I have been afflicted all day long,* and punished every morning.
Had I gone on speaking this way,* I should have betrayed the generation of your
     children.
When I tried to understand these things,* it was too hard for me;
Until I entered the sanctuary of God* and discerned the end of the wicked.
Surely, you set them in slippery places;* you cast them down in ruin.
Oh, how suddenly do they come to destruction,* come to an end, and perish from
     terror!
Like a dream when one awakes, O Lord,* when you arise you make their image
     vanish.

Psalm 73:1–20

The Refrain
Help me, O LORD my God;* save me for your mercy's sake.

The Cry of the Church
O God, come to my assistance! O Lord, make haste to help me!

The Lord's Prayer

The Prayer Appointed for the Week
O God, you have taught me to keep all your commandments by loving you and
my neighbor: Grant me the grace of your Holy Spirit, that I may be devoted to
you with my whole heart, and united to others with pure affection; through
Jesus Christ our Lord, who lives and reigns with you and the Holy Spirit, one
God, for ever and ever. *Amen.†*

The Concluding Prayer of the Church
Lord God, almighty and everlasting Father, you have brought me in safety to this
new day: Preserve me with your mighty power, that I may not fall into sin, nor
be overcome by adversity; and in all I do direct me to the fulfilling of your purpose; through Jesus Christ my Lord. *Amen.†*

The Midday Office   **To Be Observed on the Hour or Half Hour**
                                     Between 11 a.m. and 2 p.m.

The Call to Prayer
Come now and look upon the works of the LORD,* what awesome things he has
done on earth.

Psalm 46:9

The Request for Presence
O LORD, I call to you; come to me quickly;* hear my voice when I cry to you.

Psalm 141:1

The Greeting
When I was in trouble, I called to the LORD;* I called to the LORD, and he answered
me.

The Refrain for the Midday Lessons
"Greatly have they oppressed me since my youth,"* let Israel now say;
"Greatly have they oppressed me since my youth,* but they have not prevailed
against me."

Psalm 129:1-2

A Reading
For I, YAHWEH, your God, I grasp you by the right hand; I tell you, 'Do not be
afraid, I will help you.'

Isaiah 41:13

The Refrain
"Greatly have they oppressed me since my youth,"* let Israel now say;
"Greatly have they oppressed me since my youth,* but they have not prevailed
against me."

The Midday Psalm   *Save Us by Your Right Hand and Answer Us*
O God, you have cast us off and broken us;* you have been angry; oh, take us back
to you again.

You have shaken the earth and split it open;* repair the cracks in it, for it totters.
You have made your people know hardship;* you have given us wine that makes
   us stagger.
You have set up a banner for those who fear you,* to be a refuge from the power of
   the bow.
Save us by your right hand and answer us,* that those who are dear to you may be
   delivered.

Psalm 60:1–5

The Refrain
"Greatly have they oppressed me since my youth,"* let Israel now say;
"Greatly have they oppressed me since my youth,* but they have not prevailed
   against me."

The Small Verse
From my secret sins cleanse me, Lord. And from all strange evils deliver me.

The Lord's Prayer

The Prayer Appointed for the Week
O God, you have taught me to keep all your commandments by loving you and
   my neighbor: Grant me the grace of your Holy Spirit, that I may be devoted to
   you with my whole heart, and united to others with pure affection; through
   Jesus Christ our Lord, who lives and reigns with you and the Holy Spirit, one
   God, for ever and ever. *Amen.*†

The Concluding Prayer of the Church
Lord Jesus Christ, by your death you took away the sting of death: Grant me to so
   follow in faith where you have led the way, that I may at length fall asleep peacefully in you and wake in your likeness; for your tender mercies' sake. *Amen.*†

The Vespers Office

**To Be Observed on the Hour or Half Hour
Between 5 and 8 p.m.**

The Call to Prayer
May these words of mine please him;* I will rejoice in the LORD.

Psalm 104:35

The Request for Presence
Remember not our past sins;* let your compassion be swift to meet us . . .
Help us, O God our Savior, for the glory of your Name;* deliver us and forgive us
   our sins, for your Name's sake.

Psalm 79:8–9

The Greeting
You are to be praised, O God, in Zion . . .
To you that hear prayer shall all flesh come,* because of their transgressions.

Psalm 65:1–2

The Hymn   *When I Survey the Wondrous Cross*
When I survey the wondrous cross
On which the Prince of glory died,
My richest gain I count but loss,
And pour contempt on all my pride.

Forbid it, Lord, that I should boast,
Save in the death of Christ, my God;
All the vain things that charm me most—
I sacrifice them to his blood.

See from his head, his hands, his feet
Sorrow and love flow mingled down.
Did ever such love and sorrow meet,
Or thorns compose so rich a crown?

Were the whole realm of nature mine,
That were a present far too small.
Love so amazing, so divine,
Demands my soul, my life, my all.

Isaac Watts

The Refrain for the Vespers Lessons
Remember not the sins of my youth and my transgressions;* remember me
according to your love and for the sake of your goodness, O Lord.

Psalm 25:6

The Vespers Psalm   *Like a Child Upon Its Mother's Breast*
O Lord, I am not proud;* I have no haughty looks.
I do not occupy myself with great matters,* or with things that are too hard for me.
But I still my soul and make it quiet, like a child upon its mother's breast,* my soul
is quieted within me.

Psalm 131:1–3

The Refrain
Remember not the sins of my youth and my transgressions;* remember me
according to your love and for the sake of your goodness, O Lord.

The Cry of the Church
Lord, have mercy on us. Christ, have mercy on us. Lord, have mercy on us.

The Lord's Prayer

The Prayer Appointed for the Week
O God, you have taught me to keep all your commandments by loving you and
my neighbor: Grant me the grace of your Holy Spirit, that I may be devoted to
you with my whole heart, and united to others with pure affection; through
Jesus Christ our Lord, who lives and reigns with you and the Holy Spirit, one
God, for ever and ever. *Amen.*†

Concluding Prayers of the Church

Almighty God, who has promised to hear the petitions of those who ask in your
Son's Name: I beseech you mercifully to incline your ear to me who have made
my prayers and supplications to you; and grant that those things which I have
faithfully asked according to your will, may effectually be obtained, to the
relief of my necessity, and to the setting forth of your glory; through Jesus
Christ my Lord. *Amen.*†

May the souls of the faithful departed, through the mercy of God, rest in eternal
peace. *Amen.*

The Morning Office　　　　　　**To Be Observed on the Hour or Half Hour
Between 6 and 9 a.m.**

The Call to Prayer

Let us give thanks to the LORD for his mercy* and the wonders he does for his children.
For he satisfies the thirsty* and fills the hungry with good things.

based on Psalm 107:8–9

The Request for Presence

Give ear to my words, O LORD;* consider my meditation.
Hearken to my cry for help, my King and my God,* for I make my prayer to you.
In the morning, LORD, you hear my voice;* early in the morning I make my appeal
and watch for you.

Psalm 5:1–3

The Greeting

Out of the mouths of infants and children, O LORD,* your majesty is praised above
the heavens.

based on Psalm 8:2

The Refrain for the Morning Lessons

I am small and of little account* yet I do not forget your commandments.

Psalm 119:141

A Reading

At this time the disciples came to Jesus and said, 'Who is the greatest in the kingdom of heaven?' So he called a little child to him whom he set among them.
Then he said, 'In truth I tell you, unless you change and become like little children you will never enter the kingdom of heaven. And so, the one who makes
himself as little as this little child is the greatest in the kingdom of heaven.'

Matthew 18:1–4

The Refrain

I am small and of little account* yet I do not forget your commandments.

The Morning Psalm   *Teach Us to Number Our Days*
The span of our life is seventy years, perhaps in strength even eighty;* yet the sum
    of them is but labor and sorrow, for they pass away quickly and we are gone.
Who regards the power of your wrath?* Who rightly fears your indignation?
So teach us to number our days* that we may apply our hearts to wisdom.

Psalm 90:10–12

The Refrain
I am small and of little account* yet I do not forget your commandments.

The Cry of the Church
O Lamb of God, that takes away the sins of the world, have mercy upon me.
O Lamb of God, that takes away the sins of the world, have mercy upon me.
O Lamb of God, that takes away the sins of the world, grant me your peace.

The Lord's Prayer

The Prayer Appointed for the Week
O God, you have taught me to keep all your commandments by loving you and
    my neighbor: Grant me the grace of your Holy Spirit, that I may be devoted to
    you with my whole heart, and united to others with pure affection; through
    Jesus Christ our Lord, who lives and reigns with you and the Holy Spirit, one
    God, for ever and ever. *Amen.*†

The Concluding Prayer of the Church
Lord God, almighty and everlasting Father, you have brought me in safety to this
    new day: Preserve me with your mighty power, that I may not fall into sin, nor
    be overcome by adversity; and in all I do direct me to the fulfilling of your pur-
    pose; through Jesus Christ my Lord. *Amen.*†

The Midday Office   **To Be Observed on the Hour or Half Hour**
Between 11 a.m. and 2 p.m.

The Call to Prayer
Ascribe to the LORD the honor due his Name;* bring offerings and come into his
    courts.

Psalm 96:8

The Request for Presence
Accept, O LORD, the willing tribute of my lips,* and teach me your judgments.

Psalm 119:108

The Greeting
I give you thanks, O God, I give you thanks,* calling upon your Name and declar-
    ing all your wonderful deeds.

based on Psalm 75:1

The Refrain for the Midday Lessons
My tongue will proclaim your righteousness all day long.

Psalm 71:24

A Reading
For YAHWEH says this to the House of Israel: Seek me out and you will
 survive . . . Seek good and not evil so that you may survive, and YAHWEH, God
 of Sabaoth, be with you as you claim he is . . . spare me the din of your chanting, let me hear none of your strumming on lyres, but let justice flow like water,
 and uprightness like a never-failing stream.

Amos 5:4ff

The Refrain
My tongue will proclaim your righteousness all day long.

The Midday Psalm   *Afterward You Will Receive Me in Glory*
Yet I am always with you;* you hold me by my right hand.
You will guide me by your counsel,* and afterwards receive me in glory.

Psalm 73:23–24

The Refrain
My tongue will proclaim your righteousness all day long.

The Gloria

The Lord's Prayer

The Prayer Appointed for the Week
O God, you have taught me to keep all your commandments by loving you and
 my neighbor: Grant me the grace of your Holy Spirit, that I may be devoted to
 you with my whole heart, and united to others with pure affection; through
 Jesus Christ our Lord, who lives and reigns with you and the Holy Spirit, one
 God, for ever and ever. *Amen.†*

The Concluding Prayer of the Church
O God, the source of eternal light: Shed forth your unending day upon all of us
 who watch for you, that our lips may praise you, our lives may bless you, and
 our worship may give you glory; through Jesus Christ our Lord. *Amen.†*

The Vespers Office   **To Be Observed on the Hour or Half Hour
Between 5 and 8 p.m.**

The Call to Prayer
Let the Name of the LORD be blessed,* from this time forth for evermore.
From the rising of the sun to its going down* let the Name of the LORD be praised.

Psalm 113:2–3

The Request for Presence
Let my cry come before you, O LORD;* give me understanding, according to your
   word.
Let my supplication come before you;* deliver me, according to your promise.

Psalm 119:169–170

The Greeting
The Lord is in his holy temple; Let all the earth keep silence before him. *Amen.*

The Hymn   *Lord of All Hopefulness*
   Lord of all hopefulness, Lord of all joy,
   Whose trust, ever childlike, no cares could destroy,
   Be there at our waking, and give us, we pray,
   Your bliss in our hearts, Lord, at the break of the day.

   Lord of all eagerness, Lord of all faith,
   Whose strong hands were skilled at the plane and the lathe,
   Be there at our labors, and give us, we pray,
   Your strength in our hearts, Lord, at the noon of the day.

   Lord of all kindliness, Lord of all grace,
   Your hands swift to welcome, your arms to embrace,
   Be there at our homing, and give us we pray,
   Your love in our hearts at the eve of the day.

   Lord of all gentleness, Lord of all calm,
   Whose voice is contentment, whose presence is balm,
   Be there at our sleeping, and give us, we pray,
   Your peace in our hearts, Lord, at the end of the day.

Jan Struther

The Refrain for the Vespers Lessons
Turn again to your rest, O my soul,* for the LORD has treated you well.

Psalm 116:6

The Vespers Psalm   *My Help Comes from the LORD*
I lift up my eyes to the hills;* from where is my help to come?
My help comes from the LORD,* the maker of heaven and earth.
He will not let your foot be moved* and he who watches over you will not fall
   asleep.
Behold, he who keeps watch over Israel* shall neither slumber nor sleep.

Psalm 121:1–4

The Refrain
Turn again to your rest, O my soul,* for the LORD has treated you well.

The Small Verse
Blessed be the Lord God of Israel for he has visited and delivered us. Alleluia,
   alleluia, alleluia.

The Lord's Prayer

The Prayer Appointed for the Week

O God, you have taught me to keep all your commandments by loving you and
my neighbor: Grant me the grace of your Holy Spirit, that I may be devoted to
you with my whole heart, and united to others with pure affection; through
Jesus Christ our Lord, who lives and reigns with you and the Holy Spirit, one
God, for ever and ever. *Amen.*†

The Concluding Prayer of the Church

Almighty God, who after the creation of the world rested from all your works and
sanctified a day of rest for all your creatures: Grant that I, putting away all
earthly anxieties, may be duly prepared for the service of public worship, and
grant as well that my Sabbath upon the earth may be a preparation for the eternal rest promised to your people in heaven; through Jesus Christ our Lord.
Amen.†

The Morning Office **To Be Observed on the Hour or Half Hour**
Between 6 and 9 a.m.

The Call to Prayer

Come, let us sing to the LORD;* let us shout for joy to the rock of our salvation.

Psalm 95:1

The Request for Presence

Hear the voice of my prayer when I cry out to you,* when I lift up my hands to
your holy of holies.

Psalm 28:2

The Greeting

The Lord is in his holy temple; let all the earth keep silence before him. *Amen.*

Traditional

The Refrain for the Morning Lessons

Blessed is he who comes in the name of the LORD;* we bless you from the house of
the LORD.

Psalm 118:26

A Reading

Jesus declared publicly: 'Whoever believes in me believes not in me but in the one
who sent me, and whoever sees me, sees the one who sent me. I have come into
the world as light, to prevent anyone who believes in me from staying in the

dark any more. If anyone hears my words and does not keep them faithfully, it is not I who shall judge such a person, since I have not come to judge the world, but to save the world: anyone who rejects me and refuses my words has his judge already: the word itself that I have spoken will be his judge on the last day. For I have not spoken of my own accord; but the Father who sent me commanded me what to say and what to speak, and I know that his commands mean eternal life. And therefore what the Father has told me is what I speak.'

John 12:44–50

The Refrain

Blessed is he who comes in the name of the LORD;* we bless you from the house of the LORD.

The Morning Psalm   *Through Your Commandments I Gain Understanding*

How sweet are your words to my taste!* they are sweeter than honey to my mouth.

Through your commandments I gain understanding;* therefore I hate every lying way.

Psalm 119:103–4

The Refrain

Blessed is he who comes in the name of the LORD;* we bless you from the house of the LORD.

The Small Verse

The Lord is my shepherd and nothing is wanting to me.* In green pastures He hath settled me.

THE SHORT BREVIARY

The Lord's Prayer

The Prayer Appointed for the Week

O Lord, mercifully receive the prayers of your servant who calls upon you, and grant that I may know and understand what things I ought to do, and that I also may have the grace and power faithfully to accomplish them; through Jesus Christ our Lord, who lives and reigns with you and the Holy Spirit, one God, for ever and ever. *Amen.*†

The Concluding Prayer of the Church

Lord God, almighty and everlasting Father, you have brought me in safety to this new day: Preserve me with your mighty power, that I may not fall into sin, nor be overcome by adversity; and in all I do direct me to the fulfilling of your purpose; through Jesus Christ my Lord. *Amen.*†

The Midday Office   **To Be Observed on the Hour or Half Hour Between 11 a.m. and 2 p.m.**

The Call to Prayer

I will call upon God,* and the LORD will deliver me.

In the evening, in the morning, and at the noonday, I will complain and lament,*
    and he will hear my voice.
He will bring me safely back . . .* God, who is enthroned of old, will hear me.

Psalm 55:17ff

The Request for Presence
Gladden the soul of your servant,* for to you, O LORD, I lift up my soul.

Psalm 86:4

The Greeting
To you I lift up my eyes,* to you enthroned in the heavens.
As the eyes of servants look to the hand of their masters,* and the eyes of a maid to
    the hand of her mistress,
So our eyes look to the LORD our God,* until he shows us his mercy.

Psalm 123:1–3

The Refrain for the Midday Lessons
Be merciful to me, O God, be merciful, for I have taken refuge in you;* in the
    shadow of your wings will I take refuge.

Psalm 57:1

A Reading
For thus says the High and Exalted One who lives eternally and whose name is
    holy. 'I live in the holy heights, but I am with the contrite and humble, to revive
    the spirit of the humble, to revive the heart of the contrite. For I do not want to
    be forever accusing nor always to be angry, or the spirit would fail under my
    onslaught, the souls that I myself have made.'

Isaiah 57:15–16

The Refrain
Be merciful to me, O God, be merciful, for I have taken refuge in you;* in the
    shadow of your wings will I take refuge.

The Midday Psalm   *He Shall Have Pity on the Lowly and Poor*
For he shall deliver the poor who cries out in distress,* and the oppressed who has
    no helper.
He shall have pity on the lowly and poor* he shall preserve the lives of the needy.
He shall redeem their lives from oppression and violence,* and dear shall their
    blood be in his sight.

Psalm 72:12–14

The Refrain
Be merciful to me, O God, be merciful, for I have taken refuge in you;* in the
    shadow of your wings will I take refuge.

The Gloria

The Lord's Prayer

The Prayer Appointed for the Week

O Lord, mercifully receive the prayers of your servant who calls upon you, and grant that I may know and understand what things I ought to do, and that I also may have the grace and power faithfully to accomplish them; through Jesus Christ our Lord, who lives and reigns with you and the Holy Spirit, one God, for ever and ever. *Amen.*†

The Concluding Prayer of the Church

O God, you make me glad with the weekly remembrance of the glorious resurrection of your Son my Lord: Give me this day such blessing through my worship of you, that the week to come may be spent in your favor; through Jesus Christ our Lord. *Amen.*†

The Vespers Office **To Be Observed on the Hour or Half Hour Between 5 and 8 p.m.**

The Call to Prayer

Give thanks to the LORD and call upon his Name;* make known his deeds among the peoples.

Psalm 105:1

The Request for Presence

Show us the light of your countenance, O God,* and come to us.

based on Psalm 67:1

The Greeting

My mouth shall recount your mighty acts and saving deeds all day long;* though I cannot know the number of them.

Psalm 71:15

The Hymn *Praise, My Soul, the King of Heaven*

Praise, my soul, the King of heaven,
To His feet thy tribute bring;
Ransomed, healed, restored, forgiven,
Who, like me, His praise should sing?
Praise Him! Praise Him! Praise Him! Praise Him!
Praise the everlasting King!

Praise Him for his grace and favor
To our fathers in distress;
Praise Him, still the same forever,
Slow to chide, and swift to bless.
Praise Him! Praise Him! Praise Him! Praise Him!
Glorious in His faithfulness!

Father-like, He tends and spares us;
Well our feeble frame He knows;
In His hands He gently bears us,
Rescues us from all foes.
Praise Him! Praise Him! Praise Him! Praise Him!
Widely as His mercy flows!

Angels, help us to adore Him—
Ye behold Him face to face;
Sun and Moon, bow down before Him;
Dwellers all in time and space,
Praise Him! Praise Him! Praise Him! Praise Him!
Praise with us the God of grace!

Henry Francis Lyte

The Refrain for the Vespers Lessons

Light has sprung up for the righteous,* and joyful gladness for those who are true-
hearted.

Psalm 97:11

The Vespers Psalm   *Righteousness and Peace Have Kissed Each Other*

I will listen to what the LORD God is saying,* for he is speaking peace to his faithful
people and to those who turn their hearts to him.
Truly his salvation is very near to those who fear him,* that his glory may dwell in
our land.
Mercy and truth have met together;* righteousness and peace have kissed each
other.
Truth shall spring up from the earth,* and righteousness shall look down from
heaven.
The LORD will indeed grant prosperity,* and our land will yield its increase.
Righteousness shall go before him,* and peace shall be a pathway for his feet.

Psalm 85:8–13

The Refrain

Light has sprung up for the righteous,* and joyful gladness for those who are true-
hearted.

The Gloria

The Lord's Prayer

The Prayer Appointed for the Week

O Lord, mercifully receive the prayers of your servant who calls upon you, and
grant that I may know and understand what things I ought to do, and that I
also may have the grace and power faithfully to accomplish them; through
Jesus Christ our Lord, who lives and reigns with you and the Holy Spirit, one
God, for ever and ever. *Amen.*†

The Concluding Prayer of the Church
Lord God, whose Son our Savior Jesus Christ, triumphed over the powers of death
and prepared us for our place in the new Jerusalem: Grant that I, who have this
day given thanks for his resurrection, may praise you in the City of which he is
the light, and where he lives and reigns for ever and ever. *Amen*.†

The Morning Office   **To Be Observed on the Hour or Half Hour
                                          Between 6 and 9 a.m.**

The Call to Prayer
Open my lips, O LORD,* and my mouth shall proclaim your praise.
Had you desired it, I would have offered sacrifice,* but you take no delight in
burnt-offerings.
The sacrifice of God is a troubled spirit;* and a broken and contrite heart, O God,
you will not despise.

Psalm 51:16–18

The Request for Presence
I call with my whole heart;* answer me, O LORD, that I may keep your statutes.

Psalm 119:145

The Greeting
Let the words of my mouth and the meditation of my heart be acceptable in your
sight,* O LORD, my strength and my redeemer.

Psalm 19:14

The Refrain for the Morning Lessons
Blessed are you, O LORD;* instruct me in your statutes.

Psalm 119:12

A Reading
Jesus taught us, saying: '. . . If your brother does something wrong, rebuke him
and, if he is sorry, forgive him. And if he wrongs you seven times a day and
seven times comes back to you and says, "I am sorry," you must forgive him.'

Luke 17:3–4

The Refrain
Blessed are you, O LORD;* instruct me in your statutes.

The Morning Psalm   *With You Is the Well of Life*
Your love, O LORD, reaches to the heavens,* and your faithfulness to the clouds.
Your righteousness is like the strong mountains, your justice like the great deep;*
you save both man and beast, O LORD.
How priceless is your love, O God!* your people take refuge under the shadow of
your wings.
They feast upon the abundance of your house;* you give them drink from the
river of your delights.
For with you is the well of life,* and in your light we see light.

Continue your loving-kindness to those who know you,* and your favor to those
who are true of heart.

Psalm 36:5–10

The Refrain
Blessed are you, O LORD;* instruct me in your statutes.

The Cry of the Church
Lord, have mercy on us. Christ, have mercy on us. Lord, have mercy on us.

The Lord's Prayer

The Prayer Appointed for the Week
O Lord, mercifully receive the prayers of your servant who calls upon you, and
grant that I may know and understand what things I ought to do, and that I
also may have the grace and power faithfully to accomplish them; through
Jesus Christ our Lord, who lives and reigns with you and the Holy Spirit, one
God, for ever and ever. *Amen.†*

The Concluding Prayer of the Church
Lord God, almighty and everlasting Father, you have brought me in safety to this
new day: Preserve me with your mighty power, that I may not fall into sin, nor
be overcome by adversity; and in all I do direct me to the fulfilling of your purpose; through Jesus Christ my Lord. *Amen.†*

The Midday Office   **To Be Observed on the Hour or Half Hour
Between 11 a.m. and 2 p.m.**

The Call to Prayer
Search for the LORD and his strength;* continually seek his face.

Psalm 105:4

The Request for Presence
Let your loving-kindness be my comfort,* as you have promised to your servant.
Let your compassion come to me, that I may live,* for your law is my delight.

Psalm 119:76–77

The Greeting
Hosanna, LORD, hosanna!* Lord, send us now success.

Psalm 118:25

The Refrain for the Midday Lessons
For he himself knows whereof we are made;* he remembers that we are but dust.

Psalm 103:14

A Reading
Let love be without any pretense. Avoid what is evil; stick to what is good. In
brotherly love let your feelings of deep affection for one another come to
expression and regard others as more important than yourself. In the service of

the Lord, work not half-heartedly, but with conscientiousness and an eager spirit. Be joyful in hope, persevere in hardship; keep praying regularly; share with any of God's holy people who are in need; look for opportunities to be hospitable.

Romans 12:9–13

The Refrain
For he himself knows whereof we are made;* he remembers that we are but dust.

The Midday Psalm   *Give Me Life in Your Ways*
Teach me, O LORD, the way of your statutes,* and I shall keep it to the end.
Give me understanding and I shall keep your law;* I shall keep it with all my heart.
Make me go in the path of your commandments,* for that is my desire.
Incline my heart to your decrees* and not just to unjust gain
Turn my eyes from watching what is worthless;* give me life in your ways.

Psalm 119:33–37

The Refrain
For he himself knows whereof we are made;* he remembers that we are but dust.

The Small Verse
I will bless the Lord at all times and his praise shall be always in my mouth. Glory to the Father and the Son and the eternal Spirit.

Traditional

The Lord's Prayer

The Prayer Appointed for the Week
O Lord, mercifully receive the prayers of your servant who calls upon you, and grant that I may know and understand what things I ought to do, and that I also may have the grace and power faithfully to accomplish them; through Jesus Christ our Lord, who lives and reigns with you and the Holy Spirit, one God, for ever and ever. *Amen.†*

The Concluding Prayer of the Church
Almighty God, to whom our needs are known before we even ask, Help me to ask only what accords with your will; and those good things which I dare not, or in my blindness I cannot ask, grant for the sake of your Son Jesus Christ our Lord. *Amen.†*

The Vespers Office   **To Be Observed on the Hour or Half Hour**
Between 5 and 8 p.m.

The Call to Prayer
Come, let us sing to the LORD;* let us shout for joy to the Rock of our salvation.
Let us come into his presence with thanksgiving* and raise a loud shout to him with psalms.

Psalm 95:1–2

The Request for Presence
I call upon you, O God, for you will answer me;* incline your ear to me and hear
my words.

Psalm 17:6

The Greeting
Out of Zion, perfect in its beauty,* God reveals himself in glory.

Psalm 50:2

The Hymn   *Come Thou Fount of Every Blessing*
Come thou fount of every blessing,   O to grace how great a debtor,
Tune my heart to sing Thy grace;   Daily I'm constrained to be!
Streams of mercy never ceasing   Let Thy goodness, like a fetter,
Call for songs of loudest praise.   Bind my wandering heart to Thee:
Teach me some melodious sonnet,   Prone to wander, Lord, I feel it,
Sung by flaming tongues above;   Prone to leave the God I love;
Praise the mount—I'm fixed upon it—   Here's my heart, O take and seal it;
Mount of Thy redeeming love.   Seal it for Thy courts above.

Robert Robinson

Here I'll raise mine Ebenezer,
Hither by Thy help I've come;
And I hope, by Thy good pleasure,
Safely to arrive at home.
Jesus sought me when a stranger,
Wandering from the fold of God;
He, to rescue me from danger,
Interposed His precious blood.

The Refrain for the Vespers Lessons
He will not let your foot be moved* and he who watches over you will not fall
asleep.
Behold, he who keeps watch over Israel* shall neither slumber nor sleep . . .

Psalm 121:3–4

The Vespers Psalm   *All Who Are True of Heart Will Glory*
The human mind and heart are a mystery;* but God will loose an arrow at them,
and suddenly they will be wounded.
He will make them trip over their tongues,* and all who see them will shake their
heads.
Everyone will stand in awe and declare God's deeds;* they will recognize his
works.
The righteous will rejoice in the Lord and put their trust in him,* and all who are
true of heart will glory.

Psalm 64:7–10

The Refrain
He will not let your foot be moved* and he who watches over you will not fall
asleep.

Behold, he who keeps watch over Israel* shall neither slumber nor sleep . . .

The Small Verse
The Lord is my shepherd and nothing is wanting to me.* In green pastures He
hath settled me.

THE SHORT BREVIARY

The Lord's Prayer

The Prayer Appointed for the Week
O Lord, mercifully receive the prayers of your servant who calls upon you, and
grant that I may know and understand what things I ought to do, and that I
also may have the grace and power faithfully to accomplish them; through
Jesus Christ our Lord, who lives and reigns with you and the Holy Spirit, one
God, for ever and ever. *Amen.*†

The Concluding Prayer of the Church
Lord Jesus, stay with me, for evening is at hand and the day is past; be my companion in the way, kindle my heart, and awaken hope, that I may know you as
you are revealed in Scripture and the breaking of the bread. Grant this for the
sake of your love. *Amen.*†

The Morning Office
**To Be Observed on the Hour or Half Hour
Between 6 and 9 a.m.**

The Call to Prayer
Sing to the LORD a new song;* sing to the LORD, all the whole earth.

Psalm 96:1

The Request for Presence
May God be merciful to us and bless us,* show us the light of his countenance and
come to us.

Psalm 67:1

The Greeting
Awesome things will you show us in your righteousness, O God of our salvation,*
O Hope of all the ends of the earth.

Psalm 65:5

The Refrain for the Morning Lessons
Your testimonies are very sure,* and holiness adorns your house, O LORD, for ever
and for evermore.

Psalm 93:6

A Reading

Jesus taught us, saying: 'The kingdom of heaven is like treasure hidden in a field
which someone has found; he hides it again, goes off in his joy, sells everything
he owns and buys the field. Again, the kingdom of heaven is like a merchant
looking for fine pearls; when he finds one of great value he goes and sells
everything he owns and buys it.'

Matthew 13:44–45

The Refrain

Your testimonies are very sure,* and holiness adorns your house, O Lord, for ever
and for evermore.

The Morning Psalm   *My Lips Will Sing with Joy*

Therefore I will praise you upon the lyre for your faithfulness, O my God;* I will
sing to you with the harp, O Holy One of Israel.

My lips will sing with joy when I play to you,* and so will my soul, which you
have redeemed.

My tongue will proclaim your righteousness all day long,* for they are ashamed
and disgraced who sought to do me harm.

Psalm 71:22–24

The Refrain

Your testimonies are very sure,* and holiness adorns your house, O Lord, for ever
and for evermore.

The Small Verse

My soul has a desire and longing for the courts of the Lord;* my heart and my
flesh rejoice in the living God.

Psalm 84:1

The Lord's Prayer

The Prayer Appointed for the Week

O Lord, mercifully receive the prayers of your servant who calls upon you, and
grant that I may know and understand what things I ought to do, and that I
also may have the grace and power faithfully to accomplish them; through
Jesus Christ our Lord, who lives and reigns with you and the Holy Spirit, one
God, for ever and ever. *Amen.*†

The Concluding Prayer of the Church

Lord God, almighty and everlasting Father, you have brought me in safety to this
new day: Preserve me with your mighty power, that I may not fall into sin, nor
be overcome by adversity; and in all I do direct me to the fulfilling of your purpose; through Jesus Christ my Lord. *Amen.*†

The Midday Office

**To Be Observed on the Hour or Half Hour
Between 11 a.m. and 2 p.m.**

The Call to Prayer
Be strong and let your heart take courage,* all you who wait for the LORD.

Psalm 31:24

The Request for Presence
With my whole heart I seek you;* let me not stray from your commandments.

Psalm 119:10

The Greeting
I cry out to you, O LORD;* I say, "You are my refuge, my portion in the land of the living."

Psalm 142:5

The Refrain for the Midday Lessons
The LORD loves those who hate evil;* he preserves the lives of the saints and delivers them from the hand of the wicked.

Psalm 97:10

A Reading
Your uprightness is too great, YAHWEH, for me to dispute with you. But I should like to discuss some points of justice with you: Why is it that the way of the wicked prospers? Why do treacherous people thrive? You plant them, they take root, they flourish, yes, and bear fruit. You are on their lips, yet far from their heart. You know me, YAHWEH, you see me, you probe my heart, which is close to yours. Drag them off like sheep for the slaughter-house, reserve them for the day of butchery. . . . For they say, 'God does not see our fate.'

Jeremiah 12:1–4

The Refrain
The LORD loves those who hate evil;* he preserves the lives of the saints and delivers them from the hand of the wicked.

The Midday Psalm   ***He Will Break Them Down and Not Build Them Up***
Do not snatch me away with the wicked or with the evildoers,* who speak peaceably to their neighbors, while strife is in their hearts.
Repay them according to their deeds,* and according to the wickedness of their actions.
According to the work of their hands repay them,* and give them their just desserts.
They have no understanding of the LORD's doings, nor of the works of his hands;* therefore he will break them down and not build them up.

Psalm 28:3–6

The Refrain
The LORD loves those who hate evil;* he preserves the lives of the saints and delivers them from the hand of the wicked.

The Cry of the Church
O God, come to my assistance! O Lord, make haste to help me!

The Lord's Prayer

The Prayer Appointed for the Week
O Lord, mercifully receive the prayers of your servant who calls upon you, and
grant that I may know and understand what things I ought to do, and that I
also may have the grace and power faithfully to accomplish them; through
Jesus Christ our Lord, who lives and reigns with you and the Holy Spirit, one
God, for ever and ever. *Amen.*†

The Concluding Prayer of the Church
Direct me, O Lord, in all my doings with your most gracious favor, and further me
with your continual help; that in all my work begun, continued, and ended in
you, I may glorify your holy name, and finally, by your mercy, obtain everlasting life; through Jesus Christ my Lord. *Amen.*†

The Vespers Office   **To Be Observed on the Hour or Half Hour**
                                  Between 5 and 8 p.m.

The Call to Prayer
God is the Lord; he has shined upon us;* form a procession with branches up to
the horns of the altar.

Psalm 118:27

The Request for Presence
Show us the light of your countenance, O God,* and come to us.

Psalm 67:1

The Greeting
O Lamb of God, that takes away the sins of the world, have mercy upon me.
O Lamb of God, that takes away the sins of the world, have mercy upon me.
O Lamb of God, that takes away the sins of the world, grant me your peace.

The Hymn   *Leaning on the Everlasting Arms*
What a fellowship, what a joy divine,
leaning on the everlasting arms;
what a blessedness, what peace is mine,
leaning on the everlasting arms.
Leaning, leaning safe and secure from all alarms;
leaning, leaning, leaning on the everlasting arms.

O how sweet to walk in this pilgrim way,
leaning on the everlasting arms;
O how bright the path grows from day to day,
leaning on the everlasting arms.
Leaning, leaning safe and secure from all alarms;
leaning, leaning, leaning on the everlasting arms.

What have I to dread, what have I to fear,
leaning on the everlasting arms?
I have blessed peace with my Lord so near,
leaning on the everlasting arms.
Leaning, leaning safe and secure from all alarms;
leaning, leaning, leaning on the everlasting arms.

Elisha Hoffman

The Refrain for the Vespers Lessons
I will listen to what the LORD God is saying,* for he is speaking peace to his faithful
people and to those who turn their hearts to him.

Psalm 85:8

The Vespers Psalm *Those Who Sowed with Tears Will Reap with Songs of Joy*
When the LORD restored the fortunes of Zion,* then were we like those who
dream.
Then was our mouth filled with laughter,* and our tongue with shouts of joy.
Then they said among the nations,* "The LORD has done great things for them."
The LORD has done great things for us,* and we are glad indeed.
Restore our fortunes, O LORD,* like the watercourses of the Negev.
Those who sowed with tears* will reap with songs of joy.
Those who go out weeping, carrying the seed,* will come again with joy, shoul-
dering their sheaves.

Psalm 126:1–7

The Refrain
I will listen to what the LORD God is saying,* for he is speaking peace to his faithful
people and to those who turn their hearts to him.

The Gloria

The Lord's Prayer

The Prayer Appointed for the Week
O Lord, mercifully receive the prayers of your servant who calls upon you, and
grant that I may know and understand what things I ought to do, and that I
also may have the grace and power faithfully to accomplish them; through
Jesus Christ our Lord, who lives and reigns with you and the Holy Spirit, one
God, for ever and ever. *Amen.*†

The Concluding Prayer of the Church
Gentle God, you remind me that you are my faithful friend, and that you will
deliver me from the chains that keep me from the fullness of life. I bless you for
this in love and in confidence in Jesus' name. *Amen.*

adapted from THE NEW COMPANION TO THE BREVIARY

The Morning Office   **To Be Observed on the Hour or Half Hour**
                                          Between 6 and 9 a.m.

The Call to Prayer
I will call upon God,* and the LORD will deliver me.
In the evening, in the morning, and at the noonday, I will complain and lament,*
    and he will hear my voice.
He will bring me safely back . . .* God, who is enthroned of old, will hear me.
Psalm 55:17ff

The Request for Presence
O God of hosts,* show us the light of your countenance, and we shall be saved.
Psalm 80:7

The Greeting
What terror you inspire!* who can stand before you when you are angry?
Psalm 76:7

The Refrain for the Morning Lessons
Our God is in heaven;* whatever he wills to do, he does.
Psalm 115:3

A Reading
Jesus taught us, saying: 'Take the fig tree as a parable: as soon as its twigs grow
    supple and its leaves come out, you know that summer is near. So with you
    when you see these things happening: know that he is near, right at the gates.
    In truth I tell you solemnly, before this generation has passed away all these
    things will have taken place. Sky and earth will pass away, but my words will
    not pass away. But as for that day or hour, nobody knows it, neither the angels
    of heaven, nor the Son; no one but the Father.'
Mark 13:28–32

The Refrain
Our God is in heaven;* whatever he wills to do, he does.

The Morning Psalm   *Let All the Earth Fear the LORD*
By the word of the LORD were the heavens made,* by the breath of his mouth all
    the heavenly hosts.
He gathers up the waters of the ocean as in a water-skin* and stores up the depths
    of the sea.
Let all the earth fear the LORD;* let all who dwell in the world stand in awe of him.
For he spoke, and it came to pass;* he commanded, and it stood fast.
The LORD brings the will of the nations to naught;* he thwarts the designs of the
    peoples.
But the LORD'S will stands fast for ever,* and the designs of his heart from age to age.
Psalm 33:6–11

The Refrain
Our God is in heaven;* whatever he wills to do, he does.

The Cry of the Church
O God, come to my assistance! O Lord, make haste to help me!

The Lord's Prayer

The Prayer Appointed for the Week
O Lord, mercifully receive the prayers of your servant who calls upon you, and
grant that I may know and understand what things I ought to do, and that I
also may have the grace and power faithfully to accomplish them; through
Jesus Christ our Lord, who lives and reigns with you and the Holy Spirit, one
God, for ever and ever. *Amen*.✝

The Concluding Prayer of the Church
Lord God, almighty and everlasting Father, you have brought me in safety to this
new day: Preserve me with your mighty power, that I may not fall into sin, nor
be overcome by adversity; and in all I do direct me to the fulfilling of your purpose; through Jesus Christ my Lord. *Amen*.✝

The Midday Office **To Be Observed on the Hour or Half Hour**
Between 11 a.m. and 2 p.m.

The Call to Prayer
Bless the LORD, you angels of his, you mighty ones who do his bidding,* and hear-
ken to the voice of his word.
Bless the LORD, all you his hosts,* you ministers of his who do his will.
Bless the LORD, all you works of his,* in all places of his dominion.

Psalm 103:20–22

The Request for Presence
Send out your light and your truth, that they may lead me,* and bring me to your
holy hill and to your dwelling.

Psalm 43:3

The Greeting
Your righteousness, O God, reaches to the heavens;* you have done great things;
who is like you, O God?

Psalm 71:19

The Refrain for the Midday Lessons
The heavens declare his righteousness,* and all the peoples see his glory.

Psalm 97:6

A Reading
Within yourself, before God, hold on to what you already believe. Blessed is the
person whose principles do not condemn his practice.

Romans 14:22

The Refrain
The heavens declare his righteousness,* and all the peoples see his glory.

The Midday Psalm   *You Are Gods, and All of You Children of the Most High*
God takes his stand in the councils of heaven;* he gives justice in the midst of the
    gods:
"How long will you judge unjustly,* and show favor to the wicked?
Save the weak and the orphan;* defend the humble and the needy;
Rescue the weak and the poor;* deliver them from the power of the wicked.
They do not know, neither do they understand; they go about in darkness;* all the
    foundations of the earth are shaken.
Now I say to you, 'You are gods,* and all of you children of the Most High;
Nevertheless, you shall die like mortals,* and fall like any prince.' "

Psalm 82:1–7

The Refrain
The heavens declare his righteousness,* and all the peoples see his glory.

The Small Verse
The Lord is my light and my salvation. Whom else have I in the land of the living.
    The Lord is the protector of my soul. Whom then should I fear?

Traditional

The Lord's Prayer

The Prayer Appointed for the Week
O Lord, mercifully receive the prayers of your servant who calls upon you, and
    grant that I may know and understand what things I ought to do, and that I
    also may have the grace and power faithfully to accomplish them; through
    Jesus Christ our Lord, who lives and reigns with you and the Holy Spirit, one
    God, for ever and ever. *Amen.*†

The Concluding Prayer of the Church
To you, O God, I lift up my heart at this midday prayer. I ask you to remember me
    and all those who are troubled at this time. Help me to reach out in justice and
    charity to those in need. Grant this though the intercession of all who served
    you in serving your poor. *Amen.*

adapted from THE NEW COMPANION TO THE BREVIARY

The Vespers Office   **To Be Observed on the Hour or Half Hour**
                                          Between 5 and 8 p.m.

The Call to Prayer
Proclaim with me the greatness of the LORD;* let us exalt his Name together.

Psalm 34:3

The Request for Presence
As the eyes of servants look to the hand of their masters,* and the eyes of a maid to
the hand of her mistress,
So my eyes look to you, O LORD, my God.

adapted from Psalm 123:2–3

The Greeting
Blessed is the LORD!* for he has heard the voice of my prayer.

Psalm 28:7

The Hymn   Break Thou the Bread of Life

Break thou the bread of life,	Bless thou the truth, dear Lord,
Dear Lord, to me,	Now unto me,
As thou didst break the loaves	As thou didst bless the bread
Beside the sea;	By Galilee;
Beyond the sacred page	Then shall all bondage cease,
I seek thee, Lord;	All fetters fall;
My spirit pants for thee,	And I will find my peace,
O living Word!	My all in all.

Mary A. Lathbury

The Refrain for the Vespers Lessons
Great peace have they who love your law;* for them there is no stumbling block.

Psalm 119:165

The Vespers Psalm   Come, Children, and Listen to Me
The young lions lack and suffer hunger,* but those who seek the LORD lack
nothing that is good.
Come, children, and listen to me;* I will teach you the fear of the LORD.
Who among you loves life* and desires long life to enjoy prosperity?
Keep your tongue from evil-speaking* and your lips from lying words.
Turn from evil and do good;* seek peace and pursue it.

Psalm 34:10–14

The Refrain
Great peace have they who love your law;* for them there is no stumbling block.

The Gloria

The Lord's Prayer

The Prayer Appointed for the Week
O Lord, mercifully receive the prayers of your servant who calls upon you, and
grant that I may know and understand what things I ought to do, and that I
also may have the grace and power faithfully to accomplish them; through
Jesus Christ our Lord, who lives and reigns with you and the Holy Spirit, one
God, for ever and ever. *Amen.*†

The Concluding Prayer of the Church

O God, the King eternal, whose light divides the day from the night and turns the
shadow of death into the morning: Drive far from me all wrong desires, incline
my heart to keep your law, and guide my feet into the way of peace; that, having done your will with cheerfulness during the day, I may, when night comes,
rejoice to give you thanks; through Jesus Christ my Lord. *Amen.*†

The Morning Office

**To Be Observed on the Hour or Half Hour
Between 6 and 9 a.m.**

The Call to Prayer

Come, let us sing to the LORD;* let us shout for joy to the Rock of our salvation.
Let us come before his presence with thanksgiving* and raise a loud shout to him
with psalms.
For the LORD is a great God,* and a great king above all gods.

Psalm 95:1–3

The Request for Presence

LORD God of hosts, hear my prayer;* hearken, O God of Jacob.

Psalm 84:7

The Greeting

I will thank you, O LORD my God, with all my heart,* and glorify your Name for
evermore.

Psalm 86:12

The Refrain for the Morning Lessons

Gracious is the LORD and righteous;* our God is full of compassion.

Psalm 116:4

A Reading

Jesus taught us, saying: 'I am the true vine, and my Father is the vinedresser.
Every branch in me that bears no fruit he cuts away, and every branch that
does bear fruit he prunes to make it bear even more. You are pruned already,
by means of the word that I have spoken to you.'

John 15:1–3

The Refrain

Gracious is the LORD and righteous;* our God is full of compassion.

The Morning Psalm   *I Shall Not Die, But Live*

The LORD is my strength and my song,* and he has become my salvation.
There is a sound of exultation and victory* in the tents of the righteous:
"The right hand of the LORD has triumphed!* The right hand of the LORD is
exalted! The right hand of the LORD has triumphed!"
I shall not die, but live,* and declare the works of the LORD.
The LORD has punished me sorely,* but he did not hand me over to death.

Psalm 118:14–18

The Refrain
Gracious is the LORD and righteous;* our God is full of compassion.

The Gloria

The Lord's Prayer

The Prayer Appointed for the Week
O Lord, mercifully receive the prayers of your servant who calls upon you, and
grant that I may know and understand what things I ought to do, and that I
also may have the grace and power faithfully to accomplish them; through
Jesus Christ our Lord, who lives and reigns with you and the Holy Spirit, one
God, for ever and ever. *Amen.*†

The Concluding Prayer of the Church
Lord God, almighty and everlasting Father, you have brought me in safety to this
new day: Preserve me with your mighty power, that I may not fall into sin, nor
be overcome by adversity; and in all I do direct me to the fulfilling of your purpose; through Jesus Christ my Lord. *Amen.*†

The Midday Office   **To Be Observed on the Hour or Half Hour**
Between 11 a.m. and 2 p.m.

The Call to Prayer
Be glad, you righteous, and rejoice in the LORD;* shout for joy, all who are true of
heart.

Psalm 32:12

The Request for Presence
Hear, O Shepherd of Israel, leading Joseph like a flock;* shine forth, you that are
enthroned upon the cherubim.

Psalm 80:1

The Greeting
"You are my God, and I will thank you;* you are my God, and I will exalt you."

Psalm 118:28

The Refrain for the Midday Lessons
The LORD is high above all nations,* and his glory above the heavens.

Psalm 113:4

A Reading
Then a voice came from the throne; it said, 'Praise our God, you servants of his
and *those who fear him, small and great alike.'* And I heard what seemed to be the
voices of a huge crowd, like the sound of the ocean or the great roar of thunder
answering, 'Alleluia! The reign of the Lord our God Almighty has begun; let us
be glad and joyful and give glory to God, because this is the time for the mar-
riage of the Lamb. His bride is ready, and she has been able to dress herself in

dazzling white linen, because her linen is made of the good deeds of saints.'
The angel said, 'Write this: Blessed are those who are invited to the wedding
feast of the Lamb,' and he added, 'These words of God are true.' Then I knelt at
his feet to worship him, but he said to me, 'Never do that: I am your fellow servant and the fellow servant of all your brothers who have in themselves the
witness of Jesus. God alone you must worship.' The witness of Jesus is the
spirit of prophesy.

Revelation 19:5–10

The Refrain
The LORD is high above all nations,* and his glory above the heavens.

The Midday Psalm *Happy Are the People Who Know the Festal Shout*
Happy are the people who know the festal shout!* they walk, O LORD, in the light
of your presence.
They daily rejoice in your Name;* they are jubilant in your righteousness.
For you are the glory of their strength,* and by your favor our might is exalted.

Psalm 89:15–17

The Refrain
The LORD is high above all nations,* and his glory above the heavens.

The Small Verse
Great are the works of the Lord and greatly to be praised among the peoples. They
are sought by all who delight in him. Alleluia. Alleluia. Alleluia.

Traditional

The Lord's Prayer

The Prayer Appointed for the Week
O Lord, mercifully receive the prayers of your servant who calls upon you, and
grant that I may know and understand what things I ought to do, and that I
also may have the grace and power faithfully to accomplish them; through
Jesus Christ our Lord, who lives and reigns with you and the Holy Spirit, one
God, for ever and ever. *Amen.*†

The Concluding Prayer of the Church
Renew in my heart, O God, the gift of your Holy Spirit, so that I may love you
fully in all that I do and love others as Christ loves me. May all that I do proclaim the good news that you are God with me. *Amen.*

adapted from THE NEW COMPANION TO THE BREVIARY

The Vespers Office **To Be Observed on the Hour or Half Hour**
Between 5 and 8 p.m.

The Call to Prayer
Praise God from whom all blessings flow; praise Him all creatures here below;
praise Him above, you heavenly hosts; praise Father, Son, and Holy Ghost.

Traditional Doxology

The Request for Presence
Give ear to my words, O Lord;* consider my meditation . . . for I make my prayer
to you.

Psalm 5:1–2

The Greeting
How glorious you are!* more splendid than the everlasting mountains!

Psalm 76:4

The Hymn   *O Lord, You Are My Chosen Portion*

O Lord, you are my chosen portion;
you are my strength and my might.
I will bless you at all times;
your praise shall be in my mouth.

Though the produce of the olive fails,
and the fields yield no food,
yet I will praise your name, O God;
I will magnify you with thanksgiving.

Though the fig tree does not blossom,
and no fruit is on the vines,
yet I will give thanks to you;
I will sing praises to you.

Though the flock is cut off from the fold,
and there is no herd in the stalls,
yet I will rejoice in you, O Lord;
I will exult you, O God of my salvation.   ❖

The Refrain for the Vespers Lessons
The Lord is my light and my salvation; whom then shall I fear?* the Lord is the
strength of my life; of whom then shall I be afraid?

Psalm 27:1

The Vespers Psalm   *He Has Not Dealt with Us According to Our Sins*
He has not dealt with us according to our sins,* nor rewarded us according to our
wickedness.
For as the heavens are high above the earth,* so is his mercy great upon those who
fear him.

Psalm 103:10–11

The Refrain
The Lord is my light and my salvation; whom then shall I fear?* the Lord is the
strength of my life; of whom then shall I be afraid?

The Cry of the Church
Lord, have mercy on us. Christ, have mercy on us. Lord, have mercy on us.

The Lord's Prayer

The Prayer Appointed for the Week
O Lord, mercifully receive the prayers of your servant who calls upon you, and
grant that I may know and understand what things I ought to do, and that I
also may have the grace and power faithfully to accomplish them; through
Jesus Christ our Lord, who lives and reigns with you and the Holy Spirit, one
God, for ever and ever. *Amen.*†

The Concluding Prayer of the Church
Protect me, Lord, as I stay awake; watch over me as I sleep, that awake I may
watch with Christ, and asleep, rest in peace. *Amen.*

The Morning Office

**To Be Observed On the Hour or Half Hour
Between 6 and 9 a.m.**

The Call to Prayer
Bless God in the congregation;* bless the LORD, you that are of the fountain of
Israel.

Psalm 68:26

The Request for Presence
Turn to me and have pity on me,* for I am left alone and in misery.
The sorrows of my heart have increased;* bring me out of my troubles.
Look upon my adversity and misery* and forgive me all my sin.

Psalm 25:15–17

The Greeting
O LORD, I cry to you for help;* in the morning my prayer comes before you.

Psalm 88:14

The Refrain for the Morning Lessons
Who is like the LORD our God, who sits enthroned on high,* but stoops to behold
the heavens and the earth?

Psalm 113:5

A Reading
Jesus taught us, saying: 'Enter by the narrow gate, since the road that leads to
destruction is wide and spacious, and many take it; but it is a narrow gate and
a hard road that leads to life, and only a few find it.'

Matthew 7:13–14

The Refrain
Who is like the LORD our God, who sits enthroned on high,* but stoops to behold
the heavens and the earth?

The Morning Psalm   *Then Would the Waters Have Overwhelmed Us*
If the LORD had not been on our side,* let Israel now say;
If the LORD had not been on our side,* when enemies rose up against us;
Then would they have swallowed us up alive* in their fierce anger toward us;
Then would the waters have overwhelmed us* and the torrent gone over us;
Then would the raging waters* have gone over us.
Blessed be the LORD!* he has not given us over to be prey for their teeth.
We have escaped like a bird from the snare of the fowler;* the snare is broken and
we have escaped.
Our help is in the Name of the LORD,* the maker of heaven and earth.

Psalm 124:1–8

The Refrain
Who is like the LORD our God, who sits enthroned on high,* but stoops to behold
the heavens and the earth?

The Gloria

The Lord's Prayer

The Prayer Appointed for the Week
O Lord, mercifully receive the prayers of your servant who calls upon you, and
grant that I may know and understand what things I ought to do, and that I
also may have the grace and power faithfully to accomplish them; through
Jesus Christ our Lord, who lives and reigns with you and the Holy Spirit, one
God, for ever and ever. *Amen.*†

The Concluding Prayer of the Church
Lord God, almighty and everlasting Father, you have brought me in safety to this
new day: Preserve me with your mighty power, that I may not fall into sin, nor
be overcome by adversity; and in all I do direct me to the fulfilling of your purpose; through Jesus Christ my Lord. *Amen.*†

The Midday Office   **To Be Observed on the Hour or Half Hour**
Between 11 a.m. and 2 p.m.

The Call to Prayer
Sing to the LORD and bless his Name;* proclaim the good news of his salvation
from day to day.
For great is the LORD and greatly to be praised;* he is more to be feared than all
gods.

Psalm 96:2, 4

The Request for Presence
O LORD, watch over us* and save us from this generation for ever.
The wicked prowl on every side,* and that which is worthless is highly praised by
everyone.

Psalm 12:7–8

The Greeting
Deliver me, O LORD, by your hand* from those whose portion in life is this
world . . .

Psalm 17:14

The Refrain for the Midday Lesson
Our iniquities you have set before you,* and our secret sins in the light of your
countenance.

Psalm 90:8

A Reading

The heart is more devious than any other thing, and is depraved; who can pierce
its secrets? I, Yahweh, search the heart, test the motives, to give each person
what his conduct and his actions deserve.

Jeremiah 17:9–10

The Refrain

Our iniquities you have set before you,* and our secret sins in the light of your
countenance.

The Midday Psalm   *It Is God Who Judges*

For judgment is neither from the east nor from the west,* nor yet from the wilderness or the mountains.

It is God who judges,* he puts down one and lifts up another.

For in the Lord's hand there is a cup, full of spiced and foaming wine, which he
pours out,* and all the wicked of the earth shall drink and drain the dregs.

Psalm 75:6–8

The Refrain

Our iniquities you have set before you,* and our secret sins in the light of your
countenance.

The Cry of the Church

O Lamb of God, that takes away the sins of the world, have mercy upon me.
O Lamb of God, that takes away the sins of the world, have mercy upon me.
O Lamb of God, that takes away the sins of the world, grant me your peace.

The Lord's Prayer

The Prayer Appointed for the Week

O Lord, mercifully receive the prayers of your servant who calls upon you, and
grant that I may know and understand what things I ought to do, and that I
also may have the grace and power faithfully to accomplish them; through
Jesus Christ our Lord, who lives and reigns with you and the Holy Spirit, one
God, for ever and ever. *Amen.*†

The Concluding Prayer of the Church

Lord Jesus Christ, by your death you took away the sting of death: Grant me to so
follow in faith where you have led the way, that I may at length fall asleep
peacefully in you and wake in your likeness; for your tender mercies' sake.
Amen.†

The Vespers Office   **To Be Observed on the Hour or Half Hour**
Between 5 and 8 p.m.

The Call to Prayer

Let my mouth be full of your praise* and your glory all the day long.
Do not cast me off in my old age;* forsake me not when my strength fails.

Psalm 71:8–9

The Request for Presence
O God, do not be silent;* do not keep still nor hold your peace, O God.

Psalm 93:1

The Greeting
You, O Lord, are my lamp;* my God, you make my darkness bright.

Psalm 18:29

The Hymn   *Forgive Our Sins as We Forgive*
"Forgive our sins as we forgive," In blazing light your cross reveals
You taught us, Lord, to pray,   The truth we dimly knew:
But you alone can grant us grace What trivial debts are owed to us,
To live the words we say.   How great our debt to you!

How can your pardon reach and bless Lord, cleanse the depths within our souls
The unforgiving heart   And bid resentment cease.
That broods on wrongs and will not let Then, bound to all in bonds of love,
Old bitterness depart?   Our lives will spread your peace.

Rosamond E. Herklots

The Refrain for the Vespers Lessons
I love the Lord, because he has heard the voice of my supplication,* because he
  has inclined his ear to me whenever I called upon him.

Psalm 116:11

The Vespers Psalm   *My Days Drift Away Like Smoke*
Lord, hear my prayer, and let my cry come before you;* hide not your face from
  me in the day of my trouble.
Incline your ear to me;* when I call, make haste to answer me,
For my days drift away like smoke,* and my bones are hot as burning coals.
My heart is smitten like grass and withered,* so that I forget to eat my bread.
Because of the voice of my groaning* I am but skin and bones.
I have become like a vulture in the wilderness,* like an owl among the ruins.
I lie awake and groan;* I am like a sparrow, lonely on a house top.

Psalm 102:1–7

The Refrain
I love the Lord, because he has heard the voice of my supplication,* because he
  has inclined his ear to me whenever I called upon him.

The Cry of the Church
In the evening, in the morning, and at noonday, I will complain and lament,* and
  he will hear my voice.

Psalm 55:18

The Lord's Prayer

The Prayer Appointed for the Week
O Lord, mercifully receive the prayers of your servant who calls upon you, and
  grant that I may know and understand what things I ought to do, and that I

also may have the grace and power faithfully to accomplish them; through
Jesus Christ our Lord, who lives and reigns with you and the Holy Spirit, one
God, for ever and ever. *Amen.*†

The Concluding Prayers of the Church

Almighty God, who has promised to hear the petitions of those who ask in your
Son's Name: I beseech you mercifully to incline your ear to me who have made
my prayers and supplications to you; and grant that those things which I have
faithfully asked according to your will, may effectually be obtained, to the
relief of my necessity, and to setting forth of your glory; through Jesus Christ
my Lord. *Amen.*†

May the souls of the faithful departed, through the mercy of God, rest in eternal
peace. *Amen.*

The Morning Office

**To Be Observed on the Hour or Half Hour
Between 6 and 9 a.m.**

The Call to Prayer

Open my lips, O Lord,* and my mouth shall proclaim your praise.
Had you desired it, I would have offered sacrifice,* but you take no delight in
burnt offerings.
The sacrifice of God is a troubled spirit;* and a broken and contrite heart, O God,
you will not despise.

Psalm 51:16–18

The Request for Presence

Help us, O God our Savior, for the glory of your Name;* deliver us and forgive us
our sins, for your Name's sake.

Psalm 79:9

The Greeting

Blessed be the Lord God, the God of Israel,* who alone does wondrous deeds!
And blessed be his glorious Name for ever!* and may all the earth be filled with
his glory. Amen. Amen.

Psalm 72:18–19

The Refrain for the Morning Lessons

Bless the LORD, O my soul,* and forget not all his benefits.

Psalm 103:2

A Reading

Jesus taught us, saying: 'Do not store up treasures for yourself on earth, where
moth and woodworm destroy them and thieves can break in and steal. But
store up treasures for yourselves in heaven, where neither moth nor woodworm destroys them and thieves cannot break in and steal. For wherever your
treasure is, there will be your heart too.'

Matthew 6:19–21

The Refrain
Bless the LORD, O my soul,* and forget not all his benefits.

The Morning Psalm   *From Age to Age You Are God*
Before the mountains were brought forth, or the land and earth were born,* from
    age to age you are God.
You turn back to dust and say,* "Go back, O child of the earth."
For a thousand years in your sight are like yesterday when it is past* and like a
    watch in the night.
You sweep us away like a dream;* we fade away suddenly like the grass.
In the morning it is green and flourishes;* in the evening it is dried up and with-
    ered.
For we consume away in your displeasure;* we are afraid because of your wrath-
    ful indignation.

                                                        Psalm 90:2–7

The Refrain
Bless the LORD, O my soul,* and forget not all his benefits.

The Cry of the Church
O God, come to my assistance! O Lord, make haste to help me!

The Lord's Prayer

The Prayer Appointed for the Week
O Lord, mercifully receive the prayers of your servant who calls upon you, and
    grant that I may know and understand what things I ought to do, and that I
    also may have the grace and power faithfully to accomplish them; through
    Jesus Christ our Lord, who lives and reigns with you and the Holy Spirit, one
    God, for ever and ever. *Amen.*†

The Concluding Prayer of the Church
Lord God, almighty and everlasting Father, you have brought me in safety to this
    new day: Preserve me with your mighty power, that I may not fall into sin, nor
    be overcome by adversity; and in all I do direct me to the fulfilling of your pur-
    pose; through Jesus Christ my Lord. *Amen.*†

The Midday Office   **To Be Observed on the Hour or Half Hour**
                                       Between 11 a.m. and 2 p.m.

The Call to Prayer
Open my lips, O Lord,* and my mouth shall proclaim your praise.
                                                        Psalm 51:16

The Request for Presence
Hearken to my voice, O LORD, when I call;* have mercy on me and answer me.
You speak in my heart and say, "Seek my face."* Your face, O LORD, will I seek.
                                                        Psalm 27:10–11

The Greeting
When your word goes forth it gives light;* it gives understanding to the simple.

Psalm 119:130

The Refrain for the Midday Lessons
Let the words of my mouth and the meditation of my heart be acceptable in your sight,* O Lord, my strength and my redeemer.

Psalm 19:14

The Reading
But I shall rejoice in Yahweh, I shall exult in God my Savior. Yahweh my Lord is my strength, he will make my feet as light as a doe's, and set my steps on the heights.

Habakkuk 3:18–19

The Refrain
Let the words of my mouth and the meditation of my heart be acceptable in your sight,* O Lord, my strength and my redeemer.

The Midday Psalm   *We Flourish Like a Flower of the Field*
Our days are like the grass;* we flourish like a flower of the field;
When the wind goes over it, it is gone,* and its place shall know it no more.
But the merciful goodness of the Lord endures for ever on those who fear him,*
and his righteousness on children's children.

Psalm 103:15–17

The Refrain
Let the words of my mouth and the meditation of my heart be acceptable in your sight,* O Lord, my strength and my redeemer.

The Small Verse
Open, Lord, my eyes that I may see. Open, Lord, my ears that I may hear. Open, Lord, my heart and my mind that I may understand. So shall I turn to you and be healed.

Traditional

The Lord's Prayer

The Prayer Appointed for the Week
O Lord, mercifully receive the prayers of your servant who calls upon you, and grant that I may know and understand what things I ought to do, and that I also may have the grace and power faithfully to accomplish them; through Jesus Christ our Lord, who lives and reigns with you and the Holy Spirit, one God, for ever and ever. *Amen.*†

The Concluding Prayer of the Church
O God, the source of eternal light: Shed forth your unending day upon all of us who watch for you, that our lips may praise you, our lives may bless you, and our worship may give you glory; through Jesus Christ our Lord. *Amen.*†

The Vespers Office   **To Be Observed on the Hour or Half Hour**
                                          Between 5 and 8 p.m.

The Call to Prayer
Praise God, from whom all blessings flow; praise him, all creatures here below;
   praise him above, you heavenly hosts; praise Father, Son, and Holy Ghost.

Traditional Doxology

The Request for Presence
Give ear, O Lord, to my prayer.

Psalm 86:6

The Greeting
Exalt yourself above the heavens, O God,* and your glory over all the earth.

Psalm 57:11

The Hymn   *All Hail the Power of Jesus' Name*

All hail the power of Jesus' name!   Let every kindred, every tribe,
Let angels prostrate fall;   On this terrestrial ball,
Bring forth the royal diadem,   To Him all majesty ascribe,
And crown him Lord of all!   And crown him Lord of all!

You chosen seed of Israel's race,   O that with yonder sacred throng
You ransomed from the fall;   We at His feet may fall,
Hail Him who saves you by his grace,   We'll join the everlasting song,
And crown him Lord of all!   And crown him Lord of all!

E. Perronet

The Refrain for the Vespers Lessons
The fear of the Lord is the beginning of wisdom;* those who act accordingly have
   a good understanding; his praise endures for ever.

Psalm 111:10

The Vespers Psalm   *What Is Man That You Should Be Mindful of Him*
When I consider your heavens, the work of your fingers,* the moon and the stars
   you have set in their courses,
What is man that you should be mindful of him?* the son of man that you should
   seek him out?
You have made him but little lower than the angels;* you adorn him with glory
   and honor;
You give him mastery over the works of your hands;* you put all things under his
   feet:
All sheep and oxen,* even the wild beasts of the field,
The birds of the air, the fish of the sea,* and whatsoever walks in the paths of the
   sea.
O Lord our Governor,* how exalted is your Name in all the world!

Psalm 8:4–10

The Refrain
The fear of the LORD is the beginning of wisdom;* those who act accordingly have
a good understanding; his praise endures for ever.

The Gloria

The Lord's Prayer

The Prayer Appointed for the Week
O Lord, mercifully receive the prayers of your servant who calls upon you, and
grant that I may know and understand what things I ought to do, and that I
also may have the grace and power faithfully to accomplish them; through
Jesus Christ my Lord, who lives and reigns with you and the Holy Spirit, one
God, for ever and ever. *Amen.*†

The Concluding Prayer of the Church
Almighty God, who after the creation of the world rested from all your works and
sanctified a day of rest for all you creatures: Grant that I, putting away all
earthly anxieties, may be duly prepared for the service of public worship, and
grant as well that my Sabbath upon the earth may be a preparation for the eternal rest promised to your people in heaven; through Jesus Christ our Lord.
Amen.†

❧

The Morning Office   **To Be Observed on the Hour or Half Hour**
                                          Between 6 and 9 a.m.

The Call to Prayer
Let all who seek you rejoice and be glad in you;* let those who love your salvation
say for ever, "Great is the LORD!"

Psalm 70:4

The Request for Presence
Satisfy us by your loving-kindness in the morning;* so shall we rejoice and be glad
all the days of our life.

Psalm 90:14

The Greeting
I will begin with the mighty works of the Lord GOD;* I will recall your righteousness, yours alone.

Psalm 71:16

The Refrain for the Morning Lessons
I am glad because of your promise* as one who finds great spoils.

Psalm 119:162

A Reading
Jesus taught us, saying: 'I am the living bread which has come down from heaven. Anyone who eats this bread will live for ever; and the bread I shall give is my flesh, for the life of the world.'

John 6:51

The Refrain
I am glad because of your promise* as one who finds great spoils.

The Morning Psalm   *You Are a Priest Forever After the Order of Melchizedek*
The LORD said to my Lord, "Sit at my right hand,* until I make your enemies your footstool."
The LORD will send the scepter of your power out of Zion,* saying, "Rule over your enemies round about you.
Princely state has been yours from the day of your birth;* in the beauty of holiness have I begotten you, like dew from the womb of the morning."
The LORD has sworn and he will not recant:* "You are a priest forever after the order of Melchizedek."
The LORD who is at your right hand will smite kings in the day of his wrath;* he will rule over the nations.

Psalm 110:1–5

The Refrain
I am glad because of your promise* as one who finds great spoils.

The Small Verse
In you, Lord, is my hope; and I shall never hope in vain.†

The Lord's Prayer

The Prayer Appointed for the Week
Almighty God, the fountain of all wisdom, you know my necessities before I ask and my ignorance in asking: Have compassion on my weakness, and mercifully give me those things which for my unworthiness I dare not, and for my blindness I cannot ask; through the worthiness of your Son Jesus Christ my Lord, who lives and reigns with you and the Holy Spirit, one God, now and for ever. *Amen.*†

The Concluding Prayer of the Church
Lord God, almighty and everlasting Father, you have brought me in safety to this new day: Preserve me with your mighty power, that I may not fall into sin, nor be overcome by adversity; and in all I do direct me to the fulfilling of your purpose; through Jesus Christ my Lord. *Amen.*†

The Midday Office   **To Be Observed on the Hour or Half Hour**
                                                Between 11 a.m. and 2 p.m.

The Call to Prayer
Come, let us sing to the LORD . . .* For the LORD is a great God,* and a great king
   above all gods.

Psalm 95:1, 3

The Request for Presence
Show your servants your works* and your splendor to their children.

Psalm 90:16

The Greeting
I will sing to you with the harp, O Holy One of Israel.
My lips will sing with joy when I play to you,* and so will my soul, which you
   have redeemed.
My tongue will proclaim your righteousness all day long. . . .

Psalm 71:22–24

The Refrain for the Midday Lessons
Hallelujah! I will give thanks to the LORD with my whole heart,* in the assembly of
   the upright, in the congregation.

Psalm 111:1

A Reading
After that I saw a huge number, impossible to count, of people from every nation,
   race, tribe and language; they were standing in front of the throne and in front
   of the Lamb, dressed in white robes and holding palms in their hands. They
   shouted in a loud voice, 'Salvation to our God, who sits on the throne, and to
   the Lamb!' And all the angels who were standing in a circle round the throne,
   surrounding the elders and the four living creatures, prostrated themselves
   before the throne, and touched the ground with their foreheads, worshipping
   God with these words:
Amen. Praise and glory and wisdom and thanksgiving and honor and power and
   strength to our God for ever and ever. Amen.
One of the elders then spoke, and asked me, 'Who are these people, dressed in
   white robes, and where have they come from?' I answered him, 'You can tell
   me, sir.' Then he said, 'These are the people who have been through the great
   trial; they have washed their robes white again in the blood of the Lamb. That
   is why they are standing in front of God's throne and serving him day and
   night in his sanctuary; and the One who sits on the throne will spread his tent
   over them. *They will never hunger or thirst* again; *the sun and scorching wind will
   never plague them,* because the Lamb who is at the heart of the throne *will be their
   shepherd and will guide them to springs of living water;* and God *will wipe away all
   tears from their eyes.'*

Revelation 7:9–17

The Refrain
Hallelujah! I will give thanks to the LORD with my whole heart,* in the assembly of the upright, in the congregation.

The Midday Psalm   *Who Is Like the LORD Our God*
Who is like the LORD our God, who sits enthroned on high,* but stoops to behold the heavens and the earth?
He takes up the weak out of the dust* and lifts the poor from the ashes.
He sets them with princes,* with princes of his people.
He makes the woman of a childless house* to be a joyful mother of children.

Psalm 113:5–8

The Refrain
Hallelujah! I will give thanks to the LORD with my whole heart,* in the assembly of the upright, in the congregation.

The Gloria

The Lord's Prayer

The Prayer Appointed for the Week
Almighty God, the fountain of all wisdom, you know my necessities before I ask and my ignorance in asking: Have compassion on my weakness, and mercifully give me those things which for my unworthiness I dare not, and for my blindness I cannot ask; through the worthiness of your Son Jesus Christ my Lord, who lives and reigns with you and the Holy Spirit, one God, now and for ever. *Amen.*†

The Concluding Prayer of the Church
O God, you make me glad with the weekly remembrance of the glorious resurrection of your Son my Lord: Give me this day such blessing through my worship of you, that the week to come may be spent in your favor; through Jesus Christ our Lord. *Amen.*†

The Vespers Office   **To Be Observed on the Hour or Half Hour**
                                                      Between 5 and 8 p.m.

The Call to Prayer
Search for the LORD and his strength;* continually seek his face.

Psalm 105:4

The Request for Presence
O LORD, do not forsake me;* be not far from me, O my God.
Make haste to help me,* O Lord of my salvation.

Psalm 38:21–22

The Greeting
You strengthen me more and more;* you enfold and comfort me.

Psalm 71:21

The Hymn   *Abide with Me*
Abide with me: fast falls the eventide;
The darkness deepens; Lord, with me abide!
When other helpers fail and comforts flee,
Help of the helpless, O abide with me.

Swift to its close ebbs out life's little day;
Earth's joys grow dim, its glories pass away;
Change and decay in all around I see.
O thou who changest not, abide with me.

I need your presence every passing hour;
What but your grace can foil the tempter's power?
Who, like yourself, my guide and stay can be?
Through cloud and sunshine, Lord, abide with me.

Hold your cross before my closing eyes;
Shine through the gloom and point me to the skies:
Heaven's morning breaks, and earth's vain shadows flee;
In life, in death, O Lord, abide with me.

Henry Francis Lyte

The Refrain for the Vespers Lessons
My soul waits for the LORD, more than watchmen for the morning,* more than
watchmen for the morning.

Psalm 130:5

The Vespers Psalm   *My Soul Is Content, as with Marrow and Fatness*
O God, you are my God; eagerly I seek you;* my soul thirsts for you, my flesh
faints for you, as in a barren and dry land where there is no water.
Therefore I have grazed upon you in your holy place,* that I might behold your
power and your glory.
For your loving-kindness is better than life itself;* my lips shall give you praise.
So will I bless you as long as I live* and lift up my hands in your Name.
My soul is content, as with marrow and fatness,* and my mouth praises you with
joyful lips,
When I remember you upon my bed,* and meditate on you in the night watches.
For you have been my helper,* and under the shadow of your wings I will rejoice.
My soul clings to you;* your right hand holds me fast.

Psalm 63:1–8

The Refrain
My soul waits for the LORD, more than watchmen for the morning,* more than
watchmen for the morning.

The Small Verse
The Lord is my shepherd and nothing is wanting to me.* In green pastures He has
settled me.

A SHORT BREVIARY

The Lord's Prayer

The Prayer Appointed for the Week
Almighty God, the fountain of all wisdom, you know my necessities before I ask and my ignorance in asking: Have compassion on my weakness, and mercifully give me those things which for my unworthiness I dare not, and for my blindness I cannot ask; through the worthiness of your Son Jesus Christ my Lord, who lives and reigns with you and the Holy Spirit, one God, now and for ever. *Amen.†*

The Concluding Prayer of the Church
Lord God, whose Son our savior Jesus Christ, triumphed over the power of death and prepared for us our place in the new Jerusalem: Grant that I, who have this day given thanks for his resurrection, may praise you in the City of which he is the light, and where he lives and reigns for ever and ever. *Amen.†*

The Morning Office   **To Be Observed on the Hour or Half Hour Between 6 and 9 a.m.**

The Call to Prayer
Let the Name of the LORD be blessed,* from this time forth for evermore.
From the rising of the sun to its going down* let the Name of the LORD be praised.
Psalm 113:2–3

The Request for Presence
Let them know that this is your hand,* that you, O LORD, have done it.
Psalm 109:26

The Greeting
Not to us, O LORD, not to us, but to your Name give glory;* because of your love and because of your faithfulness.
Psalm 115:1

The Refrain for the Morning Lessons
It is not the healthy who need the doctor, but the sick . . . And indeed I did not come to call the virtuous, but sinners.
Matthew 9:12–13

A Reading   *In memory of Mary of Magdala, the first to see the risen Lord. Her life and witness are remembered by the Church on July 22.*

But Mary was standing outside near the tomb, weeping. Then, as she wept, she stooped to look inside, and saw two angels in white sitting where the body of Jesus had been, one at the head, the other at the feet. They said, 'Woman, why are you weeping?' 'They have taken my Lord away,' she replied, 'and I don't know where they have put him.' As she said this she turned round and saw Jesus standing there, though she did not realize that it was Jesus. Jesus said to

her, 'Woman, why are you weeping? Who are you looking for?' Supposing him
to be the gardener, she said, 'Sir, if you have taken him away, tell me where you
have put him, and I will go and remove him.' Jesus said, 'Mary!' She turned
round then and said to him in Hebrew, 'Rabbuni!'—which means Master. Jesus
said to her, 'Do not cling to me, because I have not yet ascended to the Father.
But go and find the brothers, and tell them: I am ascending to my Father and
your Father, to my God and your God.' So Mary of Magdala told the disciples,
'I have seen the Lord,' and that he had said these things to her.

John 20:11–18

The Refrain
It is not the healthy who need the doctor, but the sick . . . And indeed I did not
come to call the virtuous, but sinners.

The Morning Psalm   *My Soul Thirsts for God*
As a doe longs for running streams,* so I yearn for you, my God.
I thirst for God, the living God;* when shall I go to see the face of God?
I have no food but tears, day and night;* and all day long I am taunted, "Where is
your God?"
This I remember, as I pour out my heart,* how I used to pass under the roof of the
Most High
Used to go to the house of God,* among the cries of joy and praise, the sound of
the feast.
Why be so downcast, why all these sighs?* Hope in God: I will praise him still, my
Savior, my God.

Psalm 42:1–6 NJB

The Refrain
It is not the healthy who need the doctor, but the sick . . . And indeed I did not
come to call the virtuous, but sinners.

The Cry of the Church
O Lamb of God, that takes away the sins of the world, have mercy upon me.
O Lamb of God, that takes away the sins of the world, have mercy upon me.
O Lamb of God, that takes away the sins of the world, grant me your peace.

The Lord's Prayer

The Prayer Appointed for the Week
Almighty God, the fountain of all wisdom, you know my necessities before I ask
and my ignorance in asking: Have compassion on my weakness, and mercifully
give me those things which for my unworthiness I dare not, and for my blindness I cannot ask; through the worthiness of your Son Jesus Christ my Lord, who
lives and reigns with you and the Holy Spirit, one God, now and for ever. *Amen.*†

The Concluding Prayers of the Church
Lord God, almighty and everlasting Father, you have brought me in safety to this
new day: Preserve me with your mighty power, that I may not fall into sin, nor

be overcome by adversity; and in all I do direct me to the fulfilling of your purpose; through Jesus Christ my Lord. *Amen.*†

Almighty God, whose blessed Son restored Mary Magdalene to health of body and of mind, and called her to be a witness of his resurrection: Mercifully grant that by your grace I may be healed from all my infirmities and know you in the power of his unending life; who with you and the Holy Spirit lives and reigns, one God, now and forever. *Amen.*†

The Midday Office   **To Be Observed on the Hour or Half Hour**
Between 11 a.m. and 2 p.m.

The Call to Prayer
Open my lips, O Lord,* and my mouth shall proclaim your praise.
Psalm 51:16

The Request for Presence
Exalt yourself above the heavens, O God,* and your glory over all the earth.

The Greeting
. . . deal with me according to your Name;* for your tender mercy's sake, deliver me.
Psalm 109:20

The Refrain for the Midday Lessons
'. . . the kingdom of heaven is like a merchant looking for fine pearls; when he finds one of great value he goes and sells everything he owns that he may buy it.'
adapted from Matthew 13:45–46

A Reading
. . . the love of Christ overwhelms us when we consider that if one man died for all, then all have died; his purpose in dying for all humanity was that those who live should live not any more for themselves, but for him who died and was raised to life for them. From now onwards, then, we do not consider anyone by human standards: even if we were once familiar with Christ according to human standards, we do not know him in that way any longer. So for anyone who is in Christ, there is a new creation; the old order is gone and a new being is there to see. It is all God's work, he reconciled us to himself through Christ and gave us the ministry of reconciliation. I mean, God was in Christ reconciling the world to himself, not holding anyone's faults against them, but entrusted to us the message of reconciliation.
2 Corinthians 5:14–19

The Refrain
'. . . the kingdom of heaven is like a merchant looking for fine pearls; when he finds one of great value he goes and sells everything he owns that he may buy it.'

The Midday Psalm   *Your Throne, O God, Endures For Ever and Ever*

My heart is stirring with a noble song; let me recite what I have fashioned for the
    king;* my tongue shall be the pen of a skilled writer.

You are the fairest of men;* grace flows from your lips, because God has blessed
    you for ever.

Strap your sword upon your thigh, O mighty warrior,* in your pride and in your
    majesty.

Ride out and conquer in the cause of truth* and for the sake of justice.

Your right hand will show you marvelous things;* your arrows are very sharp, O
    mighty warrior.

The peoples are falling at your feet,* and the king's enemies are losing heart.

Your throne, O God, endures for ever and ever,* a scepter of righteousness is the
    scepter of your kingdom; you love righteousness and hate iniquity.

Therefore, God, your God, has anointed you* with the oil of gladness above your
    fellows.

All your garments are fragrant with myrrh, aloes, and cassia,* and the music of
    strings from ivory palaces makes you glad.

Kings' daughters stand among the ladies of the court;* on your right hand is the
    queen, adorned with the gold of Ophir.

Psalm 45:1–10

The Refrain

'. . . the kingdom of heaven is like a merchant looking for fine pearls; when he finds
one of great value he goes and sells everything he owns that he may buy it.'

The Cry of the Church

O God, come to my assistance! O Lord, make haste to help me!

The Lord's Prayer

The Prayer Appointed for the Week

Almighty God, the fountain of all wisdom, you know my necessities before I ask
    and my ignorance in asking: Have compassion on my weakness, and merci-
    fully give me those things which for my unworthiness I dare not, and for my
    blindness I cannot ask; through the worthiness of your Son Jesus Christ my
    Lord, who lives and reigns with you and the Holy Spirit, one God, now and for
    ever. *Amen.*†

The Concluding Prayer of the Church

Almighty God, you have surrounded me with a great cloud of witnesses: Grant
    that I, encouraged by the good example of your servant Mary Magdalene, may
    persevere in running the race that is set before me, until at last I may with her
    attain to your eternal joy; through Jesus Christ, the pioneer and perfecter of our
    faith, who lives and reigns with you and the Holy Spirit, one God, for ever and
    ever. *Amen.*†

The Vespers Office   To Be Observed on the Hour or Half Hour
                                                    Between 5 and 8 p.m.

The Call to Prayer
Bless God in the congregation;* bless the LORD, you that are the fountain of Israel.

Psalm 68:26

The Request for Presence
So teach us to number our days* that we may apply our hearts to wisdom.

Psalm 90:12

The Greeting
A thousand years in your sight are like yesterday when it is past* and like a watch
    in the night.

Psalm 90:4

The Hymn   *Our God, Our Help in Ages Past*

Our God, our help in ages past,   Time, like an ever rolling stream,
Our hope for years to come,   Soon bears us all away;
Our shelter from the stormy blast,   We fly forgotten, as a dream
And our eternal home: Dies at the opening day.

Before the hills in order stood,   Our God, our help in ages past,
Or earth received its frame,   Our hope for years to come,
From everlasting thou art God,   Be thou our guard while life shall last,
To endless years the same.   And our eternal home.

A thousand ages in thy sight   *Isaac Watts*
Are like an evening gone;
Short as the watch that ends the night
Before the rising of the sun.

The Refrain for the Vespers Lessons
Listen, daughter, pay careful attention:* forget your nation and your ancestral
    home,
Then the king will fall in love with your beauty.* He is your master now, bow
    down to him.

Psalm 45:10–11

The Vespers Psalm   *The LORD Shall Reign For Ever*
Happy are they who have the God of Jacob for their help!* whose hope is in the
    LORD their God;
Who made the heaven and the earth, the seas, and all that is in them;* who keeps
    his promise for ever;
Who gives justice to those who are oppressed,* and food to those who hunger.
The LORD sets the prisoners free; the LORD opens the eyes of the blind;* the LORD
    lifts up those who are bowed down;

The LORD loves the righteous; the LORD cares for the stranger;* he sustains the
orphan and widow, but frustrates the way of the wicked.
The LORD shall reign for ever.* Your God, O Zion, throughout the generations.
Hallelujah!

Psalm 146:4–9

The Refrain
Listen, daughter, pay careful attention:* forget your nation and your ancestral home,
Then the king will fall in love with your beauty.* He is your master now, bow
down to him.

The Gloria

The Lord's Prayer

The Prayer Appointed for the Week
Almighty God, the fountain of all wisdom, you know my necessities before I ask
and my ignorance in asking: Have compassion on my weakness, and mercifully
give me those things which for my unworthiness I dare not, and for my blindness I cannot ask; through the worthiness of your Son Jesus Christ my Lord, who
lives and reigns with you and the Holy Spirit, one God, now and for ever. *Amen.*†

The Concluding Prayer of the Church
Almighty God, by your Holy Spirit you have made us one with your saints in
heaven and on earth: Grant that in my earthly pilgrimage I may always be sup-
ported by this fellowship of love and prayer, and know myself to be surrounded by their witness to your power and mercy. I ask this for the sake of
Jesus Christ, in whom all my intercessions are acceptable through the Spirit,
and who lives and reigns for ever and ever. *Amen.*†

The Morning Office   To Be Observed on the Hour or Half Hour
Between 6 and 9 a.m.

The Call to Prayer
Bless the LORD, you angels of his, you mighty ones who do his bidding,* and hear-
ken to the voice of his word.
Bless the LORD, all you his hosts,* you ministers of his who do his will.
Bless the LORD, all you works of his,* in all places of his dominion;

Psalm 103:20–22

The Request for Presence
Show us your mercy, O LORD,* and grant us your salvation.

Psalm 85:7

The Greeting
My mouth shall recount your mighty acts and saving deeds all day long;* though I
cannot know the number of them.

Psalm 71:15

The Refrain for the Morning Lessons
He looks at the earth and it trembles;* he touches the mountains and they smoke.

Psalm 104:33

A Reading
It happened that one day he got into a boat with his disciples and said to them,
'Let us cross over to the other side of the lake.' So they set out, and as they
sailed he fell asleep. When a squall came down on the lake the boat started
shipping water and they found themselves in danger. So they went to rouse
him saying, 'Master! Master! We are lost!' Then he woke up and rebuked the
wind and the rough water; and they subsided and it was calm again. He said to
them, 'Where is your faith?' They were awestruck and astonished and said to
one another, 'Who can this be, that gives orders even to the winds and waves
and they obey him?'

Luke 8:22–25

The Refrain
He looks at the earth and it trembles;* he touches the mountains and they smoke.

The Morning Psalm   *You Still the Roaring Seas*
Awesome things will you show us in your righteousness, O God of our salvation,*
    O Hope of all the ends of the earth and of the seas that are far away.
You make fast the mountains by your power;* they are girded about with might.
You still the roaring seas,* the roaring waves, and the clamor of their peoples.
Those who dwell at the ends of the earth will tremble at your marvelous signs.

Psalm 65:5–8

The Refrain
He looks at the earth and it trembles;* he touches the mountains and they smoke.

The Small Verse
The earth is the Lord's and all the fullness thereof, the world and we who dwell
    within. Thanks be to God.

Traditional

The Lord's Prayer

The Prayer Appointed for the Week
Almighty God, the fountain of all wisdom, you know my necessities before I ask
    and my ignorance in asking: Have compassion on my weakness, and merci-
    fully give me those things which for my unworthiness I dare not, and for my
    blindness I cannot ask; through the worthiness of your Son Jesus Christ my
    Lord, who lives and reigns with you and the Holy Spirit, one God, now and for
    ever. *Amen.*†

The Concluding Prayer of the Church
Lord God, almighty and everlasting Father, you have brought me in safety to this
    new day: Preserve me with your mighty power, that I may not fall into sin, nor

be overcome by adversity; and in all I do direct me to the fulfilling of your purpose; through Jesus Christ my Lord. *Amen.*†

The Midday Office   **To Be Observed on the Hour or Half Hour**
                                                   Between 11 a.m. and 2 p.m.

The Call to Prayer
Come, let us bow down, and bend the knee,* and kneel before the Lord, our Maker.
For he is our God,* and we are the people of his pasture and the sheep of his
    hand. . . .

Psalm 95:6–7

The Request for Presence
You are my crag and my stronghold;* for the sake of your Name, lead me and
    guide me.

Psalm 31:3

The Greeting
Hosanna, Lord, hosanna!* Lord, send us now success.
Blessed is he who comes in the name of the Lord;* we bless you from the house of
    the Lord.
God is the Lord; he has shined upon us;* form a procession with branches up to
    the horns of the altar.

Psalm 118:25–27

The Refrain for the Midday Lessons
As for God, his ways are perfect; the words of the Lord are tried in the fire;* he is a
    shield to all who trust in him.

Psalm 18:31

A Reading
Finally, brothers, let your minds be filled with everything that is true, everything
    that is honorable, everything that is upright and pure, everything that we love
    and admire—with whatever is good and praiseworthy. Keep doing everything
    you learned from me and were told by me and have heard or seen me doing.
    Then the God of peace will be with you.

Phillipians 4:8–9

The Refrain
As for God, his ways are perfect; the words of the Lord are tried in the fire;* he is a
    shield to all who trust in him.

The Midday Psalm   *The Righteous Shall Flourish Like a Palm Tree*
The righteous shall flourish like a palm tree,* and shall spread abroad like a cedar
    of Lebanon.
Those who are planted in the house of the Lord* shall flourish in the courts of our
    God;

They shall still bear fruit in old age;* they shall be green and succulent;
That they may show how upright the LORD is,* my Rock, in whom there is no fault.

Psalm 92:11–14

The Refrain
As for God, his ways are perfect; the words of the LORD are tried in the fire;* he is a shield to all who trust in him.

The Cry of the Church
Lord, have mercy on us. Christ, have mercy on us. Lord, have mercy on us.

The Lord's Prayer

The Prayer Appointed for the Week
Almighty God, the fountain of all wisdom, you know my necessities before I ask and my ignorance in asking: Have compassion on my weakness, and mercifully give me those things which for my unworthiness I dare not, and for my blindness I cannot ask; through the worthiness of your Son Jesus Christ my Lord, who lives and reigns with you and the Holy Spirit, one God, now and for ever. *Amen.*✝

The Concluding Prayer of the Church
Almighty God, to whom our needs are known before we ask: Help me to ask only what accords with your will; and those good things which I dare not, or in my blindness cannot ask, grant me for the sake of your Son Jesus Christ my Lord. *Amen.*✝

The Vespers Office   **To Be Observed on the Hour or Half Hour**
                                   Between 5 and 8 p.m.

The Call to Prayer
Bless our God, you peoples;* make the voice of his praise to be heard;
Who holds our souls in life,* and will not allow our feet to slip.

Psalm 66:7–8

The Request for Presence
Hear my prayer, O LORD,* and give ear to my cry . . .
For I am but a sojourner with you,* a wayfarer, as all my forebears were.

Psalm 39:13ff

The Greeting
O God, you have taught me since I was young,* and to this day I tell of your wonderful works.

Psalm 71:17

The Hymn   *Listen to the Lambs, All a-Cryin'*
    Listen to the lambs, all a-cryin'
    Listen to the lambs, all a-cryin'
    Listen to the lambs, all a-cryin'
    All a-cryin', all a-cryin'.

He shall feed his flock like a shepherd,
Listen to the lambs, all a-cryin';
And carry the young lambs in his bosom.
Listen to the lambs, all a-cryin';

Come on sister with your ups and downs,
Listen to the lambs, all a-cryin';
Angels waiting for to give you a crown,
Listen to the lambs, all a-cryin';

Come on, sister, and don't be ashamed,
Listen to the lambs, all a-cryin';
Angels waiting for to write your name,
Listen to the lambs, all a-cryin';

Mind out, brother, how you walk the cross,
Listen to the lambs, all a-cryin';
Foot might slip, and your soul get lost,
Listen to the lambs, all a-cryin'.

Traditional

The Refrain for the Vespers Lessons

The Lord shall watch over your going out and your coming in,* from this time
forth for evermore.

Psalm 121:8

The Vespers Psalm   The Lord Is My Shepherd

The Lord is my shepherd;* I shall not be in want.
He makes me lie down in green pastures* and leads me beside still waters.
He revives my soul* and guides me along right pathways for his Name's sake.
Though I walk through the valley of the shadow of death, I shall fear no evil;* for
    you are with me; your rod and your staff, they comfort me.
You spread a table before me in the presence of those who trouble me;* you have
    anointed my head with oil, and my cup is running over.
Surely your goodness and mercy shall follow me all the days of my life,* and I will
    dwell in the house of the Lord for ever.

Psalm 23:1–6

The Refrain

The Lord shall watch over your going out and your coming in,* from this time
    forth for evermore.

The Cry of the Church

Even so, come Lord Jesus!

The Lord's Prayer

The Prayer Appointed for the Week
Almighty God, the fountain of all wisdom, you know my necessities before I ask
and my ignorance in asking: Have compassion on my weakness, and mercifully
give me those things which for my unworthiness I dare not, and for my blindness I cannot ask; through the worthiness of your Son Jesus Christ my Lord, who
lives and reigns with you and the Holy Spirit, one God, now and for ever. *Amen.*†

The Concluding Prayer of the Church
Protect me, Lord, as I stay awake; watch over me as I sleep, that awake I may
watch with Christ, and asleep, rest in his peace. *Amen.*

The Morning Office   **To Be Observed on the Hour or Half Hour**
                                        Between 6 and 9 a.m.

The Call to Prayer
Open my lips, O Lord,* and my mouth shall proclaim your praise.
Had you desired it, I would have offered sacrifice,* but you take no delight in
burnt-offerings.
The sacrifice of God is a troubled spirit;* and a broken and contrite heart, O God,
you will not despise.

Psalm 51:16–18

The Request for Presence
You are my helper and my deliverer;* O LORD, do not tarry.

Psalm 70:6

The Greeting
Your righteousness, O God, reaches to the heavens;* you have done great things;
who is like you, O God?

Psalm 71:19

The Refrain for the Morning Lessons
Happy are the people whose strength is in you!* whose hearts are set on the pilgrim's way.

Psalm 84:4

A Reading
So he sat down, called the Twelve to him and said, 'If anyone wants to be first, he
must make himself last of all and servant of all.'

Mark 9:35

The Refrain
Happy are the people whose strength is in you!* whose hearts are set on the pilgrim's way.

The Morning Psalm   *The Chief Cornerstone*
Open for me the gates of righteousness;* I will enter them; I will offer thanks to the
LORD.

"This is the gate of the LORD;* he who is righteous may enter."
I will give thanks to you, for you answered me* and have become my salvation.
The same stone that the builders rejected* has become the chief cornerstone.
This is the LORD'S doing,* and it is marvelous in our eyes.
On this day the LORD has acted;* we will rejoice and be glad in it.

Psalm 118:19–24

The Refrain
Happy are the people whose strength is in you!* whose hearts are set on the pilgrim's way.

The Small Verse
The people that walked in darkness have seen a great light; on the inhabitants of a country in shadow dark as death a light has blazed forth.

Isaiah 9:1

The Lord's Prayer

The Prayer Appointed for the Week
Almighty God, the fountain of all wisdom, you know my necessities before I ask and my ignorance in asking: Have compassion on my weakness, and mercifully give me those things which for my unworthiness I dare not, and for my blindness I cannot ask; through the worthiness of your Son Jesus Christ my Lord, who lives and reigns with you and the Holy Spirit, one God, now and for ever. *Amen.*†

The Concluding Prayer of the Church
Lord God, almighty and everlasting Father, you have brought me in safety to this new day: Preserve me with your mighty power, that I may not fall into sin, nor be overcome by adversity; and in all I do direct me to the fulfilling of your purpose; through Jesus Christ my Lord. *Amen.*†

The Midday Office — To Be Observed on the Hour or Half Hour Between 11 a.m. and 2 p.m.

The Call to Prayer
Sing to God, O kingdoms of the earth;* sing praises to the Lord.
He rides in the heavens, the ancient heavens;* he sends forth his voice, his mighty voice.

Psalm 68:33–34

The Request for Presence
May God give his blessing,* and may all the ends of the earth stand in awe of him.

Psalm 67:7

The Greeting
Zion hears and is glad, and the cities of Judah rejoice,* because of your judgments, O LORD.

Psalm 97:8

The Refrain for the Midday Lessons
The eyes of all wait upon you, O LORD,* and you give them their food in due
season.
You open wide your hand* and satisfy the needs of every living creature.

Psalm 145:16–17

A Reading
Your dead will come back to life, your corpses will rise again. Wake up and sing,
you dwellers in the dust, for your dew will be a radiant dew but the earth will
give birth to the shades.

Isaiah 26:19

The Refrain
The eyes of all wait upon you, O LORD,* and you give them their food in due
season.
You open wide your hand* and satisfy the needs of every living creature.

The Midday Psalm   *The LORD Will Build Up Zion, and His Glory Will Appear*
You will arise and have compassion on Zion, for it is time to have mercy upon
her;* indeed, the appointed time has come.
For your servants love her very rubble,* and are moved to pity even for her dust.
The nations fear your Name, O LORD,* and all the kings of the earth your glory.
For the LORD will build up Zion,* and his glory will appear.
He will look with favor on the prayer of the homeless;* he will not despise their
plea.

Psalm 102:13–17

The Refrain
The eyes of all wait upon you, O LORD,* and you give them their food in due
season.
You open wide your hand* and satisfy the needs of every living creature.

The Cry of the Church
O God, come to my assistance! O Lord, make haste to help me!

The Lord's Prayer

The Prayer Appointed for the Week
Almighty God, the fountain of all wisdom, you know my necessities before I ask
and my ignorance in asking: Have compassion on my weakness, and mercifully give me those things which for my unworthiness I dare not, and for my
blindness I cannot ask; through the worthiness of your Son Jesus Christ my
Lord, who lives and reigns with you and the Holy Spirit, one God, now and for
ever. *Amen.†*

The Concluding Prayer of the Church
O Lord my God, accept the fervent prayers of all of us, your people; in the multitude of your mercies, look with compassion upon me and all who turn to you

for help; for you are gracious, O lover of souls, and to you we give glory, Father, Son, and Holy Spirit, now and for ever. *Amen.*†

The Vespers Office   **To Be Observed on the Hour or Half Hour**
                                          Between 5 and 8 p.m.

The Call to Prayer
Ascribe to the Lord, you families of the peoples;* ascribe to the Lord honor and power.
Worship the Lord in the beauty of holiness;* let the whole earth tremble before him.

Psalm 96:7–9

The Request for Presence
O God, be not far from me.

Psalm 71:12

The Greeting
I will praise you upon the lyre for your faithfulness, O my God;* I will sing to you with the harp, O Holy One of Israel.

Psalm 71:22

The Hymn   *The Divine Image*
   To Mercy, Pity, Peace, and Love   Then every man, of every clime,
   All pray in their distress;   That prays in his distress,
   And to these virtues of delight   Prays to the human form divine,
   Return their thankfulness.   Love, Mercy, Pity, Peace.

   For Mercy, Pity, Peace, and Love   And all must love the human form,
   Is God, our Father dear,   In heathen, Turk, or Jew;
   And Mercy, Pity, Peace and Love   Where Mercy, Love, and Pity dwell
   Is man, His child and care.   There God is dwelling too.

                                                          William Blake
   For Mercy has a human heart,
   Pity a human face,
   And Love, the human form divine,
   And Peace the human dress.

The Refrain for the Vespers Lessons
Mercy and truth have met together;* righteousness and peace have kissed each other.

Psalm 85:10

The Vespers Psalm   *He Shall Come Down like Rain upon the Mown Field*
Give the king your justice, O God,* and your righteousness to the King's son;
That he may rule your people righteously* and the poor with justice;
That the mountains may bring prosperity to the people,* and the little hills bring righteousness.

He shall defend the needy among the people;* he shall rescue the poor and crush the oppressor.

He shall live as long as the sun and moon endure,* from one generation to another.

He shall come down like rain upon the mown field,* like showers that water the earth.

In his time shall the righteous flourish;* there shall be abundance of peace till the moon shall be no more.

He shall rule from sea to sea,* and from the River to the ends of the earth.

Psalm 72:1–8

The Refrain

Mercy and truth have met together;* righteousness and peace have kissed each other.

The Small Verse

Happy are the people whose strength is in you!* whose hearts are set on the pilgrim's way,

For one day in your courts is better than a thousand in my own room,* and to stand at the threshold of the house of my God than to dwell in the tents of the wicked.

Psalm 84:4ff

The Lord's Prayer

The Prayer Appointed for the Week

Almighty God, the fountain of all wisdom, you know my necessities before I ask and my ignorance in asking: Have compassion on my weakness, and mercifully give me those things which for my unworthiness I dare not, and for my blindness I cannot ask; through the worthiness of your Son Jesus Christ my Lord, who lives and reigns with you and the Holy Spirit, one God, now and for ever. *Amen.*†

The Concluding Prayer of the Church

Hasten, O Father, the coming of your kingdom; and grant that all who now live by your faith, may with joy behold your Son at his coming in glorious majesty; even Jesus Christ, our only Mediator and Advocate. *Amen.*†

The Morning Office　　　　　　**To Be Observed on the Hour or Half Hour Between 6 and 9 a.m.**

The Call to Prayer

Worship the Lord in the beauty of holiness.

Psalm 29:2

The Request for Presence

In you, O Lord, have I taken refuge; let me never be put to shame;* deliver me in your righteousness.

Psalm 31:1

The Greeting
You, O LORD, shall give strength to your people;* the LORD shall give his people
  the blessing of peace.

based on Psalm 29:11

The Refrain for the Morning Lessons
Jesus took with him Peter and James and his brother John and led them up a high
  mountain by themselves. There in their presence he was transfigured: his face
  shone like the sun and his clothes became as dazzling as light.

Matthew 17:1–2

A Reading   *In remembrance of St. James, son of Zebedee and*
                       brother of St. John, executed by Herod the Great
                       ca. 42 a.d. and memorialized by the Church on July 25.

Then the mother of Zebedee's sons came with her sons, to make a request of him,
  and bowed low; and he said to her, 'What is it you want?' She said to him,
  'Promise that these two sons of mine may sit one at your right hand and the
  other at your left in your kingdom.' 'You do not know what you are asking.
  Can you drink the cup that I am going to drink?' They (James and John)
  replied, 'We can.' He said to them, 'Very well, you shall drink my cup, but as
  for seats at my right hand and my left, these are not mine to grant; they belong
  to those to whom they have been allotted by my Father.'
When the other ten heard this they were indignant with the two brothers. But
  Jesus called them to him and said, 'You know that among the gentiles the
  rulers lord it over them, and great men make their authority felt. Among you,
  this is not to happen. No; anyone who wants to become great among you must
  be your servant, and anyone who wants to be first among you must be your
  slave, just as the Son of man came not to be served but to serve, and to give his
  life as a ransom for many.'

Matthew 20:20–28

The Refrain
Jesus took with him Peter and James and his brother John and led them up a high
  mountain where they could be alone. There in their presence he was transfigured: his face shone like the sun and his clothes became as white as the light.

The Morning Psalm   *One Day Tells Its Tale to Another*
The heavens declare the glory of God,* and the firmament shows his handiwork.
One day tells its tale to another,* and one night imparts knowledge to another.
Although they have no words or language,* and their voices are not heard,
Their sound has gone out into all the lands,* and their message to the ends of the
  world.
In the deep has he set a pavilion for the sun;* it comes forth like a bridegroom out
  of his chamber; it rejoices like a champion to run its course.

It goes forth from the uttermost edge of the heavens and runs about to the end of it again;* nothing is hidden from its burning heat.

Psalm 19:1–6

The Refrain
Jesus took with him Peter and James and his brother John and led them up a high mountain where they could be alone. There in their presence he was transfigured: his face shone like the sun and his clothes became as white as the light.

The Gloria

The Lord's Prayer

The Prayer Appointed for the Week
Almighty God, the fountain of all wisdom, you know my necessities before I ask and my ignorance in asking: Have compassion on my weakness, and mercifully give me those things which for my unworthiness I dare not, and for my blindness I cannot ask; through the worthiness of your Son Jesus Christ my Lord, who lives and reigns with you and the Holy Spirit, one God, now and for ever. *Amen.*†

The Concluding Prayer of the Church
Lord God, almighty and everlasting Father, you have brought me in safety to this new day: Preserve me with your mighty power, that I may not fall into sin, nor be overcome by adversity; and in all I do direct me to the fulfilling of your purpose; through Jesus Christ my Lord. *Amen.*†

The Midday Office — To Be Observed on the Hour or Half Hour Between 11 a.m. and 2 p.m.

The Call to Prayer
Ascribe to the LORD, you gods,* ascribe to the LORD glory and strength.

Psalm 29:1

The Request for Presence
"Hear, O LORD, and have mercy upon me;* O LORD, be my helper."

Psalm 30:11

The Greeting
In the temple of the LORD* all are crying, "Glory!"

Psalm 29:9

The Refrain for the Midday Lessons
Their line is gone out into all the lands,* and their message to the ends of the world.

Psalm 19:4

A Reading

While they were there some prophets came down to Antioch from Jerusalem, and
one of them whose name was Agabus, seized by the Spirit, stood up and pre-
dicted that a severe and universal famine was going to happen. This in fact
happened while Claudius was emperor. The disciples decided to send relief,
each to contribute what he could afford, to the brothers living in Judaea. They
did this and delivered their contributions to the elders through the agency of
Barnabus and Saul. It was about this time that King Herod started persecuting
certain members of the Church. He had James the brother of John beheaded,
and when he saw that this pleased the Jews he went on to arrest Peter as well.

Acts 11:27–12:3

The Refrain

Their line is gone out into all the lands,* and their message to the ends of the world.

The Midday Psalm   *I Take Refuge in You*

O LORD my God, I take refuge in you;* save and deliver me from all who pursue me;
Lest like a lion they tear me in pieces* and snatch me away with none to deliver me.
O LORD my God, if I have done these things:* if there is any wickedness in my hands,
If I have repaid my friend with evil,* or plundered him who without cause is my
    enemy;
Then let my enemy pursue and overtake me,* trample my life into the ground,
    and lay my honor in the dust.
Stand up, O LORD, in your wrath;* rise up against the fury of my enemies.
Awake, O my God, decree justice;* let the assembly of the peoples gather round you.
Be seated on your lofty throne, O Most High;* O LORD, judge the nations.
Give judgment for me according to my righteousness, O LORD,* and according to
    my innocence, O Most High.
Let the malice of the wicked come to an end, but establish the righteous;* for you
    test the mind and heart, O righteous God.

Psalm 7:1–10

The Refrain

Their line is gone out into all the lands,* and their message to the ends of the
    world.

The Cry of the Church

Lord, have mercy on us. Christ, have mercy on us. Lord, have mercy on us.

The Lord's Prayer

The Prayer Appointed for the Week

Almighty God, the fountain of all wisdom, you know my necessities before I ask
    and my ignorance in asking: Have compassion on my weakness, and mercifully
    give me those things which for my unworthiness I dare not, and for my blind-
    ness I cannot ask; through the worthiness of your Son Jesus Christ my Lord, who
    lives and reigns with you and the Holy Spirit, one God, now and for ever. *Amen.*†

The Concluding Prayer of the Church
O gracious God, I remember before you today your servant and apostle James,
first among the Twelve to suffer martyrdom for the Name of Jesus Christ; and I
pray that you will pour out upon the leaders of your Church that spirit of self-
denying service by which alone they may have true authority among us;
through Jesus Christ out Lord, who lives and reigns with you and the Holy
Spirit, one God, now and for ever. *Amen.*✝

The Vespers Office   **To Be Observed on the Hour or Half Hour**
                                          Between 5 and 8 p.m.

The Call to Prayer
Ascribe to the LORD the glory due his Name.

Psalm 29:2

The Request for Presence
LORD, let me not be ashamed for having called upon you.

Psalm 31:17

The Greeting
I will exalt you, O LORD, because you have lifted me up* and have not let my enemies triumph over me.

Psalm 30:1

The Hymn
Now let the earth with joy resound
And heaven the chant re-echo round;
Nor heaven nor earth too high can raise
The great Apostles' glorious praise!

Sickness and health your voice obey,
At your command they go or stay;
From sin's disease our souls restore,
In good confirm us more and more.

So when the world is at its end
And Christ to judgment shall descend,
May we be called those joys to see
Prepared from all eternity.

Praise to the Father, with the Son
And Paraclete for ever one:
To you, O most blessed Trinity
Be our praise for all time and for eternity.

adapted from THE SHORT BREVIARY

The Refrain for the Vespers Lessons
I tell you that if these followers of mine should hold their peace, the very stones
themselves would immediately cry out for joy.

based on Luke 19:40 KJV

The Vespers Psalm   *In Keeping of These There Is Great Reward*
The law of the Lord is perfect and revives the soul;* the testimony of the Lord is
sure and gives wisdom to the innocent.
The statutes of the Lord are just and rejoice the heart;* the commandment of the
Lord is clear and gives light to the eyes.
The fear of the Lord is clean and endures for ever;* the judgments of the Lord are
true and righteous altogether.
More to be desired are they than gold, more than much fine gold,* sweeter far than
honey, than honey in the comb.
By them also is your servant enlightened,* and in keeping them there is great
reward.

Psalm 19:7-11

The Refrain
I tell you that if these followers of mine should hold their peace, the very stones
themselves would immediately cry out for joy.

The Gloria

The Lord's Prayer

The Prayer Appointed for the Week
Almighty God, the fountain of all wisdom, you know my necessities before I ask
and my ignorance in asking: Have compassion on my weakness, and mercifully give me those things which for my unworthiness I dare not, and for my
blindness I cannot ask; through the worthiness of your Son Jesus Christ my
Lord, who lives and reigns with you and the Holy Spirit, one God, now and for
ever. *Amen.*†

The Concluding Prayer of the Church
Almighty God, who gave to your servant James boldness to confess the Name of
our Savior Jesus Christ before the rulers of this world, and courage to die for
this faith: Grant that I may always be ready to give a reason for the hope that is
in me, and to suffer gladly for the sake of my Lord Jesus Christ; who lives and
reigns with you and the Holy Spirit, one God, for ever and ever. *Amen.*†

The Morning Office   **To Be Observed on the Hour or Half Hour**
                                 Between 6 and 9 a.m.

The Call to Prayer
The Lord is King; let the people tremble;* he is enthroned upon the cherubim; let
the earth shake.

Psalm 99:1

The Request for Presence
Be pleased, O God, to deliver me;* O LORD, make haste to help me.

Psalm 70:1

The Greeting
You are my hope, O Lord GOD,* my confidence since I was young.

Psalm 71:5

The Refrain for the Morning Lessons
Know this, the LORD himself is God;* he himself has made us, and we are his; we are his people and the sheep of his pasture.

Psalm 100:2

A Reading
Jesus taught us, saying: 'But in those days, after that time of distress, the sun will be darkened, the moon will not give its light, the stars will come falling out of the sky and the powers in the heavens will be shaken. And then they will see the *Son of man coming in the clouds* with great power and glory. And then he will send the angels to gather his elect from the four winds, from the ends of the world to the ends of the sky.'

Mark 13:24–27

The Refrain
Know this, the LORD himself is God;* he himself has made us, and we are his; we are his people and the sheep of his pasture.

The Morning Psalm   *The LORD Has Become My Stronghold*
Can a corrupt tribunal have any part with you,* one which frames evil into law?
They conspire against the life of the just* and condemn the innocent to death.
But the LORD has become my stronghold,* and my God the rock of my trust.
He will turn their wickedness back upon them and destroy them in their own malice;* the LORD our God will destroy them.

Psalm 94:20–23

The Refrain
Know this, the LORD himself is God;* he himself has made us, and we are his; we are his people and the sheep of his pasture.

The Cry of the Church
In the evening, in the morning, and at noonday, I will complain and lament,* and he will hear my voice.

Psalm 55:18

The Lord's Prayer

The Prayer Appointed for the Week
Almighty God, the fountain of all wisdom, you know my necessities before I ask and my ignorance in asking: Have compassion on my weakness, and mercifully give me those things which for my unworthiness I dare not, and for my

blindness I cannot ask; through the worthiness of your Son Jesus Christ my Lord, who lives and reigns with you and the Holy Spirit, one God, now and for ever. *Amen.*†

The Concluding Prayer of the Church
Lord God, almighty and everlasting Father, you have brought me in safety to this new day: Preserve me with your mighty power, that I may not fall into sin, nor be overcome by adversity; and in all I do direct me to the fulfilling of your purpose; through Jesus Christ my Lord. *Amen.*†

The Midday Office   To Be Observed on the Hour or Half Hour
Between 11 a.m. and 2 p.m.

The Call to Prayer
Ascribe to the LORD, you families of the peoples;* ascribe to the LORD honor and power.
Ascribe to the LORD the honor due his Name.

Psalm 96:7–8

The Request for Presence
You are my crag and my stronghold.
Psalm 71:3

The Greeting
You have showed me great troubles and adversities,* but you will restore my life and bring me up again from the deep places of the earth.

Psalm 71:20

The Refrain for the Midday Lessons
Hallelujah! Happy are they who fear the Lord* and have great delight in his commandments!

Psalm 112:1

A Reading
The only thing you should owe to anyone is love for one another. For to love the other person is to fulfill the law. All these: *You shall not commit adultery, you shall not kill, you shall not steal, you shall not covet,* and all the other commandments are summed up in this single phrase: *You must love your neighbor as yourself.* Love can cause no harm to your neighbor; and so love is the fulfillment of the Law.

Romans 13:8–10

The Refrain
Hallelujah! Happy are they who fear the Lord* and have great delight in his commandments!

The Midday Psalm   *Happy Are They Who Consider the Poor and Needy*
Happy are they who consider the poor and needy!* The LORD will deliver them in the time of trouble.

The LORD preserves them and keeps them alive, so that they may be happy in the
land;* he does not hand them over to the will of their enemies.
The LORD sustains them on their sickbed* and ministers to them in their illness.

Psalm 41:1–3

The Refrain
Hallelujah! Happy are they who fear the Lord* and have great delight in his commandments!

The Small Verse
Lord, be merciful to me, a sinner.   Spirit, be merciful to me, a sinner.
Christ, be merciful to me, a sinner.   Lord, be merciful to me, a sinner.
Father, be merciful to me, a sinner.   *Traditional*

The Lord's Prayer

The Prayer Appointed for the Week
Almighty God, the fountain of all wisdom, you know my necessities before I ask
and my ignorance in asking: Have compassion on my weakness, and mercifully give me those things which for my unworthiness I dare not, and for my
blindness I cannot ask; through the worthiness of your Son Jesus Christ my
Lord, who lives and reigns with you and the Holy Spirit, one God, now and for
ever. *Amen.*†

The Concluding Prayer of the Church
Lord Jesus Christ, by your death you took away the sting of death: Grant me to so
follow in faith where you have led the way, that I may at length fall asleep
peacefully in you and wake in your likeness; for your tender mercies' sake.
Amen.†

The Vespers Office   To Be Observed on the Hour or Half Hour
Between 5 and 8 p.m.

The Call to Prayer
Praise the LORD, all you nations;* laud him, all you peoples.
For his loving-kindness toward us is great,* and the faithfulness of the LORD
endures for ever.

Psalm 117:1–2

The Request for Presence
Incline your ear to me and save me.

Psalm 71:2

The Greeting
You strengthen me more and more;* you enfold and comfort me.

Psalm 71:21

The Hymn   *When the Roll Is Called Up Yonder*
When the trumpet of the Lord shall sound, and time shall be no more,
And the morning breaks, eternal, bright, and fair;
Then the saved of earth shall gather over on the other shore,
And the roll is called up yonder, I'll be there.
When the roll is called up yonder,
When the roll is called up yonder,
When the roll is called up yonder,
When the roll is called up yonder, I'll be there.

On that bright and cloudless morning when the dead in Christ shall rise,
And the glory of His resurrection share;
When His chosen ones shall gather to their home beyond the skies,
And the roll is called up yonder, I'll be there.
When the roll is called up yonder,
When the roll is called up yonder,
When the roll is called up yonder,
When the roll is called up yonder, I'll be there.

Let us labor for the Master from the dawn till setting sun,
Let us talk of all His wondrous love and care;
Then when all of life is over, and our work on earth is done,
And the roll is called up yonder, I'll be there.
When the roll is called up yonder,
When the roll is called up yonder,
When the roll is called up yonder,
When the roll is called up yonder, I'll be there.

James M. Black

The Refrain for the Vespers Lessons
Though an army should encamp against me,* yet my heart shall not be afraid;
And though war should rise up against me,* yet will I put my trust in him.

Psalm 27:3–4

The Vespers Psalm   *He Strengthens Those in Whose Way He Delights*
Our steps are directed by the LORD;* he strengthens those in whose way he
    delights.
If they stumble, they shall not fall headlong,* for the LORD holds them by the hand.
I have been young and now I am old,* but never have I seen the righteous for-
    saken . . .

Psalm 37:14–16

The Refrain
Though an army should encamp against me,* yet my heart shall not be afraid;
And though war should rise up against me,* yet will I put my trust in him.

The Cry of the Church
O God, come to my assistance! O Lord, make haste to help me!

The Lord's Prayer

The Prayer Appointed for the Week
Almighty God, the fountain of all wisdom, you know my necessities before I ask
and my ignorance in asking: Have compassion on my weakness, and mercifully give me those things which for my unworthiness I dare not, and for my
blindness I cannot ask; through the worthiness of your Son Jesus Christ my
Lord, who lives and reigns with you and the Holy Spirit, one God, now and for
ever. *Amen.*†

The Concluding Prayers of the Church
Almighty God, who has promised to hear the petitions of those who ask in your
Son's Name: I beseech you mercifully to incline your ear to me who have made
my prayers and supplications to you; and grant that those things which I have
faithfully asked according to your will, may effectually be obtained, to the
relief of my necessity, and to setting forth of your glory; through Jesus Christ
my Lord. *Amen.*†

May the souls of the faithful departed, through the mercy of God, rest in eternal
peace. *Amen.*

The Morning Office   **To Be Observed on the Hour or Half Hour**
                                      Between 6 and 9 a.m.

The Call to Prayer
Bless the LORD, O my soul,* and all that is within me, bless his holy Name.
Psalm 103:1

The Request for Presence
Set watch before my mouth, O LORD, and guard the door of my lips;* let not my
heart incline to any living thing.
Let me not be occupied in wickedness with evildoers,* nor eat of their choice foods.
Let the righteous smite me in friendly rebuke; let not the oil of the unrighteous
anoint my head;* for my prayer is continually against their wicked deeds.
Let their rulers be overthrown in stony places,* that they may know my words are
true.
Psalm 141:3–6

The Greeting
Show me your ways, O LORD,* and teach me your paths.
Lead me in your truth and teach me,* for you are the God of my salvation; in you
have I trusted all the day long.
Psalm 25:3–4

The Refrain for the Morning Lessons
Your word is a lantern to my feet* and a light upon my path.
Psalm 119:105

A Reading

With a large crowd gathering and people from every town finding their way to him, he told this parable: 'A sower went out to sow his seed. Now as he sowed, some fell on the edge of the path and was trampled on; and the birds of the air ate it up. Some seed fell on rock, and when it came up it withered away, having no moisture. Some seed fell in the middle of thorns and the thorns grew with it and choked it. And some seed fell into good soil and grew and produced its crop a hundredfold.' Saying this he cried, 'Anyone who has ears for listening, should listen!'

His disciples asked him what his parable might mean, and he said, 'To you is granted to understand the secrets of the kingdom of God; for the rest it remains in parables, so that *they may look but not perceive, listen but not understand.*

'This, then, is what the parable means: the seed is the word of God. Those on the edge of the path are people who have heard it, and then the devil comes and carries away the word from their hearts in case they should believe and be saved. Those on the rock are people who, when they first hear it, welcome the word with joy. But these have no root; they believe for a while, and in a time of trial they give up. As for the part that fell into thorns, this is people who have heard, but as they go on their way they are choked up by the worries and riches and pleasures of life and never produce any crop. As for the part in the rich soil, this is people with a noble and generous heart who have heard the word and take it to themselves and yield a harvest through their perseverance.'

Luke 8:4–15

The Refrain

Your word is a lantern to my feet* and a light upon my path.

Psalm 119:105

The Morning Psalm   *The LORD Preserves All Those Who Love Him*

The LORD is near to those who call upon him,* to all who call upon him faithfully.
He fulfills the desire of those who fear him;* he hears their cry and helps them.
The LORD preserves all those who love him,* but he destroys all the wicked.

Psalm 145:19–21

The Refrain

Your word is a lantern to my feet* and a light upon my path.

Psalm 119:105

The Small Verse

I will remember the works of the LORD,* and call to mind your wonders of old time.
I will meditate on all your acts* and ponder your mighty deeds.

Psalm 77:11–12

The Lord's Prayer

The Prayer Appointed for the Week

Almighty God, the fountain of all wisdom, you know my necessities before I ask and my ignorance in asking: Have compassion on my weakness, and mercifully give me those things which for my unworthiness I dare not, and for my blindness I cannot ask; through the worthiness of your Son Jesus Christ my Lord, who lives and reigns with you and the Holy Spirit, one God, now and for ever. *Amen.*†

The Concluding Prayer of the Church
Lord God, almighty and everlasting Father, you have brought me in safety to this new day: Preserve me with your mighty power, that I may not fall into sin, nor be overcome by adversity; and in all I do direct me to the fulfilling of your purpose; through Jesus Christ my Lord. *Amen.*†

The Midday Office
To Be Observed on the Hour or Half Hour Between 11 a.m. and 2 p.m.

The Call to Prayer
Praise God, from whom all blessings flow; praise him, all creatures here below; praise him above, you heavenly hosts; praise Father, Son and Holy Ghost.

Traditional Doxology

The Request for Presence
So teach me to number my days* that I may apply my heart to wisdom.

based on Psalm 90:12

The Greeting
There is forgiveness in you;* therefore you shall be feared.

Psalm 130:3

The Refrain for the Midday Lessons
The merciful goodness of the Lord endures for ever on those who fear him,* and his righteous children's children.

Psalm 103:17

A Reading
Having hope for what we cannot yet see, we are able to wait for it with persevering confidence. And as well as this, the Spirit too comes to help us in weakness, for when we do not know how to pray properly, then the Spirit personally makes our petitions for us in groans that cannot be put into words, and he who can see into all hearts knows what the Spirit means because the prayers that the Spirit makes for God's holy people are always in accordance with the mind of God.

Romans 8:25–27

The Refrain
The merciful goodness of the Lord endures for ever on those who fear him,* and his righteous children's children.

The Midday Psalm   *Longing for the Courts of the* LORD

How dear to me is your dwelling, O LORD of hosts!* My soul has a desire and longing for the courts of the LORD; my heart and my flesh rejoice in the living God.

The sparrow has found her a house and the swallow a nest where she may lay her
young;* by the side of your altars, O LORD of hosts, my King and my God.

Happy are they who dwell in your house!* they will always be praising you.

Happy are the people whose strength is in you!* whose hearts are set on the pilgrims' way.

Psalm 84:1–4

The Refrain

The merciful goodness of the LORD endures for ever on those who fear him,* and
his righteous children's children.

The Small Verse

The Lord is my shepherd and nothing is wanting to me.* In green pastures He
hath settled me.

THE SHORT BREVIARY

The Lord's Prayer

The Prayer Appointed for the Week

Almighty God, the fountain of all wisdom, you know my necessities before I ask
and my ignorance in asking: Have compassion on my weakness, and mercifully give me those things which for my unworthiness I dare not, and for my
blindness I cannot ask; through the worthiness of your Son Jesus Christ my
Lord, who lives and reigns with you and the Holy Spirit, one God, now and for
ever. *Amen.*†

The Concluding Prayer of the Church

O God, the source of eternal light: Shed forth your unending day upon all of us
who watch for you, that our lips may praise you, our lives may bless you, and
our worship may give you glory; through Jesus Christ our Lord. *Amen.*†

The Vespers Office   **To Be Observed on the Hour or Half Hour**
Between 5 and 8 p.m.

The Call to Prayer

Proclaim the greatness of the LORD our God and worship him upon his holy hill;*
for the LORD our God is the Holy One.

Psalm 99:9

The Request for Presence

Send out your light and your truth, that they may lead me,* and bring me to your
holy hill and to your dwelling.

Psalm 43:3

The Greeting

The LORD lives! Blessed is my Rock!* Exalted is the God of my salvation!

Psalm 18:46

The Hymn   *Come, Thou Almighty King*

Come, Thou Almighty King,   Come, holy Comforter,
Help us Thy name to sing,   Thy sacred witness bear,
Help us to praise: In this glad hour;
Father all-glorious,   Thou who almighty art,
O'er all victorious,   Now rule in every heart,
Come, and reign over us,   And never from us depart,
Ancient of days!   Spirit of power!

Come, Thou incarnate Word,   To the great One in Three,
Gird on Thy mighty sword,   The highest praises be
Our prayer attend,   Hence, evermore!
Come and Thy people bless,   His sovereign majesty
And give Thy Word success: May we in glory see,
Spirit of holiness,   And to eternity
On us descend!   Love and adore!

Charles Wesley

The Refrain for the Vespers Lessons

Behold, the eye of the LORD is upon those who fear him,* on those who wait upon
     his love,
To pluck their lives from death,* and to feed them in the time of famine.

Psalm 33:18–19

The Vespers Psalm   *Offer to God a Sacrifice of Thanksgiving*

Hear, O my people, and I will speak: "O Israel, I will bear witness against you;* for
     I am God, your God.
I do not accuse you because of your sacrifices;* your offerings are always before me.
I will take no bull-calf from your stalls,* nor he-goats out of your pens;
For all the beasts of the forest are mine,* the herds in their thousands upon the hills.
I know every bird in the sky,* and the creatures of the fields are in my sight.
If I were hungry, I would not tell you,* for the whole world is mine and all that is
     in it.
Do you think I eat the flesh of bulls,* or drink the blood of goats?
Offer to God a sacrifice of thanksgiving* and make good your vows to the Most
     High.
Call upon me in the day of trouble;* I will deliver you, and you shall honor me."

Psalm 50:7–15

The Refrain

Behold, the eye of the LORD is upon those who fear him,* on those who wait upon
     his love,
To pluck their lives from death,* and to feed them in the time of famine.

The Gloria

The Lord's Prayer

The Prayer Appointed for the Week
Almighty God, the fountain of all wisdom, you know my necessities before I ask
and my ignorance in asking: Have compassion on my weakness, and mercifully
give me those things which for my unworthiness I dare not, and for my blindness I cannot ask; through the worthiness of your Son Jesus Christ my Lord, who
lives and reigns with you and the Holy Spirit, one God, now and for ever. *Amen.*†

The Concluding Prayer of the Church
Almighty God, who after the creation of the world rested from all your works and
sanctified a day of rest for all your creatures: Grant that I, putting away all
earthly anxieties, may be duly prepared for the service of public worship, and
grant as well that my Sabbath upon earth may be a preparation for the eternal
rest promised to your people in heaven; through Jesus Christ our Lord. *Amen.*†

The Morning Office   **To Be Observed on the Hour or Half Hour
                                 Between 6 and 9 a.m.**

The Call to Prayer
Ascribe to the LORD, you families of the peoples;* ascribe to the LORD honor and
    power.
Ascribe to the LORD the honor due his Name;* bring offerings and come into his
    courts.
Worship the LORD in the beauty of holiness;* let the whole earth tremble before him.
                                                            Psalm 96:7–9

The Request for Presence
Bow your heavens, O LORD, and come down;* touch the mountains, and they shall
    smoke.
                                                            Psalm 144:5

The Greeting
My heart sings to you without ceasing;* O LORD my God, I will give you thanks
    for ever.
                                                            Psalm 30:13

The Refrain for the Morning Lessons
Who can declare the mighty acts of the LORD* or show forth all his praise?
                                                            Psalm 106:2

A Reading

Then the seventh angel blew his trumpet, and voices could be heard shouting in heaven, calling, 'The kingdom of the world has become the kingdom of our Lord and his Christ, and he will reign for ever and for ever.' The twenty-four elders enthroned in the presence of God, prostrated themselves and touched the ground with their foreheads worshipping God with these words, 'We give thanks to you, Almighty Lord God, He who is, He who was, for assuming your great power and beginning your reign. *The nations were in uproar* and now the time has come for your retribution, and for the dead to be judged, and for *your servants the prophets,* for the saints and for all *those who fear* your name, *small and great alike,* to be rewarded. The time has come to destroy those who are destroying the earth.' Then the sanctuary of God in heaven opened, and the ark of the covenant could be seen inside it. Then came flashes of lightning, peals of thunder and an earthquake, and violent hail.

Revelation 11:15–19

The Refrain

Who can declare the mighty acts of the LORD* or show forth all his praise?

Psalm 106:2

The Morning Psalm   *Let the Hills Ring Out with Joy Before the LORD*

Let the sea make a noise and all that is in it,* the lands and those that dwell therein.
Let the rivers clap their hands,* and let the hills ring out with joy before the LORD,
    when he comes to judge the earth.
In righteousness shall he judge the world* and the peoples with equity.

Psalm 98:8–10

The Refrain

Who can declare the mighty acts of the LORD* or show forth all his praise?

Psalm 106:2

The Gloria

The Lord's Prayer

The Prayer Appointed for the Week

O God, the protector of all who trust in you, without whom nothing is strong, nothing is holy: Increase and multiply upon all your faithful people your mercy; that, with you as our ruler and guide, we may so pass through things temporal, that we lose not the things eternal; through Jesus Christ our Lord, who lives and reigns with you and the Holy Spirit, one God, for ever and ever. *Amen.*†

The Concluding Prayer of the Church

Lord God, almighty and everlasting Father, you have brought me in safety to this new day: Preserve me with your mighty power, that I may not fall into sin, nor be overcome by adversity; and in all I do direct me to the fulfilling of your purpose; through Jesus Christ my Lord. *Amen.*†

The Midday Office **To Be Observed on the Hour or Half Hour**
Between 11 a.m. and 2 p.m.

The Call to Prayer
Tell it out among the nations: "The LORD is King!* he has made the world so firm
that it cannot be moved; he will judge the peoples with equity."

Psalm 96:10

The Request for Presence
Let the peoples praise you, O God;* let all peoples praise you.

Psalm 67:3

The Greeting
Awesome things will you show us in your righteousness, O God of salvation,*
O Hope of all the ends of the earth.

Psalm 65:5

The Refrain for the Midday Lessons
My soul is consumed at all times* with longing for your judgments.

Psalm 119:20

A Reading
What race deserves honor? The human race.
What race deserves honor? Those who fear the Lord.
What race deserves contempt? The human race.
What race deserves contempt? Those who break the commandments.
Among brothers the leader of them deserves honor,
and those who fear the Lord deserve honor in his sight.
Let rich and noble and poor
take pride in fearing the Lord.
It is not right to despise a poor but intelligent man,
and it is not good to honor a man who is a sinner.
Ruler, magistrate, influential man, all are to be honored,
but none of them is greater than him who fears the Lord.

Ecclesiasticus 10:19–24

The Refrain
My soul is consumed at all times* with longing for your judgments.

Psalm 119:20

The Midday Psalm *Happy Are They Who Observe His Decrees*
Happy are they whose way is blameless,* who walk in the law of the LORD!
Happy are they who observe his decrees* and seek him with all their hearts!
Who never do any wrong,* but always walk in his ways.

Psalm 119:1–3

The Refrain
My soul is consumed at all times* with longing for your judgments.

Psalm 119:20

The Small Verse

From the rising of the sun to the place of its going down, let the name of the Lord
be praised henceforth and forever more.

Traditional

The Lord's Prayer

The Prayer Appointed for the Week

O God, the protector of all who trust in you, without whom nothing is strong,
nothing is holy: Increase and multiply upon all your faithful people your mercy;
that, with you as our ruler and guide, we may so pass through things temporal,
that we lose not the things eternal; through Jesus Christ our Lord, who lives and
reigns with you and the Holy Spirit, one God, for ever and ever. *Amen.*†

The Concluding Prayer of the Church

O God, you make me glad with the weekly remembrance of the glorious resurrection of your Son my Lord: Give me this day such blessing through my worship
of you, that the week to come may be spent in your favor; through Jesus Christ
our Lord. *Amen.*†

The Vespers Office   **To Be Observed on the Hour or Half Hour**
                                                          Between 5 and 8 p.m.

The Call to Prayer

Open my lips, O Lord,* and my mouth shall proclaim your praise.

Psalm 51:16

The Request for Presence

Gladden the soul of your servant,* for to you, O Lord, I lift up my soul.

Psalm 86:4

The Greeting

Happy are the people whose strength is in you!* whose hearts are set on the pilgrims' way.

Psalm 84:4

The Reading   *A Hymn of David*

Bless the Lord, O my soul;* O Lord my God, how excellent is your greatness! You
are clothed with majesty and splendor.

You wrap yourself with light as with a cloak* and spread out the heavens as a
curtain.

You lay the beams of your chambers in the waters above;* you make the clouds
your chariot; you ride on the wings of the wind.

You make the winds your messengers* and flames of fire your servants.

You have set the earth upon its foundations,* so that it never shall move at any time.

You covered it with the Deep as with a mantle;* the waters stood higher than the
mountains.

At your rebuke they fled,* at the voice of your thunder they hastened away.
They went up into the hills and down to the valleys beneath,* to the places you
    had appointed for them.
You set the limits that they should not pass;* they shall not again cover the earth.
You send the springs into the valleys;* they flow between the mountains.
All the beasts of the wild drink their fill from them,* and the wild asses quench
    their thirst.
Beside them the birds of the air make their nests* and sing among the branches.
You water the mountains from your dwelling on high;* the earth is fully satisfied
    by the fruit of your works.
You make grass grow for flocks and herds* and plants to serve mankind;
That they may bring forth food from the earth,* and wine to gladden our hearts,
Oil to make a cheerful countenance,* and bread to strengthen the heart.
The trees of the LORD are full of sap,* the cedars of Lebanon which he planted,
In which the birds build their nests,* and in whose top the stork makes his dwelling.
The high hills are a refuge for the mountain goats,* and his stony cliffs for the rock
    badgers.
You appointed the moon to mark the seasons,* and the sun knows the time of its
    setting.
You make darkness that it may be night,* in which all the beasts of the forest prowl.
The lions roar after their prey* and seek their food from God.
The sun rises, and they slip away* and lay themselves down in their dens.
Man goes forth to his work* and to his labor until evening.
I will sing to the LORD as long as I live;* I will praise my God while I have my
    being.
May these words of mine please him;* I will rejoice in the LORD.

Psalm 104:1–24, 34–35

The Refrain for the Vespers Lessons
I will exalt you, O God my King,* and bless your Name for ever and ever.

Psalm 145:1

The Vespers Psalm   I Commune with My Heart in the Night
I consider the days of old;* I remember the years long past;
I commune with my heart in the night;* I ponder and search my mind.

Psalm 77:5–6

The Refrain
I will exalt you, O God my King,* and bless your Name for ever and ever.

The Gloria

The Lord's Prayer

The Prayer Appointed for the Week
O God, the protector of all who trust in you, without whom nothing is strong,
    nothing is holy: Increase and multiply upon all your faithful people your

mercy; that, with you as our ruler and guide, we may so pass through things temporal, that we lose not the things eternal; through Jesus Christ our Lord, who lives and reigns with you and the Holy Spirit, one God, for ever and ever. *Amen.*†

The Concluding Prayer of the Church
Lord God, whose Son our Savior Jesus Christ, triumphed over the powers of death and prepared for us our place in the new Jerusalem: Grant that I, who have this day given thanks for his resurrection, may praise you in the City of which he is the light, and where he lives and reigns for ever and ever. *Amen.*†

The Morning Office   **To Be Observed on the Hour or Half Hour Between 6 and 9 a.m.**

The Call to Prayer
Be joyful in the LORD, all you lands;* serve the LORD with gladness and come before his presence with a song.

Psalm 110:1

The Request for Presence
I have said to the LORD, "You are my God;* listen, O LORD, to my supplication."

Psalm 140:6

The Greeting
Whom have I in heaven but you?* and having you I desire nothing upon earth.

Psalm 73:25

The Refrain for the Morning Lessons
The LORD has sworn and he will not recant:* "You are a priest for ever after the order of Melchizedek."

Psalm 110:4

A Reading
And so the Lord Jesus, after he had spoken to them, was taken up into heaven: there at the right hand of God he took his place, while they, going out, preached everywhere, the Lord working with them and confirming the word by the signs that accompanied it.

Mark 16:19–20

The Refrain
The LORD has sworn and he will not recant:* "You are a priest for ever after the order of Melchizedek."

The Morning Psalm   *May All the Nations Call Him Blessed*
Long may he live! And may there be given to him gold from Arabia;* may prayer be made for him always, and may they bless him all the day long.
May there be abundance of grain on the earth, growing thick even on the hilltops;* may its fruit flourish like Lebanon, and its grain like grass upon the earth.

May his Name remain for ever and be established as long as the sun endures;*
  may all the nations bless themselves in him and call him blessed.

Psalm 72:15–17

The Refrain
The LORD has sworn and he will not recant:* "You are a priest for ever after the
  order of Melchizedek."

The Cry of the Church
Lord, have mercy on us. Christ, have mercy on us. Lord, have mercy on us.

The Lord's Prayer

The Prayer Appointed for the Week
O God, the protector of all who trust in you, without whom nothing is strong,
  nothing is holy: Increase and multiply upon all your faithful people your
  mercy; that, with you as our ruler and guide, we may so pass through things
  temporal, that we lose not the things eternal; through Jesus Christ our Lord,
  who lives and reigns with you and the Holy Spirit, one God, for ever and ever.
  Amen.†

The Concluding Prayer of the Church
Lord God, almighty and everlasting Father, you have brought me in safety to this
  new day: Preserve me with your mighty power, that I may not fall into sin, nor
  be overcome by adversity; and in all I do direct me to the fulfilling of your purpose; through Jesus Christ my Lord. *Amen.*†

The Midday Office **To Be Observed on the Hour or Half Hour
Between 11 a.m. and 2 p.m.**

The Call to Prayer
Proclaim the greatness of the LORD our God and fall down before his footstool;* he
  is the Holy One.
Proclaim the greatness of the LORD our God* and worship him upon his holy hill;
  for the LORD our God is the Holy One.

Psalm 99:5, 9

The Request for Presence
For God alone my soul in silence waits;* truly, my hope is in him.

Psalm 62:6

The Greeting
To you I lift up my eyes,* to you enthroned in the heavens.
As the eyes of servants look to the hand of their masters,* and the eyes of the maid
  to the hand of her mistress,
So our eyes look to the LORD our God,* until he shows us his mercy.

Psalm 123:1–3

The Refrain for the Midday Lessons

The LORD has sworn and he will not recant:* "You are a priest for ever after the order of Melchizedek."

Psalm 110:4

A Reading

The spirit of Lord YAHWEH is in me for YAHWEH has anointed me. He has sent me to bring good news to the afflicted, to soothe the broken-hearted, to proclaim liberty to captives, release to those in prison; to proclaim a year of favor from YAHWEH, and a day of vengeance for our God, to comfort all who mourn (to give to Zion's mourners), to give them for ashes a garland, for mourning dress, the oil of gladness, for despondency, festal attire; and they will be called 'terebinths of saving justice,' planted by YAHWEH to glorify him. They will rebuild the ancient ruins, they will raise what has long lain waste, they will restore the ruined cities, all that has lain waste for ages past.

Isaiah 61:1–4

The Refrain

The LORD has sworn and he will not recant:* "You are a priest for ever after the order of Melchizedek."

The Midday Psalm   The LORD Comes in Holiness from Sinai

The LORD gave the word;* great was the company of women who bore the tidings:
"Kings with their armies are fleeing away;* the women at home are dividing the spoils."
Though you have lingered among the sheepfolds,* you shall be like a dove whose wings are covered with silver, whose feathers like green gold.
When the Almighty scattered kings,* it was like snow falling in Zalmon.
O mighty mountain, O hill of Bashan!* O rugged mountain, O hill of Bashan!
Why do you look with envy, O rugged mountain, at the hill which God chose for his resting place?* truly, the LORD will dwell there for ever.
The chariots of God are twenty thousand, even thousands of thousands;* the LORD comes in holiness from Sinai.

Psalm 68:11–17

The Refrain

The LORD has sworn and he will not recant:* "You are a priest for ever after the order of Melchizedek."

The Cry of the Church

O Lamb of God, that takes away the sins of the world, have mercy upon me.
O Lamb of God, that takes away the sins of the world, have mercy upon me.
O Lamb of God, that takes away the sins of the world, grant me your peace.

The Lord's Prayer

The Prayer Appointed for the Week

O God, the protector of all who trust in you, without whom nothing is strong, nothing is holy: Increase and multiply upon all your faithful people your mercy; that, with you as our ruler and guide, we may so pass through things temporal, that we lose not the things eternal; through Jesus Christ our Lord, who lives and reigns with you and the Holy Spirit, one God, for ever and ever. *Amen.*✝

The Concluding Prayer of the Church

O God, you both comfort me and disturb my complacency through your Spirit. May I recognize the blind, the lame and the prisoner in the circumstances of my life, and understand my call to proclaim the good news to the poor. I ask this through Jesus who is my way, my truth and my life. *Amen.*

adapted from The New Companion to the Breviary

The Vespers Office   **To Be Observed on the Hour or Half Hour Between 5 and 8 p.m.**

The Call to Prayer

Let the heavens rejoice, and let the earth be glad; let the sea thunder and all that is in it;* let the field be joyful and all that is therein.

Then shall all the trees of the wood shout for joy before the LORD when he comes,* when he comes to judge the earth.

Psalm 96:11–12

The Request for Presence

May God be merciful to us and bless us,* show us the light of his countenance and come to us.

Psalm 67:1

The Greeting

For you alone are the Holy One, you alone are the Lord, you alone are the Most High, Jesus Christ, with the Holy Spirit, in the glory of God the Father.

The Hymn   *Hail to the Lord's Anointed*

Hail to the Lord's Anointed,
Great David's greater Son!
Hail, in the time appointed,
His reign on earth begun!
He comes to break oppression,
To set the captive free;
To take away transgression,
And rule in equity.

He comes with succor speedy
To those who suffer wrong,
To help the poor and needy,
And bid the weak be strong;
To give them songs for sighing,
Their darkness turn to light,
Whose souls, condemned and dying,
Were precious in his sight.

Hail to the Lord's Anointed,
Great David's greater Son!
Hail, in the time appointed,
His reign on earth begun!
He comes to break oppression,
To set the captive free;
To take away transgression,
And rule in equity.

James Montgomery

The Refrain for the Vespers Lessons
You strengthen me more and more;* you enfold and comfort me.

Psalm 71:21

The Vespers Psalm   *O Mighty Lord, Your Faithfulness Is All Around Us*
Who is like you, Lord God of hosts?* O mighty Lord, your faithfulness is all
    around you.
You rule the raging of the sea* and still the surging of its waves.
You have crushed Rahab of the deep with a deadly wound;* you have scattered
    your enemies with your mighty arm.
Yours are the heavens; the earth is yours also;* you laid the foundations of the
    world and all that is in it.
You have made both the north and the south;* Tabor and Hermon rejoice in your
    name.
You have a mighty arm;* strong is your hand and high is your right hand.
Righteousness and justice are the foundations of your throne;* love and truth go
    before your face.

Psalm 89:8–14

The Refrain
You strengthen me more and more;* you enfold and comfort me.

The Cry of the Church
Lord, have mercy on us. Christ, have mercy on us. Lord, have mercy on us.

The Lord's Prayer

The Prayer Appointed for the Week
O God, the protector of all who trust in you, without whom nothing is strong,
nothing is holy: Increase and multiply upon all your faithful people your
mercy; that, with you as our ruler and guide, we may so pass through things
temporal, that we lose not the things eternal; through Jesus Christ our Lord,
who lives and reigns with you and the Holy Spirit, one God, for ever and ever.
Amen.✝

The Concluding Prayer of the Church
O God, the author of peace and lover of concord, to know you is eternal life and to
serve you is perfect freedom: Defend me, your humble servant, in all the

assaults of my enemies; that I, surely trusting in your defense, may not fear the power of any adversary; through the might of Jesus Christ my Lord. *Amen.*†

The Morning Office

To Be Observed on the Hour or Half Hour Between 6 and 9 a.m.

The Call to Prayer
Be joyful to the LORD, all you lands;* serve the LORD with gladness and come before his presence with a song.

Psalm 100:1

The Request for Presence
Show us the light of your countenance, O God,* and come to us.

based on Psalm 67:1

The Greeting
Splendor and honor and kingly power are yours by right, O Lord our God . . . For you created everything that is, and by your will they were created and have their being.

Revelation 4:11, 5:9ff

The Refrain for the Morning Lessons
Great are the deeds of the LORD!* they are studied by all who delight in them.

Psalm 111:2

A Reading
Jesus taught us, saying: 'I give you a new commandment: love one another; you must love one another just as I have loved you. It is by your love for one another, that everyone will recognize you as my disciples.'

John 13:34–35

The Refrain
Great are the deeds of the LORD!* they are studied by all who delight in them.

The Morning Psalm   *This God Is Our God For Ever and Ever*
Your praise, like your Name, O God, reaches to the world's end;* your right hand is full of justice.
Let Mount Zion be glad and the cities of Judah rejoice,* because of your judgments.
Make the circuit of Zion; walk round about her;* count the number of her towers.
Consider well her bulwarks; examine her strongholds;* that you may tell those who come after.
This God is our God for ever and ever;* he shall be our guide for evermore.

Psalm 48:8–13

The Refrain
Great are the deeds of the LORD!* they are studied by all who delight in them.

The Small Verse
'I am the Alpha and the Omega,' says the Lord God, who is, who was, and who is
to come, the Almighty.

Revelation 1:8

The Lord's Prayer

The Prayer Appointed for the Week
O God, the protector of all who trust in you, without whom nothing is strong,
nothing is holy: Increase and multiply upon all your faithful people your
mercy; that, with you as our ruler and guide, we may so pass through things
temporal, that we lose not the things eternal; through Jesus Christ our Lord,
who lives and reigns with you and the Holy Spirit, one God, for ever and ever.
Amen.†

The Concluding Prayer of the Church
Lord God, almighty and everlasting Father, you have brought me in safety to this
new day: Preserve me with your mighty power, that I may not fall into sin, nor
be overcome by adversity; and in all I do direct me to the fulfilling of your purpose; through Jesus Christ my Lord. *Amen.*†

The Midday Office   **To Be Observed on the Hour or Half Hour**
Between 11 a.m. and 2 p.m.

The Call to Prayer
Sing to the LORD and bless his Name;* proclaim the good news of his salvation
from day to day.
Declare his glory among the nations* and his wonders among all the peoples.

Psalm 96:2–3

The Request for Presence
I have gone astray like a sheep that is lost;* search for your servant, for I do not
forget your commandments.

Psalm 119:176

The Greeting
Not to us, O LORD, not to us, but to your Name give glory;* because of your love
and because of your faithfulness.

Psalm 115:1

The Refrain for the Midday Lessons
He will judge the world with righteousness* and the people with his truth.

Psalm 96:13

A Reading
Bless your persecutors; never curse them, bless them. Rejoice with others when
they rejoice and be sad with those in sorrow. Give the same consideration to all

others alike. Pay no regard to social standing, but meet humble people on their own terms. Do not congratulate yourself on your own wisdom. Never try to get revenge: leave that, my dear friends, to the Retribution. As scripture says: *Vengeance is mine—I will pay them back*, the Lord promises. And more: *If your enemy is hungry, give him something to eat, if thirsty, something to drink. By this you will be heaping red-hot coals on his head*. Do not be mastered by evil, but master evil with good.

Romans 12:14–21

The Refrain
He will judge the world with righteousness* and the people with his truth.

The Midday Psalm   The Law of Their God Is in Their Heart
Turn from evil, and do good,* and dwell in the land for ever.
For the LORD loves justice;* he does not forsake his faithful ones.
They shall be kept safe for ever,* but the offspring of the wicked shall be
    destroyed.
The righteous shall possess the land* and dwell in it for ever.
The mouth of the righteous utters wisdom,* and their tongue speaks what is right.
The law of their God is in their heart,* and their footsteps shall not falter.

Psalm 37:28–33

The Refrain
He will judge the world with righteousness* and the people with his truth.

The Small Verse
Create in me a clean heart, O God,* and renew a right spirit within me.
Cast me not away from your presence* and take not your holy Spirit from me.
Give me the joy of your saving help again* and sustain me with your bountiful
    spirit.

Psalm 51:11–13

The Lord's Prayer

The Prayer Appointed for the Week
O God, the protector of all who trust in you, without whom nothing is strong,
    nothing is holy: Increase and multiply upon all your faithful people your
    mercy; that, with you as our ruler and guide, we may so pass through things
    temporal, that we lose not the things eternal; through Jesus Christ our Lord,
    who lives and reigns with you and the Holy Spirit, one God, for ever and ever.
    Amen.†

The Concluding Prayer of the Church
Almighty and eternal God, ruler of all things in heaven and earth: Mercifully
    accept the prayers of your people everywhere, and strengthen each of us to do
    your will; through Jesus Christ my Lord. *Amen.†*

The Vespers Office   **To Be Observed on the Hour or Half Hour**
                                           Between 5 and 8 p.m.

The Call to Prayer
Come, let us bow down, and bend the knee.* And kneel before the LORD our Maker.
For he is our God, and we are the people of his pasture and the sheep of his hand.*
    Oh, that today you would hearken to his voice!

Psalm 95:6–7

The Request for Presence
Remember not our past sins;* let your compassion be swift to meet us.

Psalm 79:8

The Greeting
Remember your word to your servant,* because you have given me hope.
This is my comfort in my trouble,* that your promise gives me life.

Psalm 119:49–50

The Hymn

There's a wideness in God's mercy
Like the wideness of the sea.
There's a kindness in His justice,
Which is more than liberty.

There's no place where earth's sorrows
Are felt more than they are in heaven;
There's no place where earth's failings
Have such kindly judgment given.

For the love of God is broader
Than the measures of man's mind,
And the heart of the Eternal
Is most wonderfully kind.

There is plentiful redemption
In the blood that has been shed;
There is joy for all the members
In the sorrows of the Head.

If our love were but more simple
We should take Him at His word;
And our lives would be all sunshine
In the goodness of the Lord.

Frederick W. Faber

The Refrain for the Vespers Lessons
For the LORD is good; his mercy is everlasting;* and his faithfulness endures from
    age to age.

Psalm 100:4

The Vespers Psalm   *The LORD Watches Over the Innocent*
I love the LORD, because he has heard the voice of my supplication,* because he
    has inclined his ear to me whenever I called upon him.
The cords of death entangled me; the grip of the grave took hold of me;* I came to
    grief and sorrow.
Then I called upon the Name of the LORD:* "O LORD, I pray you, save my life."
Gracious is the LORD and righteous;* our God is full of compassion.
The LORD watches over the innocent;* I was brought very low, and he helped me.

Psalm 116:1–5

The Refrain
For the LORD is good; his mercy is everlasting;* and his faithfulness endures from age to age.

The Cry of the Church
O God, come to my assistance! O Lord, make haste to help me!

The Lord's Prayer

The Prayer Appointed for the Week
O God, the protector of all who trust in you, without whom nothing is strong, nothing is holy: Increase and multiply upon all your faithful people your mercy; that, with you as our ruler and guide, we may so pass through things temporal, that we lose not the things eternal; through Jesus Christ our Lord, who lives and reigns with you and the Holy Spirit, one God, for ever and ever. *Amen.*†

The Concluding Prayer of the Church
O God, the King eternal, whose light divides the day from the night and turns the shadow of death into the morning: Drive far from me all wrong desires, incline my heart to keep your law, and guide my feet into the way of peace; that, having done your will with cheerfulness during the day, I may, when night comes, rejoice to give you thanks; through Jesus Christ my Lord. *Amen.*†

The Morning Office   **To Be Observed on the Hour or Half Hour Between 6 and 9 a.m.**

The Call to Prayer
Come, let us sing to the LORD;* let us shout for joy to the Rock of our salvation.
Let us come before his presence with thanksgiving* and raise a loud shout to him with psalms.

Psalm 95:1–2

The Request for Presence
To you I lift up my eyes,* to you enthroned in the heavens.

Psalm 123:1

The Greeting
You are the LORD most high over all the earth;* you are exalted far above all gods.

Psalm 97:9

The Refrain for the Morning Lessons
For as the heavens are high above the earth,* so is his mercy great upon those who fear him.

Psalm 103:11

A Reading
When Jesus spoke to the people again, he said: 'I am the light of the world; anyone who follows me will not be walking in the dark; but will have the light of life.'

John 8:12

The Refrain
For as the heavens are high above the earth,* so is his mercy great upon those who
fear him.

The Morning Psalm   *In the Temple of the LORD All Are Crying, "Glory!"*
Ascribe to the LORD the glory due his name;* worship the LORD in the beauty of
holiness.
The voice of the LORD is upon the waters; the God of glory thunders;* the LORD is
upon the mighty waters.
The voice of the LORD is a powerful voice;* the voice of the LORD is a voice of
splendor.
The voice of the LORD breaks cedar trees;* the LORD breaks the cedars of Lebanon;
He makes Lebanon skip like a calf,* and Mount Hermon like a young wild ox.
The voice of the LORD splits the flames of fire; the voice of the LORD shakes the
wilderness;* the LORD shakes the wilderness of Kadesh.
The voice of the LORD makes the oak trees writhe* and strips the forest bare.
And in the temple of the LORD* all are crying, "Glory!"
The LORD sits enthroned above the flood;* the LORD sits enthroned as King for
evermore.
The LORD shall give strength to his People;* the LORD shall give his people the
blessing of peace.

Psalm 29:2–11

The Refrain
For as the heavens are high above the earth,* so is his mercy great upon those who
fear him.

The Gloria

The Lord's Prayer

The Prayer Appointed for the Week
O God, the protector of all who trust in you, without whom nothing is strong,
nothing is holy: Increase and multiply upon all your faithful people your
mercy; that, with you as our ruler and guide, we may so pass through things
temporal, that we lose not the things eternal; through Jesus Christ our Lord,
who lives and reigns with you and the Holy Spirit, one God, for ever and ever.
Amen.†

The Concluding Prayer of the Church
Lord God, almighty and everlasting Father, you have brought me in safety to this
new day: Preserve me with your mighty power, that I may not fall into sin, nor
be overcome by adversity; and in all I do direct me to the fulfilling of your purpose; through Jesus Christ my Lord. *Amen.*†

The Midday Office	To Be Observed on the Hour or Half Hour
	Between 11 a.m. and 2 p.m.

The Call to Prayer
Let the sea make a noise and all that is in it,* the lands and those who dwell
    therein.
Let the rivers clap their hands,* and let the hills ring out with joy before the LORD,
    when he comes to judge the earth.
In righteousness shall he judge the world* and the peoples with equity.

Psalm 98:8–10

The Request for Presence
Make me understand the way of your commandments,* that I may meditate on
    your marvelous works.

Psalm 119:27

The Greeting
LORD you have been our refuge* from one generation to another.
Before the mountains were brought forth, or the land and the earth were born,*
    from age to age you are God.

Psalm 90:1–2

The Refrain for the Midday Lessons
Happy are they who fear the LORD,* and follow in his ways!

Psalm 128:1

A Reading
It is of the mysterious wisdom of God that we talk, the wisdom that was hidden,
    which God predestined to be for our glory before the ages began. None of the
    rulers of the age recognized it; for if they had recognized it, they would not
    have crucified the Lord of glory; but it is as scripture says: *what no eye has seen
    and no ear has heard, what the mind of man cannot visualize, all that God has prepared
    for those who love him,* to us, though, God has given revelation through the
    Spirit, for the Spirit explores the depths of everything, even the depths of God.
    After all, is there anyone who knows the qualities of anyone except his own
    spirit, within him; and in the same way, nobody knows the qualities of God
    except the Spirit of God.

I Corinthians 2:7–11

The Refrain
Happy are they who fear the LORD,* and follow in his ways!

The Midday Psalm   *Come and Listen*
Come and listen, all you who fear God,* and I will tell you what he has done for me.
I called out to him with my mouth,* and his praise was on my tongue.
If I had found evil in my heart,* the Lord would not have heard me;

But in truth God has heard me;* he has attended to the voice of my prayer.
Blessed be God, who has not rejected my prayer,* nor withheld his love from me.

Psalm 66:14–18

The Refrain
Happy are they who fear the LORD,* and follow in his ways!

The Small Verse
Into your hands I commend my spirit for you have redeemed me, O God of my life. Glory be to the Father, and to the Son and to the comforting Spirit.

Traditional

The Lord's Prayer

The Prayer Appointed for the Week
O God, the protector of all who trust in you, without whom nothing is strong, nothing is holy: Increase and multiply upon all your faithful people your mercy; that, with you as our ruler and guide, we may so pass through things temporal, that we lose not the things eternal; through Jesus Christ our Lord, who lives and reigns with you and the Holy Spirit, one God, for ever and ever. *Amen.†*

The Concluding Prayer of the Church
Almighty and everlasting God, by whose Spirit the whole body of your faithful people is governed and sanctified: Receive my supplications and prayers which I offer before you for all members of your holy Church, that in our vocation and ministry we may in truth and in godliness serve you all the days of our lives; through Jesus Christ our Lord. *Amen.†*

The Vespers Office   To Be Observed on the Hour or Half Hour Between 5 and 8 p.m.

The Call to Prayer
Oh, the majesty and magnificence of his presence!* Oh, the power and the splendor of his sanctuary!
Ascribe to the LORD, you families of the peoples;* ascribe to the LORD honor and power.

Psalm 96:6–7

The Request for Presence
Answer me when I call, O God, the defender of my cause;* you set me free when I am hard-pressed; have mercy on me and hear my prayer.

Psalm 4:1

The Greeting
In you, O LORD, have I taken refuge;* let me never be ashamed.

Psalm 71:1

The Hymn

Firmly I believe and truly	And I hold in veneration,
God is three and God is one;	For the love of him alone,
And next I acknowledge duly	Holy Church as his creation,
Manhood taken by the Son.	And her teachings as his own.
And I trust and hope most fully	Praise and thanks be ever given
In that manhood crucified;	With and through the angel host,
And I love supremely, solely	To the God of earth and heaven,
Christ who for my sins has died.	Father, Son and Holy Ghost.

John H. Newman

The Refrain for the Vespers Lessons

Among the gods there is none like you, O Lord,* nor anything like your works.

Psalm 86:8

The Vespers Psalm   *Let Them Offer a Sacrifice of Thanksgiving*

He sent forth his word and healed them* and saved them from the grave.

Let them give thanks to the Lord for his mercy* and the wonders he does for his children.

Let them offer a sacrifice of thanksgiving* and tell of his acts with shouts of joy.

Psalm 107:20–22

The Refrain

Among the gods there is none like you, O Lord,* nor anything like your works.

The Gloria

The Lord's Prayer

The Prayer Appointed for the Week

O God, the protector of all who trust in you, without whom nothing is strong, nothing is holy: Increase and multiply upon all your faithful people your mercy; that, with you as our ruler and guide, we may so pass through things temporal, that we lose not the things eternal; through Jesus Christ our Lord, who lives and reigns with you and the Holy Spirit, one God, for ever and ever. *Amen.†*

The Concluding Prayer of the Church

Save me, O Lord, while I am awake, and keep me while I sleep that I may wake in Christ and rest in peace.

adapted from The Short Breviary

The Morning Office   **To Be Observed on the Hour or Half Hour**
Between 6 and 9 a.m.

The Call to Prayer

Be joyful in the Lord, all you lands;* serve the Lord with gladness and come before his presence with a song.

Psalm 100:1–2

The Request for Presence
Turn to me and have mercy upon me;* give your strength to your servant; and
save the child of your handmaid.

Psalm 86:16

The Greeting
O Lord, what are we that you should care for us?* mere mortals that you should
think of us?
We are like a puff of wind;* our days are like a passing shadow.

Psalm 144:3–4

The Refrain for the Morning Lessons
Blessed be the Lord day by day,* the God of our salvation, who bears our burdens.

Psalm 68:19

A Reading
Jesus taught us, saying: 'Come to me, all you who labor and are overburdened,
and I will give you rest. Shoulder my yoke and learn from me, for I am gentle
and humble in heart, *and you will find rest for your souls.* Yes, my yoke is easy
and my burden light.'

Matthew 11:28

The Refrain
Blessed be the Lord day by day,* the God of our salvation, who bears our burdens.

The Morning Psalm *In the Shadow of Your Wings Will I Take My Refuge*
Be merciful to me, O God, be merciful, for I have taken refuge in you;* in the
shadow of your wings will I take refuge until the time of trouble has gone by.
I will call upon the Most High God,* the God who maintains my cause.
He will send from heaven and save me; he will confound those who trample upon
me;* God will send forth his love and his faithfulness.
I lie in the midst of lions that devour the people;* their teeth are spears and
arrows, their tongue a sharp sword.
They have laid a net for my feet, and I am bowed low;* they have dug a pit before
me, but have fallen into it themselves.

Psalm 57:1–5

The Refrain
Blessed be the Lord day by day,* the God of our salvation, who bears our burdens.

The Cry of the Church
O Lamb of God, that takes away the sins of the world, have mercy upon me.
O Lamb of God, that takes away the sins of the world, have mercy upon me.
O Lamb of God, that takes away the sins of the world, grant me your peace.

The Lord's Prayer

The Prayer Appointed for the Week
O God, the protector of all who trust in you, without whom nothing is strong, nothing is holy: Increase and multiply upon all your faithful people your mercy; that, with you as our ruler and guide, we may so pass through things temporal, that we lose not the things eternal; through Jesus Christ our Lord, who lives and reigns with you and the Holy Spirit, one God, for ever and ever. *Amen.*†

The Concluding Prayer of the Church
Lord God, almighty and everlasting Father, you have brought me in safety to this new day: Preserve me with your mighty power, that I may not fall into sin, nor be overcome by adversity; and in all I do direct me to the fulfilling of your purpose; through Jesus Christ my Lord. *Amen.*†

The Midday Office   **To Be Observed on the Hour or Half Hour Between 11 a.m. and 2 p.m.**

The Call to Prayer
Let us make a vow to the LORD our God and keep it;* let all around him bring gifts to him who is worthy to be feared.

Psalm 76:11

The Request for Presence
You are good and you bring forth good;* instruct me in your statutes.

Psalm 119:68

The Greeting
Your way, O God, is holy;* who is as great as our God?

Psalm 77:13

The Refrain for the Midday Lessons
The LORD is near to those who call upon him,* to all who call upon him faithfully.

Psalm 146:19

A Reading
But now—declares YAHWEH—come back to me with all your heart, fasting, weeping, mourning. Tear your hearts and not your clothes, and come back to YAHWEH your God, for he is gracious and compassionate, slow to anger, rich in faithful love, and he relents about inflicting disaster.

Joel 2:12–13

The Refrain
The LORD is near to those who call upon him,* to all who call upon him faithfully.

The Midday Psalm   *He Judges the People with Equity*
The LORD is enthroned for ever;* he has set up his throne for judgment.
It is he who rules the world with righteousness;* he judges the people with equity.
The LORD will be a refuge for the oppressed,* a refuge in a time of trouble.

Those who know your Name will put their trust in you,* for you never forsake those who seek you, O LORD.

Psalm 9:7–10

The Refrain
The LORD is near to those who call upon him,* to all who call upon him faithfully.

The Gloria

The Lord's Prayer

The Prayer Appointed for the Week
O God, the protector of all who trust in you, without whom nothing is strong, nothing is holy: Increase and multiply upon all your faithful people your mercy; that, with you as our ruler and guide, we may so pass through things temporal, that we lose not the things eternal; through Jesus Christ our Lord, who lives and reigns with you and the Holy Spirit, one God, for ever and ever. *Amen.*†

The Concluding Prayer of the Church
O God, who has made of one blood all the peoples of the earth, and sent your blessed Son to preach to those of us who are far off and to those of us who are near: Grant that people everywhere may seek after you and find you; bring the nations into your fold; pour out your spirit upon all flesh; and hasten the coming of your kingdom; through the same, your Son Jesus Christ our Lord. *Amen.*†

The Vespers Office **To Be Observed on the Hour or Half Hour Between 5 and 8 p.m.**

The Call to Prayer
Bless the LORD, you angels of his, you mighty ones who do his bidding,* and hearken to the voice of his word.
Bless the LORD, all you his hosts,* you ministers of his who do his will.
Bless the LORD, all you works of his, in all places of his dominion;* bless the LORD, O my soul.

Psalm 103:20–22

The Request for Presence
Show us the light of your countenance, O God,* and come to us.

based on Psalm 67:1

The Greeting
I will confess you among the peoples, O LORD;* I will sing praises to you among the nations.
For your loving-kindness is greater than the heavens,* and your faithfulness reaches to the clouds.

Psalm 108:3–4

The Hymn   ***By Thee I Would Be Blessed***

Jesu, by thee I would be blessed!   Jesu, in mercy be my guide,
Jesu, pray give my spirit rest.   Jesu, when I by grief am tried!
The springs of life I fain would know   Be thou my refuge from this day
that from thy pierced side do flow.   that I may ever near thee stay.

Jesu, when foes encompass me,   Jesu, grant me eternal bliss.
Jesu, be near to comfort me.   Jesu, I ask no joy but this:
Protect me with thy grace divine: My heart and voice on high to raise
no help avails save only thine.   To thee in never-ending praise.

Anonymous

The Refrain for the Vespers Lessons

Let my prayer be set forth in your sight as incense,* the lifting up of my hands as
the evening sacrifice.

Psalm 141:2

The Vespers Psalm   ***Enfold and Comfort Me***

Your righteousness, O God, reaches to the heavens;* you have done great things;
who is like you, O God?

You have showed me great troubles and adversities,* but you will restore my life
and bring me up again from the deep places of the earth.

You strengthen me more and more;* you enfold and comfort me.

Psalm 71:19–21

The Refrain

Let my prayer be set forth in your sight as incense,* the lifting up of my hands as
the evening sacrifice.

The Cry of the Church

O God, come to my assistance! O Lord, make haste to help me!

The Lord's Prayer

The Prayer Appointed for the Week

O God, the protector of all who trust in you, without whom nothing is strong,
nothing is holy: Increase and multiply upon all your faithful people your
mercy; that, with you as our ruler and guide, we may so pass through things
temporal, that we lose not the things eternal; through Jesus Christ our Lord,
who lives and reigns with you and the Holy Spirit, one God, for ever and ever.
Amen.†

The Concluding Prayer of the Church

O God, whose glory it is always to have mercy: Be gracious to all of us who have
gone astray from your ways, and bring us again with penitent hearts and
steadfast faith to embrace and hold fast the unchangeable truth of your Word,
Jesus Christ your Son; who with you and the Holy Spirit lives and reigns, one
God, for ever and ever. *Amen.*†

The Morning Office   **To Be Observed on the Hour or Half Hour**
                                          Between 6 and 9 a.m.

The Call to Prayer
Let all who seek you rejoice and be glad in you;* let those who love your salvation
  say for ever, "Great is the LORD!"

Psalm 70:4

The Request for Presence
But as for me, I am poor and needy;* come to me speedily, O God.

Psalm 70:5

The Greeting
O LORD, I am your servant;* I am your servant and the child of your handmaid;
  you have freed me from my bonds.

Psalm 116:14

The Refrain for the Morning Lessons
Our days are like the grass;* we flourish like a flower of the field.

Psalm 103:15

A Reading
He called the people to him again and said, 'Listen to me, all of you, and understand. Nothing that goes into someone from outside can make that person
  unclean; it is the things that come out of someone that make that person
  unclean. . . . For it is from within, from the heart, that evil intentions emerge:
  fornication, theft, murder, adultery, avarice, malice, deceit, indecency, envy,
  slander, pride, folly. All these evil things come from within and make a person
  unclean.'

Mark 7:14–15, 21–23

The Refrain
Our days are like the grass;* we flourish like a flower of the field.

The Morning Psalm   *Teach Us to Number Our Days*
Our iniquities you have set before you,* and our secret sins in the light of your
  countenance.
When you are angry, all our days are gone;* we bring our years to an end like a
  sigh.
The span of our life is seventy years, perhaps in strength even eighty;* yet the sum
  of them is but labor and sorrow, for they pass away quickly and we are gone.
Who regards the power of your wrath?* who rightly fears your indignation?
So teach us to number our days* that we may apply our hearts to wisdom.

Psalm 90:8–12

The Refrain
Our days are like the grass;* we flourish like a flower of the field.

The Cry of the Church
O Lamb of God, that takes away the sins of the world, have mercy upon me.
O Lamb of God, that takes away the sins of the world, have mercy upon me.
O Lamb of God, that takes away the sins of the world, grant me your peace.

The Lord's Prayer

The Prayer Appointed for the Week
O God, the protector of all who trust in you, without whom nothing is strong,
nothing is holy: Increase and multiply upon all your faithful people your mercy;
that, with you as our ruler and guide, we may so pass through things temporal,
that we lose not the things eternal; through Jesus Christ our Lord, who lives and
reigns with you and the Holy Spirit, one God, for ever and ever. *Amen.*†

The Concluding Prayer of the Church
Lord God, almighty and everlasting Father, you have brought me in safety to this
new day: Preserve me with your mighty power, that I may not fall into sin, nor
be overcome by adversity; and in all I do direct me to the fulfilling of your purpose; through Jesus Christ my Lord. *Amen.*†

The Midday Office   **To Be Observed on the Hour or Half Hour**
                                    Between 11 a.m. and 2 p.m.

The Call to Prayer
I will call upon God,* and the LORD will deliver me.
In the evening, in the morning, and at the noonday, I will complain and lament,*
and he will hear my voice.
He will bring me safely back . . .* God, who is enthroned of old, will hear me.

Psalm 55:17ff

The Request for Presence
Out of the depths I called to you, O LORD; LORD, hear my voice;* let your ears consider well the voice of my supplication.

Psalm 130:1

The Greeting
LORD, how great are your works!* your thoughts are very deep.
The dullard does not know, nor does the fool understand,* that though the wicked
grow like weeds, and all the workers of iniquity flourish,
They flourish only to be destroyed for ever;* but you, O LORD, are exalted for ever-
more.

Psalm 92:5–7

The Refrain for the Midday Lessons
I will cry aloud to God;* I will cry aloud, and he will hear me.

Psalm 77:1

A Reading

Heal me, YAHWEH, and I shall be healed, save me and I shall be saved, for you are
my praise.

Jeremiah 17:14

The Refrain

I will cry aloud to God;* I will cry aloud, and he will hear me.

The Midday Psalm   *Steadfast Love Is Yours, O LORD*

Put your trust in him always, O people,* pour out your hearts before him, for God
is our refuge.

Those of high degree are but a fleeting breath,* even those of low estate cannot be
trusted.

On the scale they are lighter than a breath,* all of them together.

Put no trust in extortion; in robbery take no empty pride;* though wealth increase,
set not your heart upon it.

God has spoken once, twice have I heard it,* that power belongs to God.

Steadfast love is yours, O LORD,* for you repay everyone according to his deeds.

Psalm 62:9–14

The Refrain

I will cry aloud to God;* I will cry aloud, and he will hear me.

The Cry of the Church

Even so, come Lord Jesus!

The Lord's Prayer

The Prayer Appointed for the Week

O God, the protector of all who trust in you, without whom nothing is strong,
nothing is holy: Increase and multiply upon all your faithful people your mercy;
that, with you as our ruler and guide, we may so pass through things temporal,
that we lose not the things eternal; through Jesus Christ our Lord, who lives and
reigns with you and the Holy Spirit, one God, for ever and ever. *Amen.*†

The Concluding Prayer of the Church

Lord Jesus Christ, by your death you took away the sting of death: Grant me to so
follow in faith where you have led the way, that I may at length fall asleep peacefully in you and wake in your likeness; for your tender mercies' sake. *Amen.*†

The Vespers Office   **To Be Observed on the Hour or Half Hour**
Between 5 and 8 p.m.

The Call to Prayer

Come, let us sing to the LORD;* let us shout for joy to the Rock of our salvation.

Let us come before his presence with thanksgiving* and raise a loud shout to him
with psalms.

For the LORD is a great God,* and a great king above all gods.

Psalm 95:1–3

The Request for Presence
In your righteousness, deliver me and set me free;* incline your ear to me and
save me.

Psalm 71:2

The Greeting
Your testimonies are very sure,* and holiness adorns your house, O LORD, for ever
and for evermore.

Psalm 93:6

The Hymn   *A Prayer on Freedom*
Free at last, free at last,
Thank God Almighty, I'm free at last.

I was a sinner just like you,
Thank God Almighty, I'm free at last.
I prayed and mourned till I came through,
Thank God Almighty, I'm free at last.

I never shall forget the day,
Thank God Almighty, I'm free at last.
When Jesus washed my sins away,
Thank God Almighty, I'm free at last.

The very time I thought I was lost,
Thank God Almighty, I'm free at last.
My dungeon shook and my chains fell off
Thank God Almighty, I'm free at last.

This is religion, I do know,
Thank God Almighty, I'm free at last.
For I never felt such a love before,
Thank God Almighty, I'm free at last.

Traditional

The Refrain for the Vespers Lessons
God is my shield and defense;* he is the savior of the true in heart.

Psalm 7:11

The Vespers Psalm   *You Are My Refuge, My Portion in the Land of the Living*
I cry to you, O LORD;* I say, "You are my refuge, my portion in the land of the living."
Listen to my cry for help, for I have been brought very low;* save me from those
who pursue me, for they are too strong for me.
Bring me out of prison, that I may give thanks to your Name;* when you have
dealt bountifully with me, the righteous will gather around me.

Psalm 142:5–7

The Refrain
God is my shield and defense;* he is the savior of the true in heart.

The Gloria

The Lord's Prayer

The Prayer Appointed for the Week
O God, the protector of all who trust in you, without whom nothing is strong,
    nothing is holy: Increase and multiply upon all your faithful people your mercy;
    that, with you as our ruler and guide, we may so pass through things temporal,
    that we lose not the things eternal; through Jesus Christ our Lord, who lives and
    reigns with you and the Holy Spirit, one God, for ever and ever. *Amen.†*

The Concluding Prayers of the Church
Almighty God, who has promised to hear the petitions of those who ask in your
    Son's Name: I beseech you mercifully to incline your ear to me who have made
    my prayers and supplications to you; and grant that those things which I have
    faithfully asked according to your will, may effectually be obtained, to the
    relief of my necessity, and to the setting forth of your glory; through Jesus
    Christ my Lord. *Amen.†*

May the souls of the faithful departed, through the mercy of God, rest in eternal
    peace. *Amen.*

The Morning Office   **To Be Observed on the Hour or Half Hour**
                                       Between 6 and 9 a.m.

The Call to Prayer
Be joyful in God, all you lands;* sing the glory of his name; sing the glory of his
    praise.
Say to God, "How awesome are your deeds! All the earth bows down before you,*
    sings to you, sings out your Name."

Psalm 66:1–3

The Request for Presence
Let your loving-kindness, O LORD, be upon us,* as we have put our trust in you.

Psalm 33:22

The Greeting
For you have made me glad by your acts, O LORD;* and I shout for joy because of
    the works of your hands.

Psalm 92:4

The Refrain for the Morning Lessons
He who dwells in the shelter of the Most High,* abides under the shadow of the
    Almighty.

Psalm 91:1

A Reading

Jesus taught us, saying: 'Peace I bequeath to you, my own peace I give you, a peace which the world cannot give, this is my gift to you. Do not let your hearts be troubled or afraid. You heard me say: I am going away, and shall return.'

John 14:27–28

The Refrain

He who dwells in the shelter of the Most High,* abides under the shadow of the Almighty.

The Morning Psalm   *My Help Comes from the LORD*

I lift up my eyes to the hills;* from where is my help to come?
My help comes from the LORD,* the maker of heaven and earth.
He will not let your foot be moved* and he who watches over you will not fall asleep.
Behold, he who keeps watch over Israel* shall neither slumber nor sleep;
The LORD himself watches over you;* the LORD is your shade at your right hand,
So that the sun shall not strike you by day,* nor the moon by night.
The LORD shall preserve you from all evil;* it is he who shall keep you safe.
The LORD shall watch over your going out and your coming in,* from this time forth for evermore.

Psalm 121

The Refrain

He who dwells in the shelter of the Most High,* abides under the shadow of the Almighty.

The Small Verse

May God himself order my days and make them acceptable in his sight. Blessed is the Lord always, my strength and my redeemer.

Traditional

The Lord's Prayer

The Prayer Appointed for the Week

O God, the protector of all who trust in you, without whom nothing is strong, nothing is holy: Increase and multiply upon all your faithful people your mercy; that, with you as our ruler and guide, we may so pass through things temporal, that we lose not the things eternal; through Jesus Christ our Lord, who lives and reigns with you and the Holy Spirit, one God, for ever and ever. *Amen.*†

The Concluding Prayer of the Church

Lord God, almighty and everlasting Father, you have brought me in safety to this new day: Preserve me with your mighty power, that I may not fall into sin, nor be overcome by adversity; and in all I do direct me to the fulfilling of your purpose; through Jesus Christ my Lord. *Amen.*†

The Midday Office　　　　　　　**To Be Observed on the Hour or Half Hour**
　　　　　　　　　　　　　　　　　　Between 11 a.m. and 2 p.m.

The Call to Prayer
Enter his gates with thanksgiving; go into his courts with praise;* give thanks to
　　him and call upon his Name.

Psalm 100:3

The Request for Presence
Test me, O Lord, and try me;* examine my heart and mind.
For your love is before my eyes;* I have walked faithfully with you.
I have not sat with the worthless,* nor do I consort with the deceitful.
I have hated the company of evildoers;* I will not sit down with the wicked.
I will wash my hands in innocence, O Lord,* that I may go in procession round
　　your altar,
Singing aloud a song of thanksgiving* and recounting all your wonderful deeds.

Psalm 26:2–7

The Greeting
It is a good thing to give thanks to the Lord,* and to sing praises to your Name, O
　　Most High;
To tell of your loving-kindness early in the morning* and of your faithfulness in
　　the night season.

Psalm 92:1–2

The Refrain for the Midday Lessons
Everyday will I bless you* and praise your Name for ever and ever.

Psalm 145:2

A Reading
If you refrain from breaking the Sabbath, and from taking your own pleasure on
　　my holy day, if you call the Sabbath 'Delightful,' and the day sacred to Yahweh
　　'Honorable,' if you honor it by abstaining from travel, from seeking your own
　　pleasure and from too much talk, then you will find true happiness in Yahweh,
　　and I shall lead you in triumph over the heights of the land. I shall feed you on
　　the heritage of your father Jacob, for the mouth of Yahweh has spoken.

Isaiah 58:13–14

The Refrain
Every day will I bless you* and praise your Name for ever and ever.

The Midday Psalm Let Everything That Has Breath Praise the Lord
Hallelujah! Praise God in his holy temple;* praise him in the firmament of his
　　power.
Praise him for his mighty acts;* praise him for his excellent greatness.

Praise him with the blast of the ram's-horn;* praise him with lyre and harp.
Praise him with timbrel and dance;* praise him with strings and pipe.
Praise him with resounding cymbals;* praise him loud-clanging cymbals.
Let everything that has breath* praise the LORD. Hallelujah!

Psalm 150:1–6

The Refrain
Every day will I bless you* and praise your Name for ever and ever.

The Gloria

The Lord's Prayer

The Prayer Appointed for the Week
O God, the protector of all who trust in you, without whom nothing is strong,
nothing is holy: Increase and multiply upon all your faithful people your mercy;
that, with you as our ruler and guide, we may so pass through things temporal,
that we lose not the things eternal; through Jesus Christ our Lord, who lives and
reigns with you and the Holy Spirit, one God, for ever and ever. *Amen.*†

The Concluding Prayer of the Church
O God, the source of eternal light: Shed forth your unending day upon all of us
who watch for you, that our lips may praise you, our lives may bless you, and
our worship may give you glory; through Jesus Christ our Lord. *Amen.*†

The Vespers Office **To Be Observed on the Hour or Half Hour
Between 5 and 8 p.m.**

The Call to Prayer
Open my lips, O LORD,* and my mouth shall proclaim your praise.

Psalm 51:16

The Request for Presence
Let your countenance shine upon your servant* and teach me your statutes.

Psalm 119:135

The Greeting
Oh, the majesty and magnificence of his presence!* Oh, the power and the
splendor of his sanctuary!

Psalm 96:6

The Hymn   *The Canticle of St. Patrick*
   I arise today
   Through the strength of heaven:
   Light of the sun,
   Radiance of the moon,
   Splendor of fire,
   Speed of lightning,
   Swiftness of wind,
   Depth of sea,
   Stability of earth,
   Firmness of rock.

   I arise today
   Through God's strength to pilot me:
   God's might to uphold me,
   God's wisdom to guide me,
   God's eye to look before me,
   God's ear to hear me,
   God's word to speak for me,
   God's hand to guard me,
   God's way to lie before me,
   God's shield to protect me,
   God's hosts to save me,
   From snares of devils,
   . . . From everyone who shall wish me ill.
   Afar or near,
   Alone and in a multitude. . . .

   Christ with me, Christ before me, Christ behind me,
   Christ in me, Christ beneath me, Christ above me,
   Christ on my right, Christ on my left,
   Christ when I lie down, Christ when I sit down, Christ when I arise,
   Christ in the heart of everyone who thinks of me,
   Christ in the mouth of everyone who speaks of me,
   Christ in every eye that sees me,
   Christ in the ear that hears me.

                                          St. Patrick

The Refrain for the Vespers Lessons
I will sing to the LORD as long as I live;* I will praise my God while I have my being.
                                          Psalm 104:34

The Vespers Psalm   *I Begin with the Mighty Works of the Lord GOD*
But I shall always wait in patience,* and shall praise you more and more.
My mouth shall recount your mighty acts and saving deeds all day long;* though I
   cannot know the number of them.

I begin with the mighty works of the Lord GOD:* I will recall your righteousness, yours alone.

O God, you have taught me since I was young,* and to this day I tell of your wonderful works.

Psalm 71:14–17

The Refrain
I will sing to the LORD as long as I live;* I will praise my God while I have my being.

The Small Verse
Keep me, Lord, as the apple of your eye and carry me under the shadow of your wings.

Traditional

The Lord's Prayer

The Prayer Appointed for the Week
O God, the protector of all who trust in you, without whom nothing is strong, nothing is holy: Increase and multiply upon all your faithful people your mercy; that, with you as our ruler and guide, we may so pass through things temporal, that we lose not the things eternal; through Jesus Christ our Lord, who lives and reigns with you and the Holy Spirit, one God, for ever and ever. *Amen.*✝

The Concluding Prayer of the Church
Almighty God, who after the creation of the world rested from all your works and sanctified a day of rest for all your creatures: Grant that I, putting away all earthly anxieties, may be duly prepared for the service of public worship, and grant as well that my Sabbath upon earth may be a preparation for the eternal rest promised to your people in heaven; through Jesus Christ our Lord. *Amen.*✝

July Compline

Sunday
The Night Office   **To Be Observed Before Retiring**

The Call to Prayer
May the Lord Almighty grant me and those I love a peaceful night and a perfect
end. *Amen.*†

The Request for Presence
Our help is in the Name of the Lord;* the maker of heaven and earth.

Psalm 124:8

The Greeting
Almighty God, my heavenly Father: I have sinned against you, through my own
fault, in thought, and word, and deed, and in what I have left undone. For the
sake of your Son our Lord Jesus Christ, forgive me all my offenses; and grant
that I may serve you in newness of life, to the glory of your Name. *Amen.*†

The Reading   *A Canticle of the Mystery*
I write this to you in the hope that I may be able to come to you soon; but in case I
should be delayed, I want you to know . . . [that] Without any doubt, the mystery of our religion is very deep indeed: He was made visible in the flesh, justified in the Spirit, seen by angels, proclaimed to the gentiles, believed in
throughout the world, taken up in glory.

I Timothy 3:14–16

The Gloria

The Psalm   *Bless the Lord, All You His Hosts*
Bless the Lord, you angels of his, you mighty ones who do his bidding,* and hear-
ken to the voice of his word.
Bless the Lord, all you his hosts,* you ministers of his who do his will.
Bless the Lord, all you works of his, in all places of his dominion;* bless the Lord,
O my soul.

Psalm 103:20–22

The Gloria

The Small Verse
Into your hands, O Lord, I commend my spirit; for you have redeemed me, O
Lord, O God of truth. Keep me, O Lord, as the apple of your eye; hide me
under the shadow of your wings.†

The Lord's Prayer

The Petition
Lord, hear my prayers; And let my cry come to you.†

The Final Thanksgiving
Lord, you now have set your servant free to go in peace as you have promised; for
these eyes of mine have seen the Savior, whom you have prepared for all the

world to see: a Light to enlighten the nations, and the glory of your people Israel. Glory to the Father, and to the Son, and to the Holy Spirit: as it was in the beginning, is now, and will be for ever. *Amen.*

⁊❊⳾

Monday
The Night Office   **To Be Observed Before Retiring**

The Call to Prayer
May the Lord Almighty grant me and those I love a peaceful night and a perfect end. *Amen.*†

The Request for Presence
Our help is in the Name of the Lord;* the maker of heaven and earth.

Psalm 124:8

The Greeting
Almighty God, my heavenly Father: I have sinned against you, through my own fault, in thought, and word, and deed, and in what I have left undone. For the sake of your Son our Lord Jesus Christ, forgive me all my offenses; and grant that I may serve you in newness of life, to the glory of your Name. *Amen.*†

The Reading
I believe in God, the Father almighty,
  creator of heaven and earth.
I believe in Jesus Christ, his only Son, our Lord.
  He was conceived by the power of the Holy Spirit and born of the Virgin
    Mary.
  He suffered under Pontius Pilate, was crucified, died, and was buried.
  He descended to the dead.
  On the third day he rose again.
  He ascended into heaven, and is seated at the right hand of the Father.
  He will come again to judge the living and the dead.
I believe in the Holy Spirit,
  the holy universal Church,
  the communion of saints,
  the forgiveness of sins,
  the resurrection of the body,
  and the life everlasting. *Amen.*

The Apostles' Creed

The Gloria

The Psalm   *I Will Dwell in Your House For Ever*
For you have been my refuge,* a strong tower against the enemy.
I will dwell in your house for ever;* I will take refuge under the cover of your
     wings.
For you, O God, have heard my vows;* you have granted me the heritage of those
     who fear your Name.

                                                              Psalm 61:3–5

The Gloria

The Small Verse
Into your hands, O Lord, I commend my spirit; For you have redeemed me, O
     Lord, O God of truth. Keep me, O Lord, as the apple of your eye; Hide me
     under the shadow of your wings.†

The Lord's Prayer

The Petition
Lord, hear my prayers; And let my cry come to you.†

The Final Thanksgiving
Lord, you now have set your servant free to go in peace as you have promised; for
     these eyes of mine have seen the Savior, whom you have prepared for all the
     world to see: a Light to enlighten the nations, and the glory of your people
     Israel. Glory to the Father, and to the Son, and to the Holy Spirit: as it was in the
     beginning, is now, and will be for ever. *Amen.*

৵৺৲

Tuesday
The Night Office   **To Be Observed Before Retiring**

The Call to Prayer
May the Lord Almighty grant me and those I love a peaceful night and a perfect
     end. *Amen.*†

The Request for Presence
Our help is in the Name of the Lord;* the maker of heaven and earth.

                                                              Psalm 124:8

The Greeting
Almighty God, my heavenly Father: I have sinned against you, through my own
     fault, in thought, and word, and deed, and in what I have left undone. For the
     sake of your Son our Lord Jesus Christ, forgive me all my offenses; and grant
     that I may serve you in newness of life, to the glory of your Name. *Amen.*†

The Reading
From the heart of the tempest . . . YAHWEH said, 'Who is this, obscuring my intentions with his ignorant words? Brace yourself like a fighter; I am going to ask the questions, and you are to inform me! Where were you when I laid the earth's foundations? Tell me since you are so well-informed! Who decided the dimensions, do you know? Or who stretched the measuring line across it? What supports its pillars at their bases? Who laid its cornerstone to the joyful concert of the morning stars and unanimous acclaim of the sons of God? Who pent up the sea behind closed doors when it leapt tumultuous from the womb, when I wrapped it in a robe of mist and made black clouds its swaddling bands; when I cut out the place I had decreed for it and imposed gates and a bolt? "Come so far," I said, "and no further; here your proud waves must break!" '

Job 38:1–11

The Gloria

The Psalm   *Praise Him in the Heights*
Hallelujah! Praise the LORD from the heavens;* praise him in the heights.
Praise him, all you angels of his;* praise him, all his host.
Praise him, sun and moon;* praise him, all you shining stars.
Praise him, heaven of heavens,* and you waters above the heavens.
Let them praise the Name of the LORD;* for he commanded, and they were created.
He made them stand fast for ever and ever;* he gave them a law which shall not pass away.

Psalm 148:1–6

The Gloria

The Small Verse
Into your hands, O Lord, I commend my spirit; For you have redeemed me, O Lord, O God of truth. Keep me, O Lord, as the apple of your eye; Hide me under the shadow of your wings.†

The Lord's Prayer

The Petition
Lord, hear my prayers; And let my cry come to you.†

The Final Thanksgiving
Lord, you now have set your servant free to go in peace as you have promised; for these eyes of mine have seen the Savior, whom you have prepared for all the world to see: a Light to enlighten the nations, and the glory of your people Israel. Glory to the Father, and to the Son, and to the Holy Spirit: as it was in the beginning, is now, and will be for ever. *Amen.*

༄

Wednesday
The Night Office   To Be Observed Before Retiring

The Call to Prayer
May the Lord Almighty grant me and those I love a peaceful night and a perfect
    end. *Amen.*†

The Request for Presence
Our help is in the Name of the LORD;* the maker of heaven and earth.
                                                            Psalm 124:8

The Greeting
Almighty God, my heavenly Father: I have sinned against you, through my own
    fault, in thought, and word, and deed, and in what I have left undone. For the
    sake of your Son our Lord Jesus Christ, forgive me all my offenses; and grant
    that I may serve you in newness of life, to the glory of your Name. *Amen.*†

The Reading
I have been crucified with Christ and yet I am alive; yet it is no longer I, but Christ
    living in me.
The life that I am now living, subject to the limitation of human nature, I am living
    in faith, faith in the Son of God who loved me and gave himself for me.
                                                            Galatians 2:20–21

The Gloria

The Psalm   *I Have Said, "You Are My God"*
. . . as for me, I have trusted in you, O LORD,* I have said, "You are my God.
My times are in your hand;* rescue me from the hand of my enemies, and from
    those who persecute me.
Make your face to shine upon your servant,* and in your loving-kindness save
    me."
LORD, let me not be ashamed for having called upon you . . .
                                                            Psalm 31:14–17

The Gloria

The Small Verse
Into your hands, O Lord, I commend my spirit; For you have redeemed me, O
    Lord, O God of truth. Keep me, O Lord, as the apple of your eye; Hide me
    under the shadow of your wings.†

The Lord's Prayer

The Petition
Lord, hear my prayers; And let my cry come to you.†

The Final Thanksgiving
Lord, you now have set your servant free to go in peace as you have promised; for these eyes of mine have seen the Savior, whom you have prepared for all the world to see: a Light to enlighten the nations, and the glory of your people Israel. Glory to the Father, and to the Son, and to the Holy Spirit: as it was in the beginning, is now, and will be for ever. *Amen.*

Thursday
The Night Office   **To Be Observed Before Retiring**

The Call to Prayer
May the Lord Almighty grant me and those I love a peaceful night and a perfect end. *Amen.*†

The Request for Presence
Our help is in the Name of the LORD;* the maker of heaven and earth.

Psalm 124:8

The Greeting
Almighty God, my heavenly Father: I have sinned against you, through my own fault, in thought, and word, and deed, and in what I have left undone. For the sake of your Son our Lord Jesus Christ, forgive me all my offenses; and grant that I may serve you in newness of life, to the glory of your Name. *Amen.*†

The Reading
On the last day, the great day of the festival, Jesus stood and cried out: 'Let anyone who is thirsty come to me! Let anyone who believes in me come and drink! As scripture says, "From his heart shall flow streams of living water." ' He was speaking of the Spirit which those who believed in Him were to receive; for there was no Spirit as yet because Jesus had not yet been glorified.

John 7:37–39

The Gloria

The Psalm   *My Help Comes from the LORD*
I lift up my eyes to the hills;* from where is my help to come?
My help comes from the LORD,* the maker of heaven and earth.

He will not let your foot be moved* and he who watches over you will not fall
asleep.

Behold, he who keeps watch over Israel* shall neither slumber nor sleep;

Psalm 121:1–4

The Gloria

The Small Verse

Into your hands, O Lord, I commend my spirit; For you have redeemed me, O
Lord, O God of truth. Keep me, O Lord, as the apple of your eye; Hide me
under the shadow of your wings.†

The Lord's Prayer

The Petition

Lord, hear my prayers; And let my cry come to you.†

The Final Thanksgiving

Lord, you now have set your servant free to go in peace as you have promised; for
these eyes of mine have seen the Savior, whom you have prepared for all the
world to see: a Light to enlighten the nations, and the glory of your people
Israel. Glory to the Father, and to the Son, and to the Holy Spirit: as it was in the
beginning, is now, and will be for ever. *Amen.*

‿❊♪

Friday
The Night Office   **To Be Observed Before Retiring**

The Call to Prayer

May the Lord Almighty grant me and those I love a peaceful night and a perfect
end. *Amen.*†

The Request for Presence

Our help is in the Name of the LORD;* the maker of heaven and earth.

Psalm 124:8

The Greeting

Almighty God, my heavenly Father: I have sinned against you, through my own
fault, in thought, and word, and deed, and in what I have left undone. For the
sake of your Son our Lord Jesus Christ, forgive me all my offenses; and grant
that I may serve you in newness of life, to the glory of your Name. *Amen.*†

The Reading

Listen, my God, listen to us. . . . Relying not on our upright deeds but on your
great mercy, we pour out our plea to you. Listen, Lord! Forgive, Lord! Hear,
Lord, and act! For your own sake, my God, do not delay—since your city and
your people alike bear your name.

Daniel 9:18ff

The Gloria

The Psalm   *Do Not Tarry, O My God*

Let all who seek you rejoice in you and be glad;* let those who love your salvation
continually say, "Great is the LORD!"
Though I am poor and afflicted,* the LORD will have regard for me.
You are my helper and my deliverer;* do not tarry, O my God.

Psalm 40:17–19

The Gloria

The Small Verse

Into your hands, O Lord, I commend my spirit; for you have redeemed me, O
Lord, O God of truth. Keep me, O Lord, as the apple of your eye; hide me
under the shadow of your wings.†

The Lord's Prayer

The Petition

Lord, hear my prayers; And let my cry come to you.†

The Final Thanksgiving

Lord, you now have set your servant free to go in peace as you have promised; for
these eyes of mine have seen the Savior, whom you have prepared for all the
world to see: a Light to enlighten the nations, and the glory of your people
Israel. Glory to the Father, and to the Son, and to the Holy Spirit: as it was in the
beginning, is now, and will be for ever. *Amen.*

❧

Saturday
The Night Office   **To Be Observed Before Retiring**

The Call to Prayer

May the Lord Almighty grant me and those I love a peaceful night and a perfect
end. *Amen.*†

The Request for Presence

Our help is in the Name of the LORD;* the maker of heaven and earth.

Psalm 124:8

The Greeting

Almighty God, my heavenly Father: I have sinned against you, through my own
fault, in thought, and word, and deed, and in what I have left undone. For the
sake of your Son our Lord Jesus Christ, forgive me all my offenses; and grant
that I may serve you in newness of life, to the glory of your Name. *Amen.*†

The Reading   *Teach Us to Number Our Days, O LORD*

In all generations, O LORD,
You have been our dwelling place.
Before the mountains were brought forth,
Or ever you had formed the earth and the world,
From everlasting to everlasting you are God.
A thousand years in your sight
Are like yesterday when it is past,
Or like a watch in the night.
But the days of our life are seventy years,
Or perhaps eighty, if we are strong.
Even then their span is toil and trouble.
They are soon gone, and we fly away.
We are like a dream
Or like grass that is renewed in the morning.
In the morning it flourished;
In the evening it fades and withers.
So our years come to an end like a sigh,
and you turn us back to dust.
You say, "Turn back, you mortals,"
And you sweep us away.
So teach us to number our days, O LORD,
That we may gain a wise heart.   ❖

The Gloria

The Psalm   *For God Alone, My Soul in Silence Waits*

For God alone, my soul in silence waits;* from him comes my salvation.
He alone is my rock and my salvation,* my stronghold, so that I shall not be
greatly shaken.

Psalm 62:1–2

The Gloria

The Small Verse

Into your hands, O Lord, I commend my spirit; For you have redeemed me, O
Lord, O God of truth. Keep me, O Lord, as the apple of your eye; Hide me
under the shadow of your wings.†

The Lord's Prayer

The Petition

Lord, hear my prayers; And let my cry come to you.†

The Final Thanksgiving

Lord, you now have set your servant free to go in peace as you have promised; for
these eyes of mine have seen the Savior, whom you have prepared for all the
world to see: a Light to enlighten the nations, and the glory of your people
Israel. Glory to the Father, and to the Son, and to the Holy Spirit: as it was in the
beginning, is now, and will be for ever. *Amen.*

The Gloria
Glory be to God the Father, God the Son, and God the Holy Spirit. As it was
in the beginning, so it is now and so it shall ever be, world without end.
Alleluia. *Amen.*

The Lord's Prayer
Our Father, who art in heaven, hallowed be your Name.
May your kingdom come, and your will be done, on earth as in heaven.
Give us today our daily bread.
Forgive us our sins as we forgive those who sin against us.
Lead us not into temptation, but deliver us from evil;
for yours are the kingdom and the power and the glory
forever and ever. *Amen.*

Compline Prayers for August Are Located on Page 487

The Following Holy Days Occur in August:
The Transfiguration of our Lord Jesus Christ: *August 6*
The Feast of Mary, the Virgin: *August 15*
The Feast of St. Bartholomew: *August 24*

August

The Morning Office   **To Be Observed on the Hour or Half Hour**
                                      Between 6 and 9 a.m.

The Call to Prayer
Clap your hands all you peoples;* shout to God with a cry of joy.

Psalm 47:1

The Request for Presence
Hear my voice, O LORD, according to your loving-kindness;* according to your
    judgments, give me life.

Psalm 119:149

The Greeting
How priceless is your love, O God!* your people take refuge under the shadow of
    your wings.
They feast upon the abundance of your house;* you give them drink from the
    river of your delights.
For with you is the well of life,* and in your light we see light.

Psalm 36:7–9

The Refrain for the Morning Lessons
Glory in his holy Name;* let the hearts of those who seek the LORD rejoice.

Psalm 105:3

A Reading
Jesus taught us, saying: 'Do not let your hearts be troubled. You trust in God, trust
    also in me. In my Father's house there are many places to live in; otherwise, I
    would have told you. I am going now to prepare a place for you, and after I
    have gone and prepared a place for you, I shall return to take you to myself, so
    that you may be with me where I am.'

John 14:1–3

The Refrain
Glory in his holy Name;* let the hearts of those who seek the LORD rejoice.

The Morning Psalm   *He Has Led Captivity Captive*
The Lord gave the word;* great was the company of women who bore the tidings:
"Kings with their armies are fleeing away;* the women at home are dividing the
    spoils."
Though you lingered among the sheepfolds,* you shall be like a dove whose
    wings are covered with silver, whose feathers are like green gold.
When the Almighty scattered kings,* it was like snow falling in Zalmon.
O mighty mountain, O hill of Bashan!* O rugged mountain, O hill of Bashan!
Why do you look with envy, O rugged mountain, at the hill which God chose for
    his resting place?* truly, the Lord will dwell there for ever.
The chariots of God are twenty thousand, even thousands of thousands;* the Lord
    comes in holiness from Sinai.

You have gone up on high and led captivity captive; you have received gifts even
from your enemies,* that the Lord God might dwell among them.
Blessed be the Lord day by day,* the God of our salvation, who bears our burdens.
He is our God, the God of our salvation;* God is the Lord, by whom we escape
death.

Psalm 68:11–20

The Refrain
Glory in his holy Name;* let the hearts of those who seek the Lord rejoice.

The Gloria

The Lord's Prayer

The Prayer Appointed for the Week
Let your continual mercy, O Lord, cleanse and defend your Church; and, because
it cannot continue in safety without your help, protect and govern it always by
your goodness; through Jesus Christ our Lord, who lives and reigns with you
and the Holy Spirit, one God, for ever and ever. *Amen.*†

The Concluding Prayer of the Church
Lord God, almighty and everlasting Father, you have brought me in safety to this
new day: Preserve me with your mighty power, that I may not fall into sin, nor
be overcome by adversity; and in all I do direct me to the fulfilling of your purpose; through Jesus Christ my Lord. *Amen.*†

The Midday Office | **To Be Observed on the Hour or Half Hour**
Between 11 a.m. and 2 p.m.

The Call to Prayer
Sing to God, sing praises to his Name; exalt him who rides upon the heavens;*
Yahweh is his Name, rejoice before him!

Psalm 68:4

The Request for Presence
Send forth your strength, O God;* establish, O God, what you have wrought for us.

Psalm 68:28

The Greeting
I give you thanks, O God, I give you thanks,* calling upon your Name and declaring all your wonderful deeds.

Psalm 75:1

The Refrain for the Midday Lessons
The Lord is gracious and full of compassion,* slow to anger and of great kindness.
The Lord is loving to everyone* and his compassion is over all his works.

Psalm 145:8–9

A Reading

How rich and deep are the wisdom and knowledge of God! We cannot reach to the root of his decisions or his ways. *Who has ever known the mind of the Lord? Who has ever been his adviser? Who has given anything to him, so that his presents come only as a debt returned?* Everything there is comes from him and is caused by him and exists for him. To him be glory forever! *Amen.*

Romans 11:33–36

The Refrain

The LORD is gracious and full of compassion,* slow to anger and of great kindness. The LORD is loving to everyone* and his compassion is over all his works.

The Midday Psalm   Sing Praises to Our King

God has gone up with a shout,* the LORD with the sound of the ram's-horn. Sing praises to God, sing praises;* sing praises to our King, sing praises. For God is King of all the earth;* sing praises with all your skill. God reigns over the nations;* God sits upon his holy throne.

Psalm 47:5–8

The Refrain

The LORD is gracious and full of compassion,* slow to anger and of great kindness. The LORD is loving to everyone* and his compassion is over all his works.

The Small Verse

Thanks be to you, O Lord, maker of heaven and earth. Thanks be to you.

Traditional

The Lord's Prayer

The Prayer Appointed for the Week

Let your continual mercy, O Lord, cleanse and defend your Church; and, because it cannot continue in safety without your help, protect and govern it always by your goodness; through Jesus Christ our Lord, who lives and reigns with you and the Holy Spirit, one God, for ever and ever. *Amen.*†

The Concluding Prayer of the Church

O God, you make me glad with the weekly remembrance of the glorious resurrection of your Son my Lord: Give me this day such blessing through my worship of you, that the week to come may be spent in your favor; through Jesus Christ our Lord. *Amen.*†

The Vespers Office   To Be Observed on the Hour or Half Hour
Between 5 and 8 p.m.

The Call to Prayer

Open my lips, O Lord,* and my mouth shall proclaim your praise.

Psalm 51:16

The Request for Presence
Show me the light of your countenance, O God,* and come to me.

based on Psalm 57:1

The Greeting
O gracious Light, pure brightness of the everlasting Father in heaven, O Jesus
Christ, holy and blessed!
Now as I come to the setting of the sun, and my eyes behold the vesper light, I sing
your praises, O God: Father, Son and Holy Spirit.
You are worthy at all times to be praised by happy voices, O Son of God, O giver
of life, and to be glorified through all the worlds.

based on Phos Hilaron

The Hymn

Take my life, and let it be
Consecrated, Lord, to thee.
Take my moments and my days,
Let them flow in ceaseless praise.

Take my hands and let them move
At the impulse of your love;
Take my feet and let them be
Swift and beautiful for thee.

Take my voice, and let me sing
Always, only for my King;
Take my intellect, and use
Every power as you shall choose.

Take my will, and make it thine,
It shall be no longer mine;
Take myself, and I will be
Ever, only, all for thee.

Frances R. Havergal

The Refrain for the Vespers Lessons
My eyes are open in the night watches,* that I may meditate upon your promise.

Psalm 119:148

The Vespers Psalm   *You Know My Sitting Down and My Rising Up*
LORD, you have searched me out and known me;* you know my sitting down and
my rising up; you discern my thoughts from afar.
You trace my journeys and my resting-places* and are acquainted with all my ways.
Indeed, there is not a word on my lips,* but you, O LORD, know it altogether.
You press upon me behind and before* and lay your hand upon me.
Such knowledge is too wonderful for me;* it is so high that I cannot attain it.

Psalm 139:1–5

The Refrain
My eyes are open in the night watches,* that I may meditate upon your promise.

The Cry of the Church
Lord, have mercy on us. Christ, have mercy on us. Lord, have mercy on us.

The Lord's Prayer

The Prayer Appointed for the Week
Let your continual mercy, O Lord, cleanse and defend your Church; and, because
it cannot continue in safety without your help, protect and govern it always by

your goodness; through Jesus Christ our Lord, who lives and reigns with you and the Holy Spirit, one God, for ever and ever. *Amen.*†

The Concluding Prayer of the Church

Lord God, whose Son our Savior Jesus Christ, triumphed over the powers of death and prepared for us our place in the new Jerusalem: Grant that I, who have this day given thanks for his resurrection, may praise you in the City of which he is the light, and where he lives and reigns for ever and ever. *Amen.*†

The Morning Office   To Be Observed on the Hour or Half Hour
Between 6 and 9 a.m.

The Call to Prayer
Let the Name of the Lord be blessed,* from this time forth for evermore.
From the rising of the sun to its going down* let the Name of the Lord be praised.

Psalm 113:2–3

The Request for Presence
Who is like the Lord our God, who sits enthroned on high,* but stoops to behold the heavens and the earth.

Psalm 113:5

The Greeting
One day in your courts is better than a thousand in my own room,* and to stand at the threshold of the house of my God than to dwell in the tents of the wicked.

Psalm 84:9

The Refrain for the Morning Lessons
'This is my Son, the Chosen One. Listen to him.'

Luke 9:35

A Reading   *On August 6 the Church rejoices in the Transfiguration on Mount Tabor of our Lord, the Christ.*

Now about eight days after this had been said, he took with him Peter, John and James and went up the mountain to pray. And it happened that, as he was praying, the aspect of his face was changed and his clothing became sparkling white. And suddenly there were two men talking to him; they were Moses and Elijah appearing in glory, and they were speaking of his passing which he was to accomplish in Jerusalem. Peter and his companions were heavy with sleep, but they woke up and saw his glory and the two men standing with him. As these were leaving him, Peter said to Jesus, 'Master, it is wonderful for us to be here; so let us make three shelters, one for you, one for Moses and one for Elijah.' He did not know what he was saying. As he was saying this, a cloud came and covered them with shadow; and when they went into the cloud the disciples were afraid. And a voice came from the cloud saying, 'This is my Son, the Chosen

One. Listen to him.' And after the voice had spoken, Jesus was found alone. The
disciples kept silence and at that time, told no one what they had seen.

Luke 9:28–36

The Refrain
'This is my Son, the Chosen One. Listen to him.'

The Morning Psalm   *Let the People Tremble*
The LORD is King; let the people tremble;* he is enthroned upon the cherubim; let
the earth shake.
The LORD is great in Zion;* he is high above all peoples.
Let them confess his Name, which is great and awesome;* he is the Holy One.
"O mighty King, lover of justice, you have established equity;* you have executed
justice and righteousness in Jacob."

Psalm 99:1–4

The Refrain
'This is my Son, the Chosen One. Listen to him.'

The Gloria

The Lord's Prayer

The Prayer Appointed for the Week
Let your continual mercy, O Lord, cleanse and defend your Church; and, because
it cannot continue in safety without your help, protect and govern it always by
your goodness; through Jesus Christ our Lord, who lives and reigns with you
and the Holy Spirit, one God, for ever and ever. *Amen.*†

The Concluding Prayer of the Church
Lord God, almighty and everlasting Father, you have brought me in safety to this
new day: Preserve me with your mighty power, that I may not fall into sin, nor
be overcome by adversity; and in all I do direct me to the fulfilling of your purpose; through Jesus Christ my Lord. *Amen.*†

The Midday Office   **To Be Observed on the Hour or Half Hour**
Between 11 a.m. and 2 p.m.

The Call to Prayer
Praise the LORD, all you nations;* laud him, all you peoples.
For his loving-kindness toward us is great,* and the faithfulness of the LORD
endures for ever. Hallelujah!

Psalm 117

The Request for Presence
Even so, come, Lord Jesus, come.
based on Revelation 22:20

The Greeting
For you are the LORD, most high over all the earth;* you are exalted far above all
    gods.

Psalm 97:9

The Refrain for the Midday Lessons
'This is my Son, the Chosen One. Listen to him.'

Luke 9:35

A Reading
When we told you about the power and the coming of our Lord Jesus Christ we
    were not slavishly repeating cleverly invented myths; no, we had seen his
    majesty with our own eyes. He was honored and glorified by God the Father,
    when a voice came to him from the transcendent Glory, 'This is my Son, the
    Beloved; he enjoys my favor.' We ourselves heard this voice from heaven,
    when we were with him on the holy mountain.

2 Peter 1:16–18

The Refrain
'This is my Son, the Chosen One. Listen to him.'

The Midday Psalm   *Princely States Are Yours*
The LORD said to my Lord, "Sit at my right hand,* until I make your enemies your
    footstool."
The LORD will send the scepter of your power out of Zion,* saying, "Rule over
    your enemies round about you.
Princely state has been yours from the day of your birth;* in the beauty of holiness
    have I begotten you, like dew from the womb of the morning."
The LORD has sworn and he will not recant:* "You are a priest for ever after the
    order of Melchizedek."
The Lord who is at your right hand will smite kings in the day of his wrath;* he
    will rule over the nations.
He will drink from the brook beside the road;* therefore he will lift high his head.

Psalm 110:1–5, 7

The Refrain
'This is my Son, the Chosen One. Listen to him.'

The Gloria

The Lord's Prayer

The Prayer Appointed for the Week
Let your continual mercy, O Lord, cleanse and defend your Church; and, because
    it cannot continue in safety without your help, protect and govern it always by
    your goodness; through Jesus Christ our Lord, who lives and reigns with you
    and the Holy Spirit, one God, for ever and ever. *Amen.*†

The Concluding Prayer of the Church
O God, who on holy Tabor revealed to the chosen witnesses your well-beloved
  Son, wonderfully transfigured white and glistening: Mercifully grant that I and
  all your church, being delivered from the disquietude of this world, may by
  faith behold the King in his beauty; who with you, O Father, and you, O Holy
  Spirit, lives and reigns, one God, for ever and ever. *Amen.*†

The Vespers Office   **To Be Observed on the Hour or Half Hour**
                                              Between 5 and 8 p.m.

The Call to Prayer
Rejoice in the LORD, you righteous,* and give thanks to his holy Name.
                                                        Psalm 97:12

The Request for Presence
"O mighty King, lover of justice, you have established equity;* you have executed
  justice and righteousness in Jacob."
                                                        Psalm 99:4

The Greeting
Zion hears and is glad, and the cities of Judah rejoice,* because of your judgments,
  O LORD.
                                                        Psalm 97:8

The Hymn   *All Hail the Power*

All hail the power of Jesus' Name!   Sinners, whose love can never forget
Let angels prostrate fall;   the wormwood and the gall,
bring forth the royal diadem,   go, spread your trophies at his feet,
and crown him Lord of all!   and crown him Lord of all!

Hail him, the Heir of David's line,   Let every kindred, every tribe,
whom David Lord did call,   on this terrestrial ball,
the God incarnate, Man divine,   to him all majesty ascribe,
and crown him Lord of all!   and crown him Lord of all!

                                              Edward Perronet

You heirs of Israel's chosen race,
you ransomed of the fall,
hail him who saves you by his grace
and crown him Lord of all!

The Refrain for the Vespers Lessons
'This is my Son, the Chosen One. Listen to him.'
                    Luke 9:35

The Vespers Psalm   *All the People See His Glory*

The LORD is King; let the earth rejoice;* let the multitude of the isles be glad.

Clouds and darkness are round about him,* righteousness and justice are the
   foundations of his throne.

A fire goes before him* and burns up his enemies on every side.

His lightnings light up the world;* the earth sees it and is afraid.

The mountains melt like wax at the presence of the LORD,* at the presence of the
   Lord of the whole earth.

The heavens declare his righteousness,* and all the peoples see his glory.

Light has sprung up for the righteous,* and joyful gladness for those who are true-
   hearted.

Psalm 97:1–6, 11

The Refrain

'This is my Son, the Chosen One. Listen to him.'

The Gloria

The Lord's Prayer

The Prayer Appointed for the Week

Let your continual mercy, O Lord, cleanse and defend your Church; and, because
   it cannot continue in safety without your help, protect and govern it always by
   your goodness; through Jesus Christ our Lord, who lives and reigns with you
   and the Holy Spirit, one God, for ever and ever. *Amen.*†

The Concluding Prayer of the Church
   All glory, Lord, to you I pay,
   Transfigured on the Mount today;
   All glory, as is ever meet,
   To Father and to Paraclete. *Amen.*
               THE SHORT BREVIARY

The Morning Office   **To Be Observed on the Hour or Half Hour
                                            Between 6 and 9 a.m.**

The Call to Prayer

Let the heavens rejoice, and let the earth be glad; let the sea thunder and all that is
   in it;* let the field be joyful and all that is therein.

Then shall all the trees of the wood shout for joy before the LORD when he comes,*
   when he comes to judge the earth.

Psalm 96:11–12

The Request for Presence

Let me hear of your loving-kindness in the morning, for I put my trust in you;*
   show me the road that I must walk, for I lift up my soul to you.

Psalm 143:8

The Greeting
Blessed be the LORD, the God of Israel, from everlasting and to everlasting;* and
let all the people say, "Amen!" Hallelujah!

Psalm 106:48

The Refrain for the Morning Lessons
The LORD is my strength and my song,* and he has become my salvation.

Psalm 118:14

A Reading
. . . everyone in the crowd was trying to touch him because power came out of him
that cured them all. Then fixing his eyes on his disciples he said: 'How happy
are you who are poor: the kingdom of God is yours. Blessed are you who are
hungry now: you shall have your fill. Blessed are you who are weeping now:
you shall laugh. Blessed are you when people hate you, drive you out, abuse
you, denounce your name as criminal, on account of the Son of Man. Rejoice
when that day comes and dance for joy, look!—your reward will be great in
heaven. This was the way their ancestors treated the prophets. But alas for you
who are rich: you are having your consolation now. Alas for you who have
plenty to eat now: you shall go hungry. Alas for you who are laughing now:
you shall mourn and weep. Alas for you when everyone speaks well of you!
This was the way their ancestors treated the false prophets.'

Luke 6:19–26

The Refrain
The LORD is my strength and my song,* and he has become my salvation.

The Morning Psalm   **They Shall Bear Fruit in Due Season**
Happy are they who have not walked in the counsel of the wicked,* nor lingered
in the way of sinners, nor sat in the seats of the scornful!
Their delight is in the law of the LORD,* and they meditate on his law day and
night.
They are like trees planted by streams of water, bearing fruit in due season, with
leaves that do not wither;* everything they do shall prosper.
It is not so with the wicked;* they are like the chaff which the wind blows away.
Therefore the wicked shall not stand upright when judgment comes,* nor the sinner in the council of the righteous.
For the LORD knows the way of the righteous,* but the way of the wicked is
doomed.

Psalm 1

The Refrain
The LORD is my strength and my song,* and he has become my salvation.

The Gloria

The Lord's Prayer

The Prayer Appointed for the Week
Let your continual mercy, O Lord, cleanse and defend your Church; and, because
 it cannot continue in safety without your help, protect and govern it always by
 your goodness; through Jesus Christ our Lord, who lives and reigns with you
 and the Holy Spirit, one God, for ever and ever. *Amen.*†

The Concluding Prayer of the Church
Lord God, almighty and everlasting Father, you have brought me in safety to this
 new day: Preserve me with your mighty power, that I may not fall into sin, nor
 be overcome by adversity; and in all I do direct me to the fulfilling of your purpose; through Jesus Christ my Lord. *Amen.*†

The Midday Office   **To Be Observed on the Hour or Half Hour**
Between 11 a.m. and 2 p.m.

The Call to Prayer
Praise the LORD, for the LORD is good;* sing praises to his Name, for it is lovely.
Psalm 135:3

The Request for Presence
Remember your congregation that you purchased long ago,* the tribe you
 redeemed to be your inheritance . . .
Psalm 74:2

The Greeting
You, O God, have heard my vows;* you have granted me the heritage of those
 who fear your Name.
Psalm 61:5

The Refrain for the Midday Lessons
Unless the LORD builds the house,* their labor is in vain who build it.
Psalm 127:1

A Reading
I, the prisoner of the Lord, urge you therefore to lead a life worthy of the vocation
 to which you were called. With all humility and gentleness, and with patience
 support each other in love. Take every care to preserve the unity of the Spirit by
 the peace that binds you together. There is one Body, one Spirit, just as one
 hope is the goal of your calling by God. There is one Lord, one faith, one baptism, and one God and Father of all, over all, through all and within all.
Ephesians 4:1–6

The Refrain
Unless the LORD builds the house,* their labor is in vain who build it.

The Midday Psalm   *How Good and Pleasant It Is*

Oh, how good and pleasant it is,* when brethren live together in unity!
It is like fine oil upon the head* that runs down upon the beard,
Upon the beard of Aaron,* and runs down upon the collar of his robe.
It is like the dew of Hermon* that falls upon the hills of Zion.
For there the LORD has ordained the blessing:* life for evermore.

Psalm 133

The Refrain
Unless the LORD builds the house,* their labor is in vain who build it.

The Small Verse
My soul has a desire and longing for the courts of the LORD;* my heart and my
flesh rejoice in the living God.

Psalm 84:1

The Lord's Prayer

The Prayer Appointed for the Week
Let your continual mercy, O Lord, cleanse and defend your Church; and, because
it cannot continue in safety without your help, protect and govern it always by
your goodness; through Jesus Christ our Lord, who lives and reigns with you
and the Holy Spirit, one God, for ever and ever. *Amen.*†

The Concluding Prayer of the Church
Lord Jesus Christ, you have prepared a quiet place for us in your Father's eternal
home. Watch over our welfare on this perilous journey, shade us from the
burning heat of day, and keep our lives free of evil until the end. *Amen.*

THE LITURGY OF THE HOURS, VOL. II

The Vespers Office   **To Be Observed on the Hour or Half Hour**
Between 5 and 8 p.m.

The Call to Prayer
Let the peoples praise you, O God;* let all the peoples praise you.
Let the nations be glad and sing for joy,* for you judge the peoples with equity and
guide all nations upon the earth.
Let the peoples praise you, O God;* let all the peoples praise you.

Psalm 67:3–5

The Request for Presence
Remember me, O LORD, with the favor you have for your people,* and visit me
with your saving help;
That I may see the prosperity of your elect and be glad with the gladness of your
people,* that I may glory with your inheritance.

Psalm 106:4–5

The Greeting
Praise God from whom all blessings flow; praise Him all creatures here below;
  praise Him above, you heavenly hosts; praise Father, Son and Holy Ghost.

Traditional

The Hymn   ***In Christ There Is No East or West***
In Christ there is no east or west,   Join hands, disciples of the faith,
In him no south or north;   Whatever your race may be.
But one great fellowship of love   All children of the living God
Throughout the whole wide earth.   Are surely kin to me.

In Christ shall true hearts everywhere   In Christ now meet both east and west,
Their high communion find;   In him meet south and north;
His service is the golden cord   All Christly souls are one in him
Close-binding humankind.   Throughout the whole wide earth.

John Oxenham

The Refrain for the Vespers Lessons
My mouth shall speak praise of the Lord;* let all flesh bless his holy Name for ever
  and ever.

Psalm 145:22

The Vespers Psalm   ***Those Who Lead a Shameless Life Shall Be My Servants***
My eyes are upon the faithful in the land, that they may dwell with me,* and only
  those who lead a shameless life shall be my servants.
Those who act deceitfully shall not dwell in my house,* and those who tell lies
  shall not continue in my sight.

Psalm 101:6–7

The Refrain
My mouth shall speak praise of the Lord;* let all flesh bless his holy Name for ever
  and ever.

The Gloria

The Lord's Prayer

The Prayer Appointed for the Week
Let your continual mercy, O Lord, cleanse and defend your Church; and, because
  it cannot continue in safety without your help, protect and govern it always by
  your goodness; through Jesus Christ our Lord, who lives and reigns with you
  and the Holy Spirit, one God, for ever and ever. *Amen.†*

The Concluding Prayer of the Church
Save me, O Lord, while I am awake, And keep me while I sleep That I may wake
  in Christ and rest in peace.

The Short Breviary

The Morning Office **To Be Observed on the Hour or Half Hour**
Between 6 and 9 a.m.

The Call to Prayer
Let Israel rejoice in its Maker;* let the children of Zion be joyful in their king.
For the LORD takes pleasure in his people* and adorns the poor with victory.

Psalm 149:2, 4

The Request for Presence
Show your goodness, O LORD, to those who are good* and to those who are true of
heart.

Psalm 125:4

The Greeting
Blessed be the LORD God, the God of Israel,* who alone does wondrous deeds!
And blessed be his glorious Name for ever!* and may all the earth be filled with
his glory. Amen. Amen.

Psalm 72:18–19

The Refrain for the Morning Lessons
May the LORD increase you more and more,* you and your children after you.

Psalm 115:14

A Reading
Jesus made a tour through all the towns and villages, teaching in their synagogues, proclaiming the Good News of the kingdom and curing all kinds of
diseases and all kinds of illness. And when he saw the crowds he felt sorry for
them because they were harassed and dejected, like sheep without a shepherd.
Then he said to his disciples, 'The harvest is rich but the laborers are few, so ask
the Lord of the harvest to send out laborers to his harvest.'

Matthew 9:35–37

The Refrain
May the LORD increase you more and more,* you and your children after you.

The Morning Psalm *Tremble, O Earth, at the Presence of the LORD*
Hallelujah! When Israel came out of Egypt,* the house of Jacob from a people of
strange speech,
Judah became God's sanctuary* and Israel his dominion.
The sea beheld it and fled;* Jordan turned and went back.
The mountains skipped like rams,* and the little hills like young sheep.
What ailed you, O sea, that you fled?* O Jordan, that you turned back?
You mountains, that you skipped like rams?* you little hills like young sheep?
Tremble, O earth, at the presence of the Lord,* at the presence of the God of Jacob,
Who turned the hard rock into a pool of water* and flint-stone into a flowing
spring.

Psalm 114

The Refrain

May the LORD increase you more and more,* you and your children after you.

The Gloria

The Lord's Prayer

The Prayer Appointed for the Week

Let your continual mercy, O Lord, cleanse and defend your Church; and, because it cannot continue in safety without your help, protect and govern it always by your goodness; through Jesus Christ our Lord, who lives and reigns with you and the Holy Spirit, one God, for ever and ever. *Amen.*†

The Concluding Prayer of the Church

Lord God, almighty and everlasting Father, you have brought me in safety to this new day: Preserve me with your mighty power, that I may not fall into sin, nor be overcome by adversity; and in all I do direct me to the fulfilling of your purpose; through Jesus Christ my Lord. *Amen.*†

The Midday Office   **To Be Observed on the Hour or Half Hour**
                            Between 11 a.m. and 2 p.m.

The Call to Prayer

Give thanks to the LORD, for he is good,* and his mercy endures for ever.
Let all those whom the LORD has redeemed proclaim* that he redeemed them from the hand of the foe.
He gathered them out of the lands;* from the east and from the west, from the north and from the south.

Psalm 107:1–3

The Request for Presence

Teach me your way, O LORD, and I will walk in your truth;* knit my heart to you that I may fear your Name.

Psalm 86:11

The Greeting

I am bound by the vow I made to you, O God;* I will present to you thank-offerings;
For you have rescued my soul from death and my feet from stumbling,* that I may walk before God in the light of the living.

Psalm 56:11–12

The Refrain for the Midday Lessons

I long for your salvation, O LORD,* and your law is my delight.

Psalm 119:174

A Reading

YAHWEH then said to Moses, 'Put these words in writing, for they are the terms of the covenant I have made with you and with Israel.' He stayed there with YAHWEH for forty days and forty nights, eating and drinking nothing and on the tablets he wrote the words of the Covenant—the Ten Words. When Moses came down from Mount Sinai with the two tablets of the Testimony in his hands, as he was coming down the mountain, Moses did not know that the skin of his face was radiant because he had been talking to him. And when Aaron and all the Israelites saw Moses, the skin on his face was so radiant that they were afraid to go near him. But Moses called to them, and Aaron with all the leaders of the community rejoined him; and Moses talked to them, after which all the Israelites came closer, and he passed on to them all the orders that YAHWEH had given to him on Mount Sinai. Once Moses had finished speaking to them, he put a veil over his face. Whenever he went into YAHWEH's presence to speak to him, he took off the veil until he came out again. And when he came out, he would tell the Israelites what orders he had been given, and the Israelites would see Moses' face radiant. Then Moses would put the veil back over his face until he went in to speak to him next time.

Exodus 34:28–35

The Refrain
I long for your salvation, O LORD,* and your law is my delight.

The Midday Psalm   *There Is a River Whose Streams Make Glad the City of God*
There is a river whose streams make glad the city of God,* the holy habitation of the Most High.
God is in the midst of her; she shall not be overthrown;* God shall help her at the break of day.
The nations make much ado, and the kingdoms are shaken;* God has spoken, and the earth shall melt away.
The LORD of hosts is with us;* the God of Jacob is our stronghold.

Psalm 46:5–8

The Refrain
I long for your salvation, O LORD,* and your law is my delight.

The Small Verse
My soul thirsts for the strong, living God. And all that is within me cries out to him.

Traditional

The Lord's Prayer

The Prayer Appointed for the Week
Let your continual mercy, O Lord, cleanse and defend your Church; and, because it cannot continue in safety without your help, protect and govern it always by your goodness; through Jesus Christ our Lord, who lives and reigns with you and the Holy Spirit, one God, for ever and ever. *Amen.*†

The Concluding Prayer of the Church
Let us bless the Lord God living and true! Let us always render him praise, glory, honor, blessing, and all good things! Amen. Amen. So be it! So be it!

St. Francis

The Vespers Office	To Be Observed on the Hour or Half Hour
	Between 5 and 8 p.m.

The Call to Prayer
Hallelujah! Give praise, you servants of the LORD;* praise the Name of the LORD.
Let the Name of the LORD be blessed,* from this time forth for evermore.
From the rising of the sun to its going down* let the Name of the LORD be praised.

Psalm 113:1–3

The Request for Presence
Rouse yourself, come to my side, and see;* for you, LORD God of hosts, are Israel's
    God.

Psalm 59:5

The Greeting
I am the LORD your God, who brought you out of the land of Egypt and said,*
    "Open your mouth wide, and I will fill it."

Psalm 81:10

The Hymn   *Go into the Wilderness*
    If you want to find Jesus,
    go into the wilderness,
    go into the wilderness, Mourning Brother,
    go into the wilderness,
    I wait upon the Lord,
    I wait upon the Lord,
    I wait upon the Lord, my God,
    who takes away the sin of the world.

    If you want to be a Christian,
    go into the wilderness,
    go into the wilderness, Mourning Sister,
    go into the wilderness,
    I wait upon the Lord,
    I wait upon the Lord,
    I wait upon the Lord, my God,
    who takes away the sin of the world.

    You want to get religion,
    go into the wilderness,
    go into the wilderness, Mourning Friends,
    go into the wilderness,
    I wait upon the Lord,
    I wait upon the Lord,
    I wait upon the Lord, my God,
    who takes away the sin of the world.

If you sped' to be connected,
go into the wilderness,
go into the wilderness, Mourning Children,
go into the wilderness,
I wait upon the Lord,
I wait upon the Lord,
I wait upon the Lord, my God,
who takes away the sin of the world.

African-American Spiritual

The Refrain for the Vespers Lessons
For he shall give his angels charge over you,* to keep you in all your ways.

Psalm 91:11

The Vespers Psalm   *Into Your Hands I Commend My Spirit*
In you, O LORD, have I taken refuge; let me never be put to shame;* deliver me in
 your righteousness.
Incline your ear to me;* make haste to deliver me.
Be my strong rock, a castle to keep me safe, for you are my crag and my strong-
 hold;* for the sake of your Name, lead me and guide me.
Take me out of the net that they have secretly set for me,* for you are my tower of
 strength.
Into your hands I commend my spirit, for you have redeemed me,* O LORD, O
 God of truth.

Psalm 31:1–5

The Refrain
For he shall give his angels charge over you,* to keep you in all your ways.

The Cry of the Church
In the evening, in the morning, and at noonday, I will complain and lament,* and
 he will hear my voice.

Psalm 55:18

The Lord's Prayer

The Prayer Appointed for the Week
Let your continual mercy, O Lord, cleanse and defend your Church; and, because
 it cannot continue in safety without your help, protect and govern it always by
 your goodness; through Jesus Christ our Lord, who lives and reigns with you
 and the Holy Spirit, one God, for ever and ever. *Amen.*†

The Concluding Prayer of the Church
May Almighty God grant me a peaceful night and a perfect end. *Amen.*

The Morning Office To Be Observed on the Hour or Half Hour
Between 6 and 9 a.m.

The Call to Prayer
Let the righteous be glad and rejoice before God;* let them be merry and joyful.

Psalm 68:3

The Request for Presence
Rise up, O Lord; lift up your hand, O God . . .

Psalm 10:12

The Greeting
Be exalted, O Lord, in your might;* we will sing and praise your power.

Psalm 21:14

The Refrain for the Morning Lessons
Sing to the Lord a new song,* for he has done marvelous things.

Psalm 98:1

A Reading
Blessed be the Lord, God of Israel, for he has visited his people, he has *set them free,*
and he has established for us a saving power in the House of his servant David,
just as he proclaimed, by the mouth of his holy prophets from ancient times.

Luke 1:68–70

The Refrain
Sing to the Lord a new song,* for he has done marvelous things.

The Morning Psalm *The Trees of the Lord Are Full of Sap*
The trees of the Lord are full of sap,* the cedars of Lebanon which he planted,
In which the birds build their nests,* and in whose top the stork makes his
dwelling.
The high hills are a refuge for the mountain goats,* and his stony cliffs for rock
badgers.

Psalm 104:17–19

The Refrain
Sing to the Lord a new song,* for he has done marvelous things.

The Small Verse
Lift up your heads, O gates, and be lifted up, you mighty doors* and the king of
glory shall come in!
Who is the king of glory?* The Lord strong and mighty, the Lord of hosts is his
name. He is the king of glory.

based on Psalm 24:7–10

The Lord's Prayer

The Prayer Appointed for the Week
Let your continual mercy, O Lord, cleanse and defend your Church; and, because
it cannot continue in safety without your help, protect and govern it always by

your goodness; through Jesus Christ our Lord, who lives and reigns with you
and the Holy Spirit, one God, for ever and ever. *Amen.*†

The Concluding Prayer of the Church

Lord God, almighty and everlasting Father, you have brought me in safety to this
new day: Preserve me with your mighty power, that I may not fall into sin, nor
be overcome by adversity; and in all I do direct me to the fulfilling of your purpose; through Jesus Christ my Lord. *Amen.*†

The Midday Office　　　　　　　**To Be Observed on the Hour or Half Hour**
Between 11 a.m. and 2 p.m.

The Call to Prayer

Sing to him, sing praise to him,* and speak of all his marvelous works.

Psalm 105:2

The Request for Presence

Give ear to my words, O LORD;* consider my meditation.

Psalm 5:1

The Greeting

The LORD will make good his purpose for me;* O LORD, your love endures for
ever; do not abandon the works of your hands,

Psalm 138:9

The Refrain for the Midday Lessons

Blessed be the Lord for evermore!* Amen, I say, Amen.

Psalm 89:32

A Reading

Jesus, are you not my mother? Are you not even more than my mother? My
human mother after all laboured in giving birth to me for only a day or a night;
You, my tender and beautiful Lord, laboured for me for over thirty years. . . .
Oh with what measureless love you laboured for me! . . . But when the time
was ripe for you to be delivered, your labor pains were so terrible your holy
sweat was like great drops of blood that ran from your body onto the earth. . . .
Who ever saw a mother endure so dreadful a birth? When the time of your
delivery came, you were nailed to the hard bed of the Cross . . . and your
nerves and all your veins were broken. How could anyone be surprised that
your veins broke open when in one day you gave birth to the whole world?

Marguerite of Oingt

The Refrain

Blessed be the Lord for evermore!* Amen, I say, Amen.

The Midday Psalm　　　　*I Have Been Entrusted to You Ever Since I Was Born*

But as for me, I am a worm and no man,* scorned by all and despised by the people.
All who see me laugh to scorn;* they curl their lips and wag their heads, saying,

"He trusted in the Lord; let him deliver him;* let him rescue him, if he delights in him."

Yet you are he who took me out of the womb,* and kept me safe upon my mother's breast.

I have been entrusted to you ever since I was born;* you were my God when I was still in my mother's womb.

Be not far from me, for trouble is near,* and there is none to help.

Psalm 22:6–11

The Refrain
Blessed be the Lord for evermore!* Amen, I say, Amen.

The Cry of the Church
Lord, have mercy on us. Christ, have mercy on us. Lord, have mercy on us.

The Lord's Prayer

The Prayer Appointed for the Week
Let your continual mercy, O Lord, cleanse and defend your Church; and, because it cannot continue in safety without your help, protect and govern it always by your goodness; through Jesus Christ our Lord, who lives and reigns with you and the Holy Spirit, one God, for ever and ever. *Amen.*†

The Concluding Prayer of the Church
Almighty God, to whom my needs are known before I ask: Help me to ask only what accords with your will; and those good things which I dare not, or in my blindness cannot ask, grant me for the sake of your Son Jesus Christ our Lord. *Amen.*†

The Vespers Office   **To Be Observed on the Hour or Half Hour
Between 5 and 8 p.m.**

The Call to Prayer
Come, let us sing to the Lord . . .

Psalm 95:1

The Request for Presence
May God give us his blessing,* and may all the ends of the earth stand in awe of him.

Psalm 67:7

The Greeting
You are God: we praise you; you are the Lord: we acclaim you; you are the eternal Father: all creation worships you. To you all angels, all the powers of heaven, Cherubim and Seraphim, sing in endless praise: Holy, holy, holy Lord, God of power and might, heaven and earth are full of your glory.

The Hymn   *Lord of All Being, Throned Afar*
> Lord of all being, throned afar,
> Your glory flames from sun and star;
> Center and soul of every sphere,
> And yet to loving hearts how near.

> Sun of life, your living ray
> Sheds on our path the glow of day;
> Star of our hope, your gentle light
> Shall ever cheer the longest night.

> Lord of all life, below, above,
> Whose light is truth, whose warmth is love;
> Before the brilliance of your throne
> We ask no luster of our own.

> Give us your grace to make us true,
> And kindling hearts that burn for you,
> Till all your living altars claim
> One holy light, one heavenly flame.

> > *Oliver W. Holmes*

The Refrain for the Vespers Lessons
May the graciousness of the LORD our God be upon us;* prosper the work of our
hands; prosper our handiwork.

> > *Psalm 90:17*

The Vespers Psalm   *Happy Are the People Whose God Is the LORD*
May our sons be like plants well nurtured from their youth,* and our daughters
like sculptured corners of a palace.
May our barns be filled to overflowing with all manner of crops;* may the flocks
in our pastures increase by thousands and tens of thousands; may our cattle be
fat and sleek.
May there be no breaching of the walls, no going into exile,* no wailing in the pub-
lic squares.
Happy are the people of whom this is so!* happy are the people whose God is the
LORD!

> > *Psalm 144:13–16*

The Refrain
May the graciousness of the LORD our God be upon us;* prosper the work of our
hands; prosper our handiwork.

The Gloria

The Lord's Prayer

The Prayer Appointed for the Week
Let your continual mercy, O Lord, cleanse and defend your Church; and, because
it cannot continue in safety without your help, protect and govern it always by

your goodness; through Jesus Christ our Lord, who lives and reigns with you
and the Holy Spirit, one God, for ever and ever. *Amen.*†

The Concluding Prayer of the Church
May Almighty God grant me a peaceful night and a perfect end. *Amen.*

The Morning Office　　　　　　　　**To Be Observed on the Hour or Half Hour**
　　　　　　　　　　　　　　　　　　　　Between 6 and 9 a.m.

The Call to Prayer
Ascribe power to God;* his majesty is over Israel; . . .
How wonderful is God in his holy places! . . . * Blessed be God!
Psalm 68:35–36

The Request for Presence
Look well whether there be any wickedness in me* and lead me in the way that is
　everlasting.
Psalm 139:23

The Greeting
Restore us, O God of hosts;* show the light of your countenance, and we shall be
　saved.
Psalm 80:3

The Refrain for the Morning Lessons
I will meditate on your commandments* and give attention to your ways.
Psalm 119:15

A Reading
Jesus taught us, saying: 'Make a tree sound and its fruit will be sound; make a tree
　rotten and its fruit will be rotten. For the tree can be told by its fruit. You brood
　of vipers, how can your speech be good when you are evil? For words flow out
　of what fills the heart. Good people draw good things from their store of good-
　ness; and bad people draw bad things from their store of badness. So I tell you
　this, that for every unfounded word people utter they will answer on
　Judgment Day, since it is by your words you will be justified, and by your
　words condemned.'
Matthew 12:33–37

The Refrain
I will meditate on your commandments* and give attention to your ways.

The Morning Psalm　　　　　　　*The Just Shall Not Put Their Hands to Evil*
Those who trust the LORD are like Mount Zion,* which cannot be moved, but
　stands fast for ever.
The hills stand about Jerusalem;* so does the LORD stand round his people, from
　this time forth for evermore.

The scepter of the wicked shall not hold sway over the land allotted to the just,* so that the just shall not put their hands to evil.

Psalm 125:1–3

The Refrain
I will meditate on your commandments* and give attention to your ways.

The Cry of the Church
Even so, come Lord Jesus!

The Lord's Prayer

The Prayer Appointed for the Week
Let your continual mercy, O Lord, cleanse and defend your Church; and, because it cannot continue in safety without your help, protect and govern it always by your goodness; through Jesus Christ our Lord, who lives and reigns with you and the Holy Spirit, one God, for ever and ever. *Amen.*†

The Concluding Prayer of the Church
Lord God, almighty and everlasting Father, you have brought me in safety to this new day: Preserve me with your mighty power, that I may not fall into sin, nor be overcome by adversity; and in all I do direct me to the fulfilling of your purpose; through Jesus Christ my Lord. *Amen.*†

The Midday Office
To Be Observed on the Hour or Half Hour Between 11 a.m. and 2 p.m.

The Call to Prayer
I will call upon God,* and the LORD will deliver me.
In the evening, in the morning, and at the noonday, I will complain and lament,* and he will hear my voice.
He will bring me safely back . . . * God, who is enthroned of old, will hear me.

Psalm 55:17ff

The Request for Presence
Bow down your ear, O LORD, and answer me,* for I am poor and in misery.

Psalm 86:1

The Greeting
I love you, O LORD of my strength,* O LORD my stronghold, my crag, and my haven.

Psalm 18:1

The Refrain for the Midday Lessons
Though my flesh and heart should waste away,* God is the strength of my heart and my portion for ever.

Psalm 73:26

A Reading

How often have we rebelled against you and our sins bear witness against us. Our
rebellious acts are indeed with us, we are well aware of our guilt: rebellion and
denial of Yahweh, turning our back on God, talking violence and revolt, mur-
muring lies in our heart. Fair judgment is driven away and saving justice stands
aloof; for good faith has stumbled in the street and sincerity cannot enter.

Isaiah 59:12–14

The Refrain

Though my flesh and heart should waste away,* God is the strength of my heart
and my portion for ever.

The Midday Psalm   Your Love, O Lord, Upheld Me

If the Lord had not come to my help,* I should soon have dwelt in the land of
silence.
As often as I said, "My foot has slipped,"* your love, O Lord, upheld me.
When many cares fill my mind,* your consolations cheer my soul.

Psalm 94:17–19

The Refrain

Though my flesh and heart should waste away,* God is the strength of my heart
and my portion for ever.

The Cry of the Church

Lord, have mercy on us. Christ, have mercy on us. Lord, have mercy on us.

The Lord's Prayer

The Prayer Appointed for the Week

Let your continual mercy, O Lord, cleanse and defend your Church; and, because
it cannot continue in safety without your help, protect and govern it always by
your goodness; through Jesus Christ our Lord, who lives and reigns with you
and the Holy Spirit, one God, for ever and ever. *Amen.*†

The Concluding Prayer of the Church

Lord Jesus Christ, by your death you took away the sting of death: Grant me to so
follow in faith where you have led the way, that I may at length fall asleep
peacefully in you and wake in your likeness; for your tender mercies' sake.
Amen.†

The Vespers Office   To Be Observed on the Hour or Half Hour
                                         Between 5 and 8 p.m.

The Call to Prayer

Tremble, then, and do not sin;* speak to your heart in silence upon your bed.
Offer the appointed sacrifices* and put your trust in the Lord.

Psalm 4:4–5

The Request for Presence
You are my helper and my deliverer;* do not tarry, O my God.

> *Psalm 40:19*

The Greeting
My very bones will say, "Lord, who is like you?* You deliver the poor from those who are too strong for them, the poor and needy from those who rob them."

> *Psalm 35:10*

The Hymn **Pass Me Not**

Pass me not, O gentle Savior,
Hear my humble cry;
While on others you are calling,
Do not pass me by.
Savior, Savior, Hear my humble cry.

Let me at your throne of mercy
Find a sweet relief;
Kneeling there in deep contrition
Help my unbelief.
Savior, Savior, Hear my humble cry.

Trusting only in Your merit,
Would I seek Your face;
Heal my wounded, broken spirit,
Save me by Your grace.
Savior, Savior, Hear my humble cry.

You the Spring of all my comfort,
More than life to me,
Whom have I on earth beside Thee?
Whom in heaven but Thee?
Savior, Savior, Hear my humble cry.

> *Fanny J. Crosby*

The Refrain for the Vespers Lessons
The Lord is faithful in all his words* and merciful in all his deeds.

> *Psalm 145:14*

The Vespers Psalm ***Show Me the Road That I Must Walk***
My spirit faints within me;* my heart within me is desolate.
I remember the time past; I muse upon all your deeds;* I consider the works of your hands.
I spread out my hands to you;* my soul gasps to you like a thirsty land.
O Lord, make haste to answer me; My spirit fails me;* do not hide your face from me or I shall be like those who go down to the Pit.
Let me hear of your loving-kindness in the morning, for I put my trust in you;* show me the road that I must walk, for I lift up my soul to you.

> *Psalm 143:4–8*

The Refrain
The Lord is faithful in all his words* and merciful in all his deeds.

The Cry of the Church
O Lamb of God, that takes away the sins of the world, have mercy upon me.
O Lamb of God, that takes away the sins of the world, have mercy upon me.
O Lamb of God, that takes away the sins of the world, grant me your peace.

The Lord's Prayer

The Prayer Appointed for the Week
Let your continual mercy, O Lord, cleanse and defend your Church; and, because
it cannot continue in safety without your help, protect and govern it always by
your goodness; through Jesus Christ our Lord, who lives and reigns with you
and the Holy Spirit, one God, for ever and ever. *Amen*.†

The Concluding Prayers of the Church
Almighty God, who has promised to hear the petitions of those who ask in your
Son's Name: I beseech you mercifully to incline your ear to me who have made
my prayers and supplications to you; and grant that those things which I have
faithfully asked according to your will, I may effectually obtain, to the relief of
my necessity, and to setting forth of your glory; through Jesus Christ my Lord.
Amen.†

May the souls of the faithful departed, through the mercy of God, rest in eternal
peace. *Amen*.

The Morning Office   **To Be Observed on the Hour or Half Hour**
                                                    Between 6 and 9 a.m.

The Call to Prayer
Blessed be the Lord, the God of Israel, from everlasting and to everlasting;* and
let all the people say, "Amen!" Hallelujah!

Psalm 106:48

The Request for Presence
Open my eyes, that I may see* the wonders of your law.

Psalm 119:18

The Greeting
I am bound by the vow I made to you, O God;* I will present to you thank-
offerings;
For you have rescued my soul from death and my feet from stumbling,* that I may
walk before God in the light of the living.

Psalm 56:11–12

The Refrain for the Morning Lessons
Those who trust in the Lord are like Mount Zion,* which cannot be moved, but
stands fast for ever.

Psalm 125:1

A Reading
As he was walking by the Lake of Galilee he saw two brothers, Simon, who was
called Peter, and his brother Andrew; they were making a cast into the lake
with their net, for they were fishermen. And he said to them, 'Come after me
and I will make you fishers of people.' And at once they left their nets and followed him.

Matthew 4:18–20

The Refrain
Those who trust in the LORD are like Mount Zion,* which cannot be moved, but
stands fast for ever.

The Morning Psalm   *To You, O My Strength, Will I Sing*
The ungodly go to and fro in the evening;* they snarl like dogs and run about the
city.
They forage for food,* and if they are not filled, they howl.
For my part, I will sing of your strength;* I will celebrate your love in the morning;
For you have become my stronghold,* a refuge in my day of trouble.
To you, O my Strength, will I sing;* for you, O God, are my stronghold and my
merciful God.

Psalm 59:16–20

The Refrain
Those who trust in the LORD are like Mount Zion,* which cannot be moved, but
stands fast for ever.

The Small Verse
Come forth, O Christ, and help me. For your name's sake deliver me.

The Lord's Prayer

The Prayer Appointed for the Week
Let your continual mercy, O Lord, cleanse and defend your Church; and, because
it cannot continue in safety without your help, protect and govern it always by
your goodness; through Jesus Christ our Lord, who lives and reigns with you
and the Holy Spirit, one God, for ever and ever. *Amen.*†

The Concluding Prayer of the Church
Lord God, almighty and everlasting Father, you have brought me in safety to this
new day: Preserve me with your mighty power, that I may not fall into sin, nor
be overcome by adversity; and in all I do direct me to the fulfilling of your purpose; through Jesus Christ my Lord. *Amen.*†

The Midday Office   **To Be Observed on the Hour or Half Hour
                                               Between 11 a.m. and 2 p.m.**

The Call to Prayer
Bless the LORD, you angels of his, you mighty ones who do his bidding,* and hear-
ken to the voice of his word.
Bless the LORD, all you his hosts,* you ministers of his who do his will.
Bless the LORD, all you works of his, in all places of his dominion;* bless the LORD,
O my soul.

Psalm 103:20–22

The Request for Presence
Give ear to my words, O LORD;* consider my meditation . . . for I make my prayer
to you.

Psalm 5:1–2

The Greeting
One generation shall praise your works to another* and shall declare your power.

Psalm 145:4

The Refrain for the Midday Lessons
As a father cares for his children,* so does the LORD care for those who fear him.

Psalm 103:13

A Reading
We have been given possession of an unshakable kingdom. Let us therefore be
grateful and use our gratitude to worship God in the way that pleases him, in
reverence and fear. For our God is a *consuming fire.*

Hebrews 12:28–29

The Refrain
As a father cares for his children,* so does the LORD care for those who fear him.

The Midday Psalm   *Where Can I Flee from Your Presence*
Where can I go then from your spirit?* where can I flee from your presence?
If I climb up to heaven, you are there;* if I make the grave my bed, you are there
also.
If I take the wings of morning* and dwell in the uttermost parts of the sea,
Even there your hand will lead me* and your right hand will hold me fast.

Psalm 139:6–9

The Refrain
As a father cares for his children,* so does the LORD care for those who fear him.

The Cry of the Church
Lord, have mercy on us. Christ, have mercy on us. Lord, have mercy on us.

The Lord's Prayer

The Prayer Appointed for the Week
Let your continual mercy, O Lord, cleanse and defend your Church; and, because
it cannot continue in safety without your help, protect and govern it always by
your goodness; through Jesus Christ our Lord, who lives and reigns with you
and the Holy Spirit, one God, for ever and ever. *Amen.*†

The Concluding Prayer of the Church
O God, the source of eternal light: Shed forth your unending day upon all of us
who watch for you, that our lips may praise you, our lives may bless you, and
our worship may give you glory; through Jesus Christ our Lord. *Amen.*†

The Vespers Office

**To Be Observed on the Hour or Half Hour
Between 5 and 8 p.m.**

The Call to Prayer
Behold now, bless the LORD, all you servants of the LORD,* you that stand by night
 in the house of the LORD.
Lift up your hands in the holy place and bless the LORD;* the LORD who made
 heaven and earth bless you out of Zion.

Psalm 134

The Request for Presence
Let those who seek you rejoice and be glad in you;* let those who love your salva-
 tion say for ever, "Great is the LORD!"
But as for me, I am poor and needy;* come to me speedily, O God.
You are my helper and my deliverer;* O LORD, do not tarry.

Psalm 70:4–6

The Greeting
You have put gladness in my heart,* more than when grain and wine and oil
 increase.
I lie down in peace; at once I fall asleep;* for only you, LORD, make me dwell in
 safety.

Psalm 4:7–8

The Hymn   *The Humble Heart*

Whence comes the bright celestial light,
What cause produces this?
A heaven opens to my sight,
Bright scenes of joy and bliss.
O Lord Jehovah art Thou here?
This light proclaims Thou art.
"I am indeed, I'm always near
Unto the humble heart.

"The proud and lofty I despise,
And bless the meek and low,
I hear the humble soul that cries,
And comfort I bestow.
Of all the trees among the wood
I've chosen one little vine,
The meek and low are nigh to me,
The humble heart is mine.

"Tall cedars fall before the wind,
The tempest breaks the oak,
While slender vines will bow and bend
And rise beneath the stroke.
I've chosen me one pleasant grove
And set my lovely vine,
Here in my vineyard I will rove,
The humble heart is mine.

"Of all the fowls that beat the air
I've chosen one little dove,
I've made her spotless white and fair,
The object of my love.
Her feathers are like the purest gold,
With glory she does shine,
She is a beauty to behold,
Her humble heart is mine.

"Of all kinds that range at large
I've chosen one little flock,
And those I make my lovely charge,
Before them I will walk.
Their constant shepherd I will be,
And all their ways refine,
And they shall serve and reverence me,
The humble heart is mine.

"Of all the sects that fill the land
One little band I chose,
And led them forth by my right hand
And placed my love on those.
The lovely object of my love,
Around my heart shall twine
My flock, my vineyard and my dove,
The humble heart is mine."

Traditional Shaker Hymn

The Refrain for the Vespers Lessons
I will sing of mercy and justice;* to you, O Lord, will I sing praises.

Psalm 101:1

The Vespers Psalm   *My Boundaries Enclose a Pleasant Land*
O Lord, you are my portion and my cup;* it is you who uphold my lot.
My boundaries enclose a pleasant land;* indeed I have a goodly heritage.
I will bless the Lord who gives me counsel;* my heart teaches me, night after night.
I have set the Lord always before me;* because he is at my right hand I shall not fall.
My heart, therefore, is glad, and my spirit rejoices;* my body also shall rest in hope.
For you will not abandon me to the grave,* nor let your holy one see the Pit.
You will show me the path of life;* in your presence there is a fullness of joy, and in
    your right hand are pleasures for evermore.

Psalm 16:5–11

The Refrain
I will sing of mercy and justice;* to you, O Lord, will I sing praises.

The Small Verse
The Lord is my shepherd and nothing is wanting to me. In green pastures He hath
    settled me.

The Short Breviary

The Lord's Prayer

The Prayer Appointed for the Week
Let your continual mercy, O Lord, cleanse and defend your Church; and, because
    it cannot continue in safety without your help, protect and govern it always by
    your goodness; through Jesus Christ our Lord, who lives and reigns with you
    and the Holy Spirit, one God, for ever and ever. *Amen.*†

The Concluding Prayer of the Church
Almighty God, who after the creation of the world rested from all your works and
    sanctified a day of rest for all your creatures: Grant that I, putting away all
    earthly anxieties, may be duly prepared for the service of public worship, and
    grant as well that my Sabbath upon earth may be a preparation for the eternal
    rest promised to your people in heaven; through Jesus Christ our Lord. *Amen.*†

❧

The Morning Office   **To Be Observed on the Hour or Half Hour**
Between 6 and 9 a.m.

The Call to Prayer
Sing to the LORD, a new song,* for he has done marvelous things.
With his right hand and his holy arm* has he won himself the victory.
Psalm 98:1–2

The Request for Presence
Show us the light of your countenance, O God,* and come to us.
based on Psalm 67:1

The Greeting
How deep I find your thoughts, O God!* how great is the sum of them!
Psalm 139:16

The Refrain for the Morning Lessons
On this day the LORD has acted;* we will rejoice and be glad in it.
Psalm 118:24

A Reading
And when the day came for them to be purified in keeping with the Law of Moses,
they took him up to Jerusalem to present him to the Lord—observing what is
written in the Law of the Lord: *Every first-born male must be consecrated to the
Lord*—and also to offer in sacrifice, in accordance with what is said in the Law
of the Lord, *a pair of turtledoves or two young pigeons.* Now in Jerusalem there
was a man named Simeon. He was an upright and devout man; he looked forward to the restoration of Israel and the Holy Spirit rested on him. It had been
revealed to him by the Holy Spirit that he would not see death until he had set
eyes on Christ the Lord. Prompted by the Spirit he came to the Temple; and
when the parents brought in the child Jesus to do for him what the Law
required, he took him into his arms and blessed God; and he said: 'Now,
Master, you are letting your servant go in peace, as you promised; for my eyes
have seen the salvation which you have made ready in the sight of the nations;
a light of revelation for the gentiles and glory for your people Israel.' As the
child's father and mother were wondering at the things that were being said
about him, Simeon blessed them and said to Mary his mother, 'Look, he is destined for the fall and for the rise of many in Israel, destined to be a sign that is
opposed—and a sword will pierce your soul too—so that the secret thoughts of
many may be laid bare.'
Luke 2:22–35

The Refrain
On this day the Lord has acted;* we will rejoice and be glad in it.

The Morning Psalm   **He Has Raised Up Strength for His People**
Praise the Lord from the earth,* you sea-monsters and all deeps;
Fire and hail, snow and fog,* tempestuous wind, doing his will;
Mountains and all hills,* fruit trees and all cedars;
Wild beasts and all cattle,* creeping things and winged birds;
Kings of earth and all peoples,* princes and all rulers of the world;
Young men and maidens,* old and young together.
Let them praise the Name of the Lord,* for his Name only is exalted, his splendor
    is over earth and heaven.
He has raised up strength for his people and praise for all his loyal servants,* the
    children of Israel, a people who are near him. Hallelujah!

Psalm 148:7–14

The Refrain
On this day the Lord has acted;* we will rejoice and be glad in it.

The Small Verse
My soul magnifies the Lord and rejoices in God my Savior.

The Lord's Prayer

The Prayer Appointed for the Week
Grant to me, Lord. I pray, the spirit to think and do always those things that are
    right, that I, who cannot exist without you, may by you be enabled to live
    according to your will; through Jesus Christ my Lord, who lives and reigns
    with you and the Holy Spirit, one God, for ever and ever. *Amen.*†

The Concluding Prayer of the Church
Lord God, almighty and everlasting Father, you have brought me in safety to this
    new day: Preserve me with your mighty power, that I may not fall into sin, nor
    be overcome by adversity; and in all I do direct me to the fulfilling of your pur-
    pose; through Jesus Christ my Lord. *Amen.*†

The Midday Office   **To Be Observed on the Hour or Half Hour**
                                         Between 11 a.m. and 2 p.m.

The Call to Prayer
The Lord is King; let the earth rejoice;* let the multitude of the isles be glad.

Psalm 97:1

The Request for Presence
Open my lips, O Lord,* and my mouth shall proclaim your praise.

Psalm 51:16

The Greeting

I give thanks to you, O LORD, with my whole heart;* I will tell of all your marvelous works.

I will be glad and rejoice in you;* I will sing your Name, O Most High.

Psalm 9:1–2

The Refrain for the Midday Lessons

Oh, the majesty and magnificence of his presence!* Oh, the power and the splendor of his sanctuary!

Psalm 96:6

A Reading

. . . He loves us and has washed away our sins with his blood, and made us a *kingdom of priests to serve* his God and Father, to him; then, be glory and power for
ever and ever. Amen.

Revelation 1:5–6

The Refrain

Oh, the majesty and magnificence of his presence!* Oh, the power and the splendor of his sanctuary!

The Midday Psalm   *Who Can Ascend the Hill of the LORD?*

The earth is the LORD's and all that is in it,* the world and all who dwell therein.
For it is he who founded it upon the seas* and made it firm upon the rivers of the
deep.
"Who can ascend the hill of the LORD?* and who can stand in his holy place?"
"Those who have clean hands and a pure heart,* who have not pledged them-
selves to falsehood, nor sworn by what is fraud.
They shall receive a blessing from the LORD* and a just reward from the God of
their salvation."
Such is the generation of those who seek him,* of those who seek your face, O God
of Jacob.

Psalm 24:1–6

The Refrain

Oh, the majesty and magnificence of his presence!* Oh, the power and the splendor of his sanctuary!

The Gloria

The Lord's Prayer

The Prayer Appointed for the Week

Grant to me, Lord. I pray, the spirit to think and do always those things that are
right, that I, who cannot exist without you, may by you be enabled to live
according to your will; through Jesus Christ my Lord, who lives and reigns
with you and the Holy Spirit, one God, for ever and ever. *Amen.*†

The Concluding Prayer of the Church

O God, you make me glad with the weekly remembrance of the glorious resurrection of your Son my Lord: Give me this day such blessing through my worship of you, that the week to come may be spent in your favor; through Jesus Christ our Lord. *Amen.*†

The Vespers Office **To Be Observed on the Hour or Half Hour Between 5 and 8 p.m.**

The Call to Prayer

Sing praise to the LORD who dwells in Zion:* proclaim to the peoples the things he has done.

Psalm 9:11

The Request for Presence

I call aloud upon the LORD,* and he answers me from his holy hill;
I lie down and go to sleep;* I wake again, because the LORD sustains me.

Psalm 3:4–5

The Greeting

You, O LORD, are a shield about me;* you are my glory, the one who lifts up my head.

Psalm 3:3

The Hymn *By All Your Saints*

By all your saints still striving,
for all your saints at rest,
your holy Name, O Jesus
for evermore be blessed.
You rose, our King victorious,
that they might wear the crown
and ever shine in splendor:
reflected from your throne.

We sing with joy of Mary
whose heart with awe was stirred
when, youthful and unready,
she heard the angel's word;
yet she her voice upraises,
God's glory to proclaim,
as once for our salvation
your mother she became.

Then let us praise the Father
and worship God the Son
and sing to God the Spirit,
eternal Three in One,
till all the ransomed number
who stand before the throne
ascribe all power and glory
and praise to God alone.

Horatio Nelson

The Refrain for the Vespers Lessons

Lift up your hands in the holy place and bless the LORD;* the LORD who made heaven and earth bless you out of Zion.

The Vespers Psalm   *Like a Child Upon Its Mother's Breast*
O LORD, I am not proud;* I have no haughty looks.
I do not occupy myself with great matters,* or with things that are too hard for me.
But I still my soul and make it quiet, like a child upon its mother's breast,* my soul
    is quieted within me.

Psalm 131:1–3

The Refrain
Lift up your hands in the holy place and bless the LORD;* the LORD who made
    heaven and earth bless you out of Zion.

The Small Verse
The Lord is King. He has put on glorious apparel. Let all the nations praise him.
    Let those of every tongue bow before him. Alleluia, alleluia, alleluia.

The Lord's Prayer

The Prayer Appointed for the Week
Grant to me, Lord. I pray, the spirit to think and do always those things that are
    right, that I, who cannot exist without you, may by you be enabled to live
    according to your will; through Jesus Christ my Lord, who lives and reigns
    with you and the Holy Spirit, one God, for ever and ever. *Amen.*†

The Concluding Prayer of the Church
Lord God, whose Son our Savior Jesus Christ, triumphed over the powers of death
    and prepared for us our place in the new Jerusalem: Grant that I, who have this
    day given thanks for his resurrection, may praise you in the City of which he is
    the light, and where he lives and reigns for ever and ever. *Amen.*†

The Morning Office   **To Be Observed on the Hour or Half Hour**
                                          Between 6 and 9 a.m.

The Call to Prayer
Worship the LORD in the beauty of holiness;* let the whole earth tremble before him.

Psalm 96:9

The Request for Presence
Hear, O Shepherd of Israel, leading Joseph like a flock;* shine forth, you that are
    enthroned upon the cherubim.

Psalm 80:1

The Greeting
Out of Zion, perfect in its beauty,* God reveals himself in glory.

Psalm 50:2

The Refrain for the Morning Lessons
The Lord himself shall give you a sign; behold, a virgin shall conceive, and bear a
    son, and shall call his name Immanuel.

Isaiah 7:14 KJV

A Reading   On August 15 of each year, the Church celebrates the life
                      and assumption of the Blessed Virgin, Mother of our Lord.

I will greatly rejoice in the LORD, my soul shall be joyful in my God; for he has
  clothed me with the garments of salvation, he has covered me with the robe of
  righteousness, as a bridegroom decks himself with ornaments, and as a bride
  adorns herself with jewels.
For as the earth brings forth her bud, and as the garden causes the things that are
  sown in it to spring forth; so the Lord GOD will cause righteousness and praise
  to spring forth before all nations.

                                                        based on Isaiah 61:10–11 KJV

The Refrain
The Lord himself shall give you a sign; behold, a virgin shall conceive, and bear a
  son, and shall call his name Immanuel.

The Morning Psalm   *Proclaim with Me the Greatness of the* LORD
I will bless the LORD at all times;* his praise shall ever be in my mouth.
I will glory in the LORD;* let the humble hear and rejoice.
Proclaim with me the greatness of the LORD;* let us exalt his Name together.
I sought the LORD, and he answered me* and delivered me out of all my terror.
Look upon him and be radiant,* and let not your faces be ashamed.
I called in my affliction and the LORD heard me* and saved me from my troubles.
The angel of the LORD heard me* and saved me from all my troubles.
The angel of the LORD encompasses those who fear him,* and he will deliver them.
Taste and see that the LORD is good;* happy are they who trust in him!

                                                        Psalm 34:1–8

The Refrain
The Lord himself shall give you a sign; behold, a virgin shall conceive, and bear a
  son, and shall call his name Immanuel.

The Gloria

The Lord's Prayer

The Prayer Appointed for the Week
Grant to me, Lord. I pray, the spirit to think and do always those things that are
  right, that I, who cannot exist without you, may by you be enabled to live
  according to your will; through Jesus Christ my Lord, who lives and reigns
  with you and the Holy Spirit, one God, for ever and ever. *Amen.*✝

The Concluding Prayer of the Church
Lord God, almighty and everlasting Father, you have brought me in safety to this
  new day: Preserve me with your mighty power, that I may not fall into sin, nor
  be overcome by adversity; and in all I do direct me to the fulfilling of your purpose; through Jesus Christ my Lord. *Amen.*✝

The Midday Office   **To Be Observed on the Hour or Half Hour**
Between 11 a.m. and 2 p.m.

The Call to Prayer
Come, let us sing to the LORD;* let us shout for joy to the Rock of our salvation.
Let us come before his presence with thanksgiving* and raise a loud shout to him
    with psalms.

Psalm 95:1–2

The Request for Presence
Protect me, O God, for I take refuge in you;* I have said to the LORD, "You are my
    Lord, my good above all other."

Psalm 16:1

The Greeting
Let all who seek you rejoice and be glad in you;* let those who love your salvation
    say for ever, "Great is the LORD!"

Psalm 70:4

The Refrain for the Midday Lessons
The Lord himself shall give you a sign; behold, a virgin shall conceive, and bear a
    son, and shall call his name Immanuel.

Isaiah 7:14 KJV

A Reading
. . . when the completion of the time came, God sent his Son, born of a woman,
    born a subject of the Law, to redeem the subjects of the Law and so that we
    could receive adoption as sons. As you are sons, God has sent into our hearts
    the Spirit of his Son crying, 'Abba, Father,' and so you are no longer a slave, but
    a son . . .

Galatians 4:4–7

The Refrain
The Lord himself shall give you a sign; behold, a virgin shall conceive, and bear a
    son, and shall call his name Immanuel.

The Midday Psalm   *The Song of King Uzziah*
'May you be blessed, my daughter, by God Most High,
    beyond all women on earth;
    and blessed be the Lord God,
    Creator of heaven and earth, . . .
    The trust which you have shown
    will not pass from human hearts,
    as they commemorate
    the power of God for evermore.
    God grant you may always be held in honor,
    and rewarded with blessings,

since you did not consider your own life
when our nation was brought to its knees,
but warded off our ruin
walking in the upright path before our God.'
. . . 'Amen! Amen!'

Judith 13:23–26

The Refrain
The Lord himself shall give you a sign; behold, a virgin shall conceive, and bear a
son, and shall call his name Immanuel.

The Gloria

The Lord's Prayer

The Prayer Appointed for the Week
Grant to me, Lord. I pray, the spirit to think and do always those things that are
right, that I, who cannot exist without you, may by you be enabled to live
according to your will; through Jesus Christ my Lord, who lives and reigns
with you and the Holy Spirit, one God, for ever and ever. *Amen.*†

The Concluding Prayer of the Church
O God, you have taken to yourself the blessed Virgin Mary, mother of your incarnate Son: Grant that all your people, redeemed by his blood, may share with
her the glory of your eternal kingdom; through Jesus Christ our Lord, who
lives and reigns with you, in the unity of the Holy Spirit, one God, now and
forever. *Amen.*†

The Vespers Office   **To Be Observed on the Hour or Half Hour**
Between 5 and 8 p.m.

The Call to Prayer
Bless the LORD, you angels of his, you mighty ones who do his bidding,* and hear-
ken to the voice of his word.
Bless the LORD, all you his hosts,* you ministers of his who do his will.
Bless the LORD, all you works of his, in all places of his dominion;* bless the LORD,
O my soul.

Psalm 103:20–22

The Request for Presence
O God be merciful to us and bless us,* show us the light of your countenance and
come to us.
Let your ways be known upon the earth,* your saving health among all nations.

based on Psalm 67:1–2

The Greeting
Hosanna, LORD, hosanna!* LORD, send us now success.

Psalm 118:25

The Hymn   *Mary the Dawn*

Mary the dawn, Christ the Perfect Day;
Mary the gate, Christ the Heavenly Way!

Mary the root, Christ the Mystic Vine;
Mary the grape, Christ the Sacred Wine!

Mary the wheat, Christ the Living Bread;
Mary the stem, Christ the Rose blood-red!

Mary the font, Christ the Cleansing flood;
Mary the cup, Christ the Saving Blood!

Mary the temple, Christ the temple's Lord;
Mary the shrine, Christ the God adored!

Mary the beacon, Christ the Haven's Rest;
Mary the mirror, Christ the Vision Blest!

Mary the mother, Christ the mother's Son
By all things blessed while endless ages run.

                 The Dominican Sisters of Summit

The Refrain for the Vespers Lessons

The Lord himself shall give you a sign; behold, a virgin shall conceive, and bear a
son, and shall call his name Immanuel.

                                      Isaiah 7:14 KJV

The Vespers Psalm   The Fruit of the Womb Is a Gift

Unless the Lord builds the house,* their labor is in vain who build it.
Unless the Lord watches over the city,* in vain the watchmen keep their vigil.
It is in vain that you rise so early and go to bed so late;* vain, too, to eat the bread
of toil, for he gives his beloved sleep.
Children are a heritage from the Lord,* and the fruit of the womb is a gift.
Like arrows in the hand of a warrior* are the children of one's youth.

                                    Psalm 127:1–5

The Refrain

The Lord himself shall give you a sign; behold, a virgin shall conceive, and bear a
son, and shall call his name Immanuel.

The Gloria

The Lord's Prayer

The Prayer Appointed for the Week

Grant to me, Lord. I pray, the spirit to think and do always those things that are
right, that I, who cannot exist without you, may by you be enabled to live
according to your will; through Jesus Christ my Lord, who lives and reigns
with you and the Holy Spirit, one God, for ever and ever. *Amen.†*

The Concluding Prayer of the Church

O God, you have taken to yourself the blessed Virgin Mary, mother of your incarnate Son: Grant that all your people, redeemed by his blood, may share with her the glory of your eternal kingdom; through Jesus Christ our Lord, who lives and reigns with you, in the unity of the Holy Spirit, one God, now and forever. *Amen.*†

The Morning Office   **To Be Observed on the Hour or Half Hour**
Between 6 and 9 a.m.

The Call to Prayer

Give thanks to the LORD, for he is good,* for his mercy endures for ever.
Give thanks to the God of gods,* for his mercy endures for ever.
Give thanks to the Lord of lords,* for his mercy endures for ever.

Psalm 136:1–3

The Request for Presence

Bow down your ear, O LORD, and answer me . . . * Keep watch over my life, for I am faithful.

Psalm 86:1–2

The Greeting

The LORD, the God of gods, has spoken;* he has called the earth from the rising of the sun to its setting.
Out of Zion, perfect in its beauty,* God reveals himself in glory.
Our God will come and will not keep silence;* before him there is a consuming flame, and round about him a raging storm.

Psalm 50:1–3

The Refrain for the Morning Lessons

The LORD has sworn an oath to David;* in truth, he will not break it:
"A son, fruit of your body* will I set upon your throne."

Psalm 132:11–12

A Reading

Every year his parents used to go to Jerusalem for the feast of the Passover. When he was twelve years old, they went up for the feast as usual. When the days of the feast were over and they set off home, the boy Jesus stayed behind in Jerusalem without his parents knowing it. They assumed he was somewhere in the party, and it was only after a day's journey that they went to look for him among their relations and acquaintances. When they failed to find him they went back to Jerusalem, looking for him everywhere. It happened that, three days later, they found him in the Temple, sitting among the teachers, listening to them, and asking them questions; and all those who heard him were astounded at his intelligence and his replies. They were overcome when they saw him, and his mother said to him, 'My child, why have you done this to us? See how worried your father and I have been, looking for you.' 'Why were you looking for me?' he replied. 'Did you not know that I must be in my Father's house?' But they did not understand what he meant. He went down with them and came to Nazareth and lived under their authority. His mother stored up all these things in her heart. And Jesus increased in wisdom, in stature, and in favor with God and with people.

Luke 2:41–52

The Refrain
The LORD has sworn an oath to David;* in truth, he will not break it:
"A son, fruit of your body* will I set upon your throne."

The Morning Psalm   *This Day Have I Begotten You*
Let me announce the decree of the LORD:* he said to me, "You are my Son; this day have I begotten you.
Ask of me, and I will give you the nations for your inheritance* and the ends of the earth for your possession.

Psalm 2:7–8

The Refrain
The LORD has sworn an oath to David;* in truth, he will not break it:
"A son, fruit of your body* will I set upon your throne."

The Cry of the Church
Even so come, Lord Jesus!

The Lord's Prayer

The Prayer Appointed for the Week
Grant to me, Lord. I pray, the spirit to think and do always those things that are right, that I, who cannot exist without you, may by you be enabled to live according to your will; through Jesus Christ my Lord, who lives and reigns with you and the Holy Spirit, one God, for ever and ever. *Amen.*†

The Concluding Prayer of the Church
Lord God, almighty and everlasting Father, you have brought me in safety to this new day: Preserve me with your mighty power, that I may not fall into sin, nor be overcome by adversity; and in all I do direct me to the fulfilling of your purpose; through Jesus Christ my Lord. *Amen.*†

The Midday Office   **To Be Observed on the Hour or Half Hour**
                                         Between 11 a.m. and 2 p.m.

The Call to Prayer
Hallelujah! Praise the Name of the LORD;* give praise, you servants of the LORD!

Psalm 135:1

The Request for Presence
Be seated on your lofty throne, O Most High;* O LORD, judge the nations.

Psalm 7:8

The Greeting

I will confess you among the peoples, O LORD;* I will sing praise to you among the
  nations.
For your loving-kindness is greater than the heavens,* and your faithfulness
  reaches to the clouds.

Psalm 57:9–10

The Refrain for the Midday Lessons

Light has sprung up for the righteous,* and joyful gladness for those who are true
  hearted.

Psalm 97:11

A Reading

He had shown himself alive to them after his Passion by many demonstrations;
  for forty days he had continued to appear to them and tell them about the
  kingdom of God. As he said this he was lifted up while they looked on, and a
  cloud took him from their sight. They were still staring into the sky as he went
  when suddenly two men in white were standing beside them and they said,
  'Why are you Galileans standing here looking into the sky? Jesus who has been
  taken up from you into heaven will come back in the same way as you have
  seen him go to heaven.' So from the Mount of Olives, as it is called, they went
  back to Jerusalem, a short distance away, no more than a Sabbath walk; and
  when they reached the city they went to the upper room where they were staying; there were Peter and John, James and Andrew, Philip and Thomas,
  Bartholomew and Matthew, James son of Alphaeus and Simon the Zealot, and
  Jude son of James.

Acts 1:3, 9–14

The Refrain

Light has sprung up for the righteous,* and joyful gladness for those who are true
  hearted.

The Midday Psalm   *That the Generations to Come Might Know*

That which we have heard and known, and what our forefathers have told us,* we
  will not hide from their children.
We will recount for generations to come the praiseworthy deeds and power of the
  LORD,* and the wonderful works he has done.
He gave his decrees to Jacob and established a law for Israel,* which he com-
  manded them to teach their children;
That the generations to come might know, and the children yet unborn;* that they
  in their turn might tell it to their children;
So that they might put their trust in God,* and not forget the deeds of God, but
  keep his commandments;
And not be like their forefathers, a stubborn and rebellious generation,* a genera-
  tion whose heart was not steadfast, and whose spirit was not faithful to God.

Psalm 78:3–8

The Refrain

Light has sprung up for the righteous,* and joyful gladness for those who are true
hearted.

The Gloria

The Lord's Prayer

The Prayer Appointed for the Week

Grant to me, Lord. I pray, the spirit to think and do always those things that are
right, that I, who cannot exist without you, may by you be enabled to live
according to your will; through Jesus Christ my Lord, who lives and reigns
with you and the Holy Spirit, one God, for ever and ever. *Amen.*†

The Concluding Prayer of the Church

May God himself order my days
And make them acceptable in his sight.
Blessed is the Lord always,
My strength and my redeemer.

Traditional

The Vespers Office   **To Be Observed on the Hour or Half Hour**
Between 5 and 8 p.m.

The Call to Prayer

Great is the LORD and greatly to be praised;* there is no end to his greatness.

Psalm 145:3

The Request for Presence

I am a stranger here on earth;* do not hide your commandments from me.

Psalm 119:19

The Greeting

You, O LORD, are my lamp;* my God, you make my darkness bright.

Psalm 18:29

The Hymn   ***God Moves in Mysterious Ways***

God moves in a mysterious way   Judge not the Lord by feeble sense,
His wonders to perform;   But trust him for his grace;
He plants his footstep in the sea,   Behind a frowning providence
And rides upon the storm.   He hides a smiling face.

Deep in unfathomable mines   His purposes will ripen fast,
Of never-failing skill   Unfolding every hour;
He treasures up his bright designs,   The bud may have a bitter taste,
And works his sovereign will.   But sweet will be the flower.

Blind unbelief is sure to err,
And scan his work in vain;
God is his own interpreter,
And he will make it plain.

William Cowper

The Refrain for the Vespers Lessons

The fool has said in his heart, "There is no God."*

Psalm 53:1

The Vespers Psalm   *His Piercing Eye Beholds Our Worth*

The LORD is in his holy temple;* the LORD's throne is in heaven.

His eyes behold the inhabited world;* his piercing eye beholds our worth.

The LORD weighs the righteous as well as the wicked,* but those who delight in violence he abhors.

For the LORD is righteous; he delights in righteous deeds;* and the just shall see his face.

Psalm 11:4–8

The Refrain

The fool has said in his heart, "There is no God."*

The Small Verse

The Lord is my shepherd and nothing is wanting to me. In green pastures He hath settled me.

THE SHORT BREVIARY

The Lord's Prayer

The Prayer Appointed for the Week

Grant to me, Lord. I pray, the spirit to think and do always those things that are right, that I, who cannot exist without you, may by you be enabled to live according to your will; through Jesus Christ my Lord, who lives and reigns with you and the Holy Spirit, one God, for ever and ever. *Amen.*†

The Concluding Prayer of the Church

Drop thy still dews of quietness,
Till all our strivings cease;
Take from our souls the strain and stress,
And let our ordered lives confess
The beauty of thy peace.

John G. Whittier

The Morning Office   **To Be Observed on the Hour or Half Hour**
                                         Between 6 and 9 a.m.

The Call to Prayer
Bless the LORD, O my soul,* and all that is within me, bless his holy Name.
Bless the LORD, O my soul,* and forget not all his benefits.

Psalm 103:1–2

The Request for Presence
Satisfy us by your loving-kindness in the morning;* so shall we rejoice and be glad
all the days of our life.

Psalm 90:14

The Greeting
The words of the LORD are pure words,* like silver refined from ore and purified
seven times in fire.

Psalm 12:6

The Refrain for the Morning Lessons
The earth, O LORD, is full of your love;* instruct me in your statutes.

Psalm 119:64

A Reading
Jesus taught us, saying: 'Sell your possessions and give to those in need. Get yourselves purses that do not wear out, treasure that will not fail you, in heaven
where no thief can reach it and no moth destroy it. For where your treasure is,
there is where your heart will be too.'

Luke 12:33–34

The Refrain
The earth, O LORD, is full of your love;* instruct me in your statutes.

The Morning Psalm   *May the LORD Strengthen You Out of Zion*
May the LORD answer you in the day of trouble,* the Name of the God of Jacob
defend you;
Send you help from this holy place* and strengthen you out of Zion;
Remember all your offerings* and accept you burnt sacrifice;
Grant you your heart's desire* and prosper all your plans.
We will shout for joy at your victory and triumph in the Name of our God;* may
the LORD grant all your requests.

Psalm 20:1–5

The Refrain
The earth, O LORD, is full of your love;* instruct me in your statutes.

The Gloria

The Lord's Prayer

The Prayer Appointed for the Week
Grant to me, Lord. I pray, the spirit to think and do always those things that are
right, that I, who cannot exist without you, may by you be enabled to live
according to your will; through Jesus Christ my Lord, who lives and reigns
with you and the Holy Spirit, one God, for ever and ever. *Amen.*†

The Concluding Prayer of the Church
Lord God, almighty and everlasting Father, you have brought me in safety to this
new day: Preserve me with your mighty power, that I may not fall into sin, nor
be overcome by adversity; and in all I do direct me to the fulfilling of your purpose; through Jesus Christ my Lord. *Amen.*†

The Midday Office   **To Be Observed on the Hour or Half Hour**
Between 11 a.m. and 2 p.m.

The Call to Prayer
I will call upon the LORD,* and so shall I be saved from my enemies.
Psalm 18:3

The Request for Presence
Save me, O God, by your Name;* in your might, defend my cause.
Hear my prayer, O God;* give ear to the words of my mouth.
Psalm 54:1–2

The Greeting
To you, O LORD, I lift up my soul; my God, I put my trust in you;* let me not be
humiliated, nor let my enemies triumph over me.
Let none who look to you be put to shame;* let the treacherous be disappointed in
their schemes.
Psalm 25:1–2

The Refrain for the Midday Lessons
Protect my life and deliver me;* let me not be put to shame, for I have trusted in
you.
Psalm 25:19

A Reading   *A Canticle of Isaiah, the Prophet*
Thus says YAHWEH: . . . 'There is no other god besides me, no saving God, no
Savior except me! Turn to me and you will be saved, all you ends of the earth,
for I am God and there is no other. By my own self I swear it: what comes from
my mouth is saving justice, it is an irrevocable word: All shall bend the knee to
me, by me every tongue shall swear, saying, "In YAHWEH alone are saving justice and strength." '
Isaiah 45:14, 21–24

The Refrain
Protect my life and deliver me;* let me not be put to shame, for I have trusted in you.

The Midday Psalm   *They Have Not Prevailed Against Me*

"Greatly have they oppressed me since my youth,"* let Israel now say;

"Greatly have they oppressed me since my youth,* but they have not prevailed
against me."

The plowmen plowed upon my back* and made their furrows long.

The LORD, the righteous one,* has cut the cords of the wicked.

Let them be put to shame and thrown back,* all those who are enemies of Zion.

Let them be like grass upon the housetops,* which withers before it can be
plucked;

Which does not fill the hand of the reaper,* nor the bosom of him who binds the
sheaves;

So that those who go by say not so much as, "The LORD prosper you.* We wish you
well in the Name of the LORD."

Psalm 129

The Refrain

Protect my life and deliver me;* let me not be put to shame, for I have trusted in you.

The Cry of the Church

Lord, have mercy on us. Christ, have mercy on us. Lord, have mercy on us.

The Lord's Prayer

The Prayer Appointed for the Week

Grant to me, Lord. I pray, the spirit to think and do always those things that are
right, that I, who cannot exist without you, may by you be enabled to live
according to your will; through Jesus Christ my Lord, who lives and reigns
with you and the Holy Spirit, one God, for ever and ever. *Amen.*†

The Concluding Prayer of the Church

Lord Jesus Christ, you have prepared a quiet place for us in your Father's eternal
home. Watch over my welfare on this perilous journey, shade me from the
burning heat of day, and keep my life free of evil until the end. *Amen.*

THE LITURGY OF THE HOURS, VOL. III

The Vespers Office   **To Be Observed on the Hour or Half Hour**
Between 5 and 8 p.m.

The Call to Prayer

Hallelujah! Give thanks to the LORD for he is good,* for his mercy endures for ever.

Psalm 106:1

The Request for Presence

Give ear, O LORD, to my prayer,* and attend to the voice of my supplications.

Psalm 86:6

The Greeting
You are my hiding-place; you preserve me from trouble;* you surround me with
shouts of deliverance.

Psalm 32:8

The Hymn   ***Take My Hand, Precious Lord***
Take my hand, Precious Lord,
Lead me on, let me stand.
I am tired, I am weak, I am worn.
Through the storm, through the night,
lead me on to the light.
Take my hand, Precious Lord, lead me home.

When my way grows dear,
Precious Lord, linger near
When my life is almost gone.
Hear my cry, hear my call,
hold my hand lest I fall.
Take my hand, Precious Lord, lead me home.

When the darkness appears
And the night draws near
At the river I stand,
Guide my feet, hold my hand
Take my hand, Precious Lord, lead me home.

Thomas A. Dorsey

The Refrain for the Vespers Lessons
In God, the Lord, whose word I praise, in God I trust and will not be afraid,* for
what can mortals do to me?

Psalm 56:10

The Vespers Psalm   ***He Gives to His Beloved Sleep***
Unless the Lord builds the house,* their labor is in vain who build it.
Unless the Lord watches over the city,* in vain the watchman keeps his vigil.
It is vain that you rise so early and go to bed so late;* vain, too, to eat the bread of
toil, for he gives to his beloved sleep.

Psalm 127:1–3

The Refrain
In God, the Lord, whose word I praise, in God I trust and will not be afraid,* for
what can mortals do to me?

The Cry of the Church
O God, come to my assistance! O Lord, make haste to help me!

The Lord's Prayer

The Prayer Appointed for the Week
Grant to me, Lord. I pray, the spirit to think and do always those things that are right, that I, who cannot exist without you, may by you be enabled to live according to your will; through Jesus Christ my Lord, who lives and reigns with you and the Holy Spirit, one God, for ever and ever. *Amen.*†

The Concluding Prayer of the Church
May Almighty God grant me a peaceful night and a perfect end. *Amen.*

The Morning Office   **To Be Observed on the Hour or Half Hour Between 6 and 9 a.m.**

The Call to Prayer
Sing with joy to God our strength* and raise a loud shout to the God of Jacob.
Psalm 81:1

The Request for Presence
Our God will come and will not keep silence;* before him there is a consuming flame, and round about him a raging storm.
Psalm 50:3

The Greeting
I will give thanks for what you have done* and declare the goodness of your Name in the presence of the godly.
Psalm 52:9

The Refrain for the Morning Lessons
I am like a green olive tree in the house of God;* I trust in the mercy of God for ever and ever.
Psalm 52:8

A Reading
Jesus taught us, saying: 'Do not imagine that I have come to abolish the Law or the Prophets. I have come not to abolish but to complete them. In truth I tell you, till heaven and earth disappear, not one dot, not one little stroke, is to disappear from the Law until all its purpose is achieved. Therefore, anyone who infringes even one of the least of these commandments and teaches others to do the same will be considered the least in the kingdom of heaven; but the person who keeps them and teaches them will be considered great in the kingdom of heaven.'
Matthew 5:17–19

The Refrain
I am like a green olive tree in the house of God;* I trust in the mercy of God for ever and ever.

The Morning Psalm   *He Declares His Word to Jacob*
Worship the LORD, O Jerusalem;* praise your God, O Zion;
For he has strengthened the bars of your gates;* he has blessed your children within you.

He has established peace on your borders;* he satisfies you with the finest wheat.

He sends out his command to the earth,* and his word runs very swiftly.

He gives snow like wool;* he scatters hoarfrost like ashes.

He scatters his hail like bread crumbs;* who can stand against his cold?

He sends forth his word and melts them;* he blows with his wind, and the waters flow.

He declares his word to Jacob,* his statutes and his judgments to Israel.

He has not done so to any other nation;* to them he has not revealed his judgments. Hallelujah!

Psalm 147:13–21

The Refrain
I am like a green olive tree in the house of God;* I trust in the mercy of God for ever and ever.

The Gloria

The Lord's Prayer

The Prayer Appointed for the Week
Grant to me, Lord. I pray, the spirit to think and do always those things that are right, that I, who cannot exist without you, may by you be enabled to live according to your will; through Jesus Christ my Lord, who lives and reigns with you and the Holy Spirit, one God, for ever and ever. *Amen.*†

The Concluding Prayer of the Church
Lord God, almighty and everlasting Father, you have brought me in safety to this new day: Preserve me with your mighty power, that I may not fall into sin, nor be overcome by adversity; and in all I do direct me to the fulfilling of your purpose; through Jesus Christ my Lord. *Amen.*†

The Midday Office   **To Be Observed on the Hour or Half Hour Between 11 a.m. and 2 p.m.**

The Call to Prayer
Clap your hands, all you peoples;* shout to God with a cry of joy.

Psalm 47:1

The Request for Presence
Be exalted, O Lord, in your might;* we will sing and praise your power.

Psalm 21:14

The Greeting
Exalt yourself above the heavens, O God,* and your glory over all the earth.

Psalm 108:5

The Refrain for the Midday Lessons
The LORD shall reign forever,* your god, O Zion, throughout all generations. Hallelujah!

Psalm 146:9

A Reading
Thus says YAHWEH, the Creator of the heavens—he is God, who shaped the earth and made it, who set it firm, he did not create it to be chaos, he formed it to be lived in: I am YAHWEH: and there is no other, I have not spoken in secret, in some dark corner of the underworld. I did not say, 'Offspring of Jacob, search for me in chaos!' I am YAHWEH: I proclaim saving justice, what I say is true. Assemble, come, all of you gather round, survivors of the nations. They have no knowledge, those who parade their wooden idols and pray to a god that cannot save.

Isaiah 45:18–20

The Refrain
The LORD shall reign forever,* your god, O Zion, throughout all generations. Hallelujah!

The Midday Psalm   *The Fool Has Said in His Heart, "There Is No God."*
The fool has said in his heart, "There is no God."* All are corrupt and commit abominable acts; there is none who does any good.
The LORD looks down from heaven upon us all,* to see if there is any who is wise, if there is one who seeks after God.
Every one has proved faithless; all alike have turned bad;* there is none who does good; no, not one.
Have they no knowledge, all those evildoers* who eat up my people like bread and do not call upon the LORD?
See how they tremble with fear,* because God is in the company of the righteous.
Their aim is to confound the plans of the afflicted,* but the LORD is their refuge.
Oh, that Israel's deliverance would come out of Zion!* When the LORD restores the fortunes of his people, Jacob will rejoice and Israel will be glad.

Psalm 14

The Refrain
The LORD shall reign forever,* your god, O Zion, throughout all generations. Hallelujah!

The Cry of the Church
Even so, come Lord Jesus.

The Lord's Prayer

The Prayer Appointed for the Week
Grant to me, Lord. I pray, the spirit to think and do always those things that are right, that I, who cannot exist without you, may by you be enabled to live according to your will; through Jesus Christ my Lord, who lives and reigns with you and the Holy Spirit, one God, for ever and ever. *Amen.*†

The Concluding Prayer of the Church
Lord, my God, King of heaven and earth, for this day please direct and sanctify,
set right and govern my heart and body, my sentiments, my words and my
actions in conformity with Your law and Your commandments. Thus I shall be
able to attain salvation and deliverance, in time and in eternity, by Your help, O
Savior of the world, who lives and reigns forever. *Amen.*

adapted from The Divine Office, *II*

The Vespers Office   **To Be Observed on the Hour or Half Hour**
                                    Between 5 and 8 p.m.

The Call to Prayer
Come, let us sing to the Lord;* let us shout for joy to the Rock of our salvation.

Psalm 95:1

The Request for Presence
You have set up a banner for those who fear you,* to be a refuge from the power of
the bow.
Save us by your right hand and answer us,* that those who are dear to you may be
delivered.

Psalm 60:4–5

The Greeting
You are my refuge and shield;* my hope is in your word.

Psalm 119:114

The Hymn
   O God, creation's secret force,
   Yourself unmoved but all motion's source;
   Who, from the morn till the evening's ray,
   Through all its changes guide the day.

   Come, Holy Ghost, with God the Son,
   And God the Father ever one;
   Shed forth your grace within my breast,
   And dwell with me a ready guest.

   By every power, by heart and tongue,
   By act and deed your praise be sung;
   Inflame with perfect love each sense
   That others' souls may kindle thence.

   O Father, grant what I ask be done
   Through Jesus Christ your only Son.
   Who, with the Holy Ghost and you as three
   Lives and reigns eternally. *Amen.*

adapted from The Short Breviary

The Refrain for the Vespers Lessons
Your righteousness, O God, reaches to the heavens;* you have done great things;
who is like you, O God?

Psalm 71:19

The Vespers Psalm   *LORD, Who May Dwell in Your Tabernacle?*
LORD, who may dwell in your tabernacle?* who may abide upon your holy hill?
Whoever leads a blameless life and does what is right,* who speaks the truth from
his heart.
There is no guile upon his tongue; he does no evil to his friend;* he does not heap
contempt upon his neighbor.
In his sight the wicked is rejected,* but he honors those who fear the LORD.
He has sworn to do no wrong* and does not take back his word.
He does not give his money in hope of gain,* nor does he take a bribe against the
innocent.
Whoever does these things* shall never be overthrown.

Psalm 15:1–7

The Refrain
Your righteousness, O God, reaches to the heavens;* you have done great things;
who is like you, O God?

The Cry of the Church
O God, come to my assistance! O Lord, make haste to help me!

The Lord's Prayer

The Prayer Appointed for the Week
Grant to me, Lord. I pray, the spirit to think and do always those things that are
right, that I, who cannot exist without you, may by you be enabled to live
according to your will; through Jesus Christ my Lord, who lives and reigns
with you and the Holy Spirit, one God, for ever and ever. *Amen.*†

The Concluding Prayer of the Church
O God, the King eternal, whose light divides the day from the night and turns the
shadow of death into the morning: Drive far from me all wrong desires, incline
my heart to keep your law, and guide my feet into the way of peace; that, having done your will with cheerfulness during the day, I may, when night comes,
rejoice to give you thanks; through Jesus Christ my Lord. *Amen.*†

The Morning Office   **To Be Observed on the Hour or Half Hour**
Between 6 and 9 a.m.

The Call to Prayer
Love the LORD, all you who worship him;* the LORD protects the faithful, but
repays to the full those who act haughtily.

Psalm 31:23

The Request for Presence
Hear, O Lord, and have mercy upon me;* Lord, be my helper.

Psalm 30:11

The Greeting
As the deer longs for the water-brooks,* so longs my soul for you, O God.

Psalm 42:1

The Refrain for the Midday Lessons
One thing have I asked of the Lord; one thing I seek;* that I may dwell in the
house of the Lord all the days of my life . . .

Psalm 27:5

A Reading
He called the people and his disciples to him and said, 'If anyone wants to be a follower of mine, let him renounce himself and take up his cross and follow me.
Anyone who wants to save his life will lose it; but anyone who loses his life for
my sake, and for the sake of the gospel, will save it. What gain, then, is it for
anyone to win the whole world and forfeit his life? And indeed what can a man
offer in exchange for his life? For if anyone in this adulterous and sinful generation is ashamed of me and my words, the Son of Man will also be ashamed of
him when he comes in the glory of his Father with the holy angels.'

Mark 8:34–38

The Refrain
One thing have I asked of the Lord; one thing I seek;* that I may dwell in the
house of the Lord all the days of my life . . .

The Midday Psalm   *All That Is Within Me, Bless His Holy Name*
Bless the Lord, O my soul,* and all that is within me, bless his holy Name.
Bless the Lord, O my soul,* and forget not all his benefits.
He forgives all your sins* and heals all your infirmities;
He redeems your life from the grave* and crowns you with mercy and loving-
kindness;
He satisfies you with good things,* and your youth is renewed like an eagle's.

Psalm 103:1–5

The Refrain
One thing have I asked of the Lord; one thing I seek;* that I may dwell in the
house of the Lord all the days of my life . . .

The Cry of the Church
Lord, have mercy on us. Christ, have mercy on us. Lord, have mercy on us.

The Lord's Prayer

The Prayer Appointed for the Week
Grant to me, Lord. I pray, the spirit to think and do always those things that are
right, that I, who cannot exist without you, may by you be enabled to live

according to your will; through Jesus Christ my Lord, who lives and reigns with you and the Holy Spirit, one God, for ever and ever. *Amen.*†

The Concluding Prayer of the Church

Lord God, almighty and everlasting Father, you have brought me in safety to this new day: Preserve me with your mighty power, that I may not fall into sin, nor be overcome by adversity; and in all I do direct me to the fulfilling of your purpose; through Jesus Christ my Lord. *Amen.*†

The Midday Office   **To Be Observed on the Hour or Half Hour**
                                          Between 11 a.m. and 2 p.m.

The Call to Prayer

Ascribe to the LORD the honor due his Name;* bring offerings and come into his courts.

Psalm 96:8

The Request for Presence

Remember not our past sins;* let your compassion be swift to meet us . . .
Help us, O God our Savior, for the glory of your Name;* deliver us and forgive us our sins, for your Name's sake.

Psalm 79:8–9

The Greeting

For your Name's sake, O LORD,* forgive my sin, for it is great.

Psalm 25:10

The Refrain for the Midday Lessons

When I was in trouble, I called to the LORD;* I called to the LORD, and he answered me.

Psalm 120:1

A Reading   A Canticle of Tobias

Blessed be God who lives for ever, for his reign endures throughout all ages! For he both punishes and pardons; he sends people down to the depths of the underworld and draws them up from utter Destruction; no one can escape his hand . . . Extol him before all the living; he is our Lord and he is our God and he is our Father and he is God for ever and ever . . . Consider how well he has treated you; loudly give him thanks. Bless the Lord of Justice and extol the King of the ages. I for my part sing his praise in the country of my exile; I make his power and greatness known to a nation that has sinned. Sinners, return to him; let your conduct be upright before him; perhaps he will be gracious to you and take pity on you. I for my part extol God and my soul rejoices in the King of heaven. Let his greatness be on every tongue his praises be sung in Jerusalem.

Tobit 13:1ff

The Refrain

When I was in trouble, I called to the LORD;* I called to the LORD, and he answered me.

The Midday Psalm   *He Knows the Secrets of the Heart*

If we have forgotten the Name of our God,* or stretched out our hands to some strange god,

Will not God find it out?* for he knows the secrets of the heart.

Indeed for your sake we are killed all the day long;* we are accounted as sheep for the slaughter.

Awake, O Lord! why are you sleeping?* Arise! do not reject us for ever.

Why have you hidden your face* and forgotten our affliction and oppression?

We sink down into the dust;* our body cleaves to the ground.

Rise up, and help us,* and save us, for the sake of your steadfast love.

Psalm 44:20–26

The Refrain

When I was in trouble, I called to the LORD;* I called to the LORD, and he answered me.

The Cry of the Church

In the evening, in the morning, and at noonday, I will complain and lament,* and he will hear my voice.

Psalm 55:18

The Lord's Prayer

The Prayer Appointed for the Week

Grant to me, Lord. I pray, the spirit to think and do always those things that are right, that I, who cannot exist without you, may by you be enabled to live according to your will; through Jesus Christ my Lord, who lives and reigns with you and the Holy Spirit, one God, for ever and ever. *Amen.†*

The Concluding Prayer of the Church

Lord Jesus Christ, by your death you took away the sting of death: Grant me to so follow in faith where you have led the way, that I may at length fall asleep peacefully in you and wake in your likeness; for your tender mercies' sake. *Amen.*

The Vespers Office   To Be Observed on the Hour or Half Hour
Between 5 and 8 p.m.

The Call to Prayer

O tarry and await the LORD's pleasure; be strong, and he shall comfort your heart;* wait patiently for the LORD.

Psalm 27:18

The Request for Presence
Let your loving-kindness be my comfort,* as you have promised to your servant.
Let your compassion come to me, that I may live,* for your law is my delight.

Psalm 119:76–77

The Greeting
To you, O Lord, I lift up my soul;* my God I put my trust in you . . .

Psalm 2:1

The Hymn   *All the Way My Savior Leads Me*

All the way my Savior leads me,
What have I to ask beside?
Can I doubt His tender mercies,
Who through life has been my guide?
Heavenly peace, divinest comfort,
Here by faith in Him to dwell,
For I know whatever befall me,
Jesus does all things well.

All the way my Savior leads me,
O the fullness of His love!
Perfect rest to me is promised
In my Father's house above;
When my spirit, clothed, immortal,
Wings its flight to realms of day,
This my song through endless ages—
Jesus led me all the way.

Fanny J. Crosby

All the way my Savior leads me,
Cheers each winding path I tread,
Gives me grace for every trial,
Feeds me with the living bread,
Though my weary steps may falter,
And my soul athirst may be,
Gushing from the Rock before me,
Lo! A spring of joy I see.

The Refrain for the Vespers Lessons
Bless the Lord, O my soul,* and forget not all his benefits.

Psalm 103:2

The Vespers Psalm   *The Lord Accepts My Prayer*
Lord, do not rebuke me in your anger;* do not punish me in your wrath.
Have pity on me, Lord, for I am weak;* heal me, Lord, for my bones are racked.
My spirit shakes with terror;* how long, O Lord, how long?
Turn, O Lord, and deliver me;* save me for your mercy's sake.
For in death no one remembers you;* and who will give you thanks in the grave?
I grow weary because of my groaning;* every night I drench my bed and flood my
    couch with tears.
My eyes are wasted with grief* and worn away because of all my enemies.
Depart from me, all evildoers,* for the Lord has heard the sound of my weeping.
The Lord has heard my supplication;* the Lord accepts my prayer.
All my enemies shall be confounded and quake with fear;* they shall turn back
    and suddenly be put to shame.

Psalm 6

The Refrain
Bless the LORD, O my soul,* and forget not all his benefits.

The Cry of the Church
O Lamb of God, that takes away the sins of the world, have mercy upon me.
O Lamb of God, that takes away the sins of the world, have mercy upon me.
O Lamb of God, that takes away the sins of the world, grant me your peace.

The Lord's Prayer

The Prayer Appointed for the Week
Grant to me, Lord. I pray, the spirit to think and do always those things that are
   right, that I, who cannot exist without you, may by you be enabled to live
   according to your will; through Jesus Christ my Lord, who lives and reigns
   with you and the Holy Spirit, one God, for ever and ever. *Amen.*†

The Concluding Prayers of the Church
Almighty God, who has promised to hear the petitions of those who ask in your
   Son's Name: I beseech you mercifully to incline your ear to me who have made
   my prayers and supplications to you; and grant that those things which I have
   faithfully asked according to your will, I may effectually obtain, to the relief of
   my necessity, and to the setting forth of your glory; through Jesus Christ my
   Lord. *Amen.*†

May the souls of the faithful departed, through the mercy of God, rest in eternal
   peace. *Amen.*

The Morning Office   **To Be Observed on the Hour or Half Hour**
                                          Between 6 and 9 a.m.

The Call to Prayer
Proclaim with me the greatness of the LORD;* let us exalt his Name together.

                                                                  Psalm 34:3

The Request for Presence
May God be merciful to us and bless us,* show us the light of his countenance and
   come to us.

                                                                  Psalm 67:1

The Greeting
All who take refuge in you will be glad;* they will sing out their joy forever.
You will shelter them,* so that those who love your Name may exult in you.
For you, O LORD, will bless the righteous;* you will defend them with your favor
   as with a shield.

                                                                  Psalm 5:13–15

The Refrain for the Morning Lessons
"Be still, then, and know that I am God;* I will be exalted among the nations; I will
be exalted in the earth."

Psalm 46:11

A Reading
He told them another parable, 'The kingdom of heaven is like the yeast a woman
took and mixed in with three measures of flour till it was leavened all through.'

Matthew 13:33

The Refrain
"Be still, then, and know that I am God;* I will be exalted among the nations; I will
be exalted in the earth."

The Morning Psalm   *The LORD Shall Reign For Ever*
Happy are they who have the God of Jacob for their help!* whose hope is in the
   LORD their God;
Who made heaven and earth, the seas, and all that is in them;* who keeps his
   promise for ever;
Who gives justice to those who are oppressed,* and food to those who hunger.
The LORD sets prisoners free; the LORD opens the eyes of the blind;* the LORD lifts
   up those who are bowed down;
The LORD loves the righteous; the LORD cares for the stranger;* he sustains the
   orphan and the widow, but frustrates the way of the wicked.
The LORD shall reign for ever,* your God, O Zion, throughout all generations.
   Hallelujah!

Psalm 146:4–9

The Refrain
"Be still, then, and know that I am God;* I will be exalted among the nations; I will
be exalted in the earth."

The Small Verse
The Lord is my shepherd and nothing is wanting to me. In green pastures He hath
settled me.

THE SHORT BREVIARY

The Lord's Prayer

The Prayer Appointed for the Week
Grant to me, Lord. I pray, the spirit to think and do always those things that are
   right, that I, who cannot exist without you, may by you be enabled to live
   according to your will; through Jesus Christ my Lord, who lives and reigns
   with you and the Holy Spirit, one God, for ever and ever. *Amen.*†

The Concluding Prayer of the Church
Lord God, almighty and everlasting Father, you have brought me in safety to this
   new day: Preserve me with your mighty power, that I may not fall into sin, nor

be overcome by adversity; and in all I do direct me to the fulfilling of your purpose; through Jesus Christ my Lord. *Amen.*†

The Midday Office
**To Be Observed on the Hour or Half Hour
Between 11 a.m. and 2 p.m.**

The Call to Prayer
Praise God from whom all blessings flow; praise Him all creatures here below; praise Him above, you heavenly hosts; praise Father, Son, and Holy Ghost.

The Request for Presence
Send out your light and your truth, that they may lead me,* and bring me to your holy hill and to your dwelling;
That I may go to the altar of God, to the God of my joy and gladness;* and on the harp I will give thanks to you, O God, my God.

Psalm 43:3–4

The Greeting
Yours is the day, yours also the night;* you established the moon and the sun.
You fixed all the boundaries of the earth;* you made both summer and winter.

Psalm 74:15–16

The Refrain for the Midday Lessons
It is a good thing to give thanks to the LORD,* and to sing praises to your Name, O Most High . . .

Psalm 92:1

A Reading
A Canticle of Jeremiah, the Prophet
They will come shouting for joy on the heights of Zion, thronging towards YAHWEH's lavish gifts, for wheat, new wine and oil, sheep and cattle; they will be like a well-watered garden, they will sorrow no more. The young girl will then take pleasure in the dance and young men and old alike; I will change their mourning into gladness, comfort them, give them joy after their troubles, I shall refresh my priests with rich food, and see my people will gorge themselves on my lavish gifts—YAHWEH declares.

Jeremiah 31:12–14

The Refrain
It is a good thing to give thanks to the LORD,* and to sing praises to your Name, O Most High . . .

The Midday Psalm
In His Hand Are the Caverns of the Earth
Let us come before his presence with thanksgiving* and raise a loud shout to him with psalms.
For the LORD is a great God,* and a great King above all gods.
In his hand are the caverns of the earth,* and the heights of the hills are his also.
The sea is his, for he made it,* and his hands have molded the dry land.

Psalm 95:2–5

The Refrain

It is a good thing to give thanks to the LORD,* and to sing praises to your Name, O Most High . . .

The Gloria

The Lord's Prayer

The Prayer Appointed for the Week

Grant to me, Lord, I pray, the spirit to think and do always those things that are right, that I, who cannot exist without you, may by you be enabled to live according to your will; through Jesus Christ my Lord, who lives and reigns with you and the Holy Spirit, one God, for ever and ever. *Amen.*†

The Concluding Prayer of the Church

O God, the source of eternal light: Shed forth your unending day upon all of us who watch for you, that our lips may praise you, our lives may bless you, and our worship may give you glory; through Jesus Christ our Lord. *Amen.*†

The Vespers Office   **To Be Observed on the Hour or Half Hour**
                                          Between 5 and 8 p.m.

The Call to Prayer

Let those who favor my cause sing out with joy and be glad;* let them say always, "Great is the LORD, who desires the prosperity of his servant."
And my tongue shall be talking of your righteousness* and of your praise all the day long.

Psalm 35:27–28

The Request for Presence

Accept, O LORD, the willing tribute of my lips,* and teach me your judgments.

Psalm 119:108

The Greeting

I will give you thanks in the great congregation;* I will praise you in the mighty throng.

Psalm 35:18

The Hymn   There Is a Balm in Gilead

There is a balm in Gilead,	Don't ever be discouraged,
To make the wounded whole,	For Jesus is your friend,
There is a balm in Gilead,	And if you lack for knowledge,
To heal the sin-sick soul.	He'll never refuse to lend.
Sometimes I feel discouraged,	If you cannot preach like Peter,
And think my work's in vain,	If you cannot pray like Paul,
But then the Holy Spirit	You can tell the love of Jesus,
Revives my soul again.	And say He died for all.

Traditional

The Refrain for the Vespers Lessons
Glorious things are spoken of you,* O city of our God.

Psalm 87:2

The Vespers Psalm   *Let My Right Hand Forget Its Skill*
By the waters of Babylon we sat down and wept,* when we remembered you, O
Zion.
As for our harps, we hung them up* on the trees in the midst of that land.
For those who led us away captive asked us for a song, and our oppressors called
for mirth:* "Sing us one of the songs of Zion."
How shall we sing the LORD's songs* upon an alien soil?
If I forget you, O Jerusalem,* let my right hand forget its skill.
Let my tongue cleave to the roof of my mouth if I do not remember you,* if I do
not set Jerusalem above my highest joy.

Psalm 137:1–6

The Refrain
Glorious things are spoken of you,* O city of our God.

The Gloria

The Lord's Prayer

The Prayer Appointed for the Week
Grant to me, Lord. I pray, the spirit to think and do always those things that are
right, that I, who cannot exist without you, may by you be enabled to live
according to your will; through Jesus Christ my Lord, who lives and reigns
with you and the Holy Spirit, one God, for ever and ever. *Amen.*†

The Concluding Prayer of the Church
Almighty God, who after the creation of the world rested from all your works and
sanctified a day of rest for all your creatures: Grant that I, putting away all
earthly anxieties, may be duly prepared for the service of public worship, and
grant as well that my Sabbath upon earth may be a preparation for the eternal
rest promised to your people in heaven; through Jesus Christ our Lord. *Amen.*†

✥

The Morning Office   **To Be Observed on the Hour or Half Hour**
Between 6 and 9 a.m.

The Call to Prayer
Be joyful in the LORD, all you lands;* serve the LORD with gladness and come
before his presence with a song.

Know this: The LORD himself is God;* he himself has made us, and we are his; we
  are his people and the sheep of his pasture.
Enter his gates with thanksgiving;* go into his courts with praise; give thanks to
  him and call upon his Name.
For the LORD is good; his mercy is everlasting;* and his faithfulness endures from
  age to age.

Psalm 100

The Request for Presence
Early in the morning I cry out to you,* for in your words is my trust.

Psalm 119:147

The Greeting
You have made me glad by your acts, O LORD;* and I shout for joy because of the
  works of your hands.

Psalm 92:4

The Refrain for the Morning Lessons
I wait for the LORD; my soul waits for him;* in his word is my hope.

Psalm 130:4

A Reading
Jesus taught us, saying: 'Ask, and it will be given to you; search, and you will find;
  knock, and the door will be opened to you. Everyone who asks receives; everyone who searches finds; everyone who knocks will have the door opened. Is
  there anyone among you who would hand his son a stone when he asked for
  bread? Or would hand him a snake when he asked for fish? If you, then, evil as
  you are, know how to give your children what is good, how much more will
  your Father in heaven give good things to those who ask him!'

Matthew 7:7–11

The Refrain
I wait for the LORD; my soul waits for him;* in his word is my hope.

The Morning Psalm   *Bring Me to Your Holy Hill*
Send out your light and truth, that they may lead me,* and bring me to your holy
  hill and to your dwelling;
That I may go to the altar of God, to the God of my joy and gladness;* and on the
  harp I will give thanks to you, O God my God.
Why are you so full of heaviness, O my soul?* and why are you so disquieted
  within me?
Put your trust in God;* for I will yet give thanks to him, who is the help of my
  countenance, and my God.

Psalm 43:3–6

The Refrain
I wait for the LORD; my soul waits for him;* in his word is my hope.

The Cry of the Church
Even so come, Lord Jesus!

The Lord's Prayer

The Prayer Appointed for the Week
Almighty God, who has given your only Son to be unto us both a sacrifice for sin
and also an example of his godly life: Give me grace that I may always most
thankfully receive that his inestimable benefit and also daily endeavor myself
to follow the blessed steps of his most holy life; through the same your Son
Jesus Christ our Lord, who lives and reigns with you and the Holy Spirit, one
God, now and for ever. *Amen.*†

The Concluding Prayer of the Church
Lord God, almighty and everlasting Father, you have brought me in safety to this
new day: Preserve me with your mighty power, that I may not fall into sin, nor
be overcome by adversity; and in all I do direct me to the fulfilling of your purpose; through Jesus Christ my Lord. *Amen.*†

The Midday Office   **To Be Observed on the Hour or Half Hour**
Between 11 a.m. and 2 p.m.

The Call to Prayer
Praise the LORD, for the LORD is good;* sing praises to his Name, for it is lovely.
Psalm 135:3

The Request for Presence
Show us the light of your countenance, O God,* and come to us.
based on Psalm 67:1

The Greeting
My God, My rock in whom I put my trust,* my shield, the horn of my salvation,
and my refuge; you are worthy of my praise.
Psalm 18:2

The Refrain for the Midday Lessons
All nations you have made will come and worship you, O LORD,* and glorify your
Name.
Psalm 86:9

A Reading
He was made visible in the flesh, justified in the Spirit, seen by angels, proclaimed
to the gentiles, believed in throughout the world, taken up in glory and at the
due time will be revealed by God, the blessed and only Ruler of all, the King of
kings and the Lord of lords, who alone is immortal, whose home is in inaccessi-
ble light, whom no human being has seen or is able to see; to him be honor and
everlasting power. Amen.
1 Timothy 3:16, 6:15–16

The Refrain
All nations you have made will come and worship you, O LORD,* and glorify your
Name.

The Midday Psalm   *There Are the Thrones of Judgment*
I was glad when they said to me,* "Let us go to the house of the LORD."
Now our feet are standing* within your gates, O Jerusalem.
Jerusalem is built as a city* that is at unity with itself;
To which the tribes go up, the tribes of the LORD,* the assembly of Israel, to praise
the Name of the LORD.
For there are the thrones of judgment,* the thrones of the house of David.
Pray for the peace of Jerusalem:* "May they prosper who love you.
Peace be within your walls* and quietness within your towers.
For my brethren and companions' sake,* I pray for your prosperity.
Because of the house of the LORD our God,* I will seek to do you good."

Psalm 122

The Refrain
All nations you have made will come and worship you, O LORD,* and glorify your
Name.

The Gloria

The Lord's Prayer

The Prayer Appointed for the Week
Almighty God, who has given your only Son to be unto us both a sacrifice for sin
and also an example of his godly life: Give me grace that I may always most
thankfully receive that his inestimable benefit and also daily endeavor myself
to follow the blessed steps of his most holy life; through the same your Son
Jesus Christ our Lord, who lives and reigns with you and the Holy Spirit, one
God, now and for ever. *Amen.*†

The Concluding Prayer of the Church
O God, you make me glad with the weekly remembrance of the glorious resurrection of your Son my Lord: Give me this day such blessing through my worship
of you, that the week to come may be spent in your favor; through Jesus Christ
our Lord. *Amen.*†

The Vespers Office   **To Be Observed on the Hour or Half Hour**
Between 5 and 8 p.m.

The Call to Prayer
Worship the LORD in the beauty of holiness;* let the whole earth tremble before
him.
Let the heavens rejoice, and let the earth be glad; let the sea thunder and all that is
in it;* let the field be joyful and all that is therein.

Psalm 96:9, 11

The Request for Presence
As the eyes of servants look to the hand of their masters,* and the eyes of a maid
    look to the hand of her mistress,
So my eyes look to you, O LORD my God . . .

based on Psalm 123:2–3

The Greeting
. . . O LORD my God, how excellent is your greatness!* You are clothed with
    majesty and splendor.

Psalm 104:1

The Hymn   *Jesus, the Very Thought of Thee*

Jesus, the very thought of Thee   O Hope of every contrite heart!
With sweetness fills my breast;   O Joy of all the meek!
But sweeter far Thy face to see,   To those who fall, how kind thou art!
And in Thy presence rest.   How good to those who seek!

No voice can sing, no heart can frame,   But what to those who find? Ah! This,
Or can the memory find   No tongue or pen can show
A sweeter sound than Jesus' name,   The love of Jesus, what it is
O Savior of mankind.   None but His loved ones know.

Bernard of Clairvaux

The Refrain for the Vespers Lessons
The LORD himself watches over you;* the LORD is your shade at your right hand,
So that the sun shall not strike you by day,* nor the moon by night.

Psalm 121:5–6

The Vespers Psalm   *I Will Dwell in Your House For Ever*
For you have been my refuge,* a strong tower against the enemy.
I will dwell in you house for ever;* I will take refuge under the cover of your wings.
For you, O God, have heard my vows;* you have granted me the heritage of those
    who fear your Name.

Psalm 61:3–5

The Refrain
The LORD himself watches over you;* the LORD is your shade at your right hand,
So that the sun shall not strike you by day,* nor the moon by night.

The Cry of the Church
Lord, have mercy on us. Christ, have mercy on us. Lord, have mercy on us.

The Lord's Prayer

The Prayer Appointed for the Week
Almighty God, who has given your only Son to be unto us both a sacrifice for sin
    and also an example of his godly life: Give me grace that I may always most
    thankfully receive that his inestimable benefit and also daily endeavor myself
    to follow the blessed steps of his most holy life; through the same your Son

Jesus Christ our Lord, who lives and reigns with you and the Holy Spirit, one God, now and for ever. *Amen.*†

The Concluding Prayer of the Church
Lord God, whose Son our Savior Jesus Christ, triumphed over the powers of death and prepared for us our place in the new Jerusalem: Grant that I, who have this day given thanks for his resurrection, may praise you in the City of which he is the light, and where he lives and reigns for ever and ever. *Amen.*†

The Morning Office **To Be Observed on the Hour or Half Hour Between 6 and 9 a.m.**

The Call to Prayer
Hallelujah! How good it is to sing praises to our God!* how pleasant it is to honor him with praise!

Psalm 147:1

The Request for Presence
Hear the voice of my prayer when I cry out to you,* when I lift up my hands to your holy of holies.

Psalm 28:2

The Greeting
It is a good thing to give thanks to the LORD,* and to sing praises to your Name, O Most High;
To tell of your loving-kindness early in the morning* and of your faithfulness in the night season;

Psalm 92:1–2

The Refrain for the Morning Lessons
For we are your people and the sheep of your pasture;* we will give you thanks for ever and show forth your praise from age to age.

Psalm 79:13

A Reading
Jesus taught us, saying: '. . . In all truth I tell you, I am the gate of the sheepfold. All who have come before me are thieves and bandits; but the sheep took no notice of them. I am the gate. Anyone who enters through me will be safe: such a one will go in and out and will find pasture.'

John 10:7–9

The Refrain
For we are your people and the sheep of your pasture;* we will give you thanks for ever and show forth your praise from age to age.

The Morning Psalm   *The LORD Is My Shepherd*
The LORD is my shepherd;* I shall not want.
He makes me lie down in green pastures* and leads me beside still waters.

He revives my soul* and guides me along right pathways for his Name's sake.

Though I walk through the valley of the shadow of death, I shall fear no evil;* for you are with me; your rod and your staff, they comfort me.

You spread a table before me in the presence of those who trouble me;* you have anointed my head with oil, and my cup is running over.

Surely your goodness and mercy shall follow me all the days of my life,* and I will dwell in the house of the LORD for ever.

Psalm 23

The Refrain

For we are your people and the sheep of your pasture;* we will give you thanks for ever and show forth your praise from age to age.

The Cry of the Church

O God, come to my assistance! O Lord, make haste to help me!

The Lord's Prayer

The Prayer Appointed for the Week

Almighty God, who has given your only Son to be unto us both a sacrifice for sin and also an example of his godly life: Give me grace that I may always most thankfully receive that his inestimable benefit and also daily endeavor myself to follow the blessed steps of his most holy life; through the same your Son Jesus Christ our Lord, who lives and reigns with you and the Holy Spirit, one God, now and for ever. *Amen.*†

The Concluding Prayer of the Church

Lord God, almighty and everlasting Father, you have brought me in safety to this new day: Preserve me with your mighty power, that I may not fall into sin, nor be overcome by adversity; and in all I do direct me to the fulfilling of your purpose; through Jesus Christ my Lord. *Amen.*†

The Midday Office **To Be Observed on the Hour or Half Hour Between 11 a.m. and 2 p.m.**

The Call to Prayer

Let us come before his presence with thanksgiving* and raise a loud shout to him with psalms.

Psalm 95:2

The Request for Presence

O LORD, my God, my Savior,* by day and night I cry to you.

Let my prayer enter into your presence;* incline your ear to my lamentation.

Psalm 88:1–2

The Greeting

O LORD our governor,* how exalted is your Name in all the world.

Psalm 8:1

The Refrain for the Midday Lessons
I will walk in the presence of the LORD* in the land of the living.
Psalm 116:8

A Reading
Blessed be God the Father of our Lord Jesus Christ, who has blessed us with all the
spiritual blessings of heaven in Christ. Thus he chose us in Christ, before the
world was made to be holy and faultless before him in love, marking us out
beforehand, to be adopted sons, through Jesus Christ such was his purpose
and good pleasure, to the praise and glory of his grace, his free gift to us in the
Beloved.
Ephesians 1:3–6

The Refrain
I will walk in the presence of the LORD* in the land of the living.
Psalm 116:8

The Midday Psalm   ***My Mouth Shall Recount Your Mighty Acts***
I shall always wait in patience,* and shall praise you more and more.
My mouth shall recount your mighty acts and saving deeds all day long;* though I
cannot know the number of them.
I will begin with the mighty works of the Lord God;* I will recall your righteous-
ness, yours alone.
O God, you have taught me since I was young,* and to this day I tell of your won-
derful works.
Psalm 71:14–17

The Refrain
I will walk in the presence of the LORD* in the land of the living.
Psalm 116:8

The Gloria

The Lord's Prayer

The Prayer Appointed for the Week
Almighty God, who has given your only Son to be unto us both a sacrifice for sin
and also an example of his godly life: Give me grace that I may always most
thankfully receive that his inestimable benefit and also daily endeavor myself
to follow the blessed steps of his most holy life; through the same your Son
Jesus Christ our Lord, who lives and reigns with you and the Holy Spirit, one
God, now and for ever. *Amen.*†

The Concluding Prayer of the Church
O Lord my God, to you and your service I devote myself, body, soul, and spirit.
Fill my memory with the record of your mighty works; enlighten my understanding with the light of your Holy Spirit; and make all the desires of my
heart and will center in what you would have me do. Make me an instrument
of your salvation for the people entrusted to my care, and let me by my life and

speaking set forth your true and living Word. Be always with me in carrying out the duties of my vocation; in praises heighten my love and gratitude; in speaking of You give me readiness of thought and expression; and grant that, by the clearness and brightness of your holy Word, all the world may be drawn to your blessed kingdom. All this I ask for the sake of your Son my Savior Jesus Christ. *Amen.*†

The Vespers Office   **To Be Observed on the Hour or Half Hour**
                                          Between 5 and 8 p.m.

The Call to Prayer
Come, let us bow down, and bend the knee,* and kneel before the Lord, our Maker.
For he is our God,* and we are the people of his pasture and the sheep of his hand.

Psalm 95:6–7

The Request for Presence
Test me, O Lord, and try me;* examine my heart and mind.
For your love is before my eyes . . .

Psalm 26:2–3

The Greeting
You, O Lord, are my lamp;* my God, you make my darkness bright.

Psalm 18:29

The Hymn   *Breathe on Me, Breath of God*

Breathe on me, Breath of God,   Breathe on me, Breath of God,
Fill me with life anew,   Until my heart is pure,
That I may love what you love,   Until this earthly part of me
And do what You would do.   Glows with Your fire divine.

Breathe on me, Breath of God,   Breathe on me, Breath of God,
Until my heart is pure,   So I will never die,
Until with You I will one will,   But live with You the perfect life
To do and to endure.   Of Your eternity.

Edwin Hatch

The Refrain for the Vespers Lessons
You have showed me great troubles and adversities,* but you will restore my life
and bring me up again from the deep places of the earth.

Psalm 71:20

The Vespers Psalm   *You Hold Me by My Right Hand*
When my mind became embittered,* I was sorely wounded in my heart.
I was stupid and had no understanding;* I was like a brute beast in your presence.
Yet I am always with you;* you hold me by my right hand.
You will guide me by your counsel,* and afterwards receive me in glory.

Psalm 73:21–24

The Refrain
You have showed me great troubles and adversities,* but you will restore my life
and bring me up again from the deep places of the earth.

The Cry of the Church
O God, come to my assistance! O Lord, make haste to help me!

The Lord's Prayer

The Prayer Appointed for the Week
Almighty God, who has given your only Son to be unto us both a sacrifice for sin
and also an example of his godly life: Give me grace that I may always most
thankfully receive that his inestimable benefit and also daily endeavor myself
to follow the blessed steps of his most holy life; through the same your Son
Jesus Christ our Lord, who lives and reigns with you and the Holy Spirit, one
God, now and for ever. *Amen.*†

The Concluding Prayer of the Church
May Almighty God grant me a peaceful night and a perfect end. *Amen.*

The Morning Office   **To Be Observed on the Hour or Half Hour**
Between 6 and 9 a.m.

The Call to Prayer
Be strong and let your heart take courage,* all you who wait for the LORD.

Psalm 31:24

The Request for Presence
O LORD, I call to you; come to me quickly;* hear my voice when I cry to you.
Let my prayer be set forth in your sight as incense,

Psalm 141:1–2

The Greeting
Let the words of my mouth and the meditation of my heart be acceptable in your
sight,* O LORD, my strength and my redeemer.

Psalm 19:14

The Refrain for the Morning Lessons
"I have made a covenant with my chosen one;* I have sworn an oath to David my
servant:
'I will establish your line for ever,* and preserve your throne for all generations.' "

Psalm 89:3–4

A Reading
Jesus taught us, saying: 'I shall ask the Father, and he will give you another
Paraclete to be with you for ever, the Spirit of truth whom the world can never
accept since it neither sees nor knows him; but you know him, because he is
with you, he is in you.'

John 14:16–17

The Refrain
"I have made a covenant with my chosen one;* I have sworn an oath to David my
    servant:
'I will establish your line for ever,* and preserve your throne for all generations.' "

The Morning Psalm   *This Is My Prayer to You*
But as for me, this is my prayer to you,* at the time you have set, O LORD:
"In your great mercy, O God,* answer me with your unfailing help.
Save me from the mire; do not let me sink;* let me be rescued from those who hate
    me and out of the deep waters.
Let not the torrent of waters wash over me,* neither let the deep swallow me up;
    do not let the Pit shut its mouth upon me.
Answer me, O LORD, for your love is kind;* in your great compassion, turn to me."

Psalm 69:14–18

The Refrain
"I have made a covenant with my chosen one;* I have sworn an oath to David my
    servant:
'I will establish your line for ever,* and preserve your throne for all generations.' "

The Cry of the Church
O God, come to my assistance! O Lord, make haste to help me!

The Lord's Prayer

The Prayer Appointed for the Week
Almighty God, who has given your only Son to be unto us both a sacrifice for sin
    and also an example of his godly life: Give me grace that I may always most
    thankfully receive that his inestimable benefit and also daily endeavor myself
    to follow the blessed steps of his most holy life; through the same your Son
    Jesus Christ our Lord, who lives and reigns with you and the Holy Spirit, one
    God, now and for ever. *Amen.*†

The Concluding Prayer of the Church
Lord God, almighty and everlasting Father, you have brought me in safety to this
    new day: Preserve me with your mighty power, that I may not fall into sin, nor
    be overcome by adversity; and in all I do direct me to the fulfilling of your pur-
    pose; through Jesus Christ my Lord. *Amen.*†

The Midday Office   **To Be Observed on the Hour or Half Hour
                                              Between 11 a.m. and 2 p.m.**

The Call to Prayer
The LORD is my strength and my shield;* my heart trusts him, and I have been
    helped;
Therefore my heart dances for joy,* and in my song I will praise him.

Psalm 28:8–9

The Request for Presence
Save us, O LORD our God, and gather us from among the nations,* that we may
give thanks to your holy Name and glory in your praise.

Psalm 106:47

Greeting
I long for your salvation, O LORD,* and your law is my delight.
Let me live, and I will praise you,* and let your judgments help me.

Psalm 119:174–75

The Refrain for the Midday Lessons
I will lift up my hands to your commandments,* and I will meditate on your statutes.

Psalm 119:48

A Reading
"Because you have kept my commandment to persevere, I will keep you safe in
the time of trial which is coming for the whole world, to put the people of the
world to the test. I am coming soon: hold firmly to what you already have, and
let no one take your victor's crown away from you. Anyone who proves victorious I will make into a pillar in the sanctuary of my God, and it will stay there
for ever; I will inscribe on it the name of my God and the name of the city of my
God, the new Jerusalem which is coming down from my God in heaven, and
my own new name as well. Let anyone who can hear, listen to what the Spirit is
saying to the churches."

Revelation 3:10–13

The Refrain
I will lift up my hands to your commandments,* and I will meditate on your statutes.

The Midday Psalm   *I Have Kept the Ways of the LORD*
The LORD rewarded me because of my righteous dealing;* because my hands were
clean he rewarded me;
For I have kept the ways of the LORD* and have not offended against my God;
For all his judgments are before my eyes,* and his decrees I have not put away
from me;
For I have been blameless with him* and have kept myself from iniquity;
Therefore the LORD rewarded me according to my righteous dealing,* because of
the cleanness of my hands in his sight.

Psalm 18:21–25

The Refrain
I will lift up my hands to your commandments,* and I will meditate on your statutes.

The Small Verse
Lead me not into temptation. Deliver me from evil. Yours are the kingdom and the
glory.

The Lord's Prayer

The Prayer Appointed for the Week

Almighty God, who has given your only Son to be unto us both a sacrifice for sin and also an example of his godly life: Give me grace that I may always most thankfully receive that his inestimable benefit and also daily endeavor myself to follow the blessed steps of his most holy life; through the same your Son Jesus Christ our Lord, who lives and reigns with you and the Holy Spirit, one God, now and for ever. *Amen.*†

The Concluding Prayer of the Church

Blessed be God, who has not rejected my prayer,* nor withheld his love from me.

Psalm 66:18

The Vespers Office

To Be Observed on the Hour or Half Hour Between 5 and 8 p.m.

The Call to Prayer

Bless the LORD, you angels of his, you mighty ones who do his bidding,* and hearken to the voice of his word.
Bless the LORD, all you his hosts,* you ministers of his who do his will.
Bless the LORD, all you works of his, in all places of his dominion;* bless the LORD, O my soul.

Psalm 103:20–22

The Request for Presence

Show us the light of your countenance, O God,* and come to us.

based on Psalm 67:1

The Greeting

I will confess you among the peoples, O LORD;* I will sing praises to you among the nations.

Psalm 108:3

The Hymn

Now let the earth with joy resound
And heaven the chant re-echo round;
Nor heaven nor earth too high can raise
The great Apostles' glorious praise!

Sickness and health your voice obey,
At your command they go or stay;
From sin's disease our souls restore,
In good confirm us more and more.

So when the world is at its end
And Christ to judgment shall descend,
May we be called those joys to see
Prepared from all eternity.

All honor, praise and glory be
O Jesus, Virgin-born, to Thee;
All glory, as is ever meet,
To Father and to Paraclete.

THE SHORT BREVIARY

The Refrain for the Vespers Lessons

Into your hands I commend my spirit,* for you have redeemed me, O LORD, O God of truth.

Psalm 31:5

The Vespers Psalm   *My Merciful God Comes to Meet Me*

The ungodly go to and fro in the evening;* they snarl like dogs and run about the
    city.

Behold, they boast with their mouths, and taunts are on their lips;* "For who,"
    they say, "will hear us?"

But you, O LORD, you laugh at them;* you laugh all the ungodly to scorn.

My eyes are fixed on you, O my Strength;* for you, O God, are my stronghold.

My merciful God comes to meet me . . .

Psalm 59:7–11

The Refrain

Into your hands I commend my spirit,* for you have redeemed me, O LORD, O
    God of truth.

The Gloria

The Lord's Prayer

The Prayer Appointed for the Week

Almighty God, who has given your only Son to be unto us both a sacrifice for sin
    and also an example of his godly life: Give me grace that I may always most
    thankfully receive that his inestimable benefit and also daily endeavor myself
    to follow the blessed steps of his most holy life; through the same your Son
    Jesus Christ our Lord, who lives and reigns with you and the Holy Spirit, one
    God, now and for ever. *Amen.*†

The Concluding Prayer of the Church

Protect us, Lord, as we stay awake; watch over us as we sleep, that awake we may
    watch with Christ, and asleep, rest in his peace. *Amen.*

The Morning Office   **To Be Observed on the Hour or Half Hour**
                                      Between 6 and 9 a.m.

The Call to Prayer

Sing to the LORD and bless his Name;* proclaim the good news of his salvation
    from day to day.

Declare his glory among the nations* and his wonders among all peoples.

Psalm 96:2–3

The Request for Presence

Help us, O God our Savior, for the glory of your Name;* deliver us and forgive us
    our sins, for your Name's sake.

Psalm 79:9

The Greeting

Seven times a day do I praise you,* because of your righteous judgments.

Psalm 119:164

The Refrain for the Morning Lessons
Righteousness and justice are the foundations of your throne;* love and truth go
before your face.

Psalm 89:14

A Reading
Jesus taught us, saying: 'But I say this to you who are listening: Love your enemies, do good to those who hate you, bless those who curse you, pray for those
who treat you badly. To anyone who slaps you on one cheek, present the other
cheek as well; to anyone who takes your cloak from you, do not refuse your
tunic. Give to everyone who asks you, and do not ask for property back from
someone who takes it. Treat others as you would like people to treat you.'

Luke 6:27–31

The Refrain
Righteousness and justice are the foundations of your throne;* love and truth go
before your face.

The Morning Psalm   *I Will Walk with Sincerity of Heart Within My House*
I will sing of mercy and justice;* to you, O LORD, will I sing praises.
I will strive to follow a blameless course; oh, when will you come to me?* I will
walk with sincerity of heart within my house.
I will set no worthless thing before my eyes;* I hate the doers of evil deeds; they
shall not remain with me.
A crooked heart shall be far from me;* I will not know evil.
Those who in secret slander their neighbors I will destroy;* those who have a
haughty look and a proud heart I cannot abide.

Psalm 101:1–5

The Refrain
Righteousness and justice are the foundations of your throne;* love and truth go
before your face.

The Cry of the Church
Even so, come, Lord Jesus.

The Lord's Prayer

The Prayer Appointed for the Week
Almighty God, who has given your only Son to be unto us both a sacrifice for sin
and also an example of his godly life: Give me grace that I may always most
thankfully receive that his inestimable benefit and also daily endeavor myself
to follow the blessed steps of his most holy life; through the same your Son
Jesus Christ our Lord, who lives and reigns with you and the Holy Spirit, one
God, now and for ever. *Amen.*†

The Concluding Prayer of the Church
Lord God, almighty and everlasting Father, you have brought me in safety to this
new day: Preserve me with your mighty power, that I may not fall into sin, nor

be overcome by adversity; and in all I do direct me to the fulfilling of your purpose; through Jesus Christ my Lord. *Amen.*†

The Midday Office   **To Be Observed on the Hour or Half Hour**
                                              Between 11 a.m. and 2 p.m.

The Call to Prayer
I will call upon God,* and the LORD will deliver me.
In the evening, in the morning, and at the noonday, I will complain and lament,*
    and he will hear my voice.
He will bring me safely back. . . .* God who is enthroned of old will hear me.

Psalm 55:17ff

The Request for Presence
Arise, O God, maintain your cause;* remember how the fools revile you all day
    long.

Psalm 74:21

The Greeting
In you, O LORD, have I taken refuge;* let me never be put to shame; deliver me in
    your righteousness.

Psalm 31:1

The Refrain for the Midday Lessons
Deliverance belongs to the LORD.* Your blessing be upon your people!

Psalm 3:8

A Reading
Can anything cut us off from the love of Christ—can hardships or distress, or persecution, or lack of food or clothes, or threats or violence. As scripture says: *For your sake we are being massacred all day long, treated as sheep to be slaughtered?* No; we come through all these things triumphantly victorious, by the power of him who loved us. For I am certain of this: neither death nor life, no angel, no prince, nothing that exists, nothing still to come, not any power, or height or depth, nor any created thing, can ever come between us and the love of God made visible in Christ Jesus our Lord.

Romans 8:35–39

The Refrain
Deliverance belongs to the LORD.* Your blessing be upon your people!

The Midday Psalm   *Surely There Is a God Who Rules in the Earth*
Do you indeed decree righteousness, you rulers?* do you judge the peoples with
    equity?
No; you devise evil in your hearts,* and your hands deal out violence in the land.
The wicked are perverse from the womb;* liars go astray from their birth.
They are venomous as a serpent,* they are like the deaf adder which stops its ears,

Which does not heed the voice of the charmer,* no matter how skillful his charming.
O God, break their teeth in their mouths;* pull the fangs of the young lions, O LORD.
Let them vanish like water that runs off;* let them wither like trodden grass.
Let them be like the snail that melts away,* like a stillborn child that never sees the sun.
Before they bear fruit, let them be cut down like a briar;* like thorns and thistles let them be swept away.
The righteous will be glad . . . and they will say, "Surely, there is a reward for the righteous;* surely, there is a God who rules in the earth."

Psalm 58

The Refrain
Deliverance belongs to the LORD.* Your blessing be upon your people!

The Cry of the Church
Lord, have mercy on us. Christ, have mercy on us. Lord, have mercy on us.

The Lord's Prayer

The Prayer Appointed for the Week
Almighty God, who has given your only Son to be unto us both a sacrifice for sin and also an example of his godly life: Give me grace that I may always most thankfully receive that his inestimable benefit and also daily endeavor myself to follow the blessed steps of his most holy life; through the same your Son Jesus Christ our Lord, who lives and reigns with you and the Holy Spirit, one God, now and for ever. *Amen.*†

The Concluding Prayer of the Church
Lord Jesus Christ, you have prepared a quiet place for us in your Father's eternal home. Watch over our welfare on this perilous journey, shade us from the burning heat of day, and keep our lives free of evil until the end. *Amen.*

THE LITURGY OF THE HOURS, VOL. III

The Vespers Office　　　　　**To Be Observed on the Hour or Half Hour Between 5 and 8 p.m.**

The Call to Prayer
May these words of mine please him;* I will rejoice in the LORD.

Psalm 104:35

The Request for Presence
Restore us, O God of hosts;* show the light of your countenance, and we shall be saved.

Psalm 80:7

The Greeting
The Lord is in his holy temple; let all the earth keep silence before him. Amen.

Traditional Greeting

The Hymn   *Mother of Christ*
Mother of Christ, Mother of Christ,
The world will bid Him flee,
Too busy to heed His gentle voice,
Too blind His charms to see.

Then, Mother of Christ, Mother of Christ,
Come with thy Babe to me;
Though the world be cold, my heart shall hold
A shelter for Him and for Thee.

A Notre Dame Hymn

The Refrain for the Vespers Lessons
I commune with my heart in the night;* I ponder and search my mind.

Psalm 77:6

The Vespers Psalm   *I Will Thank You Because I Am Marvelously Made*
For you yourself created my inmost parts;* you knit me together in my mother's
    womb.
I will thank you because I am marvelously made;* your works are wonderful, and
    I know it well.
My body was not hidden from you,* while I was being made in secret and woven
    in the depths of the earth.
Your eyes beheld my limbs, yet unfinished in the womb; all of them were written
    in your book;* they were fashioned day by day, when as yet there was one of
    them.
How deep I find your thoughts, O God!* how great is the sum of them!
If I were to count them, they would be more in number than the sand;* to count
    them all, my life span would need to be like yours.

Psalm 139:12–17

The Refrain
I commune with my heart in the night;* I ponder and search my mind.

The Small Verse
The Lord is my shepherd and nothing is wanting to me. In green pastures He hath
    settled me.

THE SHORT BREVIARY

The Lord's Prayer

The Prayer Appointed for the Week
Almighty God, who has given your only Son to be unto us both a sacrifice for sin
    and also an example of his godly life: Give me grace that I may always most
    thankfully receive that his inestimable benefit and also daily endeavor myself
    to follow the blessed steps of his most holy life; through the same your Son
    Jesus Christ our Lord, who lives and reigns with you and the Holy Spirit, one
    God, now and for ever. *Amen.*†

The Concluding Prayer of the Church
Protect us, Lord, as we stay awake; watch over us as we sleep, that awake we may
  watch with Christ, and asleep, rest in his peace. *Amen.*

The Morning Office **To Be Observed on the Hour or Half Hour**
Between 6 and 9 a.m.

The Call to Prayer
Open my lips, O Lord,* and my mouth shall proclaim your praise.
Had you desired it, I would have offered sacrifice,* but you take no delight in
  burnt-offerings.
The sacrifice of God is a troubled spirit;* a broken and contrite heart, O God, you
  will not despise.

Psalm 51:16–18

The Request for Presence
"Hide not your face from your servant;* be swift and answer me . . .
Draw near to me and redeem me . . .

Psalm 69:19–20

The Greeting
O Lord, I cry to you for help;* in the morning my prayer comes before you.

Psalm 88:14

The Refrain for the Morning Lessons
Blessed be the Lord day by day,* the God of our salvation, who bears our burdens.
He is our God, the God of our salvation;* God is the Lord, by whom we escape
  death.

Psalm 68:19–20

A Reading
When Jesus was at dinner in his [Matthew's] house, a number of tax collectors and
  sinners were also sitting at the table with Jesus and his disciples; for there were
  many of them among his followers. When the scribes of the Pharisee party saw
  him eating with sinners and tax collectors, they said to his disciples, 'Why does
  he eat with tax collectors and sinners?' When Jesus heard this he said to them,
  'It is not the healthy who need the doctor, but the sick. I did not come to call the
  upright, but sinners.'

Mark 2:15–17

The Refrain
Blessed be the Lord day by day,* the God of our salvation, who bears our burdens.
He is our God, the God of our salvation;* God is the Lord, by whom we escape
  death.

The Morning Psalm   *In God Is My Safety and Honor*

For God alone my soul in silence waits;* truly, my hope is in him.

He alone is my rock and my salvation,* my stronghold, so that I shall not be shaken.

In God is my safety and my honor;* God is my strong rock and my refuge.

Psalm 62:6–8

The Refrain

Blessed be the Lord day by day,* the God of our salvation, who bears our burdens.

He is our God, the God of our salvation;* God is the LORD, by whom we escape death.

The Gloria

The Lord's Prayer

The Prayer Appointed for the Week

Almighty God, who has given your only Son to be unto us both a sacrifice for sin and also an example of his godly life: Give me grace that I may always most thankfully receive that his inestimable benefit and also daily endeavor myself to follow the blessed steps of his most holy life; through the same your Son Jesus Christ our Lord, who lives and reigns with you and the Holy Spirit, one God, now and for ever. *Amen.*†

The Concluding Prayer of the Church

Lord God, almighty and everlasting Father, you have brought me in safety to this new day: Preserve me with your mighty power, that I may not fall into sin, nor be overcome by adversity; and in all I do direct me to the fulfilling of your purpose; through Jesus Christ my Lord. *Amen.*†

The Midday Office   **To Be Observed on the Hour or Half Hour**
                                     Between 11 a.m. and 2 p.m.

The Call to Prayer

Open my lips, O Lord,* and my mouth shall proclaim your praise.

Psalm 51:16

The Request for Presence

I call upon you, O God, for you will answer me;* incline your ear to me and hear my words.

Psalm 17:6

The Greeting

Had you desired it, I would have offered sacrifice,* but you take no delight in burnt-offerings.

The sacrifice of God is a troubled spirit;* a broken and contrite heart, O God, you will not despise.

Psalm 51:17–18

The Refrain for the Midday Lessons
The fool has said in his heart, "There is no God."

Psalm 14:1

A Reading
Never desire to be the object of praise or love above others, for that belongs only to
God, who has none like Himself. Neither desire that anyone's heart be set on
you, and do not set your heart on the love of anyone, but let Jesus be in you
and in every good man and woman.

Thomas à Kempis

The Refrain
The fool has said in his heart, "There is no God."

The Midday Psalm　　　　　　　　*Let Me Know My End and the Number of My Days*
I said, "I will keep watch upon my ways,* so that I do not offend with my tongue.
I will put a muzzle on my mouth* while the wicked are in my presence."
So I held my tongue and said nothing;* I refrained from rash words; but my pain
became unbearable.
My heart was hot within me; while I pondered, the fire burst into flame;* I spoke
out with my tongue:
LORD, let me know my end and the number of my days,* so that I may know how
short my life is.
You have given me a mere handful of days, and my lifetime is as nothing in your
sight;* truly, even those who stand erect are but a puff of wind.
We walk about like a shadow, and in vain we are in turmoil;* we heap up riches
and cannot tell who will gather them.
And now, what is my hope?* O Lord, my hope is in you.
Deliver me from all my transgressions* and do not make me the taunt of the fool.

Psalm 39:1–9

The Refrain
The fool has said in his heart, "There is no God."

The Cry of the Church
Even so, come Lord Jesus.

The Lord's Prayer

The Prayer Appointed for the Week
Almighty God, who has given your only Son to be unto us both a sacrifice for sin
and also an example of his godly life: Give me grace that I may always most
thankfully receive that his inestimable benefit and also daily endeavor myself
to follow the blessed steps of his most holy life; through the same your Son
Jesus Christ our Lord, who lives and reigns with you and the Holy Spirit, one
God, now and for ever. *Amen.*†

The Concluding Prayer of the Church
O God, who has made of one blood all the peoples of the earth, and sent your
blessed Son to preach to those of us who are far off and to those who are near:
Grant that people everywhere may seek after you and find you; bring the
nations into your fold; pour out your Spirit upon all flesh; and hasten the coming of your kingdom; through the same your Son Jesus Christ our Lord. *Amen.*†

The Vespers Office   **To Be Observed on the Hour or Half Hour**
Between 5 and 8 p.m.

The Call to Prayer
Every day will I bless you* and praise your Name for ever and ever.
Psalm 145:2

The Request for Presence
My soul waits for the LORD, more than watchmen for the morning,* more than
watchmen for the morning.
Psalm 130:5

The Greeting
Let my prayer be set forth in your sight as incense,* the lifting up of my hands as
the evening sacrifice.
Psalm 141:2

The Hymn   *Fairest Lord Jesus*

Fairest Lord Jesus,   Fair is the sunshine,
Ruler of all nature,   Fairer still the moonlight
O Thou of God and man the Son;   And all the twinkling, starry host;
Thee will I cherish,   Jesus shines brighter,
Thee will I honor,   Jesus shines purer,
Thou my soul's glory, joy and crown. Than all the angels heaven can boast.
German, Traditional

Fair are the meadows,
Fairer still the woodlands,
Robed in the blooming garb of spring;
Jesus is fairer,
Jesus is purer,
Who makes the woeful heart to sing.

The Refrain for the Vespers Lessons
The LORD is King; he has put on splendid apparel;* the LORD has put on his
apparel and girded himself with strength.
He has made the whole world so sure* that it cannot be moved.
Psalm 93:1–2

The Vespers Psalm   *Your Loving-Kindness Is Greater Than the Heavens*
Be merciful to me, O God, be merciful, for I have taken refuge in you;* in the
    shadow of your wings will I take refuge until this time of trouble has gone by.
My heart is firmly fixed, O God, my heart is fixed;* I will sing and make melody.
Wake up, my spirit; awake, lute and harp;* I myself will waken the dawn.
I will confess you among the peoples, O LORD;* I will sing praise to you among the
    nations.
For your loving-kindness is greater than the heavens,* and your faithfulness
    reaches to the clouds.
Exalt yourself above the heavens, O God,* and your glory over all the earth.

Psalm 57:1ff

The Refrain
The LORD is King; he has put on splendid apparel;* the LORD has put on his
    apparel and girded himself with strength.
He has made the whole world so sure* that it cannot be moved.

The Cry of the Church
Even so come, Lord Jesus!

The Lord's Prayer

The Prayer Appointed for the Week
Almighty God, who has given your only Son to be unto us both a sacrifice for sin
    and also an example of his godly life: Give me grace that I may always most
    thankfully receive that his inestimable benefit and also daily endeavor myself
    to follow the blessed steps of his most holy life; through the same your Son
    Jesus Christ our Lord, who lives and reigns with you and the Holy Spirit, one
    God, now and for ever. *Amen.*†

The Concluding Prayer of the Church
Save me, O Lord, while I am awake, and keep me while I sleep that I may wake in
    Christ and rest in peace.

adapted from THE SHORT BREVIARY

The Morning Office   **To Be Observed on the Hour or Half Hour**
Between 6 and 9 a.m.

The Call to Prayer
But I will call upon God,* and the LORD will deliver me.
In the evening, in the morning, and at noonday, I will complain and lament,* and
    he will hear my voice.
He will bring me safely back . . .* God, who is enthroned of old, will hear me.

Psalm 55:17ff

The Request for Presence
O LORD, I call to you; my Rock, do not be deaf to my cry;* lest, if you do not hear me, I become like those who go down to the Pit.

Psalm 28:1

The Greeting
I put my trust in your mercy;* my heart is joyful because of your saving help.

Psalm 13:5

The Refrain for the Morning Lessons
Happy are they whose transgressions are forgiven,* and whose sin is put away!
Happy are they to whom the LORD imputes no guilt,* and in whose spirit there is no guile!

Psalm 32:1–2

A Reading
In the due course John the Baptist appeared; he proclaimed this message in the desert of Judaea: 'Repent, for the kingdom of Heaven is close at hand.'

Matthew 3:1–2

The Refrain
Happy are they whose transgressions are forgiven,* and whose sin is put away!
Happy are they to whom the LORD imputes no guilt* and in whose spirit there is no guile!

The Morning Psalm   *There Is a Voice of Rebellion Deep in the Heart of the Wicked*
There is a voice of rebellion deep in the heart of the wicked;* there is no fear of God before his eyes.
He flatters himself in his own eyes* that his hateful sin will not be found out.
The words of his mouth are wicked and deceitful,* he has left off acting wisely and doing good.
He thinks up wickedness upon his bed and has set himself in no good way;* he does not abhor that which is evil.

Psalm 36:1–4

The Refrain
Happy are they whose transgressions are forgiven,* and whose sin is put away!
Happy are they to whom the LORD imputes no guilt,* and in whose spirit there is no guile!

The Cry of the Church
O God, come to my assistance! O Lord, make haste to help me!

The Lord's Prayer

The Prayer Appointed for the Week
Almighty God, who has given your only Son to be unto us both a sacrifice for sin and also an example of his godly life: Give me grace that I may always most

thankfully receive that his inestimable benefit and also daily endeavor myself to follow the blessed steps of his most holy life; through the same your Son Jesus Christ our Lord, who lives and reigns with you and the Holy Spirit, one God, now and for ever. *Amen.*†

The Concluding Prayer of the Church
Lord God, almighty and everlasting Father, you have brought me in safety to this new day: Preserve me with your mighty power, that I may not fall into sin, nor be overcome by adversity; and in all I do direct me to the fulfilling of your purpose; through Jesus Christ my Lord. *Amen.*†

The Midday Office   **To Be Observed on the Hour or Half Hour**
                             Between 11 a.m. and 2 p.m.

The Call to Prayer
"Come now, let us reason together," says the Lord.
                                        Isaiah 1:18 KJV

The Request for Presence
Hear my prayer, O LORD,* and give ear to my cry . . .
For I am but a sojourner with you,* a wayfarer, as all my forebears were.
                                        Psalm 39:13–14

The Greeting
You are to be praised, O God, in Zion . . . * To you that hear prayer shall all flesh
    come . . .

                                        Psalm 65:1–2

The Refrain for the Midday Lesson
He will not let your foot be moved* and he who watches over you will not fall asleep.
                                        Psalm 121:3

A Reading
I know that whatever God does will be forever. To this there is nothing to add,
    from this there is nothing to subtract; and the way God acts inspires dread.
    What is, has already been; what will be, is already;
                                        Ecclesiastes 3:14–15

The Refrain
He will not let your foot be moved* and he who watches over you will not fall asleep.

The Midday Psalm   *We Will Not Fear, Though the Earth Be Moved*
God is our refuge and strength,* a very present help in trouble.
Therefore we will not fear, though the earth be moved,* and though the mountains be toppled into the depths of the sea;
Though its waters rage and foam,* and though the mountains tremble at its tumult.
The LORD of hosts is with us;* the God of Jacob is our stronghold.
                                        Psalm 46:1–4

The Refrain
He will not let your foot be moved* and he who watches over you will not fall asleep.

The Small Verse
From my secret sins cleanse me, Lord. And from all strange evils deliver me.

Traditional

The Lord's Prayer

The Prayer Appointed for the Week
Almighty God, who has given your only Son to be unto us both a sacrifice for sin and also an example of his godly life: Give me grace that I may always most thankfully receive that his inestimable benefit and also daily endeavor myself to follow the blessed steps of his most holy life; through the same your Son Jesus Christ our Lord, who lives and reigns with you and the Holy Spirit, one God, now and for ever. *Amen.*✝

The Concluding Prayer of the Church
Lord Jesus Christ, by your death you took away the sting of death: Grant me to so follow in faith where you have led the way, that I may at length fall asleep peacefully in you and wake in your likeness; for your tender mercies' sake. *Amen.*✝

The Vespers Office

To Be Observed on the Hour or Half Hour Between 5 and 8 p.m.

The Call to Prayer
Bless our God, you peoples;* make the voice of his praise to be heard;
Who holds our souls in life,* and will not allow our feet to slip.

Psalm 66:7–8

The Request for Presence
To you I lift up my eyes,* to you enthroned in the heavens.

Psalm 123:1

The Greeting
"You are my God, and I will thank you;* you are my God, and I will exalt you."

Psalm 118:28

The Hymn — *Trust and Obey*

When we walk with the Lord	Not a burden we bear,
In the light of his word,	Not a sorrow we share,
What a glory he sheds on our way!	But our toil he does richly repay;
While we do his good will,	Not a grief or a loss,
He abides with us still,	Not a frown or a cross,
And with all who will trust and obey.	But is blessed if we trust and obey.

But we never can prove
The delights of his love
Until all on the altar we lay;
For the favor he shows,
    For the joy he bestows,
Are for them who will trust and obey.

Trust and obey,
For there's no other way
To be happy in Jesus,
But to trust and obey.
             John H. Sammis

The Refrain for the Vespers Lessons

For God alone my soul in silence waits;* truly, my hope is in him.
He alone is my rock and my salvation,* my stronghold, so that I shall not be shaken.

                  Psalm 62:6–7

The Vespers Psalm   *You Have Set My Heart at Liberty*

My soul cleaves to the dust;* give me life according to your word.
I have confessed my ways, and you answered me;* instruct me in your statutes.
Make me understand the way of your commandments* that I may meditate on
    your marvelous works.
My soul melts away for sorrow;* strengthen me according to your word.
Take from me the way of lying;* let me find grace through your law.
I have chosen the way of faithfulness;* I have set your judgments before me.
I hold fast to your decrees;* O LORD, let me not be put to shame.
I will run the way of your commandments,* for you have set my heart at liberty.

                Psalm 119:25–32

The Refrain

For God alone my soul in silence waits;* truly, my hope is in him.
He alone is my rock and my salvation,* my stronghold, so that I shall not be shaken.

The Small Verse

Blessed be the Lord God of Israel for he has visited and delivered us. Alleluia,
    alleluia, alleluia.

                  Traditional

The Lord's Prayer

The Prayer Appointed for the Week

Almighty God, who has given your only Son to be unto us both a sacrifice for sin
    and also an example of his godly life: Give me grace that I may always most
    thankfully receive that his inestimable benefit and also daily endeavor myself
    to follow the blessed steps of his most holy life; through the same your Son
    Jesus Christ our Lord, who lives and reigns with you and the Holy Spirit, one
    God, now and for ever. *Amen.*†

The Concluding Prayers of the Church

Almighty God, who has promised to hear the petitions of those who ask in your
    Son's Name: I beseech you mercifully to incline your ear to me who have made
    my prayers and supplications to you; and grant that those things which I have

faithfully asked according to your will, I may effectually obtain, to the relief of
my necessity, and to the setting forth of your glory; through Jesus Christ my
Lord. *Amen.*†

May the souls of the faithful departed, through the mercy of God, rest in eternal
peace. *Amen.*

The Morning Office   **To Be Observed on the Hour or Half Hour**
Between 6 and 9 a.m.

The Call to Prayer
Let us come before his presence with thanksgiving* and raise a loud shout to him
    with psalms.
For the LORD is a great God,* and a great King above all gods.

Psalm 95:2–3

The Request for Presence
Show us the light of your countenance, O God,* and come to us.

based on Psalm 67:1

The Greeting
Open my eyes, that I may see* the wonders of your law.
I am a stranger here on earth;* do not hide your commandments from me.
My soul is consumed at all times* with longing for your judgments.

Psalm 119:18–20

The Refrain for the Morning Lessons
The LORD has pleasure in those who fear him,* in those who await his gracious
    favor.

Psalm 147:12

A Reading
Jesus taught us, saying: 'You have heard how it was said: *You will love your neighbor*
    and hate your enemy. But I say this to you: love your enemies and pray for
    those who persecute you; so that you may be children of your Father in
    heaven.'

Matthew 5:43–45

The Refrain
The LORD has pleasure in those who fear him,* in those who await his gracious
    favor.

The Morning Psalm   *What Is Man That You Should Be Mindful of Him?*
O LORD our Governor,* how exalted is your Name in all the world!
Out of the mouths of infants and children* your majesty is praised above the
    heavens.
You have set up a stronghold against your adversaries,* to quell the enemy and
    the avenger.

When I consider your heavens, the work of your fingers,* the moon and the stars
you have set in their courses,
What is man that you should be mindful of him?* the son of man that you should
seek him out?
You have made him but little lower than the angels;* you adorn him with glory
and honor;
You give him mastery over the works of your hands;* you put all things under his
feet:
All sheep and oxen,* even the wild beasts of the field,
The birds of the air, the fish of the sea,* and whatsoever walks in the paths of the sea.
O Lord our Governor,* how exalted is your Name in all the world!

Psalm 8:1–10

The Refrain
The Lord has pleasure in those who fear him,* in those who await his gracious
favor.

The Gloria

The Lord's Prayer

The Prayer Appointed for the Week
Almighty God, who has given your only Son to be unto us both a sacrifice for sin
and also an example of his godly life: Give me grace that I may always most
thankfully receive that his inestimable benefit and also daily endeavor myself
to follow the blessed steps of his most holy life; through the same your Son
Jesus Christ our Lord, who lives and reigns with you and the Holy Spirit, one
God, now and for ever. *Amen.†*

The Concluding Prayer of the Church
Lord God, almighty and everlasting Father, you have brought me in safety to this
new day: Preserve me with your mighty power, that I may not fall into sin, nor
be overcome by adversity; and in all I do direct me to the fulfilling of your purpose; through Jesus Christ my Lord. *Amen.†*

The Midday Office **To Be Observed on the Hour or Half Hour**
Between 11 a.m. and 2 p.m.

The Call to Prayer
Praise God, from whom all blessings flow; praise him, all creatures here below;
praise him above, you heavenly hosts; praise Father, Son, and Holy Ghost.

Traditional

The Request for Presence
Hear, O Shepherd of Israel, leading Joseph like a flock;* shine forth, you that are
enthroned upon the cherubim.

Psalm 80:1

The Greeting
I will offer you the sacrifice of thanksgiving* and call upon the Name of the Lord.

Psalm 116:15

The Refrain for the Midday Lessons
The hills stand about Jerusalem;* so does the Lord stand round about his people, from this time forth for evermore.

Psalm 125:2

A Reading
It will happen in the final days that the mountain of Yahweh's house will rise higher than the mountains and tower above the heights. All the nations will stream to it, many people will come to it and say: 'Come, let us go up to the mountain of Yahweh, to the house of the God of Jacob that he may teach us his ways so that we may walk in his paths.' For the Law will issue from Zion, and the word of Yahweh from Jerusalem. Then he will judge between the nations and arbitrate between many peoples. They will hammer their swords into plowshares and their spears into sickles. Nation will not lift sword against nation, no longer will they learn how to make war. House of Jacob, come, let us walk in Yahweh's light.

Isaiah 2:2–5

The Refrain
The hills stand about Jerusalem;* so does the Lord stand round about his people, from this time forth for evermore.

The Midday Psalm   *Lift Up Your Heads, O Gates*
Lift up your heads, O gates; lift them high, O everlasting doors;* and the King of glory shall come in.
"Who is this King of glory?* The Lord, strong and mighty, the Lord, mighty in battle."
Lift up your heads, O gates;* lift them high, O everlasting doors; and the King of glory shall come in.
"Who is he, this King of glory?* The Lord of hosts, he is the King of glory."

Psalm 24:7–10

The Refrain
The hills stand about Jerusalem;* so does the Lord stand round about his people, from this time forth for evermore.

The Small Verse
The earth is the Lord's and all the fullness thereof, the world and we who dwell within. Thanks be to God.

Traditional

The Lord's Prayer

The Prayer Appointed for the Week
Almighty God, who has given your only Son to be unto us both a sacrifice for sin and also an example of his godly life: Give me grace that I may always most

thankfully receive that his inestimable benefit and also daily endeavor myself
to follow the blessed steps of his most holy life; through the same your Son
Jesus Christ our Lord, who lives and reigns with you and the Holy Spirit, one
God, now and for ever. *Amen.*†

The Concluding Prayer of the Church
O God, the source of eternal light: Shed forth your unending day upon all of us
who watch for you, that our lips may praise you, our lives may bless you, and
our worship may give you glory; through Jesus Christ our Lord. *Amen.*†

The Vespers Office   **To Be Observed on the Hour or Half Hour**
                                          Between 5 and 8 p.m.

The Call to Prayer
Behold now, bless the LORD, all you servants of the LORD,* you that stand by night
in the house of the LORD.

Psalm 134:1

The Request for Presence
I have said to the LORD, "You are my God;* listen, O LORD, to my supplication.

Psalm 140:6

The Greeting
Remember your word to your servant,* because you have given me hope.
This is my comfort in my trouble,* that your promise gives me life.

Psalm 119:49–50

The Hymn   *Chariot's a'Coming!*
    Good news, chariot's a'coming!
    Good news, chariot's a'coming!
    Good news, chariot's a'coming!
    And I don't want her leaving me behind.

    There's a long white robe in heaven, I know.
    There's a long white robe in heaven, I know.
    There's a long white robe in heaven, I know.
    And I don't want her leaving me behind.

    There's a starry crown in heaven, I know.
    There's a starry crown in heaven, I know.
    There's a starry crown in heaven, I know.
    And I don't want her leaving me behind.

    Good news, chariot's a'coming!
    Good news, chariot's a'coming!
    Good news, chariot's a'coming!
    And I don't want her leaving me behind.

There's a golden harp in heaven, I know.
There's a golden harp in heaven, I know.
There's a golden harp in heaven, I know.
And I don't want her leaving me behind.

There's silver slippers in heaven, I know.
There's silver slippers in heaven, I know.
There's silver slippers in heaven, I know.
And I don't want her leaving me behind.

Good news, chariot's a'coming!
Good news, chariot's a'coming!
Good news, chariot's a'coming!
And I don't want her leaving me behind.

Traditional Spiritual

The Refrain for the Vespers Lessons

The LORD is my light and my salvation; whom then shall I fear?* the LORD is the strength of my life; of whom then shall I be afraid?

Psalm 27:1

The Vespers Psalm   *Praise Him in the Heights*

Hallelujah! Praise the LORD from the heavens;* praise him in the heights.
Praise him, all you angels of his;* praise him, all his host.
Praise him, sun and moon;* praise him, all you shining stars.
Praise him, heaven of heavens,* and you waters above the heavens.
Let them praise the Name of the LORD;* for he commanded, and they were created.
He made them stand fast for ever and ever;* he gave them a law which shall not pass away.

Psalm 148:1–6

The Refrain

The LORD is my light and my salvation; whom then shall I fear?* the LORD is the strength of my life; of whom then shall I be afraid?

The Gloria

The Lord's Prayer

The Prayer Appointed for the Week

Almighty God, who has given your only Son to be unto us both a sacrifice for sin and also an example of his godly life: Give me grace that I may always most thankfully receive that his inestimable benefit and also daily endeavor myself to follow the blessed steps of his most holy life; through the same your Son Jesus Christ our Lord, who lives and reigns with you and the Holy Spirit, one God, now and for ever. *Amen.*†

The Concluding Prayer of the Church
Almighty God, who after the creation of the world rested from all your works and
sanctified a day of rest for all your creatures: Grant that I, putting away all
earthly anxieties, may be duly prepared for the service of public worship, and
grant as well that my Sabbath upon earth may be a preparation for the eternal
rest promised to your people in heaven; through Jesus Christ our Lord. *Amen.*✝

✿

The Morning Office   **To Be Observed on the Hour or Half Hour**
Between 6 and 9 a.m.

The Call to Prayer
Hallelujah! Praise the LORD, O my soul!* I will praise the LORD as long as I live; I
will sing praises to my God while I have my being.

Psalm 146:1

The Request for Presence
Set a watch before my mouth, O LORD, and guard the door of my lips;* let not my
heart incline to any evil thing.
Let me not be occupied in wickedness with evildoers,* nor eat of their choice
foods.
Let the righteous smite me in friendly rebuke;* let not the oil of the unrighteous
anoint my head;

Psalm 141:3–5

The Greeting
Not to us, O LORD, not to us, but to your Name give glory;* because of your love
and because of your faithfulness.

Psalm 115:1

The Refrain for the Morning Lessons
Let the words of my mouth and the meditation of my heart be acceptable in your
sight,* O LORD, my strength and my redeemer.

Psalm 19:14

A Reading
Jesus taught us, saying: 'You are the light of the world. A city built on a hill-top
cannot be hidden. No one lights a lamp to put it under a tub; they put it on the
lamp-stand where it shines for everyone in the house. In the same way your
light must shine in people's sight, so that, seeing your good works, they give
praise to your Father in heaven.'

Matthew 5:14–16

The Refrain
Let the words of my mouth and the meditation of my heart be acceptable in your
sight,* O LORD, my strength and my redeemer.

The Morning Psalm   *I Will Lift Up the Cup of Salvation*
How shall I repay the LORD* for all the good things he has done for me?
I will lift up the cup of salvation* and call upon the Name of the LORD.
I will fulfill my vows to the LORD* in the presence of all his people.

Psalm 116:10–12

The Refrain
Let the words of my mouth and the meditation of my heart be acceptable in your
sight,* O LORD, my strength and my redeemer.

The Cry of the Church
O God, come to my assistance! O Lord, make haste to help me!

The Lord's Prayer

The Prayer Appointed for the Week
Grant, O merciful God, that your Church, being gathered together in unity by
your Holy Spirit, may show forth your power among all people, to the glory of
your Name; through Jesus Christ our Lord, who lives and reigns with you and
the Holy Spirit, one God, for ever and ever. *Amen.*†

The Concluding Prayer of the Church
Lord God, almighty and everlasting Father, you have brought me in safety to this
new day: Preserve me with your mighty power, that I may not fall into sin, nor
be overcome by adversity; and in all I do direct me to the fulfilling of your purpose; through Jesus Christ my Lord. *Amen.*†

The Midday Office   **To Be Observed on the Hour or Half Hour**
Between 11 a.m. and 2 p.m.

The Call to Prayer
God has gone up with a shout,* the LORD with the sound of the ram's-horn.
Sing praises to God, sing praises;* sing praises to our King, sing praises.
For God is King of all the earth;* sing praises with all your skill.
God reigns over the nations;* God sits upon his holy throne.

Psalm 47:5–8

The Request for Presence
Let the peoples praise you, O God;* let all the peoples praise you.

Psalm 67:3

The Greeting
For you alone are the Holy One, you alone are the Lord, you alone are the Most
High, Jesus Christ, with the Holy Spirit, in the glory of God the Father.

The Refrain for the Midday Lessons
Tell it out among the nations: "The Lord is King!* he has made the world so firm
that it cannot be moved; he will judge the peoples with equity."

Psalm 96:10

A Reading
Then, in my vision, I saw a door open in heaven and heard the same voice speaking to me, the voice like a trumpet, saying, 'Come up here: I will show you
what is to take place in the future.' With that, I fell into ecstasy and I saw a
throne standing in heaven, and the *One* who was *sitting on the throne,* and the
One sitting there looked like a diamond and a ruby. There was a rainbow
encircling the throne, and this looked like an emerald. Round the throne in a
circle were twenty-four thrones, and on them I saw twenty-four elders sitting,
dressed in white robes with golden crowns on their heads. Flashes of lightning were coming from the throne, and the sound of peals of thunder, and in
front of the throne there were seven flaming lamps burning, the seven Spirits
of God. In front of the throne was a sea as transparent as crystal. *In the middle
of* the throne and around it, were *four living creatures all studded with eyes,* in
front and behind. *The first* living creature was like *a lion, the second* like *a bull,
the third* living creature had a *human face,* and the *fourth* living creature was
like a flying *eagle. Each* of the four living creatures had *six wings* and *was studded with eyes all the way round* as well as inside; and day and night they never
stopped singing: 'Holy, Holy, Holy is the Lord God, the Almighty; he was, he is and
is to come.' Every time the living creatures glorified and honored and gave
thanks to the One sitting on the throne, *who lives for ever and ever,* the twenty-
four elders prostrated themselves before him to worship the One *who lives for
ever and ever,* and threw down their crowns in front of the throne, saying, 'You
are worthy our Lord and God to receive glory and honor and power, because
you made the whole universe; and by your will, when it did not exist, it was
created.'

Revelation 4:1–11

The Refrain
Tell it out among the nations: "The Lord is King!* he has made the world so firm
that it cannot be moved; he will judge the peoples with equity."

The Midday Psalm   *Glory in His Holy Name*
Give thanks to the Lord and call upon his Name;* make known his deeds among
the peoples.
Sing to him, sing praises to him,* and speak of all his marvelous works.
Glory in his holy Name;* let the hearts of those who seek the Lord rejoice.
Search for the Lord and his strength;* continually seek his face.
Remember the marvels he has done,* his wonders and the judgments of his
mouth,
He is the Lord our God;* his judgments prevail in all the world.

Psalm 105:1–5, 6

The Refrain

Tell it out among the nations: "The LORD is King!* he has made the world so firm
that it cannot be moved; he will judge the peoples with equity."

The Gloria

The Lord's Prayer

The Prayer Appointed for the Week

Grant, O merciful God, that your Church, being gathered together in unity by
your Holy Spirit, may show forth your power among all people, to the glory of
your Name; through Jesus Christ our Lord, who lives and reigns with you and
the Holy Spirit, one God, for ever and ever. *Amen.*†

The Concluding Prayer of the Church

O God, you make me glad with the weekly remembrance of the glorious resurrection of your Son my Lord: Give me this day such blessing through my worship
of you, that the week to come may be spent in your favor; through Jesus Christ
our Lord. *Amen.*†

The Vespers Office   **To Be Observed on the Hour or Half Hour**
                                    Between 5 and 8 p.m.

The Call to Prayer

Open my lips, O LORD,* and my mouth shall proclaim your praise.

Psalm 51:16

The Request for Presence

Be my strong rock, a castle to keep me safe,* for you are my crag and my stronghold; for the sake of your Name, lead me and guide me.

Psalm 31:3

The Greeting

O gracious Light, pure brightness of the everlasting Father in heaven, O Jesus
Christ, holy and blessed! Now as we come to the setting of the sun, and our
eyes behold the vesper light, we sing your praises O God: Father, Son and Holy
Spirit. You are worthy at all times to be praised by happy voices, O Son of God,
O giver of life, and to be glorified through all the worlds.

Phos Hilaron

The Hymn   *Hymn for Bartholomew*

For all your saints still striving,   Praise your blessed apostle
    for all your saints at rest,   surnamed Bartholomew;
your holy Name, O Jesus,   we know not his achievements
    for evermore be blessed.   but know that he was true,
You rose, our King victorious,   for he at the ascension
    that they might wear the crown   was an apostle still.
and ever shine in splendor   May we discern your presence
    reflected from your throne.   and seek, like him, your will.

Then let us praise the Father
>and worship God the Son
and sing to God the Spirit,
>eternal Three in One,
till all the ransomed number
>who stand before the throne
ascribe all power and glory
>and praise to God alone.

Horatio Nelson

The Refrain for the Vespers Lessons
You have noted my lamentation;* put my tears into your bottle; are they not
recorded in your book?

Psalm 56:8

The Vespers Psalm   *Of Whom Then Shall I Be Afraid?*
The LORD is my light and my salvation; whom then shall I fear?* the LORD is the
strength of my life; of whom then shall I be afraid?
When evildoers came upon me to eat up my flesh,* it was they, my foes and my
adversaries, who stumbled and fell.
Though an army should encamp against me,* yet my heart shall not be afraid;
And though war should rise up against me,* yet will I put my trust in him.
One thing have I asked of the LORD; one thing I seek;* that I may dwell in the
house of the LORD all the days of my life;
To behold the fair beauty of the LORD* and to seek him in his temple.
For in the day of trouble he shall keep me safe in his shelter;* he shall hide me in
the secrecy of his dwelling and set me high upon a rock.
Even now he lifts up my head* above my enemies round about me.
Therefore I will offer in his dwelling an oblation with sounds of great gladness;* I
will sing and make music to the LORD.

Psalm 27:1–9

The Refrain
You have noted my lamentation;* put my tears into your bottle; are they not
recorded in your book?

The Small Verse
Into your hands I commend my spirit for you have redeemed me, O God of my
life. Glory be to the Father, and to the Son and to the comforting Spirit.

Traditional

The Lord's Prayer

The Prayer Appointed for the Week
Grant, O merciful God, that your Church, being gathered together in unity by
your Holy Spirit, may show forth your power among all people, to the glory of
your Name; through Jesus Christ our Lord, who lives and reigns with you and
the Holy Spirit, one God, for ever and ever. *Amen.*†

The Concluding Prayer of the Church

O God, you have brought me near to an innumerable company of angels, and to
the spirits of just men made perfect: Grant me during my earthly pilgrimage to
abide in their fellowship, and in your heavenly country to become partakers of
their joy; through Jesus Christ our Lord, who lives and reigns with you and the
Holy Spirit, one God, now and for ever. *Amen.*†

The Morning Office   **To Be Observed on the Hour or Half Hour**
                                          Between 6 and 9 a.m.

The Call to Prayer

Love the Lord, all you who worship him;* the Lord protects the faithful, but
repays to the full those who act haughtily.
Be strong and let your heart take courage,* all you who wait for the Lord.

Psalm 31:23–24

The Request for Presence

Be my strong rock, a castle to keep me safe, for you are my crag and my stronghold;* for the sake of your Name, lead me and guide me.

Psalm 31:3

The Greeting

How great is your goodness, O Lord!* which you have laid up for those who fear
you; which you have done in the sight of all

Psalm 31:19

The Refrain for the Morning Lessons

Blessed be the Lord!* for he has shown me the wonders of his love in a besieged
city.

A Reading   *On August 24, the Church remembers St. Bartholomew,*
                               called Nathaniel in the Gospel of John and one of the twelve
                               apostles. Tradition says Bartholomew traveled to India and
                               founded the Church in Armenia, where he was flayed to
                               death and then beheaded for the faith.

Jesus taught the apostles, saying: 'Among the gentiles it is the kings who lord it
over them and those who have authority over them are given the title
Benefactor. With you, this must not happen. No; the greatest among you must
behave as if he were the youngest, the leader as if he were the one who serves.
For who is the greater: the one at table or the one who serves? The one at table,
surely? Yet here I am among you as one who serves! You are the men who have
stood by me faithfully in my trials; and now I confer a kingdom on you, just as
my Father conferred one on me: you will eat and drink at my table in my kingdom, and you will sit on thrones to judge the twelve tribes of Israel.'

Luke 22:25–30

The Refrain
Blessed be the Lord!* for he has shown me the wonders of his love in a besieged city.

The Morning Psalm
I believed, even when I said, "I have been brought very low."* In my distress I
    said, "No one can be trusted."
How shall I repay the Lord* for all the good things he has done for me?
I will lift up the cup of salvation* and call upon the Name of the Lord.
I will fulfill my vows to the Lord* in the presence of all his people.
Precious in the sight of the Lord* is the death of his servants.
O Lord, I am your servant;* I am your servant and the child of your handmaid;
    you have freed me from my bonds.
I will offer you the sacrifice of thanksgiving* and call upon the Name of the Lord.
I will fulfill my vows to the Lord* in the presence of all his people,
In the courts of the Lord's house,* in the midst of you, O Jerusalem. Hallelujah!

Psalm 116:9–17

The Refrain
Blessed be the Lord!* for he has shown me the wonders of his love in a besieged
    city.

The Cry of the Church
In the evening, in the morning, and at noonday, I will complain and lament,* and
    he will hear my voice.

Psalm 55:18

The Lord's Prayer

The Prayer Appointed for the Week
Grant, O merciful God, that your Church, being gathered together in unity by
    your Holy Spirit, may show forth your power among all people, to the glory of
    your Name; through Jesus Christ our Lord, who lives and reigns with you and
    the Holy Spirit, one God, for ever and ever. *Amen.*†

The Concluding Prayers of the Church
Almighty and everlasting God, who gave to your apostle Bartholomew grace
    truly to believe and to preach your Word: Grant that your Church may love
    what he believed and preach what he taught; through Jesus Christ our Lord,
    who lives and reigns with you and the Holy Spirit, one God, for ever and ever.
    Amen.

Lord God, almighty and everlasting Father, you have brought me in safety to this
    new day: Preserve me with your mighty power, that I may not fall into sin, nor
    be overcome by adversity; and in all I do direct me to the fulfilling of your pur-
    pose; through Jesus Christ my Lord. *Amen.*†

The Midday Office   To Be Observed on the Hour or Half Hour
                                 Between 11 a.m. and 2 p.m.

The Call to Prayer
Be glad, you righteous, and rejoice in the Lord;* shout for joy, all who are true of
    heart.

Psalm 32:12

The Request for Presence
Lord, hear my prayer, and let my cry come before you;* hide not your face from
    me in the day of my trouble.

Psalm 102:1

The Greeting
Into your hands I commend my spirit,* for you have redeemed me, O Lord, O
    God of truth.

Psalm 31:5

The Refrain for the Midday Lessons
My help comes from the Lord,* the maker of heaven and earth.

Psalm 121:2

A Reading
Moses taught the people, saying: 'Yahweh our God will raise up a prophet like
    me; you will listen to him. This is exactly what you asked Yahweh your God to
    do at Horeb on the day of the Assembly, when you said, "Never let me hear the
    voice of Yahweh my God or see this great fire again, or I shall die." Then
    Yahweh said to me, "What they have said is well said. From their own brothers
    I shall raise up a prophet like yourself; I shall put my words into his mouth and
    he will tell them everything I command him. Anyone who refuses to listen to
    my words, spoken by him in my name, will have to render an account to me.
    But the prophet who presumes to say something in my name which I have not
    commanded him to say, or who speaks in the name of other gods, that prophet
    must die." '

Deuteronomy 18:15–20

The Refrain
My help comes from the Lord,* the maker of heaven and earth.

The Midday Psalm
I lift up my eyes to the hills;* from where is my help to come?
My help comes from the Lord,* the maker of heaven and earth.
He will not let your foot be moved* and he who watches over you will not fall
    asleep.
Behold, he who keeps watch over Israel* shall neither slumber nor sleep;
The Lord himself watches over you;* the Lord is your shade at your right hand,
So that the sun shall not strike you by day,* nor the moon by night.

The LORD shall preserve you from all evil;* it is he who shall keep you safe.
The LORD shall watch over your going out and your coming in,* from this time
forth for evermore.

Psalm 121

The Refrain
My help comes from the LORD,* the maker of heaven and earth.

The Cry of the Church
O God, come to my assistance! O Lord, make haste to help me!

The Lord's Prayer

The Prayer Appointed for the Week
Grant, O merciful God, that your Church, being gathered together in unity by
your Holy Spirit, may show forth your power among all people, to the glory of
your Name; through Jesus Christ our Lord, who lives and reigns with you and
the Holy Spirit, one God, for ever and ever. *Amen.*†

The Concluding Prayer of the Church
Almighty and everlasting God, who has given me this day reverent and holy joy
in the remembrance of Your blessed Apostle Bartholomew, I ask you, grant
unto your Church ever to love that which he believed and to preach that which
he taught. Through our Lord. *Amen.*

adapted from THE SHORT BREVIARY

The Vespers Office   **To Be Observed on the Hour or Half Hour
Between 5 and 8 p.m.**

The Call to Prayer
Tell it out among the nations: "The LORD is King!* he has made the world so firm
that it cannot be moved; he will judge the peoples with equity."

Psalm 96:10

The Request for Presence
Restore our fortunes, O LORD,* like the watercourses of the Negev.

Psalm 126:5

The Greeting
Whom have I in heaven but you?* and having you I desire nothing upon earth.

Psalm 73:25

The Hymn

Now let the earth with joy resound
And heaven the chant re-echo round;
Nor heaven nor earth too high can raise
The great Apostle's glorious praise!

Sickness and health your voice obey,
At your command they go or stay;
From sin's disease our souls restore,
In good confirm us more and more.

So when the world is at its end
And Christ to judgment shall descend,
May we be called those joys to see
Prepared from all eternity.

Praise to the Father, with the Son
And Paraclete for ever one:
To You, O most blessed Trinity
Be our praise for all time and eternity.

adapted from The Short Breviary

The Refrain for the Vespers Lessons
Those who sowed with tears* will reap with songs of joy.
Those who go out weeping, carrying the seed,* will come again with joy, shouldering their sheaves.

Psalm 126:6–7

The Vespers Psalm   *Turn Again to Your Rest, O My Soul*
I love the Lord, because he has heard the voice of my supplication,* because he has inclined his ear to me whenever I called upon him.
The cords of death entangled me; the grip of the grave took hold of me;* I came to grief and sorrow.
Then I called upon the Name of the Lord:* "O Lord, I pray you, save my life."
Gracious is the Lord and righteous;* our God is full of compassion.
The Lord watches over the innocent;* I was brought very low, and he helped me.
Turn again to your rest, O my soul,* for the Lord has treated you well.

Psalm 116:1–6

The Refrain
Those who sowed with tears* will reap with songs of joy.
Those who go out weeping, carrying the seed,* will come again with joy, shouldering their sheaves.

The Cry of the Church
Even so come, Lord Jesus!

The Lord's Prayer

The Prayer Appointed for the Week
Grant, O merciful God, that your Church, being gathered together in unity by your Holy Spirit, may show forth your power among all people, to the glory of your Name; through Jesus Christ our Lord, who lives and reigns with you and the Holy Spirit, one God, for ever and ever. *Amen.*†

The Concluding Prayer of the Church
Almighty God, you have surrounded me with a great cloud of witnesses: Grant that I, encouraged by the good example of your servant Bartholomew; may persevere in running the race that is set before me, until at last I may with him attain to your eternal joy; through Jesus Christ, the pioneer and perfecter of our faith, who lives and reigns with you and the Holy Spirit, one God, for ever and ever. *Amen.*†

The Morning Office

To Be Observed on the Hour or Half Hour Between 6 and 9 a.m.

The Call to Prayer
Come, let us sing to the Lord;* let us shout for joy to the Rock of our salvation.

Psalm 95:1

The Request for Presence
Bow your heavens, O Lord, and come down;* touch the mountains, and they shall
   smoke.

Psalm 144:5

The Greeting
My lips will sing with joy when I play to you,* and so will my soul, which you
   have redeemed.

Psalm 71:23

The Refrain for the Morning Lessons
Your love, O Lord, for ever will I sing;* from age to age my mouth will proclaim
   your faithfulness.

Psalm 89:1

A Reading
Jesus taught us, saying: 'The Father loves me, because I lay down my life in order
   to take it up again. No one takes it from me; I lay it down of my own free will,
   and as I have power to lay it down, so I have power to take it up again; and this
   is the command I have received from my Father.'

John 10:17–18

The Refrain
Your love, O Lord, for ever will I sing;* from age to age my mouth will proclaim
   your faithfulness.

The Morning Psalm   *Keep Me as the Apple of Your Eye*
Show me your marvelous loving-kindness,* O Savior of those who take refuge at
   your right hand from those who rise up against them.
Keep me as the apple of your eye;* hide me under the shadow of your wings,
From the wicked who assault me,* from my deadly enemies who surround me.

Psalm 17:7–9

The Refrain
Your love, O Lord, for ever will I sing;* from age to age my mouth will proclaim
   your faithfulness.

The Gloria

The Lord's Prayer

The Prayer Appointed for the Week

Grant, O merciful God, that your Church, being gathered together in unity by
your Holy Spirit, may show forth your power among all people, to the glory of
your Name; through Jesus Christ our Lord, who lives and reigns with you and
the Holy Spirit, one God, for ever and ever. *Amen.*†

The Concluding Prayer of the Church

Lord God, almighty and everlasting Father, you have brought me in safety to this
new day: Preserve me with your mighty power, that I may not fall into sin, nor
be overcome by adversity; and in all I do direct me to the fulfilling of your purpose; through Jesus Christ my Lord. *Amen.*†

The Midday Office   **To Be Observed on the Hour or Half Hour
Between 11 a.m. and 2 p.m.**

The Call to Prayer

Hallelujah! Give praise, you servants of the LORD;* praise the Name of the LORD.
Psalm 113:1

The Request for Presence

Hear my voice, O LORD, according to your loving-kindness;* according to your
judgments, give me life.
Psalm 119:149

The Greeting

O LORD of hosts,* happy are they who put their trust in you!
Psalm 84:12

The Refrain for the Midday Lessons

With the faithful you show yourself faithful, O God;* with the forthright you show
yourself forthright.
With the pure you show yourself pure,* but with the crooked you are wily.
Psalm 18:26–27

A Reading

Since you have been raised up to be with Christ, you must look for the things that
are above, where Christ is, sitting at God's right hand. Let your thoughts be on
heavenly things, not on things that are on the earth, because you have died,
and now the life you have is hidden with Christ in God. But when Christ is
revealed—and he is your life—you too will be revealed in all your glory with
him.
Colossians 3:1–4

The Refrain

With the faithful you show yourself faithful, O God;* with the forthright you show
yourself forthright.
With the pure you show yourself pure,* but with the crooked you are wily.

The Midday Psalm   *Like Trees Planted by Streams of Water*
Happy are they who have not walked in the counsel of the wicked,* nor lingered
    in the way of sinners, nor sat in the seats of the scornful!
Their delight is in the law of the LORD,* and they meditate on his law day and night.
They are like trees planted by streams of water,* bearing fruit in due season, with
    leaves that do not wither; everything they do shall prosper.
It is not so with the wicked;* they are like chaff which the wind blows away.
Therefore the wicked shall not stand upright when judgment comes,* nor the sin-
    ner in the council of the righteous.
For the LORD knows the way of the righteous,* but the way of the wicked is
    doomed.

Psalm 1:1–6

The Refrain
With the faithful you show yourself faithful, O God;* with the forthright you show
    yourself forthright.
With the pure you show yourself pure,* but with the crooked you are wily.

The Cry of the Church
O God, come to my assistance! O Lord, make haste to help me!

The Lord's Prayer

The Prayer Appointed for the Week
Grant, O merciful God, that your Church, being gathered together in unity by
    your Holy Spirit, may show forth your power among all people, to the glory of
    your Name; through Jesus Christ our Lord, who lives and reigns with you and
    the Holy Spirit, one God, for ever and ever. *Amen.*†

The Concluding Prayer of the Church
O Lord, my God, accept the fervent prayers of all of us your people; in the multi-
    tude of your mercies, look with compassion upon me and all who turn to you
    for help; for you are gracious, O lover of souls, and to you we give glory,
    Father, Son, and Holy Spirit, now and forever. *Amen.*†

The Vespers Office   **To Be Observed on the Hour or Half Hour**
Between 5 and 8 p.m.

The Call to Prayer
Sing to the LORD with thanksgiving;* make music to our God upon the harp.

Psalm 147:7

The Request for Presence
Let your countenance shine upon your servant* and teach me your statutes.

Psalm 119:135

The Greeting
How glorious you are!* more splendid than the everlasting mountains!

Psalm 76:4

The Hymn   *Love Divine, All Loves Excelling*

Love Divine, all loves excelling,
Joy of heaven, to earth come down,
Fix in us your humble dwelling,
All your faithful mercies crown!
Jesus, you are all compassion,
Pure, unbounded love thou art;
Visit us with your salvation,
Enter every trembling heart.

Come, Almighty to deliver,
Let us all your life receive;
Suddenly return and never,
Nevermore your temples leave.
You we would be always blessing,
Serve you as your hosts above;
Pray, and praise you without ceasing,
Glory in your perfect love.

Finish, then, your new creation;
Pure and spotless let us be;
Let us see your great salvation
Perfectly restored in thee;
Changed from glory into glory,
Till in heaven we take our place,
Till we cast our crowns before thee,
Lost in wonder, love, and praise.

Charles Wesley

The Refrain for the Vespers Lessons
Your love, O LORD, for ever will I sing;* from age to age my mouth will proclaim
your faithfulness.

Psalm 89:1

The Vespers Psalm   *So That a People Yet Unborn May Praise the* LORD
Let this be written for a future generation,* so that a people yet unborn may praise
the LORD.
For the LORD looked down from his holy place on high;* from the heavens he
beheld the earth;
That he might hear the groan of the captive* and set free those condemned to die;
That they may declare in Zion the Name of the LORD,* and his praise in Jerusalem;
When the peoples are gathered together,* and the kingdoms also, to serve the
LORD.

Psalm 102:18–22

The Refrain
Your love, O LORD, for ever will I sing;* from age to age my mouth will proclaim
your faithfulness.

The Gloria

The Lord's Prayer

The Prayer Appointed for the Week
Grant, O merciful God, that your Church, being gathered together in unity by
your Holy Spirit, may show forth your power among all people, to the glory of
your Name; through Jesus Christ our Lord, who lives and reigns with you and
the Holy Spirit, one God, for ever and ever. *Amen.*†

The Concluding Prayer of the Church
Lord Jesus Christ, you have prepared a quiet place for us in your Father's eternal
home. Watch over our welfare on this perilous journey, shade us from the
burning heat of day, and keep our lives free of evil until the end. *Amen.*

THE LITURGY OF THE HOURS, VOL. III

The Morning Office **To Be Observed on the Hour or Half Hour**
Between 6 and 9 a.m.

The Call to Prayer
Taste and see that the LORD is good;* happy are they who trust in him!

Psalm 34:8

The Request for Presence
Gladden the soul of your servant,* for to you, O LORD, I lift up my soul.

Psalm 86:4

The Greeting
With my whole heart I seek you;* let me not stray from your commandments.

Psalm 119:10

The Refrain for the Morning Lessons
I will bear witness that the LORD is righteous;* I will praise the Name of the LORD
Most High.

Psalm 7:18

A Reading
Jesus taught us, saying: 'This is what the kingdom of God is like. A man scatters
seed on the land. Night and day, while he sleeps, when he is awake, the seed is
sprouting and growing; how, he does not know. Of its own accord the land produces first the shoot, then the ear, then the full grain in the ear. And when the
crop is ready, he loses no time: he starts to reap because the harvest has come.'

Mark 4:26–29

The Refrain
I will bear witness that the LORD is righteous;* I will praise the Name of the LORD
Most High.

The Morning Psalm *The Earth Is Fully Satisfied by the Fruit of Your Works*
You water the mountains from your dwelling on high;* the earth is fully satisfied
by the fruit of your works.
You make grass grow for flocks and herds* and plants to serve mankind;
That they may bring forth food from the earth,* and wine to gladden our hearts,
Oil to make a cheerful countenance,* and bread to strengthen the heart.
You appointed the moon to mark the seasons,* and the sun knows the time of its
setting.
You make darkness that it may be night,* in which all the beasts of the forest prowl.
The lions roar after their prey* and seek their food from God.

The sun rises, and they slip away* and lay themselves down in their dens.
Man goes forth to his work* and to his labor until the evening.

Psalm 13:16, 20–24

The Refrain
I will bear witness that the LORD is righteous;* I will praise the Name of the LORD
Most High.

The Small Verse
Let me seek the Lord while he may still be found. I will call upon his name while
he is near.

Traditional

The Lord's Prayer

The Prayer Appointed for the Week
Grant, O merciful God, that your Church, being gathered together in unity by
your Holy Spirit, may show forth your power among all people, to the glory of
your Name; through Jesus Christ our Lord, who lives and reigns with you and
the Holy Spirit, one God, for ever and ever. *Amen.*†

The Concluding Prayer of the Church
Lord God, almighty and everlasting Father, you have brought me in safety to this
new day: Preserve me with your mighty power, that I may not fall into sin, nor
be overcome by adversity; and in all I do direct me to the fulfilling of your purpose; through Jesus Christ my Lord. *Amen.*†

The Midday Office   To Be Observed on the Hour or Half Hour
Between 11 a.m. and 2 p.m.

The Call to Prayer
Bless the LORD, O my soul,* and all that is within me, bless his holy Name.

Psalm 103:1

The Request for Presence
Hearken to my voice, O LORD, when I call;* have mercy on me and answer me.
You speak in my heart and say, "Seek my face."* Your face, LORD, will I seek.
Hide not your face from me,* nor turn away your servant in displeasure.

Psalm 27:10–12

The Greeting
I restrain my feet from every evil way,* that I may keep your word.

Psalm 119:101

The Refrain for the Midday Lessons
For one day in your courts is better than a thousand in my own room,* and to stand
at the threshold of the house of my God than to dwell in the tents of the wicked.

Psalm 84:9

A Reading

I, therefore, the prisoner of the Lord, beseech you that you walk worthy of the
vocation wherewith you are called, with all lowliness, with long-suffering, for-
bearing one another in love; endeavoring to keep the unity of the Spirit in the
bond of peace.

Ephesians 4:1–4 KJV

The Refrain

For one day in your courts is better than a thousand in my own room,* and to
stand at the threshold of the house of my God than to dwell in the tents of the
wicked.

The Midday Psalm   *You Have Made the Son of Man Strong for Yourself*

Let your hand be upon the man of your right hand,* the son of man you have
made so strong for yourself.

And so will we never turn away from you;* give us life, that we may call upon
your Name.

Restore us, O LORD God of hosts;* show the light of your countenance, and we
shall be saved.

Psalm 80:16–18

The Refrain

For one day in your courts is better than a thousand in my own room,* and to
stand at the threshold of the house of my God than to dwell in the tents of the
wicked.

The Cry of the Church

O Lamb of God, that takes away the sins of the world, have mercy upon me.
O Lamb of God, that takes away the sins of the world, have mercy upon me.
O Lamb of God, that takes away the sins of the world, grant me your peace.

The Lord's Prayer

The Prayer Appointed for the Week

Grant, O merciful God, that your Church, being gathered together in unity by
your Holy Spirit, may show forth your power among all people, to the glory of
your Name; through Jesus Christ our Lord, who lives and reigns with you and
the Holy Spirit, one God, for ever and ever. *Amen.*†

The Concluding Prayer of the Church

God of justice, God of mercy, bless all those who are surprised with pain this day
from suffering caused by their own weakness or that of others. Let what we
suffer teach us to be merciful; let our sins teach us to forgive. This we ask
through the intercession of Jesus and all who died forgiving those who
oppressed them. *Amen.*

THE NEW COMPANION TO THE BREVIARY

The Vespers Office   **To Be Observed on the Hour or Half Hour**
                                       Between 5 and 8 p.m.

The Call to Prayer
Bless the LORD, you angels of his, you mighty ones who do his bidding,* and hear-
    ken to the voice of his word.
Bless the LORD, all you his hosts,* you ministers of his who do his will.
Bless the LORD, all you works of his,* in all places of his dominion;
                                                            Psalm 103:20–22

The Request for Presence
LORD God of hosts, hear my prayer;* hearken, O God of Jacob.
                                       Psalm 84:7

The Greeting
Show me your ways, O LORD,* and teach me your paths.
Lead me in your truth and teach me,* for you are the God of my salvation; in you
    have I trusted all the day long.
                                                            Psalm 25:3–4

The Hymn   *O Master, Let Me Walk With Thee*
    O Master, let me walk with thee
    In lowly paths of service free;
    Tell me your secret; help me bear
    The strain of toil, the fret of care.

    Help me the slow of heart to move
    By some clear, winning word of love;
    Teach me the wayward feet to stay,
    And guide them in some homeward way.

    Teach me your patience; still with thee
    In closer, dearer company,
    In work that keeps faith sweet and strong,
    In trust that triumphs over wrong.

    In hope that sends a shining ray
    Far down the future's broadening way;
    In peace that only you can give,
    With You, O Master, let me live.
                        Washington Gladden

The Refrain for the Vespers Lessons
But it is good for me to be near God;* I have made the Lord GOD my refuge.
                                       Psalm 73:28

The Vespers Psalm   *My Soul Is Athirst for the Living God*

As the deer longs for the water-brooks,* so longs my soul for you, O God.

My soul is athirst for God, athirst for the living God;* when shall I come to appear
before the presence of God?

My tears have been my food day and night,* while all day long they say to me,
"Where now is your God?"

I pour out my soul when I think on these things:* how I went with the multitude
and led them into the house of God,

With the voice of praise and thanksgiving,* among those who keep holy-day.

Why are you so full of heaviness, O my soul?* and why are you so disquieted
within me?

Put your trust in God;* for I will yet give thanks to him, who is the help of my
countenance, and my God.

Psalm 42:1–7

The Refrain

But it is good for me to be near God;* I have made the Lord GOD my refuge.

The Small Verse

Keep me, Lord, as the apple of your eye and carry me under the shadow of your
wings.

Traditional

The Lord's Prayer

The Prayer Appointed for the Week

Grant, O merciful God, that your Church, being gathered together in unity by
your Holy Spirit, may show forth your power among all people, to the glory of
your Name; through Jesus Christ our Lord, who lives and reigns with you and
the Holy Spirit, one God, for ever and ever. *Amen.*†

The Concluding Prayer of the Church

Protect us, Lord, as we stay awake; watch over us as we sleep, that awake we may
watch with Christ, and asleep, rest in his peace. *Amen.*

The Morning Office   **To Be Observed on the Hour or Half Hour**
Between 6 and 9 a.m.

The Call to Prayer

Sing to the LORD and bless his Name;* proclaim the good news of his salvation
from day to day.

Declare his glory among the nations* and his wonders among all peoples.

For great is the LORD and greatly to be praised;* he is more to be feared than all gods.

Psalm 96:2–4

The Request for Presence

Save me, O God,* for the waters have risen up to my neck.

Psalm 69:1

The Greeting
The LORD lives! Blessed is my Rock!* Exalted is the God of my salvation!
Psalm 18:46

The Refrain for the Morning Lessons
He looks at the earth and it trembles;* he touches the mountains and they smoke.
Psalm 104:33

A Reading
Then he got into the boat followed by his disciples. Suddenly a storm broke over
the lake, so violent that the boat was being swamped by the waves. But he was
asleep. So they went to him and woke him saying, 'Save us, Lord, we are lost!'
And he said to them, 'Why are you so frightened, you who have so little faith?'
And then he stood up and rebuked the winds and the sea; and there was a
great calm. They were astounded and said, 'Whatever kind of man is this?
Even the winds and the sea obey him.'
Matthew 8:23–27

The Refrain
He looks at the earth and it trembles;* he touches the mountains and they smoke.

The Morning Psalm   *What Ailed You, O Sea, That You Fled?*
Hallelujah! When Israel came out of Egypt,* the house of Jacob from a people of
strange speech,
Judah became God's sanctuary* and Israel his dominion.
The sea beheld it and fled;* Jordan turned and went back.
The mountains skipped like rams,* and the little hills like young sheep.
What ailed you, O sea, that you fled?* O Jordan, that you turned back?
You mountains, that you skipped like rams?* you little hills like young sheep?
Tremble, O earth, at the presence of the Lord,* at the presence of the God of Jacob,
Who turned the hard rock into a pool of water* and flint-stone into a flowing
spring.
Psalm 114:1–8

The Refrain
He looks at the earth and it trembles;* he touches the mountains and they smoke.

The Cry of the Church
O God, come to my assistance! O Lord, make haste to help me!

The Lord's Prayer

The Prayer Appointed for the Week
Grant, O merciful God, that your Church, being gathered together in unity by
your Holy Spirit, may show forth your power among all people, to the glory of
your Name; through Jesus Christ our Lord, who lives and reigns with you and
the Holy Spirit, one God, for ever and ever. *Amen.*†

The Concluding Prayer of the Church
Lord God, almighty and everlasting Father, you have brought me in safety to this
new day: Preserve me with your mighty power, that I may not fall into sin, nor
be overcome by adversity; and in all I do direct me to the fulfilling of your purpose; through Jesus Christ my Lord. *Amen.*†

The Midday Office   **To Be Observed on the Hour or Half Hour**
                                           Between 11 a.m. and 2 p.m.

The Call to Prayer
Search for the LORD and his strength;* continually seek his face.

Psalm 105:4

The Request for Presence
You are good and you bring forth good;* instruct me in your statutes.

Psalm 119:68

The Greeting
When your word goes forth it gives light;* it gives understanding to the simple.

Psalm 119:130

The Refrain for the Midday Lessons
You strengthen me more and more; you enfold and comfort me,

Psalm 71:21

A Reading
YAHWEH appeared to Solomon in a dream during the night. God said, 'Ask what you
would like me to give you.' Solomon replied, 'You showed most faithful love to
your servant David, my father . . . Now, YAHWEH my God, you have made your
servant king in succession to David my father. But I am a very young man,
unskilled in leadership. And here is your servant, surrounded with your people
whom you have chosen, a people so numerous that its number cannot be
counted or reckoned. So give your servant a heart to understand how to govern
your people, how to discern between good and evil, for how could one otherwise govern such a great people as yours?' It pleased YAHWEH that Solomon
should have asked for this. 'Since you have asked for this,' GOD said, 'and not
asked for long life for yourself or riches or the lives of your enemies, but have
asked for a discerning judgment for yourself, here and now I do what you ask, I
give you a heart wise and shrewd as no one has had before and no one will have
after you. What you have not asked I shall give you too: such riches and glory as
no other king can match. And I shall give you a long life, if you follow my ways,
keeping my laws and commandments, as your father David followed them.'
Then Solomon woke up; it had been a dream. He returned to Jerusalem and
stood before the ark of the covenant of YAHWEH; he presented burnt offerings and
communion sacrifices, and held a banquet for all those in his service.

I Kings 3:5ff

The Refrain
You strengthen me more and more;* you enfold and comfort me,

The Midday Psalm   *The Judgments of the LORD Are Sweeter Far Than Honey*
The law of the LORD is perfect and revives the soul;* the testimony of the LORD is
    sure and gives wisdom to the innocent.
The statutes of the LORD are just and rejoice the heart;* the commandment of the
    LORD is clear and gives light to the eyes.
The fear of the LORD is clean and endures for ever;* the judgments of the LORD are
    true and righteous altogether.
More to be desired are they than gold, more than much fine gold,* sweeter far than
    honey, than honey in the comb.
By them also is your servant enlightened,* and in keeping them there is great
    reward.

Psalm 19:7–11

The Refrain
You strengthen me more and more;* you enfold and comfort me,

The Gloria

The Lord's Prayer

The Prayer Appointed for the Week
Grant, O merciful God, that your Church, being gathered together in unity by
    your Holy Spirit, may show forth your power among all people, to the glory of
    your Name; through Jesus Christ our Lord, who lives and reigns with you and
    the Holy Spirit, one God, for ever and ever. *Amen.*†

The Concluding Prayer of the Church
Lord, make me according to thy heart.
Brother Lawrence

The Vespers Office   **To Be Observed on the Hour or Half Hour**
Between 5 and 8 p.m.

The Call to Prayer
Come now and see the works of God,* how wonderful he is in his doing toward
    all people.
In his might he rules for ever; his eyes keep watch over the nations;* let no rebel
    rise up against him.

Psalm 66:4, 6

The Request for Presence
Show us your mercy, O LORD,* and grant us your salvation.
Psalm 85:7

The Greeting
Praise God from whom all blessings flow; praise Him all creatures here below;
praise Him above, you heavenly hosts; praise Father, Son, and Holy Ghost.

Traditional Doxology

The Hymn   *Dear Lord and Father of Mankind*
Dear Lord and Father of mankind,
Forgive our foolish ways;
Reclothe us in our rightful mind,
In purer lives thy service find,
In deeper reverence, praise.

Drop thy still dews of quietness,
Till all our strivings cease;
Take from our souls the strain and stress,
And let our ordered lives confess
The beauty of thy peace.

Breathe through the heats of our desire
Thy coolness and thy balm;
Let sense be dumb, let flesh retire;
Speak through the earthquake, wind, and fire,
O still, small voice of calm!

John G. Whittier

The Refrain for the Vespers Lessons
Our sins are stronger than we are,* but you will blot them out.

Psalm 65:3

The Vespers Psalm   *The Lord Will Not Abandon His People*
He that planted the ear, does he not hear?* he that formed the eye, does he not see?
He who admonishes the nations, will he not punish?* he who teaches all the
world, has he no knowledge?
The Lord knows our human thoughts;* how like a puff of wind they are.
Happy are they whom you instruct, O Lord!* whom you teach out of your law;
To give them rest in evil days,* until a pit is dug for the wicked.
For the Lord will not abandon his people,* nor will he forsake his own.
For judgment will again be just,* and all the true of heart will follow it.

Psalm 94:9–15

The Refrain
Our sins are stronger than we are,* but you will blot them out.

The Small Verse
The Lord is my shepherd and nothing is wanting to me. In green pastures He hath
settled me.

The Short Breviary

The Lord's Prayer

The Prayer Appointed for the Week
Grant, O merciful God, that your Church, being gathered together in unity by
your Holy Spirit, may show forth your power among all people, to the glory of
your Name; through Jesus Christ our Lord, who lives and reigns with you and
the Holy Spirit, one God, for ever and ever. *Amen.*†

The Concluding Prayer of the Church
Help each one of us, gracious Father, to live in such magnanimity and restraint
that the Head of the Church may never have cause to say to any one of us, This
is my body, broken by you.

Prayer from China

The Morning Office   **To Be Observed on the Hour or Half Hour**
Between 6 and 9 a.m.

The Call to Prayer
Know this: The LORD himself is God;* he himself has made us, and we are his; we
are his people and the sheep of his pasture.

Psalm 100:2

The Request for Presence
Lead me, O LORD, in your righteousness, . . .* make your way straight before me.

Psalm 5:8

The Greeting
Hosannah, LORD, hosannah!* LORD, send us now success.
Blessed is he who comes in the name of the Lord;* we bless you from the house of
the LORD.
God is the LORD; he has shined upon us;* form a procession with branches up to
the horns of the altar.

Psalm 118:25–27

The Refrain for the Morning Lessons
Let not those who hope in you be put to shame through me, Lord GOD of hosts;*
let not those who seek you be disgraced because of me, O God of Israel.

Psalm 69:7

A Reading
Jesus taught us, saying: 'Disciple is not superior to teacher, nor slave to master. It
is enough for the disciple to grow to be like his teacher, and slave like
master. . . .'

Matthew 10:24–25

The Refrain
Let not those who hope in you be put to shame through me, Lord GOD of hosts;*
let not those who seek you be disgraced because of me, O God of Israel.

The Morning Psalm   *I Will Keep Your Statutes*
You laid down your commandments,* that we should fully keep them.
Oh, that my ways were made so direct* that I might keep your statutes!
Then I should not be put to shame,* when I regard all your commandments.
I will thank you with an unfeigned heart,* when I have learned your righteous
     judgments.
I will keep your statutes;* do not utterly forsake me.

Psalm 119:4–8

The Refrain
Let not those who hope in you be put to shame through me, Lord GOD of hosts;*
     let not those who seek you be disgraced because of me, O God of Israel.

The Cry of the Church
O God, come to my assistance! O Lord, make haste to help me!

The Lord's Prayer

The Prayer Appointed for the Week
Grant, O merciful God, that your Church, being gathered together in unity by
     your Holy Spirit, may show forth your power among all people, to the glory of
     your Name; through Jesus Christ our Lord, who lives and reigns with you and
     the Holy Spirit, one God, for ever and ever. *Amen.*†

The Concluding Prayer of the Church
Lord God, almighty and everlasting Father, you have brought me in safety to this
     new day:Preserve me with your mighty power, that I may not fall into sin, nor
     be overcome by adversity; and in all I do direct me to the fulfilling of your pur-
     pose; through Jesus Christ my Lord. *Amen.*†

The Midday Office   **To Be Observed on the Hour or Half Hour**
                                              Between 11 a.m. and 2 p.m.

The Call to Prayer
Give thanks to the LORD, for he is good;* his mercy endures for ever.

Psalm 118:29

The Request for Presence
You are the LORD;* do not withhold your compassion from me; let your love and
     your faithfulness keep me safe for ever,

Psalm 40:12

The Greeting
There is forgiveness with you;* therefore you shall be feared.

Psalm 130:3

The Refrain for the Midday Lessons
For you, O LORD, are good and forgiving,* and great is your love toward all who
    call upon you.

Psalm 86:5

A Reading
If we say, 'We have no sin,' we are deceiving ourselves, and truth has no place in
    us; if we acknowledge our sins, he is trustworthy and upright, so that he will
    forgive our sins and will cleanse us from all evil. If we say, 'We have never
    sinned,' we make him a liar, and his word has no place in us.

I John 1:8–10

The Refrain
For you, O LORD, are good and forgiving,* and great is your love toward all who
    call upon you.

The Midday Psalm   *He Remembers That We Are But Dust*
He has not dealt with us according to our sins,* nor rewarded us according to our
    wickedness.
For as the heavens are high above the earth,* so is his mercy great upon those who
    fear him.
As far as the east is from the west,* so far has he removed our sins from us.
As a father cares for his children,* so does the LORD care for those who fear him.
For he himself knows whereof we are made;* he remembers that we are but dust.

Psalm 103:10–14

The Refrain
For you, O LORD, are good and forgiving,* and great is your love toward all who
    call upon you.

The Cry of the Church
In the evening, in the morning, and at noonday, I will complain and lament,* and
    he will hear my voice.

Psalm 55:18

The Lord's Prayer

The Prayer Appointed for the Week
Grant, O merciful God, that your Church, being gathered together in unity by
    your Holy Spirit, may show forth your power among all people, to the glory of
    your Name; through Jesus Christ our Lord, who lives and reigns with you and
    the Holy Spirit, one God, for ever and ever. *Amen.*†

The Concluding Prayer of the Church
Lord Jesus Christ, by your death you took away the sting of death: Grant me to so
    follow in faith where you have led the way, that I may at length fall asleep
    peacefully in you and wake in your likeness; for your tender mercies' sake.
    Amen.†

The Vespers Office

To Be Observed on the Hour or Half Hour
Between 5 and 8 p.m.

The Call to Prayer
I will call upon God,* and the LORD will deliver me.
In the evening, in the morning, and at noonday, I will complain and lament,* and
    he will hear my voice.
He will bring me safely back . . .* God, who is enthroned of old, will hear me.

Psalm 55:17ff

The Request for Presence
You are the LORD; do not withhold your compassion from me;* let your love and
    your faithfulness keep me safe for ever.

Psalm 40:12

The Greeting
I remember your Name in the night, O LORD,* and dwell upon your law.

Psalm 119:55

The Hymn   *I Need Thee Every Hour*

I need Thee every hour,
Most gracious Lord;
No tender voice like Thine
Can peace afford.
I need Thee, O I need Thee;
Every hour I need Thee!
O bless me now, my Savior,
I come to Thee!

I need Thee every hour,
In joy or pain;
Come quickly and abide,
Or life is vain.
I need Thee, O I need Thee;
Every hour I need Thee!
O bless me now, my Savior,
I come to Thee!

I need Thee every hour,
Stay Thou near by;
Temptations lose their power
When Thou art nigh.
I need Thee, O I need Thee;
Every hour I need Thee!
O bless me now, my Savior,
I come to Thee!

I need Thee every hour,
Most Holy One;
O make me Thine indeed,
Thou blessed Son.
I need Thee, O I need Thee;
Every hour I need Thee!
O bless me now, my Savior,
I come to Thee!

Annie Hawks

The Refrain for the Vespers Lessons
Unless the LORD watches over the city,* in vain the watchman keeps his vigil.

Psalm 127:2

The Vespers Psalm   *We Flourish Like a Flower of the Field*
Our days are like the grass;* we flourish like a flower of the field;
When the wind goes over it, it is gone,* and its place shall know it no more.

But the merciful goodness of the LORD endures for ever on those who fear him,*
    and his righteousness on children's children;
On those who keep his covenant* and remember his commandments and do them.

Psalm 103:15–18

The Refrain
Unless the LORD watches over the city,* in vain the watchman keeps his vigil.

The Small Verse
Open, Lord, my eyes that I may see. Open, Lord, my ears that I may hear. Open,
    Lord, my heart and my mind that I may understand. So shall I turn to you and
    be healed.

Traditional

The Lord's Prayer

The Prayer Appointed for the Week
Grant, O merciful God, that your Church, being gathered together in unity by
    your Holy Spirit, may show forth your power among all people, to the glory of
    your Name; through Jesus Christ our Lord, who lives and reigns with you and
    the Holy Spirit, one God, for ever and ever. *Amen.*†

The Concluding Prayers of the Church
Almighty God, who has promised to hear the petitions of those who ask in your
    Son's Name: I beseech you mercifully to incline your ear to me who have made
    my prayers and supplications to you; and grant that those things which I have
    faithfully asked according to your will, I may effectually obtain, to the relief of
    my necessity, and to the setting forth of your glory; through Jesus Christ my
    Lord. *Amen.*†

May the souls of the faithful departed, through the mercy of God, rest in eternal
    peace. *Amen.*

The Morning Office   **To Be Observed on the Hour or Half Hour**
                                            Between 6 and 9 a.m.

The Call to Prayer
Let us bless the LORD,* from this time forth for evermore. Hallelujah!

based on Psalm 115:18

The Request for Presence
I cry out to you, O LORD;* I say, "You are my refuge, my portion in the land of the
    living."

Psalm 142:5

The Greeting
I will confess you among the peoples, O LORD;* I will sing praises to you among
    the nations.

For your loving-kindness is greater than the heavens,* and your faithfulness reaches to the clouds.

Psalm 108:3–4

The Refrain for the Morning Lessons
For the LORD God is both sun and shield;* he will give grace and glory . . .

Psalm 84:11

A Reading
Now it happened that he was praying alone, and his disciples came to him and he put this question to them, 'Who do the crowds say I am?' And they answered, 'Some say John the Baptist; others Elijah; and others again one of the ancient prophets come back to life.' 'But you,' he said to them, 'who do you say I am?' It was Peter who spoke up. 'The Christ of God,' he said. But he gave them strict orders not to say this to anyone.

Luke 9:18–21

The Refrain
For the LORD God is both sun and shield;* he will give grace and glory . . .

The Morning Psalm   *Proclaim the Greatness of Our God*
Proclaim the greatness of the LORD our God* and fall down before his footstool; he is the Holy One.

Moses and Aaron among his priests,* and Samuel among those who call upon his Name, they called upon the LORD, and he answered them.

He spoke to them out of the pillar of cloud;* they kept his testimonies and the decree that he gave them.

O LORD our God, you answered them indeed;* you were a God who forgave them, yet punished them for their evil deeds.

Proclaim the greatness of the LORD our God* and worship him upon his holy hill; for the LORD our God is the Holy One.

Psalm 99:5–9

The Refrain
For the LORD God is both sun and shield;* he will give grace and glory . . .

The Gloria

The Lord's Prayer

The Prayer Appointed for the Week
Grant, O merciful God, that your Church, being gathered together in unity by your Holy Spirit, may show forth your power among all people, to the glory of your Name; through Jesus Christ our Lord, who lives and reigns with you and the Holy Spirit, one God, for ever and ever. *Amen.*†

The Concluding Prayer of the Church
Lord God, almighty and everlasting Father, you have brought me in safety to this new day: Preserve me with your mighty power, that I may not fall into sin, nor

be overcome by adversity; and in all I do direct me to the fulfilling of your purpose; through Jesus Christ my Lord. *Amen.*†

The Midday Office   To Be Observed on the Hour or Half Hour
Between 11 a.m. and 2 p.m.

The Call to Prayer
Ascribe to the LORD, you families of the peoples;* ascribe to the LORD honor and power.
Ascribe to the LORD the honor due his Name;* bring offerings and come into his courts.
Worship the LORD in the beauty of holiness . . .
Psalm 96:7–9

The Request for Presence
For God alone my soul in silence waits;* truly, my hope is in him.
Psalm 62:6

The Greeting
Happy are the people whose strength is in you!* whose hearts are set on the pilgrims' way.
Psalm 84:4

The Refrain for the Midday Lessons
I will bless the LORD who gives me counsel;* my heart teaches me, night after night.
Psalm 16:7

A Reading
My child, if you take my words to heart, if you set store by my commandments, turning your ear to wisdom, and turning your heart to understanding, yes, if your plea is for clear perception, if you cry out for understanding, if you look for it as though for silver, and search for it as though for buried treasure, then you will understand what the fear of YAHWEH is, and discover the knowledge of God. For YAHWEH himself is the giver of wisdom, from his mouth issue knowledge and understanding. He reserves his advice for the honest, a shield to those whose ways are sound; he stands guard over the paths of equity, he keeps watch over the way of those faithful to him. Then you will understand uprightness, equity, and fair dealing, the paths that lead to happiness.
Proverbs 2:1–9

The Refrain
I will bless the LORD who gives me counsel;* my heart teaches me, night after night.

The Midday Psalm   Wait Upon the LORD
Wait upon the LORD and keep his way;* he will raise you up to possess the land, and when the wicked are cut off, you will see it.
I have seen the wicked in their arrogance,* flourishing like a tree in full leaf.

I went by, and behold, they were not there;* I searched for them, but they could not be found.

Mark those who are honest;* observe the upright; for there is a future for the peaceable.

Transgressors shall be destroyed, one and all;* the future of the wicked is cut off.

But the deliverance of the righteous comes from the LORD;* he is their stronghold in time of trouble.

The LORD will help them and rescue them;* he will rescue them from the wicked and deliver them, because they seek refuge in him.

Psalm 37:36–42

The Refrain
I will bless the LORD who gives me counsel;* my heart teaches me, night after night.

The Small Verse
Lead me not into temptation. Deliver me from evil. Yours are the kingdom and the glory.

Traditional

The Lord's Prayer

The Prayer Appointed for the Week
Grant, O merciful God, that your Church, being gathered together in unity by your Holy Spirit, may show forth your power among all people, to the glory of your Name; through Jesus Christ our Lord, who lives and reigns with you and the Holy Spirit, one God, for ever and ever. *Amen.*†

The Concluding Prayer of the Church
O God, the source of eternal light: Shed forth your unending day upon all of us who watch for you, that our lips may praise you, our lives may bless you, and our worship may give you glory; through Jesus Christ our Lord. *Amen.*†

The Vespers Office   **To Be Observed on the Hour or Half Hour**
Between 5 and 8 p.m.

The Call to Prayer
Come now and look upon the works of the LORD,* what awesome things he has done on earth.

Psalm 46:9

The Request for Presence
Hear my cry, O God,* and listen to my prayer.
I call upon you from the ends of the earth . . .

Psalm 61:1–2

The Greeting
O ruler of the universe, Lord God, great deeds are they that you have done,* surpassing human understanding.
Your ways are ways of righteousness and truth,* O King of all the ages.

The Hymn	*Not a Word*
They crucified my Lord,	They pierced him in the side
And he never said a mumbling word	And he never said a mumbling word
Not a word, not a word, not a word.	Not a word, not a word, not a word.
They nailed him to the tree	He bowed his head and died
And he never said a mumbling word	And he never said a mumbling word
Not a word, not a word, not a word.	Not a word, not a word, not a word.

Traditional

The Refrain for the Vespers Lessons

Let the sorrowful sighing of the prisoners come before you,* and by your great
might spare those who are condemned to die.

Psalm 79:11

The Vespers Psalm *They Gave Me Gall to Eat and Vinegar to Drink*

"Hide not your face from your servant;* be swift and answer me, for I am in distress.

Draw near to me and redeem me;* because of my enemies deliver me.

You know my reproach, my shame, and my dishonor;* my adversaries are all in
your sight."

Reproach has broken my heart, and it cannot be healed;* I looked for sympathy,
but there was none, for comforters, but I could find no one.

They gave me gall to eat,* and when I was thirsty, they gave me vinegar to drink.

Psalm 69:19–23

The Refrain

Let the sorrowful sighing of the prisoners come before you,* and by your great
might spare those who are condemned to die.

The Cry of the Church

Even so, come Lord Jesus!

The Lord's Prayer

The Prayer Appointed for the Week

Grant, O merciful God, that your Church, being gathered together in unity by
your Holy Spirit, may show forth your power among all people, to the glory of
your Name; through Jesus Christ our Lord, who lives and reigns with you and
the Holy Spirit, one God, for ever and ever. *Amen.*†

The Concluding Prayer of the Church

Almighty God, who after the creation of the world rested from all your works and
sanctified a day of rest for all your creatures: Grant that I, putting away all
earthly anxieties, may be duly prepared for the service of public worship, and
grant as well that my Sabbath upon earth may be a preparation for the eternal
rest promised to your people in heaven; through Jesus Christ our Lord. *Amen.*†

∾❧∾

The Morning Office To Be Observed on the Hour or Half Hour
Between 6 and 9 a.m.

The Call to Prayer
Hallelujah! I will give thanks to the LORD with my whole heart,* in the assembly of
the upright, in the congregation.

Psalm 111:1

The Request for Presence
Let them know that you, whose Name is YAHWEH,* you alone are the Most High
over all the earth.

Psalm 83:18

The Greeting
I shall always wait in patience,* and shall praise you more and more.

Psalm 71:14

The Refrain for the Morning Lessons
The same stone which the builders rejected* has become the chief cornerstone.

Psalm 118:22

A Reading
Jesus prayed, saying: 'Father, I want those you have given me to be with me where
I am, so that they may always see my glory which you have given me because
you loved me before the foundation of the world. Father, Upright One, the
world has not known you, but I have known you, and these have known that
you have sent me. I have made your name known to them and will continue to
make it known so that the love with which you loved me may be in them, and
so that I may be in them.'

John 17:24–26

The Refrain
The same stone which the builders rejected* has become the chief cornerstone.

The Morning Psalm *A Canticle of the Messiah*
The LORD said to my Lord, "Sit at my right hand,* until I make your enemies your
footstool."
The LORD will send the scepter of your power out of Zion,* saying, "Rule over
your enemies round about you.
Princely state has been yours from the day of your birth;* in the beauty of holiness
have I begotten you, like dew from the womb of the morning."
The LORD has sworn and he will not recant:* "You are a priest for ever after the
order of Melchizedek."

The Lord who is at your right hand* will smite kings in the day of his wrath; he
will rule over the nations.

Psalm 110:1–5

The Refrain
The same stone which the builders rejected* has become the chief cornerstone.

The Gloria

The Lord's Prayer

The Prayer Appointed for the Week
Lord of all power and might, the author and giver of all good things: Graft in my
heart the love of your Name; increase in me true religion; nourish me with all
goodness; and bring forth in me the fruit of good works; through Jesus Christ
our Lord, who lives and reigns with you and the Holy Spirit, one God, for ever
and ever. *Amen.*†

The Concluding Prayer of the Church
Lord God, almighty and everlasting Father, you have brought me in safety to this
new day: Preserve me with your mighty power, that I may not fall into sin, nor
be overcome by adversity; and in all I do direct me to the fulfilling of your purpose; through Jesus Christ my Lord. *Amen.*†

The Midday Office **To Be Observed on the Hour or Half Hour
Between 11 a.m. and 2 p.m.**

The Call to Prayer
Blessed be the Lord for evermore!* Amen, I say, Amen.

Psalm 89:52

The Request for Presence
May the graciousness of the Lord our God be upon us;* prosper the work of our
hands; prosper our handiwork.

Psalm 90:17

The Greeting
Blessed are you, O Lord;* instruct me in your statutes.

Psalm 119:12

The Refrain for the Midday Lessons
"I will instruct you and teach you in the way that you should go;* I will guide you
with my eye. Do not be like horse or mule, which have no understanding;*
who must be fitted with bit and bridle, or else they will not stay near you."

Psalm 32:9–10

A Reading
Dear Ones, you have been called and chosen: work all the harder to justify it.

based on 2 Peter 1:10

The Refrain
"I will instruct you and teach you in the way that you should go;* I will guide you
with my eye. Do not be like horse or mule, which have no understanding;*
who must be fitted with bit and bridle, or else they will not stay near you."

The Midday Psalm   *In God the LORD, Whose Word I Praise*
In God the LORD, whose word I praise,* in God I trust and will not be afraid, for
what can mortals do to me?
I am bound by the vow I made to you, O God;* I will present to you thank-
offerings;
For you have rescued my soul from death and my feet from stumbling,* that I may
walk before God in the light of the living.

Psalm 56:10–12

The Refrain
"I will instruct you and teach you in the way that you should go;* I will guide you
with my eye. Do not be like horse or mule, which have no understanding;*
who must be fitted with bit and bridle, or else they will not stay near you."

The Small Verse
My help is in the name of the Lord who made heaven and earth and all that is in
them. Thanks be to God.

Traditional

The Lord's Prayer

The Prayer Appointed for the Week
Lord of all power and might, the author and giver of all good things: Graft in my
heart the love of your Name; increase in me true religion; nourish me with all
goodness; and bring forth in me the fruit of good works; through Jesus Christ
our Lord, who lives and reigns with you and the Holy Spirit, one God, for ever
and ever. *Amen.*†

The Concluding Prayer of the Church
O God, you make me glad with the weekly remembrance of the glorious resurrection of your Son my Lord: Give me this day such blessing through my worship
of you, that the week to come may be spent in your favor; through Jesus Christ
our Lord. *Amen.*†

The Vespers Office   **To Be Observed on the Hour or Half Hour
                                      Between 5 and 8 p.m.**

The Call to Prayer
Let my mouth be full of your praise* and your glory all the day long.
Do not cast me off in my old age;* forsake me not when my strength fails.

Psalm 71:8–9

The Request for Presence
Let your loving-kindness, O LORD, be upon us,* as we have put our trust in you.

Psalm 33:22

The Greeting
To you I lift up my eyes,* to you enthroned in the heavens.
As the eyes of servants look to the hand of their masters,* and the eyes of a maid to
the hand of her mistress,
So my eyes look to the LORD my God,* until he shows me his mercy.

based on Psalm 123:1–3

The Hymn
O Blessed Creator of the light,
Who made the day with radiance bright,
And over the forming world did call
The light from chaos first of all;

Whose wisdom joined in sweet array
The morning and evening, naming them as day;
Night comes with all its darkling fears,
Regard your people's prayers and tears.

Lest, sunk in sin and numbed with strife,
We lose the gift of endless life;
Or while thinking but the thoughts of time
We weave new chains of woe and crime.

Hear our prayer, our mighty king!
Hear our praises too, we sing,
Adoring with all heaven's host
The Father, Son and Holy Ghost. *Amen.*

adapted from THE SHORT BREVIARY

The Refrain for the Vespers Lessons
In truth God has heard me;* he has attended to the voice of my prayer.

Psalm 66:17

The Vespers Psalm   *In the Night Season His Song Is with Me*
My soul is heavy within me;* therefore I will remember you from the land of
Jordan, and from the peak of Mizar among the heights of Hermon.
One deep calls to another in the noise of your cataracts;* all your rapids and floods
have gone over me.
The LORD grants his loving-kindness in the daytime;* in the night season his song
is with me, a prayer to the God of my life.
I will say to the God of my strength,* "Why have you forgotten me? and why do I
go so heavily while the enemy oppresses me?"
While my bones are being broken,* my enemies mock me to my face;
All day long they mock me* and say to me, "Where now is your God?"

Why are you so full of heaviness, O my soul?* and why are you so disquieted
within me?

Put your trust in God;* for I will yet give thanks to him, who is the help of my
countenance, and my God.

Psalm 42:8–15

The Refrain
In truth God has heard me;* he has attended to the voice of my prayer.

Psalm 66:17

The Cry of the Church
O Lord, hear my prayer and let my cry come unto you. Thanks be to God.

The Short Breviary

The Lord's Prayer

The Prayer Appointed for the Week
Lord of all power and might, the author and giver of all good things: Graft in my
heart the love of your Name; increase in me true religion; nourish me with all
goodness; and bring forth in me the fruit of good works; through Jesus Christ
our Lord, who lives and reigns with you and the Holy Spirit, one God, for ever
and ever. *Amen.*†

The Concluding Prayer of the Church
Lord God, whose Son our Savior Jesus Christ, triumphed over the powers of death
and prepared for us our place in the new Jerusalem: Grant that I, who have this
day given thanks for his resurrection, may praise you in the City of which he is
the light, and where he lives and reigns for ever and ever. *Amen.*†

The Morning Office   **To Be Observed on the Hour or Half Hour
Between 6 and 9 a.m.**

The Call to Prayer
Let my mouth be full of your praise* and your glory all the day long.

Psalm 71:8

The Request for Presence
Your word is a lantern to my feet* and a light upon my path.

Psalm 119:105

The Greeting
O God, you have taught me since I was young,* and to this day I tell of your
wonderful works.

Psalm 71:17

The Refrain for the Morning Lessons
This is the LORD's doing,* and it is marvelous in our eyes.

Psalm 118:23

A Reading
Jesus taught us, saying: 'For if ye forgive men their trespasses, your heavenly
Father will also forgive you: but if ye forgive not men their trespasses, neither
will your Father forgive you.'

Matthew 6:14–15 KJV

The Refrain
This is the LORD's doing,* and it is marvelous in our eyes.

The Morning Psalm   *One Day Tells Its Tale to Another*
The heavens declare the glory of God,* and the firmament shows his handiwork.
One day tells its tale to another,* and one night imparts knowledge to another.
Although they have no words or language,* and their voices are not heard,
Their sound has gone out into all lands,* and their message to the ends of the world.
In the deep has he set a pavilion for the sun;* it comes forth like a bridegroom out
of his chamber; it rejoices like a champion to run its course.
It goes forth from the uttermost edge of the heavens* and runs about to the end of
it again; nothing is hidden from its burning heat.

Psalm 19:1–6

The Refrain
This is the LORD's doing,* and it is marvelous in our eyes.

The Gloria

The Lord's Prayer

The Prayer Appointed for the Week
Lord of all power and might, the author and giver of all good things: Graft in my
heart the love of your Name; increase in me true religion; nourish me with all
goodness; and bring forth in me the fruit of good works; through Jesus Christ
our Lord, who lives and reigns with you and the Holy Spirit, one God, for ever
and ever. *Amen.*†

The Concluding Prayer of the Church
Lord God, almighty and everlasting Father, you have brought me in safety to this
new day: Preserve me with your mighty power, that I may not fall into sin, nor
be overcome by adversity; and in all I do direct me to the fulfilling of your purpose; through Jesus Christ my Lord. *Amen.*†

The Midday Office   **To Be Observed on the Hour or Half Hour**
                                              Between 11 a.m. and 2 p.m.

The Call to Prayer
Sing to the LORD a new song,* for he has done marvelous things.

Psalm 98:1

The Request for Presence
Remember me, O LORD, with the favor you have for your people,* and visit me
    with your saving help;
That I may see the prosperity of your elect* and be glad with the gladness of your
    people, that I may glory with your inheritance.

Psalm 106:4–5

The Greeting
Your righteousness, O God, reaches to the heavens;* you have done great things;
    who is like you, O God?

Psalm 71:19

The Refrain for the Midday Lessons
I will sing to the LORD as long as I live;* I will praise my God while I have my being.

Psalm 104:34

A Reading
. . . our salvation is even nearer than when we first began to believe. The night is
    nearly over, daylight is on the way; so let us throw off everything that belongs
    to darkness and equip ourselves for the light. Let us live decently, as in the
    light of day; with no orgies or drunkenness, no promiscuity or licentiousness,
    and no wrangling or jealousy.

Romans 13:11–13

The Refrain
I will sing to the LORD as long as I live;* I will praise my God while I have my
    being.

The Midday Psalm   On This Day the LORD Has Acted
Open for me the gates of righteousness;* I will enter them; I will offer thanks to the
    LORD.
"This is the gate of the LORD;* he who is righteous may enter."
I will give thanks to you, for you answered me* and have become my salvation.
The same stone which the builders rejected* has become the chief cornerstone.
This is the LORD's doing,* and it is marvelous in our eyes.
On this day the LORD has acted;* we will rejoice and be glad in it.

Psalm 118:19–24

The Refrain
I will sing to the LORD as long as I live;* I will praise my God while I have my
    being.

The Cry of the Church
Be, Lord, my helper and forsake me not. Do not despise me, O God, my savior.

THE SHORT BREVIARY

The Lord's Prayer

The Prayer Appointed for the Week
Lord of all power and might, the author and giver of all good things: Graft in my
heart the love of your Name; increase in me true religion; nourish me with all
goodness; and bring forth in me the fruit of good works; through Jesus Christ
our Lord, who lives and reigns with you and the Holy Spirit, one God, for ever
and ever. *Amen.*†

The Concluding Prayer of the Church
Direct me, O Lord, in all my doings with your most gracious favor, and further me
with your continual help; that in all my work begun, continued, and ended in
you, I may glorify your holy name, and finally, by your mercy, obtain everlasting life; through Jesus Christ my Lord. *Amen.*†

The Vespers Office   **To Be Observed on the Hour or Half Hour**
                                                           Between 5 and 8 p.m.

The Call to Prayer
Let the Name of the LORD be blessed,* from this time forth for evermore.
From the rising of the sun to its going down* let the Name of the LORD be praised.
Psalm 113:2–3

The Request for Presence
Hear my prayer, O God;* do not hide yourself from my petition.
Listen to me and answer me . . .
Psalm 55:1–2

The Greeting
The Lord is in his holy temple; let all the earth keep silence before him.
Traditional

The Hymn   *O My Soul, Bless Thou Jehovah*
O my soul, bless thou Jehovah,   He will not forever chide us,
All within me bless His name;   Nor keep anger in His mind;
Bless Jehovah, and forget not   Has not dealt as we offended,
All his mercies to proclaim.   Nor rewarded as we sinned.
For as high as is the heaven,   For as high as is the heaven,
Far above the earth below,   Far above the earth below,
Ever great to them that fear Him   Ever great to them that fear Him
Is the mercy He will ever show.   Is the mercy He will ever show.

Far as east is from west distant,
He has put away our sins;
Like the pity of a father,
Hath the Lord's compassion been.
For as high as is the heaven,
Far above the earth below,
Ever great to them that fear Him
Is the mercy He will ever show.

based on Psalm 103

The Refrain for the Vespers Lessons

Why are you so full of heaviness, O my soul?* and why are you so disquieted
within me?
Put your trust in God;* for I will yet give thanks to him, who is the help of my
countenance, and my God.

Psalm 42:6–7

The Vespers Psalm
My Soul Shall Live for Him

All the ends of the earth shall remember and turn to the Lord,* and all the families
of the nations shall bow before him.
For kingship belongs to the Lord;* he rules over the nations.
To him alone all who sleep in the earth bow down in worship;* all who go down to
the dust fall before him.
My soul shall live for him;* my descendants shall serve him; they shall be known
as the Lord's for ever.
They shall come and make known to a people yet unborn* the saving deeds that
he has done.

Psalm 22:26–30

The Refrain

Why are you so full of heaviness, O my soul?* and why are you so disquieted
within me?
Put your trust in God;* for I will yet give thanks to him, who is the help of my
countenance, and my God.

The Cry of the Church

O God, come to my assistance! O Lord, make haste to help me!

The Lord's Prayer

The Prayer Appointed for the Week

Lord of all power and might, the author and giver of all good things: Graft in my
heart the love of your Name; increase in me true religion; nourish me with all
goodness; and bring forth in me the fruit of good works; through Jesus Christ
our Lord, who lives and reigns with you and the Holy Spirit, one God, for ever
and ever. *Amen.*†

The Concluding Prayer of the Church
Save me, Lord, while I am awake and keep me while I sleep, that I may wake with
   Christ and rest in peace. *Amen.*

The Morning Office   **To Be Observed on the Hour or Half Hour**
                                           Between 6 and 9 a.m.

The Call to Prayer
Come and listen, all you who fear God,* and I will tell you what he has done for me.
                                                          Psalm 66:14

The Request for Presence
May God be merciful to us and bless us,* show us the light of his countenance and
   come to us. Let your ways be known upon earth,* your saving health among
   all nations.
                                                          Psalm 67:1–2

The Greeting
Your statutes have been like songs to me* wherever I have lived as a stranger.
                                                          Psalm 119:54

The Refrain for the Morning Lessons
Purge me from my sin, and I shall be pure;* wash me, and I shall be clean indeed.
                                                          Psalm 51:8

A Reading
Jesus knew that the Father had put everything into his hands, and that he had
   come from God and was returning to God, and he got up from table, removed
   his outer garments and, taking a towel, wrapped it round his waist; he then
   poured water into a basin and began to wash the disciples' feet and to wipe
   them with the towel he was wearing . . . When he had washed their feet and
   put on his outer garments again he went back to the table. 'Do you understand,' he said, 'what I have done to you? You call me Master and Lord, and
   rightly; so I am. If I, then, the Lord and Master have washed your feet, you
   must wash each other's feet. I have given you an example so that you may
   copy what I have done to you. In all truth I tell you, no servant is greater than
   his master, no messenger is greater than the man who sent him. Now that you
   know this, blessed are you if you behave accordingly.'
                                                          John 13:3–5, 12–17

The Refrain
Purge me from my sin, and I shall be pure;* wash me, and I shall be clean indeed.

The Morning Psalm   *Righteousness and Peace Have Kissed Each Other*
I will listen to what the LORD God is saying,* for he is speaking peace to his faithful
   people and to those who turn their hearts to him.
Truly, his salvation is very near to those who fear him,* that his glory may dwell in
   our land.

Mercy and truth have met together;* righteousness and peace have kissed each other.
Truth shall spring up from the earth,* and righteousness shall look down from
heaven.
The LORD will indeed grant prosperity,* and our land will yield its increase.
Righteousness shall go before him,* and peace shall be a pathway for his feet.

Psalm 85:8–13

The Refrain
Purge me from my sin, and I shall be pure;* wash me, and I shall be clean indeed.

The Cry of the Church
Even so come, Lord Jesus!

The Lord's Prayer

The Prayer Appointed for the Week
Lord of all power and might, the author and giver of all good things: Graft in my
heart the love of your Name; increase in me true religion; nourish me with all
goodness; and bring forth in me the fruit of good works; through Jesus Christ
our Lord, who lives and reigns with you and the Holy Spirit, one God, for ever
and ever. *Amen.†*

The Concluding Prayer of the Church
Lord God, almighty and everlasting Father, you have brought me in safety to this
new day: Preserve me with your mighty power, that I may not fall into sin, nor
be overcome by adversity; and in all I do direct me to the fulfilling of your purpose; through Jesus Christ my Lord. *Amen.†*

The Midday Office   **To Be Observed on the Hour or Half Hour**
Between 11 a.m. and 2 p.m.

The Call to Prayer
Open my lips, O Lord,* and my mouth shall proclaim your praise.

Psalm 51:16

The Request for Presence
Let my cry come before you, O LORD;* give me understanding, according to your
word.
Let my supplication come before you;* deliver me, according to your promise.

Psalm 119:169–170

The Greeting
How priceless is your love, O God!* your people take refuge under the shadow of
your wings.
They feast upon the abundance of your house;* you give them drink from the
river of your delights.
For with you is the well of life,* and in your light we see light.

Psalm 36:7–9

The Refrain for the Midday Lessons

Mercy and truth have met together;* righteousness and peace have kissed each other.

Psalm 85:10

A Reading

Someone who thinks himself important, when he is not, only deceives himself; but everyone is to examine his own achievements, then he will confine his boasting to his own achievements, not comparing them with anybody else's. Each one has his own load to carry.

Galations 6:3–5

The Refrain

Mercy and truth have met together;* righteousness and peace have kissed each other.

The Midday Psalm   ***Happy Are the People Whose God Is the LORD***

May our sons be like plants well nurtured from their youth,* and our daughters like sculptured corners of a palace.

May our barns be filled to overflowing with all manner of crops;* may the flocks in our pastures increase by thousands and tens of thousands; may our cattle be fat and sleek.

May there be no breaching of the walls, no going into exile,* no wailing in the public squares.

Happy are the people of whom this is so!* happy are the people whose God is the LORD!

Psalm 144:13–16

The Refrain

Mercy and truth have met together;* righteousness and peace have kissed each other.

The Small Verse

Lord, be merciful to me, a sinner. Christ, be merciful to me, a sinner. Father, be merciful to me, a sinner. Spirit, be merciful to me, a sinner. Lord, be merciful to me, a sinner.

Traditional

The Lord's Prayer

The Prayer Appointed for the Week

Lord of all power and might, the author and giver of all good things: Graft in my heart the love of your Name; increase in me true religion; nourish me with all goodness; and bring forth in me the fruit of good works; through Jesus Christ our Lord, who lives and reigns with you and the Holy Spirit, one God, for ever and ever. *Amen.†*

The Concluding Prayer of the Church

Let us bless the Lord God living and true! Let us always render him praise, glory, honor, blessing, and all good things! Amen. Amen. So be it! So be it!

St. Francis of Assisi

The Vespers Office   **To Be Observed on the Hour or Half Hour**
                                           Between 5 and 8 p.m.

The Call to Prayer
Give thanks to the Lord, for he is good;* his mercy endures for ever.
Let Israel now proclaim,* "His mercy endures for ever."
Let the house of Aaron now proclaim,* "His mercy endures for ever."
Let those who fear the Lord now proclaim,* "His mercy endures for ever."

Psalm 118:1–4

The Request for Presence
Show me the light of your countenance, O God,* and come to me.

based on Psalm 67:1

The Greeting
But you, O Lord, are gracious and full of compassion,* slow to anger, and full of
    kindness and truth.

Psalm 86:15

The Hymn   *Love Song*
    The love we give each other   Glory to the Father,
    Is that which builds us up.   To the Son,
    We live in one another;   And to the Holy Spirit.
    We share a common cup.   As in the beginning,
    Our loves are each a whisper   So it is now
    Of one sweet voice divine,   And so it evermore shall be.
    And when we sing together   *Haskell Miller*
    The chorus is sublime.

The Refrain for the Vespers Lessons
Remember me, O Lord, with the favor you have for your people,* and visit me
    with your saving help . . .

Psalm 106:4

The Vespers Psalm   *More Than Watchmen for the Morning*
I wait for the Lord; my soul waits for him;* in his word is my hope.
My soul waits for the Lord,* more than watchmen for the morning, more than
    watchmen for the morning.
O Israel, wait for the Lord,* for with the Lord there is mercy;
With him there is plenteous redemption,* and he shall redeem Israel from all their
    sins.

Psalm 130:4–7

The Refrain
Remember me, O Lord, with the favor you have for your people,* and visit me
    with your saving help . . .

The Small Verse

The Lord is my shepherd and nothing is wanting to me. In green pastures He hath settled me.

THE SHORT BREVIARY

The Lord's Prayer

The Prayer Appointed for the Week

Lord of all power and might, the author and giver of all good things: Graft in my heart the love of your Name; increase in me true religion; nourish me with all goodness; and bring forth in me the fruit of good works; through Jesus Christ our Lord, who lives and reigns with you and the Holy Spirit, one God, for ever and ever. *Amen.*†

The Concluding Prayer of the Church

O Lord my God, I am not worthy to have you come under my roof; yet you have called me to stand in this house, and to serve at this work. To you and to your service I devote myself, body, soul, and spirit. Fill my memory with the record of your mighty works; enlighten my understanding with the light of your Holy Spirit; and may all the desires of my heart and will center in what you would have me do. Make me an instrument of your salvation for the people entrusted to my care, and grant that by my life and teaching I may set forth your true and living Word. Be always with me in carrying out the duties of my faith. In prayer, quicken my devotion; in praises, heighten my love and gratitude; in conversation give me readiness of thought and expression; and grant that, by the clearness and brightness of your holy Word, all the world may be drawn into your blessed kingdom. All this I ask for the sake of your Son our Savior Jesus Christ. *Amen.*†

The Morning Office

To Be Observed on the Hour or Half Hour Between 6 and 9 a.m.

The Call to Prayer

My mouth shall speak the praise of the LORD;* let all flesh bless his holy Name for ever and ever.

Psalm 145:22

The Request for Presence

O Lamb of God, that takes away the sins of the world, have mercy on me. O Lamb of God, that takes away the sins of the world, have mercy on me. O Lamb of God, that takes away the sins of the world, grant me your peace.

Agnus Dei

The Greeting

Your love, O LORD, reaches to the heavens,* and your faithfulness to the clouds.

Psalm 36:5

The Refrain for the Morning Lessons
I will exalt you, O God my King,* and bless your Name for ever and ever.

Psalm 145:1

A Reading
Jesus taught us, saying: 'Is a lamp brought in to be put under a tub or under the bed? Surely to be put on the lamp-stand? For there is nothing hidden, but it must be disclosed, nothing kept secret except to be brought to light. Anyone has ears for listening should listen.'

Mark 4:21–23

The Refrain
I will exalt you, O God my King,* and bless your Name for ever and ever.

The Morning Psalm   *He Has Shown His People the Power of His Works*
Great are the deeds of the Lord!* they are studied by all who delight in them.
His work is full of majesty and splendor,* and his righteousness endures for ever.
He makes his marvelous works to be remembered;* the Lord is gracious and full
   of compassion.
He gives food to those who fear him;* he is ever mindful of his covenant.
He has shown his people the power of his works* in giving them the lands of the
   nations.
The works of his hands are faithfulness and justice;* all his commandments are sure.
They stand fast for ever and ever,* because they are done in truth and equity.
He sent redemption to his people;* he commanded his covenant for ever; holy and
   awesome is his Name.

Psalm 111:2–9

The Refrain
I will exalt you, O God my King,* and bless your Name for ever and ever.

The Cry of the Church
O God, come to my assistance! O Lord, make haste to help me!

The Lord's Prayer

The Prayer Appointed for the Week
Lord of all power and might, the author and giver of all good things: Graft in my
   heart the love of your Name; increase in me true religion; nourish me with all
   goodness; and bring forth in me the fruit of good works; through Jesus Christ
   our Lord, who lives and reigns with you and the Holy Spirit, one God, for ever
   and ever. *Amen.*†

The Concluding Prayer of the Church
Lord God, almighty and everlasting Father, you have brought me in safety to this
   new day: Preserve me with your mighty power, that I may not fall into sin, nor
   be overcome by adversity; and in all I do direct me to the fulfilling of your purpose; through Jesus Christ my Lord. *Amen.*†

The Midday Office **To Be Observed on the Hour or Half Hour**
Between 11 a.m. and 2 p.m.

The Call to Prayer
Open my lips, O Lord,* and my mouth shall proclaim your praise.
Had you desired it, I would have offered sacrifice,* but you take no delight in
burnt-offerings.
The sacrifice of God is a troubled spirit;* a broken and contrite heart, O God, you
will not despise.

Psalm 51:16–18

The Request for Presence
Let your ways be known upon earth,* your saving health among all nations.

Psalm 67:2

The Greeting
I hate those who have a divided heart,* but your law do I love.

Psalm 119:113

The Refrain for the Midday Lessons
I will listen to what the Lord God is saying,* for he is speaking peace to his faithful
people and to those who turn their hearts to him.

Psalm 85:8

A Reading
Have mercy, Lord, on the people who have invoked your name,* on Israel whom
you have treated as a first-born.
Show compassion on your holy city,* on Jerusalem the place of your rest.
Fill Zion with songs of your praise,* and your sanctuary with your glory.
Bear witness to those you created in the beginning,* and bring about what has
been prophesied in your Name.
Give those who wait for you their reward,* and let your prophets be proved wor-
thy of belief.
Grant, Lord, the prayer of your servants,* in accordance with Aaron's blessing on
your people, so that all the earth's inhabitants may acknowledge* that you are
the Lord, the everlasting God.

Ecclesiaticus 36:11–17

The Refrain
I will listen to what the Lord God is saying,* for he is speaking peace to his faithful
people and to those who turn their hearts to him.

The Midday Psalm *The Lord Is Known by His Acts of Justice*
The ungodly have fallen into the pit they dug,* and in the snare they set is their
own foot caught.
The Lord is known by his acts of justice;* the wicked are trapped in the works of
their own hands.

The wicked shall be given over to the grave,* and also all the peoples that forget God.

For the needy shall not always be forgotten,* and the hope of the poor shall not perish for ever.

Rise up, O Lord, let not the ungodly have the upper hand;* let them be judged before you.

Put fear upon them, O Lord;* let the ungodly know they are but mortal.

Psalm 9:15–20

The Refrain

I will listen to what the Lord God is saying,* for he is speaking peace to his faithful people and to those who turn their hearts to him.

The Cry of the Church

Lord, have mercy on us. Christ, have mercy on us. Lord, have mercy on us.

The Lord's Prayer

The Prayer Appointed for the Week

Lord of all power and might, the author and giver of all good things: Graft in my heart the love of your Name; increase in me true religion; nourish me with all goodness; and bring forth in me the fruit of good works; through Jesus Christ our Lord, who lives and reigns with you and the Holy Spirit, one God, for ever and ever. *Amen.*†

The Concluding Prayer of the Church

Heavenly, Father, in you I live and move and have my being: I humbly pray you so to guide and govern me by your Holy Spirit, that in all the cares and occupations of my life I may not forget you, but may remember that I am ever walking in your sight; through Jesus Christ my Lord. *Amen.*†

The Vespers Office   **To Be Observed on the Hour or Half Hour Between 5 and 8 p.m.**

The Call to Prayer

Come, let us sing to the Lord;* let us shout for joy to the Rock of our salvation.

Psalm 95:1

The Request for Presence

May the glory of the Lord endure for ever;* may the Lord rejoice in all his works.

Psalm 104:32

The Greeting

How great is your goodness, O Lord! which you have laid up for those who fear you;* which you have done in the sight of all for those who put their trust in you.

Psalm 31:19

The Hymn   *Holy Ghost, with Light Divine*

Holy Ghost, with light divine	Holy Ghost, with joy divine
Shine upon this heart of mine;	Cheer this saddened heart of mine;
Chase the shades of dark away,	Bid my many woes depart,
Turn the darkness into day.	Heal my wounded, bleeding heart.
Holy Ghost, with power divine	Holy Spirit, all divine,
Cleanse this guilty heart of mine;	Dwell within this heart of mine;
Long has sun without control,	Cast down every idol throne,
Held dominion over my soul.	Reign supreme, and reign alone.

Andrew Reed

The Refrain for the Vespers Lessons

I am small and of little account,* yet I do not forget your commandments.

Psalm 119:141

The Vespers Psalm   *The LORD Is My Shepherd*

The LORD is my shepherd;* I shall not be in want.

He makes me lie down in green pastures* and leads me beside still waters.

He revives my soul* and guides me along right pathways for his Name's sake.

Though I walk through the valley of the shadow of death, I shall fear no evil;* for
you are with me; your rod and your staff, they comfort me.

You spread a table before me in the presence of those who trouble me;* you have
anointed my head with oil, and my cup is running over.

Surely your goodness and mercy shall follow me all the days of my life,* and I will
dwell in the house of the LORD for ever.

Psalm 23:1–6

The Refrain

I am small and of little account,* yet I do not forget your commandments.

The Small Verse

Those who sowed with tears* will reap with songs of joy.

Those who go out weeping, carrying the seed,* will come again with joy, shouldering their sheaves.

Psalm 126:6–7

The Lord's Prayer

The Prayer Appointed for the Week

Lord of all power and might, the author and giver of all good things: Graft in my
heart the love of your Name; increase in me true religion; nourish me with all
goodness; and bring forth in me the fruit of good works; through Jesus Christ
our Lord, who lives and reigns with you and the Holy Spirit, one God, for ever
and ever. *Amen.*†

The Concluding Prayer of the Church

Almighty God, to whom our needs are known before we even ask, Help me to
ask only what accords with your will; and those good things which I dare not,

or in my blindness I cannot ask, grant for the sake of your Son Jesus Christ our
Lord. *Amen.*†

The Morning Office   **To Be Observed on the Hour or Half Hour**
Between 6 and 9 a.m.

The Call to Prayer
Sing with joy to God our strength* and raise a loud shout to the God of Jacob.
Raise a song and sound the timbrel,* the merry harp, and the lyre.
Blow the ram's-horn at the new moon,* and at the full moon, the day of our feast.
For this is a statute for Israel,* a law of the God of Jacob.

Psalm 81:1–4

The Request for Presence
Teach me your way, O LORD,* and I will walk in your truth; knit my heart to you
that I may fear your Name.

Psalm 86:11

The Greeting
My mouth shall recount your mighty acts* and saving deeds all day long;* though
I cannot know the number of them.

Psalm 71:15

The Refrain for the Morning Lessons
I have sworn and am determined* to keep your righteous judgments.

Psalm 119:106

A Reading
Jesus taught us, saying: 'You are the salt of the earth. But if salt loses its taste, what
can make it salty again? It is good for nothing, and can only be thrown out to
be trampled under foot by men.'

Matthew 5:13

The Refrain
I have sworn and am determined* to keep your righteous judgments.

The Morning Psalm   *The Sparrow Has Found a Nest*
. . . My soul has a desire and longing for the courts of the LORD;* my heart and my
flesh rejoice in the living God.
The sparrow has found her a house and the swallow a nest where she may lay her
young;* by the side of your altars, O LORD of hosts, my King and my God.

Psalm 84:1–2

The Refrain
I have sworn and am determined* to keep your righteous judgments.

The Gloria

The Lord's Prayer

The Prayer Appointed for the Week
Lord of all power and might, the author and giver of all good things: Graft in my
heart the love of your Name; increase in me true religion; nourish me with all
goodness; and bring forth in me the fruit of good works; through Jesus Christ
our Lord, who lives and reigns with you and the Holy Spirit, one God, for ever
and ever. *Amen.*†

The Concluding Prayer of the Church
Lord God, almighty and everlasting Father, you have brought me in safety to this
new day: Preserve me with your mighty power, that I may not fall into sin, nor
be overcome by adversity; and in all I do direct me to the fulfilling of your purpose; through Jesus Christ my Lord. *Amen.*†

The Midday Office   **To Be Observed on the Hour or Half Hour**
Between 11 a.m. and 2 p.m.

The Call to Prayer
Sing to God, O kingdoms of the earth;* sing praises to the LORD.
He rides in the heavens, the ancient heavens;* he sends forth his voice, his mighty
voice.

Psalm 68:33–34

The Request for Presence
For God alone my soul in silence waits;* from him comes my salvation.

Psalm 62:1

The Greeting
Awesome things will you show us in your righteousness,* O God of our salvation,
O Hope of all the ends of the earth . . .

Psalm 65:5

The Refrain for the Midday Lessons
Happy are they who trust in the LORD!* they do not resort to evil spirits or turn to
false gods.

Psalm 40:4

A Reading
Blessed are those who have discovered wisdom, those who have acquired understanding! Gaining her is more rewarding than silver, her yield is more valuable
than gold. She is beyond the price of pearls, nothing you could covet is her
equal. In her right hand is length of days; in her left hand, riches and honor.
Her ways are delightful ways, her paths all lead to contentment. She is a tree of
life for those who hold her fast, those who cling to her live happy lives.

Proverbs 3:13–18

The Refrain
Happy are they who trust in the LORD!* they do not resort to evil spirits or turn to
false gods.

The Midday Psalm   *Those Who Make Idols*
Their idols are silver and gold,* the work of human hands.
They have mouths, but they cannot speak;* eyes have they, but they cannot see;
They have ears, but they cannot hear;* noses, but they cannot smell;
They have hands, but they cannot feel; feet, but they cannot walk;* they make no
    sound with their throat.
Those who make them are like them,* and so are all who put their trust in them.

Psalm 115:4–8

The Refrain
Happy are they who trust in the LORD!* they do not resort to evil spirits or turn to
    false gods.

The Cry of the Church
Be, Lord, my helper and forsake me not. Do not despise me, O God, my savior.

THE SHORT BREVIARY

The Lord's Prayer

The Prayer Appointed for the Week
Lord of all power and might, the author and giver of all good things: Graft in my
    heart the love of your Name; increase in me true religion; nourish me with all
    goodness; and bring forth in me the fruit of good works; through Jesus Christ
    our Lord, who lives and reigns with you and the Holy Spirit, one God, for ever
    and ever. *Amen.*†

The Concluding Prayer of the Church
May God have mercy on me, forgive me my sins and bring me to life everlasting.
    In Jesus' name. *Amen.*

The Vespers Office   **To Be Observed on the Hour or Half Hour**
                                                        Between 5 and 8 p.m.

The Call to Prayer
Bless God in the congregation;* bless the LORD, you that are of the fountain of
    Israel.

Psalm 68:26

The Request for Presence
O LORD, watch over us* and save us from this generation for ever.
The wicked prowl on every side,* and that which is worthless is highly prized by
    everyone.

Psalm 12:7–8

The Greeting
One generation shall praise your works to another* and shall declare your power.

Psalm 145:4

The Hymn

More love to Thee, O Christ,
More love to Thee!
Hear Thou the prayer I make
On bended knee;
This is my earnest plea,
More love, O Christ, to Thee,
More love to Thee,
More love to Thee!

Once earthly joy I craved,
Sought peace and rest;
Now Thee alone I seek;
Give what is best:
This all my prayer shall be,
More love, O Christ, to Thee,
More love to Thee,
More love to Thee!

More Love to Thee

Then shall my latest breath
Whisper Thy praise;
This be the parting cry
My heart shall raise;
This still its prayer shall be,
More love, O Christ, to Thee,
More love to Thee,
More love to Thee!

Elizabeth P. Prentiss

The Refrain for the Vespers Lessons

The heaven of heavens is the LORD's,* but he entrusted the earth to its peoples.

Psalm 115:16

The Vespers Psalm   The Righteous Will Be Kept in Everlasting Remembrance

Light shines in the darkness for the upright;* the righteous are merciful and full of compassion.

It is good for them to be generous in lending* and to manage their affairs with justice.

For they will never be shaken;* the righteous will be kept in everlasting remembrance.

They will not be afraid of any evil rumors;* their heart is right; they put their trust in the Lord.

Their heart is established and will not shrink,* until they see their desire upon their enemies.

They have given freely to the poor,* and their righteousness stands fast for ever; they will hold up their head with honor.

The wicked will see it and be angry; they will gnash their teeth and pine away;* the desires of the wicked will perish.

Psalm 112:4–10

The Refrain

The heaven of heavens is the LORD's,* but he entrusted the earth to its peoples.

The Cry of the Church

Even so come, Lord Jesus!

The Lord's Prayer

The Prayer Appointed for the Week
Lord of all power and might, the author and giver of all good things: Graft in my
heart the love of your Name; increase in me true religion; nourish me with all
goodness; and bring forth in me the fruit of good works; through Jesus Christ
our Lord, who lives and reigns with you and the Holy Spirit, one God, for ever
and ever. *Amen.*†

The Concluding Prayer of the Church
Grant me, I beseech thee, O merciful God, prudently to study, rightly to understand and perfectly to fulfill that which is pleasing to thee, to the praise and
glory of thy name. Amen.

St. Thomas Aquinas

The Morning Office　　　　　　　　　**To Be Observed on the Hour or Half Hour
Between 6 and 9 a.m.**

The Call to Prayer
I will call upon God,* and the LORD will deliver me.
In the evening, in the morning, and at noonday, I will complain and lament,* and
he will hear my voice.
He will bring me safely back . . . * God, who is enthroned of old, will hear me.

Psalm 55:17ff

The Request for Presence
Be pleased, O God, to deliver me;* O LORD, make haste to help me.

Psalm 70:1

The Greeting
Happy are they whom you choose and draw to your courts to dwell there!* they
will be satisfied by the beauty of your house, by the holiness of your temple.

Psalm 65:4

The Refrain for the Morning Lessons
It is not the healthy who need the doctor, but the sick . . . And indeed I did not
come to call the virtuous, but sinners.

Matthew 9:12–13

A Reading
Jesus taught us, saying: 'Which one of you with a hundred sheep, if he lost one,
would fail to leave the ninety-nine in the desert and go after the missing one till
he found it? And when he found it, would he not joyfully take it on his shoul-
ders and then, when he got home, call together his friends and neighbors saying
to them, "Rejoice with me, I have found my sheep that was lost." In the same
way, I tell you, there will be more rejoicing in heaven over one sinner repenting
than over ninety-nine upright people who have no need of repentance.'

Luke 15:4–7

The Refrain
It is not the healthy who need the doctor, but the sick . . . And indeed I did not
    come to call the virtuous, but sinners.

The Morning Psalm   *I Am Poor and Needy*
But you, O LORD my God,* oh, deal with me according to your Name; for your ten-
    der mercy's sake, deliver me.
For I am poor and needy,* and my heart is wounded within me.
I have faded away like a shadow when it lengthens;* I am shaken off like a locust.
My knees are weak through fasting,* and my flesh is wasted and gaunt. . . .
Help me, O LORD my God;* save me for your mercy's sake.

Psalm 109:20ff

The Refrain
It is not the healthy who need the doctor, but the sick . . . And indeed I did not
    come to call the virtuous, but sinners.

The Cry of the Church
O God, come to my assistance! O Lord, make haste to help me!

The Lord's Prayer

The Prayer Appointed for the Week
Lord of all power and might, the author and giver of all good things: Graft in my
    heart the love of your Name; increase in me true religion; nourish me with all
    goodness; and bring forth in me the fruit of good works; through Jesus Christ
    our Lord, who lives and reigns with you and the Holy Spirit, one God, for ever
    and ever. *Amen.*†

The Concluding Prayer of the Church
Lord God, almighty and everlasting Father, you have brought me in safety to this
    new day: Preserve me with your mighty power, that I may not fall into sin, nor
    be overcome by adversity; and in all I do direct me to the fulfilling of your pur-
    pose; through Jesus Christ my Lord. *Amen.*†

The Midday Office   **To Be Observed on the Hour or Half Hour**
                                    Between 11 a.m. and 2 p.m.

The Call to Prayer
. . . let the righteous be glad and rejoice before God;* let them also be merry and
    joyful.

Psalm 68:3

The Request for Presence
Be my strong rock, a castle to keep me safe;* you are my crag and my stronghold.

Psalm 71:3

The Greeting
Your way, O God, is holy;* who is so great a god as our God?

Psalm 77:13

The Refrain for the Midday Lessons
He who dwells in the shelter of the Most High,* abides under the shadow of the
  Almighty.
He shall say to the LORD, "You are my refuge and my stronghold,* my God in
  whom I put my trust."

Psalm 91:1–2

A Reading
For the high priest we have is not incapable of feeling our weaknesses with us, but
  has been put to the test in exactly the same way as ourselves, apart from sin.
  Let us, then, have no fear in approaching the throne of grace to receive mercy
  and to find grace when we are in need of help.

Hebrews 4:15–16

The Refrain
He who dwells in the shelter of the Most High,* abides under the shadow of the
  Almighty.
He shall say to the LORD, "You are my refuge and my stronghold,* my God in
  whom I put my trust."

The Midday Psalm   *He Shatters the Doors of Bronze*
He led them out of darkness and deep gloom* and broke their bonds asunder.
Let them give thanks to the LORD for his mercy* and the wonders he does for his
  children.
For he shatters the doors of bronze* and breaks in two the iron bars.

Psalm 107:14–16

The Refrain
He who dwells in the shelter of the Most High,* abides under the shadow of the
  Almighty.
He shall say to the LORD, "You are my refuge and my stronghold,* my God in
  whom I put my trust."

Cry of the Church
O Lamb of God, that takes away the sins of the world, have mercy upon me.
O Lamb of God, that takes away the sins of the world, have mercy upon me.
O Lamb of God, that takes away the sins of the world, grant me your peace.

The Lord's Prayer

The Prayer Appointed for the Week
Lord of all power and might, the author and giver of all good things: Graft in my
  heart the love of your Name; increase in me true religion; nourish me with all
  goodness; and bring forth in me the fruit of good works; through Jesus Christ

our Lord, who lives and reigns with you and the Holy Spirit, one God, for ever and ever. *Amen.*†

The Concluding Prayer of the Church

Lord Jesus Christ, by your death you took away the sting of death: Grant me to so follow in faith where you have led the way, that I may at length fall asleep peacefully in you and wake in your likeness; for your tender mercies' sake. *Amen.*†

The Vespers Office **To Be Observed on the Hour or Half Hour** **Between 5 and 8 p.m.**

The Call to Prayer

Glory in his holy Name;* let the hearts of those who seek the LORD rejoice.

Psalm 105:3

The Request for Presence

Send forth your strength, O God;* establish, O God, what you have wrought for us.

Psalm 68:28

The Greeting

The LORD is my strength and my song,* and he has become my salvation.

Psalm 118:14

The Hymn   *My Jesus, I Love Thee*

My Jesus, I love Thee, I know Thou art mine,
For Thee all the follies of sin I resign;
My gracious Redeemer, my Savior art Thou;
If ever I loved Thee, my Jesus, 'tis now.

I love Thee because Thou hast first loved me,
And purchased my pardon on Calvary's tree;
I love Thee for wearing the thorns on Thy brow;
If ever I loved Thee, my Jesus, 'tis now.

I'll love Thee in life, I will love Thee in death,
And praise Thee as long as Thou lendest me breath;
And say when the death dew lies cold on my brow,
If ever I loved Thee, my Jesus, 'tis now.

In mansions of glory and endless delight
I'll ever adore Thee in heaven so bright;
I'll sing with the glittering crown on my brow,
If ever I loved Thee, my Jesus, 'tis now.

William R. Featherstone

The Refrain for the Vespers Lessons

Keep watch over my life, for I am faithful;* save your servant whose trust is in you.

based on Psalm 86:2

The Vespers Psalm   *Hosanna, Lord, Hosanna!*

Hosanna, Lord, hosanna!* Lord, send us now success.

Blessed is he who comes in the name of the Lord;* we bless you from the house of
the Lord.

God is the Lord; he has shined upon us;* form a procession with branches up to
the horns of the altar.

"You are my God, and I will thank you;* you are my God, and I will exalt you."

Give thanks to the Lord, for he is good;* his mercy endures for ever.

Psalm 118:25–29

The Refrain

Keep watch over my life, for I am faithful;* save your servant whose trust is in you.

The Small Verse

My help is in the Name of the Lord who made the heavens and the earth. What
then shall I fear, of what shall I be afraid?

Traditional

The Lord's Prayer

The Prayer Appointed for the Week

Lord of all power and might, the author and giver of all good things: Graft in my
heart the love of your Name; increase in me true religion; nourish me with all
goodness; and bring forth in me the fruit of good works; through Jesus Christ
our Lord, who lives and reigns with you and the Holy Spirit, one God, for ever
and ever. *Amen.*†

The Concluding Prayers of the Church

Almighty God, who has promised to hear the petitions of those who ask in your
Son's Name: I beseech you mercifully to incline your ear to me who have made
my prayers and supplications to you; and grant that those things which I have
faithfully asked according to your will, I may effectually obtain, to the relief of
my necessity, and to the setting forth of your glory; through Jesus Christ my
Lord. *Amen.*

May the souls of the faithful departed, through the mercy of God, rest in eternal
peace. *Amen.*

The Morning Office   **To Be Observed on the Hour or Half Hour**
Between 6 and 9 a.m.

The Call to Prayer

Sing to the Lord a new song;* sing to the Lord, all the whole earth.

Psalm 96:1

The Request for Presence

I call with my whole heart;* answer me, O Lord, that I may keep your statutes.

Psalm 119:145

The Greeting
Glory to you, Lord God of our fathers; you are worthy of praise; glory to you.
Glory to you for the radiance of your holy Name; we will praise you and
highly exalt you for ever. Glory to you in the splendor of your temple; on the
throne of your majesty, glory to you. Glory to you, seated between the
Cherubim; we will praise you and highly exalt you for ever. Glory to you,
beholding the depths; in the high vault of heaven, glory to you. Glory to you,
Father, Son, and Holy Spirit; we will praise you and highly exalt you for ever.

Te Deum

The Refrain for the Morning Lessons
Righteousness shall go before him,* and peace shall be a pathway for his feet.

Psalm 85:13

A Reading
Jesus taught us, saying: 'My food is to do the will of the one who sent me, and to
complete his work. Have you not got a saying: Four months and then the harvest? Well, I tell you: Look around you, look at the fields; already they are
white, ready for the harvest! Already the reaper is being paid his wages,
already he is bringing in the grain for eternal life, and thus sower and reaper
rejoice together. For here the proverb holds good: one sows, another reaps; I
sent you to reap a harvest you had not worked for. Others worked for it; and
you have come into the rewards of their trouble.'

John 4:34–38

The Refrain
Righteousness shall go before him,* and peace shall be a pathway for his feet.

The Morning Psalm   *Let Your Good Spirit Lead Me on Level Ground*
My spirit faints within me;* my heart within me is desolate.
I remember the time past; I muse upon all your deeds;* I consider the works of
your hands.
I spread out my hands to you;* my soul gasps to you like a thirsty land.
O Lord, make haste to answer me; my spirit fails me;* do not hide your face from
me or I shall be like those who go down to the Pit.
Let me hear of your loving-kindness in the morning, for I put my trust in you;*
show me the road that I must walk, for I lift up my soul to you. . . .
Teach me to do what pleases you, for you are my God;* let your good Spirit lead
me on level ground.
Revive me, O Lord, for your Name's sake;* for your righteousness' sake, bring me
out of trouble.

Psalm 143:4ff

The Refrain
Righteousness shall go before him,* and peace shall be a pathway for his feet.

The Gloria

The Lord's Prayer

The Prayer Appointed for the Week
Lord of all power and might, the author and giver of all good things: Graft in my heart the love of your Name; increase in me true religion; nourish me with all goodness; and bring forth in me the fruit of good works; through Jesus Christ our Lord, who lives and reigns with you and the Holy Spirit, one God, for ever and ever. *Amen.*†

The Concluding Prayer of the Church
Lord God, almighty and everlasting Father, you have brought me in safety to this new day: Preserve me with your mighty power, that I may not fall into sin, nor be overcome by adversity; and in all I do direct me to the fulfilling of your purpose; through Jesus Christ my Lord. *Amen.*†

The Midday Office   To Be Observed on the Hour or Half Hour
Between 11 a.m. and 2 p.m.

The Call to Prayer
Open my lips, O Lord,* and my mouth shall proclaim your praise.

Psalm 51:16

The Request for Presence
Look well whether there be any wickedness in me* and lead me in the way that is everlasting.

Psalm 139:23

The Greeting
O LORD, I am your servant;* I am your servant and the child of your handmaid; you have freed me from my bonds.

Psalm 116:14

The Refrain for the Midday Lessons
Unless the LORD builds the house,* their labor is in vain who build it.

Psalm 127:1

A Reading
We appeal to you, my brothers, to be considerate to those who work so hard among you as your leaders in the Lord and those who admonish you. Have the greatest respect and affection for them because of their work. Be at peace among yourselves. We urge you, brothers, to admonish those who are undisciplined, encourage the apprehensive, support the weak and be patient with everyone. Make sure that people do not try to repay evil for evil; always aim for what is best for each other and for everyone. Always be joyful; pray constantly; and for all things give thanks; this is the will of God for you in Christ Jesus.

I Thessalonians 5:12–18

The Refrain
Unless the Lord builds the house,* their labor is in vain who build it.

The Midday Psalm   *He Guides the Humble in Doing Right*
Gracious and upright is the Lord;* therefore he teaches sinners in his way.
He guides the humble in doing right* and teaches his way to the lowly.
All the paths of the Lord are love and faithfulness* to those who keep his
    covenant and his testimonies.

Psalm 25:7–9

The Refrain
Unless the Lord builds the house,* their labor is in vain who build it.

The Cry of the Church
Even so come, Lord Jesus!

The Lord's Prayer

The Prayer Appointed for the Week
Lord of all power and might, the author and giver of all good things: Graft in my
    heart the love of your Name; increase in me true religion; nourish me with all
    goodness; and bring forth in me the fruit of good works; through Jesus Christ
    our Lord, who lives and reigns with you and the Holy Spirit, one God, for ever
    and ever. *Amen.†*

The Concluding Prayer of the Church
O God, the source of eternal light: Shed forth your unending day upon all of us
    who watch for you, that our lips may praise you, our lives may bless you, and
    our worship may give you glory; through Jesus Christ our Lord. *Amen.†*

The Vespers Office   **To Be Observed on the Hour or Half Hour**
                                    Between 5 and 8 p.m.

The Call to Prayer
Give thanks to the Lord, for he is good,* and his mercy endures for ever.

Psalm 107:1

The Request for Presence
So teach us to number our days* that we may apply our hearts to wisdom.

Psalm 90:12

The Greeting
Remember not the sins of my youth and my transgressions;* remember me
    according to your love and for the sake of your goodness, O Lord.

Psalm 25:6

The Hymn   *God, Who Made the Earth and Heaven*

God, who made the earth and heaven,
Darkness and light:
You the day for work have given,
For rest the night.
May your angel guards defend us,
Slumber sweet your mercy send us,
Holy dreams and hopes attend us
All through the night.

And, when morn again shall call us
To run life's way,
May we still, whate'er befall us,
Your will obey.
From the power of evil hide us,
In the narrow pathway guide us,
Never be your smile denied us
All through the day.

Stanza 1: Reginald Heber
Stanza 2: William Mercer

The Refrain for the Vespers Lessons

Behold, God is my helper;* it is the Lord who sustains my life.

Psalm 54:4

The Vespers Psalm   *An Evening Song*

O Lord, You are my portion and my cup;* it is you who uphold my lot.

My boundaries enclose a pleasant land;* indeed, I have a goodly heritage.

I will bless the Lord who gives me counsel;* my heart teaches me, night after
night.

I have set the Lord always before me;* because he is at my right hand I shall not
fall.

My heart, therefore, is glad, and my spirit rejoices;* my body also shall rest in
hope.

For you will not abandon me to the grave,* nor let your holy one see the Pit.

You will show me the path of life;* in your presence there is fullness of joy, and in
your right hand are pleasures for evermore.

Psalm 16:5–11

The Refrain

Behold, God is my helper;* it is the Lord who sustains my life.

The Small Verse

The Lord is my shepherd and nothing is wanting to me. In green pastures He hath
settled me.

THE SHORT BREVIARY

The Lord's Prayer

The Prayer Appointed for the Week

Lord of all power and might, the author and giver of all good things: Graft in my
heart the love of your Name; increase in me true religion; nourish me with all
goodness; and bring forth in me the fruit of good works; through Jesus Christ
our Lord, who lives and reigns with you and the Holy Spirit, one God, for ever
and ever. *Amen.*†

The Concluding Prayer of the Church

Almighty God, who after the creation of the world rested from all your works and sanctified a day of rest for all your creatures: Grant that I, putting away all earthly anxieties, may be duly prepared for the service of public worship, and grant as well that my Sabbath upon earth may be a preparation for the eternal rest promised to your people in heaven; through Jesus Christ our Lord. *Amen.*†

August Compline

Sunday
The Night Office   **To Be Observed Before Retiring**

The Call to Prayer
May the Lord Almighty grant me and those I love a peaceful night and a perfect end. *Amen.*†

The Request for Presence
Our help is in the Name of the LORD;* the maker of heaven and earth.

Psalm 124:8

The Greeting
Almighty God, my heavenly Father: I have sinned against you, through my own fault, in thought, and word, and deed, and in what I have left undone. For the sake of your Son our Lord Jesus Christ, forgive me all my offenses; and grant that I may serve you in newness of life, to the glory of your Name. *Amen.*†

The Reading
Then Peter stood up with the eleven and addressed them in a loud voice: 'Men of Judaea and all you who live in Jerusalem, make no mistake about this, but listen carefully to what I say . . . Jesus the Nazarene was a man commended to you by God by the miracles and portents and signs that God worked through him when he was among you, as you know. This man, who was put into your power by the deliberate intention and foreknowledge of God, you took and had crucified and killed by men outside the Law. But God raised him to life, freeing him from the pangs of Hades; for it was impossible for him to be held in its power . . . God raised this man Jesus to life, and of that we are all witnesses. Now raised to the heights by God's right hand, he has received from the Father the Holy Spirit, who was promised, and what you see and hear is the outpouring of that Spirit.'

Acts 2:14ff

The Gloria

The Psalm   *Hosanna, LORD, Hosanna*
Hosanna, LORD, hosanna!* LORD, send us now success.
Blessed is he who comes in the name of the LORD;* we bless you from the house of the LORD.
God is the LORD; he has shined upon us;* form a procession with branches up to the horns of the altar.
"You are my God, and I will thank you;* you are my God and I will exalt you."
Give thanks to the LORD, for he is good;* his mercy endures for ever.

Psalm 118:25–29

The Gloria

The Small Verse
Into your hands, O Lord, I commend my spirit; for you have redeemed me, O
Lord, O God of truth. Keep me, O Lord, as the apple of your eye; hide me
under the shadow of your wings.†

The Lord's Prayer

The Petition
Lord, hear my prayers; And let my cry come to you.†

The Final Thanksgiving
Lord, you now have set your servant free to go in peace as you have promised; for
these eyes of mine have seen the Savior, whom you have prepared for all the
world to see: a Light to enlighten the nations, and the glory of your people
Israel. Glory to the Father, and to the Son, and to the Holy Spirit: as it was in the
beginning, is now, and will be for ever. *Amen.*

Monday
The Night Office   **To Be Observed Before Retiring**

The Call to Prayer
May the Lord Almighty grant me and those I love a peaceful night and a perfect
end. *Amen.*†

The Request for Presence
Our help is in the Name of the LORD;* the maker of heaven and earth.

Psalm 124:8

The Greeting
Almighty God, my heavenly Father: I have sinned against you, through my own
fault, in thought, and word, and deed, and in what I have left undone. For the
sake of your Son our Lord Jesus Christ, forgive me all my offenses; and grant
that I may serve you in newness of life, to the glory of your Name. *Amen.*†

The Reading   *The Nicene Creed*
We believe in one God, the Father, the Almighty, maker of heaven and earth, of all
that is, seen and unseen. We believe in one Lord, Jesus Christ. The only Son of
God, eternally begotten of the Father, God from God, Light from Light, true
God from true God, begotten, not made, of one Being with the Father. Through
him all things were made. For us and for our salvation he came down from
heaven: by the power of the Holy Spirit he became incarnate from the Virgin

Mary, and was made man. For our sake he was crucified under Pontius Pilate; he suffered death and was buried. On the third day he rose again in accordance with the Scriptures; he ascended into heaven and is seated at the right hand of the Father. He will come again in glory to judge the living and the dead, and his kingdom will have no end. We believe in the Holy Spirit, the Lord, the giver of life, who proceeds from the Father and the Son. With the Father and the Son he is worshipped and glorified. He has spoken through the Prophets. We believe in one holy, catholic and apostolic Church. We acknowledge one baptism for the forgiveness of sins. We look for the resurrection of the dead, and the life of the world to come. *Amen.*

The Gloria

The Psalm   *My Soul Is Content, As with Marrow and Fatness*
O God, you are my God; eagerly I seek you;* my soul thirsts for you, my flesh
    faints for you, as in a barren and dry land where there is no water.
Therefore I have gazed upon you in your holy place,* that I may behold your
    power and your glory.
For your loving-kindness is better than life itself;* my lips shall give you praise.
So will I bless you as long as I live* and lift up my hands to your Name.
My soul is content, as with marrow and fatness,* and my mouth praises you with
    joyful lips,
When I remember you upon my bed,* and meditate on you in the night watches.
For you have been my helper,* and under the shadow of your wings I will
    rejoice.
My soul clings to you;* your right hand holds me fast.

Psalm 63:1–8

The Gloria

The Small Verse
Into your hands, O Lord, I commend my spirit; For you have redeemed me, O
    Lord, O God of truth. Keep me, O Lord, as the apple of your eye; Hide me
    under the shadow of your wings.†

The Lord's Prayer

The Petition
Lord, hear my prayers; And let my cry come to you.†

The Final Thanksgiving
Lord, you now have set your servant free to go in peace as you have promised; for
    these eyes of mine have seen the Savior, whom you have prepared for all the
    world to see: a Light to enlighten the nations, and the glory of your people
    Israel. Glory to the Father, and to the Son, and to the Holy Spirit: as it was in the
    beginning, is now, and will be for ever. *Amen.*

Tuesday
The Night Office   **To Be Observed Before Retiring**

The Call to Prayer
May the Lord Almighty grant me and those I love a peaceful night and a perfect
end. *Amen.*†

The Request for Presence
Our help is in the Name of the LORD;* the maker of heaven and earth.

Psalm 124:8

The Greeting
Almighty God, my heavenly Father: I have sinned against you, through my own
fault, in thought, and word, and deed, and in what I have left undone. For the
sake of your Son our Lord Jesus Christ, forgive me all my offenses; and grant
that I may serve you in newness of life, to the glory of your Name. *Amen.*†

The Reading
To hallow the name of God is, in the language of the Scripture, to love him,
adore Him, and to recognize His holiness in all things. Things, like words,
do indeed proceed from the mouth of God. The events of each moment are
divine thoughts expressed by created objects. Thus, all those things by which
He makes His will known to us are so many names, so many words by which
He shows us His will. . . . To hallow the name of God is to know, adore, and
love the Ineffable One expressed by this name. It is also to know, adore and
love His blessed will at all times, in all its effects, seeing all things as so many
veils, shadows and names of this eternally holy will. It is holy in all its works,
holy in all its words, holy in all its forms of manifestation, holy in all the
names it bears.

Jean-Pierre de Caussade

The Gloria

The Psalm   *Behold, I Did Not Restrain My Lips*
I proclaimed righteousness in the great congregation;* behold, I did not restrain
my lips; and that, O LORD, you know.
Your righteousness have I not hidden in my heart; I have spoken of your faithfulness and your deliverance;* I have not concealed your love and faithfulness
from the great congregation.

Psalm 40:10–11

The Gloria

The Small Verse

Into your hands, O Lord, I commend my spirit; For you have redeemed me, O
Lord, O God of truth. Keep me, O Lord, as the apple of your eye; Hide me
under the shadow of your wings.†

The Lord's Prayer

The Petition

Lord, hear my prayers; And let my cry come to you.†

The Final Thanksgiving

Lord, you now have set your servant free to go in peace as you have promised; for
these eyes of mine have seen the Savior, whom you have prepared for all the
world to see: a Light to enlighten the nations, and the glory of your people
Israel. Glory to the Father, and to the Son, and to the Holy Spirit: as it was in the
beginning, is now, and will be for ever. *Amen.*

Wednesday
The Night Office   **To Be Observed Before Retiring**

The Call to Prayer

May the Lord Almighty grant me and those I love a peaceful night and a perfect
end. *Amen.*†

The Request for Presence

Our help is in the Name of the LORD;* the maker of heaven and earth.

Psalm 124:8

The Greeting

Almighty God, my heavenly Father: I have sinned against you, through my own
fault, in thought, and word, and deed, and in what I have left undone. For the
sake of your Son our Lord Jesus Christ, forgive me all my offenses; and grant
that I may serve you in newness of life, to the glory of your Name. *Amen.*†

The Reading   *Abou Ben Adhem*

Abou Ben Adhem (may his tribe increase!)
Awoke one night from a deep dream of peace,
And saw within the moonlight in his room,
Making it rich, and like a lily in bloom,
An Angel, writing in a book of gold;
Exceeding peace made Ben Adhem bold,
And to the presence in the room he said,

"What do you write?"—The vision raised its head,
And with a look made of all sweet accord,
Answered, "The names of those who love the Lord."
"And is mine one?" said Abou. "Nay, not so,"
Replied the angel. Abou spoke more low,
But cheerily still; and said, "I pray you, then,
Write me as one that loves his fellowmen."
The angel wrote and vanished. The next night
It came again, with a great wakening light,
And showed the names whom love of God had blessed,
And, lo! Ben Adhem's name led all the rest.

Leigh Hunt

The Gloria

The Psalm   *So That a People Yet Unborn May Praise the* LORD
Let this be written for a future generation,* so that a people yet unborn may praise
 the LORD.
For the LORD looked down from his holy place on high;* from the heavens he
 beheld the earth;
That he might hear the groan of the captive;* and set free those condemned to die;
That they may declare in Zion the Name of the LORD,* and his praise in Jerusalem;
When the peoples are gathered together,* and the kingdoms also, to serve the
 LORD.

Psalm 102:18–22

The Gloria

The Small Verse
Into your hands, O Lord, I commend my spirit; For you have redeemed me, O
 Lord, O God of truth. Keep me, O Lord, as the apple of your eye; Hide me
 under the shadow of your wings.†

The Lord's Prayer

The Petition
Lord, hear my prayers; And let my cry come to you.†

The Final Thanksgiving
Lord, you now have set your servant free to go in peace as you have promised; for
 these eyes of mine have seen the Savior, whom you have prepared for all the
 world to see: a Light to enlighten the nations, and the glory of your people
 Israel. Glory to the Father, and to the Son, and to the Holy Spirit: as it was in the
 beginning, is now, and will be for ever. *Amen.*

Thursday
The Night Office   **To Be Observed Before Retiring**

The Call to Prayer
May the Lord Almighty grant me and those I love a peaceful night and a perfect
    end. *Amen.*†

The Request for Presence
Our help is in the Name of the LORD;* the maker of heaven and earth.

Psalm 124:8

The Greeting
Almighty God, my heavenly Father: I have sinned against you, through my own
    fault, in thought, and word, and deed, and in what I have left undone. For the
    sake of your Son our Lord Jesus Christ, forgive me all my offenses; and grant
    that I may serve you in newness of life, to the glory of your Name. *Amen.*†

The Reading
'I, Wisdom, share house with Discretion, I am the mistress of the art of thought.
    YAHWEH created me, first-fruits of his fashioning, before the oldest of his
    works. From everlasting, I was firmly set, from the beginning, before the earth
    came into being. The deep was not, when I was born, nor were the springs with
    their abounding waters. Before the mountains were settled, before the hills, I
    came to birth; before he had made the earth, the countryside, and the first ele-
    ments of the world. When he fixed the heavens firm, I was there, when he drew
    a circle on the surface of the deep, when he thickened the clouds above, when
    the sources of the deep began to swell, when he assigned the sea its bound-
    aries—and the waters will not encroach on the shore—when he traced the
    foundations of the earth, I was beside the master craftsman, delighting him
    day after day, ever at play in his presence, at play everywhere on his earth,
    delighting to be with the children of men.'

Proverbs 8:12, 22–31

The Gloria

The Psalm   *The LORD Beholds All People*
The LORD looks down from heaven,* and beholds all the people in the world.
From where he sits enthroned he turns his gaze* on all who dwell on earth.
He fashions all the hearts of them* and understands all their works.

Psalm 33:13–15

The Gloria

The Small Verse
Into your hands, O Lord, I commend my spirit; For you have redeemed me, O
    Lord, O God of truth. Keep me, O Lord, as the apple of your eye; Hide me
    under the shadow of your wings.†

The Lord's Prayer

The Petition
Lord, hear my prayers; And let my cry come to you.†

The Final Thanksgiving
Lord, you now have set your servant free to go in peace as you have promised; for
these eyes of mine have seen the Savior, whom you have prepared for all the
world to see: a Light to enlighten the nations, and the glory of your people
Israel. Glory to the Father, and to the Son, and to the Holy Spirit: as it was in the
beginning, is now, and will be for ever. *Amen.*

❧

Friday
The Night Office **To Be Observed Before Retiring**

The Call to Prayer
May the Lord Almighty grant me and those I love a peaceful night and a perfect
end. *Amen.*†

The Request for Presence
Our help is in the Name of the LORD;* the maker of heaven and earth.

Psalm 124:8

The Greeting
Almighty God, my heavenly Father: I have sinned against you, through my own
fault, in thought, and word, and deed, and in what I have left undone. For the
sake of your Son our Lord Jesus Christ, forgive me all my offenses; and grant
that I may serve you in newness of life, to the glory of your Name. *Amen.*†

The Reading *Hail, Holy Queen!*
Hail, holy Queen, Mother of mercy, our life, our sweetness, and our hope. To you
do we cry, poor banished children of Eve, to you do we send up our sighs,
mourning and weeping in this vale of tears. Turn, then, most gracious advocate, your eyes of mercy toward us; and after this our exile, show unto us the
blessed fruit of your womb, Jesus. O clement, O loving, O sweet Virgin Mary.
Pray for us, O holy Mother of God, that we may be made worthy of the promises
of Christ.
Almighty and everlasting God, who by the cooperation of the Holy Spirit prepared
the body and soul of the glorious Virgin-Mother Mary to be a fit dwelling for
your Son, grant that we who rejoice in her memory may be freed by her kindly
prayers both from present ills and from eternal death; through the same Christ
our Lord. Amen.

Traditional

The Gloria

The Psalm   *Those Who Sowed with Tears Will Reap with Songs of Joy*
When the LORD restored the fortunes of Zion,* then were we like those who dream.
Then was our mouth filled with laughter,* and our tongue with shouts of joy.
Then they said among the nations,* "The LORD has done great things for them."
The LORD has done great things for us,* and we are glad indeed.
Restore our fortunes, O LORD,* like the watercourses of the Negev.
Those who sowed with tears* will reap with songs of joy.
Those who go out weeping, carrying the seed,* will come again with joy, shoul-
    dering the sheaves.

Psalm 126:1–7

The Gloria

The Small Verse
Into your hands, O Lord, I commend my spirit; for you have redeemed me, O
    Lord, O God of truth. Keep me, O Lord, as the apple of your eye; Hide me
    under the shadow of your wings.†

The Lord's Prayer

The Petition
Lord, hear my prayers; And let my cry come to you.†

The Final Thanksgiving
Lord, you now have set your servant free to go in peace as you have promised; for
    these eyes of mine have seen the Savior, whom you have prepared for all the
    world to see: a Light to enlighten the nations, and the glory of your people
    Israel. Glory to the Father, and to the Son, and to the Holy Spirit: as it was in the
    beginning, is now, and will be for ever. *Amen.*

~❧~

Saturday
The Night Office   **To Be Observed Before Retiring**

The Call to Prayer
May the Lord Almighty grant me and those I love a peaceful night and a perfect
    end. *Amen.*†

The Request for Presence
Our help is in the Name of the LORD;* the maker of heaven and earth.

Psalm 124:8

The Greeting
Almighty God, my heavenly Father: I have sinned against you, through my own fault, in thought, and word, and deed, and in what I have left undone. For the sake of your Son our Lord Jesus Christ, forgive me all my offenses; and grant that I may serve you in newness of life, to the glory of your Name. *Amen.*†

The Reading
Finally, brothers, let your minds be filled with everything that is true, everything that is honorable, everything that is upright and pure, everything that we love and admire—with whatever is good and praiseworthy. Keep doing everything you learnt from me and were told by me and have heard or seen me doing. Then the God of peace will be with you.

Philippians 4:8–9

The Gloria

The Psalm   *The Eyes of the LORD Are Upon the Righteous*
The eyes of the LORD are upon the righteous,* and his ears are open to their cry.
The face of the LORD is against those who do evil,* to root out the remembrance of them from the earth.
The righteous cry, and the LORD hears them* and delivers them from all their troubles.
The Lord is near to the brokenhearted* and will save those whose spirits are crushed.
Many are the troubles of the righteous,* but the LORD will deliver him out of them all.

Psalm 34:15–19

The Gloria

The Small Verse
Into your hands, O Lord, I commend my spirit; For you have redeemed me, O Lord, O God of truth. Keep me, O Lord, as the apple of your eye; Hide me under the shadow of your wings.†

The Lord's Prayer

The Petition
Lord, hear my prayers; And let my cry come to you.†

The Final Thanksgiving
Lord, you now have set your servant free to go in peace as you have promised; for these eyes of mine have seen the Savior, whom you have prepared for all the world to see: a Light to enlighten the nations, and the glory of your people Israel. Glory to the Father, and to the Son, and to the Holy Spirit: as it was in the beginning, is now, and will be for ever. *Amen.*

The Gloria

Glory be to God the Father, God the Son, and God the Holy Spirit. As it was in the beginning, so it is now and so it shall ever be, world without end. Alleluia. *Amen.*

The Lord's Prayer

Our Father, who art in heaven, hallowed be your Name.
May your kingdom come, and your will be done, on earth as in heaven.
Give us today our daily bread.
Forgive us our sins as we forgive those who sin against us.
Lead us not into temptation, but deliver us from evil;
for yours are the kingdom and the power and the glory
forever and ever. *Amen.*

Compline Prayers for September Are Located on Page 631

The Following Holy Days Occur in September:
Holy Cross Day: *September 14*
The Feast of St. Matthew: *September 21*
The Feast of St. Michael and All Angels: *September 29*

September

The Morning Office   **To Be Observed on the Hour or Half Hour**
                                          Between 6 and 9 a.m.

The Call to Prayer
Be glad, you righteous, and rejoice in the LORD;* shout for joy, all who are true of
    heart.

Psalm 32:12

The Request for Presence
May God be merciful to us and bless us,* show us the light of his countenance and
    come to us.

Psalm 67:1

The Greeting
Out of Zion, perfect in its beauty,* God reveals himself in glory.

Psalm 50:2

The Refrain for the Morning Lessons
Let the words of my mouth and the meditation of my heart be acceptable in your
    sight,* O LORD, my strength and my redeemer.

Psalm 19:14

A Reading
Jesus said: 'It is for judgment that I have come into this world, so that those with-
    out sight may see and those with sight may become blind.' Hearing this, some
    Pharisees who were present said to him, 'So we are blind, are we?' Jesus
    replied: 'If you were blind, you would not be guilty, but since you say, "We can
    see," your guilt remains.'

John 9:39–41

The Refrain
Let the words of my mouth and the meditation of my heart be acceptable in your
    sight,* O LORD, my strength and my redeemer.

The Morning Psalm   *I Will Show the Salvation of God*
But to the wicked God says:* "Why do you recite my statutes, and take my
    covenant upon your lips;
Since you refuse discipline,* and toss my words behind your back?
When you see a thief, you make him your friend,* and you cast in your lot with
    adulterers.
You have loosed your lips for evil,* and harnessed your tongue to a lie.
You are always speaking evil of your brother* and slandering your own mother's
    son.
These things you have done, and I kept still,* and you thought that I am like you.
I have made my accusation;* I have put my case in order before your eyes.
Consider this well, you who forget God,* lest I rend you and there be none to
    deliver you.

Whoever offers me the sacrifice of thanksgiving honors me;* but to those who
keep in my way will I show the salvation of God."

Psalm 50:16–24

The Refrain
Let the words of my mouth and the meditation of my heart be acceptable in your
sight,* O Lord, my strength and my redeemer.

The Small Verse
Blessed be the Lord God of Israel for he has visited and delivered us. Alleluia,
alleluia, alleluia.

Traditional

The Lord's Prayer

The Prayer Appointed for the Week
Grant me, O Lord, to trust in you with all my heart; for, as you always resist the
proud who confide in their own strength, so you never forsake those who
make their boast of your mercy; through Jesus Christ our Lord, who lives and
reigns with you and the Holy Spirit, one God, now and for ever. *Amen.*†

The Concluding Prayer of the Church
Lord God, almighty and everlasting Father, you have brought me in safety to this
new day:Preserve me with your mighty power, that I may not fall into sin, nor
be overcome by adversity; and in all I do direct me to the fulfilling of your purpose; through Jesus Christ my Lord. *Amen.*†

The Midday Office To Be Observed on the Hour or Half Hour
Between 11 a.m. and 2 p.m.

The Call to Prayer
Hallelujah! Praise the Name of the Lord;* give praise, you servants of the Lord,
You who stand in the house of the Lord,* in the courts of the house of our God.
Praise the Lord, for the Lord is good;* sing praises to his Name, for it is lovely.

Psalm 135:1–3

The Request for Presence
Let them know that you, whose Name is Yahweh,* you alone are the Most High
over all the earth.

Psalm 83:18

The Greeting
. . . My heart sings to you without ceasing;* O Lord my God, I will give you
thanks for ever.

Psalm 30:13

The Refrain for the Midday Lessons
When I called, you answered me;* you increased my strength within me.

Psalm 138:4

A Reading   *The Song of Hannah*
My heart exults in YAHWEH, in my God is my strength lifted up, my mouth derides
my foes, for I rejoice in your deliverance.
There is no Holy One like YAHWEH, (indeed, there is none but you) no Rock like
our God . . .
. . . The bow of the mighty has been broken but those who were tottering are now
braced with strength. The full fed are hiring themselves out for bread but the
hungry need labor no more; the barren woman bears sevenfold, but the mother
of many is left desolate.
YAHWEH gives death and life, brings down to Sheol and draws up; YAHWEH makes
poor and rich, he humbles and also exalts.
He raises the poor from the dust, he lifts the needy from the dunghill to give them
a place with princes, to assign them a seat of honor; for to YAHWEH belong the
pillars of the earth, on these he has poised the world.
He safeguards the steps of the faithful but the wicked vanish in darkness (for
human strength can win no victories). YAHWEH, his enemies are shattered, the
Most High thunders in the heavens.
YAHWEH judges the end of the earth, he endows his king with power, he raises up
the strength of his Anointed.

I Samuel 2:1–10

The Refrain
When I called, you answered me;* you increased my strength within me.

The Midday Psalm   *He Put a New Song in My Mouth*
I waited patiently upon the LORD;* he stooped to me and heard my cry.
He lifted me out of the desolate pit, out of the mire and clay;* he set my feet upon a
high cliff and made my footing sure.
He put a new song in my mouth, a song of praise to our God;* many shall see, and
stand in awe, and put their trust in the LORD.

Psalm 40:1–3

The Refrain
When I called, you answered me;* you increased my strength within me.

The Gloria

The Lord's Prayer

The Prayer Appointed for the Week
Grant me, O Lord, to trust in you with all my heart; for, as you always resist the
proud who confide in their own strength, so you never forsake those who
make their boast of your mercy; through Jesus Christ our Lord, who lives and
reigns with you and the Holy Spirit, one God, now and for ever. *Amen.*†

The Concluding Prayer of the Church

O God, you make me glad with the weekly remembrance of the glorious resurrection of your Son my Lord: Give me this day such blessing through my worship
of you, that the week to come may be spent in your favor; through Jesus Christ
our Lord. *Amen.*✝

The Vespers Office   **To Be Observed on the Hour or Half Hour**
                                          Between 5 and 8 p.m.

The Call to Prayer

Enter his gates with thanksgiving; go into his courts with praise;* give thanks to
him and call upon his Name.

Psalm 100:3

The Request for Presence

May God give us his blessing,* and may all the ends of the earth stand in awe of
him.

Psalm 67:7

The Greeting

We give you thanks, O God, we give you thanks,* calling upon your Name and
declaring all your wonderful deeds.

Psalm 75:1

The Hymn   *Blessed Be the Tie That Binds*

Blessed be the tie that binds   We share each other's woes,
our hearts in Christian love;   our mutual burdens bear;
the fellowship of kindred minds   and often for each other flows
is like to that above.   the sympathizing tear.

Before our Father's throne   When we asunder part,
we pour our ardent prayers;   it gives us inward pain;
our fears, our hopes, our aims are one,   but we shall still be joined in heart,
our comforts and our cares.   and hope to meet again.

John Fawcett

The Refrain for the Vespers Lessons

I will fulfill my vows to the LORD* in the presence of all his people,

Psalm 116:16

The Vespers Psalm   *Gather Before Me Those Who Have Made a Covenant with Me*

The LORD, the God of gods, has spoken;* he has called the earth from the rising of
the sun to its setting.

Out of Zion, perfect in its beauty,* God reveals himself in glory.

Our God will come and will not keep silence;* before him there is a consuming
flame, and round about him a raging storm.

He calls the heavens and the earth from above* to witness the judgment of his
people.
"Gather before me my loyal followers,* those who have made a covenant with me
and sealed it with sacrifice."
Let the heavens declare the rightness of his cause;* for God himself is judge.

Psalm 50:1–6

The Refrain
I will fulfill my vows to the LORD* in the presence of all his people.

The Gloria

The Lord's Prayer

The Prayer Appointed for the Week
Grant me, O Lord, to trust in you with all my heart; for, as you always resist the
proud who confide in their own strength, so you never forsake those who
make their boast of your mercy; through Jesus Christ our Lord, who lives and
reigns with you and the Holy Spirit, one God, now and for ever. *Amen.*†

The Concluding Prayer of the Church
Lord God, whose Son our Savior Jesus Christ, triumphed over the powers of death
and prepared for us our place in the new Jerusalem: Grant that I, who have this
day given thanks for his resurrection, may praise you in the City of which he is
the light, and where he lives and reigns for ever and ever. *Amen.*†

The Morning Office   **To Be Observed on the Hour or Half Hour
Between 6 and 9 a.m.**

The Call to Prayer
Bless God in the congregation;* bless the LORD, you that are of the fountain of
Israel.

Psalm 68:26

The Request for Presence
Look upon your covenant;* the dark places of the earth are haunts of violence.

Psalm 74:19

The Greeting
Deliver me, O LORD, by your hand* from those whose portion in life is this world.

Psalm 17:14

The Refrain for the Morning Lessons
The fool has said in his heart, "There is no God."* All are corrupt and commit
abominable acts; there is none who does any good.

Psalm 53:1

A Reading

Jesus taught us, saying: 'So stay awake, because you do not know the day when your master is coming. You may be quite sure of this that if the householder had known at what time of the night the burglar would come, he would have stayed awake and would not have allowed anyone to break through the wall of his house. Therefore, you too must stand ready because the Son of man is coming at an hour you do not expect.'

Matthew 24:42–44

The Refrain

The fool has said in his heart, "There is no God."* All are corrupt and commit abominable acts; there is none who does any good.

The Morning Psalm   The LORD Laughs at the Wicked

In a little while the wicked shall be no more;* you shall search out their place, but they will not be there.

But the lowly shall possess the land;* they will delight in abundance of peace.

The wicked plot against the righteous* and gnash at them with their teeth.

The Lord laughs at the wicked,* because he sees that their day will come.

The wicked draw their sword and bend their bow* to strike down the poor and needy, to slaughter those who are upright in their ways.

Their sword shall go through their own heart,* and their bow shall be broken.

The little that the righteous has* is better than great riches of the wicked.

For the power of the wicked shall be broken,* but the LORD upholds the righteous.

Psalm 37:11–18

The Refrain

The fool has said in his heart, "There is no God."* All are corrupt and commit abominable acts; there is none who does any good.

The Cry of the Church

Even so come, Lord Jesus!

The Lord's Prayer

The Prayer Appointed for the Week

Grant me, O Lord, to trust in you with all my heart; for, as you always resist the proud who confide in their own strength, so you never forsake those who make their boast of your mercy; through Jesus Christ our Lord, who lives and reigns with you and the Holy Spirit, one God, now and for ever. *Amen.*†

The Concluding Prayer of the Church

Lord God, almighty and everlasting Father, you have brought me in safety to this new day: Preserve me with your mighty power, that I may not fall into sin, nor be overcome by adversity; and in all I do direct me to the fulfilling of your purpose; through Jesus Christ my Lord. *Amen.*†

The Midday Office   **To Be Observed on the Hour or Half Hour
Between 11 a.m. and 2 p.m.**

The Call to Prayer
Blessed be the Lord, the God of Israel, from everlasting and to everlasting;* and
let all the people say, "Amen!" Hallelujah!

Psalm 106:48

The Request for Presence
Turn to me and have mercy upon me;* give your strength to your servant; and
save the child of your handmaid.

Psalm 86:16

The Greeting
O Lord, your love endures for ever;* do not abandon the works of your hands.

Psalm 138:9

The Refrain for the Midday Lessons
The fear of the Lord is the beginning of wisdom;* those who act accordingly have
a good understanding; his praise endures for ever.

Psalm 111:10

A Reading
Rid yourselves, then, of all spite, or deceit, or hypocrisy, or envy and carping criti-
cism. Like newborn babies all your longing should be for milk—the unadulter-
ated spiritual milk—which will help you grow to salvation, at any rate if you
have *tasted the goodness of the Lord.*

1 Peter 2:1–3

The Refrain
The fear of the Lord is the beginning of wisdom;* those who act accordingly have
a good understanding; his praise endures for ever.

The Midday Psalm   *Sustain Me with Your Bountiful Spirit*
Create in me a clean heart, O God,* and renew a right spirit within me.
Cast me not away from your presence* and take not your holy Spirit from me.
Give me the joy of your saving help again* and sustain me with your bountiful
Spirit.
I shall teach your ways to the wicked,* and sinners shall return to you.

Psalm 51:11–14

The Refrain
The fear of the Lord is the beginning of wisdom;* those who act accordingly have
a good understanding; his praise endures for ever.

The Small Verse
The Lord is my shepherd and nothing is wanting to me. In green pastures He hath
settled me.

The Short Breviary

The Lord's Prayer

The Prayer Appointed for the Week
Grant me, O Lord, to trust in you with all my heart; for, as you always resist the
proud who confide in their own strength, so you never forsake those who
make their boast of your mercy; through Jesus Christ our Lord, who lives and
reigns with you and the Holy Spirit, one God, now and for ever. *Amen.*†

The Concluding Prayer of the Church
Heavenly Father, you have promised to hear what we ask in the Name of your
Son: Accept and fulfill my petitions, I pray, not as I ask in my ignorance, nor as
I deserve in my sinfulness, but as you know and love me in your Son Jesus
Christ our Lord. *Amen.*†

The Vespers Office   **To Be Observed on the Hour or Half Hour
                                          Between 5 and 8 p.m.**

The Call to Prayer
Be joyful in God, all you lands;* sing the glory of his Name; sing the glory of his
praise.
Say to God, "How awesome are your deeds! . . .
All the earth bows down before you,* sings to you, sings out your Name."
Psalm 66:1–3

The Request for Presence
Let your loving-kindness, O LORD, be upon us,* as we have put our trust in you.
Psalm 33:22

The Greeting
Blessed is the LORD!* for he has heard the voice of my prayer.
Psalm 28:7

The Hymn   *Leaning on the Everlasting Arms*
    What a fellowship, what a joy divine,
    Leaning on the everlasting arms;
    What a blessedness, what a peace is mine,
    Leaning on the everlasting arms.
    Leaning, leaning,
    Safe and secure from all alarms;
    Leaning, leaning,
    Leaning on the everlasting arms.

What have I to dread, what have I to fear
Leaning on the everlasting arms?
I have blessed peace with my Lord so near,
Leaning on the everlasting arms.
Leaning, leaning,
Safe and secure from all alarms;
Leaning, leaning,
Leaning on the everlasting arms.

Elisha Hoffman

The Refrain for the Vespers Lessons

Turn again to your rest, O my soul,* for the Lord has treated you well.
For you have rescued my life from death,* my eyes from tears, and my feet from
stumbling.

Psalm 116:6–7

The Vespers Psalm   *With You Is the Well of Life*

Your love, O Lord, reaches to the heavens,* and your faithfulness to the clouds.
Your righteousness is like the strong mountains, your justice like the great deep;*
you save both man and beast, O Lord.
How priceless is your love, O God!* your people take refuge under the shadow of
your wings.
They feast upon the abundance of your house;* you give them drink from the
river of your delights.
For with you is the well of life,* and in your light we see light.
Continue your loving-kindness to those who know you,* and your favor to those
who are true of heart.

Psalm 36:5–10

The Refrain

Turn again to your rest, O my soul,* for the Lord has treated you well.
For you have rescued my life from death,* my eyes from tears, and my feet from
stumbling.

The Cry of the Church

O Lord, hear my prayer and let my cry come unto you. Thanks be to God.

The Lord's Prayer

The Prayer Appointed for the Week

Grant me, O Lord, to trust in you with all my heart; for, as you always resist the
proud who confide in their own strength, so you never forsake those who
make their boast of your mercy; through Jesus Christ our Lord, who lives and
reigns with you and the Holy Spirit, one God, now and for ever. *Amen.*†

The Concluding Prayer of the Church
Grant me and all of your people the gift of your Spirit, that we may know Christ
and make him known; and through him, at all times and in all places, may give
thanks to you in all things. *Amen.*†

The Morning Office   **To Be Observed on the Hour or Half Hour**
                                           Between 6 and 9 a.m.

The Call to Prayer
Open my lips, O Lord,* and my mouth shall proclaim your praise.
Psalm 51:16

The Request for Presence
Open my eyes, that I may see* the wonders of your law.
Psalm 119:18

The Greeting
I will thank you, O LORD my God, with all my heart,* and glorify your Name for
evermore.
Psalm 86:12

The Refrain for the Morning Lessons
For who is God, but the LORD?* who is the Rock, except our God?
Psalm 18:32

A Reading
Jesus taught us, saying: 'If I were to seek my own glory my glory would be worth
nothing; in fact, my glory is conferred by the Father, by the one of whom you
say, "He is our God" although you do not know him. But I know him, and if I
were to say: I do not know him, I should be a liar. . . . But I do know him, and I
keep his word.'
John 8:54–56

The Refrain
For who is God, but the LORD?* who is the Rock, except our God?

The Morning Psalm   *The Dullard Does Not Know*
LORD, how great are your works!* your thoughts are very deep.
The dullard does not know, nor does the fool understand,* that though the wicked
grow like weeds, and all the workers of iniquity flourish,
They flourish only to be destroyed for ever;* but you, O LORD, are exalted for
evermore.
Psalm 92:5–7

The Refrain
For who is God, but the LORD?* who is the Rock, except our God?

The Small Verse
O Lamb of God, that takes away the sins of the world, have mercy upon me.
O Lamb of God, that takes away the sins of the world, have mercy upon me.
O Lamb of God, that takes away the sins of the world, grant me your peace.

The Lord's Prayer

The Prayer Appointed for the Week
Grant me, O Lord, to trust in you with all my heart; for, as you always resist the
proud who confide in their own strength, so you never forsake those who
make their boast of your mercy; through Jesus Christ our Lord, who lives and
reigns with you and the Holy Spirit, one God, now and for ever. *Amen.*†

The Concluding Prayer of the Church
Lord God, almighty and everlasting Father, you have brought me in safety to this
new day: Preserve me with your mighty power, that I may not fall into sin, nor
be overcome by adversity; and in all I do direct me to the fulfilling of your purpose; through Jesus Christ my Lord. *Amen.*†

The Midday Office   **To Be Observed on the Hour or Half Hour**
                                          Between 11 a.m. and 2 p.m.

The Call to Prayer
Hallelujah! Sing to the Lord a new song;* sing his praise in the congregation of the
faithful.

Psalm 149:1

The Request for Presence
Hear, O Shepherd of Israel, leading Joseph like a flock;* shine forth, you that are
enthroned upon the cherubim.

Psalm 80:1

The Greeting
The Lord is in his holy temple; let all the earth keep silence before him. *Amen.*

Traditional

The Refrain for the Midday Lessons
The Lord shall watch over your going out and your coming in* from this time
forth for evermore.

Psalm 121:8

A Reading
Something which has existed since the beginning, which we have heard, which
we have seen with our own eyes; which we have watched and touched with
our hands: the Word of life—this is our theme. That life was made visible: we
saw it and are giving our testimony, declaring to you the eternal life which was
present to the Father and has been revealed to us. We are declaring to you what
we have seen and heard so that you too may share our life. Our life is shared

with the Father and with his Son Jesus Christ. We are writing this to you so that our joy may be complete.

I John 1:1–4

The Refrain
The LORD shall watch over your going out and your coming in,* from this time forth for evermore.

The Midday Psalm   *Great Things Are They That You Have Done, O LORD My God!*
Great things are they that you have done, O LORD my God! how great your wonders and your plans for us!* there is none who can be compared with you.

Oh, that I could make them known and tell them!* but they are more than I can count.

In sacrifice and offering you take no pleasure* (you have given me ears to hear you);

Burnt-offering and sin-offering you have not required,* and so I said, "Behold, I come.

In the roll of the book it is written concerning me:* I love to do your will, O my God; your law is deep in my heart."

Psalm 40:5–9

The Refrain
The LORD shall watch over your going out and your coming in,* from this time forth for evermore.

The Gloria

The Lord's Prayer

The Prayer Appointed for the Week
Grant me, O Lord, to trust in you with all my heart; for, as you always resist the proud who confide in their own strength, so you never forsake those who make their boast of your mercy; through Jesus Christ our Lord, who lives and reigns with you and the Holy Spirit, one God, now and for ever. *Amen.*†

The Concluding Prayer of the Church
Let us bless the Lord God living and true! Let us always render him praise, glory, honor, blessing, and all good things! Amen. Amen. So be it! So be it!

St. Francis of Assisi

The Vespers Office   To Be Observed on the Hour or Half Hour Between 5 and 8 p.m.

The Call to Prayer
Praise the LORD, all you nations;* laud him, all you peoples.

For his loving-kindness toward us is great,* and the faithfulness of the LORD endures for ever. . . .

Psalm 117:1–2

The Request for Presence
O LORD, do not forsake me;* be not far from me, O my God.
Make haste to help me,* O Lord of my salvation.

Psalm 38:21–22

The Greeting
You are my refuge and shield;* my hope is in your word.

Psalm 119:114

The Hymn   *Love Lifted Me*

   I was sinking deep in sin,
   Far from the peaceful shore,
   Very deeply stained within,
   Sinking to rise no more;
   But the Master of the sea
   Heard my despairing cry,
   From the waters lifted me,
   Now safe am I,
   Love lifted me! Love lifted Me!
   When nothing else could help, Love lifted me!

   All my heart to Him I gave,
   Ever to Him I'll cling,
   In His blessed presence live,
   Ever His praises sing.
   Love so mighty and so true
   Merits my soul's best songs,
   Faithful, loving service, too,
   To Him belongs.
   Love lifted me! Love lifted Me!
   When nothing else could help, Love lifted me!

   Souls in danger, look above,
   Jesus completely saves;
   He will lift you by His love
   Out of the angry waves.
   He's the Master of the sea
   Billows His will obey;
   He your Savior wants to be—
   Be saved today!
   Love lifted me! Love lifted Me!
   When nothing else could help, Love lifted me!

James Rowe

The Refrain for the Vespers Lessons
. . . it is good for me to be near God;* I have made the Lord GOD my refuge.

Psalm 73:28

The Vespers Psalm   *I Will Call Upon God*

My heart quakes within me,* and the terrors of death have fallen upon me.

Fear and trembling have come over me,* and horror overwhelms me.

And I said, "Oh, that I had wings like a dove!* I would fly away and be at rest.

I would flee to a far-off place* and make my lodging in the wilderness.

I would hasten to escape* from the stormy wind and tempest."

Swallow them up, O Lord; confound their speech;* for I have seen violence and strife in the city.

Day and night the watchmen make their rounds upon her walls,* but trouble and misery are in the midst of her.

There is corruption at her heart;* her streets are never free of oppression and deceit.

But I will call upon God,* and the LORD will deliver me.

He will bring me safely back . . .* God, who is enthroned of old, will hear me . . .

Psalm 55:5 ff

The Refrain

. . . it is good for me to be near God;* I have made the Lord GOD my refuge.

The Cry of the Church

Lord, have mercy on us. Christ, have mercy on us. Lord, have mercy on us.

The Lord's Prayer

The Prayer Appointed for the Week

Grant me, O Lord, to trust in you with all my heart; for, as you always resist the proud who confide in their own strength, so you never forsake those who make their boast of your mercy; through Jesus Christ our Lord, who lives and reigns with you and the Holy Spirit, one God, now and for ever. *Amen.*†

The Concluding Prayer of the Church

Save me, O Lord, while I am awake, and keep me while I sleep that I may wake in Christ and rest in peace.

adapted from THE SHORT BREVIARY

The Morning Office   **To Be Observed on the Hour or Half Hour**
                                  Between 6 and 9 a.m.

The Call to Prayer

Praise God from whom all blessings flow; praise him, all creatures here below; praise him above, you heavenly hosts; praise Father, Son and Holy Ghost.

Doxology

The Request for Presence

Send out your light and your truth, that they may lead me,* and bring me to your holy hill and to your dwelling;

That I may go to the altar of God, to the God of my joy and gladness;* and on the
harp I will give thanks to you, O God my God.

Psalm 43:3–4

The Greeting

Splendor and honor and kingly power* are yours by right, O Lord our God,
For you created everything that is,* and by your will they were created and have
their being;

A Song to the Lamb

The Refrain for the Morning Lessons

For one day in your courts is better than a thousand in my own room,* and to
stand at the threshold of the house of my God than to dwell in the tents of the
wicked.

Psalm 84:9

A Reading

Of the early Church, it is written: 'The whole group of believers was united, heart
and soul; no one claimed for his own use anything that he had, as everything
they owned was held in common.

The apostles continued to testify to the resurrection of the Lord Jesus with great
power, and they were all given great respect.

None of their members was ever in want, as all those who owned land or houses
would sell them, and bring the money from them, to present it to the apostles;
it was then distributed to any members who might be in need.'

Acts 4:32–35

The Refrain

For one day in your courts is better than a thousand in my own room,* and to
stand at the threshold of the house of my God than to dwell in the tents of the
wicked.

The Morning Psalm   The Earth Is the Lord's

The earth is the Lord's and all that is in it,* the world and all who dwell therein.
For it is he who founded it upon the seas* and made it firm upon the rivers of the
deep.
"Who can ascend the hill of the Lord?* and who can stand in his holy place?"
"Those who have clean hands and a pure heart,* who have not pledged them-
selves to falsehood, nor sworn by what is a fraud.
They shall receive a blessing from the Lord* and a just reward from the God of
their salvation."
Such is the generation of those who seek him,* of those who seek your face, O God
of Jacob.

Psalm 24:1–6

The Refrain

For one day in your courts is better than a thousand in my own room,* and to stand at the threshold of the house of my God than to dwell in the tents of the wicked.

The Small Verse

The people that walked in darkness have seen a great light; on those who live in a land of deep shadow a light has shone.

Isaiah 9:1

The Lord's Prayer

The Prayer Appointed for the Week

Grant me, O Lord, to trust in you with all my heart; for, as you always resist the proud who confide in their own strength, so you never forsake those who make their boast of your mercy; through Jesus Christ our Lord, who lives and reigns with you and the Holy Spirit, one God, now and for ever. *Amen.*†

The Concluding Prayer of the Church

Lord God, almighty and everlasting Father, you have brought me in safety to this new day: Preserve me with your mighty power, that I may not fall into sin, nor be overcome by adversity; and in all I do direct me to the fulfilling of your purpose; through Jesus Christ my Lord. *Amen.*†

The Midday Office
To Be Observed on the Hour or Half Hour Between 11 a.m. and 2 p.m.

The Call to Prayer

Come, let us sing to the LORD;* let us shout for joy to the Rock of our salvation.
Let us come before his presence with thanksgiving* and raise a loud shout to him with psalms.
For the LORD is a great God,* and a great King above all gods.
In his hand are the caverns of the earth,* and the heights of the hills are his also.
The sea is his, for he made it,* and his hands have molded the dry land.

Psalm 95:1–5

The Request for Presence

Remember not our past sins;* let your compassion be swift to meet us.

Psalm 79:8

The Greeting

Zion hears and is glad, and the cities of Judah rejoice,* because of your judgments, O LORD.

Psalm 97:8

The Refrain for the Midday Lessons

I will listen to what the Lord God is saying,* for he is speaking peace to his faithful
people and to those who turn their hearts to him.

Psalm 85:8

A Reading

When the Lord has given you the bread of suffering and the water of distress, he
who is your teacher will hide no longer, and you will see your teacher with
your own eyes. . . . He will send rain for the seed you sow in the ground, and
the bread that the ground provides will be rich and nourishing. That day, your
cattle will graze in wide pastures. Oxen and donkeys that work the land will
eat for fodder wild sorrel, spread by the shovel-load and fork-load. On every
lofty mountain, on every high hill there will be streams and watercourses. . . .
Then moonlight will be bright as sunlight and sunlight itself be seven times
brighter—like the light of seven days in one—on the day Yahweh dresses his
people's wound and heals the scars of the blows they have received.

Isaiah 30:20 ff

The Refrain

I will listen to what the Lord God is saying,* for he is speaking peace to his faithful
people and to those who turn their hearts to him.

The Midday Psalm   Let the Earth Be Glad

Let the heavens rejoice, and let the earth be glad; let the sea thunder and all that is
in it;* let the field be joyful and all that is therein.
Then shall all the trees of the wood shout for joy before the Lord when he comes,*
when he comes to judge the earth.
He will judge the world with righteousness* and the peoples with his truth.

Psalm 96:11–13

The Refrain

I will listen to what the Lord God is saying,* for he is speaking peace to his faithful
people and to those who turn their hearts to him.

The Gloria

The Lord's Prayer

The Prayer Appointed for the Week

Grant me, O Lord, to trust in you with all my heart; for, as you always resist the
proud who confide in their own strength, so you never forsake those who
make their boast of your mercy; through Jesus Christ our Lord, who lives and
reigns with you and the Holy Spirit, one God, now and for ever. *Amen.*†

The Concluding Prayer of the Church

Direct me, O Lord, on all my doings with your most gracious favor, and further
me with your continual help; that in all my work begun, continued, and ended

in you, I may glorify your holy name, and finally, by your mercy, obtain everlasting life; through Jesus Christ my Lord. *Amen.†*

The Vespers Office **To Be Observed on the Hour or Half Hour**
Between 5 and 8 p.m.

The Call to Prayer
Sing to the LORD, you servants of his;* give thanks for the remembrance of his
   holiness.
For his wrath endures but the twinkling of an eye,* his favor for a lifetime.
Psalm 30:4–5

The Request for Presence
Show us the light of your countenance, O God,* and come to us.
based on Psalm 67:1

The Greeting
Your statutes have been like songs to me* wherever I have lived as a stranger.
I remember your Name in the night, O LORD,* and dwell upon your law.
This is how it has been with me,* because I have kept your commandments.
Psalm 119:54–56

The Hymn   *O God of Truth*
O God of truth, O Lord of might,   Grant this, O Father ever one
Disposing time and change aright,   With Jesus Christ Your only Son
Who clothes the splendid morning ray   And Holy Ghost, whom all adore,
And gives the heat at noon of day: Reigning and blessed forevermore.

Extinguish now each sinful fire   *adapted from A SHORT BREVIARY*
And banish every ill desire;
And while You keep the body whole
Shed forth Your peace upon the soul.

The Refrain for the Vespers Lessons
Righteousness shall go before him,* and peace shall be a pathway for his feet.
Psalm 85:13

The Vespers Psalm   *Turn Again to Your Rest, O My Soul*
The LORD watches over the innocent;* I was brought very low, and he helped me.
Turn again to your rest, O my soul,* for the LORD has treated you well.
For you have rescued my life from death,* my eyes from tears, and my feet from
   stumbling.
I will walk in the presence of the LORD* in the land of the living.
Psalm 116:5–8

The Refrain
Righteousness shall go before him,* and peace shall be a pathway for his feet.

The Cry of the Church
Even so come, Lord Jesus!

The Lord's Prayer

The Prayer Appointed for the Week
Grant me, O Lord, to trust in you with all my heart; for, as you always resist the
    proud who confide in their own strength, so you never forsake those who
    make their boast of your mercy; through Jesus Christ our Lord, who lives and
    reigns with you and the Holy Spirit, one God, now and for ever. *Amen.*†

The Concluding Prayer of the Church
May Almighty God grant me a peaceful night and a perfect end. *Amen.*

The Morning Office   **To Be Observed on the Hour or Half Hour**
                                                 Between 6 and 9 a.m.

The Call to Prayer
Open my lips, O Lord,* and my mouth shall proclaim your praise.
                                                              Psalm 51:16

The Request for Presence
Bow down your ear, O Lord, and answer me . . .
Keep watch over my life, for I am faithful.
                                                     Psalm 86:1–2

The Greeting
Lord, you have been our refuge* from one generation to another.
Before the mountains were brought forth, or the land and the earth were born,*
    from age to age you are God.
                                                              Psalm 90:1–2

The Refrain for the Morning Lessons
Truly, his salvation is very near to those who fear him,* that his glory may dwell in
    our land.
                                                              Psalm 85:9

A Reading
His mother and his brothers came looking for him, but they could not get to him
    because of the crowd. He was told, 'Your mother and brothers are standing
    outside and want to see you.' But he said in answer, 'My mother and my broth-
    ers are those who hear the word of God and put it into practice.'
                                                              Luke 8:19–21

The Refrain
Truly, his salvation is very near to those who fear him,* that his glory may dwell in
    our land.

The Morning Psalm   *O Israel, If You Would But Listen to Me*

Hear, O my people, and I will admonish you:* O Israel, if you would but listen to
   me!

There shall be no strange god among you;* you shall not worship a foreign god.

I am the LORD your God, who brought you out of the land of Egypt and said,*
   "Open your mouth wide, and I will fill it."

Psalm 81:8–10

The Refrain

Truly, his salvation is very near to those who fear him,* that his glory may dwell in
   our land.

The Cry of the Church

Be, Lord, my helper and forsake me not. Do not despise me, O God, my savior.

THE SHORT BREVIARY

The Lord's Prayer

The Prayer Appointed for the Week

Grant me, O Lord, to trust in you with all my heart; for, as you always resist the
   proud who confide in their own strength, so you never forsake those who
   make their boast of your mercy; through Jesus Christ our Lord, who lives and
   reigns with you and the Holy Spirit, one God, now and for ever. *Amen.*†

The Concluding Prayer of the Church

Lord God, almighty and everlasting Father, you have brought me in safety to this
   new day: Preserve me with your mighty power, that I may not fall into sin, nor
   be overcome by adversity; and in all I do direct me to the fulfilling of your purpose; through Jesus Christ my Lord. *Amen.*†

The Midday Office   To Be Observed on the Hour or Half Hour
Between 11 a.m. and 2 p.m.

The Call to Prayer

God has gone up with a shout,* the LORD with the sound of the ram's-horn.

Sing praises to God, sing praises;* sing praises to our King, sing praises.

For God is King of all the earth;* sing praises with all your skill.

God reigns over the nations;* God sits upon his holy throne.

Psalm 47:5–8

The Request for Presence

Answer me when I call, O God, defender of my cause;* you set me free when I am
   hard-pressed; have mercy on me and hear my prayer.

Psalm 4:1

The Greeting

Deliver me, my God, from the hand of the wicked,* from the clutches of the evil-
   doer and the oppressor.

For you are my hope, O Lord GOD,* my confidence since I was young.
I have been sustained by you ever since I was born;* from my mother's womb you
have been my strength; my praise shall be always of you.

Psalm 71:4–6

The Refrain for the Midday Lessons
Your love, O LORD, for ever will I sing;* from age to age my mouth will proclaim
your faithfulness.

Psalm 89:1

A Reading
I myself shall go before you, I shall level the heights, I shall shatter the bronze
gateways, I shall smash the iron bars. I shall give you hidden treasures and
hidden hoards of wealth, so that you will know that I am YAHWEH, the God of
Israel. It is for the sake of my servant Jacob and of Israel my chosen one, that I
have called you by your name, have given you a title though you do not know
me. I am YAHWEH, and there is no other; there is no other God except me.
Though you do not know me, I have armed you so that it may be known from
east to west that there is no one except me. I am YAHWEH, and there is no other,
I form the light and create the darkness, I make well being and create disaster,
I, YAHWEH, do all these things.
Rain down, you heavens, from above and let the clouds pour down saving justice,
let the earth open up and blossom with salvation, and let justice sprout up with
it; I, YAHWEH, do all these things.

Isaiah 45:2–8

The Refrain
Your love, O LORD, for ever will I sing;* from age to age my mouth will proclaim
your faithfulness.

The Midday Psalm   *Surely There Is a God Who Rules in the Earth*
Do you indeed decree righteousness, you rulers?* do you judge the peoples with
equity?
No; you devise evil in your hearts,* and your hands deal out violence in the land.
The wicked are perverse from the womb;* liars go astray from their birth.
They are as venomous as a serpent,* they are like the deaf adder which stops its
ears,
Which does not heed the voice of the charmer,* no matter how skillful his
charming.
O God, break their teeth in their mouths;* pull the fangs of the young lions, O
LORD.
Let them vanish like water that runs off;* let them wither like trodden grass.
Let them be like the snail that melts away,* like a stillborn child that never sees the
sun.

Before they bear fruit, let them be cut down like a brier;* like thorns and thistles let
them be swept away.
The righteous will be glad when they see the vengeance;* they will bathe their feet
in the blood of the wicked.
And they will say, "Surely, there is a reward for the righteous;* surely, there is a
God who rules in the earth."

Psalm 58:1–11

The Refrain
Your love, O Lord, for ever will I sing;* from age to age my mouth will proclaim
your faithfulness.

The Gloria

The Lord's Prayer

The Prayer Appointed for the Week
Grant me, O Lord, to trust in you with all my heart; for, as you always resist the
proud who confide in their own strength, so you never forsake those who
make their boast of your mercy; through Jesus Christ our Lord, who lives and
reigns with you and the Holy Spirit, one God, now and for ever. *Amen.*†

The Concluding Prayer of the Church
In truth God has heard me; he has attended the voice of my prayer. Thanks be to
God. *Amen.*

based on Psalm 66:17

The Vespers Office   To Be Observed on the Hour or Half Hour
                                              Between 5 and 8 p.m.

The Call to Prayer
God is the Lord; he has shined upon us;* form a procession with branches up to
the horns of the altar.

Psalm 118:27

The Request for Presence
Hear the voice of my prayer when I cry out to you,* when I lift up my hands to
your holy of holies.

Psalm 28:2

The Greeting
All your works praise you, O Lord,* and your faithful servants bless you.
They make known the glory of your kingdom and speak of your power . . .* and
the glorious splendor of your kingdom.

Psalm 145:10–12

The Hymn *God, Who Made the Earth and Heaven*

Guard us waking, guard us sleeping,	Holy Father, throned in heaven,
And, when we die,	All holy Son,
May we in your mighty keeping	Holy Spirit, freely given,
All peaceful lie.	Blessed Three in One:
When the last dread call shall wake us,	Grant us grace, we now implore you,
Then, O Lord, do not forsake us,	Till we lay our crowns before you
But to reign in glory take us	And in worthier strains adore you
With you on high.	While ages run.

Stanza 1: Richard Whately
Stanza 2: William Mercer

The Refrain for the Vespers Lessons
Those who trust in the LORD are like Mount Zion,* which cannot be moved, but
stands fast for ever.

Psalm 125:1

The Vespers Psalm *May the LORD Strengthen You Out of Zion*
May the LORD answer you in the day of trouble,* the Name of the God of Jacob
defend you;
Send you help from his holy place* and strengthen you out of Zion;
Remember all your offerings* and accept your burnt sacrifice;
Grant you your heart's desire* and prosper all your plans.
We will shout for joy at your victory and triumph in the Name of our God;* may
the LORD grant all your requests.

Psalm 20:1–5

The Refrain
Those who trust in the LORD are like Mount Zion,* which cannot be moved, but
stands fast for ever.

The Small Verse
The earth is the Lord's and all the fullness thereof, the world and we who dwell
within. Thanks be to God.

Traditional

The Lord's Prayer

The Prayer Appointed for the Week
Grant me, O Lord, to trust in you with all my heart; for, as you always resist the
proud who confide in their own strength, so you never forsake those who
make their boast of your mercy; through Jesus Christ our Lord, who lives and
reigns with you and the Holy Spirit, one God, now and for ever. *Amen.*†

The Concluding Prayer of the Church
May God himself order my days and make them acceptable in his sight. Blessed is
the Lord always, my strength and my redeemer.

Traditional

The Morning Office   **To Be Observed on the Hour or Half Hour**
Between 6 and 9 a.m.

The Call to Prayer
Hallelujah! Praise the Name of the Lord;* give praise, you servants of the Lord,
You who stand in the house of the Lord,* in the courts of the house of our God.
Praise the Lord, for the Lord is good;* sing praises to his Name, for it is lovely.

Psalm 136:1–3

The Request for Presence
I have said to the Lord, "You are my God;* listen, O Lord, to my supplication."

Psalm 140:6

The Greeting
You are the Lord, most high over all the earth;* you are exalted far above all gods.

Psalm 97:9

The Refrain for the Morning Lessons
The human mind and heart are a mystery; but God will loose an arrow at them,*
and suddenly they will be wounded.

Psalm 64:7

A Reading
Jesus taught us, saying: 'Watch yourselves, or your hearts will be coarsened by
debauchery and drunkenness and the cares of life, and that day will come
upon you unexpectedly, like a trap. For it will come down on all those living on
the face of the earth. Stay awake, praying at all times for the strength to survive
all that is going to happen, and to hold your ground before the Son of man.'

Luke 21:34–36

The Refrain
The human mind and heart are a mystery; but God will loose an arrow at them,*
and suddenly they will be wounded.

The Morning Psalm   *All of You Are Children of the Most High*
God takes his stand in the council of heaven;* he gives judgment in the midst of
the gods:
"How long will you judge unjustly,* and show favor to the wicked?
Save the weak and the orphan;* defend the humble and needy;
Rescue the weak and the poor;* deliver them from the power of the wicked.
They do not know, neither do they understand; they go about in darkness;* all the
foundations of the earth are shaken.
Now I say to you, 'You are gods,* and all of you children of the Most High;
Nevertheless, you shall die like mortals,* and fall like any prince.' "
Arise, O God, and rule the earth,* for you shall take all nations for your own.

Psalm 82

The Refrain
The human mind and heart are a mystery; but God will loose an arrow at them,*
and suddenly they will be wounded.

The Cry of the Church
O God, come to my assistance! O Lord, make haste to help me!

The Lord's Prayer

The Prayer Appointed for the Week
Grant me, O Lord, to trust in you with all my heart; for, as you always resist the
proud who confide in their own strength, so you never forsake those who
make their boast of your mercy; through Jesus Christ our Lord, who lives and
reigns with you and the Holy Spirit, one God, now and for ever. *Amen.*†

The Concluding Prayer of the Church
Lord God, almighty and everlasting Father, you have brought me in safety to this
new day: Preserve me with your mighty power, that I may not fall into sin, nor
be overcome by adversity; and in all I do direct me to the fulfilling of your purpose; through Jesus Christ my Lord. *Amen.*†

The Midday Office **To Be Observed on the Hour or Half Hour**
Between 11 a.m. and 2 p.m.

The Call to Prayer
Sing to the LORD with thanksgiving;* make music to our God upon the harp.

Psalm 147:7

The Request for Presence
Hear, O Shepherd of Israel, leading Joseph like a flock;* shine forth, you that are
enthroned upon the cherubim.

Psalm 80:1

The Greeting
Exalt yourself above the heavens, O God,* and your glory over all the earth.

Psalm 57:6

The Refrain for the Midday Lessons
The LORD has sworn and he will not recant:* "You are a priest for ever after the
order of Melchizedek."

Psalm 110:4

A Reading
When Abram returned from defeating Chedor-Laomer and the kings who had
been on his side, the king of Sodom came to meet him in the Valley of Shaveh
(that is the Valley of the King). Melchizedek king of Salem brought bread and
wine; he was a priest of God Most High. He pronounced this blessing: 'Blessed
be Abram by God Most High, creator of heaven and earth, and blessed be God

Most High for putting your enemies into your clutches.' And Abram gave him a tenth of everything.

Genesis 14:17–20

The Refrain
The LORD has sworn and he will not recant:* "You are a priest for ever after the order of Melchizedek."

The Midday Psalm — *My Tongue Shall Be the Pen of a Skilled Writer*
My heart is stirring with a noble song; let me recite what I have fashioned for the king;* my tongue shall be the pen of a skilled writer.

You are the fairest of men;* grace flows from your lips, because God has blessed you for ever.

Strap your sword upon your thigh, O mighty warrior,* in your pride and in your majesty.

Ride out and conquer in the cause of truth* and for the sake of justice.

Your right hand will show you marvelous things;* your arrows are very sharp, O mighty warrior.

The peoples are falling at your feet,* and the king's enemies are losing heart.

Your throne, O God, endures for ever and ever,* a scepter of righteousness is the scepter of your kingdom; you love righteousness and hate iniquity.

Therefore God, your God, has anointed you* with the oil of gladness above your fellows.

All your garments are fragrant with myrrh, aloes, and cassia,* and the music of strings from ivory palaces makes you glad.

Psalm 45:1–9

The Refrain
The LORD has sworn and he will not recant:* "You are a priest for ever after the order of Melchizedek."

The Cry of the Church
Even so come, Lord Jesus!

The Lord's Prayer

The Prayer Appointed for the Week
Grant me, O Lord, to trust in you with all my heart; for, as you always resist the proud who confide in their own strength, so you never forsake those who make their boast of your mercy; through Jesus Christ our Lord, who lives and reigns with you and the Holy Spirit, one God, now and for ever. *Amen.*†

The Concluding Prayer of the Church
Lord Jesus Christ, by your death you took away the sting of death: Grant me to so follow in faith where you have led the way, that I may at length fall asleep peacefully in you and wake in your likeness; for your tender mercies' sake. *Amen.*†

The Vespers Office   **To Be Observed on the Hour or Half Hour**
Between 5 and 8 p.m.

The Call to Prayer
Behold now, bless the Lord, all you servants of the Lord,* you that stand by night
in the house of the Lord.
Lift up your hands in the holy place and bless the Lord;* the Lord who made
heaven and earth bless you out of Zion.

Psalm 134

The Request for Presence
Look upon me and answer me, O Lord my God;* give light to my eyes, lest I sleep
in death.

Psalm 13:3

The Greeting
O Lord, I am not proud;* I have no haughty looks.
I do not occupy myself with great matters,* or with things that are too hard for me.
But I still my soul and make it quiet, like a child upon its mother's breast;* my soul
is quieted within me.

Psalm 131:1–3

The Hymn   *Lord Jesus, Think on Me*

Lord Jesus, think on me,   Lord Jesus, think on me,
And purge away my sin;   Nor let me go astray;
From earth-born passions set me free,   Through darkness and perplexity
And make me pure within.   Point thou the heavenly way.

Lord Jesus, think on me,   Lord Jesus, think on me,
Amid all the battle's strife;   That, when this life is past,
In all my pain and misery   I may the eternal brightness see,
Be thou my health and life.   And share thy joy at last.

Synesius of Cyrene

The Refrain for the Vespers Lessons
Those who are planted in the house of the Lord* shall flourish in the courts of our
God.

Psalm 92:12

The Vespers Psalm   *Your Love Is Before My Eyes*
Test me, O Lord, and try me;* examine my heart and my mind.
For your love is before my eyes;* I have walked faithfully with you.
I have not sat with the worthless,* nor do I consort with the deceitful.
I have hated the company of evildoers;* I will not sit down with the wicked.
I will wash my hands in innocence, O Lord,* that I may go in procession round
your altar,
Singing aloud a song of thanksgiving* and recounting all your wonderful deeds.

Psalm 26:2–7

The Refrain

Those who are planted in the house of the LORD* shall flourish in the courts of our God;

The Small Verse

The Lord is my shepherd and nothing is wanting to me. In green pastures He has settled me.

The Short Breviary

The Lord's Prayer

The Prayer Appointed for the Week

Grant me, O Lord, to trust in you with all my heart; for, as you always resist the proud who confide in their own strength, so you never forsake those who make their boast of your mercy; through Jesus Christ our Lord, who lives and reigns with you and the Holy Spirit, one God, now and for ever. *Amen.*†

The Concluding Prayers of the Church

Almighty God, who has promised to hear the petitions of those who ask in your Son's Name: I beseech you mercifully to incline your ear to me who have made my prayers and supplications to you; and grant that those things which I have faithfully asked according to your will, I may effectually obtain, to the relief of my necessity, and to the setting forth of your glory; through Jesus Christ my Lord. *Amen.*†

May the souls of the faithful departed, through the mercy of God, rest in eternal peace. *Amen.*

The Morning Office

To Be Observed on the Hour or Half Hour Between 6 and 9 a.m.

The Call to Prayer

Come now and look upon the works of the LORD,* what awesome things he has done on earth.

Psalm 46:9

The Request for Presence

O LORD . . . answer us when we call.

Psalm 20:9

The Greeting

My eyes are fixed on you, O my Strength;* for you, O God, are my stronghold.

Psalm 59:10

The Refrain for the Morning Lessons

Our days are like the grass;* we flourish like a flower of the field;
When the wind goes over it, it is gone,* and its place shall know it no more.

Psalm 103:15–16

A Reading

Jesus taught us, saying: 'Take care not to be deceived, because many will come using my name and saying, "I am the one" and "The time is near at hand." Refuse to join them. And when you hear of wars and revolutions, do not be terrified, for this is something that must happen first, but the end will not come at once . . .

There will be signs in the sun and moon and stars; on earth nations in agony, bewildered by the turmoil of the ocean and its waves; men fainting away with terror and fear at what menaces the world, for the powers of heaven will be shaken. And then they will see the *Son of man coming in a cloud* with power and great glory. When these things begin to take place, stand erect, hold your heads high, because your liberation is near at hand . . .

So with you when you see these things happening: know that the kingdom of God is near. In truth I tell you, before this generation has passed away all will have taken place. Sky and earth will pass away, but my words will never pass away.'

Luke 21:8ff

The Refrain

Our days are like the grass;* we flourish like a flower of the field;
When the wind goes over it, it is gone,* and its place shall know it no more.

The Morning Psalm   *Yours Is the Day*

God is my King from ancient times,* victorious in the midst of the earth.
You divided the sea by your might* and shattered the heads of the dragons upon the waters;
You crushed the heads of Leviathan* and gave him to the people of the desert for food.
You split open spring and torrent;* you dried up ever-flowing rivers.
Yours is the day, yours also the night;* you established the moon and the sun.
You fixed all the boundaries of the earth;* you made both summer and winter.

Psalm 74:11–16

The Refrain

Our days are like the grass;* we flourish like a flower of the field;
When the wind goes over it, it is gone,* and its place shall know it no more.

The Cry of the Church

Lord, have mercy on us. Christ, have mercy on us. Lord, have mercy on us.

The Lord's Prayer

The Prayer Appointed for the Week

Grant me, O Lord, to trust in you with all my heart; for, as you always resist the proud who confide in their own strength, so you never forsake those who make their boast of your mercy; through Jesus Christ our Lord, who lives and reigns with you and the Holy Spirit, one God, now and for ever. *Amen.†*

The Concluding Prayer of the Church

Lord God, almighty and everlasting Father, you have brought me in safety to this new day: Preserve me with your mighty power, that I may not fall into sin, nor be overcome by adversity; and in all I do direct me to the fulfilling of your purpose; through Jesus Christ my Lord. *Amen.*†

The Midday Office   **To Be Observed on the Hour or Half Hour**
Between 11 a.m. and 2 p.m.

The Call to Prayer

Bless our God, you peoples;* make the voice of his praise to be heard;
Who holds our souls in life,* and will not allow our feet to slip.

Psalm 66:7–8

The Request for Presence

Let your ways be known upon earth,* your saving health among all nations.

Psalm 67:2

The Greeting

How great is your goodness, O LORD! which you have laid up for those who fear you;* which you have done in the sight of all for those who put their trust in you.

Psalm 31:19

The Refrain for the Midday Lessons

Your love, O LORD, reaches to the heavens,* and your faithfulness to the clouds.

Psalm 36:5

A Reading

When God made the promise to Abraham, he *swore by his own self,* since there was no one greater he could swear by: *I will shower blessings on you and give you many descendants.* Because of that, Abraham persevered and received fulfillment of the promise. Human beings, of course, swear an oath by something greater than themselves, and between them, confirmation by an oath puts an end to all dispute. In the same way, when God wanted to show the heirs to the promise even more clearly how unalterable his plan was, he conveyed this by an oath so that through two unalterable factors in which God could not be lying, we who have fled to him might have a vigorous encouragement to grasp the hope held out to us. This is the anchor our souls have, as sure as it is firm, reaching right *through inside the curtain* where Jesus had entered as a forerunner on our behalf, having become a high *priest for ever, of the order of Melchizedek.*

Hebrews 6:13–20

The Refrain

Your love, O LORD, reaches to the heavens,* and your faithfulness to the clouds.

The Midday Psalm　　　　　*We Will Recount the Praiseworthy Deeds of the* LORD
That which we have heard and known, and what our forefathers have told us,* we
　　will not hide from their children.
We will recount to generations to come the praiseworthy deeds and the power of
　　the LORD,* and the wonderful works he has done.
He gave his decrees to Jacob and established a law for Israel,* which he com-
　　manded them to teach their children;
That the generations to come might know, and the children yet unborn;* that they
　　in their turn might tell it to their children;
So that they might put their trust in God,* and not forget the deeds of God, but
　　keep his commandments;
And not be like their forefathers, a stubborn and rebellious generation,* a genera-
　　tion whose heart was not steadfast.

Psalm 78:3–8

The Refrain
Your love, O LORD, reaches to the heavens,* and your faithfulness to the clouds.

The Small Verse
My help is in the name of the Lord who made heaven and earth and all that is in
　　them. Thanks be to God.

Traditional

The Lord's Prayer

The Prayer Appointed for the Week
Grant me, O Lord, to trust in you with all my heart; for, as you always resist the
　　proud who confide in their own strength, so you never forsake those who
　　make their boast of your mercy; through Jesus Christ our Lord, who lives and
　　reigns with you and the Holy Spirit, one God, now and for ever. *Amen.*✝

The Concluding Prayer of the Church
O God, the source of eternal light: Shed forth your unending day upon all of us
　　who watch for you, that our lips may praise you, our lives may bless you, and
　　our worship may give you glory; through Jesus Christ our Lord. *Amen.*✝

The Vespers Office　　　　　**To Be Observed on the Hour or Half Hour**
Between 5 and 8 p.m.

The Call to Prayer
Let everything that has breath* praise the LORD. Hallelujah!

Psalm 150:6

The Request for Presence
O God, you are my God; eagerly I seek you;* my soul thirsts for you, my flesh
　　faints for you, as in a barren and dry land where there is no water.

Therefore I have gazed upon you in your holy place,* that I might behold your
   power and your glory.

Psalm 63:1–2

The Greeting
Your loving-kindness is better than life itself;* my lips shall give you praise.
So will I bless you as long as I live* and lift up my hands in your Name.

Psalm 63:3–4

The Hymn   *Swing Low, Sweet Chariot*
   Swing low, sweet chariot
   Comin' for to carry me home.

   I looked over Jordan and what did I see,
   Comin' for to carry me home?
   A band of angels comin' after me,
   Comin' for to carry me home.

   Swing low, sweet chariot
   Comin' for to carry me home.

   If you get there before I do
   Comin' for to carry me home.
   Tell all my friends I'm comin' too
   Comin' for to carry me home.

   Swing low, sweet chariot
   Comin' for to carry me home.

   Sometimes I'm up, sometimes I'm down,
   Comin' for to carry me home.
   Yet still my soul feels heavenly bound,
   Comin' for to carry me home.

   Swing low, sweet chariot
   Comin' for to carry me home.
African American Spiritual

The Refrain for the Vespers Lessons
The LORD is my light and my salvation; whom then shall I fear?* the LORD is the
   strength of my life; of whom then shall I be afraid?

Psalm 27:1

The Vespers Psalm   *I Lift Up My Eyes to the Hills*
I lift up my eyes to the hills;* from where is my help to come?
My help comes from the LORD,* the maker of heaven and earth.
He will not let your foot be moved* and he who watches over you will not fall
   asleep.

Behold, he who keeps watch over Israel* shall neither slumber nor sleep;
The LORD himself watches over you;* the LORD is your shade at your right hand,
So that the sun shall not strike you by day,* nor the moon by night.
The LORD shall preserve you from all evil;* it is he who shall keep you safe.
The LORD shall watch over your going out and your coming in,* from this time
   forth for evermore.

Psalm 121

The Refrain
The LORD is my light and my salvation; whom then shall I fear?* the LORD is the
   strength of my life; of whom then shall I be afraid?

The Cry of the Church
O Lamb of God, that takes away the sins of the world, have mercy upon me.
O Lamb of God, that takes away the sins of the world, have mercy upon me.
O Lamb of God, that takes away the sins of the world, grant me your peace.

The Lord's Prayer

The Prayer Appointed for the Week
Grant me, O Lord, to trust in you with all my heart; for, as you always resist the
   proud who confide in their own strength, so you never forsake those who
   make their boast of your mercy; through Jesus Christ our Lord, who lives and
   reigns with you and the Holy Spirit, one God, now and for ever. *Amen.*†

The Concluding Prayer of the Church
Almighty God, who after the creation of the world rested from all your works and
   sanctified a day of rest for all your creatures: Grant that I, putting away all
   earthly anxieties, may be duly prepared for the service of public worship, and
   grant as well that my Sabbath upon earth may be a preparation for the eternal
   rest promised to your people in heaven; through Jesus Christ our Lord. *Amen.*†

❧

The Morning Office   **To Be Observed on the Hour or Half Hour**
                                Between 6 and 9 a.m.

The Call to Prayer
I will sing of mercy and justice;* to you, O LORD, will I sing praises.

Psalm 101:1

The Request for Presence
But as for me, O Lord, I cry to you for help;* in the morning my prayer comes
before you.

Psalm 88:14

The Greeting
Your testimonies are very sure,* and holiness adorns your house, O Lord, for ever
and for evermore.

Psalm 93:6

The Refrain for the Morning Lessons
This is the Lord's doing,* and it is marvelous in our eyes.

Psalm 118:23

A Reading
Jesus taught us, saying: 'No one has gone up to heaven except the one who came
down from heaven, the Son of man; as Moses lifted up the snake in the desert,
so must the Son of man be lifted up so that everyone who believes may have
eternal life in him. For this is how God loved the world: he gave his only Son,
so that everyone who believes in him may not perish but may have eternal life.'

John 3:13–16

The Refrain
This is the Lord's doing,* and it is marvelous in our eyes.

The Morning Psalm   *This God Is Our God For Ever and Ever*
Your praise, like your Name, O God, reaches to the world's end;* your right hand
is full of justice.
Let Mount Zion be glad and the cities of Judah rejoice,* because of your
judgments.
Make the circuit of Zion; walk round about her;* count the number of her towers.
Consider well her bulwarks; examine her strongholds;* that you may tell those
who come after.
This God is our God for ever and ever;* he shall be our guide for evermore.

Psalm 48:9–13

The Refrain
This is the Lord's doing,* and it is marvelous in our eyes.

The Gloria

The Lord's Prayer

The Prayer Appointed for the Week
O God, because without you we are not able to please you, mercifully grant that
your Holy Spirit may in all things direct and rule my heart; through Jesus
Christ our Lord, who lives and reigns with you and the Holy Spirit, one God,
now and for ever. *Amen.*†

The Concluding Prayer of the Church
Lord God, almighty and everlasting Father, you have brought me in safety to this
new day: Preserve me with your mighty power, that I may not fall into sin, nor
be overcome by adversity; and in all I do direct me to the fulfilling of your purpose; through Jesus Christ my Lord. *Amen.*†

The Midday Office **To Be Observed on the Hour or Half Hour**
Between 11 a.m. and 2 p.m.

The Call to Prayer
In the temple of the LORD* all are crying, "Glory!"

Psalm 29:9

The Request for Presence
Fight those who fight me, O LORD;* attack those who are attacking me. . . . say to
my soul, "I am your salvation."

Psalm 35:1, 3

The Greeting
Blessed be the Lord GOD, the God of Israel,* who alone does wondrous deeds!
And blessed be his glorious Name for ever!* and may all the earth be filled with
his glory. Amen. Amen.

Psalm 72:18–19

The Refrain for the Midday Lessons
Blessed be the LORD God of Israel,* from age to age. Amen. Amen.

Psalm 41:13

A Reading
They left Mount Hor by the road to the Sea of Suph, to skirt around Edom. On the
way the people lost patience. They spoke against God and against Moses,
'Why did you bring us out of Egypt to die in the desert? For there is neither
bread nor water here; we are sick of this meager diet.' At this, God sent fiery
serpents among the people; their bite brought death to many in Israel. The people came and said to Moses, 'We have sinned by speaking against YAHWEH and
against you. Intercede for us with YAHWEH to save us from these serpents.'
Moses interceded for the people, and YAHWEH replied, 'Make a fiery serpent
and raise it as a standard. Anyone who is bitten and looks at it will survive.'
Moses then made a serpent out of bronze and raised it as a standard, and anyone who was bitten by a serpent and looked at the bronze serpent survived.

Numbers 21:4–9

The Refrain
Blessed be the LORD God of Israel,* from age to age. Amen. Amen.

The Midday Psalm *He Shall Deliver You from the Daily Pestilence*
He who dwells in the shelter of the Most High,* abides under the shadow of the
Almighty.

He shall say to the Lord,* "You are my refuge and my stronghold, my God in
  whom I put my trust."
He shall deliver you from the snare of the hunter* and from the deadly pestilence.
He shall cover you with his pinions, and you shall find refuge under his wings;*
  his faithfulness shall be a shield and buckler.
You shall not be afraid of any terror by night,* nor of the arrow that flies by day;
Of the plague that stalks in the darkness,* nor of the sickness that lays waste at
  mid-day.
A thousand shall fall at your side and ten thousand at your right hand,* but it shall
  not come near you.
Your eyes have only to behold* to see the reward of the wicked.
Because you have made the Lord your refuge,* and the Most High your
  habitation,
There shall no evil happen to you,* neither shall any plague come near your
  dwelling.

Psalm 91:1–10

The Refrain
Blessed be the Lord God of Israel,* from age to age. Amen. Amen.

The Cry of the Church
Lord, have mercy on us. Christ, have mercy on us. Lord, have mercy on us.

The Lord's Prayer

The Prayer Appointed for the Week
O God, because without you we are not able to please you, mercifully grant that
  your Holy Spirit may in all things direct and rule my heart; through Jesus
  Christ our Lord, who lives and reigns with you and the Holy Spirit, one God,
  now and for ever. *Amen.*†

The Concluding Prayer of the Church
O God, you make me glad with the weekly remembrance of the glorious resurrection of your Son my Lord: Give me this day such blessing through my worship
  of you, that the week to come may be spent in your favor; through Jesus Christ
  our Lord. *Amen.*†

The Vespers Office 　　　　**To Be Observed on the Hour or Half Hour
                                Between 5 and 8 p.m.**

The Call to Prayer
Hallelujah! Praise the Lord from the heavens;* praise him in the heights.

Psalm 148:1

The Request for Presence
You are my helper and my deliverer;* O Lord, do not tarry.

Psalm 70:6

The Greeting

O LORD, I am your servant;* I am your servant and the child of your handmaid;
you have freed me from my bonds.

Psalm 116:14

The Hymn   *Let Us Worship and Bow Down*

O come, let us worship and bow down,
let us kneel before the Lord, our Maker!
For we are the people of his pasture,
and the sheep of his hand.

Do not put your trust in princes,
in mortals, in whom there is no help.
When their breath departs, they return to the earth;
on that very day their plans perish.

Our help is the name of the Lord,
who made heaven and earth.
Great is our Lord, and abundant in power;
his understanding is beyond measure. ❖

The Refrain for the Vespers Lessons

Turn again to your rest, O my soul,* for the LORD has treated you well.

Psalm 116:6

The Vespers Psalm   *Happy Are They All Who Take Refuge in Him*

Why are the nations in an uproar?* Why do the peoples mutter empty threats?
Why do the kings of the earth rise up in revolt, and the princes plot together,*
    against the LORD and against his Anointed?
"Let us break their yoke," they say;* "let us cast off their bonds from us."
He whose throne is in heaven is laughing;* the Lord has them in derision.
Then he speaks to them in his wrath,* and his rage fills them with terror.
"I myself have set my king* upon my holy hill of Zion."
Let me announce the decree of the LORD:* he said to me, "You are my Son; this day
    have I begotten you.
Ask of me, and I will give you the nations for your inheritance* and the ends of the
    earth for your possession.
You shall crush them with an iron rod* and shatter them like a piece of pottery."
And now, you kings, be wise;* be warned, you rulers of the earth.
Submit to the LORD with fear,* and with trembling bow before him;
Lest he be angry and you perish;* for his wrath is quickly kindled.
Happy are they all* who take refuge in him!

Psalm 2

The Refrain

Turn again to your rest, O my soul,* for the LORD has treated you well.

The Gloria

The Lord's Prayer

The Prayer Appointed for the Week
O God, because without you we are not able to please you, mercifully grant that
   your Holy Spirit may in all things direct and rule my heart; through Jesus
   Christ our Lord, who lives and reigns with you and the Holy Spirit, one God,
   now and for ever. *Amen.*†

The Concluding Prayer of the Church
Lord God, whose Son our Savior Jesus Christ, triumphed over the powers of death
   and prepared for us our place in the new Jerusalem: Grant that I, who have this
   day given thanks for his resurrection, may praise you in the City of which he is
   the light, and where he lives and reigns for ever and ever. *Amen.*†

The Morning Office　　　　**To Be Observed on the Hour or Half Hour**
Between 6 and 9 a.m.

The Call to Prayer
Sing to the LORD and bless his Name;* proclaim the good news of his salvation
   from day to day.　Declare his glory among the nations* and his wonders among
   all peoples.

Psalm 96:2–3

The Request for Presence
In the morning, LORD, you hear my voice;* early in the morning I make my appeal
   and watch for you.

Psalm 5:3

The Greeting
Be exalted, O LORD, in your might;* we will sing and praise your power.

Psalm 21:14

The Refrain for the Morning Lessons
Then shall all the trees of the wood shout for joy before the LORD when he comes,*
   when he comes to judge the earth.

A Reading　　　　　　　*Holy Cross Day, celebrated by much of Western
Christianity on September 14, commemorates
the public exhibiting in Jerusalem in 629 a.d.
by the Emperor Heraclius of the supposedly
true cross, after his recovery of it from the
Persians.*

Jesus taught the crowds, saying: 'The light will be with you only a little longer
   now. Go on your way while you have the light, or darkness will overtake you,

and nobody who walks in the dark knows where he is going. While you still
have the light, believe in the light so that you may become the children of
light.' Having said this, Jesus left them and was hidden from their sight.

John 12:35–36

The Refrain
Then shall all the trees of the wood shout for joy before the LORD when he comes,*
when he comes to judge the earth.

The Morning Psalm   *How Good It Is to Sing Praises*
Hallelujah! How good it is to sing praises to our God!* how pleasant it is to honor
him with praise!
The LORD rebuilds Jerusalem;* he gathers the exiles of Israel.
He heals the brokenhearted* and binds up their wounds.
He counts the number of the stars* and calls them all by their names.
Great is our LORD and mighty in power;* there is no limit to his wisdom.
The LORD lifts up the lowly,* but casts the wicked to the ground.
Sing to the LORD with thanksgiving;* make music to our God upon the harp.
He covers the heavens with clouds* and prepares rain for the earth;
He makes grass to grow upon the mountains* and green plants to serve mankind.
He provides food for flocks and herds* and for the young ravens when they cry.
He is not impressed by the might of a horse;* he has no pleasure in the strength of
a man . . .

Psalm 147:1–11

The Refrain
Then shall all the trees of the wood shout for joy before the LORD when he comes,*
when he comes to judge the earth.

The Cry of the Church
Even so come, Lord Jesus!

The Lord's Prayer

The Prayer Appointed for the Week
O God, because without you we are not able to please you, mercifully grant that
your Holy Spirit may in all things direct and rule my heart; through Jesus
Christ our Lord, who lives and reigns with you and the Holy Spirit, one God,
now and for ever. *Amen.*†

The Concluding Prayers of the Church
Lord God, almighty and everlasting Father, you have brought me in safety to this
new day: Preserve me with your mighty power, that I may not fall into sin, nor
be overcome by adversity; and in all I do direct me to the fulfilling of your purpose; through Jesus Christ my Lord. *Amen.*†

Almighty God, whose Son our Savior Jesus Christ was lifted high upon the cross
that he might draw the whole world to himself: Mercifully grant that we who

glory in the mystery of our redemption may have the grace to take up our cross and follow him; who lives and reigns with you and the Holy Spirit, one God, in glory everlasting. *Amen.*

The Midday Office   **To Be Observed on the Hour or Half Hour**
                                                         Between 11 a.m. and 2 p.m.

The Call to Prayer
Sing to the LORD with the harp,* with the harp and the voice of song.
With trumpets and the sound of the horn* shout with joy before the King, the
   LORD.

Psalm 98:6–7

The Request for Presence
Show us the light of your countenance, O God,* and come to us.
based on Psalm 67:1

The Greeting
O LORD, what are we that you should care for us?* mere mortals that you should
   think of us?
We are like a puff of wind;* our days are like a passing shadow.

Psalm 144:3–4

The Refrain for the Midday Lessons
Shout with joy to the LORD, all you lands;* lift up your voice, rejoice, and sing.
Psalm 98:5

A Reading
Make your own the mind of Christ Jesus: Who, being in the form of God, did not count equality with God something to be grasped. But he emptied himself, taking the form of a slave, becoming as human beings are; and being in every way like a human being, he was humbler yet, even to accepting death, death on a cross. And for this God raised him high, and gave him the name which is above all other names; so that *all beings* in the heavens, on earth and in the underworld, *should bend the knee* at the name of Jesus and that *every tongue should acknowledge* Jesus Christ as Lord, to the glory of God the Father.

Philippians 2:5–11

The Refrain
Shout with joy to the LORD, all you lands;* lift up your voice, rejoice, and sing.

The Midday Psalm   *He Has Won for Himself the Victory*
Sing to the LORD a new song,* for he has done marvelous things.
With his right hand and his holy arm* has he won for himself the victory.
The LORD has made known his victory;* his righteousness has he openly shown in
   the sight of the nations.

He remembers his mercy and faithfulness to the house of Israel,* and all the ends
of the earth have seen the victory of our God.

Psalm 98:1–4

The Refrain
Shout with joy to the Lord, all you lands;* lift up your voice, rejoice, and sing.

The Gloria

The Lord's Prayer

The Prayer Appointed for the Week
O God, because without you we are not able to please you, mercifully grant that
your Holy Spirit may in all things direct and rule my heart; through Jesus
Christ our Lord, who lives and reigns with you and the Holy Spirit, one God,
now and for ever. *Amen.*†

The Concluding Prayer of the Church
Almighty and everlasting God, who willed that our Savior should take upon Him
our flesh and suffer death upon the Cross, that all mankind should follow the
example of His great humility, mercifully grant that we may both follow the
example of His patience and also be made partakers of His resurrection.
Through the same Jesus Christ. *Amen.*

adapted from The Short Breviary

The Vespers Office   **To Be Observed on the Hour or Half Hour
Between 5 and 8 p.m.**

The Call to Prayer
Sing to the Lord a new song;* sing to the Lord, all the whole earth.
For great is the Lord and greatly to be praised;* he is more to be feared than all gods.

Psalm 96:1, 4

The Request for Presence
Give ear, O Lord, to my prayer,* and attend to the voice of my supplications.

Psalm 86:6

The Greeting
Your way, O God, is holy;* who is so great a god as our God?

Psalm 77:13

The Hymn

Lofty Tree, bend down your branches   Tree which solely was found worthy
To embrace your sacred load: Earth's great Victim to sustain,
Oh, relax the native tension   Harbor from the raging tempest,
Of that all too rigid wood;   Ark, that saved the world again,
Gently, gently bear the members   Tree with sacred Blood anointed
Of your dying King and God.   Of the Lamb for sinners slain.

Honor, blessing everlasting
To the immortal Deity:
To the Father, Son and Spirit
Equal praises ever be:
Glory through the earth and heaven
To Trinity in Unity. Amen.

adapted from The Short Breviary

The Refrain for the Vespers Lessons

He will judge the world with righteousness* and the peoples with his truth.

Psalm 96:13

The Vespers Psalm   *What Is Man That You Should Be Mindful of Him?*

O Lord our Governor,* how exalted is your Name in all the world!

Out of the mouths of infants and children* your majesty is praised above the heavens.

You have set up a stronghold against your adversaries,* to quell the enemy and the avenger.

When I consider your heavens, the work of your fingers,* the moon and the stars you have set in their courses,

What is man that you should be mindful of him?* the son of man that you should seek him out?

You have made him but little lower than the angels;* you adorn him with glory and honor;

You give him mastery over the works of your hands;* you put all things under his feet:

All sheep and oxen,* even the wild beasts of the field,

The birds of the air, the fish of the sea,* and whatsoever walks in the paths of the sea.

O Lord our Governor,* how exalted is your Name in all the world!

Psalm 8

The Refrain

He will judge the world with righteousness* and the peoples with his truth.

The Gloria

The Lord's Prayer

The Prayer Appointed for the Week

O God, because without you we are not able to please you, mercifully grant that your Holy Spirit may in all things direct and rule my heart; through Jesus Christ our Lord, who lives and reigns with you and the Holy Spirit, one God, now and for ever. *Amen.*†

The Concluding Prayer of the Church

Almighty God, whose beloved Son willingly endured the agony and shame of the

cross for our redemption: Give me courage to take up my cross and follow him;
who lives and reigns with you and the Holy Spirit, one God, now and for ever.
Amen.†

The Morning Office   **To Be Observed on the Hour or Half Hour**
                                           Between 6 and 9 a.m.

The Call to Prayer
Come, let us sing to the Lord;* let us shout for joy to the Rock of our salvation.
Let us come before his presence with thanksgiving* and raise a loud shout to him
    with psalms.

Psalm 95:1–2

The Request for Presence
Show us the light of your countenance, O God,* and come to us.
based on Psalm 67:1

The Greeting
To you I lift up my eyes,* to you enthroned in the heavens.
As the eyes of servants look to the hand of their masters,* and the eyes of a maid to
    the hand of her mistress,
So our eyes look to the Lord our God,* until he shows us his mercy.

Psalm 123:1–3

The Refrain for the Morning Lessons
I will bear witness that the Lord is righteous;* I will praise the Name of the Lord
    Most High.

Psalm 7:18

A Reading
He then took a little child, whom set him among them and embraced, and he said
    to them, 'Anyone who welcomes a little child such as this in my name, wel-
    comes me; and anyone who welcomes me, welcomes not me but the one who
    sent me.'

Mark 9:36–37

The Refrain
I will bear witness that the Lord is righteous;* I will praise the Name of the Lord
    Most High.

The Morning Psalm   *Sing Praises to His Name*
Sing to God, sing praises to his Name; exalt him who rides upon the heavens;*
    Yahweh is his Name, rejoice before him!
Father of orphans, defender of widows,* God in his holy habitation!

Psalm 68:4–5

The Refrain
I will bear witness that the LORD is righteous;* I will praise the Name of the LORD
  Most High.

The Small Verse
Keep me, Lord, as the apple of your eye and carry me under the shadow of your
  wings.

Traditional

The Lord's Prayer

The Prayer Appointed for the Week
O God, because without you we are not able to please you, mercifully grant that
  your Holy Spirit may in all things direct and rule my heart; through Jesus
  Christ our Lord, who lives and reigns with you and the Holy Spirit, one God,
  now and for ever. *Amen.*†

The Concluding Prayer of the Church
Lord God, almighty and everlasting Father, you have brought me in safety to this
  new day: Preserve me with your mighty power, that I may not fall into sin, nor
  be overcome by adversity; and in all I do direct me to the fulfilling of your purpose; through Jesus Christ my Lord. *Amen.*†

The Midday Office   **To Be Observed on the Hour or Half Hour**
Between 11 a.m. and 2 p.m.

The Call to Prayer
Open my lips, O Lord,* and my mouth shall proclaim your praise.

Psalm 51:16

The Request for Presence
You are my helper and my deliverer;* do not tarry, O my God.

Psalm 40:19

The Greeting
Hosanna, LORD, hosanna!* LORD, send us now success.
Blessed is he who comes in the name of the Lord;* we bless you from the house of
  the LORD.

Psalm 118:25–26

The Refrain for the Midday Lessons
. . . You hold me by my right hand.
You will guide me by your counsel,* and afterwards receive me with glory.

Psalm 73:23–24

A Reading
But as for me, it is out of the question that I should boast at all, except of the cross
  of our Lord Jesus Christ, through whom the world has been crucified to me,

and I to the world. It is not being circumcised or uncircumcised that matters; but what matters is a new creation. Peace and mercy to all who follow this as their rule and to the Israel of God. After this let no one trouble me; I carry branded on my body the marks of Jesus. The grace of our Lord Jesus Christ be with your spirit, my brothers. Amen.

Galatians 6:14–18

The Refrain
. . . You hold me by my right hand.
You will guide me by your counsel,* and afterwards receive me with glory.

The Midday Psalm   *You Are My Crag and My Stronghold*
In you, O Lord, have I taken refuge;* let me never be ashamed.
In your righteousness, deliver me and set me free;* incline your ear to me and save me.
Be my strong rock, a castle to keep me safe;* you are my crag and my stronghold.

Psalm 71:1–3

The Refrain
. . . You hold me by my right hand.
You will guide me by your counsel,* and afterwards receive me with glory.

The Small Verse
My help is in the Name of the Lord who made the heavens and the earth. What then shall I fear, of what shall I be afraid?

Traditional

The Lord's Prayer

The Prayer Appointed for the Week
O God, because without you we are not able to please you, mercifully grant that your Holy Spirit may in all things direct and rule my heart; through Jesus Christ our Lord, who lives and reigns with you and the Holy Spirit, one God, now and for ever. *Amen.*†

The Concluding Prayer of the Church
Direct me, O Lord, in all my doings with your most gracious favor, and further me with your continual help; that in all my work begun, continued, and ended in you, I may glorify your holy name, and finally, by your mercy, obtain everlasting life; through Jesus Christ my Lord. *Amen.*

The Vespers Office   **To Be Observed on the Hour or Half Hour
Between 5 and 8 p.m.**

The Call to Prayer
Praise God, from whom all blessings flow; praise him, all creatures here below; praise him above, you heavenly hosts; praise Father, Son and Holy Ghost.

Doxology

The Request for Presence

Show your goodness, O LORD, to those who are good* and to those who are true of
heart.

Psalm 125:4

The Greeting

Out of the mouths of infants and children* your majesty is praised above the
heavens.

Psalm 8:2

The Hymn   *Let Us Kneel Before the Lord*

Our help is in the name of the Lord,
who made heaven and earth.
Great is our Lord, and abundant in power;
his understanding is beyond measure.

His delight is not in the strength of the horse,
nor his pleasure in the speed of the runner;
But the Lord takes pleasure in those who fear him,
in those who hope in his steadfast love.

O come, let us worship and bow down,
let us kneel before the Lord, our Maker!
For we are the people of his pasture,
and the sheep of his hand. ❖

The Refrain for the Vespers Lessons

We have heard with our ears, O God, our forefathers have told us,* the deeds you
did in their days, in the days of old.

Psalm 44:1

The Vespers Psalm   *The Just Shall See His Face*

The LORD is in his holy temple;* the LORD's throne is in heaven.
His eyes behold the inhabited world;* his piercing eye weighs our worth.
The LORD weighs the righteous as well as the wicked,* but those who delight in
violence he abhors.
For the LORD is righteous; he delights in righteous deeds;* and the just shall see his
face.

Psalm 11:4ff

The Refrain

We have heard with our ears, O God, our forefathers have told us,* the deeds you
did in their days, in the days of old.

The Gloria

The Lord's Prayer

The Prayer Appointed for the Week

O God, because without you we are not able to please you, mercifully grant that your Holy Spirit may in all things direct and rule my heart; through Jesus Christ our Lord, who lives and reigns with you and the Holy Spirit, one God, now and for ever. *Amen.†*

The Concluding Prayer of the Church

Almighty and eternal God, ruler of all things in heaven and earth: Mercifully accept my prayer, and strengthen me to do your will; through Jesus Christ our Lord. *Amen.†*

The Morning Office   **To Be Observed on the Hour or Half Hour Between 6 and 9 a.m.**

The Call to Prayer

Let us make a vow to the LORD our God and keep it;* let all around him bring gifts to him who is worthy to be feared.

Psalm 76:11

The Request for Presence

Let my cry come before you, O LORD;* give me understanding, according to your word.

Let my supplication come before you;* deliver me, according to your promise.

Psalm 119:169–70

The Greeting

I will offer you a freewill sacrifice* and praise your Name, O LORD, for it is good.

Psalm 54:6

The Refrain for the Morning Lessons

How sweet are your words to my taste!* they are sweeter than honey to my mouth.

Psalm 119:103

A Reading

Jesus taught us, saying: 'In truth I tell you, there is no one who has left house, brothers, sisters, father, children or land for my sake and for the sake of the gospel who will not receive a hundred times as much, houses, brothers, sisters, mothers, children and land—and persecutions too—now in this present time and, in the world to come, eternal life. Many who are first will be last, and the last, first.'

Mark 10:29–31

The Refrain

How sweet are your words to my taste!* they are sweeter than honey to my mouth.

The Morning Psalm   *I Shall Not Die, But Live*

The LORD is my strength and my song,* and he has become my salvation.

There is a sound of exultation and victory* in the tents of the righteous:
"The right hand of the LORD has triumphed!* the right hand of the LORD is exalted!
  the right hand of the LORD has triumphed!"
I shall not die, but live,* and declare the works of the LORD.

Psalm 118:14–17

The Refrain
How sweet are your words to my taste!* they are sweeter than honey to my mouth.

The Cry of the Church
O God, come to my assistance! O Lord, make haste to help me!

The Lord's Prayer

The Prayer Appointed for the Week
O God, because without you we are not able to please you, mercifully grant that
  your Holy Spirit may in all things direct and rule my heart; through Jesus
  Christ our Lord, who lives and reigns with you and the Holy Spirit, one God,
  now and for ever. *Amen.*†

The Concluding Prayer of the Church
Lord God, almighty and everlasting Father, you have brought me in safety to this
  new day: Preserve me with your mighty power, that I may not fall into sin, nor
  be overcome by adversity; and in all I do direct me to the fulfilling of your purpose; through Jesus Christ my Lord. *Amen.*†

The Midday Office   **To Be Observed on the Hour or Half Hour
                                Between 11 a.m. and 2 p.m.**

The Call to Prayer
Let Israel rejoice in his Maker;* let the children of Zion be joyful in their King.

Psalm 149:2

The Request for Presence
Make me understand the way of your commandments,* that I may meditate on
  your marvelous works.

Psalm 119:27

The Greeting
How deep I find your thoughts, O God!* how great is the sum of them!

Psalm 139:16

The Refrain for the Midday Lessons
Keep watch over my life, for I am faithful;* save your servant whose trust is in
  you.

based on Psalm 86:2

A Reading
Do you not realize that your body is the temple of the Holy Spirit, who is in you

and whom you received from God? You are not your own property, then; you have been bought at a price. So use your body for the glory of God.

I Corinthians 6:19–20

The Refrain
Keep watch over my life, for I am faithful;* save your servant whose trust is in you.

The Midday Psalm   *We Are His*
Be joyful in the Lord, all you lands;* serve the Lord with gladness and come before his presence with a song.

Know this: The Lord himself is God;* he himself has made us, and we are his; we are his people and the sheep of his pasture.

Enter his gates with thanksgiving; go into his courts with praise;* give thanks to him and call upon his Name.

For the Lord is good; his mercy is everlasting;* and his faithfulness endures from age to age.

Psalm 100:1–4

The Refrain
Keep watch over my life, for I am faithful;* save your servant whose trust is in you.

The Cry of the Church
Lord, have mercy on us. Christ, have mercy on us. Lord, have mercy on us.

The Lord's Prayer

The Prayer Appointed for the Week
O God, because without you we are not able to please you, mercifully grant that your Holy Spirit may in all things direct and rule my heart; through Jesus Christ our Lord, who lives and reigns with you and the Holy Spirit, one God, now and for ever. *Amen.*†

The Concluding Prayer of the Church
O Lord my God, to you and your service I devote myself, body, soul, and spirit. Fill my memory with the record of your mighty works; enlighten my understanding with the light of your Holy Spirit; and may all the desires of my heart and will center in what you would have me do. Make me an instrument of your salvation for the people entrusted to my care, and let me by my life and speaking set forth your true and living Word. Be always with me in carrying out the duties of my vocation; in praises heighten my love and gratitude; in speaking of You give me readiness of thought and expression; and grant that, by the clearness and brightness of your holy Word, all the world may be drawn to your blessed kingdom. All this I ask for the sake of your Son my Savior Jesus Christ. *Amen.*†

The Vespers Office	**To Be Observed on the Hour or Half Hour**
	Between 5 and 8 p.m.

The Call to Prayer

Praise the LORD, all you nations;* laud him, all you peoples.
For his loving-kindness toward us is great,* and the faithfulness of the LORD
    endures for ever. Hallelujah!

Psalm 117

The Request for Presence

Gladden the soul of your servant,* for to you, O LORD, I lift up my soul.

Psalm 86:4

The Greeting

One generation shall praise your works to another* and shall declare your power.

Psalm 145:4

The Hymn   *That Old-Time Religion*

Gimme that old-time religion,   It'll do when I'm dying.
Gimme that old-time religion,   It'll do when I'm dying.
Gimme that old-time religion,   It'll do when I'm dying.
It's good enough for me.   And it's good enough for me.

It was good for all our mothers.   It'll take us all to heaven.
It was good for all our mothers.   It'll take us all to heaven.
It was good for all our mothers.   It'll take us all to heaven.
And it's good enough for me.   And it's good enough for me.

Makes me love everybody.   Yes, Lord, it's that old-time religion,
Makes me love everybody.   And it's good enough for me.
Makes me love everybody.   *Traditional*
And it's good enough for me.

It has saved our fathers.
It has saved our fathers.
It has saved our fathers.
And it's good enough for me.

The Refrain for the Vespers Lessons

Happy are they all who fear the LORD,* and who follow in his ways!

Psalm 128:1

The Vespers Psalm   *Life For Evermore*

Oh, how good and pleasant it is,* when brethren live together in unity!
It is like fine oil upon the head* that runs down upon the beard,
Upon the beard of Aaron,* and runs down upon the collar of his robe.

It is like the dew of Hermon* that falls upon the hills of Zion.
For there the LORD has ordained the blessing:* life for evermore.

Psalm 133

The Refrain
Happy are they all who fear the LORD,* and who follow in his ways!

The Gloria

The Lord's Prayer

The Prayer Appointed for the Week
O God, because without you we are not able to please you, mercifully grant that
your Holy Spirit may in all things direct and rule my heart; through Jesus
Christ our Lord, who lives and reigns with you and the Holy Spirit, one God,
now and for ever. *Amen.*†

The Concluding Prayer of the Church
May Almighty God grant me a peaceful night and a perfect end. *Amen.*

The Morning Office

**To Be Observed on the Hour or Half Hour
Between 6 and 9 a.m.**

The Call to Prayer
Come, let us bow down, and bend the knee,* and kneel before the LORD our
Maker.
For he is our God,* and we are the people of his pasture and the sheep of his
hand . . .

Psalm 95:6–7

The Request for Presence
So teach us to number our days* that we may apply our hearts to wisdom.

Psalm 90:12

The Greeting
My God, my rock in whom I put my trust,* my shield, the horn of my salvation,
and my refuge; you are worthy of praise.

Psalm 18:2

The Refrain for the Morning Lessons
My eyes are upon the faithful in the land, that they may dwell with me . . .

Psalm 101:6

A Reading
Jesus taught us, saying: 'And so I tell you this: use money, tainted as it is, to win
you friends, and thus make sure that when it fails you, they will welcome you
into eternal dwellings. Anyone who is trustworthy in little things is trustworthy in great; anyone who is dishonest in little things is dishonest in great. If

then you are not trustworthy with money, that tainted thing, who will trust you with genuine riches? And if you are not trustworthy with what is not yours, who will give you what is your very own? No servant can be the slave of two masters: he will either hate the first and love the second, or be attached to the first and despise the second. You cannot be the slave of both God and of money.'

Luke 16:9–13

The Refrain

My eyes are upon the faithful in the land, that they may dwell with me . . .

The Morning Psalm   *Our Days Are Like the Grass*

Our days are like the grass;* we flourish like a flower of the field;
When the wind goes over it, it is gone,* and its place shall know it no more.
But the merciful goodness of the LORD endures for ever on those who fear him,*
  and his righteousness on children's children;
On those who keep his covenant* and remember his commandments and do
  them.

Psalm 103:15–18

The Refrain

My eyes are upon the faithful in the land, that they may dwell with me . . .

The Cry of the Church

O God, come to my assistance! O Lord, make haste to help me!

The Lord's Prayer

The Prayer Appointed for the Week

O God, because without you we are not able to please you, mercifully grant that
  your Holy Spirit may in all things direct and rule my heart; through Jesus
  Christ our Lord, who lives and reigns with you and the Holy Spirit, one God,
  now and for ever. *Amen.*†

The Concluding Prayer of the Church

Lord God, almighty and everlasting Father, you have brought me in safety to this
  new day: Preserve me with your mighty power, that I may not fall into sin, nor
  be overcome by adversity; and in all I do direct me to the fulfilling of your purpose; through Jesus Christ my Lord. *Amen.*†

The Midday Office   **To Be Observed on the Hour or Half Hour**
Between 11 a.m. and 2 p.m.

The Call to Prayer

Glory in his holy Name;* let the hearts of those who seek the LORD rejoice.

Psalm 105:3

The Request for Presence
Let your compassion come to me, that I may live,* for your law is my delight.

Psalm 119:77

The Greeting
Your righteousness, O God, reaches to the heavens;* you have done great things;
who is like you, O God?

Psalm 71:19

The Refrain for the Midday Lessons
"I will instruct you and teach you in the way that you should go;* I will guide you
with my eye. Do not be like horse or mule, which have no understanding;*
who must be fitted with bit and bridle, or else they will not stay near you."

Psalm 32:9–10

A Reading
Thus says YAHWEH, 'Let the sage boast no more of wisdom, nor the valiant of
valor, nor the wealthy of riches! But let anyone who wants to boast, boast of
this: of understanding and knowing me. For I am YAHWEH, who acts with faithful love, justice and uprightness on earth; yes, these are what please me'—
YAHWEH declares.

Jeremiah 9:22–24

The Refrain
"I will instruct you and teach you in the way that you should go;* I will guide you
with my eye. Do not be like horse or mule, which have no understanding;*
who must be fitted with bit and bridle, or else they will not stay near you."

The Midday Psalm   *Come, Children, and Listen to Me*
The young lions lack and suffer hunger,* but those who seek the LORD lack
nothing that is good.
Come, children, and listen to me;* I will teach you the fear of the LORD.
Who among you loves life* and desires long life to enjoy prosperity?
Keep your tongue from evil-speaking* and your lips from lying words.
Turn from evil and do good;* seek peace and pursue it.

Psalm 34:10–14

The Refrain
"I will instruct you and teach you in the way that you should go;* I will guide you
with my eye. Do not be like horse or mule, which have no understanding;*
who must be fitted with bit and bridle, or else they will not stay near you."

The Cry of the Church
Lord, have mercy on us. Christ, have mercy on us. Lord, have mercy on us.

The Lord's Prayer

The Prayer Appointed for the Week
O God, because without you we are not able to please you, mercifully grant that

your Holy Spirit may in all things direct and rule my heart; through Jesus
Christ our Lord, who lives and reigns with you and the Holy Spirit, one God,
now and for ever. *Amen.*†

The Concluding Prayer of the Church

Open, Lord my eyes that I may see. Open, Lord, my ears that I may hear. Open,
Lord, my heart and my mind that I may understand. So shall I turn to you and
be healed.

Traditional

The Vespers Office To Be Observed on the Hour or Half Hour Between 5 and 8 p.m.

The Call to Prayer

Blessed be the LORD, the God of Israel, from everlasting and to everlasting;* and
let all the people say, "Amen!" Hallelujah!

Psalm 106:48

The Request for Presence

Send forth your strength, O God;* establish, O God, what you have wrought for us.

Psalm 68:28

The Greeting

My heart is firmly fixed, O God, my heart is fixed;* I will sing and make melody.

Psalm 57:7

The Hymn *All Nature's Works His Praise Declare*

All nature's works His praise declare,
to Whom they all belong;
There is a voice in every star,
in every breeze a song.
Sweet music fills the world abroad
with strains of love and power;
The stormy sea sings praise to God,
the thunder and the shower.

To God the tribes of ocean cry,
and birds upon the wing;
To God the powers that dwell on high
their tuneful tribute bring.
Like them, let us the throne surround,
with them the chorus raise,
While instruments of loftier sound
assist our feeble praise.

Great God, to Thee we consecrate
our voices and our skill;
We bid the pealing organ wait
to speak alone Thy will.
Lord, while the music round us floats
may earth-born passions die;
O grant its rich and swelling notes
may lift our souls on high!

Henry Ware, Jr.

The Refrain for the Vespers Lessons
But I am like a green olive tree in the house of God;* I trust in the mercy of God for
ever and ever.
I will give you thanks for what you have done* and declare the goodness of your
Name in the presence of the godly.

Psalm 52:8–9

The Vespers Psalm   ***Bless the*** L**ORD**, ***All You Servants of the*** L**ORD**
Behold now, bless the LORD, all you servants of the LORD,* you that stand by night
in the house of the LORD.
Lift up your hands in the holy place and bless the LORD;* the LORD who made
heaven and earth bless you out of Zion.

Psalm 134

The Refrain
But I am like a green olive tree in the house of God;* I trust in the mercy of God for
ever and ever.
I will give you thanks for what you have done* and declare the goodness of your
Name in the presence of the godly.

The Cry of the Church
Even so, come Lord Jesus!

The Lord's Prayer

The Prayer Appointed for the Week
O God, because without you we are not able to please you, mercifully grant that
your Holy Spirit may in all things direct and rule my heart; through Jesus
Christ our Lord, who lives and reigns with you and the Holy Spirit, one God,
now and for ever. *Amen.*†

The Concluding Prayer of the Church
Almighty God, whose loving hand has given me all that I possess: Grant me grace
that I may honor you with my substance, and, remembering the account which
I must one day give, may be a faithful steward of your bounty, through Jesus
Christ our Lord. *Amen.*†

The Morning Office   **To Be Observed on the Hour or Half Hour**
Between 6 and 9 a.m.

The Call to Prayer
Search for the LORD and his strength;* continually seek his face.

Psalm 105:4

The Request for Presence
O Lamb of God, that takes away the sins of the world, have mercy upon me.
O Lamb of God, that takes away the sins of the world, have mercy upon me.
O Lamb of God, that takes away the sins of the world, grant me your peace.

The Greeting
O God, you know my foolishness,* and my faults are not hidden from you.

Psalm 69:6

The Refrain for the Morning Lessons
Our sins are stronger than we are,* but you will blot them out.

Psalm 65:3

A Reading
Jesus taught us, saying: 'No one lights a lamp and puts it in some hidden place or
under a tub; they put it on the lamp-stand so that people may see the light
when they come in. The lamp of the body is your eye. When your eye is clear,
your whole body, too, is filled with light; but when it is diseased your body,
too, will be darkened. See to it then that the light inside you is not darkness. If,
therefore, your whole body is filled with light, and not darkened at all, it will
be light entirely, as when the lamp shines on you with its rays.'

Luke 11:33–36

The Refrain
Our sins are stronger than we are,* but you will blot them out.

The Morning Psalm   ***Against You Only Have I Sinned***
Have mercy on me, O God, according to your loving-kindness;* in your great
compassion blot out my offenses.
Wash me through and through from my wickedness* and cleanse me from my sin.
For I know my transgressions,* and my sin is ever before me.
Against you only have I sinned* and done what is evil in your sight.
And so you are justified when you speak* and upright in your judgment.

Psalm 51:1–5

The Refrain
Our sins are stronger than we are,* but you will blot them out.

The Cry of the Church
O God, come to my assistance! O Lord, make haste to help me!

The Lord's Prayer

The Prayer Appointed for the Week
O God, because without you we are not able to please you, mercifully grant that
your Holy Spirit may in all things direct and rule my heart; through Jesus
Christ our Lord, who lives and reigns with you and the Holy Spirit, one God,
now and for ever. *Amen.*†

The Concluding Prayer of the Church
Lord God, almighty and everlasting Father, you have brought me in safety to this
new day: Preserve me with your mighty power, that I may not fall into sin, nor
be overcome by adversity; and in all I do direct me to the fulfilling of your purpose; through Jesus Christ my Lord. *Amen.*†

The Midday Office   To Be Observed on the Hour or Half Hour
Between 11 a.m. and 2 p.m.

The Call to Prayer
Bless God in the congregation;* bless the LORD, you that are of the fountain of
Israel.

Psalm 68:26

The Request for Presence
Accept, O LORD, the willing tribute of my lips,* and teach me your judgments.

Psalm 119:108

The Greeting
Let the words of my mouth and the meditation of my heart be acceptable in your
sight,* O LORD, my strength and my redeemer.

Psalm 19:14

The Refrain for the Midday Lessons
Hallelujah! Happy are they who fear the Lord* and have great delight in his
commandments.

Psalm 112:1

A Reading   *A Song of Baruch*
She is the book of God's commandments, the Law that stands for ever; those who
keep her shall live, those who desert her shall die. Turn back, Jacob, seize her,
in her radiance make your way to light: do not yield your glory to another,
your privilege to a people not your own. Israel, blessed are we: what pleases
God has been revealed to us.

Baruch 4:1–4

The Refrain
Hallelujah! Happy are they who fear the Lord* and have great delight in his
commandments.

The Midday Psalm   *Offer to God a Sacrifice of Thanksgiving*
Hear, O my people, and I will speak: "O Israel, I will bear witness against you;* for
I am God, your God.
I do not accuse you because of your sacrifices;* your offerings are always before me.
I will take no bull-calf from your stalls,* nor he-goats out of your pens;
For all the beasts of the forest are mine,* the herds in their thousands upon the
hills.
I know every bird in the sky,* and the creatures of the fields are in my sight.
If I were hungry, I would not tell you,* for the whole world is mine and all that is
in it.
Do you think I eat the flesh of bulls,* or drink the blood of goats?

Offer to God a sacrifice of thanksgiving* and make good your vows to the Most
   High.
Call upon me in the day of trouble;* I will deliver you, and you shall honor me."

Psalm 50:7–15

The Refrain
Hallelujah! Happy are they who fear the Lord* and have great delight in his commandments.

The Cry of the Church
O Lord, hear my prayer and let my cry come unto you. Thanks be to God.

THE SHORT BREVIARY

The Lord's Prayer

The Prayer Appointed for the Week
O God, because without you we are not able to please you, mercifully grant that
   your Holy Spirit may in all things direct and rule my heart; through Jesus
   Christ our Lord, who lives and reigns with you and the Holy Spirit, one God,
   now and for ever. *Amen.*†

The Concluding Prayer of the Church
Lord Jesus Christ, by your death you took away the sting of death: Grant me to so
   follow in faith where you have led the way, that I may at length fall asleep
   peacefully in you and wake in your likeness; for your tender mercies' sake.
   Amen.†

The Vespers Office   **To Be Observed on the Hour or Half Hour**
                                        Between 5 and 8 p.m.

The Call to Prayer
Taste and see that the LORD is good;* happy are they who trust in him!

Psalm 34:8

The Request for Presence
Turn to me and have pity on me . . .*
The sorrows of my heart have increased . . .*
Look upon my adversity and misery* and forgive me all my sin.

Psalm 25:15–17

The Greeting
It is a good thing to give thanks to the LORD,* and to sing praises to your Name, O
   Most High;
To tell of your loving-kindness early in the morning* and of your faithfulness in
   the night season . . .

Psalm 92:1–2

The Hymn　　　　　　　*What a Friend We Have in Jesus*

What a friend we have in Jesus,	Are we weak and heavy laden,
All our sins and griefs to bear!	Cumbered with a load of care?
What a privilege to carry	Precious Savior, still our refuge—
Everything to God in Prayer!	Take it to the Lord in prayer!
O what peace we often forfeit,	Do your friends despise, forsake you?
O what needless pain we bear,	Take it to the Lord in prayer!
All because we do not carry	In his arms he'll take and shield you,
Everything to God in prayer!	You will find your solace there.

Joseph Scriven

The Refrain for the Vespers Lessons

When I was in trouble, I called to the LORD;* I called to the LORD, and he
answered me.

Psalm 120:1

The Vespers Psalm　　　　　　*Our Help Is in the Name of the LORD*

If the LORD had not been on our side,* let Israel now say;
If the LORD had not been on our side,* when enemies rose up against us;
Then would they have swallowed us up alive* in their fierce anger toward us;
Then would the waters have overwhelmed us* and the torrent gone over us;
Then would the raging waters* have gone right over us.
Blessed be the LORD!* he has not given us over to be a prey for their teeth.
We have escaped like a bird from the snare of the fowler;* the snare is broken, and
we have escaped.
Our help is in the Name of the LORD,* the maker of heaven and earth.

Psalm 124

The Refrain

When I was in trouble, I called to the LORD;* I called to the LORD, and he
answered me.

The Cry of the Church

Be, Lord, my helper and forsake me not. Do not despise me, O God, my savior.

THE SHORT BREVIARY

The Lord's Prayer

The Prayer Appointed for the Week

O God, because without you we are not able to please you, mercifully grant that
your Holy Spirit may in all things direct and rule my heart; through Jesus
Christ our Lord, who lives and reigns with you and the Holy Spirit, one God,
now and for ever. *Amen.*†

The Concluding Prayers of the Church

Almighty God, who has promised to hear the petitions of those who ask in your
Son's Name: I beseech you mercifully to incline your ear to me who have made
my prayers and supplications to you; and grant that those things which I have

faithfully asked according to your will, I may effectually obtain, to the relief of my necessity, and to the setting forth of your glory; through Jesus Christ my Lord. *Amen.*✝

May the souls of the faithful departed, through the mercy of God, rest in eternal peace. *Amen.*

The Morning Office

To Be Observed on the Hour or Half Hour Between 6 and 9 a.m.

The Call to Prayer
Bless the LORD, you angels of his, you mighty ones who do his bidding,* and hearken to the voice of his word.
Bless the LORD, all you his hosts,* you ministers of his who do his will.
Bless the LORD, all you works of his, in all places of his dominion;* bless the LORD, O my soul.

Psalm 103:20–22

The Request for Presence
Show me the light of your countenance, O God,* and come to me.

based on Psalm 67:1

The Greeting
As the deer longs for the water-brooks,* so longs my soul for you, O God.

Psalm 42:1

The Refrain for the Morning Lessons
The same stone which the builders rejected* has become the chief cornerstone.
This is the LORD's doing,* and it is marvelous in our eyes.

Psalm 118:22–23

A Reading
Jesus taught us, saying: 'In truth I tell you, if you do not eat the flesh of the Son of man and drink his blood, you have no life in you. Anyone who does eat my flesh and drink my blood has eternal life, and I shall raise that person up on the last day. For my flesh is real food and my blood is real drink. Whoever eats my flesh and drinks my blood lives in me and I live in that person. As the living Father sent me, and I draw life from the Father, so whoever eats me will draw life from me. This is the bread which has come down from heaven; it is not like the bread our ancestors ate: they are dead, but anyone who eats this bread will live for ever.'

John 6:53–58

The Refrain
The same stone which the builders rejected* has become the chief cornerstone.
This is the LORD's doing,* and it is marvelous in our eyes.

The Morning Psalm   *I Will Establish His Throne as the Days of Heaven*

You spoke once in a vision and said to your faithful people:* "I have set the crown
　　upon a warrior and have exalted one chosen out of the people.
I have found David my servant;* with my holy oil have I anointed him.
My hand will hold him fast* and my arm will make him strong.
No enemy shall deceive him,* nor any wicked man bring him down.
I will crush his foes before him* and strike down those who hate him.
My faithfulness and love shall be with him,* and he shall be victorious through
　　my Name.
I shall make his dominion extend* from the Great Sea to the River.
He will say to me, 'You are my Father,* my God, and the rock of my salvation.'
I will make him my firstborn* and higher than the kings of the earth.
I will keep my love for him for ever,* and my covenant will stand firm for him.
I will establish his line for ever* and his throne as the days of heaven."

Psalm 89:19–29

The Refrain

The same stone which the builders rejected* has become the chief cornerstone.
This is the LORD's doing,* and it is marvelous in our eyes.

The Gloria

The Lord's Prayer

The Prayer Appointed for the Week

O God, because without you we are not able to please you, mercifully grant that
　　your Holy Spirit may in all things direct and rule my heart; through Jesus
　　Christ our Lord, who lives and reigns with you and the Holy Spirit, one God,
　　now and for ever. *Amen.*†

The Concluding Prayer of the Church

Lord God, almighty and everlasting Father, you have brought me in safety to this
　　new day: Preserve me with your mighty power, that I may not fall into sin, nor
　　be overcome by adversity; and in all I do direct me to the fulfilling of your pur-
　　pose; through Jesus Christ my Lord. *Amen.*†

The Midday Office   **To Be Observed on the Hour or Half Hour**
Between 11 a.m. and 2 p.m.

The Call to Prayer

Be strong and let your heart take courage,* all you who wait for the LORD.

Psalm 31:24

The Request for Presence

Give ear to my words, O LORD;* consider my meditation.
Hearken to my cry for help, my King and my God,* for I make my prayer to you.

Psalm 5:1–2

The Greeting

    You are God; we praise you;
    You are the Lord: we acclaim you;
    You are the eternal Father:
    All creation worships you.
    To you all angels, all powers of heaven,
    Cherubim and Seraphim, sing in endless praise:
    Holy, holy, holy Lord, God of power and might,
    heaven and earth are full of your glory.

The Refrain for the Midday Lessons

Great peace have they who love your law;* for them there is no stumbling block.

                                    Psalm 119:165

A Reading

There are six things that YAHWEH hates, seven that he abhors: a haughty look, a
    lying tongue, hands that shed innocent blood, a heart that weaves wicked
    plots, feet that hurry to do evil, a false witness who lies with every breath, a
    man who sows dissension among brothers.

                                    Proverbs 6:16–19

The Refrain

Great peace have they who love your law;* for them there is no stumbling block.

The Midday Psalm   *Let the Words of My Mouth Be Acceptable in Your Sight*

Who can tell how often he offends?* cleanse me from my secret faults.
Above all, keep your servant from presumptuous sins; let them not get dominion
    over me;*
then shall I be whole and sound, and innocent of a great offense.
Let the words of my mouth and the meditation of my heart be acceptable in your
    sight,* O LORD,
my strength and my redeemer.

                                    Psalm 19:12–14

The Refrain

Great peace have they who love your law;* for them there is no stumbling block.

The Cry of the Church

O Lord, hear my prayer and let my cry come unto you. Thanks be to God.

                                  THE SHORT BREVIARY

The Lord's Prayer

The Prayer Appointed for the Week

O God, because without you we are not able to please you, mercifully grant that
    your Holy Spirit may in all things direct and rule my heart; through Jesus
    Christ our Lord, who lives and reigns with you and the Holy Spirit, one God,
    now and for ever. *Amen*.†

The Concluding Prayer of the Church

O God, the source of eternal light: Shed forth your unending day upon all of us who watch for you, that our lips may praise you, our lives may bless you, and our worship may give you glory; through Jesus Christ our Lord. *Amen.*†

The Vespers Office To Be Observed on the Hour or Half Hour Between 5 and 8 p.m.

The Call to Prayer

Behold now, bless the LORD, all you servants of the LORD,* you that stand by night in the house of the LORD.

Psalm 134:1

The Request for Presence

My soul waits for the LORD, more than watchmen for the morning,* more than watchmen for the morning.

Psalm 130:5

The Greeting

You, O LORD, are my lamp;* my God, you make my darkness bright.
With you I will break down an enclosure;* with the help of my God I will scale any wall.

Psalm 18:29–30

The Hymn *Let Us Break Bread Together*

Let us break bread together on our knees;
Let us break bread together on our knees;
When I fall on my knees,
With my face to the rising sun,
O Lord, have mercy on me.

Let us drink wine together on our knees;
Let us drink wine together on our knees;
When I fall on my knees,
With my face to the rising sun,
O Lord, have mercy on me.

Let us praise God together on our knees;
Let us praise God together on our knees;
When I fall on my knees,
With my face to the rising sun,
O Lord, have mercy on me.

African American, Traditional

The Refrain for the Vesper Lessons

I lie down and go to sleep;* I wake again, because the LORD sustains me.

Psalm 3:5

The Vespers Psalm   *Let Us Go to the House of the* Lord

I was glad when they said to me,* "Let us go to the house of the Lord."

Now our feet are standing* within your gates, O Jerusalem.

Jerusalem is built as a city* that is at unity with itself;

To which the tribes go up, the tribes of the Lord,* the assembly of Israel, to praise
   the Name of the Lord.

For there are the thrones of judgment,* the thrones of the house of David.

Pray for the peace of Jerusalem:* "May they prosper who love you.

Peace be within your walls* and quietness within your towers.

For my brethren and companions' sake,* I pray for your prosperity.

Because of the house of the Lord our God,* I will seek to do you good."

Psalm 122

The Refrain

I lie down and go to sleep;* I wake again, because the Lord sustains me.

The Cry of the Church

O Lamb of God, that takes away the sins of the world, have mercy upon me.

O Lamb of God, that takes away the sins of the world, have mercy upon me.

O Lamb of God, that takes away the sins of the world, grant me your peace.

The Lord's Prayer

The Prayer Appointed for the Week

O God, because without you we are not able to please you, mercifully grant that
   your Holy Spirit may in all things direct and rule my heart; through Jesus
   Christ our Lord, who lives and reigns with you and the Holy Spirit, one God,
   now and for ever. *Amen.*†

The Concluding Prayer of the Church

Almighty God, who after the creation of the world rested from all your works and
   sanctified a day of rest for all your creatures: Grant that I, putting away all
   earthly anxieties, may be duly prepared for the service of public worship, and
   grant as well that my Sabbath upon earth may be a preparation for the eternal
   rest promised to your people in heaven; through Jesus Christ our Lord. *Amen.*†

❧

The Morning Office   **To Be Observed on the Hour or Half Hour**
                                        Between 6 and 9 a.m.

The Call to Prayer

Sing to the Lord a new song,* for he has done marvelous things.

Psalm 98:1

The Request for Presence
Create in me a clean heart, O God,* and renew a right spirit within me.

Psalm 51:11

The Greeting
I am small and of little account,* yet I do not forget your commandments.

Psalm 119:141

The Refrain for the Morning Lessons
For you are my hope, O Lord God,* my confidence since I was young.

Psalm 71:5

A Reading
Then people brought little children to him, for him to lay his hands on them and pray. The disciples scolded them, but Jesus said, 'Let the little children alone, and do not stop them from coming to me; for it is to such as these that the kingdom of Heaven belongs.' Then he laid hands on them and went on his way.

Matthew 19:13–15

The Refrain
For you are my hope, O Lord God,* my confidence since I was young.

The Morning Psalm   The Sparrow Has Found a Nest
. . . My soul has a desire and longing for the courts of the Lord;* my heart and my flesh rejoice in the living God.
The sparrow has found her a house and the swallow a nest where she may lay her young;* by the side of your altars, O Lord of hosts, my King and my God.

Psalm 84:1–2

The Refrain
For you are my hope, O Lord God,* my confidence since I was young.

The Cry of the Church
O Lord, hear my prayer and let my cry come unto you. Thanks be to God.

The Short Breviary

The Lord's Prayer

The Prayer Appointed for the Week
Grant that I, Lord, may not be anxious about earthly things, but love things heavenly; and even now, while I am placed among things that are passing away, hold fast to those that shall endure; through Jesus Christ our Lord, who lives and reigns with you and the Holy Spirit, one God, for ever and ever. *Amen.*†

The Concluding Prayer of the Church
Lord God, almighty and everlasting Father, you have brought me in safety to this new day: Preserve me with your mighty power, that I may not fall into sin, nor

be overcome by adversity; and in all I do direct me to the fulfilling of your purpose; through Jesus Christ my Lord. *Amen.*†

The Midday Office   **To Be Observed on the Hour or Half Hour**
Between 11 a.m. and 2 p.m.

The Call to Prayer
God is the Lord; he has shined upon us;* form a procession with branches up to
the horns of the altar.

Psalm 118:27

The Request for Presence
Open my lips, O Lord* and my mouth shall proclaim your praise.

Psalm 51:16

The Greeting
Let all who seek you rejoice and be glad in you;* let those who love your salvation
say for ever, "Great is the Lord!"

Psalm 70:4

The Refrain for the Midday Lessons
The words of the Lord are tried in the fire;* he is a shield to all who trust in him.

Psalm 18:31

A Reading
You must keep to what you have been taught and know to be true; remember who
your teachers were, and how, ever since you were a child, you have known the
holy scriptures—from these you can learn the wisdom that leads to salvation
through faith in Christ Jesus. All scripture is inspired by God and useful for
refuting error, for guiding people's lives and teaching them to be upright. This
is how someone who is dedicated to God becomes fully equipped and ready
for any good work.

2 Timothy 3:14–17

The Refrain
The words of the Lord are tried in the fire;* he is a shield to all who trust in him.

The Midday Psalm   *Give Me Life in Your Ways*
Teach me, O Lord, the way of your statutes,* and I shall keep it to the end.
Give me understanding, and I shall keep your law;* I shall keep it with all my heart.
Make me go in the path of your commandments,* for that is my desire.
Incline my heart to your decrees* and not to unjust gain.
Turn my eyes from watching what is worthless;* give me life in your ways.

Psalm 119:33–37

The Refrain
The words of the Lord are tried in the fire;* he is a shield to all who trust in him.

The Small Verse
Blessed be the Lord God of Israel for he has visited and delivered us. Alleluia, alleluia, alleluia.

Traditional

The Lord's Prayer

The Prayer Appointed for the Week
Grant that I, Lord, may not be anxious about earthly things, but love things heavenly; and even now, while I am placed among things that are passing away, hold fast to those that shall endure; through Jesus Christ our Lord, who lives and reigns with you and the Holy Spirit, one God, for ever and ever. *Amen.*†

The Concluding Prayer of the Church
O God, you make me glad with the weekly remembrance of the glorious resurrection of your Son my Lord: Give me this day such blessing through my worship of you, that the week to come may be spent in your favor; through Jesus Christ our Lord. *Amen.*†

The Vespers Office　　　　　**To Be Observed on the Hour or Half Hour**
Between 5 and 8 p.m.

The Call to Prayer
Open my lips, O Lord,* and my mouth shall proclaim your praise.

Psalm 51:16

The Request for Presence
Hear, O LORD, and have mercy upon me;* O LORD, be my helper.

Psalm 30:11

The Greeting
Blessed be the Lord God, the God of Israel,* who alone does wondrous deeds! And blessed be his glorious Name for ever!* and may all the earth be filled with his glory. Amen. Amen.

Psalm 72:18–19

The Hymn
By all your saints still striving,
for all your saints at rest,
your holy name, O Jesus,
for evermore be blessed.
You rose, our King victorious,
that they might wear the crown
and ever shine in splendor
reflected from your throne.

We praise you, Lord, for Matthew,
whose gospel words declare
that, worldly gain forsaking,
your path of life we share.
From all unrighteous mammon,
O raise our eyes anew,
that we, whate'er our station,
may rise and follow you.

Then let us praise the Father
and worship God the Son
and sing to God the Spirit,
eternal Three in one
till all the ransomed number
who stand before the throne
ascribe all power and glory
and praise to God alone.

Horatio Nelson

The Refrain for the Vespers Lessons

It is better to rely on the LORD* than to put any trust in flesh.
It is better to rely on the LORD* than to put any trust in rulers.

Psalm 118:8–9

The Vespers Psalm

How Shall We Sing the LORD's Song

By the waters of Babylon we sat down and wept,* when we remembered you, O
Zion.
As for our harps, we hung them up* on the trees in the midst of that land.
For those who led us away captive asked us for a song, and our oppressors called
for mirth:* "Sing us one of the songs of Zion."
How shall we sing the LORD's song* upon an alien soil?
If I forget you, O Jerusalem,* let my right hand forget its skill.
Let my tongue cleave to the roof of my mouth if I do not remember you,* if I do
not set Jerusalem above my highest joy.

Psalm 137:1–6

The Refrain

It is better to rely on the LORD* than to put any trust in flesh.
It is better to rely on the LORD* than to put any trust in rulers.

The Small Verse

Their sound goes forth to all the earth and their speech to the end of the world.

adapted from THE SHORT BREVIARY

The Lord's Prayer

The Prayer Appointed for the Week

Grant that I, Lord, may not be anxious about earthly things, but love things heavenly; and even now, while I am placed among things that are passing away, hold fast to those that shall endure; through Jesus Christ our Lord, who lives and reigns with you and the Holy Spirit, one God, for ever and ever. *Amen.*†

The Concluding Prayer of the Church

Lord God, whose Son our Savior Jesus Christ, triumphed over the powers of death and prepared for us our place in the new Jerusalem: Grant that I, who have this day given thanks for his resurrection, may praise you in the City of which he is the light, and where he lives and reigns for ever and ever. *Amen.*†

The Morning Office

**To Be Observed on the Hour or Half Hour
Between 6 and 9 a.m.**

The Call to Prayer

Bless the LORD, O my soul,* and all that is within me, bless his holy Name.
Bless the LORD, O my soul,* and forget not all his benefits.

Psalm 103:1–2

The Request for Presence

Protect me, O God, for I take refuge in you;* I have said to the LORD, "You are my Lord, my good above all other."

Psalm 16:1

The Greeting

I love you, O LORD my strength,* O LORD my stronghold, my crag, and my haven.

Psalm 18:1

The Refrain for the Morning Lessons

Purge me from my sin, and I shall be pure;* wash me, and I shall be clean indeed.

Psalm 51:8

A Reading

In Western Christianity, September 21 is the feast of St. Matthew. Jesus' calling of Matthew, a publican and tax collector, scandalized the Pharisees and left the Church lasting proof of His saving compassion.

As Jesus was walking on from there he saw a man named Matthew sitting at the tax office, and he said to him, 'Follow me.' And he got up and followed him. Now while he was at table in the house it happened that a number of tax collectors and sinners came to sit at the table with Jesus and his disciples. When the Pharisees saw this, they said to his disciples, 'Why does your master eat with tax collectors and sinners?' When he heard this he replied, 'It is not the healthy who need the doctor, but the sick. Go and learn the meaning of the words: *Mercy is what pleases me, not sacrifice.* And indeed I came to call not the upright, but sinners.'

Matthew 9:9–13

The Refrain

Purge me from my sin, and I shall be pure;* wash me, and I shall be clean indeed.

The Morning Psalm

Give Me Life in Your Ways

Teach me, O LORD, the way of your statutes,* and I shall keep it to the end.
Give me understanding, and I shall keep your law;* I shall keep it with all my heart.
Make me go in the path of your commandments,* for that is my desire.

Incline my heart to your decrees* and not to unjust gain.

Turn my eyes from watching what is worthless;* give me life in your ways.

Fulfill your promise to your servant,* which you make to those who fear you.

Turn away the reproach which I dread,* because your judgments are good.

Behold, I long for your commandments;* in your righteousness preserve my life.

Psalm 119:33–40

The Refrain

Purge me from my sin, and I shall be pure;* wash me, and I shall be clean indeed.

The Cry of the Church

O Lamb of God, that takes away the sins of the world, have mercy upon me.

O Lamb of God, that takes away the sins of the world, have mercy upon me.

O Lamb of God, that takes away the sins of the world, grant me your peace.

The Lord's Prayer

The Prayer Appointed for the Week

Grant that I, Lord, may not be anxious about earthly things, but love things heavenly; and even now, while I am placed among things that are passing away, hold fast to those that shall endure; through Jesus Christ our Lord, who lives and reigns with you and the Holy Spirit, one God, for ever and ever. *Amen.*†

The Concluding Prayer of the Church

Lord God, almighty and everlasting Father, you have brought me in safety to this new day: Preserve me with your mighty power, that I may not fall into sin, nor be overcome by adversity; and in all I do direct me to the fulfilling of your purpose; through Jesus Christ my Lord. *Amen.*†

The Midday Office   **To Be Observed on the Hour or Half Hour Between 11 a.m. and 2 p.m.**

The Call to Prayer

Bless the LORD, you angels of his, you mighty ones who do his bidding,* and hearken to the voice of his word.

Bless the LORD, all you his hosts,* you ministers of his who do his will.

Bless the LORD, all you works of his, in all places of his dominion;* bless the LORD, O my soul.

Psalm 103:20–22

The Request for Presence

I am a stranger here on earth;* do not hide your commandments from me.

Psalm 119:19

The Greeting

I am bound by the vow I made to you, O God;* I will present to you thank-offerings;

For you have rescued my soul from death and my feet from stumbling,* that I may
walk before God in the light of the living.

Psalm 56:11–12

The Refrain for the Midday Lessons

Glory be to him whose power, working in us, can do infinitely more than we can
ask or imagine; glory be to him from generation to generation in the Church
and in Christ Jesus for ever and ever. Amen.

Ephesians 3:20–21

A Reading

So you are no longer aliens or foreign visitors: you are fellow-citizens with the
holy people of God and part of God's household. You are built upon the foundations of the apostles and prophets, and Christ Jesus himself is the cornerstone. Every structure knit together in him grows into a holy temple in the
Lord; and you too, in him, are being built up into a dwelling-place of God in
the Spirit.

Ephesians 2:19–22

The Refrain

Glory be to him whose power, working in us, can do infinitely more than we can
ask or imagine; glory be to him from generation to generation in the Church
and in Christ Jesus for ever and ever. Amen.

The Midday Psalm   *All Who Are True of Heart Will Glory*

The human mind and heart are a mystery;* but God will loose an arrow at them,
and suddenly they will be wounded.
He will make them trip over their tongues,* and all who see them will shake their
heads.
Everyone will stand in awe and declare God's deeds;* they will recognize his works.
The righteous will rejoice in the LORD and put their trust in him,* and all who are
true of heart will glory.

Psalm 64:7–10

The Refrain

Glory be to him whose power, working in us, can do infinitely more than we can
ask or imagine; glory be to him from generation to generation in the Church
and in Christ Jesus for ever and ever. Amen.

The Gloria

The Lord's Prayer

The Prayer Appointed for the Week

Grant that I, Lord, may not be anxious about earthly things, but love things heavenly; and even now, while I am placed among things that are passing away,
hold fast to those that shall endure; through Jesus Christ our Lord, who lives
and reigns with you and the Holy Spirit, one God, for ever and ever. *Amen.†*

The Concluding Prayer of the Church
I thank you, heavenly Father, for the witness of your apostle and evangelist
Matthew to the Gospel of your Son my Savior; and I pray that after his example, I may with ready will and heart obey the calling of my Lord, who lives and
reigns with you and the Holy Spirit, one God, now and for ever. *Amen.*†

The Vespers Office   **To Be Observed on the Hour or Half Hour**
Between 5 and 8 p.m.

The Call to Prayer
Sing to the LORD and bless his Name;* proclaim the good news of his salvation
from day to day.
Declare his glory among the nations* and his wonders among all peoples.

Psalm 96:2–3

The Request for Presence
Save us, O LORD our God, and gather us from among the nations,* that we may
give thanks to your holy Name and glory in your praise.

Psalm 106:47

The Greeting
I will give you thanks for what you have done* and declare the goodness of your
Name in the presence of the godly.

Psalm 52:9

The Hymn

Now let the earth with joy resound
And heaven the chant re-echo round;
Nor heaven nor earth too high can raise
The great Apostles' glorious praise!

Sickness and health your voice obey,
At your command they go or stay;
From sin's disease our souls restore,
In good confirm us more and more.

So when the world is at its end
And Christ to judgment shall descend,
May we be called those joys to see
Prepared from all eternity.

Praise to the Father, with the Son
And Paraclete for ever one:
To Thee, O holy Trinity
Be praise for all eternity. Amen.

THE SHORT BREVIARY

The Refrain for the Vespers Lessons
Let the faithful rejoice in triumph;* let them be joyful on their beds.

Psalm 149:5

The Vespers Psalm   *You Know My Sitting Down and My Rising Up*
LORD, you have searched me out and known me;* you know my sitting down and
my rising up; you discern my thoughts from afar.
You trace my journeys and my resting-places* and are acquainted with all my ways.
Indeed, there is not a word on my lips,* but you, O LORD, know it altogether.

You press upon me behind and before* and lay your hand upon me.
Such knowledge is too wonderful for me;* it is so high that I cannot attain to it.

Psalm 139:1–5

The Refrain
Let the faithful rejoice in triumph;* let them be joyful on their beds.

The Cry of the Church
O Lord, hear my prayer and let my cry come unto you. Thanks be to God.

THE SHORT BREVIARY

The Lord's Prayer

The Prayer Appointed for the Week
Grant that I, Lord, may not be anxious about earthly things, but love things heavenly; and even now, while I am placed among things that are passing away, hold fast to those that shall endure; through Jesus Christ our Lord, who lives and reigns with you and the Holy Spirit, one God, for ever and ever. *Amen.*†

The Concluding Prayer of the Church
I beseech You, O Lord, let the prayers of blessed Matthew Your Apostle and evangelist assist me, that those things which by myself I cannot obtain may be granted me by his intercession. Through our Lord. *Amen.*

adapted from THE SHORT BREVIARY

The Morning Office **To Be Observed on the Hour or Half Hour Between 6 and 9 a.m.**

The Call to Prayer
Love the LORD, all you who worship him;* the LORD protects the faithful, but repays to the full those who act haughtily.

Psalm 31:23

The Request for Presence
Early in the morning I cry out to you,* for in your word is my trust.

Psalm 119:147

The Greeting
"You are my God, and I will thank you;* you are my God, and I will exalt you."

Psalm 118:28

The Refrain for the Morning Lessons
I hate those who have a divided heart,* but your law do I love.

Psalm 119:113

A Reading
Now his mother and brothers arrived and, standing outside, sent in a message asking for him. A crowd was sitting round him at the time the message was passed to him, 'Look, your mother and brothers and sisters are outside asking

for you.' He replied, 'Who are my mother and my brothers?' And looking at
those sitting in a circle round him, he said, 'Here are my mother and my brothers. Anyone who does the will of God, that person is my brother and sister and
mother.'

Mark 3:31–35

The Refrain

I hate those who have a divided heart,* but your law do I love.

The Morning Psalm   *The LORD Preserves All Those Who Love Him*

The LORD is near to those who call upon him,* to all who call upon him faithfully.
He fulfills the desire of those who fear him;* he hears their cry and helps them.
The LORD preserves all those who love him,* but he destroys all the wicked.

Psalm 145:19–21

The Refrain

I hate those who have a divided heart,* but your law do I love.

The Cry of the Church

Lord, have mercy on us. Christ, have mercy on us. Lord, have mercy on us.

The Lord's Prayer

The Prayer Appointed for the Week

Grant that I, Lord, may not be anxious about earthly things, but love things heavenly; and even now, while I am placed among things that are passing away,
hold fast to those that shall endure; through Jesus Christ our Lord, who lives
and reigns with you and the Holy Spirit, one God, for ever and ever. *Amen.*†

The Concluding Prayer of the Church

Lord God, almighty and everlasting Father, you have brought me in safety to this
new day: Preserve me with your mighty power, that I may not fall into sin, nor
be overcome by adversity; and in all I do direct me to the fulfilling of your purpose; through Jesus Christ my Lord. *Amen.*†

The Midday Office   **To Be Observed on the Hour or Half Hour**
Between 11 a.m. and 2 p.m.

The Call to Prayer

Praise Him from whom all blessings flow; praise Him all creatures here below;
praise Him above you heavenly hosts; praise Father, Son and Holy Ghost.

Traditional

The Request for Presence

Be my strong rock, a castle to keep me safe, for you are my crag and my stronghold;* for the sake of your Name, lead me and guide me.

Psalm 31:3

The Greeting

To you, O LORD, I lift up my soul;* my God, I put my trust in you . . .

Psalm 25:1

The Refrain for the Midday Lessons

Happy are they all who fear the LORD,* and who follow in his ways!

Psalm 28:1

A Reading

As David's life drew to its close he laid this charge on his son Solomon, 'I am going the way of all the earth. Be strong and show yourself a man. Observe the injunctions of YAHWEH your God, following his ways and keeping his laws, his commandments, his ordinances and his decrees, as stands written in the Law of Moses, so that you may be successful in everything you do and undertake, and that YAHWEH may fulfil the promise he made me, "If your sons are careful how they behave, and walk loyally before me with all their heart and soul, you will never want for a man on the throne of Israel." '

I Kings 2:1–4

The Refrain

Happy are they all who fear the LORD,* and who follow in his ways!

The Midday Psalm   *Righteousness and Justice Are the Foundations of His Throne*

The LORD is King; let the earth rejoice;* let the multitude of the isles be glad.
Clouds and darkness are round about him,* righteousness and justice are the
    foundations of his throne.
A fire goes before him* and burns up his enemies on every side.
His lightnings light up the world;* the earth sees it and is afraid.
The mountains melt like wax at the presence of the LORD,* at the presence of the
    Lord of the whole earth.
The heavens declare his righteousness,* and all the peoples see his glory.

Psalm 97:1–6

The Refrain

Happy are they all who fear the LORD,* and who follow in his ways!

The Small Verse

The Lord is king. He has put on glorious apparel. Let all the nations praise him.
    Let those of every tongue bow before him. Alleluia, alleluia, alleluia.

Traditional

The Lord's Prayer

The Prayer Appointed for the Week

Grant that I, Lord, may not be anxious about earthly things, but love things heav-
    enly; and even now, while I am placed among things that are passing away,
    hold fast to those that shall endure; through Jesus Christ our Lord, who lives
    and reigns with you and the Holy Spirit, one God, for ever and ever. *Amen.*†

The Concluding Prayer of the Church
Come forth, O Christ, and help me. For your name's sake deliver me.

Traditional

The Vespers Office **To Be Observed on the Hour or Half Hour Between 5 and 8 p.m.**

The Call to Prayer
Open my lips, O Lord,* and my mouth shall proclaim your praise.
Had you desired it, I would have offered sacrifice,* but you take no delight in
burnt-offerings.
The sacrifice of God is a troubled spirit;* a broken and contrite heart, O God, you
will not despise.

Psalm 51:16–18

The Request for Presence
Out of the depths have I called to you, O LORD; LORD, hear my voice;* let your ears
consider well the voice of my supplication.

Psalm 130:1

The Greeting
You have put gladness in my heart,* more than when grain and wine and oil
increase.
I lie down in peace; at once I fall asleep;* for only you, LORD, make me dwell in
safety.

Psalm 4:7–8

The Hymn *Turn Your Eyes Upon Jesus*
Turn your eyes upon Jesus,
Look full in His wonderful face,
And the things of earth
Will grow strangely dim
In the light of His glory and grace.

Helen K. Hemmel

The Refrain for the Vespers Lessons
The LORD has sworn an oath to David;* in truth, he will not break it:
"A son, the fruit of your body* will I set upon your throne."

Psalm 132:11–12

The Vespers Psalm *My Heart Shall Meditate on Understanding*
Hear this, all you peoples; hearken, all you who dwell in the world,* you of high
degree and low, rich and poor together.
My mouth shall speak of wisdom,* and my heart shall meditate on understanding.
I will incline my ear to a proverb* and set forth my riddle upon the harp.
Why should I be afraid in evil days,* when the wickedness of those at my heels
surrounds me,

The wickedness of those who put their trust in their goods,* and boast of their
  great riches?
We can never ransom ourselves,* or deliver to God the price of our life;
For the ransom of our life is so great,* that we should never have enough to pay it,
But God will ransom my life;* he will snatch me from the grasp of death.
Do not be envious when some become rich,* or when the grandeur of their house
  increases;
For they will carry nothing away at their death,* nor will their grandeur follow
  them.
Though they thought highly of themselves while they lived,* and were praised for
  their success,
They shall join the company of their forebears,* who will never see the light again.
Those who are honored, but have no understanding,* are like the beasts that perish.

Psalm 49:1–7, 15–20

The Refrain
The LORD has sworn an oath to David;* in truth, he will not break it:
"A son, the fruit of your body* will I set upon your throne."

The Gloria

The Lord's Prayer

The Prayer Appointed for the Week
Grant that I, Lord, may not be anxious about earthly things, but love things heavenly; and even now, while I am placed among things that are passing away,
  hold fast to those that shall endure; through Jesus Christ our Lord, who lives
  and reigns with you and the Holy Spirit, one God, for ever and ever. *Amen.*†

The Concluding Prayer of the Church
As my heart opens up
  under your touch
    I hear your call to death, Jesus,
      faint,
        whispering in peace
          offering my flesh in sacrifice
            waiting,
              waiting tenderly for my hour
          knowing that I am
            hidden
          in the hand
        the heart
      the womb
    of your father
  I await in silence
the wedding.

Jean Vanier

The Morning Office   **To Be Observed on the Hour or Half Hour
                                           Between 6 and 9 a.m.**

The Call to Prayer
Worship the LORD in the beauty of holiness;* let the whole earth tremble before him.
Psalm 96:9

The Request for Presence
Show us the light of your countenance, O God,* and come to us.
based on Psalm 67:1

The Greeting
Seven times a day do I praise you,* because of your righteous judgments.
Psalm 119:164

The Refrain for the Morning Lessons
Protect my life and deliver me;* let me not be put to shame, for I have trusted in
    you.
Let integrity and uprightness preserve me,* for my hope has been in you.
Psalm 25:19–20

A Reading
Jesus taught us, saying: 'No one who prefers father or mother to me is worthy of
    me. No one who prefers son or daughter to me is worthy of me. Anyone who
    does not take his cross and follow in my footsteps is not worthy of me. Anyone
    who finds his life will lose it; anyone who loses his life for my sake will find it.'
Matthew 10:37–39

The Refrain
Protect my life and deliver me;* let me not be put to shame, for I have trusted in you.
Let integrity and uprightness preserve me,* for my hope has been in you.

The Morning Psalm   ***Righteousness and Peace Have Kissed Each Other***
I will listen to what the LORD God is saying,* for he is speaking peace to his faithful
    people and to those who turn their hearts to him.
Truly, his salvation is very near to those who fear him,* that his glory may dwell in
    our land.
Mercy and truth have met together;* righteousness and peace have kissed each
    other.
Truth shall spring up from the earth,* and righteousness shall look down from
    heaven.
The LORD will indeed grant prosperity,* and our land will yield its increase.
Righteousness shall go before him,* and peace shall be a pathway for his feet.
Psalm 85:8–13

The Refrain
Protect my life and deliver me;* let me not be put to shame, for I have trusted in you.
Let integrity and uprightness preserve me,* for my hope has been in you.

The Cry of the Church
O Lamb of God, that takes away the sins of the world, have mercy upon me.
O Lamb of God, that takes away the sins of the world, have mercy upon me.
O Lamb of God, that takes away the sins of the world, grant me your peace.

The Lord's Prayer

The Prayer Appointed for the Week
Grant that I, Lord, may not be anxious about earthly things, but love things heavenly; and even now, while I am placed among things that are passing away,
hold fast to those that shall endure; through Jesus Christ our Lord, who lives
and reigns with you and the Holy Spirit, one God, for ever and ever. *Amen.*†

The Concluding Prayer of the Church
Lord God, almighty and everlasting Father, you have brought me in safety to this
new day: Preserve me with your mighty power, that I may not fall into sin, nor
be overcome by adversity; and in all I do direct me to the fulfilling of your purpose; through Jesus Christ my Lord. *Amen.*†

The Midday Office

**To Be Observed on the Hour or Half Hour
Between 11 a.m. and 2 p.m.**

The Call to Prayer
"Come now, let us reason together," says the Lord.
Isaiah 1:18 KJV

The Request for Presence
O LORD, I call to you; come to me quickly;* hear my voice when I cry to you.
Psalm 141:1

The Greeting
In you, O LORD, have I taken refuge;* let me never be ashamed.
Psalm 71:1

The Refrain for the Midday Lessons
Happy are they all who fear the LORD,* and who follow in his ways!
Psalm 128:1

A Reading
By his divine power, he has lavished on us all the things that we need for life and
for true devotion, through the knowledge of him who has called us by his own
glory and goodness. Through these, the greatest and the priceless promises
have been lavished on us, that through them you should share the divine
nature and escape the corruption rife in the world through disordered passion.
With this in view, do your utmost to support your faith with goodness, goodness with understanding, understanding with self control, self control with
perseverance, perseverance with devotion, devotion with kindness to the

brothers, and kindness to the brothers with love. The possession and growth of these qualities will prevent your knowledge of our Lord Jesus Christ from being ineffectual and unproductive. But without them a person is blind or short-sighted, forgetting how the sins of the past were washed away.

2 Peter 1:3–9

The Refrain
Happy are they all who fear the LORD,* and who follow in his ways!

The Midday Psalm   *Who Can Ascend the Hill of the LORD?*
"Who can ascend the hill of the LORD?* and who can stand in his holy place?"
"Those who have clean hands and a pure heart,* who have not pledged them-
selves to falsehood, nor sworn by what is a fraud.
They shall receive a blessing from the LORD* and a just reward from the God of
their salvation."
Such is the generation of those who seek him,* of those who seek your face, O God
of Jacob.

Psalm 24:3–6

The Refrain
Happy are they all who fear the LORD,* and who follow in his ways!

The Cry of the Church
Be, Lord, my helper and forsake me not. Do not despise me, O God, my savior.
THE SHORT BREVIARY

The Lord's Prayer

The Prayer Appointed for the Week
Grant that I, Lord, may not be anxious about earthly things, but love things heavenly; and even now, while I am placed among things that are passing away,
hold fast to those that shall endure; through Jesus Christ our Lord, who lives
and reigns with you and the Holy Spirit, one God, for ever and ever. *Amen.*†

The Concluding Prayer of the Church
Direct me, O Lord, in all my doings with your most gracious favor, and further me
with your continual help; that in all my work begun, continued, and ended in
you, I may glorify your holy name, and finally, by your mercy, obtain everlasting life; through Jesus Christ our Lord. *Amen.*†

The Vespers Office   **To Be Observed on the Hour or Half Hour**
Between 5 and 8 p.m.

The Call to Prayer
But I will call upon God,* and the LORD will deliver me.
In the evening, in the morning, and at noonday, I will complain and lament,* and
he will hear my voice.

He will bring me safely back . . .
God, who is enthroned of old, will hear me.

Psalm 55:17ff

The Request for Presence
I cry out to you, O LORD;* I say, "You are my refuge, my portion in the land of the
living."

Psalm 142:5

The Greeting
I will confess you among the peoples, O LORD;* I will sing praises to you among
the nations.

Psalm 108:3

The Hymn   Stand By Me
When the storms of life are raging,   In the midst of faults and failures,
Stand by me;   Stand by me;
When the world is tossing me,   When I do the best I can,
Like a ship upon the sea;   And my friends misunderstand,
You who rule the wind and water,   You who know all about me,
Stand by me.   Stand by me.

In the midst of tribulation,   When I'm growing old and feeble,
Stand by me;   Stand by me;
When the hosts of hell assail,   When my life becomes a burden,
And my strength begins to fail,   And I'm nearing chilly Jordan,
You who never lost a battle,   O You "Lily of the Valley,"
Stand by me.   Stand by me.

Charles A. Tindley

The Refrain for the Vespers Lessons
The LORD will hear the desire of the humble;* you will strengthen their heart and
your ears shall hear . . .

Psalm 10:18

The Vespers Psalm   We Wish You Well in the Name of the LORD
"Greatly have they oppressed me since my youth,"* let Israel now say;
"Greatly have they oppressed me since my youth,* but they have not prevailed
against me."
The plowmen plowed upon my back* and made their furrows long.
The LORD, the Righteous One,* has cut the cords of the wicked.
Let them be put to shame and thrown back,* all those who are enemies of Zion.
Let them be like grass upon the housetops,* which withers before it can be
plucked;
Which does not fill the hand of the reaper,* nor the bosom of him who binds the
sheaves;

So that those who go by say not so much as,* "The Lord prosper you. We wish you
well in the Name of the Lord."

Psalm 129

The Refrain
The Lord will hear the desire of the humble;* you will strengthen their heart and
your ears shall hear . . .

The Small Verse
The Lord is my shepherd and nothing is wanting to me. In green pastures He hath
settled me.

THE SHORT BREVIARY

The Lord's Prayer

The Prayer Appointed for the Week
Grant that I, Lord, may not be anxious about earthly things, but love things heavenly; and even now, while I am placed among things that are passing away,
hold fast to those that shall endure; through Jesus Christ our Lord, who lives
and reigns with you and the Holy Spirit, one God, for ever and ever. *Amen.*†

The Concluding Prayer of the Church
Lead me not into temptation. Deliver me from evil. Yours are the kingdom and the
glory.

The Morning Office	**To Be Observed on the Hour or Half Hour Between 6 and 9 a.m.**

The Call to Prayer
Know this: The Lord himself is God;* he himself has made us, and we are his; we
are his people and the sheep of his pasture.

Psalm 100:2

The Request for Presence
For God alone my soul in silence waits;* truly, my hope is in him.

Psalm 62:6

The Greeting
Your testimonies are very sure,* and holiness adorns your house, O Lord, for ever
and for evermore.

Psalm 93:6

The Refrain for the Morning Lessons
Blessed is he who comes in the name of the Lord;* we bless you from the house of
the Lord.

Psalm 118:26

A Reading

Again he said, 'What shall I compare the kingdom of God with? It is like the yeast a woman took and mixed in with three measures of flour till it was all leavened all through.'

Luke 13:20–21

The Refrain

Blessed is he who comes in the name of the Lord;* we bless you from the house of the LORD.

The Morning Psalm   *What Is Man That You Should Be Mindful of Him?*

When I consider your heavens, the work of your fingers,* the moon and the stars you have set in their courses,

What is man that you should be mindful of him?* the son of man that you should seek him out?

You have made him but little lower than the angels;* you adorn him with glory and honor;

You give him mastery over the works of your hands;* you put all things under his feet:

All sheep and oxen,* even the wild beasts of the field,

The birds of the air, the fish of the sea,* and whatsoever walks in the paths of the sea.

O LORD our Governor,* how exalted is your Name in all the world!

Psalm 8:4–10

The Refrain

Blessed is he who comes in the name of the Lord;* we bless you from the house of the LORD.

The Cry of the Church

O God, come to my assistance! O Lord, make haste to help me!

The Lord's Prayer

The Prayer Appointed for the Week

Grant that I, Lord, may not be anxious about earthly things, but love things heavenly; and even now, while I am placed among things that are passing away, hold fast to those that shall endure; through Jesus Christ our Lord, who lives and reigns with you and the Holy Spirit, one God, for ever and ever. *Amen.*†

The Concluding Prayer of the Church

Lord God, almighty and everlasting Father, you have brought me in safety to this new day: Preserve me with your mighty power, that I may not fall into sin, nor be overcome by adversity; and in all I do direct me to the fulfilling of your purpose; through Jesus Christ my Lord. *Amen.*†

The Midday Office To Be Observed on the Hour or Half Hour
Between 11 a.m. and 2 p.m.

The Call to Prayer
Come, let us sing to the LORD;* let us shout for joy to the Rock of our salvation.
Let us come before his presence with thanksgiving* and raise a loud shout to him
    with psalms.
For the LORD is a great God,* and a great King above all gods.

Psalm 95:1–3

The Request for Presence
Let the peoples praise you, O God;* let all the peoples praise you.

Psalm 67:3

The Greeting
You have made me glad by your acts, O LORD;* and I shout for joy because of the
    works of your hands.

Psalm 92:4

The Refrain for the Midday Lessons
Yours are the heavens; the earth also is yours;* you laid the foundations of the
    world and all that is in it.

Psalm 89:11

A Reading
Land, do not be afraid; be glad, rejoice, for YAHWEH has done great things. Wild
    animals, do not be afraid; the desert pastures are green again, the trees bear
    fruit, vine and fig tree yield their riches. Sons of Zion, be glad, rejoice in
    YAHWEH your God; for he has given you autumn rain as justness demands, and
    he will send the rains down for you, the autumn and spring rain as of old. The
    threshing-floors will be full of grain, the vats overflow with wine and oil.

Joel 2:21–24

The Refrain
Yours are the heavens; the earth also is yours;* you laid the foundations of the
    world and all that is in it.

The Midday Psalm *You Crown the Year with Your Goodness*
Awesome things will you show us in your righteousness, O God of our salvation,*
    O Hope of all the ends of the earth and of the seas that are far away.
You make fast the mountains by your power;* they are girded about with might.
You still the roaring of the seas,* the roaring of their waves, and the clamor of the
    peoples.
Those who dwell at the ends of the earth will tremble at your marvelous signs;*
    you make the dawn and the dusk to sing for joy.
You visit the earth and water it abundantly; you make it very plenteous;* the river
    of God is full of water.

You prepare the grain,* for so you provide for the earth.
You drench the furrows and smooth out the ridges;* with heavy rain you soften
the ground and bless its increase.
You crown the year with your goodness,* and your paths overflow with plenty.
May the fields of the wilderness be rich for grazing,* and the hills be clothed with
joy.
May the meadows cover themselves with flocks, and the valleys cloak themselves
with grain;* let them shout for joy and sing.

Psalm 65:5–14

The Refrain
Yours are the heavens; the earth also is yours;* you laid the foundations of the
world and all that is in it.

The Gloria

The Lord's Prayer

The Prayer Appointed for the Week
Grant that I, Lord, may not be anxious about earthly things, but love things heavenly; and even now, while I am placed among things that are passing away,
hold fast to those that shall endure; through Jesus Christ our Lord, who lives
and reigns with you and the Holy Spirit, one God, for ever and ever. *Amen.†*

The Concluding Prayer of the Church
Let us bless the Lord God living and true! Let us always render him praise, glory,
honor, blessing, and all good things! Amen. Amen. So be it! So be it!

St. Francis of Assisi

The Vespers Office **To Be Observed on the Hour or Half Hour
Between 5 and 8 p.m.**

The Call to Prayer
Let us come before his presence with thanksgiving* and raise a loud shout to him
with psalms.

Psalm 95:2

The Request for Presence
Remember not our past sins; let your compassion be swift to meet us;* for we have
been brought very low.
Help us, O God our Savior, for the glory of your Name;* deliver us and forgive us
our sins, for your Name's sake.

Psalm 79:8–9

The Greeting
Exalt yourself above the heavens, O God,* and your glory over all the earth.

Psalm 57:11

The Hymn   *Hail to the Lord's Anointed*

Hail to the Lord's anointed, great David's greater Son!
Hail in the time appointed, His reign on earth begun!
He comes to break oppression, to set the captive free;
To take away transgression and rule in equity.

He comes with succor speedy to those who suffer wrong;
To help the poor and needy, and bid the weak be strong;
To give them songs for sighing, their darkness turn to light,
Whose souls, condemned and dying, are precious in His sight.

He shall come down like showers upon the fruitful earth;
Love, joy, and hope, like flowers, spring in His path to birth.
Before Him, on the mountains, shall peace, the herald, go,
And righteousness, in fountains, from hill to valley flow.

Arabia's desert ranger to Him shall bow the knee;
The Ethiopian stranger His glory come to see;
With offerings of devotion ships from the isles shall meet,
To pour the wealth of oceans in tribute at His feet.

Kings shall fall down before Him, and gold and incense bring;
All nations shall adore Him, His praise all people sing;
For Him shall prayer unceasing and daily vows ascend;
His kingdom still increasing, a kingdom without end.

O'er every foe victorious, He on His throne shall rest;
From age to age more glorious, all blessing and all blessed.
The tide of time shall never His covenant remove;
His Name shall stand forever, His changeless Name of love.

James Montgomery

The Refrain for the Vespers Lessons

The fool has said in his heart, "There is no God."* All are corrupt and commit
abominable acts; there is none who does any good.

Psalm 14:1

The Vespers Psalm   *All My Fresh Springs Are in You*

On the holy mountain stands the city he has founded;* the Lord loves the gates of
Zion more than all the dwellings of Jacob.
Glorious things are spoken of you,* O city of our God.
I count Egypt and Babylon among those who know me;* behold Philistia, Tyre,
and Ethiopia: in Zion were they born.
Of Zion it shall be said, "Everyone was born in her,* and the Most High himself
shall sustain her."
The Lord will record as he enrolls the peoples,* "These also were born there."
The singers and the dancers will say,* "All my fresh springs are in you."

Psalm 87

The Refrain
The fool has said in his heart, "There is no God."* All are corrupt and commit abominable acts; there is none who does any good.

The Gloria

The Lord's Prayer

The Prayer Appointed for the Week
Grant that I, Lord, may not be anxious about earthly things, but love things heavenly; and even now, while I am placed among things that are passing away, hold fast to those that shall endure; through Jesus Christ our Lord, who lives and reigns with you and the Holy Spirit, one God, for ever and ever. *Amen*.†

The Concluding Prayer of the Church
Blessed be the Lord God of Israel for he has visited and delivered us. Alleluia, alleluia, alleluia.

Traditional

The Morning Office   **To Be Observed on the Hour or Half Hour Between 6 and 9 a.m.**

The Call to Prayer
Search for the Lord and his strength;* continually seek his face.
Psalm 105:4

The Request for Presence
Hearken to my voice, O Lord, when I call;* have mercy on me and answer me.
You speak in my heart and say, "Seek my face."* Your face, Lord, will I seek.
Hide not your face from me,* nor turn away your servant in displeasure.
Psalm 27:10–12

The Greeting
What terror you inspire!* who can stand before you when you are angry?
Psalm 76:7

The Refrain for the Morning Lessons
I sought the Lord, and he answered me* and delivered me out of all my terror.
Psalm 34:4

A Reading
Through towns and villages he went teaching, making his way to Jerusalem. Someone said to him, 'Sir, will there be only a few saved?' He said to them, 'Try your hardest to enter by the narrow door, because, I tell you, many will try to

enter and will not succeed. Once the master of the house has got up and locked the door, you may find yourself standing outside knocking on the door, saying, "Lord, open to us," but he will answer, "I do not know where you come from." Then you will start saying, "We once ate and drank in your company; you taught in our streets," but he will reply, "I do not know where you come from. *Away from me, all evil doers!*" Then there will be weeping and grinding of teeth, when you see Abraham and Isaac and Jacob and all the prophets in the kingdom of God, and yourselves thrown out. And people from east and west, from north and south, will come and sit down at the feast in the kingdom of God. Look, there are those now last who will be first, and those now first who will be last.'

Luke 13:22–30

The Refrain
I sought the LORD, and he answered me* and delivered me out of all my terror.

The Morning Psalm   *I Did Not Conceal My Guilt*
While I held my tongue, my bones withered away,* because of my groaning all day long.

For your hand was heavy upon me day and night;* my moisture was dried up as in the heat of summer.

Then I acknowledged my sin to you,* and did not conceal my guilt.

I said, "I will confess my transgressions to the LORD."* Then you forgave me the guilt of my sin.

Therefore all the faithful will make their prayers to you in time of trouble;* when the great waters overflow, they shall not reach them.

Psalm 32:3–7

The Refrain
I sought the LORD, and he answered me* and delivered me out of all my terror.

The Cry of the Church
Lord, have mercy on us. Christ, have mercy on us. Lord, have mercy on us.

The Lord's Prayer

The Prayer Appointed for the Week
Grant that I, Lord, may not be anxious about earthly things, but love things heavenly; and even now, while I am placed among things that are passing away, hold fast to those that shall endure; through Jesus Christ our Lord, who lives and reigns with you and the Holy Spirit, one God, for ever and ever. *Amen.*†

The Concluding Prayer of the Church
Lord God, almighty and everlasting Father, you have brought me in safety to this new day: Preserve me with your mighty power, that I may not fall into sin, nor

be overcome by adversity; and in all I do direct me to the fulfilling of your purpose; through Jesus Christ my Lord. *Amen.*✝

The Midday Office   **To Be Observed on the Hour or Half Hour**
                                          Between 11 a.m. and 2 p.m.

The Call to Prayer
Ascribe to the LORD the honor due his Name;* bring offerings and come into his
    courts.

                                                                    Psalm 96:8

The Request for Presence
Let your countenance shine upon your servant* and teach me your statutes.

                                                                  Psalm 119:135

The Greeting
I will give thanks to you, O LORD, with my whole heart;* I will tell of all your marvelous works.

                                                                    Psalm 9:1

The Refrain for the Midday Lessons
Among the gods there is none like you, O LORD,* nor anything like your works.

                                                                    Psalm 86:8

A Reading
These are the last words of David: 'Thus speaks David son of Jesse, thus speaks
    the man raised to eminence, the anointed of the God of Jacob, the singer of the
    songs of Israel: The spirit of YAHWEH speaks through me, his word is on my
    tongue; the God of Jacob has spoken, the Rock of Israel has said to me: He
    whose rule is upright on earth, who rules in the fear of God, is like the morning
    light at sunrise (on a cloudless morning) making the grass of the earth sparkle
    after rain. Yes, my House stands firm with God: he has made an eternal
    covenant with me, all in order, well assured; does he not bring to fruition my
    every victory and desire? But men of Belial he rejects like thorns, for these are
    never taken up in the hand: no one touches them except with a pitchfork or
    spear-shaft, and then only to burn them to nothing!'

                                                              2 Samuel 23:1–7

The Refrain
Among the gods there is none like you, O LORD, * nor anything like your works.

The Midday Psalm   *Hear My Teaching, O My People*
Hear my teaching, O my people;* incline your ears to the words of my mouth.
I will open my mouth in a parable;* I will declare the mysteries of ancient times.
That which we have heard and known, and what our forefathers have told us,* we
    will not hide from their children.

We will recount to generations to come the praiseworthy deeds and the power of
the LORD,* and the wonderful works he has done.
He gave his decrees to Jacob and established a law for Israel,* which he commanded them to teach their children;
That the generations to come might know, and the children yet unborn;* that they
in their turn might tell it to their children;
So that they might put their trust in God,* and not forget the deeds of God, but
keep his commandments.

Psalm 78:1–7

The Refrain
Among the gods there is none like you, O LORD,* nor anything like your works.

The Cry of the Church
Even so come, Lord Jesus!

The Lord's Prayer

The Prayer Appointed for the Week
Grant that I, Lord, may not be anxious about earthly things, but love things heavenly; and even now, while I am placed among things that are passing away,
hold fast to those that shall endure; through Jesus Christ our Lord, who lives
and reigns with you and the Holy Spirit, one God, for ever and ever. *Amen.*†

The Concluding Prayer of the Church
Lord Jesus Christ, by your death you took away the sting of death: Grant me to so
follow in faith where you have led the way, that I may at length fall asleep
peacefully in you and wake in your likeness; for your tender mercies' sake.
Amen.†

The Vespers Office   **To Be Observed on the Hour or Half Hour**
Between 5 and 8 p.m.

The Call to Prayer
I will call upon the LORD,* and so shall I be saved from my enemies.

Psalm 18:3

The Request for Presence
I have said to the LORD, "You are my God;* Listen, O LORD, to my supplication."

Psalm 140:6

The Greeting
But you, O Lord my GOD, oh, deal with me according to your Name;* for your ten-
der mercy's sake, deliver me.
For I am poor and needy,* and my heart is wounded within me.

Psalm 109:20–21

The Hymn	*The Dismissal of the Great "I"*
Go off great "I", and come not nigh	I now disclaim that great big name
But quit my habitation	And all my title to it
And come no more within my door	That great big "I", I'll mortify
Corrupting my sensation	No pity will I show it
Depart, I say, flee far away	It may elope but need not hope
Your ways no more I'll practice	To share in my salvation
For all who try to be great "I"	Though near of kin, a natural twin
Are vicious, proud and fractious.	By Adam's old relation.

Early Shaker Anthem

The Refrain for the Vespers Lessons

For the LORD has heard the sound of my weeping. The LORD has heard my supplication;* the LORD accepts my prayer.

Psalm 6:8–9

The Vespers Psalm	*Whoever Does These Things Shall Never Be Overthrown*

LORD, who may dwell in your tabernacle?* who may abide upon your holy hill?

Whoever leads a blameless life and does what is right,* who speaks the truth from his heart.

There is no guile upon his tongue; he does no evil to his friend;* he does not heap contempt upon his neighbor.

In his sight the wicked is rejected,* but he honors those who fear the LORD.

He has sworn to do no wrong* and does not take back his word.

He does not give his money in hope of gain,* nor does he take a bribe against the innocent.

Whoever does these things* shall never be overthrown.

Psalm 15

The Refrain

For the LORD has heard the sound of my weeping. The LORD has heard my supplication;* the LORD accepts my prayer.

The Cry of the Church

Be, Lord, my helper and forsake me not. Do not despise me, O God, my savior.

THE SHORT BREVIARY

The Lord's Prayer

The Prayer Appointed for the Week

Grant that I, Lord, may not be anxious about earthly things, but love things heavenly; and even now, while I am placed among things that are passing away, hold fast to those that shall endure; through Jesus Christ our Lord, who lives and reigns with you and the Holy Spirit, one God, for ever and ever. *Amen.†*

The Concluding Prayers of the Church

Almighty God, who has promised to hear the petitions of those who ask in your Son's Name: I beseech you mercifully to incline your ear to me who have made my prayers and supplications to you; and grant that those things which I have faithfully asked according to your will, I may effectually obtain, to the relief of my necessity, and to the setting forth of your glory; through Jesus Christ my Lord. *Amen.*†

May the souls of the faithful departed, through the mercy of God, rest in eternal peace. *Amen.*

The Morning Office   **To Be Observed on the Hour or Half Hour**
                               Between 6 and 9 a.m.

The Call to Prayer
Proclaim with me the greatness of the LORD;* let us exalt his Name together.
Psalm 34:3

The Request for Presence
Open my eyes, that I may see* the wonders of your law.
Psalm 119:18

The Greeting
I will confess you among the peoples, O LORD;* I will sing praise to you among the nations.
For your loving-kindness is greater than the heavens,* and your faithfulness reaches to the clouds.
Psalm 57:9–10

The Refrain for the Morning Lessons
Happy are those who act with justice* and always do what is right!
Psalm 106:3

A Reading
This, too, he said to me, 'Do not keep the prophesies in this book a secret, because the Time is close. Meanwhile let the sinner continue sinning, and the unclean continue to be unclean; let the upright continue in his uprightness, and those who are holy continue to be holy. *Look, I am coming soon, and my reward is with me, to repay everyone as their deeds deserve.* I am the Alpha and the Omega, *the First and the Last,* the Beginning and the End. Blessed are those who will have washed their robes clean, so that they will have the right to feed on the tree of life and can come through the gates into the city. Others must stay outside: dogs, fortune-tellers, and the sexually immoral, murderers, idolaters, and everyone of false speech and false life.'
Revelation 22:10–15

The Refrain
Happy are those who act with justice* and always do what is right!

The Morning Psalm   *Let All the Earth Fear the* LORD

By the word of the LORD were the heavens made,* by the breath of his mouth all
the heavenly hosts.

He gathers up the waters of the ocean as in a water-skin* and stores up the depths
of the sea.

Let all the earth fear the LORD;* let all who dwell in the world stand in awe of him.

For he spoke, and it came to pass;* he commanded, and it stood fast.

The LORD brings the will of the nations to naught;* he thwarts the designs of the
peoples.

But the LORD's will stands fast for ever,* and the designs of his heart from age to
age.

Psalm 33:6–11

The Refrain

Happy are those who act with justice* and always do what is right!

The Gloria

The Lord's Prayer

The Prayer Appointed for the Week

Grant that I, Lord, may not be anxious about earthly things, but love things heavenly; and even now, while I am placed among things that are passing away,
hold fast to those that shall endure; through Jesus Christ our Lord, who lives
and reigns with you and the Holy Spirit, one God, for ever and ever. *Amen.*†

The Concluding Prayer of the Church

Lord God, almighty and everlasting Father, you have brought me in safety to this
new day: Preserve me with your mighty power, that I may not fall into sin, nor
be overcome by adversity; and in all I do direct me to the fulfilling of your purpose; through Jesus Christ my Lord. *Amen.*†

The Midday Office   **To Be Observed on the Hour or Half Hour**
Between 11 a.m. and 2 p.m.

The Call to Prayer

May these words of mine please him;* I will rejoice in the LORD.

Psalm 104:35

The Request for Presence

Set a watch before my mouth, O LORD, and guard the door of my lips;* let not my
heart incline to any evil thing.

Let me not be occupied in wickedness with evildoers,* nor eat of their choice
foods.

Let the righteous smite me in friendly rebuke;* let not the oil of the unrighteous
anoint my head;

Psalm 141:3–5

The Greeting

I long for your salvation, O LORD,* And your law is my delight.
Let me live, and I will praise you,* and let your judgments help me.

Psalm 119:174–75

The Refrain for the Midday Lessons

O God, you have taught me since I was young,* and to this day I tell of your wonderful works.

Psalm 71:17

A Reading

Whatever your work is, put your heart into it as done for the Lord and not for
human beings, knowing that the Lord will repay you by making you his heirs.
It is Christ the Lord that you are serving. Anyone who does wrong will be
repaid in kind. For there is no favoritism.

Colossians 3:23–25

The Refrain

O God, you have taught me since I was young,* and to this day I tell of your wonderful works.

The Midday Psalm   *Let the Hills Ring Out with Joy Before the LORD*

Let the sea make a noise and all that is in it,* the lands and those who dwell
therein.
Let the rivers clap their hands,* and let the hills ring out with joy before the LORD,
when he comes to judge the earth.
In righteousness shall he judge the world* and the peoples with equity.

Psalm 98:8–10

The Refrain

O God, you have taught me since I was young,* and to this day I tell of your wonderful works.

The Small Verse

Into your hands I commend my spirit for you have redeemed me, O God of my
life. Glory be to the Father, and to the Son and to the comforting Spirit.

Traditional

The Lord's Prayer

The Prayer Appointed for the Week

Grant that I, Lord, may not be anxious about earthly things, but love things heavenly; and even now, while I am placed among things that are passing away,
hold fast to those that shall endure; through Jesus Christ our Lord, who lives
and reigns with you and the Holy Spirit, one God, for ever and ever. *Amen.*†

The Concluding Prayer of the Church

O God, the source of eternal light: Shed forth your unending day upon all of us who watch for you, that our lips may praise you, our lives may bless you, and our worship may give you glory; through Jesus Christ our Lord. *Amen.*†

The Vespers Office   **To Be Observed on the Hour or Half Hour**
                                          Between 5 and 8 p.m.

The Call to Prayer
Bless our God, you peoples;* make the voice of his praise to be heard;
Who holds our souls in life,* and will not allow our feet to slip.

Psalm 66:7–8

The Request for Presence
O God of hosts;* show us the light of your countenance, and we shall be saved.

Psalm 80:7

The Greeting
As the eyes of servants look to the hand of their masters,* and the eyes of a maid to
    the hand of her mistress,
So my eyes look to you, O Lord my God.

based on Psalm 123:2–3

The Hymn   *Trust and Obey*
When we walk with the Lord   But we never can prove
In the light of his word,   The delights of his love
What a glory he sheds on our way!   Until all on the altar we lay;
While we do his good will,   For the favor he shows,
He abides with us still,   For the joy he bestows,
And with all who will trust and obey. Are for them who will trust and obey.

Not a burden we bear,   Trust and obey,
Not a sorrow we share,   For there's no other way
But our toil he does richly repay;   To be happy in Jesus,
Not a grief or a loss,   But to trust and obey.
Not a frown or a cross   *John H. Sammis*
But is blessed if we trust and obey.

The Refrain for the Vespers Lessons
For I am but a sojourner with you,* a wayfarer, as all my forebears were.

Psalm 39:14

The Vespers Psalm   Lord, *Let Me Know How Short My Life Is*
I said, "I will keep watch upon my ways,* so that I do not offend with my tongue.
I will put a muzzle on my mouth* while the wicked are in my presence."
So I held my tongue and said nothing;* I refrained from rash words; but my pain
    became unbearable.

My heart was hot within me;* while I pondered, the fire burst into flame; I spoke
out with my tongue:

Lord, let me know my end and the number of my days,* so that I may know how
short my life is.

You have given me a mere handful of days, and my lifetime is as nothing in your
sight;* truly, even those who stand erect are but a puff of wind.

We walk about like a shadow, and in vain we are in turmoil;* we heap up riches
and cannot tell who will gather them.

And now, what is my hope?* O Lord, my hope is in you.

Deliver me from all my transgressions* and do not make me the taunt of the fool.

Psalm 39:1–9

The Refrain

For I am but a sojourner with you,* a wayfarer, as all my forebears were.

The Cry of the Church

Even so come, Lord Jesus!

The Lord's Prayer

The Prayer Appointed for the Week

Grant that I, Lord, may not be anxious about earthly things, but love things heavenly; and even now, while I am placed among things that are passing away,
hold fast to those that shall endure; through Jesus Christ our Lord, who lives
and reigns with you and the Holy Spirit, one God, for ever and ever. *Amen.*†

The Concluding Prayer of the Church

Almighty God, who after the creation of the world rested from all your works and
sanctified a day of rest for all your creatures: Grant that I, putting away all
earthly anxieties, may be duly prepared for the service of public worship, and
grant as well that my Sabbath upon earth may be a preparation for the eternal
rest promised to your people in heaven; through Jesus Christ our Lord. *Amen.*†

✺

The Morning Office **To Be Observed on the Hour or Half Hour
Between 6 and 9 a.m.**

The Call to Prayer

Sing to the Lord and bless his Name;* proclaim the good news of his salvation
from day to day.

Declare his glory among the nations* and his wonders among all peoples.
For great is the LORD and greatly to be praised;* he is more to be feared than all
gods.

Psalm 96:2–4

The Request for Presence
Satisfy us by your loving-kindness in the morning;* so shall we rejoice and be glad
all the days of our life.

Psalm 90:14

The Greeting
Awesome things will you show us in your righteousness, O God of our salvation,*
O Hope of all the ends of the earth and of the seas that are far away.

Psalm 65:5

The Refrain for the Morning Lessons
For he shall give his angels charge over you,* to keep you in all your ways.

Psalm 91:11

A Reading
Jesus taught us, saying: 'And if anyone says to you then, "Look, here is the Christ"
or "Look, he is there," do not believe it; for false Christs and false prophets will
arise and produce signs and portents to deceive the elect, if that were possible.
You, therefore, must be on your guard. I have given you full warning. But in
those days, after that time of distress, the sun will be darkened, the moon will
not give its light, the stars will come falling out of the sky and the powers in the
heavens will be shaken. And then they will see the *Son of man coming in the
clouds* with great power and glory. And then he will send the angels to gather
his elect from the four winds, from the ends of the world to the ends of the sky.'

Mark 13:21–27

The Refrain
For he shall give his angels charge over you,* to keep you in all your ways.

The Morning Psalm   *The LORD Will Make Good His Purpose*
I will give thanks to you, O LORD, with my whole heart;* before the gods I will sing
your praise.
I will bow down toward your holy temple and praise your Name,* because of
your love and faithfulness;
For you have glorified your Name* and your word above all things.
When I called, you answered me;* you increased my strength within me.
All the kings of the earth will praise you, O LORD,* when they have heard the
words of your mouth.
They will sing of the ways of the LORD,* that great is the glory of the LORD.
Though the LORD be high, he cares for the lowly;* he perceives the haughty from
afar.

Though I walk in the midst of trouble, you keep me safe;* you stretch forth your
   hand against the fury of my enemies; your right hand shall save me.
The LORD will make good his purpose for me;* O LORD, your love endures for
   ever; do not abandon the works of your hands.

Psalm 138

The Refrain
For he shall give his angels charge over you,* to keep you in all your ways.

The Cry of the Church
O Lord, hear my prayer and let my cry come unto you. Thanks be to God.

THE SHORT BREVIARY

The Lord's Prayer

The Prayer Appointed for the Week
O God, you declare your almighty power chiefly in showing mercy and pity:
   Grant me the fullness of your grace, that I, running to obtain your promises,
   may become a partaker of your heavenly treasure; through Jesus Christ our
   Lord, who lives and reigns with you and the Holy Spirit, one God, for ever and
   ever. *Amen.*†

The Concluding Prayer of the Church
Lord God, almighty and everlasting Father, you have brought me in safety to this
   new day: Preserve me with your mighty power, that I may not fall into sin, nor
   be overcome by adversity; and in all I do direct me to the fulfilling of your purpose; through Jesus Christ my Lord. *Amen.*†

The Midday Office   **To Be Observed on the Hour or Half Hour
                                Between 11 a.m. and 2 p.m.**

The Call to Prayer
Come and listen, all you who fear God,* and I will tell you what he has done for me.

Psalm 66:14

The Request for Presence
I call upon you, O God, for you will answer me;* incline your ear to me and hear
   my words.

Psalm 17:6

The Greeting
The Lord is in his holy temple; let all the earth keep silence before him. Amen.

Traditional

The Refrain for the Midday Lessons
The LORD is my strength and my song,* and he has become my salvation.

Psalm 118:14

A Reading

Jacob left Beersheba and set out for Haran. When he had reached a certain place he
stopped there for the night, since the sun had set. Taking one of the stones of
that place, he made it his pillow and lay down where he was. He had a dream:
there was a ladder, planted on the ground with its top reaching to heaven; and
God's angels were going up and down on it. And there was YAHWEH, beside
him, saying, 'I, YAHWEH, am the God of Abraham your father, and the God of
Isaac. The land on which you are lying I shall give to you and your descendants. Your descendants will be as plentiful as the dust on the ground; you will
spread to west and to east, to north and to south, and all clans on earth will
bless themselves by you and your descendants. Be sure, I am with you; I shall
keep you safe wherever you go, and bring you back to this country, for I shall
never desert you until I have done what I have promised you.' Then Jacob
awoke from his sleep and said, 'Truly, YAHWEH is in this place and I did not
know!' He was afraid and said, 'How awe-inspiring this place is! This is
nothing less than the abode of God, and this is the gate of heaven!'

Genesis 28:10–17

The Refrain

The Lord is my strength and my song,* and he has become my salvation.

The Midday Psalm   *The Angel of the LORD Encompasses Those Who Fear Him*

I sought the LORD, and he answered me* and delivered me out of all my terror.
Look upon him and be radiant,* and let not your faces be ashamed.
I called in my affliction and the LORD heard me* and saved me from all my troubles.
The angel of the LORD encompasses those who fear him,* and he will deliver them.
Taste and see that the LORD is good;* happy are they who trust in him!

Psalm 34:4–8

The Refrain

The Lord is my strength and my song,* and he has become my salvation.

The Gloria

The Lord's Prayer

The Prayer Appointed for the Week

O God, you declare your almighty power chiefly in showing mercy and pity:
Grant me the fullness of your grace, that I, running to obtain your promises,
may become a partaker of your heavenly treasure; through Jesus Christ our
Lord, who lives and reigns with you and the Holy Spirit, one God, for ever and
ever. *Amen.*†

The Concluding Prayer of the Church

O God, you make me glad with the weekly remembrance of the glorious resurrection of your Son my Lord: Give me this day such blessing through my worship
of you, that the week to come may be spent in your favor; through Jesus Christ
our Lord. *Amen.*†

The Vespers Office   **To Be Observed on the Hour or Half Hour**
                                          Between 5 and 8 p.m.

The Call to Prayer
Sing praise to the LORD who dwells in Zion;* proclaim to the peoples the things he
has done.

Psalm 9:11

The Request for Presence
To you I lift up my eyes,* to you enthroned in the heavens.

Psalm 123:1

The Greeting
I put my trust in your mercy;* my heart is joyful because of your saving help.

Psalm 13:5

The Hymn   *O You Immortal Throng of Angels*

O you immortal throng
of angels round the throne,
join with our earth-bound song
to make the Savior known.
On earth you knew
his wondrous grace,
his beauteous face
in heaven you view.

You saw the heaven-born child
in human flesh arrayed,
so innocent and mild
while in the manger laid.
"Glory to God
and peace on earth,"
for such a birth
you sang aloud.

You in the wilderness
beheld the Tempter spoiled,
unmasked in every dress,
in every combat foiled.
With great delight
You crowned his head
when Satan fled
the Savior's might.

You thronged to Calvary
and pressed with sad desire
that awful sight to see—
the Lord of life expire.
Even angel eyes
slow tears did shed:
you mourned the dead
in sad surprise.

Around his sacred tomb
a willing watch you kept;
till out from death's vast room,
up from the grave he leapt.
You rolled the stone,
and all adored
your rising Lord
with joy unknown.

When all arrayed in light
the shining conqueror rode,
you hailed his wondrous flight
up to the throne of God.
And waved around
your golden wings,
and struck your strings
of sweetest sound.

The joyous notes pursue
and louder anthems raise;
while mortals sing with you
their own Redeemer's praise.
With equal flame
and equal art,
do you my heart
extol his Name.

Philip Doddridge

The Refrain for the Vespers Lessons
The angel of the LORD encompasses those who fear him,* and he will deliver them.

Psalm 34:7

The Vespers Psalm   *Put Your Trust in God*
Why are you so full of heaviness, O my soul?* and why are you so disquieted
    within me?
Put your trust in God;* for I will yet give thanks to him, who is the help of my
    countenance, and my God.

Psalm 43:5–6

The Refrain
The angel of the LORD encompasses those who fear him,* and he will deliver them.

The Cry of the Church
Lord, have mercy on us. Christ, have mercy on us. Lord, have mercy on us.

The Lord's Prayer

The Prayer Appointed for the Week
O God, you declare your almighty power chiefly in showing mercy and pity:
    Grant me the fullness of your grace, that I, running to obtain your promises,
    may become a partaker of your heavenly treasure; through Jesus Christ our
    Lord, who lives and reigns with you and the Holy Spirit, one God, for ever and
    ever. *Amen.*†

The Concluding Prayer of the Church
Lord God, whose Son our Savior Jesus Christ, triumphed over the powers of death
    and prepared for us our place in the new Jerusalem: Grant that I, who have this
    day given thanks for his resurrection, may praise you in the City of which he is
    the light, and where he lives and reigns for ever and ever. *Amen.*†

The Morning Office   To Be Observed on the Hour or Half Hour
Between 6 and 9 a.m.

The Call to Prayer
Bless the LORD, you angels of his, you mighty ones who do his bidding,* and hearken to the voice of his word.

Bless the LORD, all you his hosts,* you ministers of his who do his will.
Bless the LORD, all you works of his,* in all places of his dominion . . .

Psalm 103:20–22

The Request for Presence
Be seated on your lofty throne, O Most High;* O LORD, judge the nations.

Psalm 7:8

The Greeting
Not to us, O LORD, not to us, but to your Name give glory;* because of your love
and because of your faithfulness.

Psalm 115:1

The Refrain for the Morning Lessons
On this day the LORD has acted;* we will rejoice and be glad in it.

Psalm 118:24

A Reading   *On September 29, the Church celebrates the role and presence of
angels in the divine plan. Of these thousands, only four are named
in Scripture—Michael, Gabriel, Uriel, and Raphael—among
whom Michael is the chief. It is he who wards off evil for the faithful and who delivers divine peace to them at the end of mortal life.*

The next day, after Jesus had decided to leave for Galilee, he met Philip and said,
'Follow me.' Philip came from the same town, Bethsaida, as Andrew and Peter.
Philip found Nathaniel and said to him, 'We have found the one of whom
Moses in the Law and the prophets wrote, Jesus son of Joseph, from Nazareth.'
Nathaniel said to him, 'From Nazareth? Can anything good come from that
place?' Phillip replied, 'Come and see.' When Jesus saw Nathaniel coming he
said of him, 'There, truly, is an Israelite in whom there is no deception.'
Nathaniel asked, 'How do you know me?' Jesus replied, 'Before Philip came to
call you, I saw you under the fig tree.' Nathaniel answered, 'Rabbi, you are the
Son of God, you are the King of Israel.' Jesus replied, 'You believe that just
because I said: I saw you under the fig tree. You are going to see greater things
than that.' And then he added, 'In truth I tell you, you will see heaven open
and the angels of God ascending and descending over the Son of man.'

John 1:43–51

The Refrain
On this day the LORD has acted;* we will rejoice and be glad in it.

The Morning Psalm   *Bless the LORD, You Angels of His*
Bless the LORD, you angels of his, you mighty ones who do his bidding,* and hear-
ken to the voice of his word.
Bless the LORD, all you his hosts,* you ministers of his who do his will.
Bless the LORD, all you works of his, in all places of his dominion;* bless the LORD,
O my soul.

Psalm 103:20–22

The Refrain
On this day the Lord has acted;* we will rejoice and be glad in it.

The Cry of the Church
Let us praise the Lord, whom the Angels are praising, whom the Cherubim and
Seraphim proclaim: Holy, holy, holy!

THE SHORT BREVIARY

The Lord's Prayer

The Prayer Appointed for the Week
O God, you declare your almighty power chiefly in showing mercy and pity:
Grant me the fullness of your grace, that I, running to obtain your promises,
may become a partaker of your heavenly treasure; through Jesus Christ our
Lord, who lives and reigns with you and the Holy Spirit, one God, for ever and
ever. *Amen.*†

The Concluding Prayers of the Church
Lord God, almighty and everlasting Father, you have brought me in safety to this
new day: Preserve me with your mighty power, that I may not fall into sin, nor
be overcome by adversity; and in all I do direct me to the fulfilling of your purpose; through Jesus Christ my Lord. *Amen.*†

O God, who in a wonderful order has established the ministry of Angels and of
men, mercifully grant that even as Your holy Angels ever do You service in
heaven, so at all times they may defend us on earth. Through our Lord. *Amen.*

THE SHORT BREVIARY

The Midday Office   **To Be Observed on the Hour or Half Hour
Between 11 a.m. and 2 p.m.**

The Call to Prayer
Tremble, then, and do not sin;* speak to your heart in silence upon your bed.
Offer the appointed sacrifices* and put your trust in the Lord.

Psalm 4:4–5

The Request for Presence
In your righteousness, deliver me and set me free,* incline your ear to me and
save me.

Psalm 71:2

The Greeting
Exalt yourself above the heavens, O God,* and your glory over all the earth.

Psalm 108:5

The Refrain for the Midday Lessons
"Be still, then, and know that I am God;* I will be exalted among the nations; I will
be exalted in the earth."

Psalm 46:11

A Reading
At that time Michael will stand up, the great prince who mounts guard over your
people. There is going to be a time of great distress, unparalleled since nations
first came into existence. When that time comes, your own people will be
spared, all those whose names are written in the Book. Of those who lie sleeping in the dust of the earth many will awake, some to everlasting life, some to
shame and everlasting disgrace. The learned will shine as brightly as the vault
of heaven, and those who have instructed many in virtue, as bright as stars for
all eternity.

Daniel 12:1–3

The Refrain
"Be still, then, and know that I am God,* I will be exalted among the nations; I will
be exalted in the earth."

The Midday Psalm   *Praise Him, All You Angels of His*
Hallelujah! Praise the LORD from the heavens;* praise him in the heights.
Praise him, all you angels of his;* praise him, all his host.
Praise him, sun and moon;* praise him, all you shining stars.
Praise him, heaven of heavens,* and you waters above the heavens.
Let them praise the Name of the LORD;* for he commanded, and they were created.
He made them stand fast for ever and ever;* he gave them a law which shall not
pass away.

Psalm 148:1–6

The Refrain
"Be still, then, and know that I am God;* I will be exalted among the nations; I will
be exalted in the earth."

The Cry of the Church
Michael, Gabriel,
Cherubim and Seraphim
cease not to cry daily:
You are worthy, O Lord,
to receive glory, alleluia.
   THE SHORT BREVIARY

The Lord's Prayer

The Prayer Appointed for the Week
O God, you declare your almighty power chiefly in showing mercy and pity:

Grant me the fullness of your grace, that I, running to obtain your promises, may become a partaker of your heavenly treasure; through Jesus Christ our Lord, who lives and reigns with you and the Holy Spirit, one God, for ever and ever. *Amen.*†

The Concluding Prayer of the Church

Everlasting God, you have ordained and constituted the ministries of the angels and men in a wonderful order. Mercifully grant now that, as your holy angels always serve and worship you in heaven, so by your appointment they may help and defend us on earth; through Jesus Christ our Lord, who lives and reigns with you and the Holy spirit, one God, for ever and ever. *Amen.*†

The Vespers Office — To Be Observed on the Hour or Half Hour Between 5 and 8 p.m.

The Call to Prayer

Come now and look upon the works of the LORD,* what awesome things he has done on earth.

Psalm 46:9

The Request for Presence

May God be merciful to us and bless us,* show us the light of his countenance and come to us.
Let your ways be known upon earth,* your saving health among all nations.

Psalm 67:1–2

The Greeting

O LORD of hosts,* happy are they who put their trust in you!

Psalm 84:12

The Hymn

The Guardians of our race, our Angel guides we hail;
Our Father sends them forth to aid our nature frail
These heavenly friends, lest we should suffer overthrow
       Through cunning of our subtle foe.

O watchful Guardians, spread your wings and cleave the air,
Haste hither to our home committed to your care;
Drive thence each noxious ill that might the soul infest,
       Nor suffer danger here to rest.

Now to the holy Three your praise devoutly pour;
His glorious Godhead guides and governs evermore
This triple frame: to Him ascribe we all our praise
       who reigns through everlasting days.

adapted from THE SHORT BREVIARY

The Refrain for the Vespers Lessons
Bless the LORD, you angels of his, you mighty ones who do his bidding,* and hearken to the voice of his word.

Psalm 103:20

The Vespers Psalm   *He Shall Give His Angels Charge Over You*
He who dwells in the shelter of the Most High,* abides under the shadow of the
    Almighty.
He shall say to the LORD, "You are my refuge and my stronghold,* my God in
    whom I put my trust."
He shall deliver you from the snare of the hunter* and from the deadly pestilence.
He shall cover you with his pinions, and you shall find refuge under his wings;*
    his faithfulness shall be a shield and buckler.
You shall not be afraid of any terror by night,* nor of the arrow that flies by day;
Of the plague that stalks in the darkness,* nor of the sickness that lays waste at
    mid-day.
A thousand shall fall at your side and ten thousand at your right hand,* but it shall
    not come near you.
Your eyes have only to behold* to see the reward of the wicked.
Because you have made the LORD your refuge,* and the Most High your
    habitation,
There shall no evil happen to you,* neither shall any plague come near your
    dwelling.
For he shall give his angels charge over you,* to keep you in all your ways.
They shall bear you in their hands,* lest you dash your foot against a stone.
You shall tread upon the lion and adder;* you shall trample the young lion and the
    serpent under your feet.

Psalm 91:1–13

The Refrain
Bless the LORD, you angels of his, you mighty ones who do his bidding,* and hearken to the voice of his word.

The Small Verse
In the sight of the Angels I praise You.
I adore at Your holy temple and give praise to Your Name.

adapted from THE SHORT BREVIARY

The Lord's Prayer

The Prayer Appointed for the Week
O God, you declare your almighty power chiefly in showing mercy and pity:
    Grant me the fullness of your grace, that I, running to obtain your promises,
    may become a partaker of your heavenly treasure; through Jesus Christ our
    Lord, who lives and reigns with you and the Holy Spirit, one God, for ever and
    ever. *Amen.*†

The Concluding Prayer of the Church

O God, who in Your ineffable providence has designed to send Your holy Angels to watch over us, grant to Your suppliants always to find safety in their protection and in eternity to share their happiness. Through our Lord.

THE SHORT BREVIARY

The Morning Office   To Be Observed on the Hour or Half Hour
                                       Between 6 and 9 a.m.

The Call to Prayer

God has gone up with a shout,* the LORD with the sound of the ram's-horn.
Sing praises to God, sing praises;* sing praises to our King, sing praises.
For God is King of all the earth;* sing praises with all your skill.
God reigns over the nations;* God sits upon his holy throne.

Psalm 47:5–8

The Request for Presence

Let all who seek you rejoice and be glad in you;* let those who love your salvation say for ever, "Great is the LORD!"

Psalm 70:4

The Greeting

Out of Zion, perfect in its beauty,* God reveals himself in glory.

Psalm 50:2

The Refrain for the Morning Lessons

The fool has said in his heart, "There is no God."

Psalm 14:1

A Reading

And now war broke out in heaven, when Michael with his angels attacked the dragon. The dragon fought back with his angels, but they were defeated and driven out of heaven. The great dragon, the primeval serpent, known as the devil or Satan, who had led all the world astray, was hurled down to the earth and his angels were hurled down with him. Then I heard a voice shout from heaven, 'Salvation and power and empire for ever have been won by our God, and all authority for his Christ, now that the accuser, who accused our brothers day and night before our God, has been brought down. They have triumphed over him by the blood of the Lamb and by the blood to which they bore witness, because even in the face of death they did not cling to life. So let the heavens rejoice and all who live there; but for you, earth and sea, disaster is coming—because the devil has gone down to you in a rage, knowing that he has little time left.'

Revelation 12:7–12

The Refrain

The fool has said in his heart, "There is no God."

The Morning Psalm   *In the Temple of the LORD All Are Crying, "Glory!"*

Ascribe to the LORD the glory due his Name;* worship the LORD in the beauty of
  holiness.

The voice of the LORD is upon the waters; the God of glory thunders;* the LORD is
  upon the mighty waters.

The voice of the LORD is a powerful voice;* the voice of the LORD is a voice of
  splendor.

The voice of the LORD breaks the cedar trees;* the LORD breaks the cedars of
  Lebanon;

He makes Lebanon skip like a calf,* and Mount Hermon like a young wild ox.

The voice of the LORD splits the flames of fire; the voice of the LORD shakes the
  wilderness;* the LORD shakes the wilderness of Kadesh.

The voice of the LORD makes the oak trees writhe* and strips the forests bare.

And in the temple of the LORD* all are crying, "Glory!"

The LORD sits enthroned above the flood;* the LORD sits enthroned as King for
  evermore.

The LORD shall give strength to his people;* the LORD shall give his people the
  blessing of peace.

Psalm 29:2–11

The Refrain
The fool has said in his heart, "There is no God."

The Gloria

The Lord's Prayer

The Prayer Appointed for the Week
O God, you declare your almighty power chiefly in showing mercy and pity:
  Grant me the fullness of your grace, that I, running to obtain your promises,
  may become a partaker of your heavenly treasure; through Jesus Christ our
  Lord, who lives and reigns with you and the Holy Spirit, one God, for ever and
  ever. *Amen.*†

The Concluding Prayer of the Church
Lord God, almighty and everlasting Father, you have brought me in safety to this
  new day: Preserve me with your mighty power, that I may not fall into sin, nor
  be overcome by adversity; and in all I do direct me to the fulfilling of your purpose; through Jesus Christ my Lord. *Amen.*†

The Midday Office   **To Be Observed on the Hour or Half Hour**
                                   Between 11 a.m. and 2 p.m.

The Call to Prayer
Praise God from whom all blessings flow; praise him, all creatures here below;
  praise him above, you heavenly hosts; praise Father, Son and Holy Ghost.

Doxology

The Request for Presence

May the glory of the LORD endure for ever;* may the LORD rejoice in all his works.

Psalm 104:32

The Greeting

Hosanna, LORD, hosanna!* LORD, send us now success.
Blessed is he who comes in the name of the Lord . . .
God is the LORD; he has shined upon us;* form a procession with branches up to
the horns of the altar.

Psalm 118:25–27

The Refrain for the Midday Lessons

I will walk in the presence of the LORD* in the land of the living.

Psalm 116:8

A Reading

To which of you angels, then, has God ever said: *You are my Son, today I have
fathered you,* or: *I shall be a father to him and he a son to me.* Again, when he brings
the First-born into the world, he says: *Let all the angels of God pay him homage.*
To the angels, he says: *appointing the winds his messengers and flames of fire his
servants,* but to the Son he says: *Your throne, God, is for ever and ever;* and: *the
scepter of his kingdom is a scepter of justice; you love uprightness and detest evil. This
is why God, your God, has anointed you with the oil of gladness, as none of your
rivals.* And again: *Long ago, Lord, you laid earth's foundations, the heavens are the
work of your hands. They pass away but you remain, they all wear out like a garment.
Like a cloak, you will roll them up,* like a garment, and *they will be changed. But
you never alter and your years are unending.* To which of you angels has God ever
said: *Take your seat at my right hand till I have made your enemies your footstool.*
Are they not all ministering spirits, sent to serve for the sake of those who are
to inherit salvation.

Hebrews 1:5–12

The Refrain

I will walk in the presence of the LORD* in the land of the living.

The Midday Psalm   *You Have Made Him But Little Lower Than Angels*

O LORD our Governor,* how exalted is your Name in all the world!
Out of the mouths of infants and children* your majesty is praised above the
heavens.
You have set up a stronghold against your adversaries,* to quell the enemy and
the avenger.
When I consider your heavens, the work of your fingers,* the moon and the stars
you have set in their courses,
What is man that you should be mindful of him?* the son of man that you should
seek him out?
You have made him but little lower than the angels;* you adorn him with glory
and honor;

You give him mastery over the works of your hands;* you put all things under his feet:
All sheep and oxen,* even the wild beasts of the field,
The birds of the air, the fish of the sea,* and whatsoever walks in the paths of the sea.
O LORD our Governor,* how exalted is your Name in all the world!

Psalm 8

The Refrain
I will walk in the presence of the LORD* in the land of the living.

The Cry of the Church
Even so come, Lord Jesus!

The Lord's Prayer

The Prayer Appointed for the Week
O God, you declare your almighty power chiefly in showing mercy and pity: Grant me the fullness of your grace, that I, running to obtain your promises, may become a partaker of your heavenly treasure; through Jesus Christ our Lord, who lives and reigns with you and the Holy Spirit, one God, for ever and ever. *Amen.*†

The Concluding Prayer of the Church
Almighty and eternal God, ruler of all things in heaven and earth: Mercifully accept the prayers of your people everywhere, and strengthen each of us to do your will; through Jesus Christ my Lord. *Amen.*†

The Vespers Office   **To Be Observed on the Hour or Half Hour Between 5 and 8 p.m.**

The Call to Prayer
Come, let us bow down, and bend the knee,* and kneel before the LORD our Maker.
For he is our God,* and we are the people of his pasture and the sheep of his hand.

Psalm 95:6–7

The Request for Presence
O LORD, watch over us* and save us from this generation for ever.
The wicked prowl on every side,* and that which is worthless is highly prized by everyone.

Psalm 12:7–8

The Greeting
How glorious you are!* more splendid than the everlasting mountains!

Psalm 76:4

The Hymn   *Sing to God, O Kingdoms of the Earth*
Sing to God, O kingdoms of the earth;
sing praises to the Lord.
Sing to the Lord a new song,
his praise to the end of the earth.

For justice is the foundation of his throne,
and steadfast love goes before him.
He shall judge between the nations,
and shall arbitrate for many peoples.

They shall beat their swords into plowshares,
and their spears into pruning hooks;
Nation shall not lift up sword against nation,
neither shall they learn war any more.

O praise the Lord, all you nations;
extol him, all you peoples!
For great is his steadfast love toward us,
and his faithfulness endures forever. ❖

The Refrain for the Vespers Lessons
Tell it among the nations: "The Lord is King!"
Psalm 96:10

The Vespers Psalm   *Let Them Praise the Name of the* LORD
Praise the LORD from the earth,* you sea-monsters and all deeps;
Fire and hail, snow and fog,* tempestuous wind, doing his will;
Mountains and all hills,* fruit trees and all cedars;
Wild beasts and all cattle,* creeping things and winged birds;
Kings of the earth and all peoples,* princes and all rulers of the world;
Young men and maidens,* old and young together.
Let them praise the Name of the LORD,* for his Name only is exalted, his splendor
   is over earth and heaven.
He has raised up strength for his people and praise for all his loyal servants,* the
   children of Israel, a people who are near him. Hallelujah!
Psalm 148:7–14

The Refrain
Tell it among the nations: "The Lord is King!"

The Gloria

The Lord's Prayer

The Prayer Appointed for the Week
O God, you declare your almighty power chiefly in showing mercy and pity:
   Grant me the fullness of your grace, that I, running to obtain your promises,
   may become a partaker of your heavenly treasure; through Jesus Christ our

Lord, who lives and reigns with you and the Holy Spirit, one God, for ever and ever. *Amen.*†

The Concluding Prayer of the Church
Blessed be God, who has not rejected my prayer,* nor withheld his love from me.

Psalm 66:18

The Morning Office   **To Be Observed on the Hour or Half Hour**
                                                     Between 6 and 9 a.m.

The Call to Prayer
But I will call upon God,* and the LORD will deliver me.
In the evening, in the morning, and at noonday,* I will complain and lament,
He will bring me safely back . . .* God, who is enthroned of old, will hear me . . .

Psalm 55:17ff

The Request for Presence
Save me, O God, by your Name;* in your might, defend my cause.
Hear my prayer, O God;* give ear to the words of my mouth.

Psalm 54:1–2

The Greeting
I will offer you the sacrifice of thanksgiving* and call upon the Name of the LORD.

Psalm 116:15

The Refrain for the Morning Lessons
The LORD is near to those who call upon him,* to all who call upon him faithfully.

Psalm 145:19

A Reading
Jesus taught us, saying: 'And when you pray, do not imitate the hypocrites: they love to say their prayers standing up in the synagogues and at street corners for people to see them. In truth I tell you, they have had their reward. But when you pray, *go to your private room*, shut yourself in, and so pray to your Father who is in that secret place, and your Father who sees all that is done in secret will reward you.'

Matthew 6:5–6

The Refrain
The LORD is near to those who call upon him,* to all who call upon him faithfully.

The Morning Psalm   *I Am Bound by the Vow I Made to You, O God*
In God the LORD, whose word I praise, in God I trust and will not be afraid,* for what can mortals do to me?
I am bound by the vow I made to you, O God;* I will present to you thank-offerings;
For you have rescued my soul from death and my feet from stumbling,* that I may walk before God in the light of the living.

Psalm 56:10–12

The Refrain
The LORD is near to those who call upon him,* to all who call upon him faithfully.

The Cry of the Church
O Lord, hear my prayer and let my cry come unto you. Thanks be to God.

THE SHORT BREVIARY

The Lord's Prayer

The Prayer Appointed for the Week
O God, you declare your almighty power chiefly in showing mercy and pity:
Grant me the fullness of your grace, that I, running to obtain your promises,
may become a partaker of your heavenly treasure; through Jesus Christ our
Lord, who lives and reigns with you and the Holy Spirit, one God, for ever and
ever. *Amen.*†

The Concluding Prayer of the Church
Lord God, almighty and everlasting Father, you have brought me in safety to this
new day: Preserve me with your mighty power, that I may not fall into sin, nor
be overcome by adversity; and in all I do direct me to the fulfilling of your purpose; through Jesus Christ my Lord. *Amen.*†

The Midday Office **To Be Observed on the Hour or Half Hour**
Between 11 a.m. and 2 p.m.

The Call to Prayer
Hallelujah! Praise the Lord, O my soul!* I will praise the LORD as long as I live; I
will sing praises to my God while I have my being.

Psalm 146:1

The Request for Presence
Remember me, O LORD, with the favor you have for your people,* and visit me
with your saving help;
That I may see the prosperity of your elect and be glad with the gladness of your
people,* that I may glory with your inheritance.

Psalm 106:4–5

The Greeting
You are to be praised, O God, in Zion; . . .
To you that hear prayer shall all flesh come,* because of their transgressions.

Psalm 65:1–2

The Refrain for the Midday Lessons
Your statutes have been like songs to me* wherever I have lived like a stranger.

Psalm 119:54

A Reading

So, with her daughters-in-law, she left the place where she was living and they
took the road back to Judah. Naomi said to her two daughters-in-law, 'Go back,
each of you to your mother's house. May YAHWEH show you faithful love as
you have done to those who have died and to me. YAHWEH grant that you may
each find happiness with a husband!' She then kissed them . . . Orpah then
kissed her mother-in-law and went back to her people. But Ruth stayed with
her. Naomi then said, 'Look, your sister-in-law has gone back to her people
and to her god. Go home, too; follow your sister-in-law.' But Ruth said, 'Do not
press me to leave you and to stop going with you, for wherever you go, I shall
go, wherever you live, I shall live. Your people will be my people, and your
God will be my God. Where you die, I shall die and there I shall be buried. Let
YAHWEH bring unnameable ills on me and worse ills, too, if anything but death
should part me from you!' Seeing that Ruth was determined to go with her,
Naomi said no more.

The two of them went on until they came to Bethlehem. Their arrival set the whole
town astir, . . . This was how Naomi came home with her daughter-in-law,
Ruth the Moabitess. They arrived in Bethlehem at the beginning of the barley
harvest.

Ruth 1:7ff

The Refrain

Your statutes have been like songs to me* wherever I have lived like a stranger.

The Midday Psalm   *The LORD Is a Friend to Those Who Fear Him*

Who are they who fear the LORD?* he will teach them the way that they should
choose.

They shall dwell in prosperity,* and their offspring shall inherit the land.

The LORD is a friend to those who fear him* and will show them his covenant.

Psalm 25:11–13

The Refrain

Your statutes have been like songs to me* wherever I have lived like a stranger.

The Small Verse

Keep me, Lord, as the apple of your eye and carry me under the shadow of your
wings.

Traditional

The Lord's Prayer

The Prayer Appointed for the Week

O God, you declare your almighty power chiefly in showing mercy and pity:
Grant me the fullness of your grace, that I, running to obtain your promises,
may become a partaker of your heavenly treasure; through Jesus Christ our

Lord, who lives and reigns with you and the Holy Spirit, one God, for ever and ever. *Amen.*†

The Concluding Prayer of the Church
May God himself order my days and make them acceptable in his sight. Blessed be the Lord always, my strength and my redeemer.

Traditional

The Vespers Office   **To Be Observed on the Hour or Half Hour**
                Between 5 and 8 p.m.

The Call to Prayer
Come, let us sing to the Lord;* let us shout for joy to the Rock of our salvation.
Let us come before his presence with thanksgiving* and raise a loud shout to him with psalms.
For the Lord is a great God,* and a great King above all gods.
In his hand are the caverns of the earth,* and the heights of the hills are his also.
The sea is his, for he made it,* and his hands have molded the dry land.

Psalm 95:1–5

The Request for Presence
May God be merciful to us and bless us,* show us the light of his countenance and come to us.

Psalm 67:1

The Greeting
Exalt yourself above the heavens, O God,* and your glory over all the earth.

Psalm 57:6

The Hymn   *Stand Up, Stand Up for Jesus*
Stand up, stand up, for Jesus, You soldiers of the cross;
Lift high His royal banner, it must not suffer loss;
From victory unto victory, His army shall He lead,
Till every foe is vanquished and Christ is Lord indeed.

Stand up, stand up, for Jesus, the trumpet call obey;
Forth to the mighty conflict in this His glorious day;
You that are His now serve Him against unnumbered foes;
Let courage rise with danger, and strength to strength oppose.

Stand up, stand up, for Jesus; stand in His strength alone;
The arm of flesh will fail you, you dare not trust your own;
Put on the gospel armor, and watching unto prayer,
When duty calls, or danger, be never wanting there.

Stand up, stand up, for Jesus; the strife will not be long;
This day, the noise of battle; the next, the victor's song.
To valiant hearts triumphant, a crown of life shall be;
They with the King of glory shall reign eternally.

George Duffield

The Refrain for the Vespers Lessons

Those who trust in the Lord are like Mount Zion,* which cannot be moved, but
stands fast for ever.

Psalm 125:1

The Vespers Psalm   Sing Praises to God, Sing Praises

Clap your hands, all you peoples;* shout to God with a cry of joy.
God has gone up with a shout,* the LORD with the sound of the ram's-horn.
Sing praises to God, sing praises;* sing praises to our King, sing praises.
For God is King of all the earth;* sing praises with all your skill.
God reigns over the nations;* God sits upon his holy throne.
The nobles of the peoples have gathered together* with the people of the God of
Abraham.
The rulers of the earth belong to God,* and he is highly exalted.

Psalm 47:1, 5–10

The Refrain

Those who trust in the Lord are like Mount Zion,* which cannot be moved, but
stands fast for ever.

The Gloria

The Lord's Prayer

The Prayer Appointed for the Week

O God, you declare your almighty power chiefly in showing mercy and pity:
Grant me the fullness of your grace, that I, running to obtain your promises,
may become a partaker of your heavenly treasure; through Jesus Christ our
Lord, who lives and reigns with you and the Holy Spirit, one God, for ever and
ever. *Amen.*†

The Concluding Prayer of the Church

Protect us, Lord, as we stay awake; watch over us as we sleep, that awake we may
watch with Christ, and asleep, rest in peace. *Amen.*

The Morning Office   **To Be Observed on the Hour or Half Hour**
Between 6 and 9 a.m.

The Call to Prayer

Rejoice in the LORD, you righteous,* and give thanks to his holy Name.

Psalm 97:12

The Request for Presence
Bow down your ear, O Lord, and answer me,* for I am poor and in misery.
Keep watch over my life, for I am faithful;* save your servant who puts his trust in
you.

Psalm 86:1–2

The Greeting
Blessed is the Lord!* for he has heard the voice of my prayer.

Psalm 28:7

The Refrain for the Morning Lessons
Blessed are they which do hunger and thirst after righteousness: for they shall be
filled.

Matthew 5:6 KJV

A Reading
He spoke the following parable to some people who prided themselves on being
upright and despised everyone else, 'Two men went up to the Temple to
pray, one a Pharisee, the other a tax collector. The Pharisee stood there and
said this prayer to himself, "I thank you, God, that I am not grasping, unjust,
adulterous like everyone else, and particularly that I am not like this tax collector here. I fast twice a week; I pay tithes on all I get." The tax collector
stood some distance away, not daring even to raise his eyes to heaven; but he
beat his breast and said, "God, be merciful to me, a sinner." This man, I tell
you, went home again justified; the other did not. For everyone who raises
himself up will be humbled, but anyone who humbles himself will be
raised up.'

Luke 18:9–14

The Refrain
Blessed are they which do hunger and thirst after righteousness: for they shall be
filled.

The Morning Psalm   *Who Is Like You, O God?*
Your righteousness, O God, reaches to the heavens;* you have done great things;
who is like you, O God?
You have showed me great troubles and adversities,* but you will restore my life
and bring me up again from the deep places of the earth.
You strengthen me more and more;* you enfold and comfort me,
Therefore I will praise you upon the lyre for your faithfulness, O my God;* I will
sing to you with the harp, O Holy One of Israel.
My lips will sing with joy when I play to you,* and so will my soul, which you
have redeemed.
My tongue will proclaim your righteousness all day long,* for they are ashamed
and disgraced who sought to do me harm.

Psalm 71:19–24

The Refrain
Blessed are they which do hunger and thirst after righteousness: for they shall be filled.

The Small Verse
My soul thirsts for the strong, living God and all that is within me cries out to him.

Traditional

The Lord's Prayer

The Prayer Appointed for the Week
O God, you declare your almighty power chiefly in showing mercy and pity: Grant me the fullness of your grace, that I, running to obtain your promises, may become a partaker of your heavenly treasure; through Jesus Christ our Lord, who lives and reigns with you and the Holy Spirit, one God, for ever and ever. *Amen.*†

The Concluding Prayer of the Church
Lord God, almighty and everlasting Father, you have brought me in safety to this new day: Preserve me with your mighty power, that I may not fall into sin, nor be overcome by adversity; and in all I do direct me to the fulfilling of your purpose; through Jesus Christ my Lord. *Amen.*†

The Midday Office
To Be Observed on the Hour or Half Hour Between 11 a.m. and 2 p.m.

The Call to Prayer
Praise God from whom all blessings flow; praise him, all creatures here below; praise him, you heavenly hosts; praise Father, Son and Holy Ghost.

Traditional

The Request for Presence
Hear my prayer, O Lord,* and give ear to my cry . . .
For I am but a sojourner with you,* a wayfarer, as all my forebears were.

Psalm 39:13–14

The Greeting
With my whole heart I seek you;* let me not stray from your commandments.

Psalm 119:10

The Refrain for the Midday Lessons
The Lord loves those who hate evil; he preserves the lives of his saints* and delivers them from the hand of the wicked.

Psalm 97:10

A Reading
Moses taught the children of Israel, saying: 'Yahweh set his heart on you and chose you not because you were the most numerous of all peoples—for indeed

you were the smallest of all—but because he loved you and meant to keep the oath which he swore to your ancestors: that was why Yahweh brought you out with his mighty hand and redeemed you from the place of slave-labor, from the power of Pharaoh king of Egypt. From this you can see that Yahweh your God is the true God, the faithful God who, though he is true to his covenant and his faithful love for a thousand generations as regards those who love him and keep his commandments, punishes in their own persons those that hate him . . . Hence, you must keep and observe the commandments, laws and customs which I am laying down for you today.'

Deuteronomy 7:7–11

The Refrain
The Lord loves those who hate evil; he preserves the lives of his saints* and delivers them from the hand of the wicked.

The Midday Psalm   *O God, When You Went Forth Before Your People*
O God, when you went forth before your people,* when you marched through the wilderness,

The earth shook, and the skies poured down rain, at the presence of God, the God of Sinai,* at the presence of God, the God of Israel.

You sent a gracious rain, O God, upon your inheritance;* you refreshed the land when it was weary.

Your people found their home in it;* in your goodness, O God, you have made provision for the poor.

Psalm 68:7–10

The Refrain
The Lord loves those who hate evil; he preserves the lives of his saints* and delivers them from the hand of the wicked.

The Cry of the Church
O God, come to my assistance! O Lord, make haste to help me!

The Lord's Prayer

The Prayer Appointed for the Week
O God, you declare your almighty power chiefly in showing mercy and pity: Grant me the fullness of your grace, that I, running to obtain your promises, may become a partaker of your heavenly treasure; through Jesus Christ our Lord, who lives and reigns with you and the Holy Spirit, one God, for ever and ever. *Amen.*†

The Concluding Prayer of the Church
Almighty and everlasting God, by whose Spirit the whole body of your faithful is governed and sanctified: Receive my supplications and prayers which I offer before you for all members of your holy Church, that in our vocation and ministry we all may truly serve you through our Lord and Savior Jesus Christ. *Amen.*†

The Vespers Office   **To Be Observed on the Hour or Half Hour**
                                              Between 5 and 8 p.m.

The Call to Prayer
Behold now, bless the Lord, all you servants of the LORD,* you that stand by night
in the house of our LORD.

Psalm 134:1

The Request for Presence
For God alone my soul in silence waits;* from him comes my salvation.

Psalm 62:1

The Greeting
Yours is the day, yours also the night;* you established the moon and the sun.
You fixed all the boundaries of the earth;* you made both summer and winter.

Psalm 74:15–16

The Hymn   *All Things Bright and Beautiful*

Each little flower that opens,   The tall trees in the green wood,
Each little bird that sings,   The meadows where we play,
God made their glowing colors,   The rushes by the water,
And made their tiny wings.   We gather every day.
All things bright and beautiful,   All things bright and beautiful,
All creatures great and small,   All creatures great and small,
All things wise and wonderful: All things wise and wonderful:
The Lord God made them all.   The Lord God made them all.

The purple headed mountains,   God gave us eyes to see them,
The river running by,   And lips that we might tell
The sunset and the morning   How great is God Almighty,
That brightens up the sky.   Who has made all things well.
All things bright and beautiful,   All things bright and beautiful,
All creatures great and small,   All creatures great and small,
All things wise and wonderful: All things wise and wonderful:
The Lord God made them all.   The Lord God made them all.

                                                   Cecil Alexander

The cold wind in the winter,
The pleasant summer sun,
The ripe fruits in the garden:
God made them every one.
All things bright and beautiful,
All creatures great and small,
All things wise and wonderful:
The Lord God made them all.

The Refrain for the Vespers Lessons
The LORD's will stands fast for ever,* and the designs of his heart from age to age.

Psalm 33:11

The Vespers Psalm   *O LORD, How Manifold Are Your Works*
O LORD, how manifold are your works!* in wisdom you have made them all; the
    earth is full of your creatures.
Yonder is the great and wide sea with its living things too many to number,* crea-
    tures both small and great.
There move the ships, and there is that Leviathan,* which you have made for the
    sport of it.
All of them look to you* to give them their food in due season.
You give it to them; they gather it;* you open your hand, and they are filled with
    good things.
You hide your face, and they are terrified; you take away their breath,* and they
    die and return to their dust.
You send forth your Spirit, and they are created;* and so you renew the face of the
    earth.

Psalm 104:25–31

The Refrain
The LORD's will stands fast for ever,* and the designs of his heart from age to age.

The Gloria

The Lord's Prayer

The Prayer Appointed for the Week
O God, you declare your almighty power chiefly in showing mercy and pity:
    Grant me the fullness of your grace, that I, running to obtain your promises,
    may become a partaker of your heavenly treasure; through Jesus Christ our
    Lord, who lives and reigns with you and the Holy Spirit, one God, for ever and
    ever. *Amen.*†

The Concluding Prayer of the Church
May Almighty God grant me a peaceful night and a perfect end. *Amen.*

The Morning Office   **To Be Observed on the Hour or Half Hour
                                          Between 6 and 9 a.m.**

The Call to Prayer
Come now and see the works of God,* how wonderful he is in his doing toward
    all people.

Psalm 66:4

The Request for Presence

Show me your marvelous loving-kindness,* O Savior of those who take refuge at
your right hand from those who rise up against them.
Keep me as the apple of your eye;* hide me under the shadow of your wings,

Psalm 17:7–8

The Greeting

Hosanna, LORD, hosanna! . . . Blessed is he who comes in the name of the LORD;*
we bless you from the house of the LORD.

Psalm 118:25–26

The Refrain for the Morning Lessons

For God, who commanded the light to shine out of darkness, hath shined in our
hearts, to give the light of the knowledge of the glory of God in the face of Jesus
Christ.

II Corinthians 4:6

A Reading

Philip said, 'Lord, show us the Father and then we shall be satisfied.' Jesus said to
him, 'Have I been with you all this time, Philip, and you still do not know me?
Anyone who has seen me has seen the Father, so how can you say, "Show us
the Father"? Do you not believe that I am in the Father and the Father is in me?
What I say to you I do not speak of my own accord: it is the Father, living in me,
who is doing his works.'

John 14:8–11

The Refrain

For God, who commanded the light to shine out of darkness, hath shined in our
hearts, to give the light of the knowledge of the glory of God in the face of Jesus
Christ.

The Morning Psalm   *A Canticle of the Messiah*

The LORD said to my Lord, "Sit at my right hand,* until I make your enemies your
footstool."
The LORD will send the scepter of your power out of Zion,* saying, "Rule over
your enemies round about you.
Princely state has been yours from the day of your birth;* in the beauty of holiness
have I begotten you, like dew from the womb of the morning."
The LORD has sworn and he will not recant:* "You are a priest for ever after the
order of Melchizedek."

Psalm 110:1–4

The Refrain

For God, who commanded the light to shine out of darkness, hath shined in our
hearts, to give the light of the knowledge of the glory of God in the face of Jesus
Christ.

The Gloria

The Lord's Prayer

The Prayer Appointed for the Week
O God, you declare your almighty power chiefly in showing mercy and pity: Grant me the fullness of your grace, that I, running to obtain your promises, may become a partaker of your heavenly treasure; through Jesus Christ our Lord, who lives and reigns with you and the Holy Spirit, one God, for ever and ever. *Amen.*†

The Concluding Prayer of the Church
Lord God, almighty and everlasting Father, you have brought me in safety to this new day: Preserve me with your mighty power, that I may not fall into sin, nor be overcome by adversity; and in all I do direct me to the fulfilling of your purpose; through Jesus Christ my Lord. *Amen.*†

The Midday Office   **To Be Observed on the Hour or Half Hour Between 11 a.m. and 2 p.m.**

The Call to Prayer
Let us bless the LORD, from this time forth for evermore. Hallelujah!
based on Psalm 115:18

The Request for Presence
Send forth your strength, O God;* establish, O God, what you have wrought for us.
Psalm 68:28

The Greeting
I will thank you, O LORD my God, with all my heart,* and glorify your Name for evermore.
Psalm 86:12

The Refrain for the Midday Lessons
This is the LORD's doing,* and it is marvelous in our eyes.
Psalm 118:23

A Reading
We are well aware . . . that the Son of God has come, and has given us understanding so that we may know the One who is true. We are in the One who is true, as we are in his Son, Jesus Christ. He is the true God, and this is eternal life. Children, be on your guard against false gods.
I John 5:20–21

The Refrain
This is the LORD's doing,* and it is marvelous in our eyes.

The Midday Psalm   *He Redeems Your Life from the Grave*

Bless the LORD, O my soul,* and all that is within me, bless his holy Name.

Bless the LORD, O my soul,* and forget not all his benefits.

He forgives all your sins* and heals all your infirmities;

He redeems your life from the grave* and crowns you with mercy and loving-
    kindness;

He satisfies you with good things,* and your youth is renewed like an eagle's.

Psalm 103:1–5

The Refrain

This is the LORD's doing,* and it is marvelous in our eyes.

The Cry of the Church

O Lord, hear my prayer and let my cry come unto you. Thanks be to God.

THE SHORT BREVIARY

The Lord's Prayer

The Prayer Appointed for the Week

O God, you declare your almighty power chiefly in showing mercy and pity:
    Grant me the fullness of your grace, that I, running to obtain your promises,
    may become a partaker of your heavenly treasure; through Jesus Christ our
    Lord, who lives and reigns with you and the Holy Spirit, one God, for ever and
    ever. *Amen.*†

The Concluding Prayer of the Church

Lord Jesus Christ, by your death you took away the sting of death: Grant me to so
    follow in faith where you have led the way, that I may at length fall asleep
    peacefully in you and wake in your likeness; for your tender mercies' sake.
    Amen.†

The Vespers Office   **To Be Observed on the Hour or Half Hour
                                            Between 5 and 8 p.m.**

The Call to Prayer

The LORD is my strength and my shield;* my heart trusts in him, and I have been
    helped;

Therefore my heart dances for joy,* and in my song will I praise him.

Psalm 28:8–9

The Request for Presence

I have gone astray like a sheep that is lost;* search for your servant, for I do not
    forget your commandments.

Psalm 119:176

The Greeting

How great is your goodness, O LORD! which you have laid up for those who fear
  you;* which you have done in the sight of all for those who put their trust in you.

Psalm 31:19

The Hymn   *Old Rugged Cross*

On a hill far away stood an old rugged cross,
  the emblem of suffering and shame;
  and I love that old cross where the dearest and best
  for a world of lost sinners was slain.
  So I'll cherish the old rugged cross,
  till my trophies at last I lay down;
  I will cling to that old rugged cross,
  and exchange it some day for a crown.

O that old rugged cross, so despised by the world
  has a wondrous attraction for me;
  for the dear Lamb of God left his glory above
  to bear it to dark Calvary.
  So I'll cherish the old rugged cross,
  till my trophies at last I lay down;
  I will cling to that old rugged cross,
  and exchange it some day for a crown.

In that old rugged cross, stained with blood so divine,
  a wondrous beauty I see,
  for 'twas on that old rugged cross Jesus suffered and died,
  to pardon and sanctify me.
  So I'll cherish the old rugged cross,
  till my trophies at last I lay down;
  I will cling to that old rugged cross,
  and exchange it some day for a crown.

To that old rugged cross I will ever be true,
  its shame and reproach gladly bear;
  then he'll call me some day to my home far away,
  where his glory forever I'll share.
  So I'll cherish the old rugged cross,
  till my trophies at last I lay down;
  I will cling to that old rugged cross,
  and exchange it some day for a crown.

George Bennard

The Refrain for the Vespers Lessons

Mercy and truth have met together;* righteousness and peace have kissed each
  other.

Psalm 85:10

The Vespers Psalm   *Save Us by Your Right Hand*

O God, you have cast us off and broken us;* you have been angry; oh, take us back
    to you again.
You have shaken the earth and split it open;* repair the cracks in it, for it totters.
You have made your people know hardship;* you have given us wine that makes
    us stagger.
You have set up a banner for those who fear you,* to be a refuge from the power of
    the bow.
Save us by your right hand and answer us,* that those who are dear to you may be
    delivered.

Psalm 60:1–5

The Refrain

Mercy and truth have met together;* righteousness and peace have kissed each
    other.

The Small Verse

My help is in the Name of the Lord who made heaven and earth and all that is in
    them. Thanks be to God.

Traditional

The Lord's Prayer

The Prayer Appointed for the Week

O God, you declare your almighty power chiefly in showing mercy and pity:
    Grant me the fullness of your grace, that I, running to obtain your promises,
    may become a partaker of your heavenly treasure; through Jesus Christ our
    Lord, who lives and reigns with you and the Holy Spirit, one God, for ever and
    ever. *Amen.*†

The Concluding Prayers of the Church

Almighty God, who has promised to hear the petitions of those who ask in your
    Son's Name: I beseech you mercifully to incline your ear to me who have made
    my prayers and supplications to you; and grant that those things which I have
    faithfully asked according to your will, I may effectually obtain, to the relief of
    my necessity, and to the setting forth of your glory; through Jesus Christ my
    Lord. *Amen.*†

May the souls of the faithful departed, through the mercy of God, rest in eternal
    peace. *Amen.*

The Morning Office   **To Be Observed on the Hour or Half Hour**
                                            Between 6 and 9 a.m.

The Call to Prayer

Wake up, my spirit; awake, lute and harp;* I myself will waken the dawn.

Psalm 57:8

The Request for Presence

O Lamb of God, that takes away the sins of the world, have mercy upon me.
O Lamb of God, that takes away the sins of the world, have mercy upon me.
O Lamb of God, that takes away the sins of the world, grant me your peace.

The Greeting

For you alone are the Holy One, you alone are the Lord, you alone are the Most
High, Jesus Christ, with the Holy Spirit, in the Glory of God the Father.

The Refrain for the Morning Lessons

Into your hands I commend my spirit,* for you have redeemed me, O LORD, O
God of truth.

Psalm 31:5

A Reading

Jesus taught us, saying: 'You are my friends, if you do what I command you. I
shall no longer call you servants, because a servant does not know his master's
business; I call you friends, because I have made known to you everything I
have learned from my Father. You did not choose me, no, I chose you; and I
commissioned you to go out and bear fruit, fruit that will last; so that the
Father will give you anything you ask him in my name. My command to you is
to love one another.'

John 15:14–17

The Refrain

Into your hands I commend my spirit,* for you have redeemed me, O LORD, O
God of truth.

The Morning Psalm   *I Will Fulfill My Vows to the LORD*

O LORD, I am your servant;* I am your servant and the child of your handmaid;
you have freed me from my bonds.
I will offer you the sacrifice of thanksgiving* and call upon the Name of the LORD.
I will fulfill my vows to the LORD* in the presence of all his people,
In the courts of the LORD's house,* in the midst of you, O Jerusalem. Hallelujah!

Psalm 116:14–17

The Refrain

Into your hands I commend my spirit,* for you have redeemed me, O LORD, O
God of truth.

The Cry of the Church

Even so come, Lord Jesus!

The Lord's Prayer

The Prayer Appointed for the Week

O God, you declare your almighty power chiefly in showing mercy and pity:
Grant me the fullness of your grace, that I, running to obtain your promises,

may become a partaker of your heavenly treasure; through Jesus Christ our
Lord, who lives and reigns with you and the Holy Spirit, one God, for ever and
ever. *Amen.*†

The Concluding Prayer of the Church
Lord God, almighty and everlasting Father, you have brought me in safety to this
new day: Preserve me with your mighty power, that I may not fall into sin, nor
be overcome by adversity; and in all I do direct me to the fulfilling of your purpose; through Jesus Christ my Lord. *Amen.*†

The Midday Office
**To Be Observed on the Hour or Half Hour
Between 11 a.m. and 2 p.m.**

The Call to Prayer
'Come, we will go up to YAHWEH's mountain, to the Temple of the God of Jacob so
that he may teach us his ways and we may walk in his paths . . .'

Micah 4:2

The Request for Presence
Hear, O Shepherd of Israel, leading Joseph like a flock;* shine forth, you that are
enthroned upon the cherubim.

Psalm 80:1

The Greeting
The LORD lives! Blessed is my Rock!* Exalted is the God of my salvation!

Psalm 18:46

The Refrain for the Midday Lessons
"I will appoint a time," says God;* "I will judge with equity. . . ."

Psalm 75:2

A Reading
But in days to come YAHWEH's Temple Mountain will tower above the mountains,
rise higher than the hills. Then peoples will stream to it, then many nations will
come and say, 'Come, we will go up to YAHWEH's mountain, to the Temple of
the God of Jacob so that he may teach us his ways and we may walk in his
paths; for the Law issues from Zion, and YAHWEH's word from Jerusalem. He
will judge between many peoples and arbitrate between mighty nations. They
will hammer their swords into plowshares, and their spears into bill-hooks.
Nation will not lift sword against nation, or ever again be trained to make war.'

Micah 4:1–4

The Refrain
"I will appoint a time," says God;* "I will judge with equity. . . ."

The Midday Psalm
The LORD *Comes in Holiness from Sinai*
The Lord gave the word;* great was the company of women who bore the tidings:

"Kings with their armies are fleeing away;* the women at home are dividing the
   spoils."
Though you lingered among the sheepfolds,* you shall be like a dove whose
   wings are covered with silver, whose feathers are like green gold.
When the Almighty scattered kings,* it was like snow falling in Zalmon.
O mighty mountain, O hill of Bashan!* O rugged mountain, O hill of Bashan!
Why do you look with envy, O rugged mountain,* at the hill which God chose for
   his resting place? truly, the LORD will dwell there for ever.
The chariots of God are twenty thousand, even thousands of thousands;* the Lord
   comes in holiness from Sinai.

Psalm 68:11–17

The Refrain
"I will appoint a time," says God;* "I will judge with equity. . . ."

The Gloria

The Lord's Prayer

The Prayer Appointed for the Week
O God, you declare your almighty power chiefly in showing mercy and pity:
   Grant me the fullness of your grace, that I, running to obtain your promises,
   may become a partaker of your heavenly treasure; through Jesus Christ our
   Lord, who lives and reigns with you and the Holy Spirit, one God, for ever and
   ever. *Amen.*†

The Concluding Prayer of the Church
O God, the source of eternal light: Shed forth your unending day upon all of us
   who watch for you, that our lips may praise you, our lives may bless you, and
   our worship may give you glory; through Jesus Christ our Lord. *Amen.*†

The Vespers Office   **To Be Observed on the Hour or Half Hour**
                                        Between 5 and 8 p.m.

The Call to Prayer
Come, let us sing to the LORD;* let us shout for joy to the Rock of our salvation.
Let us come before his presence with thanksgiving* and raise a loud shout to him
   with psalms.
For the LORD is a great God,* and a great king above all gods.

Psalm 95:1–3

The Request for Presence
Send out your light and your truth, that they may lead me,* and bring me to your
   holy hill and to your dwelling;

Psalm 43:3

The Greeting
You, O LORD, are my lamp;* my God, you make my darkness bright.

Psalm 18:29

The Hymn   *We Gather Together*

We gather together to ask the Lord's blessing;
He chastens and hastens His will to make known.
The wicked oppressing now cease from distressing.
Sing praises to His Name, He forgets not His own.

Beside us to guide us, our God with us joining,
Ordaining, maintaining His kingdom divine;
So from the beginning the fight we were winning;
Thou, Lord, were at our side, all glory be Thine!

We all do extol Thee, Thou leader triumphant,
And pray that Thou still our defender will be.
Let Thy congregation escape tribulation;
Thy name be ever praised! O Lord, make us free!

Theodore Baker

The Refrain for the Vespers Lessons

Seven times a day do I praise you,* because of your righteous judgments.
Great peace have they who love your law;* for them there is no stumbling block.

Psalm 119:164–65

The Vespers Psalm   *How Shall We Sing the LORD's Song upon an Alien Soil*

By the waters of Babylon we sat down and wept,* when we remembered you, O
     Zion.
As for our harps, we hung them up* on the trees in the midst of that land.
For those who led us away captive asked us for a song, and our oppressors called
     for mirth:* "Sing us one of the songs of Zion."
How shall we sing the LORD's song* upon an alien soil?
If I forget you, O Jerusalem,* let my right hand forget its skill.
Let my tongue cleave to the roof of my mouth if I do not remember you,* if I do
     not set Jerusalem above my highest joy.
Remember the day of Jerusalem, O LORD, against the people of Edom,* who said,
     "Down with it! down with it! even to the ground!"
O Daughter of Babylon, doomed to destruction,* happy the one who pays you
     back for what you have done to us!
Happy shall he be who takes your little ones,* and dashes them against the rock!

Psalm 137

The Refrain

Seven times a day do I praise you,* because of your righteous judgments.
Great peace have they who love your law;* for them there is no stumbling block.

The Gloria

The Lord's Prayer

The Prayer Appointed for the Week

O God, you declare your almighty power chiefly in showing mercy and pity:
Grant me the fullness of your grace, that I, running to obtain your promises,
may become a partaker of your heavenly treasure; through Jesus Christ our
Lord, who lives and reigns with you and the Holy Spirit, one God, for ever and
ever. *Amen.*†

The Concluding Prayer of the Church

Almighty God, who after the creation of the world rested from all your works and
sanctified a day of rest for all your creatures: Grant that I, putting away all
earthly anxieties, may be duly prepared for the service of public worship, and
grant as well that my Sabbath upon earth may be a preparation for the eternal
rest promised to your people in heaven; through Jesus Christ our Lord. *Amen.*†

September Compline

Sunday
The Night Office   **To Be Observed Before Retiring**

The Call to Prayer
May the Lord Almighty grant me and those I love a peaceful night and a perfect
end. *Amen.*†

The Request for Presence
Our help is in the Name of the LORD;* the maker of heaven and earth.

Psalm 124:8

The Greeting
Almighty God, my heavenly Father: I have sinned against you, through my own
fault, in thought, and word, and deed, and in what I have left undone. For the
sake of your Son our Lord Jesus Christ, forgive me all my offenses; and grant
that I may serve you in newness of life, to the glory of your Name. *Amen.*†

The Reading
YAHWEH says this, 'Accursed be anyone who trusts in human beings, who relies on
human strength and whose heart turns from YAHWEH. Such a person is like
scrub in the wastelands: when good comes, it does not affect him since he lives
in the parched places of the desert, uninhabited, salt land. Blessed is anyone
who trusts in YAHWEH, with YAHWEH for his reliance. He is like a tree by the
waterside that thrusts its roots into the stream: when the heat comes, it has
nothing to fear, its foliage stays green; untroubled in a year of drought, it never
stops bearing fruit.'

Jeremiah 17:5–8

The Gloria

The Psalm   *My Soul Has a Desire and Longing for the Courts of the* LORD
How dear to me is your dwelling, O LORD of hosts!* My soul has a desire and long-
ing for the courts of the LORD; my heart and my flesh rejoice in the living God.
The sparrow has found her a house and the swallow a nest where she may lay her
young;* by the side of your altars, O LORD of hosts, my King and my God.
Happy are they who dwell in your house!* They will always be praising you.
Happy are the people whose strength is in you! Whose hearts are set on the pil-
grims' way.

Psalm 84:1–4

The Gloria

The Small Verse
Into your hands, O Lord, I commend my spirit; for you have redeemed me, O
Lord, O God of truth. Keep me, O Lord, as the apple of your eye; hide me
under the shadow of your wings.†

The Lord's Prayer

The Petition
Lord, hear my prayers; And let my cry come to you.†

The Final Thanksgiving
Lord, you now have set your servant free to go in peace as you have promised; for
these eyes of mine have seen the Savior, whom you have prepared for all the
world to see: a Light to enlighten the nations, and the glory of your people
Israel. Glory to the Father, and to the Son, and to the Holy Spirit: as it was in the
beginning, is now, and will be for ever. *Amen.*

⚜

Monday
The Night Office   **To Be Observed Before Retiring**

The Call to Prayer
May the Lord Almighty grant me and those I love a peaceful night and a perfect
end. *Amen.*†

The Request for Presence
Our help is in the Name of the LORD;* the maker of heaven and earth.

                                                          Psalm 124:8

The Greeting
Almighty God, my heavenly Father: I have sinned against you, through my own
fault, in thought, and word, and deed, and in what I have left undone. For the
sake of your Son our Lord Jesus Christ, forgive me all my offenses; and grant
that I may serve you in newness of life, to the glory of your Name. *Amen.*†

The Reading
Stand firm, then, brothers and keep the traditions that we taught you, whether by
word of mouth or by letter. May our Lord Jesus Christ himself, and God our
Father who has given us his love and, through his grace, such ceaseless encouragement and such sure hope, encourage you and strengthen you in every good
word and deed.

                                                  Thessalonians 2:15–17

The Gloria

The Psalm   *The Law of Their God Is in Their Heart*
Turn from evil, and do good,* and dwell in the land for ever.
For the Lord loves justice;* he does not forsake his faithful ones.
They shall be kept safe for ever,* but the offspring of the wicked shall be
destroyed.

The righteous shall possess the land* and dwell in it for ever.
The mouth of the righteous utters wisdom,* and their tongue speaks what is right.
The Law of their God is in their heart, and their footsteps shall not falter.

Psalm 37:28–33

The Gloria

The Small Verse
Into your hands, O Lord, I commend my spirit; For you have redeemed me, O
Lord, O God of truth. Keep me, O Lord, as the apple of your eye; Hide me
under the shadow of your wings.†

The Lord's Prayer

The Petition
Lord, hear my prayers; And let my cry come to you.†

The Final Thanksgiving
Lord, you now have set your servant free to go in peace as you have promised; for
these eyes of mine have seen the Savior, whom you have prepared for all the
world to see: a Light to enlighten the nations, and the glory of your people
Israel. Glory to the Father, and to the Son, and to the Holy Spirit: as it was in the
beginning, is now, and will be for ever. *Amen.*

Tuesday
The Night Office   To Be Observed Before Retiring

The Call to Prayer
May the Lord Almighty grant me and those I love a peaceful night and a perfect
end. *Amen.*†

The Request for Presence
Our help is in the Name of the Lord;* the maker of heaven and earth.

Psalm 124:8

The Greeting
Almighty God, my heavenly Father: I have sinned against you, through my own
fault, in thought, and word, and deed, and in what I have left undone. For the
sake of your Son our Lord Jesus Christ, forgive me all my offenses; and grant
that I may serve you in newness of life, to the glory of your Name. *Amen.*†

The Reading
Then he said to his disciples, 'That is why I am telling you not to worry about your
life and what you are to eat, nor about your body and how you are to clothe it.

For life is more than food, and the body more than clothing. Think of the ravens. They do not sow or reap; they have no storehouses and no barns; yet God feeds them. And how much more you are worth than the birds! Can any of you, however much you worry, add a single cubit to your span of life? If a very small thing is beyond your powers, why worry about the rest? Think how the flowers grow, they never have to spin or weave; yet, I assure you, not even Solomon in all his royal robes was clothed like one of them. Now if that is how God clothes a flower which is growing wildly today and is thrown into the furnace tomorrow, how much more will he look after you, who have so little faith! But you must not set your hearts on things to eat and things to drink; nor must you worry. It is the gentiles of this world who set their hearts on all these things. Your Father well knows you need them. No; set your hearts on his kingdom, and these other things will be given you as well. There is no need to be afraid, little flock, for it has pleased the Father to give you the kingdom.'

Luke 12:22–32

The Gloria

The Psalm   *Come and Listen*
Come and listen, all you who fear God,* and I will tell you what he has done for me.
I called out to him with my mouth,* and his praise was on my tongue.
If I had found evil in my heart,* the LORD would not have heard me;
But in truth God has heard me;* he has attended to the voice of my prayer.
Blessed be God, who has not rejected my prayer,* nor withheld his love from me.

Psalm 66:14–18

The Gloria

The Small Verse
Into your hands, O Lord, I commend my spirit; For you have redeemed me, O
Lord, O God of truth. Keep me, O Lord, as the apple of your eye; Hide me
under the shadow of your wings.†

The Lord's Prayer

The Petition
Lord, hear my prayers; And let my cry come to you.†

The Final Thanksgiving
Lord, you now have set your servant free to go in peace as you have promised; for
these eyes of mine have seen the Savior, whom you have prepared for all the
world to see: a Light to enlighten the nations, and the glory of your people
Israel. Glory to the Father, and to the Son, and to the Holy Spirit: as it was in the
beginning, is now, and will be for ever. *Amen.*

Wednesday
The Night Office   To Be Observed Before Retiring

The Call to Prayer
May the Lord Almighty grant me and those I love a peaceful night and a perfect
  end. *Amen.*†

The Request for Presence
Our help is in the Name of the LORD;* the maker of heaven and earth.
                                                            Psalm 124:8

The Greeting
Almighty God, my heavenly Father: I have sinned against you, through my own
  fault, in thought, and word, and deed, and in what I have left undone. For the
  sake of your Son our Lord Jesus Christ, forgive me all my offenses; and grant
  that I may serve you in newness of life, to the glory of your Name. *Amen.*†

The Reading   *A Holy Mind*
There is a great difference between a clever mind, a great mind and a holy mind.
  The clever mind is pleasing because of its charm. The great mind excites our
  admiration because of its depth. But only a right spirit can save and make us
  happy through its constancy and uprightness. Do not conform your ideas to
  those of the world. Distrust the mind as much as the world esteems it.
                                                       François Fénelon

The Gloria

The Psalm   *Put Your Trust in Him Always, O People*
For God alone my soul in silence waits;* truly my hope is in him.
He alone is my rock and my salvation,* my stronghold, so that I shall not be
  shaken.
In God is my safety and my honor;* God is my strong rock and my refuge.
Put your trust in him always, my people,* pour out your hearts before him, for
  God is our refuge.
Those of high decree are but a fleeting breath,* all of them together.
Put no trust in extortion; in robbery take no empty pride;* though wealth increase,
  set not your heart upon it.
God has spoken once, twice have I heard it,* that power belongs to God.
Steadfast love is yours, O LORD,* for you repay everyone according to his deeds.
                                                           Psalm 62:6–14

The Gloria

The Small Verse
Into your hands, O Lord, I commend my spirit; For you have redeemed me, O
  Lord, O God of truth. Keep me, O Lord, as the apple of your eye; Hide me
  under the shadow of your wings.†

The Lord's Prayer

The Petition
Lord, hear my prayers; And let my cry come to you.†

The Final Thanksgiving
Lord, you now have set your servant free to go in peace as you have promised; for
these eyes of mine have seen the Savior, whom you have prepared for all the
world to see: a Light to enlighten the nations, and the glory of your people
Israel. Glory to the Father, and to the Son, and to the Holy Spirit: as it was in the
beginning, is now, and will be for ever. *Amen.*

◈

Thursday
The Night Office   **To Be Observed Before Retiring**

The Call to Prayer
May the Lord Almighty grant me and those I love a peaceful night and a perfect
end. *Amen*†

The Request for Presence
Our help is in the Name of the LORD;* the maker of heaven and earth.
                                                              Psalm 124:8

The Greeting
Almighty God, my heavenly Father: I have sinned against you, through my own
fault, in thought, and word, and deed, and in what I have left undone. For the
sake of your Son our Lord Jesus Christ, forgive me all my offenses; and grant
that I may serve you in newness of life, to the glory of your Name. *Amen.*†

The Reading
You are God: we praise you;
You are the Lord: we acclaim you;
You are the eternal Father:
All creation worships you.
To you all angels, all the powers of heaven,
Cherubim and Seraphim, sing in endless praise:
Holy, holy, holy Lord, God of power and might,
heaven and earth are full of your glory.
The glorious company of apostles praise you.
The noble fellowship of prophets praise you.
The white-robed army of martyrs praise you.
Throughout the world the holy Church acclaims you;
Father, of majesty unbounded,

your true and only Son, worthy of all worship,
and the Holy Spirit, advocate and guide.
You, Christ, are the king of glory,
the eternal Son of the Father.
When you became man you set us free
you did not shun the virgin's womb.
You overcame the sting of death
and opened the kingdom of heaven to all believers.
You are seated at God's right hand in glory.
We believe that you will come and be our judge.
Come then, Lord, and help your people,
bought with the price of your own blood,
and bring us with your saints
to glory everlasting.

Te Deum

The Gloria

The Psalm *Let Everything That Has Breath Praise the LORD*
Hallelujah! Praise God in his holy temple;* praise him in the firmament of his
   power.
Praise him for his mighty acts;* praise him for his excellent greatness.
Praise him with the blast of the ram's-horn;* praise him with lyre and harp.
Praise him with timbrel and dance;* praise him with strings and pipe.
Praise him with resounding cymbals;* praise him with loud clanging cymbals.
Let everything that has breath* praise the LORD. Hallelujah!

The Gloria

The Small Verse
Into your hands, O Lord, I commend my spirit; For you have redeemed me, O
   Lord, O God of truth. Keep me, O Lord, as the apple of your eye; Hide me
   under the shadow of your wings.†

The Lord's Prayer

The Petition
Lord, hear my prayers; And let my cry come to you.†

The Final Thanksgiving
Lord, you now have set your servant free to go in peace as you have promised; for
   these eyes of mine have seen the Savior, whom you have prepared for all the
   world to see: a Light to enlighten the nations, and the glory of your people
   Israel. Glory to the Father, and to the Son, and to the Holy Spirit: as it was in the
   beginning, is now, and will be for ever. *Amen.*†

Friday
The Night Office   To Be Observed Before Retiring

The Call to Prayer
May the Lord Almighty grant me and those I love a peaceful night and a perfect
    end. *Amen.*†

The Request for Presence
Our help is in the Name of the Lord;* the maker of heaven and earth.

Psalm 124:8

The Greeting
Almighty God, my heavenly Father: I have sinned against you, through my own
    fault, in thought, and word, and deed, and in what I have left undone. For the
    sake of your Son our Lord Jesus Christ, forgive me all my offenses; and grant
    that I may serve you in newness of life, to the glory of your Name. *Amen.*†

The Reading
What is a human being, what purpose does he serve? What is good and what is
    bad for him? The length of his life: a hundred years at most. Like a drop of
    water from the sea, or a grain of sand, such are these few years compared with
    eternity. This is why the Lord is patient with them and pours out his mercy on
    them. He sees and recognizes how wretched their end is, and so makes his for-
    giveness greater. Human compassion extends to neighbors, but the Lord's
    compassion extends to everyone; rebuking, correcting and teaching, bringing
    them back as a shepherd brings his flock. He has compassion on those who
    accept correction, and who fervently search for his judgments.

Ecclesiasticus 18:8–14

The Gloria

The Psalm   *That Which We Have Heard and Known*
That which we have heard and known, and what our forefathers have told us,* we
    will not hide from their children.
We will recount to generations to come the praiseworthy deeds and the power of
    the Lord,* and the wonderful works he has done.
He gave his decrees to Jacob and established a law for Israel,* which he com-
    manded them to teach their children;
That the generation to come might know, and the children yet unborn;* that they
    in their turn might tell it to their children;
So that they might put their trust in God,* and not forget the deeds of God, but
    keep his commandments;
And not be like their forefathers, a stubborn and rebellious generation,* a genera-
    tion whose heart was not steadfast, and whose spirit was not faithful to God.

Psalm 78:3–8

The Gloria

The Small Verse

Into your hands, O Lord, I commend my spirit; for you have redeemed me, O
Lord, O God of truth. Keep me, O Lord, as the apple of your eye; hide me
under the shadow of your wings.†

The Lord's Prayer

The Petition

Lord, hear my prayers; And let my cry come to you.†

The Final Thanksgiving

Lord, you now have set your servant free to go in peace as you have promised; for
these eyes of mine have seen the Savior, whom you have prepared for all the
world to see: a Light to enlighten the nations, and the glory of your people
Israel. Glory to the Father, and to the Son, and to the Holy Spirit: as it was in the
beginning, is now, and will be for ever. *Amen.*

Saturday
The Night Office   **To Be Observed Before Retiring**

The Call to Prayer

May the Lord Almighty grant me and those I love a peaceful night and a perfect
end. *Amen.*†

The Request for Presence

Our help is in the Name of the Lord;* the maker of heaven and earth.

Psalm 124:8

The Greeting

Almighty God, my heavenly Father: I have sinned against you, through my own
fault, in thought, and word, and deed, and in what I have left undone. For the
sake of your Son our Lord Jesus Christ, forgive me all my offenses; and grant
that I may serve you in newness of life, to the glory of your Name. *Amen.*†

The Reading

All that happens to me becomes bread to nourish me, soap to cleanse me, fire to
purify me, a chisel to carve heavenly features on me. Everything is a channel of
grace for my needs. The very thing I sought everywhere else seeks me inces-
santly, and gives itself to me by means of all created things.

Jean-Pierre de Caussade

The Gloria

The Psalm   *Where Can I Flee from Your Presence*

Where can I go then from your spirit?* Where can I flee from your presence?

If I climb up to heaven, you are there;* if I make the grave my bed, you are there also.

If I take the wings of morning* and dwell in the uttermost parts of the sea,

Even there your hand will lead me* and your right hand will hold me fast.

Psalm 139:6–9

The Gloria

The Small Verse

Into your hands, O Lord, I commend my spirit; For you have redeemed me, O Lord, O God of truth. Keep me, O Lord, as the apple of your eye; Hide me under the shadow of your wings.†

The Lord's Prayer

The Petition

Lord, hear my prayers; And let my cry come to you.†

The Final Thanksgiving

Lord, you now have set your servant free to go in peace as you have promised; for these eyes of mine have seen the Savior, whom you have prepared for all the world to see: a Light to enlighten the nations, and the glory of your people Israel. Glory to the Father, and to the Son, and to the Holy Spirit: as it was in the beginning, is now, and will be for ever. *Amen.*

Index of Authors

Acknowledgments

"Be for Us a Moon of Joy," from *An African Prayer Book* by Desmond Tutu. Copyright © 1997 by Doubleday. Used by permission.

"For Protection This Day" by Jacob Boehme, from *Sacred Poems and Prayers of Love*, edited by Mary Ford-Grabowsky. Copyright © 1998 by Doubleday. Used by permission.

"Forth in the Peace of Christ We Go," from *Amazing Grace: Hymn Texts for Devotional Use*, edited by Polman, Stulken, and Sydnor (Westminster John Knox Press, 1994). Copyright © 1969 by Geoffrey Chapman Books. Used by permission of Geoffrey Chapman Books, a division of Cassell PLC.

"Help each one of us, gracious Father," prayer from China, from *Another Day: Prayers of the Human Family*, compiled by John Carden. Copyright © 1986 by Church Missionary Society.

"How Precious Is Your Steadfast Love," from *Awake My Heart* by Fred Bassett. Copyright © 1998 by Paraclete Press. Used by permission.

"Listen, Lord—A Prayer," from *God's Trombones* by James Weldon Johnson. Copyright © 1927 by The Viking Press, renewed © 1955 by Grace Nail Johnson. Used by permission of Viking Penguin, a division of Penguin Putnam Inc.

Excerpts from *The Hours of the Divine Office in English and Latin*, prepared by the staff of Liturgical Press. Copyright © 1963 The Liturgical Press. Used by permission.

Excerpts from *Imitation of Christ* (Thomas à Kempis), edited by Hal M. Helms. Copyright © 1982 by Paraclete Press. Used by permission.

Excerpts from *The Joy of Full Surrender* (Jean-Pierre de Caussade), edited by Hal M. Helms. Copyright © 1986 by Paraclete Press. Used by permission.

Excerpts from *Liturgy of the Hours, Vol. III* by International Commission on English in the Liturgy. Copyright © 1974 by International Commission on English in the Liturgy. Used by permission.

Excerpts from *New Companion to the Breviary*. Copyright © 1988 by the Carmelites of Indianapolis, Indiana. Used by permission.

Excerpts from *A Short Breviary*, edited by The Monks of St. John's Abbey. Copyright © 1949 by St. John's Abbey. Used by permission of The Liturgical Press.

All verses, other than Psalms, are excerpted from *The New Jerusalem Bible* unless otherwise noted.

All verses from Psalms are excerpted from *The Book of Common Prayer* unless otherwise noted.

KJV refers to verses excerpted from the King James Version of the Bible.

PHYLLIS TICKLE has been reporting on religion for *Publishers Weekly* for many years and is currently Contributing Editor in Religion for the journal. One of the most respected authorities and popular speakers on religion in America today, she is frequently quoted and interviewed both in print media, including the *New York Times, Washington Post, Newsweek,* and *Time,* and in electronic media, such as CNN, C-SPAN, BBC, and "Voice of America." She appears frequently on the Odyssey Channel and is a regular guest on PBS's "Religion and Ethics NewsWeekly." She is the author of over two dozen books, including the recently published *God-Talk in America.* She lives in the rural community of Lucy, Tennessee.